the Textbook of Theatrical Combat

*a handbook for stagecraft generals
and footlight warriors*

*choosing props and preparing actors
for theatrical violence*

Richard Pallaziol

Why have I written this book?

I've had the pleasure of working with some wonderful artists and technicians who work indefatigably to create the joy and magic that is live theatre. These are people who work for nationally respected operas, professional theatre companies, high school drama clubs, middle school literature programs, and community theatre troupes of every size and composition. I greatly respect and am in awe of the talent and energy found at every level of this nation's theatrical community. But as anyone who has seen a goodly amount of theatre can empathize, I have also felt the embarrassed pain of seeing and being involved with a lot of shows that miss the mark. Sometimes a rumbling train wreck of a show has no hope of salvation; sometimes the lack of talent in key segments of the production team destroys any spark of intelligence that might have been possible. But sometimes it is the more insidious wearing down of the audience, chipping away at their patience and tolerance until they can't say that they have seen a bad show, but they are clearly dissatisfied with the overall result. Sometimes these irritants are unavoidable, and they certainly pop-up in any style of theatre. Sometimes the flaws are from lack of research; sometimes from unfamiliarity with the subject. For example, it always grieves me to see versions of *Evita.* The show is set in Argentina, but the tango singer is invariably wearing a ruffled shirt from Cuba and is backed up by two flamenco dancers of Spain, and is not even singing a tango. But theatrical flaws seem to strike with their most cruel vengeance in period plays.

I'm sure you have seen what I have seen: American actors as a group have a tremendous difficulty doing anything outside of modern realism. We often don't know how to stand or speak or walk in a way that convinces audiences that they are watching a slice of life of a previous time.

Then there are the fight scenes, most of which seem as though the acting stops while we watch some people fight, and once that's over the play resumes again. It's as though there is a disconnect between violence and the world of theatre. Although these two characteristics would at first appear to be unrelated, I've come to see that they have the same root cause.

I've spent most of my adult life trying to help actors and directors deal with creating scenes of violence on stage. I've found that, while the techniques of stage combat are what I was expected to teach, the most important lessons I gave were on <u>why</u> a character fought or dressed or stood in a certain way. The blending of period weaponry as it relates to period style provides a foundation upon which the artist can create not only an exciting fight, but make believable characters within the setting of the play.

Wearing the weapon is usually an afterthought for most costumers, treated as an embellishment to the clothing (in their view something which the properties master should be handling anyway). In studying the development of personal weapons and clothing, however, we find that it is often a change in fighting style that changes a sword choice, which itself dictates a change in general movement to accommodate the same, and then finally a change in fashion to accommodate the movement. Even when not wearing the weapon, effect on the basic daily stance remains. If an actor can understand why he is expected to stand or walk in a certain way, rather than just told "that's how it was done", he is much more likely to be able to incorporate those movements and stances as part of his character from the earliest rehearsal, rather than as an affectation.

The props themselves often add their own headaches. Very little information is out there concerning the specifics of weapons for stage. Period style books rarely cover swords and guns, and directors and even hired "experts" give contradictory, unsupported, and sometimes just flat out wrong information on what kind of weapon is required for the play. It's one thing to have to use whatever prop you can find due to budgetary constraints, but how disappointing when a different prop at the same price could have contributed to the story, rather than detract from it. Then there are the horror stories about weapons that are brought on stage which are actually dangerous to the actors, on occasion leading to serious injury.

The magnitude of this last problem was brought home to me shortly after I started my rental company, Weapons of Choice. I quickly learned that the vast majority of my clients had no knowledge about the items they were renting. Imagine opening a car rental company in a land where most of your customers not only have never driven a car, or even ridden in a car, but the only knowledge they have of automobiles is having seen car chases in action movies. And I'm not talking here only about community or high school theatre. I've seen this lack of knowledge among the very finest directors and properties masters at some of our nation's most famous and well-regarded theatre companies.

Who am I to give advice?

Excellent question. You've perhaps not heard my name before, and I haven't worked on Broadway or on major motion pictures. Instead I've mostly worked where you work; in the minimal budget, poorly staffed, under-appreciated reality that is theatre for 99% of us trying to make a living in this business.

But I have worked there for a long time, as actor, dancer, director, fight instructor and dramaturge. And I've also choreographed my share of fights; over three hundred shows, as well as a handful of independent films and a couple of video games. Since 1990 I have also owned and operated Weapons of Choice, the nation's largest theatrical weapons rental company. In that last capacity I've supervised the construction of the weapons used for nearly thirty thousand shows. Over the years I've learned a thing or two that others may find helpful. This book is a compilation of the information I wish I had had when I first got involved in theatre nearly half a century ago. The questions answered, problems solved, research compiled, and injuries avoided tend to be the same ones show after show, so maybe some of this information can help you in your next production.

What is this book?

It is not a book about props, but it does describe how to select, maintain and use the implements of violence necessary for many of the shows currently performed on the American stage.

It is not a book about costumes, but it does show a good deal about the wearing of weaponry for various times and places.

It is not a book on period style, but it will help actors portray the users of weapons throughout history, even if they aren't using the weapons.

It is not a military history book, but it places the weapons and warriors within a historical context useful to theatre professionals.

It is, simply, an attempt to fill the knowledge gap that exists between theatre folk and the violent props they use. The gift of theatre is that it gives us hope that by exploring the human condition in all of its many disguises we can expose the true essence of humanity - the depravity along with the majesty, the brutality and the gracious forbearance, the villainy and the nobility - and finally perhaps become better people ourselves through that exploration. I am certainly not an apologist for violence in the media, but since we are first and last artists and storytellers, we need to understand all aspects of what it is that makes this species tick. For good or ill, it includes the frequent use of violence.

So what this has become is a handbook, a quick reference guide to things not found in other theatre books. It's the book I could have used when I got into the business many decades ago. Some things I'll touch on briefly or not at all. For example, castle defenses and siege weapons are a fascinating study, but of very little use in theatre. Where it directly concerns the actor trying to feel comfortable with a part, I'll spend more time on what may seem trivial but can really help to ground the performer within the costume, rather than in spite of it.

You'll notice that I break the first rule in writing, namely, I don't write in the third person. I know that its use is intended to show that the writer is being objective and balanced, but *this* writer is neither, and the third person format can't hide that. Besides, I think most readers realize that a person is writing the book; after all, the name is right there on the cover. So I've dropped the artifice and will write to you directly. If you find statements with which you disagree or don't understand, well, they came from me directly, not the all-knowing third person, so I'll own up to them. Drop me a note and I'll be glad to rethink my position, explain my conclusions, or include more material in subsequent editions.

I also tend to write of the actors as being male, but this is only because most parts requiring the handling of weapons or the use of violence are written about male characters. This is unfortunate, for in my experience it is generally female actors who perform staged combat more effectively than do their male counterparts. Whether it is because they tend to have had more dance training or have become more attuned to the concept of performing movement rather than pretending to fight, I couldn't say. But when directors ask me how they should cast the fight parts in shows, I always tell them to find the best actor first, then I'll teach them the fight. If that means slapping a mustache on a female playing Richard III, so be it. None the less, demonstrative physical violence was and is predominantly a male-centered activity.

Lastly, alas, you will find no bibliography. The information that follows has come largely from my poor memory and some random notes. I wish that I could remember which books I have read over the past fifty years that have contributed to my education in theatre, history and combat, but that information is now long lost. But I do know that I am deeply indebted to, among others, the Society of American Fight Directors for stage combat techniques, and perhaps more especially to Douglas Russell of the American Conservatory Theatre for teaching that literature, art, history, science, music, physics, archeology, politics, economics - all of these are necessary study for the artist. His book, *Period Style For The Theatre*, is the finest introduction to the subject, and should be mandatory reading for all theatre artists.

Richard Pallaziol
Weapons of Choice
Napa, CA

Copyright 2009. All rights are reserved by the author. No part of this book may be reproduced or utilized in any form or by any means, electronic or mechanical, including photocopying, scanning, recording, or by any information storage or retrieval system, without the express prior permission in writing from the author.

All images in this book are either of items from the author's collection or were created by the author for this book. Certain sections of this book were previously published by Weapons of Choice.

The Way of The Warrior   9
A (very brief and brisk) history of weapons and combatants
- Non-Western Civilizations   16
- Growth of Western Development   34
- The Thin Blue Line: The Development of Civilian Police Forces   101

Weapons Defined   107
A Specialized Dictionary

Weapons Explained   144
The Nature of Violent Props
- Swords   146
- Knives and Daggers   165
- Guns   171
- Other Practical Weapons   213

Staging Violence   219
The Acting of Angry Actions
- Unarmed   234
- Edged Weapons   295
- Quarterstaff and Other Impact Weapons   350
- Guns On-Stage   362
- Choreography Basics and Acting the Fight   372

Violence on Stage   377
Specific Scenes in Some Common Plays
- Acting in Period Plays   378
- Specific Scenes from Specific Shakespeare Plays   386
- Shifting Weapons to Match Design Concepts   399
- Specific Scenes from Other Plays   402

Some Final Words   446

The Way of The Warrior
A (very brief and brisk) history of weapons and combatants

In portraying characters of other times, we run into the problem of how to recreate the style of the period. Not only to breathe life into the characters we portray, but also to convince the audience that they are witnessing a slice of history come to life. Too often, the actor views this as simply adding on mannerisms that he has been told are right for the time, without understanding why the character would have moved or even stood in a certain way. So in addition to having the right costume for the character, the actor needs to have some understanding of the way that people viewed themselves and the world they lived in. The study of how the external aspects of a people develop out of the historic underpinnings in which they lived is called *period style*. For the purpose of this book, I'm centering our focus on those elements relating to how a society demonstrates violent actions.

Obviously we're going to have to stick to broad generalities in this book, so the specific trends that might have also occurred in any given century or decade will not be mentioned here, although it might be critical to the play you could be working on. So don't think that by reading an applicable section in this chapter you need not do your regular homework in preparing for a specific play. Even so, it is important to know the general pattern before one can appreciate the variations.

Also, I'm trying to provide information for the shows most likely to be seen on stage in the United States. For that reason, while an in-depth study of Jivaro headhunters is fascinating, this section is heavily Eurocentric.

For deeper information, try to find source material from the time you are studying. Newspapers, photographs, diaries of course, but for earlier times a careful examination of visual art can lead to clues as to the way people moved and stood. Make sure that you are viewing as close to original source material as possible. A painting about an occurrence in 1252 but drawn in 1544 may tell you something about the 16th century but very little about the 13th. Also keep in mind that the artist may have his own idiosyncratic habits and may not be an expert in warfare or period style. The Bayeux Tapestry depicts the Norman Conquest of 1066, and was probably made only a decade after the event, but has many inaccuracies, so many that the work cannot by itself be used as a template of how soldiers fought or even what they wore.

Before we start, it is important to remember that whenever we try to re-create another culture or period on stage, we not only have to mimic those attributes which may be different from our own, but also cast aside those which are distinctly modern. We have many modern mannerisms that are so ingrained that we fail to notice them, so I would like to point out the most glaring ones that can interfere with trying to develop a period or character style:

♦ Voice - In the late twentieth and now twenty-first century we have become a more visual and less verbal society. Previous societies had the patience and auditory dexterity to follow long speeches and stories, even if they couldn't read them. The wealth of vocabulary used by even the uneducated was also combined with a tendency to speak faster than we do now. Our daily speech by comparison is almost exclusively monosyllabic and bisyllabic, and we use a truncated, limited sentence structure. With only a rudimentary development of expression and limited pitch variation, our university graduates would be considered by other societies to be congenitally "slow".

♦ Posture/Movement - Our daily normal stance and seated positions, unconsciously designed to make us disappear in a crowd, are best described as apologetic. They give the appearance of trying to withdraw from a room, seeming fearful of standing out and being noticed. Prior peoples had an open way of standing or sitting that freed them up to the entire space they were in, whether in or out of doors. A grouping of modern people by comparison usually looks as though they are each afraid that someone will call on them to perform some onerous task.

♦ Relaxation - We moderns confuse relaxing with collapsing; we slump into a chair, rolling the shoulders inward and retreating from the room. Prior peoples could relax while still staying open to the environment.

♦ Focus - More subtle is where we moderns direct our focus, not only where we look but how far we stretch our perception and our "energy". We no longer enter and "take" all corners of a room with our presence. Outdoors we tend to look down and away from others, keeping our "essence" within a narrow circle a mere few feet around our bodies, almost as though we have something to be ashamed of.

These four aspects of our current body language and expression show up any time you work with modern actors. They are especially the hallmarks of young, untrained American actors, so working to clear these habits can improve the general polish of performances in any show, period piece or not.

Many times for one reason or another a director will try to set a play in what is variously called "no-period", "universal", "eclectic" (or, more honestly, "no budget"). When confronted with this lack of direction, actors would be especially well advised to work on the same four points.

I should be fair and point out that often the rational for trying to set a play in "no period" is due to a laudable effort to strip away all of the time-sensitive cues that allow an audience to pigeonhole a work of art, separating themselves from the world of the play. By attempting a nonspecific period look, the hope is to present the play in a pure form, devoid of considerations of time or place. Laudable, but ultimately futile. The factors of what we call period style cannot be so easily erased. Every "modern" piece is itself set in a period, for the playwright and director cannot divorce themselves of their own history. Every actor cannot help but be a product of his or her upbringing, and all of this manifests on stage. There are tons of plays that have been performed on completely bare stages, with actors wearing all black and their hair pulled straight back. But in watching filmed versions, one can still narrow down when it was performed to within the decade. There are a hundred subtleties of expression, movement, posture and voice that shout out the where and when of every performance.

How this chapter is set-up

Where possible, and especially when looking at Western civilizations, each section will try to cover the following four categories:

Politics/Economics – an overview of the trends which place the individual in the larger society.

We make broad assumptions on what is "normal" based on the society in which we have been raised. We Americans especially have a hard time understanding the points of view that exist in other countries, let alone other periods in time. But a people's assumptions about themselves are a result of their view of the universe, of power, of religion, of work.

Fashion/Style/Manners – the expectation of the individual when in the company of his peers.

For our purposes we are defining fashion not as the seasonal trends that are on display at Bloomingdale's, or a review of what has come down the runway in Paris. Rather, we're looking for the longer baseline for "normality" in any given culture or subculture. One can dress away from that baseline and be considered abnormal, or blend in with it and be largely accepted by your subculture. In that sense, no one is more "fashion conscious" than the 14 year-old boy on the first day of school. Every item of his couture is carefully calibrated to project the right image.

Clothing is an outward manifestation of the face we give to the world, but is also a reflection of how we feel about ourselves. Clothes may not make the man, but it reflects something of the thought process that both selected the items for purchase, and then selected which items would be worn on a particular day. Inside anyone's closet the full range of articles to be worn for leisure, for formal occasions, for various social occasions, etc., represent the complete boundaries of that person's self image. Indeed, we can learn volumes about someone by noticing what is <u>not</u> in his closet. Then, from that selection of the possible, each person daily selects what representation of himself he chooses to show to the world. The choice may not be conscious, but will reflect upbringing, personality, mood, social level, and aspirations.

The same is true of the way we stand, walk, and speak. The choices are less obvious, and for that reason more telling.

<u>Civilian Conflict</u> – or, fighting off the battlefield.

This will cover both the dueling weapons and fighting styles of the non-soldier. While weapons for armies are usually a matter of improvements in technology, the choice of civilian weapons is much more restricted by social mores.

At the very end of the entire chapter is a section discussing Western police forces and the changes they have gone through.

<u>Warfare</u> – a look at the weapons and fighting methods for the soldier of the period.

The weapons mentioned in each section are meant to only give a quick overview of the most common weapons to which most combatants would have had access. That's not the same as the date that the items were invented, for there is often quite a lag time between development of a weapon and its acceptance by the intended users. Naturally, when designing a show, it is important to remember that as new weapons are invented, the older styles don't simply disappear, but often continue to be used for several generations.

Since most plays deal with the soldier who must confront another soldier on the field of battle, that's what will be described. With few exceptions, the focus here will be on land fighters, not sailors or airmen. Interestingly, most armed confrontations throughout history are centered on the taking of a city or other fortified position, but there will be no discussion here on siege warfare here, nor of bombardment. Those topics don't provide enough helpful material for the actor trying to create a character, so we will concern ourselves with the frontline troops.

Frontline soldiers throughout history have had to face the same basic challenge - attempting to kill other human beings while putting themselves in direct and immediate danger of being killed. It shouldn't be surprising that the response has been universally similar. Fear is pervasive. Training and experience can help deal with it, but it never disappears. The immediate motivation always comes down to the camaraderie built between soldiers ("you don't fight for your country; you fight for your buddy"). Other powerful motivations are often based on appeals to elitism ("the Few, the Proud, the Marines") and also on precedent (what other soldiers have done in the past). And these qualities are often blended with a heady and romantic picture of military life.

Not all soldiers in the same army will fight in the same way, and their use in battle is traditionally prescribed by the best attribute which they bring as a unit onto the field. They fall broadly into one of two categories - infantry or cavalry, and each of these is further divided into light and heavy. Although any unit might find itself fighting against any part of an opposing army, each has certain inherent strengths and weaknesses that play an important role in how a battle is fought:

• Heavy Infantry - The basic foot soldier, the grunt, the dog-face. It is his job to take the battlefield. Soldier to soldier fighting is usually borne by the heavy infantry. He is effective when working within a large controlled group and while protected with armor and heavy weapons. Because of this he usually has limited mobility while engaged in the fight. Battles are won or lost based on the outcome of the fight of the heavy infantry. A traditional battle is not considered won until they can take and control the area. Heavy infantry can normally defend itself against heavy cavalry, but can be attacked successfully by light infantry or light cavalry.

• Light Infantry - This is another foot soldier, but lightly armored for better mobility, and instead of going toe-to-toe with the enemy he has some sort of longer distance [projectile] weapon. His job is to use his mobility to stay just outside of the fight, all the while using his primary weapon to attack and weaken the opposing heavy infantry. Light infantry can be used to defend against the light cavalry, but can be attacked by heavy cavalry.

• Heavy Cavalry - The horseman. Heavy cavalry uses the greatest available method of battle transportation and combines it with heavy armor and a close-in ["shock"] weapon. He can quickly take advantage of battlefield disorganization to move in and strike, although a united heavy infantry can hold him off. Heavy cavalry can rout out light infantry, but is easily attacked by light cavalry.

• Light Cavalry - He has even better mobility than the heavy cavalry, for his weapon and armor are lighter. Instead of closing in with the enemy, he has the more difficult task of using projectile weapons that are fired while moving. Light cavalry can stay just out of range of the heavy cavalry and infantry, all the while weakening them with their distance weapons. They can be kept at bay by light infantry.

Each division will have its own weapon system, different training, and different skills.

The Types of War

War is physical violence between two politically recognizable groups. The reasons for war are varied, but we are concerned here only with how, not with why. We're going to use some terms and loose definitions to try to categorize different forms of warfare that have sprouted up through history. This is not exhaustive and certainly not definitive, but is used here to suit our limited purpose of understanding how different societies have fought their battles.

√ Raiding - A sudden surprise attack on an unsuspecting settlement, usually with the intent of driving off or stealing from the defenders. More rarely seen is the raid with intent of annihilation or extinction of the settlement.

√ Ritual - The combatants conform to a carefully prescribed set of actions in which the winner is determined without the majority of combatants ever having to come to blows.

√ Champion - Battle between opposing warriors of similar high standing. The outcome of their battles in some societies was enough to establish victory for the entire group, but not always. The battle of champions could also be found in either ritual or as part of decisive warfare.

√ Decisive - The pitched battle, in which all forces are brought to bear with the purpose of killing as many of the enemy as possible in order to secure victory. It is the type of warfare with which we are familiar. Indeed, most people in the world today are unaware of any other style of fighting.

√ Provocative - Attacks meant to bring about a political response, usually from a larger or more powerful opponent. We are currently living in a time in which we are seeing a general shift from decisive to provocative warfare.

These differing styles are not mutually exclusive, and one style is not necessarily less bloody than another. In the West, since the time of the ancient Greeks we have thought of war as being only the decisive variety. (Champion warfare is almost unheard of in Western history, and yet is the common convention of stage and cinema representations of real battles). What some sociologists refer to as "primitive war" is usually a combination of the first three forms, but is also a group fighting style which emphasizes using missile weapons (arrows and thrown spears), only limited hand-to-hand engagement, and retreat when convenient. "Fighting to the last man" as an honorable outcome is a purely Western idea, and (with the exception of the Japanese) has no parallel in other cultures.

* * *

Pre-History   [Before Metal Technology]

Obviously anything that we might say about the earliest cultures is purely based on surmise, but the best thinking on the subject suggests that personal disagreements as well as tribal conflicts were found even at the first stages of human development. Indeed, even baboons and chimps will attack other "tribes". So it is very likely that the early hominids did the same, and used stones and sharpened sticks, progressing to the stone ax, and for some societies the sling and bow and arrow.

It has until recent years been common in anthropology to take a look at previously isolated but still living "untouched" tribal groups and assume that they provide a glimpse into the lifestyles of the earliest humans. Unfortunately, it has become apparent that in almost all cases, these primitive tribes have been found to have not had a completely isolated lineage. Most were originally part of a larger bronze-aged (and in Africa, even steel-aged) kingdom. When the larger units fragmented, some of the smallest clans drifted off to the outskirts of the kingdom, slowly reverting to a simpler and impoverished state. They can hardly be considered to be representative of an "unspoiled" past. How the earliest humans regulated their societies and fought their battles must still be largely left to guesswork.

Permit a slight digression. It is usually assumed that warfare began as an extension of hunting, as both are concerned with killing. Most anthropologists are now questioning that position. Hunting large game for food throughout the world usually has had the following characteristics: tracking a herd, identifying an easy target, separating it from the group, allowing the group to disperse while the individual target is trapped and killed.

Battles are another thing entirely. The group to be attacked has a home location which is well known, the specific target is the strongest individual instead of the weakest, and then the target is killed or separated before the main objective can be reached, which is the containment of the group to either capture or kill as many as possible. These are not the skills learned by hunter/gatherers, who actually do very poorly in traditional battles. No, these battle skills seem far more closely related to those involved in the domestication of herd animals. A group of farmer/pastoralists that can surround and contain a herd, isolate and capture its alpha leader, and then dominate the remaining members has learned all of the basics of battle. Also, hunting best takes place with few members. Every additional member added to the hunting party increases the chance of spooking the quarry without increasing the chance of success. Capturing and controlling a herd, on the other hand, can use all of the available manpower working in concerted union. This requires discipline and a certain command structure, and so is also excellent training for war.

Additionally, weapons development and construction for hunter/gather societies are very simple, and usually the spear heads, arrowheads and knives are made of stone, flint, or obsidian. Nothing more is really needed to bring down even large game. Farmers, on the other hand, need much stronger tools in order to break and till the soil. Hoes must be made of metal, so as societies move to agriculture they need to invent new technologies to create strong metal tools. When primary arable land becomes scarce, ever stronger tools are needed to work ever tougher soil. These same tools and materials, only slightly modified, are the ones we see used as weapons on the battlefield.

The hunter/gatherer usually does not consider land to be ownable in the Western sense. Indeed, it is most often a part of his mythos that the natural and spiritual world are indivisible, and that one can no more possess a patch of ground than one can own a portion of sky. But a plot of land cultivated for food production becomes valuable if for no other reason than one has invested a year's worth of time in order to produce a single harvest. Though the hunter/gatherer may prefer certain areas over others in his quest for food, strategic retreats to other zones do not impose a severe hardship to him. The farmer is much more likely to think of his land as worth fighting for.

This is not to say that agriculture created war. Hunter/gatherer societies were just as capable of killing their neighbors as brutally as any modern army can. It matters not whether the society was technologically primitive or advanced nor what type of social structure they followed, nor where or when those societies existed. Throughout time and geography, every society has either fed or had to forcefully repress its continued desire to bring violence to another. But with very few exceptions the pre-agri groups limited themselves to raiding and ritual rather than to decisive warfare for material gain. What distinguished the agriculturalists was their innovation of weaponry and finally their concept of what it means to wage war and how to define victory.

With the surplus in food that agriculture provided, societies could not only more densely populate a given region, but also afford to have some members of their group step away from the daily toil involved in food procurement. They could instead devote themselves as craftsmen, warriors, religious leaders, and finally as political leaders. It is at this stage, the final turning point from tribal chieftain to agriculture-based kingdoms, that the modern notion of war has its genesis. Kings could command others to die, and populations readily accepted the sacrifice, not for self-defense nor to stave off starvation, but merely so that the group could maintain or expropriate a particular plot of land. From that point on, land has had more value than the humans on it.

* * *

Non-Western Civilizations

Africa

The birthplace of humanity is found in the plains of the great continent, and with the earliest human fossilized remains we find the first tools - and the first weapons. A full survey of all of the cultures, empires, and battles of Africa is beyond the scope of this (or any single) book, so I'll just point out a couple of examples.

Raiding parties. Before the conquest of the continent during European colonization, most coastal kingdoms and tribes conducted trade with neighboring tribes, and with a certain frequency would conduct raids on their neighbors as well. Though many achieved great wealth and oftimes the subjugation of tribes within a large area, the action of raiding warfare followed the broad basic strategy as the same raids seen in pre-iron cultures the world over. The specific intent was usually to steal cattle, food, or even land, and a side benefit was the taking of captives both male and female for use as slaves. A number of the most physically fit members of the tribe would attack either isolated members of the opposing tribe or attack at a time when the population would not be able to mount a counter attack. Should they find themselves confronted with serious resistance, the raid would be abandoned. If the tribes were of relatively equal strength or size, each raid would in time lead to a reprisal raid. Deaths were not planned, but were hardly unknown. The most isolated tribes still retain some aspects of this raiding warfare style to this day, especially where grazing land is scarce due to the thickness of flora or paucity of arable land.

Weapons were universally spears, knives, axes, and clubs. It is interesting to note that Sub-Saharan Africa never went through a bronze age, their first metal for tools being iron, usually of exceptional quality. Iron (and then steel) full length swords were introduced very early on in those areas in the north and east that had trade contact with the Middle East and the Mediterranean (Sudan being the best example), but the trend didn't extend into the south, center, or west of the continent. An exception is the Masai, who have beautiful elongated leaf-shaped blades on simple handles with no guards. But then again these nomads of Kenya originated in Sudan, and brought their technology with them.

Much of Northern Africa maintained extensive trade with the Middle East, India, and China, so a variety of weapons are found amoung these post-Carthage, post-Pharaohic kingdoms. As several had access to and bred exceptional stocks of horses, many also adapted fighting with lance and archery from horseback.

Attempts to include regional differences in weaponry when mounting a show is laudable, but can be very difficult, for the vast majority of weapons that are in museums have turned out to be purely ceremonial or were constructed for trade between tribes, so either way were never intended for battle. For example, the vast collection of "throwing" knives that intrigued the European explorers of the 19th century have turned out to have been either used as currency or were hacking tools, never thrown. The exception is among certain tribes in the Congo, especially around Zaire (most strikingly the Zande tribe) and southern Sudan, where knives were thrown, and it seems only for two distinct purposes:

1] As the Saharan warriors often had horses and lances, the large throwing knives, thrown frisbee-like rather than overhand, would have been an extremely effective weapon against a mounted combatant, better than a thrown spear. It is certainly possible that the throwing knives were developed near the Saharan border and then the practice migrated south.

2] Be that as it may, for the tribes of the Kongo kingdom (modern Zaire) these weapons were part of their ritual warfare. When fighting against other non-horsed tribes, the throwing knifes and spears were used on behalf of the chief for their set-piece battles, never for raiding. The defense against the missiles consisted of using a very large wicker shield to deflect the higher missiles and very athletic leaps if the knives were thrown low. Many of these moves survive in their traditional battle dances.

The great generalization can be made that the areas of savanna and desert tend to have nomadic herders, while the tribes dwelling in jungle and woodland tended towards agriculture. The herders tended toward more practical weapons, while the farmers/gatherers tended to the more ceremonial and ornate. But throughout, there are few weapons that can be described as swords. Shorter edged weapons were definitely daggers, and the longer pieces were more like impaling or puncturing weapons and are akin to short pikes. These are also seen with greater frequency among the cattle herding tribes of central Africa.

The countries with direct access to the Mediterranean and to the Red Sea had the edged sword very early on, often purchasing full length blades from Middle Eastern manufacturers and then fitting their own hilts, but based on existing European and Arabian layouts. What we would consider single hand medieval broadswords were in common use throughout Northern Africa, and indeed were more common than curved blades. Curved weapons, however, were usually much more exaggerated than Arab designs, with many interesting shapes and more severe curvatures in the blades.

Of special interest to fight choreographers is that Sudanese nomads often wore an arm dagger, strapped to the left forearm with the blade tip at the elbow. From that placement we can assume that the knife was pulled and used by the right hand in a standard overhand grip. From this we must also deduce that it was a defensive tool, a weapon of last resort.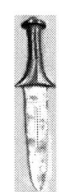

In areas where cattle were raised in larger numbers, raiding existed along with "primitive" warfare. From time immemorial, the essential pattern of warfare in the South African region was a ritualized affair, either as an escalation of several raids or as a result of insults, perceived or otherwise. For these larger set-piece battles, warriors consisted of virtually the entire tribal population, meeting at opposite ends of a prearranged field. The bravest male contingencies from both sides would stand in the front lines, hurling occasional spears and a constant shower of verbal invective. Bravery was proven by standing in the middle of the spear and arrow landing zone and evading the projectiles at the last moment. If anyone's arrow or spear actually killed someone, the fighter who threw the spear would immediately withdraw from the battlefield and perform a purification ritual. Most of the spears could be safely evaded, and after a time one side would seem to have demonstrated more martial spirit, intimidating the other side into submission. For the most part these were civilized and quite bloodless affairs. Thus it might have remained were it not for one brilliant and ruthless ruler.

Shaka Zulu was born an illegitimate and early on was cast out with his mother to a neighboring tribe. Once he began military training he convinced the chief to allow him to lead one small band of warriors in a training program of his own devising. Every aspect of tactics, strategy and materials was overhauled. The thin sandals, which he felt gave poor footing, were discarded and his warriors went barefoot. The spear was reduced to four feet long, but now fitted with a heavy foot-long cutting head.

The shield was given a new pointed elliptical shape. His warriors were also specifically drilled in conditioning exercises as well as detailed martial arts training.

The first battle with his new army was a terrifying spectacle. Shaka's troops charged the opposing force, ignoring the few spears which were thrown at them and holding onto [not throwing] their own. As soon as they reached the front line, they used the points of their shields to scoop up the shields of their opponents, exposing the lower torso, into which was thrust the heavy tip of the new spear, instantly disemboweling the enemy. (The new spears were named "iklwa" - an approximation of the sound made when thrusting and pulling it out of the enemy's body) The destruction of the enemy was total, as was the terror of the survivors who fled the field.

Shaka went on to become a general of his adoptive tribe, then conqueror and chief of his birth tribe, and finally emperor of the vast area known as Zululand. During his reign from 1816 to 1828, his enemies tried to adapt to the new battle style, but he adapted faster. Turning his attention from tactics to strategy, he developed a battle formation of a central powerful line supported by two faster moving wings, which he referred to as the "horns of the bull". The horns were used to control the movement of the enemy, and then finally crush the opposing army in what was known in Europe as a pincer movement.

As Shaka increased in power so did his ruthlessness and his insistence on absolute discipline. To make sure that his warriors had toughened the soles of their feet sufficiently, he tested them by having them dance barefoot in a kraal covered with nettles. Any soldier who so much as flinched was instantly killed with a spear.

One can only guess as to what might have been the future of the region had not the English arrived in force in the late 1800's. Perhaps the creation of another Rome or China. But the rapid fire machine guns and accurate rifles of the Europeans soon led to the destruction of Zulu control of their empire, though not before giving the English their worst fear of their sub-Saharan campaign.

By the time Europeans began carving up the continent to secure slaves, diamonds and gold, native resistance throughout Africa followed a familiar pattern. Most insurgents, although large in number, fought with spear and sword. Although possessing a fair number of trade rifles, the quality of the firearms sold to natives was usually at least one generation behind whatever the invading Europeans were using. Spare parts were nonexistent as were quality gunpowder and bullets. Many native contingents never mastered firing from the shoulder, preferring to fire from the hip or from outstretched arms to avoid painful recoil, but this also meant that shots rarely found their mark. Their most successful tactic was usually the massed infantry charge, but even when fully armed with modern repeating rifles and capable of implementing sophisticated tactics, they were no match against cannon, artillery and machine guns.

North American Indigenous Cultures

<u>Politics/Economics</u> – Speaking of course in generalizations and outrageous simplification, societal structure was chieftain tribal, meaning that the leadership of the group was by a respected elder with the tacit approval of the majority of tribal members. These chieftains were not necessarily warriors, for the primary decisions of leadership were in coordinating hunting and communal activities as well as mediating in intratribal disputes. Chiefs did not hold an office in the political sense; instead they were valued for the practical knowledge and advice that they could dispense which could keep the tribe prosperous and safe. Achieving chieftain status was neither by election, power struggle, nor heredity. One simply and slowly "became" chief as tribal members developed trust in that

man's ability to show wisdom in making decisions. Religious duties were often guided by other specialists ("medicine men", "shamans"), but these would rarely have any more or less say in tribal decisions than any other member.

There was no separation of the religious and the profane, and there was no concept of private ownership of land, whether by an individual nor by a tribe nor country. These values were so diametrically the opposite of those of the European settlers that it would lead again and again to misunderstandings and mistreatment.

Although each tribe would understand that its own members came from a common set of ancestors, there did also exist larger confederations of similar linguistically bound tribes. These "nations" rarely had any real cohesion besides limited alliances for a specific purpose, such as the defense against other nonaffiliated tribes or nations, or in settling intertribal conflicts. Trade between all groups was common, and led to widely understood sign languages covering huge areas.

Warfare –   The technological sophistication in pre-colonial America was similar to that of pre-colonial African nations, and as expected weapons development was roughly the same. But there were two key differences. The bow and arrow were nearly nonexistent in sub-Saharan Africa, while in the Americas its use was widespread. The bow was relatively weak, but after the introduction of the Spanish horse, the plains tribes' warriors learned to accurately shoot while in full gallop. This delivery system meant that the effective range of the arrow could be greatly extended.

The more important difference was the lack of domestic metal production. The few cultures that produced copper in any quantity did not (with two minor exceptions) fabricate effective weapons with them, and so remained essentially in the Stone Age. By the early nineteenth century most tribes had embraced the weaponry and tools of the white settlers, incorporating steel and rifles to their traditional stone implements. But as they did not have access to the means of production for these machines, trade with the encroaching settlers was always necessary to repair and reload their firearms.

The spear was found in all areas, and after the introduction of the horse by Europeans it became the lance, the difference being that a spear is thrown but a lance is held during a charge from horseback. By far the most common weapon was the small ax and club, at first in stone and later in iron. The method of battle for the most part was based on the techniques of raiding, and in some areas this was mixed with elements of ritualized warfare. This would lead to the destruction of the Native American civilizations in less than 200 years of contact with the Europeans.

In North America, the pattern of colonial European advance, native response, and European follow-up was repeated over and over again in the rapid progression from east to west. As settlers encroached on favored lands, Indian tribes would respond the way they always had - a raid. An isolated group of the enemy would be attacked by a raiding party, some members would be taken captive, a house might be burned down, and on occasion a male enemy might be killed. To the natives, this was the civilized way to handle the dispute. It would normally have been enough to have the enemy either move on or, worst case, a reprisal raid could be expected. They never imagined that the retaliation would be a wave of soldiers intent on obliterating every individual in the offending tribe.

By the time the expansion reached the Great Plains, the settlers came across warriors who were mounted and well armed with rifles, but the pattern remained the same. Finally, by the late 1800's, many of these tribes attempted direct confrontation with the army bent on their destruction. The US soldiers, trained in Western warfare, used the same tactics developed in European wars, while for the most part the native warriors continued with their traditional methods. Although many native chiefs would develop elaborate battlefield strategies, on the day of battle nothing could prevent the individual warriors from ignoring the plan and breaking ranks in order to "count coup".

Counting coup was how a warrior would prove his bravery in battle. It was the act of running or riding up to an opponent and striking him, and then returning back to your comrades. Killing or even hurting the opponent was not necessary to count coup (in fact, killing was of much less value than striking in terms of building a warrior's reputation within the tribe) and this corresponds to an ancient style of ritual warfare which provided honor to the combatants without devastating the population. Unfortunately, it proved to be an inadequate tactic when dealing with a modern army.

The US Army mounted cavalry quickly learned that the tribal warrior's skill in fighting one-on-one was at par with his excellent horsemanship. Plains Indians in particular learned how to ride as soon as they could walk, and a warrior could fire rifle or arrow from full gallop with accuracy. Some tribes, most notably the Apache, discarded counting coup completely and attacked to kill, becoming superb guerrilla fighters. But even then the warrior's fighting style was always intrinsically individualistic. And even when they were able to achieve victories, they were ultimately doomed to lose to an enemy that had unlimited resources and could attack their food supply and noncombatants with impunity.

<u>Weapons available</u> –   Certainly the bow and arrow, which before the introduction of the horse was truly a longbow. The spear also made the transition to lance for the same reason. A small axe (tomahawk) and large knife. The tribes of the Eastern coast used a war club, as most of their fighting was in heavily wooded areas and on foot. Flintlock muskets were available to them from the earliest contact with Europeans, whereas out West and in the plains areas, the tribes went from bow and arrow to lever-action repeating rifle in one step.

Meso and Southern American Empires
Mayans, Aztecs, and Incas

It is grossly unfair to lump these three empires together, separated as they were by time and geography. But they are distinct from other native North American cultures, in that these all had centralized governments led by emperors considered to be divine with assistance from a well developed hereditary bureaucracy. Wealth to maintain power came both from agricultural production and tribute from both allied and conquered lesser kingdoms. Dominion was periodically reestablished by use of large scale raiding wars.

In studying them as warriors they show remarkable similarities as well. All three great empires used no metal weapons nor ever developed the wheel into a method of transportation. This is especially surprising for the Incas, as they were expert in all aspects of metal working, save that of iron.

Raiding wars within these cultures were driven by ritual. Only worthy warriors would engage in battle, and the object was to take live prisoners of as high rank as possible. The captives were not returned after payment of ransom, as a matter of fact they were not returned at all. We know from Aztec documentation that the captives were feted and honored by their captors for several days, even referred to as "son", and the village would make a public show of mourning their soon-to-be deaths. The majority of the captives were sacrificed outright in a ceremony that theatrically created an idealized version of the submission and destruction of the enemy. Captive warriors of high rank would be subjected to a ritual of gladiatorial combat, tied to a central disk and given blunted clubs, fighting against heavily armored warriors using sharpened weapons. To die in such a manner was considered by both victor and victim to be highly honorable.

On the battlefield, set-piece battles would start with archers and slingers showering missiles into the enemy, containing the movement of the enemy to prevent encirclement. The elite warriors would fight in the center with spears or clubs meant to break a man's leg or knock him unconscious so he could be taken away as a captive. The most feared weapon, used by both the Mayans and the Aztecs, was the *macuahuitl*, a wooden club lined on both edges with obsidian. Such a weapon combined the attributes of both battle ax and broadsword, and accounts from the Conquistadors describe warriors cleaving horses in two with a single stroke of this sword/club. Unfortunately, no macuahuitl survives.

Use of a wooden shield strapped to the forearm was common. Only the victors would be allowed to keep the captives after the fight. Any captives taken by the losing side were immediately released. The destruction of an opposing tribe was never the intention of battle, although a great many warriors might die. Once a battle was won, the vanquished would return to their village or city, and the specifics of tribute payment would be worked out by emissaries. None of this prevented many battles from being bloody affairs.

It is very easy to ascribe the downfall of the Aztecs and Inca to the Spanish superiority of weapons, armor, and horses. In truth, the Spanish were even more assisted by the virulence of European bacteria, the treachery of local client kingdoms against their overlords, and the unwillingness of the warriors to simply overwhelm the Spanish with shear numbers or fight with the intent of killing. In the one battle in which the Aztecs did change their tactics and fought to kill, the Spaniards quickly lost and were nearly wiped out. If the Aztecs had fought for only one more day using the same methods, the later history of Mesoamerica might be completely different.

Weapons available –   Aztec and Mayan - Spears with heads made of hard stone, especially obsidian, or wooden heads lined with obsidian. Macuahuitl, single or double-hand. Slings, bows and arrows. No metal weapons used for battle.

Incas - No true spear, but a long dart launched with the aid of a spear thrower. Stones thrown by hand. Wooden and composite maces. T-shaped stone axe-head lashed onto a wooden shaft, wielded much like a battle-ax or halberd.

Among the tropical forest tribes outside of the influence of empires, simple spears, usually thrown, and sharpened stone club/daggers. Also what the Spanish would term the *macana*, a double-edged, single handed hardwood club found from the Caribbean to the Amazon headwaters. The blowgun, common among Amazon River basin tribes, could shoot out a poison-tipped dart with accuracy to about 30 to 60 feet, but these were hunting instruments, not used in warfare. The amount of poison on the dart would be enough to kill a bird or small monkey, but hardly sufficient to slow down a human.

Polynesia

The varied cultures of the South Pacific islands were for the most part tribal/chieftain with some attaining the complexity of hereditary kingship. Warfare was generally raiding or cyclical retaliation and for some developed into ritual as the primary purpose. What they all had in common was a near absence of metal. With bone, stone, and hardwood being the only hard materials available, weapons were almost universally spears, knives and clubs.

By the 1500's invasions from India brought metal to most of the South Sea islands, so traditional forms were maintained but with steel blades. Many are still worn by non-governmental fighters, who often will wear a traditional knife tucked into their sash or belt while carrying an AK-47.

Possibly because of the dense vegetation growth in most of the Pacific Islands, warfare involved fewer participants than let's say in Southern Africa, where spears could be thrown at just in-range distance between what was in essence the entire assembled male population. Instead, battles for Polynesians were made up of individual combat with held spears and sharpened war clubs. The intent was to kill, not capture.

In the Hawaiian archipelago there existed a complex social/political structure based on hereditary class divisions. Beneath the king (mo'i) and his immediate advisors were the lords (ali'i). All below this level were required to bow or even prostrate themselves in the presence of the ali'i, and not even allow their shadows to land on an ali'i. Ali'i were attended by servants at all times. Beneath them were the kahuna, the highly skilled craftsmen and priests, and below them in turn were the vast majority of people, the common workers (maka'ainana). A very small group of outcasts also existed, the kauwa. All positions were determined by heredity.

Taxes were paid yearly, and the ali'i or the mo'i could call everyone to fight in wars. Just as in the rest of Polynesia, battles were close-in and brutal, although Hawaiians did developed a sling for rock throwing. The common weapons were the stone club, axe, spear, and dagger, some lined with shark's teeth, just as in the rest of the South Sea islands. The Hawaiians did have one unique weapon, however: a weight tied to a length of rope, thrown at an opponent's legs in order to trip them.

In order to maintain battle readiness, all members of society were encouraged to practice and compete in a wide variety of sports that would have been commonly seen at the ancient or modern Olympics, including wrestling, javelin toss, sprinting, and boxing. Many also practiced an indigenous martial arts system known as lua, mostly taught in private to select warriors. From all of this and from local oral history we can deduce that Hawaiian warfare combined a brief but effective initial use of thrown projectiles that supported primarily close-in, brutal, hand-to-hand fighting.

Asia

Ancient India

The Asian subcontinent has had an amazing history of repeated invasions and a staggering array of weapons development - most of which I'm going to ignore due to the practical limitations of this book.

I will mention that due to the waves of invaders that periodically swept in from both Persia and from the Asian steppes, India was exposed to every type of weapon and fighting style that existed in the rest of the world. Each new weapon was incorporated into the local fighting traditions, and then improved upon. And once the spread of Buddhism moved northward, the unarmed and sword fighting styles of India traveled along with it. Thus the development of karate, judo, bushido, kung-fu, kendo tae-kwon-do; in a word all Asian fighting styles had their genesis in India.

Traditional Hindu society has, since possibly 2000 BC, been divided into four classes or castes:

Brahmins - priests and religious teachers
Ksatriyas - kings, warriors, aristocrats
Vaisyas - merchants and professional trades
Sudras - laborers, servants, field workers

As such, it was only among the Ksatriyas who trained for and fought in the innumerable wars and conflicts of the subcontinent. In 1463, a new monotheistic religion - Sihkism - was created in the Punjab. Sihks broke completely with the past, denouncing the caste system as immoral.

As soon as the sword was introduced into any area of India, it became the primary weapon of battle from that point forward. The earliest sword (seen from at least 100 AD) was the straight-edged two handed broadsword, later joined by a short curved sword with a cutting edge on the inside curve somewhat like the kukri, around 400 AD. Except for the spear, no other weapons are seen until contact is made with invading Persian and Mongol armies in the late thirteenth century. By the 500's, a huge variety of weapons were absorbed and made Indian. Interestingly, the swords, whether straight or curved, were always fought as exclusively cutting weapons, thrusting being restricted to daggers and spears. Ksatriya took great pride in their sword training that emphasized cutting and evading, rarely using the sword to block. As such, the blade could be made thinner and sharper than European counterparts.

<u>Weapons available</u> –

There are precious few opportunities for American actors to work with a show using a traditional Indian setting, but on rare occasions a Shakespeare company will perform a "Bollywood" Romeo and Juliet. So on the off-chance that you might be involved in such a production, here are some of the weapons you might encounter:

Swords and daggers - no thin-bladed dueling rapiers, but a wide range of straight and curved swords of war. Most were used in single hand mode, often in conjunction with a shield or buckler. A peculiar variant from one Hindi princedom was the *pata* [gauntlet-sword], something like a very long punch-dagger [the *katar*, also from India]. The pata, although straight edged and seemingly perfect for thrusting, was used as a full arm swinging cutting weapon, especially effective from horseback. The Talwar is the most popular sword of India, with a curved blade of Persia on a distinctively shaped small grip. Curved blades came into widespread use throughout India during the sixteenth century. Many Americans are confused by the scabbards of Indian swords, which are seen with either two rings or one. The two ring styles are meant to hang from a belt in European fashion, and are generally for mounted cavalry. The single ring scabbard is meant to be tucked into a waist fabric sash, the single ring fastened onto a hidden hook for security. Daggers, with exception of the katar, seem to be directly copied from Persian styles.

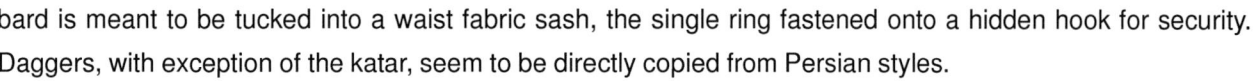

Spears/maces/axes - Anything found in medieval Europe was also found in India, but the construction tended to be much lighter. Since they generally used less wood and more steel for the shafts, they also tended to be more durable. Maces often had sword hilts for hand protection, something no European ever thought of. (A creative theatrical production might even throw in an *ankus*, the elephant hook used by the mahout. These are often included in British compendiums of Indian weapons, although there is no evidence that they were ever used that way.)

Quoits - Specifically a Sihk weapon, these flat rings of steel had razor-sharp edges and were thrown like Frisbees. Although the iconography seems to shows the quoits being spun on the index finger before being thrown, such a launch would provide very little distance. There is no indication that they were especially effective as battlefield weapons.

Siam (Thailand)

It is difficult to find much information on true Siamese weapons. Most of the pieces picked up by British travelers during the 19th century were produced specifically for what was then the "tourist trade", and Western museums were not very diligent in researching the provenance or the items they acquired. In addition, modern Thai practitioners of Muay Thai enjoy promulgating a rich sword history in their ancient and regal past, were none really seems to have existed. That all males were expected to join in battle was certainly true, and Siam did not have a standing army. Martial arts training was extensive, both unarmed and with quarterstaff and short bamboo "swords", but the metal weapons themselves were limited in number and in style.

The weapons of Siam were for the most part directly borrowed from the Indian subcontinent, but as they did not have much access to quality iron were usually limited in quantity. The very high humidity also meant that rust was a constant problem. Spears were the most important weapon, as spear heads can be made very thick and do not need to be tempered, so were always the first choice for practical weapons that would survive for many years.

Straight edged short swords could also be made with thick blades, thus getting around some of the rust, and tempering weakness of longer Indian swords. Blades were usually straight, or no more than slightly curved, and the overall sword was about two feet long. Hilts were small, usually no more than 4 to 6 inches across or just a simple disk of also 4 " in diameter.

One interesting note is that the Siamese did produce a curved sword of about three feet in length. Due to poor materials and bad tempering skills, the swords were quite inferior in warfare. Very weak and prone to sudden bending and breaking in battle, the form of the sword still showed excellent design attributes. It was later adopted by the Japanese and became the samurai katana, perhaps the finest sword ever produced.

China

Once again, a hugely important region historically and politically that will be getting painfully short shrift here. Although the unbroken written history of China goes back to 2000 BC (and distinct and complex civilizations are in evidence all the way back to 7000 BC), we are merely going to show the historical development of weaponry up to the Qing Dynasty at the turn of the century.

1700 BC - bows and arrows, spears, short knives, and the *ge*, a short spiked dagger blade mounted at right angles to a staff. The weapon heads were jade and other hard minerals, bronze coming later in the period.

800 BC - exposure to nomadic raiding trips of the Central steppe (Middle Eastern) raiding tribes (attacking with chariots). Therefore Chinese tribes went immediately from foot warriors using short utilitarian bronze knives (but of high quality) to horsemanship and the bronze sword. Sword lengths were still quite short, about 14 to 18 inches long, double-edged and slightly leaf shaped or simply straight edged. Therefore, the sword could not have been used while the fighter was mounted. Instead, the horse was used to move the warrior quickly into the field of battle, at which point he would dismount to fight. Chariots, too, were used primarily for quick transport, not as a fighting platform.

By 300 BC, the sword length had increased to over three feet in length. Certainly by this time the sword was used by both mounted cavalry and infantry, for the size of the standing army had increased to allow for differentiation of duties. Unlike Western swords of the same period, these full length singlehand bronze swords - *jian* - were of excellent quality. Although the Chinese by this time were fully capable of producing iron, they felt no need to do so.

200 BC - unification of China - a sudden jump from bronze to steel, by-passing iron, in sword making. Sword blades now could be made just as long, but lighter and stronger than bronze. In response to repeated nomadic invasions, the army was now composed of diverse specialized units. Foot soldiers were used primarily for defense. The heavy infantry was used for close fighting (using primarily the *ge*) and masses of light infantry firing crossbows or bow and arrow, but in primarily a defensive role. The primary threat (and final defeat) was from nomadic cavalry (using composite bow, lance, and sword) always fighting while mounted. As such, heavy cavalry (armed with *ge*, swords), light cavalry (with sword and crossbow) became the primary offensive arms. For both the light infantry and light cavalry, crossbows were preferred over simple bows, as they had a longer range than did the simple bows of the invaders. Chariots continued to be used, and were expanded from their role of mere delivery vehicles to a variety of uses, including mobile fighting platforms.

500 AD - introduction of curved sword from Turkmenistan. From then on it - called the *dao* - is used along with the straight sword.

618 to 907 AD - Tang Dynasty - The dao becomes standard for cavalry, jian for infantry. Tang dynasty is at a golden age - the height of empire in which Chinese weaponry, language, written characters, culture, religion spread out rather than continue to borrow from others. Here is also where improvements in steel manufacturing enabled the production of very high quality weapons. Periodic conscription of soldiers for a three year tour of duty is discontinued in favor of a professional permanent force for the standing army. A turn as well away from feudalism to a centralized Confucian bureaucracy. From this point forward, all of those that would conquer China would leave intact the massive bureaucracy necessary to run it, and in the process adopt the ways and culture of classical China of the Tang.

908 to 1644 AD. While this period includes the Ming Dynasty, for our purposes I only will note that the sword becomes relegated to a ceremonial position, and became rarely used in battle, supplanted by the halberd. Most serious fighting strategy revolved around the lance and bow and arrow. To take better use of the halberd and pike bearing heavy infantry, the battlefield formation known as the phalanx was used. The sword in China begins its long descent to a weapon of romance and legend.

1368 to 1911 AD - Qing Dynasty, although we know it better as the period of Manchu rule. These Mongolian invaders did impose some elements of Manchurian dress and tradition (especially the distinctive pigtail) on China, although after a time they too adopted traditional Chinese language and culture, and the same military format. The standard sword was a rather short, straight edged sword, much like the archers sword of medieval Europe - not considered during military planning, but still issued as a weapon of last resort. But while the sword was rarely used in combat, there was a large production of them for export as well as non-military purchase within the country. These swords differed substantially from the swords of earlier eras in that they tended to be more fanciful and of poorer quality. As they were untested in battle it didn't matter much, but the styles still survive in what around the world are now considered traditional Chinese weapons. Especially distinctive are the butterfly knives, paired swords, exaggerated dao shapes and fanciful halberd shapes. These forms have become popular among modern practitioners of Chinese martial arts. Although not used by the standing army, they do have an important role in one moment in history - The Boxer Rebellion.

In 1900, China was on the verge of being completely dominated by foreign powers. A series of attacks against Europeans living in China by peasants escalated into a full anti-imperialist rebellion, aided by the tacit approval of the Empress and by the direct military support of the Chinese Army. The rebels called themselves the "Fists of Righteous and Harmonious Society Movement", which the English simplified to "Boxers". Boxers believed in using only traditional weapons, especially spears and halberds, although they certainly did nothing to dissuade the Chinese army from using rifles and artillery against the "foreign devils". While the rebellion lasted nearly two years, it only lasted that long because resupplying the colonial troops proved difficult. Once in place, the combined foreign powers put down the Boxer rebellion rather easily.

At the end of the rebellion, the Qing empress had lost any real power. Dissatisfaction against the minority rule of the Manchu led to the creation of the Republic of China. Militarily, all vestiges of traditional weapons disappeared as the warlords in command of each warring faction procured the latest weaponry of the period.

Japan

While it is fairly common for many Shakespeare plays to be set in a generic "Medieval Japan", it is important to know that the civilization developed slowly.

We forget (and many modern Japanese choose to ignore) that the people we think of as culturally and distinct Japanese were not the original inhabitants of the islands. During the Kofun Period (aprox 300-700 AD) and Nara Period (aprox 700-794) various clans that had migrated from the Korean peninsula and from the Chinese mainland slowly grew in power. These warlike chieftain-led clans brought with them the cultural influences of China, along with iron swords, armor, and war horses. They began in the southern islands and moved slowly northward, and in doing so subjugating or eliminating the aboriginal inhabitants, the Ainu. By the Nara period, a common overlord was recognized as emperor. The swords were single edged and straight, with simple wooden or bone handles and blade lengths of anywhere from 12 to 30 inches.

The Heian Period (794-1184) saw the rise of the powerful monasteries and development of the locally produced artifacts. Although still influenced by China, life in court, literature, art, and fashion began to become distinctly Japanese. Although ancient tribes still continued to exist as they always had, fishing, growing rice, and occasionally raiding each other under small-time warlords, class divisions began to harden. Slowly, the military guards and mounted warlords became what would be known as the samurai, or aristocracy. The warrior-priests used both swords and polearms, and generally had better martial training than did the common warrior, who had access to nothing more sophisticated than spears and farm implements. While most wealthy warlords might have a straight-edged Chinese sword, many were switching to the local curved sword. The transition from straight to curved took place slowly, beginning at first with a straight blade with merely a sudden curve at the hilt. The sword during this period seems to have been used only by the mounted warlord, therefore worn as a *tachi*, with the blade edge down. In this position, the sword is less likely to fall out of a scabbard while the warrior is galloping across a field. Other auxiliary swords and daggers might also be worn, tucked into the obi, or waist belt. One dagger in particular was the *metezashi*, worn on the right side with edge leading and the handle pointing straight up. It was grasped by right hand in an underhand grip, so that the blade could rise up in one motion to cut a combatant's throat or slice up underneath the side of his armor.

But far more important militarily than the sword was the bow, for this was the weapon that, fired from horseback, could do the most damage to opponents before closing with the sword. What battlefield strategy there was was still based loosely on early Chinese models, but centuries of fighting only other warlords meant that most battles were massed episodes of largely single combat. It also included the Chinese practice of often deciding victory by counting the decapitated heads of combatants. It must be noted that the Japanese gave this custom their own twist. A special sword, shorter than the tachi, was used for the job of beheading the dead. Each warrior took great care that his own hair and skin be carefully tended and perfumed so as to present a worthy head if so taken in battle.

Kamakura Period (1185-1331) Just as in Europe, feudalism replaced tribalism. A powerful central commanding emperor used his more powerful warriors as tax collectors, and these same warriors soon carved up the islands forming their own fiefdoms. The construction of swords dramatically improved, finally achieving the graceful even curve of the *katana*. It is here that the permanent warrior class is effectively cemented into society, and along with it the nascent warrior code. The term "bushido" means "way of the warrior", but also translates from an earlier form of Japanese to "way of the horse and bow".

The country enjoyed relatively peaceful times internally. Samurai were legally required to practice martial arts, and laws were passed removing the right of any but samurai to wear the *tachi*, although other swords were still permissible. Due to the strength of a strong central shogun, there was a certain internal stability that would have limited further military advances. So it was an exterior threat that changed martial practice. Although the two great Mongol invasions (in 1274 and 1281) were both successfully repulsed, the success was due more to timely storms rather than excellent strategy. Indeed, the Japanese saw for the first time such innovations as regiments drilled in battle formations, encirclements, firing volley of arrows from infantry bowmen rather than on horseback. The samurai realized that their accustomed way of approaching battle, with shouts and challenges followed by a headlong rush on horseback into what was really a mass of single combat, was obsolete. The Japanese had fought as brave warriors: the Mongols fought as a disciplined army.

By the end of the period, Japanese warfare moved away from light raiding tactics utilizing what was primarily light cavalry. Instead, the samurai transformed themselves into a mix of heavy infantry and heavy cavalry, using spears and poleweapons in organized formations. The bow was reduced to a subsidiary role, and the sword was now the primary weapon for combat, but on ground, not from horseback. As such, the sword is worn edge up, allowing for an easy draw.

Muromachi Period (1332-1573) A period of almost unending battles between the various feudal lords. Also the time of the finest sword blade manufacture and the full development of every variety of polearm. Primary weapon for the mounted samurai remained the spear, while fighting on the ground was best performed while wielding a new sword - the *seoi tachi*. With a blade length of 40 inches or more, it was often slung on the back until drawn for battle. The scabbard was most often disposable, made of cheap bamboo, straw, or even simply paper.

Peasants were the vast majority of the foot soldiers, using the polearms in order to take a battlefield or cut down approaching cavalry. Although their function was critical to military success, during the first half of this period they were still expected to do agricultural work when not engaged in battle. Known as Ashigaru, these were conscripts armed with a long spear as the primary weapon, and a mass-produced sword (quite inferior compared to the katana and tachi of the samurai) as a close-in weapon. Ashigaru had limited training, and were specifically told not to attempt the moves they might observe from the samurai, but to sweep at the legs of the enemy.

Life for the samurai became more dangerous. Intrigue and direct attacks were a constant threat. The wearing of two swords, the full length katana and the shorter wakizashi, became fashionable to wear when out of doors, but it was the wakizashi that became the constant companion during every hour of the day. The wakizashi was worn when eating, at meditation, when in private with his family, and was even by his side when bathing or sleeping.

This was also the time when many of the practices and arts associated with the study of Zen had their inception. The tea ceremony, Noh theatre, flower arranging, landscape gardening, sumi-e painting, swordsmanship - all were practiced not with the intent of the activity itself, but to achieve spiritual enlightenment. The very end of this time also marks the first contact with Europeans (Portuguese and Spaniards)

Momoyama Period (1574-1602) The very end of the Age of the Warring Land also brought about the highest development of all of the arts, as the country became unified under Oda Nobuaga. Weapons in this period are expected to be perfect - strong, flexible, light, and beautiful. The prior Portuguese contact also led to musket development - revolutionizing warfare. At the end of this period, ashigaru (foot soldiers) were recognized as being of samurai status rather than merely peasants. In 1588 the shogun (overlord) enacted the first of two ordinances that were to have a huge influence on the definition of a samurai. The first was the 'Sword Hunt', by which all weapons were confiscated from the peasantry and placed in the hands of the daimyô (warlords) and their increasingly professional armies. The Separation Edict, which followed in 1591, completed the process. The peasants had been disarmed, and there was now to be a total separation between the military function and the agricultural function on pain of death or banishment. Thus ended the possibility of peasants joining an army to rise in social rank, and firmly established the ashigaru as permanent standing armies.

Tokugawa Period (1603-1867) Also known as the Edo Period. A long period of stability both politically and socially, a time almost without war. The class system became firmly entrenched and rigid. As usual, the warriors were at the highest level. But unlike other societies, the peasants were at the next highest rank, as it was recognized that they produced the food, therefore the wealth, on which all of the others depended. Below them were the artisans, who created things of value and beauty but only from the raw materials that others had produced. Lowest in rank and virtually disdained by all were the merchants, who were thought to be necessary in order to move products around the country, but produced nothing of value themselves.

Ironically, it was the merchants who benefited most from the strict separation, at least materially. The towns that grew near the protection of fortified castles slowly gained the most wealth, and the merchants had little competition and could operate in greater safety. Several became extremely wealthy by providing loans to samurai families.

Politically, the country was under strict totalitarian Shogun control. This was accomplished by the complete isolation of the islands from Westerners, and the near hostage situation of the various daimyôs' families, as well as the emperor himself, residing at Edo, the Emperor's capital city (later known as Tokyo). In what is called the Alternate Attendance System, every one of the 264 daimyô had to live every other year in Edo, and his principle wife and his first born son had to reside there permanently. This ushered in a number of momentous changes in Japan. First, it quickly pacified the previously contentious samurai class. Secondly, it also transferred huge amounts of wealth to the capitol city. Lastly, and unexpectedly, it meant that by the 18th century, every daimyô had been born and raised in Edo, felt himself to be a native of that city, and began to look with disdain at those denizens of the far flung castles.

With all of these disruptions and the slow loss of true power, it was natural that most of the country began turning ever towards nostalgia and romanticizing of samurai traditions. The Japanese literature for the samurai composed "Arthurian/fairy tale" views of medieval warriors, while their actual battlefield skills began to diminish. Most everything that Westerners recognize as being "samurai" is from this period. Sadly, most modern Japanese share the same view. The iconography of the sword (the way of the sword as being identical with *bushido*, the way of the warrior) springs from this era. It is the time of the great swordsmen and schools of swordplay. It also is the time of many samurai being displaced, in effect "fired" from their employment under the daimyô as financial resources shift from maintaining battle readiness at their family castles to maintaining the social position of their families at Edo. Large numbers of these former warriors became *ronin,* masterless samurai. But whereas in the past they could simply be hired by other daimyô, these ronin had few opportunities for gainful employment, and many became thieves. The warriors in the film *The Seven Samurai* are all ronin, and it is possible to view the thief in *Roshamon* as being one as well.

Meiji Restoration (1868-1945). A return to a centralized monarchy, away from the power of the Shogun. This was in large measure a direct response to foreign contact, specifically the threat of American domination. It also ushered in intense modernization and industrialization in a successful attempt to leap into the European twentieth century. By the turn of the century Japan was recognized as one of a dozen world powers. This was aided by the disarming of the samurai, and then the complete dismantling of the feudal system. The samurai attitudes and culture remained strong, and were especially promoted within the military, which in itself was no small feat considering that the modern military required conscripting large numbers of soldiers from the peasant and merchant class. Liberalism and individualism grew along with the economy.

Post-War Japan (1945 - present). An imposed shift to a constitutional and democratic republic, followed by a rapid development as an economic and technological powerhouse. Samurai and bushido fade to legend and fable.

Ok, that was the history lesson.

Fashion/Manners – The code of Bushido is described as being of "willingness". Generally it means a willingness to serve others in a way appropriate to one's station as a warrior. But bushido also was supposed to provide a template of actions off of the battlefield and even in private. A budo [warrior] was to be unflinchingly stoic in the face of pain or danger, demonstrate an unswerving loyalty to his superior, and of course to be expert in all matters military. By the time of the Momoyama Period, budo were also supposed to have not merely an appreciation of the arts, but also demonstrate a proficiency in at least some art forms [painting, music] and be fully versed in all cultural ceremonies and etiquette. Indeed, making a mistake in a social activity such as the service of tea was considered not just ignorant but deliberately insulting.

Westerners are intrigued by one aspect in particular of bushido that we call "harry carry". What we are mispronouncing is *hara kiri,* which specifically means belly cutting, and is only one aspect of *seppuku* - the act of "noble" suicide by one's own hand. *Seppuku* did not necessarily have to lead to death, although the performer of the act should have had no expectation of surviving. *Seppuku* was any extremely admirable deed of bravery from a samurai who knew he was defeated, disgraced, or mortally wounded. It meant that he could end his days with his transgressions wiped away and with his reputation not merely intact but actually enhanced. The cutting of the abdomen which is hara kiri was the most extreme form, and was thought to release the samurai's spirit in the most dramatic fashion possible. It was an extremely painful and unpleasant way to die, and sometimes the samurai who was performing the act asked a loyal comrade to cut off his head at the moment of agony. Unspoken but understood was that the attendant was also expected to do the same in case the samurai's nerve should falter, preventing a disgrace to the samurai's entire family.

Seppuku and *hara kiri* are not to be confused with the suicide missions of the kamikaze dive-bombers during WWII. Those human bombs thought that they were contributing to victory rather than atoning for failure.

Seiza

The kneeling/sitting position of rest (seiza) is difficult for Western adults to do if not accustomed to it from years of practice, but there are no shortcuts in performing it. From standing, first the left knee goes to the ground, then the right. The order is important, for it keeps the bottom of the scabbard from awkwardly driving forward and bouncing on the ground. Once on your knees, point the toes so that the tops of the feet are flat against the floor as you lower the buttocks onto your heels. The big toes may touch, but they should not cross one over the other. The head and torso should be erect, shoulders relaxed with the hands on the thighs. For many adult Westerners, the legs will fall asleep after only a few minutes in this position.

When bowing in seiza, the right hand reaches out to the ground first, then the left, forming a slight triangle. The head goes as far down towards the floor as is possible without raising the buttocks off of the feet. Better to perform a shallow bow than an ungainly one. After the bow, the left hand is removed first, followed by the right. To rise up from seiza, the right leg comes up first, followed by the left, with the torso staying straight as you stand.

In formal court situations, samurai were not allowed to stand in the presence of the emperor (not out of respect, but because it's difficult to assassinate the emperor from seiza). Once the emperor entered a room, they had to know how to "walk" while never rising up from seiza if they needed to approach. Known as *shikkô aruki,* it is great exercise, so give it a try. While still kneeling, bring one knee up and put the foot down in front of you, while simultaneously turning the other knee out to the side, forming a stable three-point base. To step forward, roll over the ball of the lead foot until the knee comes down to the floor. Then turn the knee quickly off to the side while the trailing knee rises up and forward and the next foot is placed down in front. Quickly tuck the trailing heel forward underneath the buttocks. You get the idea: swing out, step forward, swing out, step forward, all the while trying to maintain a solid triangle stance from which you can rise at any moment to defend yourself. When perfected, the torso moves gracefully across the floor without bobbing.

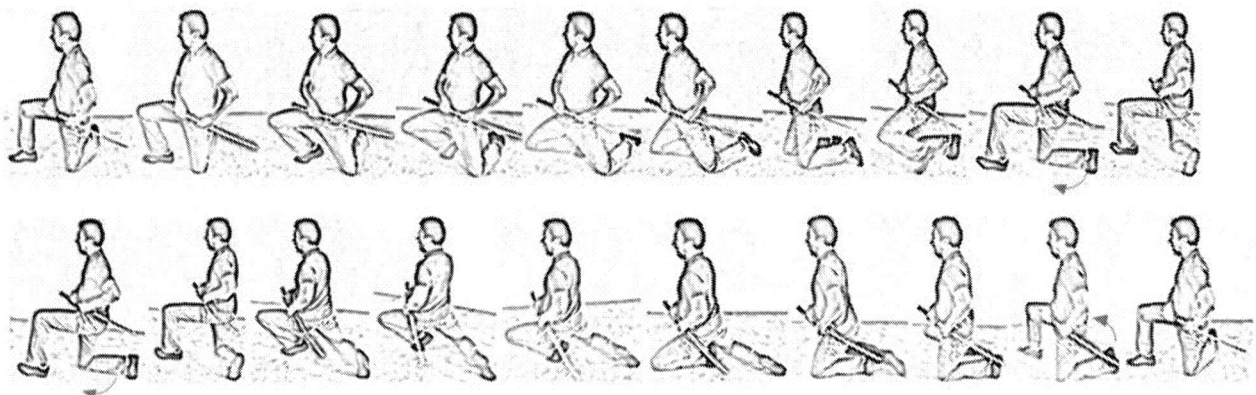

General standing and movement. It is often written in fencing guides of the period that movement while fighting must be the same as when walking, that there should be no difference between fighting movement and everyday movement. The idea here is that just as one should always be prepared for attack, not just on a battlefield or when facing a known opponent, but in every moment of the day or night. And if one trains with one stance yet lives with another, one is always unprepared..

While this may be true, it is also true that the constant and punishing training for these military men meant that the body changed in response to these exercises. With time, the legs naturally develop a slight turn out at the knees. The daily stance and walk of the warrior often show one of two distinguishing features: either the legs stay further apart than shoulder distance, or by necessity they become slightly bow legged, the outside edges of the feet digging into the ground. Naturally, you don't want your actors to turn their legs and feet this way for performance, but it is good to have them emulate some of the weight and solidity one sees in the Japanese prints of the period.

Civilian Conflict – It was expected that a duel between two of the samurai class would be a fight using the katana (though in reality most disputes were settled by hired assassins). There was no protocol for dueling beyond the agreement of time and place, and usually a day was given between challenge and confrontation. This allowed for either man to simply not show up at the appointed time, with loss of face but saving of life.

The following is perhaps the favorite story concerning Japan's most famous swordmaster, Myamoto Musashi, author of the Book of Five Rings. He declared that he was undefeated in over fifty combats. Musashi did not tell this tale - but it later became part of his legend.

Musashi was challenged by a very boastful local expert. An agreement was made to meet in the morning on a sandy shoal at a beach nearby. The expert arrived on time, but Musashi was nowhere to be found. Hours passed by until finally a very disheveled Musashi approached without his sword and obviously hung-over. Some mention was made by observers that perhaps the fight should be postponed to another day, but Musashi insisted that he was able to fight and the only reason to postpone would be the cowardice of his challenger. His challenger immediately drew his katana and threw the scabbard into the ocean, yelling out, "From this spot I shall not leave without his blood on my sword!" Musashi turned to the crowd and, just loud enough for his opponent to hear, muttered, "He must not think much of his chances today if he throws away a perfectly good scabbard."

But Musashi had no sword. He staggered to a small fishing boat anchored on the beach, pulled out a short oar made of pine, and with his knife rough-shaped it until he had a reasonable approximation of a katana-length club. The crowd became silent as the two men approached each other. When they were less than two sword lengths away, both men stood as still as statues.

For what seemed an eternity the two men stood with their weapons pointing at each others' faces, the only sound being the steady fall of each gentle wave collapsing on the sand. Both men seemed to be utterly relaxed, and yet intensely focused. Suddenly, with a fury that shook the air, both men leaped at each other as they swung their weapons down, Musashi slightly slower than his opponent, and in almost the same instant both men jumped back to their ready stance.

The onlookers at first could not understand what they saw, if indeed that they actually saw anything at all, so suddenly had the moment exploded and then gone back to stillness. Then a slight wind revealed that Musashi's headband had been neatly sliced by the downstroke of his opponent, and as the headband fell to the ground a single cut on his forehead began to bleed. Then is when his opponent fell to the ground, fatally wounded from a blow to the head. Musashi had expertly timed his leap so that his opponent's sword would be a hair's width away from killing him, and in that moment that the sword passed his face he would be close enough to deliver a death blow to his challenger's head.

Again, Musashi never told this story himself, but did admit to having used an oar in a fight at least once. Many versions of the tale abound, and the details seem to cover every imaginative conceit. But if the story is apocryphal, it does illustrate some important truths about the nature of single combat in this period, namely winning with whatever weapon was at hand, not allowing emotion to rule the movements of the fight, waiting for the single perfect moment for a decisive all-or-nothing attack, and the fact that most fights were over in the space of one or two moves.

[I never quite understood how much energy could be delivered from a standing start until I had the opportunity to attend a seminar in traditional Japanese swordplay conducted by Masayuki Shimabukuro Hanshi, 8th dan (level) iaido master. Iaido is taught and practiced using only sharpened blades, and we dutifully practiced for two days the various draws and attacks at a slow and deliberate pace. Finally, he demonstrated what a simple attack would look like at regular speed. He squared off against a 3rd dan guest instructor, and both were completely relaxed. When the guest instructor began to inhale, Shimabukuro leaped forward, his entire body moving in like a freight train, the sword crashing down to a centimeter above the other's forehead. The room reverberated from the sound of his shout, which was closer to the compressed roar of a lion than a human sound. So sudden and powerful was the attack that the guest instructor had no time to even raise his weapon, and the color drained from his face when he realized how easily this grand master could take someone's life at will.]

To coolly face death without fear or concern over defeat required an incredible self discipline and control over emotions, and the Japanese form of Buddhism known as Zen perfectly fit those requirements. While Shinto, the native religion based on deity and ancestor worship and respect, remained popular, Zen gave its practitioners a practical tool in preparing the mental toughness and self control necessary to not be overwhelmed by external events. Both religions [and a few others] coexisted in Japan. Even though several governments tried to separate and regulate the different sects, it is interesting that the vast majority of Japanese today consider themselves Buddhist but also believe in and practice at least some level of Shinto.

When not a duel, a fight of anger between two civilians of any status might of course be fought with any found object, edged weapon, or even unarmed. As all of the samurai class were expected to be expert in the use of all weapons, we would expect that they would have fought with a high degree of skill. If the lower classes had any martial arts training, they still would not have had the luxury of being able to devote several hours to daily practice. Having said that, it is worthy of note that unarmed fight training among the peasant class was fairly common in at least the area of Okinawa, said training that we would later recognize as *karate*.

Modern karate was developed during the twentieth century and the word translates as "open hand". But before then the term, although pronounced the same, was originally written with different ideograms, and meant "Chinese hands", reflecting the origin of the art. The original unarmed fighting style made no distinction between punching and kicking (karate) throwing and grappling (judo) or traps and releases (aikido). All were taught according to the ability of the instructor, and there was no hesitation to use a weapon if one was handy. The idea of learning unarmed fighting skills so as to be more "gentle" or nonlethal is a peculiarly Western concept. These skills were taught in Japan in order to be able to quickly kill an opponent and avoid being killed.

<u>Warfare</u> – It is interesting to note how Japanese warfare differed from the feudal wars of Europe. Although both were led by a mounted warrior-class nobility who far exceeded the average foot soldier in training and skill, there were also key differences. European knights fought almost exclusively as heavy cavalry, the primary weapon being the couched lance driven at full gallop. They then closed with the sword, although still while on horseback. Samurai used arrows, not lances, from horseback and so first could act as a light cavalry before switching to heavy cavalry tactics with the sword. And although their European counterparts fought dismounted only reluctantly, samurai felt no disgrace in taking to the field on foot with a sword or pike. They were much more disciplined than were knights, and therefore would easily shift their fighting styles to accommodate the orders of their leaders.

Until the end of the Muromachi period, common warriors were generally issued the naginata, a two foot sword blade mounted on a long wooden shaft, creating an effective eight foot polearm. Such a weapon could be held and swung with little training, and yet still could be used against both the massed foot soldiers and the mounted samurai. Warfare centered on being able to position the entire battle formation to best advantage, and then close in and allow each warrior to fight to the best of his ability. Prisoners were rarely taken for ransom, although sometimes were taken for prisoner exchange of high ranking family members. Head hunting on the battlefield was practiced through most of Japanese history until about the mid 1600's. Unlike China, only the opposing general and senior military staff, especially if members of the daimyô family, were singled out for this treatment. This was done to provide irrefutable proof that the enemy had been defeated. [This makes an interesting parallel with the "Highlander" movies and even with "Macbeth" - that the enemy is not dead until head is removed.]

The changes that came in the Momoyama period were dramatic. First was the decision to create a permanent lower level warrior class in order to remove all weapons from the hands of the peasantry. Very quickly, daimyôs were able to create specialized divisions within their standing armies, specially trained in the skills necessary to conduct complex battlefield tactics. Field combat changed from individual actions to group (volley) combat and maintaining tight formations.

The Meiji Restoration not only brought down the Shogunate but also ushered in Japan's entry as a modern military power. In an astoundingly short period of time, they created a military force the equal of any in Europe, in weaponry, tactics, and organization. Continuing to the present day, the military has remained modern, and decidedly Western, in every aspect.

Cradle of Western Civilization

The Chariot Empires

Mesopotamia

Time Frame – roughly 3100 B.C. to 600 B.C.

Politics/Economics – Instead of trying to expound on each empire and kingdom, we're going to go for the larger view of the commonalities found in the non-Egyptian cultures of the Middle East and Asia Minor. The time frame is also rather broad, covering the beginning of the Bronze Age and written history in the area all the way to the fall of Assyria, at which point the Persians and Greeks began to dominate.

From the earliest inscriptions, these societies seem to have been true kingdoms, each ruled by a single autocratic ruler. The power of the kingdom depended largely on the sagacity, ambition, and personal energy of the king. A weak king could easily loose all of the gains of even a powerful empire. Kings were often considered to be appointed agents of the local god, but not gods themselves or even necessarily having a special relationship with a deity. The basic economy was based on agricultural output, although a vast trade network throughout the area meant that wealth could be enhanced through the selling of especially prized commodities.

Although reading the inscriptions left behind by these kingdoms leaves the impression that all were in a constant state of war, this of course is not possible, for constant warfare is extremely expensive and would drain the coffers of these primarily agricultural societies. Having said that, it is true that certain energetic rulers could sustain prolonged military campaigns through the subjugation of neighboring tribes. Those with especially fertile and extensive plains were constantly at the mercy of raiding parties. A particularly capable leader could protect his kingdom by establishing a defensible perimeter, and with time the further frontiers of that kingdom would have to be protected as well. Standing armies would need to be provided for, requiring more land to produce more surpluses. More wealth meant more threats from kingdoms even further off, leading to further increases in the size of the army and the necessity to launch preemptive strikes. The cycle of expansion, perceived or real threat, and further expansion led to the creation of some of the most powerful kingdoms of the ancient world.

Warfare – The most powerful kingdoms used the chariot as a mobile fighting platform, usually with one driver, one archer, and one shield bearer who, armed with a sword or axe, would also defend the chariot against any enemy who approached too closely. Chariots were a nearly unstoppable force on the battle field, something that the later Persians would find out to be true as well. Moving quickly to the front lines, the chariot archer could fire a quick succession of arrows, and then the chariot itself could break through the formations of infantry and scatter the soldiers. Chariot cavalry tended to come from the upper levels of society.

The vast majority of warriors were infantry, normally using the spear, arrows, and axe. Infantry were either conscripted farmers, paid foreign mercenaries, vanquished enemies, or some combination of the three depending on the economic resources available. For what little information is available, it is most likely that the soldiers were massed into a battle line, arrows and thrown weapons were launched as soon as distance permitted. If that was enough to weaken the enemy line, the chariots would move in to take advantage of the breaks. If not, the lines would close in and infantry fought hand-to-hand.

Some regional differences should be noted:

♦ Sumerians: The earliest of the great kingdoms, from which we get the Epic of Gilgamesh, they were the first to use bronze weapons, the war chariot, and the massed infantry line (perhaps even formed as a disciplined phalanx) but had no archers.

♦ Babylonians: Renowned for their skill as archers, almost all soldiers, cavalry and infantry, carried bows in battle. There is nothing to indicate that they would close in with anything like a heavy infantry. Babylon had one of the few feudal levies of the area, where land was granted in exchange for service in the army.

♦ Nubians: Never completely united in their own territory, but also never conquered by Egypt, they conducted numerous raids as loose infantry units while armed with only the bow or spear. These groups sometimes reached impressive numbers, and their skills as fighters were highly respected. Large contingents of captured Nubian soldiers were often used by the Egyptians as mercenary/slaves. But even as slaves, they were fairly well paid as guards during peacetime and irregular infantry during war.

♦ Ethiopians: More feared than the Nubians because of their tight battlefield formations. They seem to have used heavy spear and javelins, along with some archers.

♦ Arabs: Exclusively nomadic, they fought completely unarmoured and used only the bow. It seems that they fought mounted from camels, two soldiers per animal. We may assume that one guided the camel while the other fired the arrows.

♦ Israelites: While never wealthy enough to support a large standing army, they were able to summon respectfully large numbers through their use of a compulsory rotating citizen levy, with active duty for one month of the year and the other time being held as reservists. It was primarily an infantry army, mainly due to the financial inability to purchase and maintain large numbers of war horses.

Egypt

Time Frame – aprox 3000 BC to 30 BC

Politics/Economics – Although the history of Ancient Egypt went through many dramatic changes during the 3000 years until its fall to Rome, the many dynasties did share some overarching similarities. First, a sustained shift to urban, rather than rural, forms of living. Secondly was the creation of substantial agricultural surplus due in large part to the bounty of the Nile valley. This provided wealth which allowed it to also thrive as a trading and war power. Lastly, the creation of the pharaoh. Although several societies developed systems of power based on the idea of a god/king, a pharaoh was not only a divine being but also "the high priest of all temples". As such, all religious activity, public and private, was directed through his person. He was the earthly mediator for all things secular and sacred. Combined with the wealth and military might, he had a power within the country far greater than any emperor.

That isn't to say that all was harmonious during those three thousand years. Many dynasties lost power through both foreign conquest and civil wars. But even though several pharaohs were usurped and even brutally murdered, the presumption that pharaohic culture would continue was never questioned. Each new ruler took on the title and power of the conquered kingdom, leaving the political and religious bureaucracy largely intact. And it was that higher conservative and efficient bureaucracy that largely kept the empire prosperous.

Two periods in ancient Egypt's history are particularly noteworthy for theatre. The New Kingdom (1540 BC to 1070 BC) was Egypt at the height of power, establishing itself as a nearly indomitable empire. It also was the period of greatest construction and highest achievement in art. When shows are set in "Ancient Egypt", this era is usually chosen. The glory of the prior classical period was reestablished during this time of domestic peace and tremendous wealth, when the great pyramids were already a thousand years old.

The reign of the Ptolemys (332 BC to 30 BC) was another era of rebuilding former glory. But these kings were all descendants of one of Alexander the Great's generals, so the influence was heavily Greek. Although most of the external trappings remain the same, the artwork and culture become increasingly Hellenistic. It is important to note that by the time of Cleopatra's rule, the society had lost most of its regional power. The kingdom that remained for another three hundred years under direct Roman rule was nothing but a shadow of the superpower it once was.

<u>Fashion/Manners</u> – It seems that the more we know about ancient Egypt, the less we know about how people acted. More and more information is unearthed every year as to daily activities, but we cannot tell how they moved, how they stood, or how they treated each other.

The temple and papyrus drawings that remain are apparently not attempts at realism, but rely on certain artistic conventions. The same conventions lasted some three thousand years. For instance, we see a drawing of a pharaoh holding the hair of a kneeling prisoner with the left hand, while an axe is held high with right. Obviously this king is shown in the moment before an execution. But we cannot assume that this king actually performed that action, for the same drawing appears at the end of many chronicles of victorious battles thousands of years before. On yet another pictorial representation, the same pose is shown of another pharaoh about to behead a prisoner - while single-handedly driving a chariot. Sometimes the same image is included in a specific commemoration of a military victory, with the same accompanying description of victorious carnage, even though in actuality a peace treaty had been negotiated before a battle even took place. (It is interesting to note that this same artistic convention also appears in the art of several of Egypt's neighbors, and is even seen in the carvings on Central American Mayan pyramids - a half a world away!)

What can be gleaned from these drawings is what they considered to be *not* important. Although we see images of enemy prisoners kneeling before the pharaoh, regular servants are seen standing fully upright, without even a lowering of the head. There would seem to be no tradition of bowing before the king at every occasion, as would later develop in both Europe and Asia. Also, whenever the pharaoh and his family are shown seated or reclined they are extraordinarily relaxed, shoulders rounded and completely without a trace of trying to appear "royal". When standing, the posture of all figures is shown to be "casually proud", in that the shoulders are straight but with none of the self-consciousness seen in Greek or Roman statuary.

Compare Egyptian art with that of some of their contemporaries. Assyrian, Babylonian, Sumerian depictions of kings and warriors all show them as men of great physical strength as well as having political power, as though having the first attribute validates having achieved the other. It is a conceit that is common throughout time and geography, a necessity to prove to the viewer the physical prowess of the leader. There seems to be no such imperative in Egyptian art. The Pharaohs are never shown with body language that would indicate a need to "awe" his own citizens.

To better understand this casualness, we are helped by comparing other cultures. When there exists a very real threat that the lower nobility or even the lowly workers might take arms against the rulers (i.e. Medieval Japan, Middle Age Europe), then elaborate manners in the presence of the king are required to establish every possible form of obedience from their subjects. It also becomes necessary to provide visual representations of the personal power of the rulers, reminding the viewer that it would be unwise to oppose him. It is reasonable to infer that in such a stable society as was Egypt, these considerations were nearly unknown. All of those movie scenes with servants groveling in front of the pharaoh may be way off the mark. A ruler who is supremely self-confident about his power and place in the universe might have no need to demand outward displays of obedience.

Civilian Conflict – We really have nothing which tells us anything about civilian interaction, but isn't it fascinating to note that in the period artwork no civilian is ever shown using, much less wearing, a weapon? The tight control of the ruling power may not only have tightly clamped down on representations of individual discord, but may also have had an effect on the actions themselves. Although thievery and other forms of social disruption had to have occurred (otherwise why hire Nubian guards to patrol the open marketplaces?) it is possible that within the urban areas taking justice into your own hands was fairly uncommon.

Warfare – The army of Egypt was largely an infantry army, although by the late New Kingdom there was also a significant cavalry contingent. The cavalry, as for all Middle East Bronze Age cultures, was the chariot, not a mounted rider on a horse. Therefore the chariot provided Egypt with the equivalent of a light cavalry. The bulk of the fighting was performed by heavy infantry - armed during the later periods with the kopesh but far more commonly with the small axe (daggers are found, but in small numbers). Additional weapons included the javelin, light wooden shields, and archers to provide covering fire, or to take out lightly armored forces. The archery contingent, providing a light infantry role, were not arrayed near the heavy infantry, but kept at a distance, forming a natural reserve. Egyptian bows were notoriously weak compared to those of their neighbors.

The consensus has been that Egyptian battlefield formations were rigidly controlled, and that soldiers were drilled to fight in near machine-like precision. But this assumption comes from viewing tomb paintings - not a reliable source of realistic practice.

All young males were required to serve a two year military service, but only the best prospects were actually recruited after a short period of training and testing. A military career provided significant possibilities of advancement, for able soldiers and administrators were promoted regardless of the status of their birth. The pharaoh himself led the army into battle, and was supposed to be expert in handling the chariot and in firing the bow. Some artwork show him driving the chariot and firing the bow at once - not terribly likely. Most chariots had two people on it. A driver would wear a shield, protecting the left (blind) side o the archer. The chariot would be driven directly to the front line, charge the infantry, fire the bow a few times, then turn *to the right* for an escape back to safety, keeping the shield towards the enemy.

Large contingents of mercenary soldiers, especially from the Nubian kingdom, were employed, and these foreign troops were allowed to use their own weapons, mainly spears and large shields, and fight in their own style, although controlled by an Egyptian general.

No sheaths are seen on any drawings, and none have been found in any archeological digs. We may surmise that weapons were carted to the battlefield en mass and distributed to soldiers only when battle appeared to be imminent. It is safe to assume that the daggers, swords, and small axes were simply never worn. Even archers had no arrow quivers, but merely marched into battle with a good bunch of loose arrows held in the right hand and the bow held in the left. That is clear from many tomb and obelisk drawings, But did the archers transfer the arrows to the left hand, holding both the bow and the extra arrows in one hand as they fired? Or did they stick the arrows into the ground near their feet in the medieval style? We just don't know.

Weapons available –   The very stability and continuity of the Pharaonic bureaucracy also made it susceptible to a systemic rigidity. They were very slow to adopt the chariot, doing so only after coming out of a long period of Hyksos domination. They were likewise very resistant to replacing their bronze weapons with iron, although they certainly had the wealth to be able to purchase what they could not produce. They only began to produce full swords after the nearly disastrous confrontation with waves of immigrants collectively known as the "Sea People". But even then the swords were still made out of heavy bronze and the military planners were never able to effectively incorporate them into Egyptian battle tactics.

There is some evidence that at least a few soldiers wore a short knife either tucked into the fold of fabric at the waist or strapped onto the left forearm without a sheath, but these seem to be personal items, not part of the issued weaponry.

Islamic Middle East

Rise of Empire (622 – 750)

It is customary to mark the beginnings of Islam with the Hijrah *[Hegira]*, the movement of Mohammed and his followers from Mecca to Medina, at which point the organization of Islam expanded beyond merely the ties of immediate relatives. This simple shift provided the framework which would allow Mohammed to capitalize on a series of battlefield and diplomatic victories that led to the establishment of a unified Islamic state in Arabia, where before there had been a collection of warring cities.

After his death in 632, his successors expanded the extent of Muslim rule, confronting the Persians, Byzantines, Egyptians and various smaller powers. In 661 the power center shifted to Damascus, and during the next ninety years the empire would expand deep into Europe, North Africa and pressing into the Byzantine territories. Interestingly, during this time and also during the following "Golden Age", conquests were conducted with what for the time passed for remarkable tolerance, with religious conversion not being made a requirement, and a great deal of respect given to Christian and Jewish residents within the empire. Much of this tolerance was because of the continuing influence of the great former Persian emperor Cyrus II.

Golden Age (750 – 1220)

The overthrow of the ruling Umayyads by the 'Abbasids, meant a change of capital to Baghdad for the next 500 years, and with it a re-energizing of Persian culture. Continued success into Christian states was not only from aggressive military campaigns, but also from the support of Christian communities tired of heavy-handed Byzantine control. The 'Abbasids, although constantly under attack from other independent Muslim caliphates, established a network of trade routes that encouraged the unrestricted movements of goods from Spain to China, from the Philippines and India to West Africa. To facilitate trade, borders were open and a series of inspectors made sure that weights and standards were uniform throughout.

This wealth combined with a thriving intellectual life, and the advances in medicine, art, science, architecture and learning, along with a continued tolerance of other monotheistic faiths, made Baghdad the center of civilized living after the fall of Rome. Their libraries held possibly the largest store of human knowledge at the time, with scholars combing the world "as far as China" for all surviving scientific and philosophical information. Long before the crusades, many of the material and intellectual benefits of the Islamic empire were percolating up to Southern Europe, and would provide the raw intellectual material for the Renaissance.

For Western Europe, the three most important of the independent Muslim kingdoms of this period were the Seljuks of Turkey, the Ayyubids of Egypt, and the Andalusian kings of Spain. If Europeans actually saw Muslims, they were more than likely from one of these three client states. It was the Seljuks during the 11th and 12th centuries that weakened the Byzantine Empire, the Ayyubids that conducted most of the war against the Crusaders, and the Andalusians who transformed Latin Spain into one of the glittering centers of Muslim power in Europe. Such was the wealth in Spain that after the fall of the last Muslim king, a re-Christianized Spain could instantly begin ambitious worldwide maritime exploration and become a dominant European power.

As far as the crusades are concerned, from the Muslim point of view they were a minor concern, of no more long term importance than any of the periodic uprisings and challenges to military power.

Mongol Invasions (1220 – 1380)

When Genghis Khan swept in from the east, the obliteration of the 'Abbisids in Persia was so complete that even the great city of Baghdad was reduced to rubble and ruin. As the Mongols conquered through intimidation and fear, one of their tactics after a successful invasion was to kill leaders and scholars and destroy the collected works of art and science. Only in Egypt were the Mongols defeated and finally rolled back by a concerted effort of the soldier/slaves known as the Mamluks.

Mamluks [Arabic: "white slave"] were prisoners primarily from the Caucuses, trained as cavalry soldiers and converted to Islam, then maintained as an independent fighting force. In Egypt, they attained such power that, while technically still slave, they overthrew the Ayyubids and establish their own autonomous sultanate stretching across northern Africa. Mamluks became the defacto aristocracy, and maintained power in Egypt until massacred in 1811.

Ottoman Empire (1300 – 1922)

One of the remnant emirates in Turkey that survived the Sulyuk collapse were mounted warriors converted to Islam. But the Ottomans were not only fearsome warriors but also skilled bureaucrats. Taking advantage of a weak Byzantium and Persia, at the height of its powers in 1566 it controlled all of the Balkans, coastal Northern Africa, and all of Persia. It completely surrounded the Black and Red Seas, extended to the Caspian Sea and the Persian Gulf, and controlled 3/4 of the perimeter of the Mediterranean. They effectively controlled all land and sea routes allowing trade between Europe and Asia. It was this monopoly of wealth and the constant threat of conquest that turned out to be the impetus for some of the most history-making decisions for Europe.

In order to find a way to the rich India spice trade, many European kingdoms funded the age of naval exploration that would lead to Magellan's circumnavigation and Columbus' accidental discovery of the New World. It was to protect its ships that the merchants of Venice built their city in the natural protection of marshland. Large numbers of Jews, persecuted in Europe, found safety within the Islamic Empire. For most Europeans, their only knowledge of Islam or Muslims would be that which filtered through contact with the Ottomans. That "eastern" culture was quite a mix of Persian, Greek, Arab, and Turkic elements.

The court life, limited as it was to outsiders' view, provided some of the imagery that would intrigue Western imagination to this day. The image of a turbaned Sultan surrounded by his harem, protected by eunuchs and attended by slaves - all have an element of truth, but as is usual, the truth is a bit more complicated. The harem consisted of not only the Sultans wives, but also other female relatives and their children (up to the age of sixteen, for boys). The palace quarters for the harem (the *seraglio*) were kept separated from the rest of the palace, but it was not a prison nor brothel. Eunuchs worked both within the seraglio ("black eunuchs") and in the political administration of the palace at large ("white eunuchs"). Although slaves, members of both groups could rise within their respective bureaucracies to achieve great national power. Slavery was a fact of life within the empire, always taken from the population of defeated captives of non-Muslim countries. It is estimated that perhaps one fifth of the Ottoman population at any given time were slaves.

One group of slaves, the Janissary, became the most significant part of the Empire's standing army. Recruited as young boys from among Christian captives, they were sequestered from the general population, endured harsh training, and were considered the personal slaves of the regiment and of the Sultan. But once attaining full status as Janissaries, they received regular pay, were allowed to marry, and achieved a high social standing. Janissaries had to convert to Islam, and were not allowed to wear beards, which is why they are always shown with full mustaches but clean chins. They were an infantry corps, and used muskets as their primary weapon as early as the 16th century.

Once Western Europe was able to establish its own trading routes to India by sailing around Africa, the wealth of the spice trade began to diminish. The reduction in revenue, increasing power of the Janissaries, fragmentation within the Empire by semi-autonomous local rulers, a steady line of ineffective sultans, all finally led to the long decline of the power. As allies of Germany during WWI, the loss in that war led to the final collapse of an empire that lasted six hundred years, supplanted by the modern republic of Turkey.

Modern Era (1922 – present)

Although the discovery of vast quantities of oil in the region in 1908 could have propelled another period of Islamic power, the area was already politically fragmented, most of it divided up into European colonies. Even when these achieved nation-state status, their leaders were too easily under the influence of Western political and economic interests. Many Persian and Arab leaders achieved fabulous personal wealth, but were unwilling or unable to translate that into political power, and certainly nothing approaching the creation of a Pan-Arab state.

<u>Manners</u> – From the beginning, and continuing still today, it is appropriate for Muslim to greet Muslim with "Salaam" ("peace") or the complete ""*Assalamu Alikum.*" The protocol for who greets who first is as follows: the one who comes greets the Muslims that are present, those who ride greet those who walk, one who is walking

greets one who is sitting, a smaller group greets the larger group, and younger always greets elder. It is not appropriate to offer salaam to non-Muslims.

The following gestures and manners are not specifically Islamic, but rather Arab. But as Islam began in Arabia, these gestures are now commonly practiced throughout much of the Middle East:

The right hand is used for eating, the left for personal hygiene. Therefore, by extension, all gestures toward another person, the serving of food, and the taking of food must be performed with the right hand. Using the left is taken as an insult or at best a measure of disgustingly bad manners.

Pointing a finger at someone is a sign of contempt, inferring that the person is less than human. Therefore to gesture for someone to approach the entire open hand is used, fingers together, and with the palm facing down in a gentle sweeping motion inward.

Tilting of the head slightly back, especially when combined with a "tsk" sound, signals that what the other person has said is not believed (the same is common in most of Latin Europe, as well).

Moving the open palm from right to left, thumb up, as if closing a door, means "no".

Shaking hands is common at each greeting and departure, and again only with the right hand, not adding the left as we might in the West. Immediately placing the hand over the heart after a handshake is a sign of respect and sincere honor. When the same gesture directly follows the offering of food or other item of use, it shows sincerity on the part of the giver.

The highest gesture of respect on greeting is to kiss the hand, forehead or nose of the person being greeted.

In refusing the offering of food, the heart is patted several times, indicating that the offer is greatly appreciated, but that you have had enough.

Hugging or clasping the upper arms (with both hands) upon greeting is usually reserved for a close friendship. Between men, kissing a cheek means the same, and it can also be used in business circumstances to indicate that both sides have reached a "meeting of the minds".

Especially in initial meeting, the distance between two men is very close, usually only a foot apart. This establishes trust, and may be accompanied by touching.

Touching noses together three times is a specifically Bedouin tradition, still common, but rarely seen outside of the Arabian dessert countries.

The "OK" sin, the "thumbs up" sign, and striking the left open palm with the right fist are all deeply insulting obscene gestures. When seated, the soles of the feet or shoes must never be facing another person, for to do so indicates that you are metaphorically stomping them to the ground.

To show open palms to someone expresses great approval to what they have said or done.

To kiss your hand then raise it slightly expresses thanks. Even more respectful is to touch the hand to the forehead with a slight bow. To show the highest amount of sincere thanks, the hand might first touch the heart (sincerity), then touch the lips (thanks) and then finally touch the forehead (humility).

Other signs of sincerity, especially when performed when making a promise, include touching the nose or eyes, and stroking the beard or mustache.

Warfare –   We in the West have an image of Islamic weaponry and tactics that is loosely based on fact, but even more on a combination of European revisionism and modern popular culture. Middle Eastern warriors are almost always depicted as using a single-edged curved sabre called a scimitar, and wearing little armor compared to the European knights. While this has a great deal of truth, it is also woefully simplistic.

It is true that curved swords were always more popular in the Middle East than they were in Europe, but straight swords actually have a longer history in the area. The swords particularly associated with the birth of Islam (circa 600 AD) are almost all straight double edged broadswords, swung single handedly. It is important to note that the sword is always shown as a cutting weapon, and never described in contemporary texts as being used for thrusting. While curved blades of excellent quality were produced, even as late as the 1300's both curved and straight blades were equally popular. Either way, swords were built "blade-heavy" to facilitate powerful cutting motions. Even what appear to be pommels are simply hollow flairs, never a counter weight, and the hilts are smaller and lighter as well. So by comparison, Islamic swords would be lighter than European swords, although would be heavier in feel. This means that they would be difficult to balance in preparation of a thrust, or to suddenly change direction in case one commits to a cut but suddenly needs to block. For the Muslims, the answer was simply to use the sword for attacking and ignore defense. This also led to a certain tactic which infuriated the Crusaders. Instead of closing in with the enemy and trading blows, the Arabs/Persians would harass from a distance until a distinct advantage could be discerned before attempting to close with the enemy. An attack with the sword was a single strike, all or nothing, and then step or ride out of distance. The European knights, on the other hand, wanted to close in with the enemy. Each individual was expected to find an opponent and fight until victory or defeat. In their frustration, the Europeans railed that the Muslims fought as cowards, but this was far from the case. The Muslims generals viewed their own army as a single unit with many parts. That one part should strike the enemy here and another should cut the enemy there was all one; each strike helped weaken the opponent. There was no need to have a multitude of individual battles so long as the overall battle was won.

To aid in this strategy, the Muslim generals could count on a fighting force of far superior discipline than that of the Europeans, who were often amazed at the cleanliness, quiet, and order of the Muslim army camp. This compared unfavorably with Medieval Crusader encampments, which were usually unsanitary and poorly regulated, with a high rate of disease, drunkenness, gambling, fighting, and desertion.

By 1400, with the Ottoman Turks establishing their empire, curved blades became the overwhelming standard. It is in this time that some of the curved blades developed a fattened width near the point, and this is what caught the European imagination. European depictions of swords had always emphasized sword points rather than the edge, and so they drew an exaggeration based on same.

By the sixteenth century, the blade lightened and thinned considerably, and also lost even the hollow pommel in favor of the pistol style grip. The sword became even faster in the hand. Ironically, even as the actual sword became thinner (and far lighter than comparable European cavalry sabres of the same period), the sword of European fantasy became ever more exaggerated, until the current view of the curved blade with a severe back-point below the tip nearly three times as wide as the forte of the blade has become completely ingrained in our popular image. It has even affected the concept among current inhabitants of the Middle East, with some of these exaggerated fantasy swords occasionally waived about by traditionalists even though such swords were built in response to Western expectations.

As mentioned, infantry units were largely armed with arquebus/muskets beginning as early as the mid 1400's, but even in the 1300's archery was a more valued skill among infantry than the use of the sword. So it was that the sword was relegated to a position of secondary weapon, some 300 years before the same would happen in Europe. The pistol was issued to light cavalry units, although the weapons was largely despised by the majority of soldiers.

Weapons available – The yatagan goes back to at least 1000 BC, has always been popular in the many cultures of Turkey, and the shape has also been used in some French bayonets of the late 1800's. The most recognized style of this sword has no guard and a two foot blade with a double curve, giving it the forward cutting power of a chopping tool along with the sweeping slashing edge of a sabre. Another benefit is that, since the tip of the sword ends up in a straight line with the extended arm, the weapon is perfectly made for a shortsword thrust. Surely at least some warriors would have noticed this benefit and used the weapon to its fullest advantage.

While some straight daggers existed, curved daggers were nearly universal, and every warrior wore one.

Muskets followed European designs, except that they were much lighter than their Western counterparts, due in large part to better metal working techniques that allowed for thinner, lighter barrels. These in turn could be mounted onto thinner, lighter wood stocks.

Western Development

The Phalanx, the Spear, and the concept of Unlimited War

Classical Greece

Time Frame – aprox. 500 to 300 BC

Politics/Economics – Unique for this area of the world at this time, and for reasons still unclear, the various city-states of the southern Balkan Peninsula reformed their society from the chieftain/king led tribes of its own past to a form of democratically led republics. The victory of the combined city-states against the more powerful Persian Empire led to a robust growth in trade with other countries, fueled by an unchallenged control of the Aegean Sea. With the subsequent increase in the standard of living came an astounding development in science, mathematics, art, music, philosophy - all unprecedented in that these were individual pursuits, not serving a powerful king and without serving a specific religious end.

The source of the famous myths and legends, however, come from even before the far earlier "Greek dark ages" - before 1200 B.C., a period of time in which even written language in the peninsula came to disappear altogether. The stories of the Iliad, Odyssey, the panoply of heroes and demigods converted to constellations survived only because of a strong oral tradition that survived the annihilation of the Minoan/Mycenaean civilizations. Of this earlier intermediate period we know next to nothing. [That they were technically savvy is proved by bronzework in armor and weapons that was not reproduced in classical Greece - or even today.] By the time the stories of Troy, etc., were written down, they were likely highly influenced by the intervening 700 years of progress.

Fashion/Manners – Although hardly forming a "leisure class", the average citizen could enjoy exhibitions of and even participate in what would now be called the liberal arts. The explosion of individual artistic, physical, and mental pursuits was matched by an attempt to elevate daily life, at least for landed citizens, and add a level of elegance and grace not seen in neighboring cultures. The tightly sewn garments of an earlier time gave way to a loose raiment that flowed around the body, and for some activities, even this was too constricting, nudity being preferred. From the extant artwork, we can surmise that posture and movement showed pride without arrogance, striving for an elegance not unlike that of modern dancers, but without any of the self-consciousness.

Civilian Conflict – There is no reason to believe (and no evidence exists) that Greeks, even in Sparta, wore even so much as a small knife except when traveling outside of their own state. Most men might have had some training in boxing and wrestling, but outside of the Olympian competitors, these were mere athletic exercises, not serious contests. One can surmise that most disputes which turned physical would not involve the use of a weapon.

That is not to say that violence was any less common than it is today, but that the weapons used would probably be items found near at hand.

Warfare – It is no exaggeration to say that the Greeks invented the concept of modern warfare. By that I mean that they would bring their forces to bear with the intent of winning by committing their entire assembled army to inflict the maximum number of casualties on the other side. Most of the Greek city-states depended on raising armies of heavy infantry composed of citizen/farmer-soldiers, arranged in thick lines [the phalanx] for fighting in the field. Armed with pikes, the masses of men would form a bristle-hedge of spear points which could clash and push back the opposing force. Since the assembled soldiers were only part-time warriors, training was rudimentary. By having the soldiers stand shoulder to shoulder, the overlapping shields protected them from most opposing arrows and spears, and since they were lined up several rows deep, the only place to go was forward. Since the soldiers in the back had very little to fear, there was very little desertion. The orders were simple - go forward and kill as many of the enemy as possible. While prior empires had used that phalanx, none committed to it as a decisive all-or-nothing strategy. The Persians especially saw Greek warfare as something brutal and terrifying.

The Greek heavy infantry was supported by a smaller number of soldiers [light infantry] who would throw javelins into the enemy lines and sometimes engage in hand-to-hand combat using the sword. An even smaller number of archers were employed, also to weaken the opposing force. Cavalry was so limited, both in number and in effectiveness, that it was never a factor in battle.

Soldiers were made up of only the landed citizenry, for, having a stake in the outcome of a war, they could be counted on to stay the battle better than mercenaries or slaves. They also had the financial means to provide themselves with the necessary armor and weapons. The exception was Sparta, which created a warrior society. All free-born males at birth were evaluated for physical flaws. Those deemed weak were immediately killed. At the age of seven all boys were removed from their families and began constant training in fighting and physical conditioning. At the age of eighteen they began serious military training and at twenty were taken into what was essentially a professional standing army and there remain until at least the age of thirty. The Spartans superior training, toughness and constant readiness for battle usually made them victorious in battle.

But all Greek armies operated in essentially the same way. The combination of armor, shield, pike and sword could weigh up to 70 pounds. A charge by the phalanx might be slow, but the impact on the enemy could be enough to break their line. Should the first blow be insufficient, the subsequent lines of the phalanx would quickly catch up and press against the backs of their front line compatriots, suddenly adding more and more weight and force to the contest. Pike heads might force their way between shields and cause a few casualties, but the tide would turn when one section of the phalanx could push its way through the enemy, causing a breach in the front line. This would give the leading soldiers room to thrust and hack at the now exposed "inside" of the opposing line, behind their shields. The sudden break down of the shield wall would inevitably lead to a killing zone in the area around the break, those standing firm impaled by pikes, those turning to run quickly cut down by the swords of the light infantry. When one side became the clear winner, the advantage was rarely pressed home. The winner was acknowledged and a truce often called so that both sides could gather their dead before leaving the field of battle.

Battles by necessity had to be fought on open plains in order for the Greeks to assemble the phalanx, and farmers could only be called in large numbers when planting and harvesting duties did not interfere, so quickly taking the fight to the enemy and forcing a decisive battle was crucial. The battle plan would be discussed before engaging, but there was really no way to work out even simple variations on the straight ahead slow charge, so generals always led and fought alongside their troops. Less common were battles in which a moving army was caught by surprise in a narrow defile or in a canyon trail.

Interestingly, the heroic warriors of the Homeric tales did not spring from this period of Greek wartime success, but from the far earlier time when the Greek tribes still fought in a ritualistic mode, with key warriors - champions - battling in order to determine victory for the entire tribe. While the phalanx battles of the City/States might have soldiers numbering in the several, even tens, of thousands, the earlier tribal Greek battles would have had only a few dozen actual warriors on each side. Of course, by the time the earlier fables were written down hundreds of years later, the champion warriors are placed within the context of large phalanx armies. It is analogous to the Arthurian romantic legends favored by the later Gothic medieval knights, where they would endow a near mythic early warrior with the weapons and fighting style of the later storytellers.

Weapons available –   The vast majority of warriors used only spear and shield, and uniformity was not common, as each soldier had to provide his own weaponry. Few had access to the shortsword, and few of these would actually find a use for it in battle. Thrown spears and heavy rocks were also used before the battlelines were engaged (from which we get our Olympic field events - javelin and shotput).

Rome

Time Frame – aprox 400 BC to 331 AD

Politics/Economics – Even during the height of Caesarian power, Rome maintained a working senate, with all the attendant infighting and politicizing and (usually) all of the freedoms granted under a strong respect for the rule of law. Although the later emperors ruled without the consent of the senate, they rarely interfered with the daily organization of Rome. In the earlier period, all citizens were expected to participate in politics, art, military service, and a lively social life, most of which continued until Rome's eventual fall. Citizenship was not universal, although compared to other societies was widespread and commanded several liberties and rights. The relative average income was sufficiently large that even those of modest means could afford at least one slave. The strength of the economy was based on conquest and slavery, and although certainly not unique to Rome, Rome was uniquely successful at it. People who could not be conquered were still valued as trading partners. Indeed, in some cases maintaining the independence of a rich net-importer of Roman goods was of greater value to the empire than having to provide for the infrastructure of a vassal state. Large scale public works, especially for entertainment, distribution of goods and sanitation, made Rome and its satellites the most livable of cities prior to the 20th century.

Romans held the view that every problem had a technical solution, and that Rome was unconquerable in battle. Its power was derived from the ever increasing accumulation and consumption of foreign goods, and also depended on foreign mercenaries to maintain its own security. Ironically it was those two attributes that also led to its collapse. Change the last example to using foreign companies to provide for the majority of our purchased goods, and the parallels to 20th century USA should give us pause.

Fashion/Manners – Power is the theme for this period, and it was aggressively and purposefully emphasized, from the architecture to the draping of the toga. As the upper and middle class had servants, a great deal of time could be dedicated to leisure and civic pursuits. The social designations were not absolute, and even foreign slaves could become full citizens under the right conditions.

The toga was the symbol of dignity and citizenship and was worn for public occasions. For daily wear or travel, the simple tunic under a cloak was more common. In stance and movement, the bearing of an athletic warrior was emulated by men and women alike.

Much is made of the debauchery of the Romans, but we must keep in mind that the orgiastic excesses were limited for the most part to the higher levels of Roman society, what we would consider the leisure class, and even then occurred rarely and in the later period of the Empire. We also have an exaggerated view of the level of wine consumed. Contemporary accounts do relate large volumes being consumed, but the wine served was heavily diluted and probably had only a 2 or 3% alcohol level (about half of what is found in modern beer). Drinking undiluted wine was nearly unheard of, and drinking to the point of becoming inebriated was a major societal taboo, unacceptable in any social setting.

Civilian Conflict – The sword was unknown as a civilian weapon, so violent disputes were settled by knife and fist, but again, the knife was rarely worn except by soldiers. Interestingly, although the entertainment of the Romans was often bloodthirsty and barbaric, violence in the streets was actually quite rare.

Warfare – Roman generals completely redesigned every facet of iron-aged warfare. Where other armies would merely mass their soldiers tightly together and then rush them forward to take the field, the Romans used complex battle formations that could adapt to every condition. And because they fought against armies from nearly every style of fighting, they were able to develop an organizational memory of tactics and countertactics that modern armies still study. Using professional soldiers instead of farmer/conscripts meant that the army could travel and fight during the planting and harvest seasons, and standing armies were constantly drilled in battle-tactics and fighting skills.

Other armies had almost all of their soldiers hold a long spear, knowing that if they stood shoulder to shoulder and in densely packed lines the farmer/conscripts were less likely to run away from battle. Using the sword takes even more bravery, and usually degenerates into repeated downward hacking until you or your opponent falls down. Both styles have their strength and drawbacks, so the Romans developed contingencies against both. In addition to specialization of warriors and intricate battle strategies, they also made sure that each trooper was trained to use a series of throwing and impact spears as well as the sword, dagger and shield on his own initiative as the particular situation required. Their greatest weakness was in trying to close battle with armies composed exclusively of mounted archers. Romans had cavalry, but it was not possible for them to win a battle without the use of their superb infantry.

Soldier

All Roman citizens were expected to perform at least a few years of military service, and during the initial years of the Republic all soldiers were freeborn landowners from the various Latin tribes. This changed slowly during the centuries, with the strength of the army increasing from the hiring and training of mercenary soldiers. By the later years of the Empire, the army was in fact exclusively professional. These soldiers were recruited from every corner of the globe, often from defeated armies, taught to speak and read in Latin, and underwent rigorous training. When on campaign, the basic minimal payment was usually paid at least in part by quantities of salt (from which we gain the term "salary"). Salt was easy to transport, easy to measure and divide, and accepted as a universal barter commodity no matter where in the world the soldier may find himself. It was universally recognizable, and thus more commonly accepted even than gold. An additional, and occasionally more lucrative, source of income was the distribution of whatever might be looted from defeated towns, a common practice of warfare in every century. Basic food was provided to every soldier, usually a large quantity of bread supplemented by what ever meat or vegetables could be purchased or plundered from the surrounding villages. (In a detail indicative of the planning and perspicacity of the Roman military administration, the standard loaf of bread was large enough to feed two soldiers. At mealtime, each loaf was handed out to a pair of soldiers. One soldier would cut the loaf in half; the other would take his pick of which half he wanted. Disputes over portion size were eliminated.) Clothing was provided appropriate for the terrain in which they marched, and this was probably the first army in which none of the soldiers were barefoot.

Each soldier was expected to carry 50 lbs while on the march, a number gathered from careful calculation and observation. (Interestingly, modern US soldiers are being required to carry 70 lbs, and are suffering severe maneuverability problems when on patrol).

Training for the soldiers covered three areas. Basic strength and running exercises to promote toughness and speed in battle [especially heavy during the initial months after recruitment], and then specific training in the use of sword, spear and shield. Finally, intricate drill while in unit formation created an army which could instantly respond to a general's battlefield commands.

The sword, short and stocky, was worn either on a belt at waist level, or on a sash a little higher than waist level, and worn on the right side of the body rather than on the left. In this, the Romans were unique among sword wearers the world over, but as with all other details, this was carefully thought out and based on very practical needs. Wearing the sword slightly higher than most means that it doesn't bother the legs when marching or running. Wearing the sword on the right side of the body rather than the left was a practical adaptation of the style of Roman attack.

The legionnaire might approach battle with five weapons; thee spears, a sword and a knife. The first two spears were "Pilum", light throwing spears tossed javelin-like at the opposing army to weaken the front line. The enemy was doing the same with regular spears, which the Romans would grab and throw back. But the enemy could not do the same with the pilum, for unlike a traditional spear, the pilum had a very long thin neck of iron. If a pilum struck a shield and stuck to it, the enemy couldn't simply hack off the spear. Thus the shield was instantly rendered heavy and useless. If the pilum bounced off of the shield or hit the ground, the soft iron shaft would bend, making it useless to try and throw back to the Romans. So even with an identical number of soldiers, the Romans would end up launching twice as many spears.

The third spear, heavy and traditional in construction, was used for actual engagement with the enemy. Once the lines of infantry begin to press into each other, spear to spear can quickly become shield to shield. All soldiers would lean forward with the left side of the body, since the shield can be braced against the left shoulder. But if the sword is worn on the left, as almost all other armies did, suddenly it can get pressed against the shield and made impossible to reach with the right hand. Roman soldiers, wearing the sword on the right, were not encumbered in this way, and could press forward with shield, then at the right time drop the spear, draw the sword, and start in on close fighting.

Roman soldiers were among the few to have specifically trained in using the sword in a variety of ways. Whereas most other soldiers would simply raise the sword arm high and bring it crashing down on an opponent, a favored and successful Roman tactic was to use the shield to lift up the opponent's shield and then thrust the sword into the exposed belly. [As the shortsword is very sturdy and practical in even the closest of quarters, use of the knife was not ever considered a battlefield tool and was mainly used for camp needs.] Battlefield maneuvers included not only tight formations of shield against shield for maximum defense, but also those which gave up to three feet of space between front line fighters so as to give them the most amount of space possible for individual sword fighting techniques.

But ultimately, the success of the Roman army rested on uniformity of actions by well-trained troops and the sophisticated supply and deployment of same by commander/engineers. It is interesting to note that for all its bellicosity, Rome did not value the warrior as did most other military regimes. There exist no epic poems of heroic warriors, only the paeans to victorious generals.

Gladiator

Although the gladiatorial contests began as public exhibitions of Roman army training bouts, by the time they became regularly scheduled contests at the Coliseum they were performed by disposable captives or very talented slaves and even a few prizefighting free citizens. As this was public entertainment, the types of weapons could cover anything found from any corner of the globe. It is here that the trident, casting net, club, long sword and hook are seen. Most of the serious contests would have paired fighters who had had a fair amount of training with the specific weapons they would be using. Those that survived the first season were prized for their natural fighting ability, and were given better treatment and more elaborate training. As such, they represented quite an investment by their owner/managers, so non-lethal injuries were preferred. Training therefore emphasized cuts (easier for a physician to stop bleeding) rather than thrusts. Having said that, deaths among them increased as time went on, in part to please an ever more jaded audience.

In the larger venues, gladiators would often be dressed and armed in different ways so as to provide more variety for the audience. The one we are most familiar with is the *Retiarius*, who fought with trident and net. Although it has become a movie staple to see a gladiator with net in almost every film about ancient Rome, in truth the Retiarius only fight against a *Myrmillo* (with shield and sword). The Myrmillo's helmet had a large crest in the shape of a fish, and this battle was suppose to symbolize the ancient conflict of fisherman and his prey. Quite an audience favorite, apparently. Other match ups might recreate famous battles or mythical warriors. Another crowd pleaser was to have those from exotic territories fight with the unique weapons of their home country.

If a decision to kill a defeated but not wounded gladiator went to the crowd, it is true that the spectators would show their thumbs, but as to whether it was pointed up or down is unknown (although holding the fist out with the thumb pointing up was quite an insult in ancient Rome, similar to extending the middle finger in the United State, so it was not likely to be used to spare someone's life.) The decision to execute a gladiator was usually made if he had performed particularly cowardly, not merely because he lost. Also, the old story of all gladiators entering the arena in a line and shouting to the Emperor, *"We, who are about to die, salute you!"*, is very dramatic, but also very much another Hollywood fiction. Only one warrior ever said it, and then only once, and he wasn't even in Rome.

Gladiators were slaves, but also prizefighters, and earned substantial sums from their victories. After serving for three years, or if they fought exceptionally well, they could even purchase their freedom. Many did so, yet continued to fight on, earning in the arena far more than they could ever hope to from regular employment.

Weapons available –   In general, Romans fought with weapons of inferior quality compared to those of their enemies. Romans were certainly capable of creating high quality steel, but preferred to make their weapons of a proto-steel version of iron. [Technically, the metal is still steel, but of such poor quality that I prefer to use the term iron, which better describes the nature of the finished product.] This metal made their weapons heavier and softer than their counterparts, and this was done on purpose. Why?

High quality steel takes a great deal of time to produce and then fashion into a weapon. It is the work of highly skilled specialists. The iron must be of good quality, the inclusion of carbon must be carefully calibrated, and the temperature during processing and tempering requires a well built, enclosed, and fairly large forge. Once completed, a steel sword is light, flexible, and has a resilient and tough edge. But it also is very expensive, and can chip easily and even snap in half. Repair to a finished blade is even more difficult than building a new one, so damage on the battlefield removes one warrior from the fight immediately, as a replacement sword could take several months to finish, and few were the warriors who could afford even one steel sword, let alone two.

An army on the move is better served by building its weaponry with cheap materials readily at hand. By using iron, they could be easily constructed and repaired at a regular open blacksmith's forge. Even then, Roman swords were relatively soft, so the edges might gouge and the blade might bend, but only rarely break. And no matter what the damage, they could be repaired by someone with very little technical expertise. Finally, the low cost of construction meant that large quantities of weapons could be produced as reserve items. [No Roman general ever had to call out *"My kingdom for a sword!"*.]

All soldiers were issued the standard shortsword and shield, and whatever throwing and fighting spears were necessary for the given circumstances. Longswords of about three feet in length were used only by cavalry. By the last decades of the empire, as most soldiers were hired foreign mercenaries, more and more soldiers were simply allowed to use their own tribal weapons.

Dark Ages

<u>Time Frame</u> – aprox 350 AD to 880 AD

<u>Politics/Economics</u> – With the collapse of the Roman Empire and the shift of most of its power to Greek cultured Byzantium, the ability to maintain any of the infrastructure that allowed for the "Pax Romana" disintegrated as well. Without the ability to keep large numbers of soldiers and engineers in the field, the likelihood of being attacked when traveling increased, and the slow disrepair of roads and bridges reduced travel even more. Trade decreased, and with it the dissemination of knowledge and culture. Political power devolved to that of the tribal chieftains, and while some areas developed true kingdoms, they were not monarchies, for the king himself would have only a limited power outside of his own demesne.

The tribes that inhabited the colder climates of Europe included those that gave Rome a great deal of trouble, for example the Visigoths but also Slavs, Danes, several British tribes. These, as well as ill-defined groups such as the German-speaking Franks and the vaguely Turkic Magyars, were scattered throughout the central European plains. While many of these tribes had been relatively docile during Roman occupation, all quickly took up arms to conduct raiding attacks on their neighbors. All were similar in social structure and technological development.

The disruption caused by the Roman occupation and later collapse led directly to the breakdown of what had been fairly stable and tight-knit tribal communities. These were chieftain as opposed to tribal societies, meaning that they were led by one strong central figure, usually the dominant warrior rather than an elder council. The position was not hereditary, and often was filled by a general consensus among the family heads. Rarely an occasional dynamic and charismatic leader might form a loose confederation among related tribes which could field large numbers of warriors, and some were able to mimic the battle strategies of the ancient Romans. But this was the exception rather than the rule, and the objectives they reached for were strictly military, not political. Most leaders were expected to pay their warriors handsomely with the captured wealth of other tribes, so raiding for slaves and booty was a constant feature of this warrior culture. A particularly successful leader might expect to draw followers from completely unaffiliated tribes and then raid neighboring tribes of the same clan. Fighters might travel hundreds of miles in order to serve under the command of a renowned warrior/king. But these warrior societies were never able to develop the economic resources necessary to sustain a general domestic growth in the Roman form. As soon as any charismatic leader such as Charlemagne died, any confederation would quickly collapse.

As long distance transportation of goods became more difficult, most of Europe reverted back to subsistence farming. Without a strong central government, monetary exchange was abandoned in favor of barter, further isolating most villages from their neighbors. In time, this isolation would extend to language as well, Latin breaking up into the varied romance languages of southern Europe that we know as Spanish, Italian, Portuguese, Romanian and French, among others. [In northern Europe, where Roman influence had never been quite as strong, the many Germanic and Norse Germanic languages continued to be used.]

As these were subsistence farmers, the vagaries of agricultural success in any given year could propel a normally peaceful tribe into seasonal raiding into neighboring regions. Warfare devolved as well into old-fashioned raiding parties, usually of no more than twenty or so warriors picking off a village by surprise and making off with that year's harvest. Trying to muster a defensive force from nearby villages proved useless, for the raiders would be long gone by the time an alarum could be raised. The only effective counter was to have easily defensible fortified positions - castles and walled towns. As a direct result of all of these changes, a new social construct was formed. Feudalism (possibly inherited from the Parthians) began as an understanding between a local strongman and the local agricultural workers, "I'll protect you from raids if you provide for my needs and help construct the common defense". In time this became, "All of this land is mine. I'll let you farm it if you give me a percentage of the harvest, and you fight for me when I need you to." Feudalism expanded quickly in southern Europe, whereas tribalism continued for much longer in the northern climes.

With the Bishop of Rome having lost the mechanisms for control of the population, and the Byzantine Empire being too far away to exert much influence, Christian practices began to blend with pagan local traditions. In response to and benefiting from the increased isolation from papal power, monasteries were founded that paralleled the feudal structure of the local warlords.

Fashion/Manners – The civility and simple luxuries that even middle class Romans took for granted evaporated. Life was dirty, harsh, and brutal for everyone, regardless of station. Depending on the wealth of the lord, meals were taken in a common hall, shared by his family and those of the most elevated vassals. Even sleep was largely communal, privacy being a luxury even for the comparatively rich. Peasant families of course remained in their own single room hovels.

As one would expect in such harsh conditions, clothing is a matter of practicality over elegance. Roman dress using cotton and fine linen in flowing robes and tunics are discarded in favor of heavy durable fabrics made of rough tow linen and wool. For the first time, trousers are acceptable as standard attire.

The artwork of the period shows little of what we can identify as proscribed manners. Some gestures such as extending the hand and perhaps slightly bowing are indirectly indicated, but it seems likely that what might be customary in one castle would be completely unknown a hundred miles away.

Civilian Conflict – Once the safety that had been provided by the Roman army went away, people had a not unwarranted feeling that the world was a dangerous place. Almost all men and most adult women wore an all-purpose knife, some a true dagger meant for self defense. Swords were not worn unless immanent battle was expected. It is true that Charlemagne wore his for almost all occasions, but the very fact that contemporaries wrote about it tends to confirm that the practice was exceptional rather than the rule. Considering the amount of physical labor that everyone needed to do on a daily basis, it is likely that fights were physical, brutally harsh and quick.

Warfare – Although large armies had been mustered to fight against the Romans, once that threat was gone, erstwhile allies reverted to raiding each other for cattle, grain, and tribute. Mustering an entire male population became more and more difficult, so warfare became the occupation of specialists, full time warriors supported by the local population. Gone were the sophisticated tactics of a Roman army in favor of a direct assault by what was in reality a group of individual warriors led but not necessarily controlled by the biggest, baddest fighter. The place of the warrior/king in battle was at the center of the front line, his most trusted subordinates fanning out to either side, and the ranks behind filled with less experienced warriors. Everything depended on closing quickly with the enemy and subduing him with an overwhelming attack. Sophisticated maneuvers and tactics were impossible, as each man fought as an individual. Riding into battle was common, but the heaviest fighting was done on foot. On the rare occasions when a civilian levy was formed to augment the warriors numbers, simple spears were provided to these untrained peasant farmers.

<u>Weapons available</u> –   Use of the spear declines, and ultimately disappears as the primary weapon of battle. As soldiers act primarily as individual warriors, axes predominate with swords a distant second.

As villages became ever more isolated, the technology of high quality steel making was slowly lost to the average blacksmith. Most of the skills used by the traveling craftsmen of the Roman army survived, although their priority had been on quantity, not quality. But pockets of native ingenuity produced some craftsmen capable of producing some of the finest edged weapons that Europe had ever seen. The all-iron swords were carefully crafted from dozens of individual iron strands, twisted and hammer welded to form blades of surprising strength. Many blacksmiths somehow acquired or relearned steel making techniques and became true swordsmiths, producing weapons far superior to the knives and axes made by the common village blacksmith. And it is here that the European fascination and mythology of the sword has its genesis.

Building quality steel from iron requires the removal of most of the carbon content by repeated heating and pounding, and then the reintroduction of a very small quantity of carbon or manganese into the metal. By heating and folding the metal many times, a flat bar of steel becomes lighter and far stronger than even a strong piece of iron of the same weight. An exceptional swordsmith would have the patience and knowledge to carefully fold the metal along its length perhaps hundreds of times. Some would create sword blades with layers of differing hardness, providing further resilience within the steel.

Finally the entire blade would need to be tempered, which is a process of heating and cooling the steel so as to bring about its final balance between softness and brittleness. First the blade is evenly heated at close to 1300 degrees, and then quickly quenched using a high quality oil, for water will cause the steel to crack. At this point the blade is extremely tough but very brittle. So the steel is once more heated, but this time to 900 degrees, and then allowed to slowly cool in warm air. This final step is tempering, giving the blade a spring-like flexibility. [Just as with blades, when a person, "loses his temper" he can no longer spring back to normal when faced with a problem]. Even more difficult and exceedingly rare in Europe is the process of differentially tempering different areas of the sword, but some cutlerers were even able to master this skill. If any part of the final process is incorrectly performed, if the temperatures are not exactly controlled, if the introduction of the alloy is not carefully calibrated, then months of work is wasted.

Although a swordsmith might start his career as a blacksmith, the working conditions of the two were very different. A blacksmith worked in the day in an open forge, with natural cross ventilation so as to make the workplace tolerable. Naturally, his every action was visible to any passerby, and his workshop was often conveniently near the center of the village. As his forge produced relatively low temperatures, judging the temperature of heated iron was done by a rough count, for example, so many seconds in the heat for a piece of iron of a given thickness. Quenching was done simply with water. All manner of implements were created and repaired, and virtually everyone at some point would have business there.

The swordsmith led a very different life indeed. His home was located far from the village, preferably in an area little traveled. His techniques were his trade secrets, so he rarely would have an apprentice. In order to produce the high temperatures needed for his craft, his forge was enclosed and cross currents of air strictly controlled. So as to heat the blade uniformly, some craftsmen would immerse the steel into baths of molten lead before putting the blade into the forge. In order to judge the temperature for tempering, the swordsmith could see the changes in color of the steel as the blade heated, white for the highest temperature, cherry red for the final quenching. But there are many tones and levels of brightness of steel as it heats and cools, so capturing the correct temperature required evaluating the precise shade of color. This was better done at night than during the day, and working in a forge with these high temperatures was also much more bearable in the coolness of night. Quenching was done using a variety of substances, even salt, although clarified goose oil was especially prized.

What were the local villagers to make of such a man? He worked in darkness and isolation. He bought lead but never produced any lead products, and everyone knew that lead was a popular material for alchemists. In the weeks before he would finish a sword, a number of animals would be purchased and killed, although he could hardly eat all of his killing. Surely he was making sacrifices to the old gods. Worse still was the smell of burning flesh. Were some of the sacrifices human?

Naturally, a savvy swordsmith would do nothing to downplay any such wild rumors. He probably even started a few of them, letting people assume that he was expert in the black arts. This helped keep his techniques secret, kept prying eyes at a distance, and tripled the selling price of his fine creations. So what if he could only make two or three of these weapons each year? The prices he could demand were enough to keep him well-fed indeed.

Many of these craftsmen were thought to be magicians, and certainly Merlin was such a one. To spin a fantastic tale on the origin of Excaliber and have it swallowed whole by a gullible public was good for business. But the final proof of any weapon is in battle, and a perfectly built sword that could survive with nary a scratch while hundreds of others shattered was bound to bring fame to the owner and prestige to the builder.

So the next time you read Lord of the Rings, or see a production of Camelot, or even watch Star Wars, just keep in mind that all of the "sword and sorcerer" tales come from this very ancient tradition.

Some Regional Variations:

Vikings

These were the Scandinavian raiders and traders who ran almost unchecked in Northern Europe after the collapse of Rome. Although attacking in very small numbers in only one or two ships at a time, the effects of their sporadic raids changed the face of Western civilization forever, leaving permanent changes far more profound than any caused by the Greeks or Romans. Consider the following: they established trading colonies and then permanent settlements across the width of Northern Europe, and their descendants formed all of the major royal lineages. In Eastern Europe, Swedish Vikings were known as Rus ("red" - for their red hair), later called Russians, and conquered the native Slavs. In the British Isles, descendants of Danish Vikings became the leaders of the Anglo-Saxons. In Western Europe, Norwegian Vikings were known as Norsemen, then simply as Norman, and as they settled in the continent, dominated the local population wherever they expanded. It was they who imposed the feudal system that kept them in power and established the ruling lineages that controlled all of Europe. Indeed, in the Norman conquest of England in 1066, what we think of as the last battle of a British king against French invaders, both sides were only a few generations removed from their Viking forefathers.

Viking warfare was a particularly brutal form of raiding attack. Whereas their contemporaries were content with a lightening strike to steal available grain, gold, and cattle, Vikings would first launch a direct attack on the villagers themselves. After killing off the majority of able-bodied resistance, much of the remaining population would be taken as prisoners, for the Vikings conducted a very lucrative slave-trading business. Their individual skill and prowess in face-to-face combat was widely acclaimed to be of the highest caliber. Indeed, in most cases they attacked when at a numerical disadvantage, trusting on their fighting ability to win battles against much larger forces.

Apart from warfare, there also existed a formal dueling procedure within the warrior community. Called the *homganga* ("island going"), two combatants would go to a small island so as to impede either from running away in the middle of the fight. (In later times, a simple square was roped off in any convenient flat area.) They would trade blows, one after the other, with sword or axe until blood was drawn, at which point the fight was considered won. In some variations, the disputants were allowed to bring three wooden shields each, and when the last shield broke the very next strike would obviously end the fight.

<u>Weapons available</u> – Three foot swords with very little hand protection and usually circular shields of wood. Just as common were single and double hand axes, as well as bow and arrow. Short spears were used by the few mounted warriors.

Celts

Even though Celtic peoples lived throughout Europe, for our purposes we'll focus on the pre-Anglo-Saxon tribes of the British Isles. Very little direct evidence exists as to how they lived, for the few contemporary written sources were from the Romans, not known for their scientific rigor nor dispassionate neutrality when describing their subjugated conquests. The Celts also had no written language, and although they had a strong oral tradition to transmit their legends and culture, very little of that survived their being overrun by Roman, then Anglo Saxon, then Viking, then Christian attempts to annihilate their culture, especially the repository of knowledge that was the combined memory of Druid priest/scholars. Be that as it may, it does seem that the varied tribes were led by warrior/"kings", were generally subsistence farmers and herders but still managed to maintain a class of priests and artisans. Women could achieve a level of power and respect above that found in other societies, even becoming warrior/kings themselves.

In war, all accounts agree that Celts fought primarily as complete tribes. All healthy males, and many powerful females, would join in the fray. There was no attempt at an organized attack. Instead, the king would personally lead an all-out wild charge into the middle of the assembled enemy, each warrior fighting to suit the best of his/her ability. The fighters valued bravery above all else, running into battle with one weapon in hand and no armor and usually no shield. The wealthier tribes used war chariots carrying two people - one driver and one (usually high-ranking) warrior, much as did the chariot armies of the ancient Middle East. The difference here was that the Celts used the chariot as a vehicle from which to fight using close weapons instead of as a firing platform for archers.

Celts generally had better iron and proto-steel making technologies than did their contemporaries, but due to their all-or-nothing charges, were not considered an especially troublesome adversary. The Romans in particular knew that the biggest danger came in the first moments of the initial charge of the Celts. If that could be withstood, a disciplined army could wait until the "barbarians" tired themselves out.

Weapons available – Long bladed single hand swords, and short spears and axes for ground fighting. The shield, although easily available, was considered a warrior's personal choice, rather than a soldier's essential equipment. The majority of Celts fought without shield, armour, or helmet.

Steel and the Stirrup

Steel allowed a strong sword of over four feet long to be built, and the stirrup provides a solid platform from which to swing it. The nations of Europe and all of its royal houses were built on these two tools.

Rise of Feudalism

Early Medieval (Romanesque)

Time Frame – 880 AD to 1144 AD

Politics/Economics – By the turn of the millennium the feudal system was fairly well codified, although there still existed great regional variation. For the most part it was a contract between vassal and lord, the vassal providing material and the promise of military service to the lord, the lord providing security to the vassal. In time it formed the main structure of society throughout Europe, one that served well in a time of barter rather than monetary transactions for goods and services. In theory, the scale of feudalism extended to the highest level, with regional lords owing subservience to the king. In reality, most European kings had very little recourse in trying to control a recalcitrant lord, short of calling other lords to join in a military attack. Such an action carried the risk of civil war, so most monarchs were loath to disturb the status quo. The practical result was that most lords were pretty much free to run their own counties with little interference from the monarch.

Their domination over others came from their weapons and their ability to use them on horseback. Forms of feudal society based on military service had been seen in many steppe cultures in Eastern Europe. Several were warrior societies based on fighting from horseback while well armoured, but significantly using a light lance and without the benefit of stirrups. The stirrup and the sword were costly, but allowed one armed man to control dozens of others (see Warfare, below). While this form of government is often called a plutocracy *(rule by the wealthy)* it should more accurately be called an oplocracy *(rule by the weapon)* for merely having wealth was not enough to secure power. And since the son of a lord had a natural advantage in having access to these costly implements and many opportunities to train in their use, the feudal system quickly became a hereditary one. And while there were a few variations in different pockets of Europe, the transfer of power was overwhelmingly that of agnati primogeniture - everything goes to the eldest male child.

This form of inheritance may strike us moderns as unfair, but was based on some very practical considerations. The wealth of a lord was based on a central and easily defensible position, usually a castle, and enough surrounding agricultural land to be self-sustaining and even profitable. Dividing such an entity would have been difficult, if not ruinous. The eldest son would also have been the physically strongest heir, so more likely to be able to fight off any attempts at raiding. Other sons were left to their own devices, either joining the church or by offering their services as retainer/warriors to other lords.

Because so much was at stake during this transfer of power from one generation to the next, the legitimacy of the first born son was critical. Having an uncontested heir would do much to ensure that rivals to power would be less likely to attempt a takeover. Hence, for the nobles, the question of a woman's fidelity to her husband before the birth of the first son could mean the difference between peace and war. The father's dalliances could have ramifications as well, for many an illegitimate son, if older than the "true heir", would often attempt to battle his way to his inheritance. And if the true heir was too young to be an effective warrior, such an overthrow was very easily accomplished.

Interestingly, being an illegitimate did not necessarily remove one from the ranks of the nobles, although it certainly precluded one from having a direct line to power. They were even allowed to show the family crest on their coat of arms, but by convention couldn't put it in either the main field nor in the right upper quadrant. That area was reserved for members of the "true" line. No, an illegitimate had to show that crest "with a difference", most commonly by placing the crest on the left quadrant. As the descriptions in heraldry are always in Latin, and the word *sinister* means on the left side, the word became shorthand for explaining someone's bastardy. Of course, with time it also became associated with the dubious motives of someone perhaps always plotting to take what was not rightfully his.

Fashion/Manners – Feudalism created extremely conservative societies, with little room for individual expression. What art and learning there was largely served the church. In fashion, the choice of style and fabric was unofficially but tightly regulated by custom and the weight of local pressure.

Manners at first still did not differ much from upper to lower class. Eating by all was done with spoon and hand, a knife being used to cut bread or the occasional serving of meat. At whatever level, deference was certainly given to a superior, as that person could impose severe punishment, even death, with little need to consult an outside source. But the deference was not concomitant with elaborate social rituals that had to be observed by the different strata.

With time, this changed. The Normans, having settled first in France, adopted that language as their own, and shed most of their Scandinavian traditions and religion as well. Once feudal, their further expansion through most of Europe spread Norman French as the language of the ruling class. Learning continued to be the dominion of the Church, so Latin was the language of scholars. Whatever local language survived did so at the village and worker level. These separations in society slowly created separations in expected conduct. As those of lower class might not be able to speak directly in a common language with the nobles, some non-verbal standards of greeting and general conduct were required to prove that the stranger knew his place and posed no threat. It is here that we find the beginning of the practice of bowing to a superior and doffing the hat.

Warfare – The advent of the stirrup was so startling a development that it is difficult to appreciate how profound was the effect that it had on western Europe, indeed how it still affects us to this day.

Horses had been used in combat before this time, and often in a heavy cavalry capacity. Indeed the Parthians had bred full-sized chargers, fought with a couched lance, and wore full lamellar armour and complete helmets - and all before the third century B.C. But without the stirrup there was no steady platform from which to fight while on horseback. A horseman might carry a spear, but the attack with it had to be made with an overhand throw or underhand thrust. Hold on too tightly at the moment of impact and the horseman could risk getting knocked off of his mount. Similarly, swinging the sword while on horseback gives a height advantage to be sure, but with only a rope loop for the feet there is no solid foundation from which to strike.

With the stirrup, not only is the rider more secure in the saddle, but the weight and power of the horse can be transferred through the rider and into the weapon, be it lance or sword. Each strike delivers a tremendous amount of power, far more than can be generated by a foot soldier. A single horseman could easily subdue a score of even well-armed men standing on the ground. This came at the same time that improvements in steel making allowed for longer and better tempered weapons, better suited for use on horseback. The stirrup, lance, and sword, and the armor that soon followed, couldn't be carried by a regular horse. The much larger warhorse, known as the charger, was carefully bred. But charger, sword, lance, armor, and rigging for stirrup, saddle, bridle and reins - these were all extremely expensive. Such a dynamic separation between impregnable warrior and everyone else in society further intensified the breakdown in what had been stable and more egalitarian tribal/chieftain societies.

So instead of warfare being a contest between the massed eligible fit males, it moves to battles between mounted knights, closing in at full charge and then continuing the fight with sword or ax, but still on horseback as long as possible. The larger number of peasant levies were mostly poorly armed and usually unarmoured as well. Their function was to take control of the battlefield after the initial clash of knights.

Anglo-Saxons

Although of course Angles, Saxons, and Jutes had colonized the British Isles since at least the time of the Roman evacuation, most shows that feature this culture do so set in the period of their zenith, that is, just before the Norman conquest.

These pre-Norman English had a governing system which followed Germanic traditions. The warriors below the level of high lords or king held the title of thegn, and these held their property and status directly as grants from their warlord, mostly in direct recompense for their actions as warriors. As such, the positions were not strictly hereditary. This actually improved the discipline of the fighters during battle, for title and land could be revoked at any time.

Most of the hard fighting was done by the thegns, and most war bands were limited in number to about 20 to 60 warriors. If larger numbers were needed, all able-bodied men from fifteen to sixty years of age could be called to arms, but these were usually unskilled and ill-armed farmers. Even so, they considered themselves warriors: every boy would receive a shield and spear upon coming of age (about thirteen years old). At minimum, a fighter was expected to arrive when called with shield and spear, and all would have the long knife known as the saex. Better built shields had a metal boss, a central hollow hemisphere which was used as a powerful punching weapon for close-in fighting. Thegns might also have a two-handed ax and some limited armour pieces, as well as several throwing spears. Due to the lack of a domestic steel industry, swords were relatively uncommon. Depending on access to trade with Germany, only one third to one tenth of thegns and huscarls (retinue "bodyguards" to a high noble) might have one.

The difference in fighting styles would be directly related to the weapon that each soldier had. Using a spear can keep one just out of distance to an opposing warrior, but also limits the use of the shield as a defensive weapon. Even short spears are too long to be able to pull back behind the shield, the way one can with a sword or knife, so the shield ends up protecting the left side and the center of the body, but not the right.

No matter how armed, Anglo-Saxons preferred to fight on foot, believing it to be more courageous and honorable than fighting from horseback. Discipline was high, and differed from the neighboring Celts and Vikings in their ability to maintain a "shield wall" during their attacks. Instead of a rash charge at the enemy, Anglo-Saxons would form a tight line, often three warriors deep, and interlock the shields in the Roman manner. With spears sticking out between the shields, they would march slowly and directly into the enemy formations.

Late Medieval (Gothic)

Time Frame– 1145 AD to 1350 AD

Politics/Economics – The time designation is rather arbitrary, and the starting point could have been set fifty years in either direction, but what is acknowledged is that roughly during this period Europe began to civilize itself once more, laying the groundwork for the Renaissance to come. It is also when the inhabitants began to identify themselves collectively as Europeans.

The effects of the crusades, which took place before and during this period, awakened Europeans to the larger world around them. Although material benefits were centuries away, very slowly large numbers of books were slowly making their way through the religious orders, the lost literature and study of Greece and Rome being copied page by page by monastic clerics. Roads and canals were refurbished and so travel became easier for goods and people. As suppliers could finally reach buyers further and further from their homes, surplus production could be converted to profit instead of merely being hoarded in storage. Daily trade could extend beyond the limits of daily travel. Slowly a market economy based on cash began to supplant the barter system. A distinct middle class began to develop outside of the castle centers, and the townships became the foci of a new urban culture, the larger ones even supporting the first universities.

With larger economic concerns came larger political concerns, and a recognition that trade and commerce could only be effectively conducted on a national level. By the end of the 13th century the counts and lords were more willing to cede direct power to the King's court (the Magna Carta notwithstanding), knowing that strengthening the King's hand would ultimately strengthen their wealth.

The court of the king was also the central government; his personal aides were the defacto ministers of the bureaucracy that managed the affairs of state. The national and monarchical concerns were the same. Therefore wherever the king's person was located was by definition the court, and by necessity the government moved along with the king. A specific city such as London or Paris might house the king for most of the year, but in and of themselves were not the seat of power.

Fashion/Manners – With increased prosperity came a further separation between the lives of the nobles vs. commoners. Fine fabrics, exotic foods, and elaborate social entertainments dominated courtly life. Also here we see the first stirrings of rules of etiquette. Making the sign of the cross when presented with a dish of food was considered to be not only an indication of piety, but also of good social decorum. One always dried the mouth before drinking from a shared bowl, and using two hands to hold it rather than one was further evidence of courtesy. Weapons were never worn indoors, and gloves and hoods were removed when entering the great hall. This is the setting of "fairy-tale" stories, not only in our imagination, but also in theirs. Tales of fighting dragons, rescuing damsels, magic swords, sleeping beauties awakened with a kiss - they all come from this time. The literature, dance, clothing, music, and art began to serve the ideals of the aristocracy, helping to provide the illusion of fairy-tale otherworldliness.

Some specific body postures and movement make sense when one remembers the clothing of the upper class in this period. But one must keep in mind that although the clothing became more exaggerated, the movements remained simple and direct. Fussiness must be avoided in favor of simple, long elegant movement. For example, as the shoes tended to be of extreme length and pointed, crossing the legs while seated simply looks comical. Instead, the feet should be turned out at every opportunity, and the legs apart. When out of doors, hats were not doffed, and indeed hats were removed indoors only in the presence of social equals, not as a sign of submission to authority. If the hat was off, it would usually be held in the left hand at the hip while bowing. Otherwise, both arms could freely swing down and to the side in an open gesture, palms forward, while bowing. The bow itself was simple: a slight bend at the waist while the left foot stepped back and both knees would bend, lowering the body. Seventy percent of the body weight should be on the right leg, the left being used for support only.

We have seen so many variations of a king conferring knighthood in movies that we forget how simple was the actual ceremony. The knight-to-be while standing drew his sword with his right hand, grasped the center of the blade with the left, and then knelt on both knees. Resting the hilt on his right forearm, the sword was offered to the king. The king would take the sword and touch the blade to the knight's left shoulder, and then return the sword. The knight would then rise and sheath the weapon. Movie directors like to have both shoulders touched, or even three touches, so as to draw out the moment, but Gothic ceremonies tended to be simple though solemn, with little embellishment. And although the same film directors want the knights to be on one knee only because it looks better, the ceremony was a semireligious one. As an oath before God, both knees must be on the ground.

There has also been much said of the custom of greeting by grasping the other at the forearms or at the elbows. Many posit that this precursor to the modern handshake was a way to keep someone from attacking you with a dagger in this very dangerous time. But, as lawyers would say, this assumes facts not in evidence. First, such a greeting was only done among social equals, never to mere strangers on a country road, and there is simply nothing in any historical documentation that suggests that attacks during greetings ever occurred or that anyone was ever worried about it. Second, greeting in general was very effusive compared to our modern Western timidity. Family members embraced and kissed openly during casual greetings, and knights usually embraced and kissed each other on the cheek, as is done in most of the non-Anglo/Saxon world today. Thirdly, and most tellingly, grasping another by his elbows does nothing but limit the use of your *own* hands. It leaves the other person's hands completely free to attack you with whatever weapon he wishes. Rather than an indication of wariness, I see it as a sign of great openness and trust.

Civilian Conflict – Tournaments and jousts exhibited all of the techniques of war, but to local villagers they were treated as the nearest equivalent of a grand sporting event. To the reigning monarchs, they were something of a conundrum. Although wildly popular and an excellent way of training the uninitiated into the techniques of actual battle, they could also unleash dangerous passions that could prove difficult to control. There was also the fear that the massing of so many armed men could hide an insurrection, so most kings tried to keep the tournaments under the direct control of the crown. This proved difficult, as the popularity of these events and the sudden influx of cash to the hosting city or parish meant that tournaments, legal and otherwise, were bound to pop up anywhere at almost any time.

The earliest tournaments were melees, in which two teams were formed and attacked each other using the regular weapons of war, on horseback at first but then on foot should circumstances warrant. The attendees were told to use the flats rather than the edges of their sword. As years passed, the tournament became more ceremonial and somewhat less bloody, the use of special blunted weapons doing much to reduce injuries.

Dueling as we understand it did not exist. The nearest equivalent was the right to judicial combat. This could be invoked either to establish innocence or to redress wrongs, but was considered a legal, rather than personal, action.

<u>Warfare</u> –   Warfare was still largely based on direct confrontations between mounted knights (and their men-at-arms); in other words, heavy cavalry vs. heavy cavalry. As economic conditions improved, more and better armed horsemen were available for battle. The arms and armor they used were not uniform, and limited only by the wealth of the fighter. Most aspired to sword, axe, lance, shield, full body armor and chain mail, and a fully armored war horse. While dismounting and fighting on ground was performed as situations required, the knight's greatest strength on the battlefield came from his position on horseback.

Whether or not the fully armored knight was excessively hindered by his armor has been a subject of great debate among historians. Some have suggested that once knocked from his saddle, the knight was as helpless as a turtle on its back. Others note that accounts exist of at least one knight astonishing crowds by scaling ropes and leaping over fences while wearing a full suit of armor weighing sixty pounds. We should assume that these represent the two extremes of human capability, and that the mobility of the fighter depended more on the individual's strength and ability than any inherent limitations in a suit of steel. And I can relate from experience that falling from a horse is quite a shock to the body even in the best of circumstances, let alone being battered about within a tin can. One should assume that in those several seconds of hitting the ground, gathering one's wits, and turning over to come to one's feet, the knight would be at his most vulnerable and completely defenseless. One good hit with an axe and he'd be done for.

While most of the movies we have seen show every knight in battle wearing a complete suit of armor, that was almost certainly not the case. For most humans the wearing of steel, chain mail, and the cloth padding underneath it all is stifling and dehydrating. Although some battles might have lasted for several hours, knights needed frequent rests between every few minutes of actual combat. To increase mobility and endurance, many would remove much of their armor as temperatures rose. Chain mail and helmet were considered essential, but each additional piece was up to the wearer trying to strike a balance between protection and practicality. It seems that being completely armored was more often than not taken as a sign of being untested and fearful. This is a common situation throughout history, with the greenhorns packing every possible item they can get hold of, while the veterans go into battle light and mobile.

As important now as the mounted knights were large numbers of heavily armoured men-at-arms. These infantry soldiers used pikes to break cavalry charges and also take the field in direct fighting. Usually men of proven combat experience, they were often well paid mercenary units rather than a part of the conscripted levy.

Also on the battlefield were increasing numbers of bowmen and crossbowmen. These were generally kept behind the knights or on the flanks. Their primary function was to weaken the enemy cavalry during their charge, although they could also devastate a standing infantry. Once both sides engaged, they also needed to fire into any breakaway group of riders attempting a flanking manoeuver or encirclement. These archers served as very effective light infantry so long as they could stay just out of range of the battle line. In order to move quickly so as to respond to changing battlefield conditions, bowmen were lightly armoured. In case the fight came to them, they could attempt to defend themselves with short swords and bucklers, but for them these were weapons of last resort only.

Held in especially high regard was the English longbowman. His bow was six feet long, carved from a single piece of yew trunk wood or large branch and had a draw weight of between 100 to 120 lbs (Compare that to today's hunting bows. Most draw at 45 lbs, while the most powerful max out at 75 lbs). The archer kept his shoulders relatively square to the enemy and had the left or leading foot pointed forward, unlike modern competitive archers that stand sideways to the target. It also seems that the right hand was drawn only to the front of the face, not all the way back to the right ear. Although these two techniques would seem to reduce the available power to the bow, the longbowman was still able to fire ten aimed arrows per minute at an effective range of over 200 yards. Some archers were able to provide effective fire from nearly 400 yards. Considering that a cavalry charge would take about 17 seconds to cross 200 yards, the longbowmen were an extremely effective countermeasure. Crossbows, by comparison, were only effective at about 150 yards, and the rate of fire was rarely better than twice a minute. As in modern archery, the arrow is placed on the left side of the bow for firing, although this may not have been a hard and fast rule. There were no training schools for archery, the skills being passed on from father to son and picked up around the village by watching more experienced men. It was thought to take a full three years for a young man at his full growth to be able to handle the longbow effectively.

If archers could not take a position behind the protection of a line of pikemen, they were expected to create a quick defense behind wooden spikes driven into the ground, sharpened points directed towards the enemy. For this purpose, they carried a metal headed mallet, and some carried small hatchets. Doubtless, in an extreme emergency these might be used for hand-to-hand fighting as well.

Two bits of folklore that are untrue. First, the arrow quiver was never worn on the back. That was a Victorian era conceit, made even more popular by book illustrations and film depictions of Robin Hood. Longbowmen usually carried their arrows in a cloth wrap. Once they took position on the field they would either stick the arrows in a bunch on the ground or tuck them all behind the back through the belt, points sticking out low and to the right. The cloth or leather wrapping ranged in complexity from a single square to a true back with protective rain flaps and straps from which to hang the quiver onto the waist belt. Secondly, there is an old story that the modern English insult of the "backward peace sign" comes from 14th century English archers. The idea is that the French would cut off the two draw fingers of any English bowman captured in battle, so shoving the fist upward with the two fingers pointing is something like a taunt, "I've still got mine, what are you going to do about it". The problem is that that doesn't really convey the real meaning of the gesture, and that the French didn't cut off any archers' fingers. Archers were commoners, never taken prisoner. They were simply killed outright.

Lastly in the warfare of the period were the true foot soldiers, usually untrained peasant levies. Held in utter contempt by mounted nobility, they were often used as a follow-up force. Once a break in the battle line had been formed by the knights or by the archers, the ill-armed peasants would rush in to capitalize on the break and kill as many of the enemy as possible, usually using variations of simple farming implements. Alternatively, the peasants could be used in an all-out charge into a well defended enemy position. With luck, the enemy would break their formation in order to slaughter the foot soldiers. The attacking cavalry could then take advantage of the disarray in the enemy line.

When a true heavy infantry was needed, no one depended on the peasant levy. Instead, the men-at-arms themselves would dismount and form a sturdy line, with the peasants filling in the line as necessary.

Throughout this period, the feudal system proved to be insufficient to provide fighters in sufficient quantity or skill for all of the conflicts across the continent. The ancient call to arms was increasingly ignored, with many preferring to pay a (substantial) fine rather than present themselves for war. While at first this was distressing to military commanders, it soon was found to be quite a benefit. The money raised by this "scutage" was used to pay for mercenary units, who proved to be superior warriors with well-maintained weapons and battle-honed skills and discipline. While they could prove ready to jump sides if offered better pay by the enemy, once in battle they outperformed any other units.

Weapons available – The feudal system allowed money to accumulate and centralize, allowing for more soldiers in battle and more weapons to be built. Arrows, crossbows and spears return in large numbers for the ground troops. Mounted knights and men-at-arms are generally armed with singlehand swords with cruciform style large guards. As armour plate and steel helmets become more common, impact weapons such as maces and heavy headed axes are used. Quarterstaffs, heavy walking sticks, and the ubiquitous dagger are standard weapons for a civilian walking outside of the protection of the village or township.

Byzantium

It is woefully unfair to discuss this Greek empire in the few sentences that I'll be using here, but to be honest with you there are so few productions in the USA done in this setting that it is really not worth our time to describe it in any great detail. Also, there is very little of interest here as concerns any uniqueness of Byzantine warfare or weaponry.

The empire is roughly noted as beginning circa 360 AD, concomitant with the fall of Rome, and finally ending a few years after the Ottoman invasion at around 1460 AD. So for over one thousand years, Byzantium continued to be a center of Christian power. The emperor presented himself as a direct personification of the power of the church, so even secular political activities were bathed in the light of the sacred. The city itself was remarkable to all who visited it for its fantastic wealth as well as the almost unending series of religious holidays and pageantry.

But militarily, the Byzantines were unremarkable. Their wealth enabled them to keep a standing army of mostly mercenaries throughout its history. Although their structures and clothing were outstandingly opulent, Byzantine weapons and warriors were indistinguishable from their European brethren.

The Rapier and the Rise of Individualism

The long climb out of the dark ages brings to Europe the genesis of what would become all that we consider "normal" life.

Early Renaissance
Time Frame – 1350 to 1520

Politics/Economics –

The high water mark for absolute monarchies. The feudalism of the past is too cumbersome to deal with the expanded economic opportunities made available through trade and goods from Asia, Africa, the Americas, and the Middle East. With greater economic centralization comes a lessening of the power of regional lords and a concomitant increase in the power of a reigning king.

New manufacturing and trade centers within Europe, combined with periodic drops in the population due to the plague, meant that the value of the individual worker soared. Wages tripled, and large numbers of workers could leave traditional agricultural employment for the higher pay of "factory" jobs. City populations swelled, as did their economic power. Increasingly, the middle-class burgomasters of a large township would wield more effective political power than a county lord.

Although the crusades began as an effort to subjugate the "infidel" and increase the power of Christianity, they ended by extending trade routes into Asia and the Ottoman Empire, bringing in not only goods but also knowledge in science, engineering, and philosophy long lost to Western Europe. This transfer of knowledge was further spurred by the relocation of Greek scholars from the declining Byzantine Empire to the wealthy urban centers of Italy. These parallel influences led to a sudden flourishing in the learning of and emulation of ancient Greek and Roman philosophy.

The Renaissance is also the beginning of the first wave of youth culture. This is not all that dissimilar from the Hippie movement of the 1960's. All things "old" were viewed with distrust. Only new thoughts had value. Ironically, "new" was considered the adaptation of ancient Greek philosophy, and a turning away from strict deference to church teaching. Knowledge now became something that could be found by individual intellectual pursuit, but the period is also marked by a more harsh body of critical thought, each wave of plague and each defeat at crusade further eroding the faith in an ordered world. Philosophy and art look to find a grand balance outside of the rigid framework set forth by the Vatican.

Fashion/Manners – With a higher standard of living and a much wider variety of fabrics and colors available, personal expression in attire was highly valued. The heaviness and sense of protection from nature that was suggestive in Gothic clothing gave way to apparel more open and relaxed, evocative of a person far more comfortable living in the natural world. It is a look and attitude far less fearful of the universe.

With looser and showier clothing come manners also more open and relaxed. There are no prescribed gestures or poses, but rather an easy yet proud carriage, legs generally turned out but no longer excessively so. A certain lightness of bearing was cultivated, distinctly different than that medieval stalwart stance. The look was suppose to imply that one was ready to spring at a moment to fight or dance. The bow in greeting is now used only at formal occasions, and would be performed with the back leg remaining straight and the front leg stepping forward slightly and bending at the knee (think of a very small fencer's lunge). Notice how this movement naturally opens the chest and gently propels the person forward, rather than shrinking away in fear. When not worn, the hat was generally held in front of the body, but not stiffly. Rather, the hand was relaxed, as though the hat was altogether forgotten by the owner. For a greeting between friends, the convention of the bow was eliminated altogether as too pretentious. Instead, friends, male or female, would simply join in a heartfelt handclasp.

Just as art sought balance, so did the concept of the ideal man. A gentleman of position was expected to be not only proficient in the practice of arms, but also become familiar with all areas of learning, languages, philosophy and art.

Civilian Conflict – With the exception of some larger daggers that Italians and Germans began wearing, there were no substantive changes in the way civilian disputes were settled. However, with the breakdown of ecclesiastic and manorial authority, the number of private disputes increased in many nations. In Italy especially, when a crime was committed by one individual the entire family was considered guilty, often leading to never-ending reprisals and counter reprisals.

Although there are many current plays set in this period that use civilian rapier fights, the weapon had not yet been invented. Civilian disputes were settled by knife, cudgel, or fist.

Warfare – Edged weapons for the battlefield were the same in basic layout compared to the Gothic period, although the variety expanded to fit different tactical uses. Steel became cheaper, and with the slow diffusion of technical knowledge from the Moorish cultures, far stronger swords were available.

Continuing the trend of the earlier medieval period, large numbers of mercenary companies were routinely used for war. What was new was that these units augmented the newly created and very effective native infantry units. For the first time since the ancient Greeks, large numbers of regular foot soldiers were given specific training in the use of their pole weapons and were given a primary rather than tertiary tactical assignment. By acting as a disciplined unit, a line of soldiers with spear or halberd could take the field and nullify any charge by the mounted cavalry. To aid in that task, they were given specific weapons for the job. Instead of trying to outfit them as "light-knights", their weapons were based on the agricultural implements that they already knew, but refined so as to be appropriate to the battleground.

When these units took the field (first the Swiss, then the Germans, then the rest of Europe) they became an even match for the cavalry. When combined with equally disciplined contingents of archers or crossbowmen, they were unbeatable. It was here, rather than with the introduction of gunpowder, that the mounted knight began his inexorable decline. Unable to defeat the infantry in a head-on assault, and with mobility limited by disciplined archery, the mounted cavalry lost its battlefield advantage.

Weapons Available: Every type of poleweapon, mace, axe and straight edged battle sword, both single and double handed is now seen on European battlefields.

Mannerist Renaissance
Time Frame – 1520 - 1620

Politics/Economics – A period of turmoil, where the conflict of circumstances would lead to some of the largest changes that Europe would ever see. The earlier Renaissance was a great flowering, a liberation of expression, but did not bring radical changes in thought. That change occurred in this period, what we call the Elizabethan era.

Overall standard of living rises with the influx of gold and silver from the Americas. This, along with a dramatic increase in the size and mobility of the population, moves the continent to a completely monetary economy and the creation of independent and trusted banks and exchange houses. The liberalizing of thought allowed by the Renaissance and the weakening of Catholic power after the waves of plague led directly to what would be known as Protestantism. First promulgated by Martin Luther as a challenge within the Church, it came to divide Europe politically and dynastically. When a newly powerful Germany (under Charles V) allowed its troops to sack Rome, it not only ended up strengthening Protestantism, but brought to an end the Italian Renaissance. The "accidental Protestantism" of Henry VIII and the subsequent creation of the Church of England would draw Great Britain into the center of the conflict, both within the nation in bloody civil wars and also in international intrigues.

The entire continent sees changes happening on a grand scale. The explosion of printed materials disperses knowledge, and with books becoming plentiful and remarkably inexpensive, more people of every level of society are motivated to learn to read. Not only knowledge, but opinion too can travel widely and quickly, increasing the complexity of philosophical thought and radical notions such as independent reality, humanism, and Copernican astronomy. Imagine suddenly being confronted with these two radical thoughts at the same time: that the earth is not the center of the universe, and that the Holy Roman Church is not the center of religion. Art now explores the ambiguities of life, no longer content with trying to replicate the grand classical balance of the previous period.

Just as with the beginning of the Renaissance, there is a further shift in outlook. But now it continues from criticism to pessimism. There is a general return to superstitious thought, and violent reaction against the unknown. This spurs the power of the Inquisition, and not without reason ushers in a climate of fear. With fear came violence and repression, both from the Catholic Inquisitions as well as Puritan purges.

I must make some mention here of one guy who wrote a couple of plays during this period. You might have heard of him. His name was Shakespeare (or maybe Shaksper, or Shaxpere, or Shakespere, or Shakspere). It is likely that you are reading this section in particular right now because you have a play of his coming up. So how does he fit in with the rest of the information above?

It has been said many times that Shakespeare straddled both worlds, the medieval and the modern. But just because that is almost a cliché doesn't mean that it isn't also dauntingly true. In his time he was perhaps one of the last holdouts of conservative thought. Part of this is understandable. As a successful playwright who wanted to stay successful, he made sure to play to the house and to the authorities who had the power to shut his theatre down. Throughout his plays he unquestioningly accepts the divine right of kings and shows the terrible tragedies that spring from usurping a legitimate ruler from his (or her) seat of power. He must have read the latest scientific studies of the prior fifty years, but continues to write of a universe in which the Earth is at its center, where the body is regulated by humours, and that humans are born into their natural position in society. Disrupting the natural order can bring about calamity to all. And yet ...

.... he is also undeniably a humanist, who has his central characters deal with their situations by reasoning them out. In Hamlet, other characters may call him melancholic, but he does not allow that or any other humour to rule him. We see Hamlet struggle through the right or wrong of an action by using his mental capability, even by setting up something of a scientific experiment. In Richard II, the king may have been a poor ruler, or he may have been unjustly overthrown, but Shakespeare's interest is in seeing him deconstruct his rapidly imploding universe. Using his rational thought alone, he finds a new place for himself, and a certain amount of peace, in a world that reduces him to nothingness. Every character in every play has a counterpart in the simplistic plays of Medieval Europe, and yet he endows them with understanding of their own motivations that anticipates psychological realism by centuries.

Fashion/Manners – It's not called the mannerist period for nothing. The free and easy designs and movements of the earlier Renaissance become codified and lose much of their feeling of casual elegance. German and English were more restrictive than French or Italian - they were held back by a very late entry to the benefits of the Renaissance, so much so that they still held a generally medieval outlook long after the rest of Europe flourished.

For all of Europe, the hallmarks of fashion were exaggeration, ornamentation without a conceit of utility, and a stylized, almost tortured, three dimensional embellishment. In a dramatic break from the long and loose hair of the early Renaissance, men's hair suddenly is cut much shorter. Stiff, padded, and encased, the body must conform to the new style. As dress shoes were soft and heelless, walking became slower, with the ball of the foot nearly brushing the ground in order to keep the backless shoes from falling off. Because of the wide ("pumpkin") breeches, the legs were kept at a medium-wide stance, and movement led with the hips. In addition, no man was considered completely dressed unless he also wore his rapier. It seems that all of these factors conspired to create a sort of "sailing" walking gait, a push from the hips side to side for each step forward, while trying to keep the torso level. When sitting, one would always perch on the edge of the seat, with the feet kept side by side, not crossed nor wide apart. The rapier hilt would be tilted back so that the tip of the scabbard was pointed forward, this in order to prevent anyone from tripping over it. Small wonder that many men took lessons in general movement from fencing masters.

The etiquette for greeting also became formalized. Gloves were kept on indoors and removed when offering a hand to a woman. To bow, the feet were turned outward slightly and the weight shifted to the right leg. The left leg then moved back, with the left knee now turned out even more. Keeping the back erect, both knees would bend, with the center of balance now shared by both legs. In an extreme bow, the left knee might almost touch the floor. On rising, the weight moves back to the right foot. This is what Shakespeare calls "making a leg", and is not really a bow for the restrictions of the tight doublet prevent a graceful bend at the waist. During the entire procedure the stiff ruff of the collar prevents the inclination of the head, but the hat is removed and allowed to sweep to the side.

Civilian Conflict –

To the consternation of many directors trying to set a Shakespeare play within Shakespeare's time, there are certain things that they often request that simply don't exist in the 16th century. There was no civilian pistol. There was no hunting rifle. All firearms for this period were purely military weapons, no exceptions. Hunting, for deer or boar, was done with bow and arrow (backed up with lance and sword). Bird hunting was done with light crossbows, using blunted broad bolts so as to knock birds out of the sky rather than harpooning them. No, if someone was to threaten another, it was done with the rapier.

Around 1530, the invention of the rapier provided the opportunity for any man to walk about the streets armed with a sword. Much lighter than the swords used in battle, it did not pull down at the hip as did broadswords, so one could comfortably wear it all day. It was a cut and thrust weapon, doing neither particularly well but certainly capable of doing a good deal of damage without having to have massive upper body strength. The English had a love-hate relationship with the rapier. They felt that nothing was more honorable than a simple stout English broadsword, but realized that it was not nearly so portable as the rapier. They knew that the rapier was also not only a badge of status and style but also an extraordinary weapon in case of a street attack. It was relatively expensive, so a common highwayman or street thug was not likely to have one. On the other hand, it was not restricted to the knightly class, so anyone with the money and training could wear one. The fighting style assumed that one would have a secondary weapon in the other hand, so as to knock down an opponent's weapon and provide an opening for your own thrust or cut. With so many people now fully armed, it was only natural that innumerable fencing schools popped up. Wherever the rapier flourished, so did experts charging students in its use.

It was considered a sneaky and deceitful weapon, what with the underhanded thrusts and point-tip feints and evasions. For no small reason did the English of a certain age want the rapier eradicated since it was "useless in war, and kills our youth in peace." Nationalism played a part, since most of the swordmasters were Italian or French. The traditional English weapons of stout sword and buckler or the cudgel or quarterstaff might break an arm or occasionally crack a head, but being impaled by a rapier led to deep loss of blood and often horrific delayed death from systemic infection.

Since the rapier could prove so deadly, not everyone was terribly keen to engage in a fight. Certain rules were established as to when circumstances were appropriate for a duel. The *"code duello"* or dueling protocol was a series of understandings as to the reasonableness of entering into a duel with honor, but not on how the duel itself was to take place. There were many codes, specific to different countries and often ignored or referenced as it suited the needs of one or the other party. Most held many similarities in terms of what circumstances permitted the challenge. "Giving someone the lie" (charging someone with deceit, revealing a deliberate falsehood) was clearly the most common grievance, although this could be answered back several times by counter charges and a great deal of diplomatic manoeuvering with the hope that all could be resolved or at least so confused that it could end without any confrontation at all. A private apology sent by courier could also do much to prevent bloodshed.

Because it was assume that having a rapier meant that you should know how to use it, and therefore had at least enough disposable income for the lessons so required, a challenge to a duel was generally only done among members of the middle to upper class. Using a sword against a servingman, no matter what the insult, was against civil propriety as well as legally considered murder. Beating a lower class person with a stick or with the flat of the sword was perfectly acceptable, so long as there was "justification".

A duel itself was a very straightforward affair. The use of "seconds", assistants to the participants of the duel, was not yet formalized, although it was common practice (and common sense) to bring a few friends to prevent being ambushed or other such trickery. The formal salute was also not created yet, so the two belligerents would merely arrive, draw at their pleasure, and begin. The sword was generally held with the arm fully extended and pointed at the opponent's face, and the left arm also fully extended holding the dagger. One hand might be held high and the other low, or both held out at the same height. A certain amount of changing hand positions while circling the opponent would have been common before actually beginning combat. The left, not right, foot was forward, thus bringing the dagger and sword tips at equal distance to the opponent. Among more skilled fighters, a slight standstill might occur, similar to that of samurai warriors facing off, in which one waits for the other combatant to make the first move. Then a blur of movement as one duelist quickly parries the incoming weapon with the left hand and strikes a finishing blow with the right, all in one decisive instant. The samurai would do this using the single katana; the Renaissance fighter would divert the incoming sword with his dagger and then thrust his sword towards the opponent's eye.

Historically, most fights were thus over in one or two moves. One can imagine, however, that many duels reverted to fearful slashing contests well out of range and of limited lethality until both sides could agree that honor had been served and all could return home healthy and happy.

A minor but interesting point is the symbolism of the rapier as a badge of place in society. Although anyone could wear a sword, the wearing of the rapier began to be associated with the wealthy, as it was assumed that only those with enough time and resources could afford a good sword and the lessons required to learn how to handle it. This was a very gradual process, and certainly in Shakespeare's time it was more of a generational divide rather than class, but by the 1620's certainly anyone who considered himself a gentleman or who had such aspirations owned a rapier and usually wore one in public. For many men, the only use of the rapier was to finish an elegant outfit worn for important ceremonies or exclusive entertainments. For those unwilling to spend so much money on an item of dress, "dancing swords" were available at a greatly reduced price. These were elegant hilts on false blades, worn in scabbards but never drawn, and were sufficient to meet the demands of society. Portraits of the wealthy of the period often have the subject wearing a rapier for the same reason.

One firm exception is that for the reigning monarch, always pictured wearing a sword of war but not a rapier. As a weapon of duels, rapiers decide matters of personal honor, but a king is supposed to be above such concerns. His use of the sword should only be in defense of the entire country as well as being a sword of impartial justice in domestic disputes.

Warfare – A continuation of the prior order, but with some small changes, especially the introduction of pistols as light cavalry weapons, fired with the right hand from horseback. The arquebus was used as a field artillery, something like a mobile cannon, but they were of limited range. Continuation of the same swords, although we see more contingents of sword and buckler men, very lightly armored, fighting along side either the pikemen or the archers, protecting them should the fight move their way.

The Musket and the Gunpowder Revolution

Cavalier/Baroque

Time Frame – 1600 - 1730

Politics/Economics – The final traces of medieval organization has disappeared, as countries move from being feudal monarchies to true nation-states. Instead of having a monarchy dependant on its layers of nobility for defense and administration, power is centralized so that the national government directly supports a standing army, directly manages daily administration through its own bureaucracy, and directly taxes its citizens. For the first time the aristocracy is dependant on the king, a true "absolute" monarch. The experts at this concentration of power are Louis XIV and Richelieu, and the political center of Europe shifts from Spain to France, remaining there for the next two hundred years.

With the massive increase in bureaucracy, the actual center of power is tied to a single regal court in a capital city. The daily affairs of state being far too complicated to physically move, governmental functions continue to operate in that city year-round, remaining there no matter where the king should be.

Although these changes were meant to give central governments far broader powers than they had ever had before, they also had the unintended effects of expanding citizens' rights. Up until this time commoners had to seek permission from the local lord to marry, travel, set up a business, etc., and each locality could have wildly differing standards on what it would permit. Once all of these "liberties" came under central control, nationwide standards provided a generally more permissive and certainly more efficient set of rules by which to live and work. This came as a breath of fresh air, lifting some of the dire pessimism of the previous decades.

These changes occur at the same time that the Church of Rome is struggling with the effects of the Protestant reformation and Copernican astronomy. The Counter-Reformation and the idea of an infinite universe with us not at its center leads both to an explosion of expansive art and personal expression and the fear that where one stands on any issue might need to change depending on which way the political winds blow.

Fashion/Manners – The early part of this period is called "cavalier", from the French word for "horseman", with good reason. The male ideal shifts from being a royal household courtier, decked in his court finery appropriate to his status, to being a robust adventurer, wearing clothing suitable for any occasion, indoor or out. Male movement becomes freer, the emphasis now on having a natural athletic swagger. Regular pants, practical boots and comfortable shirts and jackets allowed for a less restrained manner than the tortured costumes of the "mannerist" Elizabethan period. A man now strides into a room confidently. Gloves were worn for most occasions, and rarely removed. The courtly bow also is freer, performed with abandon. As the cavalier leaves his right foot forward and right leg straight, he steps back with his left foot and bends the left knee slightly while doffing his hat in a grand sweep. To add to the flow, he can comfortably bend at the waist and lower his head, and then dramatically sweep back up in a grand gesture. Indeed, great personal variation for the bow was acceptable, as it demonstrated the person's sense of flair and grace. The hat was returned to the head at the completion of the bow, and it is normal to keep the hat on during all occasions. With a fine plume sprouting from the brim, the hat added to the look of no longer being diminished by the world, but ready to conquer it. A man might sit sideways or even backwards on a chair, and in all circumstances giving the impression that no chair, room, or even world can contain him, for if the universe is infinite, why then so is he.

Not all of these outward changes were based on practical considerations. The high-topped cavalry boots were merely copies of what soldiers were wearing to protect their legs from pistol shots when riding in battle, and were certainly not the most comfortable things to walk around in, especially when the tops would start to sink down to the calves. But they gave a romantic look and even more swagger when walking, so civilians quickly appropriated them. In all, the people of the period reveled in a new world of extravagance and sensuality, of brilliance and exuberance.

Naturally, as the epoch progressed the free and relaxed stances of the cavalier turned into the carefully copied poses of the baroque. In the later portion of the century what had been free of affectation became strict rules of social conduct. In doffing the hat, if was gracefully lifted and then swept down to the right side, no longer across the body. A hat once doffed could not be returned to the head unless granted permission by a superior, and to fail to give permission was just as serious a breech of protocol. No one was allowed to keep the head covered in the presence of the king. The athletic stances became regimented into the ballet positions we know today, with the feet turned out at ninety degrees during every step, the ball of the foot landing before the heel. As most men wore heels, this required a strong pointing of the foot at each step.

In large social occasions, or when passing people on the street, a bow *en passant* allowed for courtesy to be extended without having to stop for conversation. It was a simple bow from the waist while allowing the back foot to drag to the forward position, never breaking stride. This passing bow could be performed either from the left or the right, with the foot nearest the person being passed allowed to drag while bowing in that same direction. Walking sticks were taller than walking canes, and allowed the user to maintain the arm at almost shoulder height, nicely mimicking the port-a-bras of classic ballet.

In sitting, the gentleman of this later period sat in the center of the cushion, neither on the edge nor fully to the back, giving the appearance of sitting regally on a throne. The handkerchief was held between the first and second fingers and allowed to drape gracefully over the back of the hand.

Most movement was still carried off with a grand flourish if possible, but here we see a dichotomy between those still influenced by the athletic swagger of the earlier period and the fops. Fops delighted in the exaggeration of clothing and movement, often walking in small, quick mincing steps and turns, the better to accentuate the bounce of the wig and clothing. The more dignified members of society kept their moves more subtle and deliberate, expansive yet solid, never fussy, heightening the illusion of power and grandeur.

Civilian Conflict –

Rapier in Transition

After the 1650's as men's fashion starts to calm down a bit and ornamentation becomes more reserved, the extreme hilt styles of the cavalier period begin to contract as well. The parts of the hilt remain, but extend away from the hand much less than before. The sword is still both a cut and thrust weapon and, with or without a secondary parrying weapon in the left hand, is still in use. But the blade of the rapier is now lighter, and the quillons smaller, leading to a faster fighting style with far more emphasis of the thrust rather than the cut, the sword being used to parry in defense rather than simply a strong block as barrier. The difference is in diverting rather than stopping the incoming thrust attack. It is not yet the smallsword, but is certainly developing in that direction.

Warfare – This is also the time known as the "gunpowder revolution", which saw the final decline of the importance of the mounted knight in battle and the elevation once again of the common foot soldier as the central focus of military planning.

Up until this time, foot soldiers (infantry) could hold off mounted knights (cavalry) by pointing long spears at the horses, but this is a defensive posture and as such it was hard for them to do much real damage if they tried to go on the offensive. Direct heavy cavalry charges could usually create openings in the line of infantry or simply work the flanks or charge from behind so as to disrupt their formations.

A smart opposing general would use either archers (light infantry) with longbows or crossbows to fire into the approaching cavalry and prevent them from reaching the infantry lines. But longbow archery, while very accurate, is a skill which requires tremendous strength and constant practice. Crossbows require less strength, but the apparatus itself breaks down frequently, requiring constant and costly repair, ad the bolts [arrows] they fire must be built by special craftsmen. So limited numbers of either of these types of archers could be brought to the field, and both suffered the same limitation of the bowstrings swelling in damp weather.

By the time Shakespeare retired to Stratford, the first practical firearm was developed that could be mass produced. The matchlock musket was a dramatic improvement over the arquebus, which had been in use since the 1400's but was notoriously underpowered. The matchlock was still an ungainly beast of a thing to load and fire, but it was finally just light enough so that a line of soldiers could load and fire at the same time. To a field general, this meant that it had infantry applications as opposed to simply another artillery piece. The matchlock musket had a lighter, longer, and thinner barrel, and could therefore be attached to less wood for the stock. So the musket, though expensive, inaccurate, and time consuming to maintain and load, was certainly far easier to maintain and repair, and required far less strength to operate than bow, pike, or sword. Although it had the same rate of fire as the crossbow, armies could muster far more of them for battle, and lead musket balls were far less expensive than arrows.

The style of firearm used by the musketeers is called the Spanish matchlock musket, so-called because it was first developed in Spain in 1567 and used a lit fuse, or "match", to set-off the explosive powder within the musket (much like a cannon). Although inoperable in the rain, the fuse could still remain lit if it were merely damp.

Due to the inaccuracy of the weapon, a line of soldiers would have to fire at the same time if they were to have any chance at hitting a column of the enemy, which meant they needed to load and aim at the same time as well. Up to thirty individual motions are required in firing each shot, and add to that the danger of carrying a lit fuse near pouches full of gunpowder and you can see why generals preferred to have well-trained and fairly intelligent men as musketeers. Their solution was to recruit among the more educated lesser nobility, and when possible to provide year-round employment for them as garrison or palace guards at a time when there were no standing armies. Remember, however, that battles were still lost or won depending on the ability of the pike men, the regular infantry, not the cavalry nor musketeers, to take and hold the field. Musketeers took the job of light infantry, protecting the pikemen from enemy cavalry.

The muskets were braced against the chest, not shoulder, in order to better absorb the shock. Also, the Spanish muskets were quite heavy, and simply could not be held in one's arms for firing. Every musketeer carried a four-foot forked pole onto which he would rest the musket before firing. It could take anywhere from one to three minutes to reload the Spanish musket, so obviously there were times when the enemy was able to reach the musketeer before he could reload. In such cases, the weapon of last defense was the sword or pistol, the sword being much preferred. Although no match against a horseman or an infantryman coming at you with a pike, it was better than nothing and at least gave the impression that you had a fighting chance.

So we begin to see the musketeer as imagined by Alexandre Dumas. Second son of a lord or perhaps son of a lesser noble, without any chance of receiving a significant inheritance, he was probably given a choice of going into the clergy or seeking his fortune in war. The cavalry positions were left to the firstborn higher nobles, so a position in the King's musketeers would be a reasonable goal to achieve. Minor military duties and much drilling occupied most of his official time, while fencing would be encouraged to provide physical stamina and a sense of warrior confidence. Of course, the sword with which he would fight his duels would not be the one he would take to war. The preferred sword for battle would be a sturdy two-edged sword that could survive clashing conflicts with armor, halberd, or shield.

Pistols were of so little power that in battle the ball could be deflected by heavy leather; hence the high topped leather boots of the period to protect the legs of the light cavalry. (Horses make a better target than people, so cavalrymen's legs were in more danger of being shot than their chest or head). Pistols continued to be used exclusively by light cavalry, who could gallop to the front line, fire a pistol, and then gallop away to safety.

Bayonets and Professional Armies

The rigid structure of the modern army, and a society which can sustain it, is born from the collapse of the old order.

Rococo

Time Frame – 1710 - 1789

Politics/Economics – The absolute monarchy is in decline. Parliaments and other forms of direct representation are either slowly and methodically, or violently and suddenly, becoming the true centers of power. The complexities of the market economy mean large numbers of middle-class managers are actually making direct decisions as to the flow of goods and services, requiring large numbers of middle-class administrators and legislators. This, and the increase in material wealth, allows the upper class to remove itself from the boring day-to-day management of politics, business, the military and even their own households. The leisure class is born.

It was also the age of enlightenment, where incredible advances in pure philosophy, in basic science, and in political theory are made all in the name of establishing an unprejudiced approach to knowledge. For example, whereas in the previous century science was a process of observing nature and then extrapolating theories based on those observations, now observation was merely the first step. Theories had to be tested and retested, proved to be viable under controlled conditions. In other words, the true scientific method was born. No idea, no matter how entrenched in society, was beyond being questioned and tested. A similar rigor was applied to all of the fields of knowledge, and quickly the concepts of democracy, of the rights of the individual, of pure human thought being able to unravel the mysteries of the universe were dusted off from Greek writings and made real. For many it was liberating, for others terrifying, for others revolutionary.

Fashion/Manners – This impulse of the upper class to separate themselves from common society had an effect on every affect. With many middle class managers achieving substantial wealth, it was almost as though the nobility had to prove that they were by their nature entitled to their vaunted position of not having to work. They did this by developing a lifestyle that they felt demonstrated their natural superiority. So their focus was on what they considered refinement, proof that they were by nature "well-bred". And in doing so created a set of social rules nearly Byzantine in complexity. But in simplified terms it came down to areas of concern: separateness of the body and elevated inclinations.

Separateness of the body is a difficult concept, although we still live with many of it's ramifications to this day. The idea is that a noble born person was literally living an elevated existence. Not sacred, but definitely on a higher plane than that of the common people, who are naturally tied to the earth. This differentiation was thought to manifest physically, so while commoners might be comfortable living an animal existence, nobles by their very nature required their bodies to be kept separate from the profane world. The Princess and the Pea story is a direct example.

That was the theory, unspoken but acted upon daily. The reality was that nobles had to work at every moment not to slip up and show any signs that they might not be as refined as their neighbors. Social occasions were filled with landmines of failure of etiquette, a thousand chances to make a mistake and act like a brute. And how the gossips would enjoy every misstep!

The marks of refinement included being embarrassed at crudity, of even denying that the body has any bodily functions at all. A refined person would want to keep his person from being touched by another, so by extension to be allowed to touch someone or even be granted close proximity was a great show of favor. Even the presenting and eating of food now required a variety of implements and procedures. In every field, one was expected to show a preference for the delicate rather than the robust, so much so that dining, traveling, viewing entertainments, all had to be performed without being sullied by the presence of commoners. Whereas prior nobles could live in an easy concourse with people of every walk of life, this generation felt that it was presumptuous of common folk to even speak out of their station. Servants were expected to not only tend to the needs of the nobility, but to isolate them from the real world and the messy parts and people of daily life. Gone were the days of travelers from all walks of life stopping at a tavern or eating a meal at an inn.

For the upper class, line, texture, and color moved to the feminine and ethereal with each passing decade. By the late 1780's pastels, lace, frills, powdered wigs and delicate patterns are the standard for high-born men and women, breaking completely with the growing middle class. And this was a conscious decision, one to create a visible gulf between have and have-nots. The more that the middle class increased in size and ability to purchase fine goods, the more the upper class felt compelled to separate itself from all aspects of daily common life. This further compelled the leisure class to develop its own forms of social customs including proscribed table manners, having elaborate coffee and tea service while entertaining guests, and even developing a style of dance - the minuet - that required time to learn and would change every few months. Only those rich enough to afford private dancing lessons and had the requisite leisure time to practice the latest version could possibly hope to present themselves at any party. And the grand opera houses and symphony halls were built as much to keep the lower classes out as to keep the finest art in.

Gone was the vigorous strength of the prior century. Instead of presenting themselves as men of power, this next generation of nobility elevated frivolity to a *raison d'état*. The world existed in order to provide them with their desires, and they existed in order to provide elegance to the world. At every turn, the artificial and ephemeral is valued over the stolid and practical.

Instead of sitting in a chair as though it were a throne, now the body is allowed to lounge gracefully, as though the body were a carefully draped fabric theatrically placed to highlight the room. The arms may drape over the back of the chair, but at no time should there be a look of collapse. Instead, every pose is calculated to give the appearance of delicately floating when lounging, sitting, standing, walking, even leaning against a door frame. It is a time of contrived casualness. And since it was so important to demonstrate that this aristocratic demeanor was completely inborn and natural and free of care, no expense was spared in hiring instructors to carefully train one in performing every possible activity. In every moment of waking life one had to move and stand as though one were being watched by the world of your peers, even when alone, for one small slip in their company could shatter your social standing.

Although men were taught to move more gracefully and lightly than before, the feet were still turned out into a ballet third position, the chest expanded and chin held high, the back straight. Interestingly, walking was finally allowed to be heel-toe for upper class men.. The arms were generally bent or occupied with some sort of prop, but never simply hanging down to the side. A certain asymmetry was always attempted, and the limbs showing graceful extension without resorting to unnatural rigidity. The bow was more relaxed, with the hat removed and swept only to waist level, the arm staying almost straight). At the same time, the right foot was extended forward and a gentle bend from the waist finished the move. Hats were removed indoors and stayed off.

It is somewhat ironic that the aristocracy, in order to fill their days now devoid of productive activity, indulged in so many activities that were oddly middle-class in nature. Playing cards, serving coffee, picnicking in a artificial "rustic" setting, and yet all still had to be performed with the same conformity to casual elegance and ultra-refined ritual.

On the positive side, the life of leisure also provided time for more productive pursuits. For those with the intellectual curiosity and mental acumen to allow it, many of the upper class seriously devoted themselves to art, literature, philosophy and science. These few were certainly not indicative of the majority of their class, but their efforts, whether working alone or in easy concourse with others across national boundaries or social barriers, in no small measure pushed advances in these fields and gave rise to the age of enlightenment.

Not to be forgotten is the tremendous growth of the middle class, both in numbers and in power. They were the ones actually running industries, operating the day-to-day functions of government. This new class and the wealth that they produced propelled cities to develop services to accommodate them. True shops, restaurants, pre-manufactured clothing and furniture become common. As usual, men's fashions ape the changes in military fashion (smaller hats, tighter sleeves, more leg covering with heavier material). In keeping with their increasing isolation from the aristocracy, the true bourgeoisie likewise did not try to emulate upper class mannerisms. They walked the streets unarmed and without turning out their feet, allowed their arms to hang at their sides if they wished, and could sit comfortably against the back of a chair with both feet on the floor without feeling ill at ease.

<u>Civilian Conflict</u> – The slow transformation of the heavy rapier to the light smallsword was helped along by the rise of the bourgeoisie. With the aristocracy responding by transforming every aspect of their daily life into something refined, the sidearm was naturally changed as well. The brutal, brawling, street fighter's tool that was the rapier was replaced with a weapon far more elegant and more suitable for a gentleman. Very little or no cutting, both thrusting and parrying with a single sword (indeed, in a single action), means that the smallsword requires intensive and expensive study, and so became exclusively the weapon of the leisure class. The hilt is reduced so that the look and movement of the sword in the scabbard while promenading allowed for a more graceful carriage than the athletic swagger of the cavalier period. It also meant that only the upper class would wear it.

For the only time in history, a weapon is designed not for function, but for fashion. The stiletto-thin smallsword cannot cut, cannot be used in battle, indeed was designed to be useless against any other type of weapon or when in the hands of someone not specifically trained in its use. The hand protection is nonfunctional, but instead made as light and elegant as possible, a badge of status. Worn from a shoulder sash and never hung from a waist belt, the scabbard moves independently of the clothing, requiring training from a dancing master to even walk the streets with grace. The very real fear of being laughed at for failure to handle the wearing of the sword with elegance led many to forego wearing the sword altogether. Use of a weapon in the left hand is considered gauche [pardon the pun] and slowly disappears. Once the waist belt goes, so must the dagger, so for the first time in European history, the dagger disappears as a normal part of a man's daily wear. Only hidden daggers used by thieves or ruffians remain.

As such, dueling becomes the activity of only the nobility. Although no longer as widespread amoung the population as it had been in the early 17th century, it became alarmingly common for young nobles to duel over imagined offences. The duel was slightly more formalized than it had been with the rapier, but there is still no salute as we see in the movies. The role of the second was tightly codified. After the initial challenge was offered, it was the seconds who would make arrangement, and all further direct contact between the duelists would cease. Seconds would make sure that the terms of the duel (to the death, first blood, etc.) were adhered to, and would no longer take up a weapon themselves to continue the fight. As dueling was legally banned in most countries, it was also the second's responsibility to maintain secrecy.

Just as in the previous century, monarchs wear a sword of war rather than a civilian sword for portraits and official functions, although now the broadsword has shrunk in size and the military sabre is seen in portraiture as well.

Warfare – In the early 1700's a fundamental shift occurred that affected weaponry, warfare, fashion, economies, governments, art, society, and philosophy to such an extent that we are still struggling with the consequences. And it all began with less than half a pound of steel. It happened once before in Western history, when the tiny stirrup shook Europe to its foundation. This time it was the lowly bayonet.

No one knows when the first bayonet was invented. In all likelihood it started as perhaps a dagger or broken sword with which the handle was simply jammed into the barrel of a malfunctioning musket, converting it into at least a heavy but practical pike. It was often a life saver, for if faced by a soldier on horseback, a long pointed stick is of infinitely more value than a sword. By the late 1600's, several companies of musketeers were actually issued plug bayonets for this purpose. [They were also used on rare occasion by the nobility when boar hunting, as the charging boar is still one of the most dangerous of game.]

On the battlefield, muskets can continue to fire so long as a line of pikemen is there to protect the musketeers from an enemy cavalry charge. Should that line be insufficient to the task, a musketeer could become part of that defense by sticking the bayonet in the barrel and pointing the weapon at the charging horses. But the plug bayonet obviously completely disables the musket, so then someone came up with the idea of attaching the bayonet underneath the barrel, instead of in it. Now the musketeers can continue to load and fire while the same muskets also act as a protective barrier of bristling spear points. Give the pikemen bayoneted muskets and you've doubled the firepower and doubled the defense with the same number of soldiers.

So soldiers were trained to hold a line with the bayoneted musket, against either a cavalry or an infantry "bayonet charge". Fire as a unit, then hold the line as a unit. Additional training (still seen today) in using the bayoneted musket as a hand-to-hand weapon was more for morale than usefulness. Once the cavalry had breached the line, the inevitable outcome was the destruction of the musketeers.

But at almost the same time, the musket itself undergoes a change. Advancements in metallurgy led to thinner, lighter barrels, which no longer required thick gunstocks, so the weight of the musket decreased in time to only a third of that of the Arquebus or the Spanish musket. Gone is the dangerous smoldering fuse of the matchlock, replaced by the much easier to operate flintlock. The gun itself had the same rough layout but instead of live embers from a burning fuse or "match", the new guns used a hammer which held a piece of flint. On squeezing the trigger, the hammer dropped the flint forward, which hit a strike plate made of rough steel, causing a shower of sparks to land on the primer powder. Musketeers could now operate their weapons even in damp weather. The misfire rate among trained soldiers dropped down to about 20%, reloading only took 30 seconds or less, and most importantly, the soldiers could now fire while standing nearly shoulder to shoulder. The effective firing distance increased slightly, from 80 yards of he matchlock to between 150 to 200 yards for the flintlock, although the order to fire was usually given at the old preferred distance of 100 yards. Firing in unison, the effect of a wall of bullets each only two feet apart flying across a field was devastating. Such a force became a combination of the best of both light and heavy infantry, and finally the lowly foot soldier could not only hold off, but even attack enemy cavalry.

To take full advantage of the improvements in firepower, soldiers had to be trained to stand as close together s possible, and march and fire as a unit. This required close-order drills of a more-or-less standing army conducted by professional army officers, rather than nobles on horseback leading hastily summoned local militias into battle. Although it took military planners another two hundred years to admit it, mounted cavalry was now obsolete. Instead, light cannons and artillery were the only effective way of softening the opposing army before attempting to take the field with your own infantry. Once engaged, winning became a matter of quickly moving the infantry into and out of position as battlefield conditions change, just as it did in Roman times. And just as the Romans learned, the only way to take full advantage of such an infantry is to train and drill on a nearly daily basis, which means a full-time standing army instead of quickly gathered levies. This also meant a professional officer class promoted due to battlefield competence rather than mere social standing. Kings were quite willing to offend the landed gentry and deny them generalships in favor of promoting lowly-born but capable fighters if it meant the difference between gaining or losing territory.

Uniformity in military dress was now crucial, not merely to identify the soldier from a distance, but in a tight formation of soldiers in drill during training to see which individual was out of step. All uniforms began to incorporate the vertical high contrast stripe on the pants' legs [that stripe is still seen on tuxedo pants, although now in black]. Along with shirts and jackets, pants and boots were tailored to be much tighter fitting. Hats were made far smaller than ever before, and the wonderful plumes stuck in the brim must disappear. Why? If the musketeers are going to be effective in holding off a cavalry charge, they have to stand, march, and fight while almost shoulder to shoulder, so the elaborate dress of the late 17th century became an encumbrance.

A popular myth is that warfare during this time became so weighed down with protocol and formality that a general would issue a written invitation to his opposite, requesting the presence of his army to meet in battle at a mutually agreed upon time and place. This story is told to demonstrate the supposed etiquette of the time, requiring fair play and honorable action, even in war. Very gentlemanly and proper and all, but a ridiculous fabrication. There were times in history where one military leader would challenge another to battle, but always because the challenger thought that he possessed a clear advantage that was unknown to the other side, an advantage that was time sensitive and might be lost if there was any delay. And there were certainly some officers who accepted the challenge, but only because they also felt that they had the upper hand, and that bringing the armies together sooner rather than later was to their benefit. This is not chivalry; it is high stakes poker playing.

It is at this time that the military salute is created. I hate to disabuse another much beloved story, one that would have us believe that the salute comes from the ancient medieval tournaments, beforewhich knights would remove their helmets or at least lift their visors. According to the tale, this allowed fellow combatants to have proof that they were fighting only fellow nobles. People who like this story enjoy the correspondence between current military practice and the romance of chivalrous protocol. There are only three problems with this story, the first of which is the rather obvious dilemma of the complete lack of saluting during the intervening 300 years, and the second being that the knights would have lifted their visors as proof of identity among equals, whereas the military salute is a demonstration of submission from inferior to superior. Third, the knights simply never did that. Knights showed up with quite a retinue days before the event, where easily recognized by everyone, and would only put on their helmets minutes before actual combat, it being too stifling to wear any longer than necessary.

In fact, the stiff-armed military salute comes from the most traditional sign of obedience there is - namely the bow. What in medieval times was a simple lowering of the head underwent many changes throughout the centuries until by the 1700's it included a graceful step back and a sweeping removal of the hat. One of lower class always bows first, bows lower, and the bow is held until acknowledged by one's superior. This civilian practice was second nature in the military, especially since officers were originally all of the upper class and soldiers were all of the lower.

Some cavalry units already had begun to forego the hat doffing when their uniform hat became the mitered cap, and especially the "shako", that extremely tall fuzzy headpiece with a tiny brim still seen on drum majors. The shako and mitre are difficult to quickly remove and replace with one hand, so the doffing was shortened to a symbolic removal, actually a mere touching of the brim showing the intent without the difficulty of the practice. This diplomatic compromise quickly became standard protocol for infantry as well, since the bowing and doffing is difficult when soldiers are standing shoulder to shoulder while wearing a sword and holding a musket.

So here we can see a direct line of descent of what was and remains a sign of respect and submission. The bow, still in full use during the cavalier period with soldiers standing far apart so as not to blow each other up, quickly is refined to the precise and snappy salute, which allows respect to be shown even in tight military formation.

Mounted cavalry could still be used on occasion to take advantage of enemy infantry or artillery errors. If a perspicacious general noted that his enemy had left a flank exposed or was lax in shifting from marching to battle formation, he might be able to call for a sudden charge by the cavalry to create an opening that the infantry could exploit. More often, a cavalry charge was aimed directly at the center of an infantry line, usually ending in the massacre of the cavalry or the infantry running in fear. Either outcome was considered glorious.

Grenadiers, Fusiliers, Dragoons - there is a litany of special units that develop during the time, usually as armies experimented with special units that could quickly ride into battle armed with firearms, but then dismount to fight. Grenadiers were trained in throwing and firing explosive grenades, fusiliers used harder to load but extremely accurate rifled muskets, and dragoons were equipped with short muskets so that they actually could fire from horseback or quickly dismount and run into battle. In some areas, local units of raiders were incorporated as special mercenaries, such as the Hussars, Cossacks, and Rangers. All were attempts to try to gain a tactical advantage by reestablishing an effective light infantry or light cavalry. But for all intents and purposes, the battlefield dynamic came down to heavy infantry vs. heavy infantry.

Although the value of a curved sword was known for thousands of years, it was only in the late 1600's that European manufacturers were able to mass produce quality curved blades of three feet in length but light enough to wield with one hand. Sabres were used for close-in fighting, replacing the military-grade rapiers and broadswords, the only exception being the Scots, who kept their basket hilt single-hand broadswords but at least changed their tactics, using them the way other armies did the sabres. Cavalry sabres were curved or straight depending on the intended use. Heavy cavalry units used a straight light blade; light cavalry units used heavy curved blades. Why? Because heavy cavalry charged at enemy infantry and impaled them as they stood or ran. Light cavalry charged at enemy cavalry and slashed and cut at them as they rode. Infantry sabres were curved for the most part, with straight blades used only on presentation dress swords. Curved sabres were preferred, as straight blades have less cutting power than curved blades at the same weight.

The military did not provide for knives for any of their soldiers. Bayonets, yes, but no knives. From the irregular units, however, many of the riflemen used a knife to carefully prepare and trim the cloth patches they used, as opposed to the rough paper cartridges used by the regular musketmen of the infantry. These specialized riflemen simply brought their own knives, and many in the regular infantry copied them and did the same, as well as bringing a variety of pocket knives for their personal use. The "rifle knives", as they were called, were usually simple butcher knives, predating the Bowie by about a hundred years, but having some of the same characteristics. Pistols were available, but still impractical enough so as to be of almost no battlefield utility. They might give a soldier a feeling of power, but they had no tactical purpose.

Sailing Ships

European monarchies were able to defeat other powers and establish colonies throughout the world primarily due to their technological advantages, especially in the production and use of firearms. But guns and soldiers need to be transported, and then local material and goods sent back to the mother country. Without the West's superior sailing vessels, each conquest could never have been exploited. A case can be made that if the West had developed steam propulsion earlier than it did, the Age of Exploration would never have happened, for steam ships require deep harbors and a supply of fuel at its destination. Only light sailing ships allowed Europeans to explore and then dominate every corner of the world, powered only by the wind.

I am unaware of any show that requires extensive knowledge of the fighting practices of the sailing vessels of the seventeenth and eighteenth centuries (lines of attack, firing cannon, etc.). But there are of course several that deal with pirates, so we will explore some of the hand weapons commonly found aboardship.

Military battles on the seas are usually attempts to sink the opposing ships, but pirates look to leave the vessel intact so they can board and loot, perhaps then take the ship and sell it, use it for themselves, or if it has little value, scuttle it. So pirates used their cannon to disable merchant vessels (striking the mast and sails, slowing the ship down) and then close in alongside. Grappling lines were thrown and the ships were pulled close together, and then the pirates would board with the idea of killing any resistance (or witnesses). None of this required any special equipment, and actually all of what we consider pirate weapons were actually developed by naval forces to *combat* piracy. It of course took very little time for them to be stolen and used by the pirates themselves.

Assuming that outrunning the pirates didn't work and then firing any defensive cannons failed to stop them, the next level of defense was preventing them from boarding. At close range, pistols and muskets were effective at killing individuals, but each firearm takes some time to reload, and firing from a tossing ship can ruin your aim. So far more practical was the blunderbuss. Not a hunting weapon at all, the blunderbuss ("thunder gun") is a very short musket with a very fat barrel and a flared barrel opening. Specifically designed as an officer's weapon to put down shipboard insurrections, it fired not a single ball, but many small pellets. The flared barrel allowed the pellets to quickly spread and cut down a large number of attackers with one shot. The pellets could be anything: gravel, ballast, glass shards, nails, tacks. A number of pirates attempting to throw grappling hooks could be disabled with one shot, even with poor aiming.

But when the grappling hooks do connect with the ship, those ropes must be cut before the ships are pulled together. A stout curved military sabre can do it, but the full length blade can easily get entangled in the ship's rigging. A shorter version of the sabre was designed, called the cutlass. Quite literally, it means "cut the rope" (lass = rope, as in lasso, windlass, etc.), but it is also a powerful killing tool. Most cutlasses were simple sabre hilts with two foot curved blades.

In the final hand-to-hand fighting, more impromptu weapons might have been added, such as knives, belaying pins, and perhaps some light fishing harpoons.

Why does the cutlass look the way it does? Even from the Middle Ages, the best seafaring generals were Moors (ipso Othello). Europeans would often hire a "Mohameten" to lead their navies. (Our word for admiral comes from the Italian "almirante" which is a corruption of the Arabic "al emir" - the prince). Europeans had the rapier and broadsword, but the Muslim nations developed the curved sabre ("saf-r" = sword), a superior weapon but again not easily swung on a ship's deck. A short curved heavy-bladed weapon is just right for tight quarters, and the guard style is merely a variant of sabre guards. Regular length sabers were, and still are, presented to naval officers as a sign of rank, but had no utility at sea. Completely useless info: Film pirates often have Gaelic accents because the Scots really were premier pirates from even centuries before the Norman Conquest ("scotti" - to plunder). Aren't you glad you're still reading this?

Wearing the cutlass was easy. Usually the pirates simply stuck it into their belt or sash, although some may actually have had scabbards for their swords. By the way, I've noticed that some people like to point out that the sword on *Captain Morgan* that used to be drawn on the rum bottle of the same name was shown with the hilt facing "the wrong way", that is to say the knucklebow facing backward, to the left. (The Captain is no longer drawn having any sword at all; probably a bow to political correctness.) Almost all swords that have a single edge are worn on the left side of the body with the edge and knucklebow going forward, as are all rapiers and smallswords. But if you think about it for a moment, that might not always be the most practical way to wear a sword. Here's why:

Both the buccaneers and the samurai warriors realized that drawing a sword might also mean having to use it even as the sword is drawn, before it is completely out of the scabbard. Grabbing the handle in the traditional manner, knucklebow and edge forward, leaves a very weak bend in the wrist until you have the chance to completely withdraw the sword and then point the blade. Wearing the sword the "wrong" way lets you immediately grab the handle using a powerful hammer grip, with no break at the wrist. The most common first attack from someone holding a weapon is to lift it high on the right and come down at an angle to the opponent's left. Even if the sword of the defender is still coming out of the scabbard, it's still possible to block that initial attack and in the same move come down with your own sword to the head of the attacker. Japanese katana are worn this way for that purpose, and it seems that for close-quarter fighting many pirates did the same.

Then why aren't all curved sabres worn "backwards"? Because in Western military usage, the curved sabre is meant to be worn and used while on horseback, and having the curve forward allows gravity to help keep the sword from bouncing out of the sheath.

NeoClassic/Empire

Time Frame – 1775-1820

Politics/Economics – At first it might seem strange to highlight such a small period of time, one that admittedly overlaps considerably and inelegantly with the previous Rococo. But it is in the tension between the two periods in this very brief slice of history, acting as giant millstones working in opposite directions, that produced the changes in society that would create what we recognize as modern life. They reverberate to almost every aspect of present day society.

The great intellectual ideas - republicanism, free market capitalism, individual rights, inherent equality without regard to ancestry - born in the previous century were now forcefully promoted by activists through Europe, and, of course, in the European colonies throughout the Americas. Whether the struggle was engaged intellectually and peaceably (as in England) or broke into violent revolution as in France and the United States, everyone realized that what was at stake was nothing less than the future of Western society.

Because the possibility of a new world order was so palpably at hand, the pressure to act out immediately was tremendous. So the natural conflict between a reasoned, intellectual examination of classical precepts and the passionate call to arms of violent overthrow often raged within nations, within cities, even within the minds of individuals. I'm not sure we can appreciate the momentous change that was happening to these people. But keep in mind that in their minds they were finally transforming human society, bringing civilization to what they considered its natural state, of being ruled by a compassionate rationalism.

To give you a sense of the emotions which reverberated underneath the cold political actions, I offer this translation of the original Argentine national anthem, written in 1813, three years before the country actually achieved its independence:

> Listen, mortals, to the sacred cry - liberty, liberty, liberty!
> Listen to the sound of broken chains, see noble equality now enthroned.
> A new and glorious nation rises to the heights of the earth,
> Its head crowned with laurels, and at her feet a Lion destroyed.
> May the laurels be eternal, that we knew how to achieve.
> Crowned with glory we shall live, or we swear to die gloriously.

Notice the quick interplay between appeals to both noble ideals and bloody action. Neither quality can sustain itself very long before being affected by the other.

Fashion/Manners – The manners and style of conduct that before was merely viewed as the difference between upper and lower classes now became markers of political affiliation in every country. To bow at the waist would show that you were a republican, while bending at the leg might disclose you as a Monarchist. A bit of lace too refined and one might be verbally attacked in a republican tea house, while failing to turn out the feet sufficiently in an elegant household might lead others to think that you had anarchic sympathies. One had to tread carefully through the minefield of dress and comportment if one had to venture in mixed company. Small wonder that as tensions rose, the members of each group would isolate themselves from the other as much as possible.

As the aristocracies fell, middle class and even lower class sympathies affected style and manners. Men now wore the trousers of the working class, cut their hair shorter in the Roman republican style, and wore simpler fashions made of less expensive fabrics. The bow was a simple bend from the waist, and shaking of hands in greeting was considered just as appropriate.

Warfare – No changes here, but it is worthy of note that by this time all armies used cloth or paper preloaded cartridges, replacing the wooden cartridges on the bandoleers of the matchlock musketeers. They could now carry thirty to fifty rounds, easily enough for one or two days of battle.

One little point of interest for those working on the American Revolution. It is not well known that the American forces were consistently underfunded and poorly supplied.

Civilian Conflict – The use of the smallsword did not alone increase the number of duels between hot-headed young men, but it did cause the number of fatalities of young noblemen to soar. In a rapier fight, some of the nastiest wounds from a cut (as opposed to a thrust) could still be patched by a skilled surgeon. The thin blade of the smallsword being unsuitable for cutting, all efforts were on the thrust, and the smallsword blade punctured more deeply than did the rapier, causing deep bleeding that was nearly impossible for the surgeons of the time to stop. Even if the bleeding could stop, the chances of systemic infection were very high and would almost certainly lead to death. Swords didn't have to be poisoned in order to kill in this pre-antibiotic age. Pistols also came into vogue as an alternative to the sword, and this in fact did lead to more duels. Many who otherwise would have found an excuse not to approach someone with sharpened steel were much more likely to show up on the field of honor with a gun.

Romantic

Time Frame – 1820 - 1865

Politics/Economics – As the century progresses, it is becoming accepted that republics either are or will be the dominant political structure for nation-states throughout the Western world. (I should define my terms: a republic is a nation ruled by a charter or constitution, a democracy is direct rule by the majority of its voting citizens. For example, the United States is a republic, for we follow the constitution that allows for democratically elected representatives. Very few, if any, countries are or were full democracies, in which whatever is voted on by the majority becomes law without restraint.) Republics have an existence that does not depend on the actions of one person, and therefore limit the power of even monarchs that remain in power. This shift in power changes the relationship of the citizens to their country. For example, in previous times one might refer to the reigning British monarch as simply "England", for the country and the ruler were one and the same. But from this time forward, it is always "the King of England", a phrase used in the prior centuries to be sure, but now with the understanding that the kingship belongs to the country, not the country to the king. Titled aristocrats may still retain many privileges, but they have lost direct control of society.

The call to pure reason could not sustain itself, and appeals to the sentimental and romantic are the hallmarks of the time. One can hear the shift take place in less than a generation in comparing the music of Beethoven to that of Mozart, and likewise the bloody excesses of armed revolutions and the studied political writings that gave them birth.

The incredible progress made in the basic sciences finally produced tangible benefits to engineering and technology. Unrestrained technology, fed by an unimpeded free market, can produce and deliver a flood of goods and services previously unavailable to middle and lower classes. Economic power begins its shift from agriculture to heavy industry.

Fashion/Manners – As the royal houses of Europe lose power, the manners and dress of the prior nobility fall from fashion. But this does nothing to squelch the desire to be in the upper class, so the newly ascendant must find another way to justify their power. The period is marked by a desperate attempt to prove a true nobility which is not tied to direct descent from a royal family, which of course few of these middle-class managers had. The concept of "nobility of sensibility" (one can be born of noble character rather than of noble lineage) leads to the disuse of ostentatiously upper class pursuits in favor of cultivating the image of natural refinement, primarily in dress and movement but also in purchasing items of distinction. This was meant to demonstrate that the truly noble could be from humble circumstances, but that they would show an intrinsic affinity to civilized things.

With increasing industrialization also came a lowering of direct employment in agriculture, therefore a migration of low income workers into cities. When combined with the dramatic rise in purchasing power, this led the newly expanded middle class to attempt to attain upper class status by proxy. Having a servant was common, and items of "culture" were bought and displayed throughout the home. Important books, musical instruments, small knickknacks to serve as "conversation pieces", all were designed to impress upon the visitor that the home was filled with people of a sensitive nature. To further that image, home life was managed so as to maintain that illusion, even if the reality was quite different. The average home, no matter how humble, was now expected to have a separate dining room and even a separate parlor, both for entertaining guests and for the devotion to leisure activities, especially reading and music. Even if a man worked by day in manual labor, he would be expected to maintain the facade of pretended leisure, and dress more befitting a gentleman once he arrived home for dinner. There was even a great proliferation in the breeding of non-working dogs, pets with no direct "job" such as catching mice or defending the livestock. Having extra things, without any true usefulness, was an important part of maintaining the facade.

The general manners of the prior period are still observed, but in a much more relaxed form. The bow is still retained for formal occasion or when greeting a woman, but the handshake becomes nearly universal. Doffing the hat is replaced by merely raising and returning it in a small and gentle motion, perhaps with a slight nod of the head. The feet may be turned out in standing or walking, but only if it should give a pleasing appearance and by no means rigidly adhered to. What was important is that there be no show of fussiness or hurry, but rather an appearance of casual elegance which could almost be called "proud neglect".

Men's fashion became middle class at all levels, starting the long slide from refinement to casualness. Laces and embellishment are considered feminine; instead - simple lines, tighter fitting coats, smaller hats, the ubiquity of trousers. By the end of the period half of all clothing is purchased pre-made. Accessories are reduced to cane, gloves, and small objects easily placed in pockets.

Warfare – Industrial progress leads to standardization of the implements of war. Vast quantities of weapons could now be built with interchangeable parts, meaning that repairs to any item could be made by the quick substitution of a spare part instead of manufacturing a specific repair. At the very end of this period rifle-barreled percussion muskets begin to replace the old flintlock smooth bores, greatly increasing the effective range. The sword is reduced to a symbol of rank or a weapon of last resort rather than a battlefield necessity. Soldiers were still trained in their use, but generals knew not to depend on them for tactical advantage. Most often, swords were used after the enemy line had been breached and the attackers were ready to crush the remaining opposition. If soldiers found that they were in a situation that required use of the sword, then the battle was almost over or something had gone terribly wrong.

Civilian Conflict – Even as the sword becomes ever more romanticized, it fades as a practical tool. Few had the leisure to practice enough to be a credible threat in a duel, and wearing a sword was considered an ostentatious affectation. Although the average man may still be armed when traveling, the single shot pocket pistol, hidden from public view, now served this function. As a result, duels of honor are now more common, but less lethal. It became easier to believe one could win, but luckily the erratic flight of round balls fired from smoothbore pistol barrels meant that most shots missed their marks.

A renewed interest in fisticuffs as a way to settle arguments led to professional prizefights utilizing a "scientific" study of the manly art of self-defense. For many, this was preferable to dueling with sword or pistol, as it was much less likely to end in death. It also brought some basic rules to a fight (no kicking, no eye gouging), and so was an exercise which even gentlemen could undertake.

Industrial Age / Rifled Breechloaders

Time Frame – 1850 - 1890

Politics/Economics – With all of the elements of the industrial revolution firmly in place, there was needed only one last component to bring it to full fruition, and that came in the laying of railway lines throughout Europe and the United States. With that, goods could be transported to an part of the country or continent within days of manufacture. In the span of one generation, a trip across the country went from taking six months to only five days. With the invention of the telegraph, news from any city could reach the furthest hamlet within minutes.

Photography changes the way humans assimilate information about the world at large. Once shown photography, they only accept reality as being that which they can confirm visually, even if only by proxy. No longer can death in battle be portrayed as something heroic - the photographs from Gettysburg are a powerful witness to the ugliness of war, giving the lie to innumerable patriotic paintings.

With Darwin's *Origin of the Species*, doubts flared again as to the legitimacy of religious authority. The heady excitement of living in the dawn of a new utopia faded as the reality of the new republics showed them to be just as liable to corruption and oppression as had the monarchies. Exuberant romanticism becomes muted, and art and science begin to look at the deficiencies of the human condition.

The response: Victorian morality. We now think of it as simply being repressively prudish, but it was far more than that. The mainstream thinking was that unrestrained passions encouraged vices that proliferate and ultimately degrade the participants. So indulging in sensual pleasures led directly to crime and unhappiness. By cultivating pastimes that both please and elevate, an individual would find not only true happiness, but society would improve as well. The basic tenet is hardly unique to this period, but had never been completely accepted as a societal norm. All aspects of living were redefined through this outlook: clothing become more somber and conservative, the dances and popular art become more pedestrian, terms of greeting become more formal, even within the confines of a private home.

Of course, when it came time to decide on the specifics, many of the mannerisms bordered on the absurd. Men are banished from being with their wives during childbirth, not because of an impropriety of seeing his wife unclothed, but that his presence among the others (doctor, midwife) was a *public* proof that he had seen his wife unclothed. (The fact that a child was emerging from the womb as evidence of the same was discreetly ignored.) Referring to chicken breasts and legs as white and dark meat was not merely to prevent offending sensitive dinner guests, but more importantly to prove that the speaker did not dwell on prurient topics.

The positive side of Victorian mores is that it brought several important societal concerns into the open. Movements against slavery, against child labor, and promoting women's rights all made great strides forward, as did the expansion of public works advancing literacy, sanitation, and the general livability of the rapidly growing cities. This was thought to be not only the job of the government, but also of all those that benefited privately from the acquisition of wealth.

An interesting counter current throughout the period is the morbid fascination with death and the paranormal, even the abnormal. Monsters, demons, ghosts had always had their part in literature, but now they inhabited the mundane world, and one did not need to have discourse with the devil in order to be in danger. The concept of evil attacking good people who have not committed any moral lapse themselves is a common theme. Melodramas are hugely popular, not because they exaggerate expressions and emotions (this was necessary when playing to large houses), but because of the unrestrained portrayal of the villain and his nearly inhuman enjoyment in committing his crimes.

Fashion/Manners – Almost all objects in daily use are now made at least in part by machine. By the end of the century only 10% of clothing will be custom made. Pre-made clothes naturally cannot be as form-fitting as their predecessors were, so male attire tended more toward the boxy, with less room for unique embellishment. Instead of individuality, men would dress largely the same, very conservatively, although with different outfits for different times of day.

More and more items are purchased without regard to their direct utility. Instead, every room and every wall is covered with bric-a-bracs and whatever opulence the household can afford. If the items don't fit to one style, so much the better, as it shows the "worldliness" of the owners. Filling a wall with photographs of one's extended family provided a faux-aristocratic lineage. *Objets d'art* are now produced to fill this middle class need to demonstrate their sensibility. Included are large numbers of landscape and still life paintings with simple domestic themes so as not to tax the average viewer.

Manners did not change, but did become more tightly restrictive. Hats and gloves were always removed when indoors. In seating, one tended to sit back in the chair, and could cross the legs at the knees, but not with the foot to the knee. Individual flair is unacceptable, and in all things the man is expected to cultivate a demeanor of being aloof and reserved, sober and conservative, the exact opposite of everything that the prior aristocracy had been before the French Revolution. Lifting the hat on a passing greeting was expected, but to engage in conversation before being formally introduced was impossible. And this last prescription was based on a very real concern of needing to identify someone's true status. Anyone could purchase the appropriate clothing of the well-to-do, and easy access to travel meant that it was now impossible to tell who was who simply by appearance. At the very least, a calling card could begin to establish one's credentials, and better yet was a letter of introduction. But at some point it was necessary to have a close associate vouch for the stranger. To do this entailed a certain social risk, for you were in effect staking your own honor on behalf of someone else.

Civilian Conflict – The sword was by now no more than a sporting diversion and only rarely a dueling weapon. For the most part it is already viewed as an anachronism. The invention of the percussion revolver, capable of firing six shots in quick succession, led to a dramatic reduction in duels. Bareknuckle fighting is replaced by gloved fighting and the Marquis of Queensbury rules of 1867, but this merely increased the number of middle and lower class prizefighters and reduced the number of gentlemen willing to "settle their differences in the ring."

At the beginning of the period, there were practical revolvers, but as they were muzzleloader/percussion guns, had several limitations. The loaded charge could fail in damp weather; and the lead ball could drop out of position if holstered for too long. Additionally, the technical limitations of the gun meant that a certain amount of pressure would be lost at the breech during firing, so the revolvers tended to be low powered and the bullets traveled with relatively slow velocity. Starting in 1875, rifles and revolvers and shotguns became available that could be loaded from the breech and fired commercially pre-loaded cartridges. Now truly anyone could pick up and fire a gun, and it required no particular skill nor strength nor even practical knowledge concerning the weapon one is holding in order to kill someone. No longer was there any need to measure out powder or set percussion caps. And since the cartridges were of brass, they effectively sealed out water vapor. Now revolvers could be left loaded indefinitely, and as the brass cartridge automatically sealed the breach, could fire bullets with a much higher flight velocity.

Metallurgical advances also permitted the overall size of the gun to be reduced. Whereas percussion pistols maxed out at .36 caliber in term of ease of use and comfort, the new cartridge revolvers at .45 caliber weighed far less and had an overall shorter length, even with a similar barrel length. As the center of balance now rested on the hand, the revolvers were no longer "barrel heavy", so were much easier to control. This meant that the guns were just as accurate, light to hold, easier to carry, easier to aim, and could fire more powerful ammunition.

The increase in power did have one drawback - the increase in recoil. Much higher powder loads combined with elimination of exhaust leaks that were endemic in the old percussion revolvers added quite a kick to the new guns. Stances were modified so that instead of the full upright posture seen in gentlemen's duels, gunfighters spread their legs and bent the knees and even the elbow of the shooting arm. Softening the joints this way allowed the entire body to act as a shock absorber to the recoil. Even then, it still took a good deal of concentration and upper body strength to keep the gun from flying up after a shot.

While the wearing of guns, even pocket pistols, was rare along the east coast states and in large cities, it was fairly common in the American west. The ubiquity of six-shot cartridge revolvers was almost matched by the tremendous popularity of lever-action rifles, which could fire up to twenty shots before reloading. Lastly, large fighting knives were commonly worn in the West and South, while discrete folding pocket knives might be carried by anyone throughout the country.

The civilian sword is now only found in the sport fencing clubs, and it is here that the downsweep of the sword is used as a salute before a practice bout or match. This "salute" is later appropriated for stage and film as a historical salute before a duel, although that is a pure fiction.

Warfare -   Interesting that at a time when civilian menswear was turning to dark and somber colors, military uniforms remained quite colorful. Part of this was to allow a certain controlled ostentation amoung the different units, but there was also a fully practical consideration. Generals often had to follow the movements of a battle line that might be as far as a half mile away and extend a mile in either direction. As warfare continued to be centered on the careful movement of ordered blocks of soldiers, recognizing the different units from the distance was critical. Having soldiers wear bright colors aided in this, and even such details as the colorful wide stripe down the pants leg would show that a unit was either marching in order or had lost discipline and was perhaps responding to a threat not visible from his position.

While warfare itself did not change during the period, one of its armaments did, catching the commanders off-guard. Starting from the 1820's, the musket went from flintlock to percussion lock, and the concomitant reduction of steps necessary for firing meant an increased rate of fire. This the generals could appreciate and quickly put to good use. But it was another change, the move from smoothbore barrels to rifled barrels, which led to catastrophic loss of life in wars of this period, especially the American Civil War.

It was long known that rifled barrels on a musket were superior to smoothbores, but it was much harder to ram a lead ball into a rifled muzzle-loader. The lead ball would have to be slightly larger than the barrel opening, so it could take the shape of the grooves in the barrel as it was being rammed in. It formed a good seal but it took some care. If the ball was too loose, the expanding gases on firing would escape past the grooves and the ball would fly without much force. So for the great mass of soldiers, the easier to load smoothbore was issued.

Then a new type of ball, the Minie bullet, was invented which was slightly smaller than the barrel diameter, so it could be rammed easily down the barrel, but once fired the flat bullet base would expand, pressing into the spaces of the lands and grooves, effectively sealing the gases so that the bullet would fly with far more force and speed than any previous ammunition. In addition, when fired from a rifled barrel the cone-shaped Minie would spin like a thrown football, giving it great stability in flight.

The changeover was not immediate, for in the initial stages of the war both sides scrambled to provide enough firearms for the thousands of mustered troops. Almost all of the armouries were filled with old style flintlock smoothbore muskets, and although these were quickly retrofitted with percussion locks, the smoothbore barrels remained the same. So although the soldiers could reload with far greater speed, the distance and accuracy of the muskets remained unchanged.

But by the second year of the war, the output of weapons was largely standardized, with smoothbores no longer being produced. Now every soldier could have a rifled-barreled musket, and could shoot with increased speed, accuracy, and especially distance. The new rifled muskets had an effective firing range of 400 yards compared to the previous smoothbores' of only 150. And this is what the generals did not consider.

The West Point trained officer corps continued to use standard military tactics learned from the Napoleonic wars, placing their troops at distances that would have been at the outer reach of the smoothbore muskets. But they were now several hundred yards inside the effective range of the new rifles. Many cavalry and infantry charges, based on calculations made from the previous era, were now doomed to fail, turning battles into massacres for both sides.

If the accuracy of fire came as a surprise to the generals, it was brutally stunning to the soldiers. So many high velocity bullets were fired in close range that in one battle an entire stand of saplings was mowed down to a height of three feet. The noise and percussive force meant that few soldiers could even distinguish the sound of their own muskets firing over the din of battle. One post-battle inspection by a reporter of the time recounted that ...

"On the field of Gettysburg there were 27,574 guns picked up and of those 24,000 were found to be loaded, and half of them were double loaded. One fourth had from three to ten loads in, and many had five or six balls to one charge of powder. In some cases the powder was above the ball, in others the

cartridges were not broken at the end, while in one musket twenty three balls, sixty two buckshot and a quantity of powder were all mixed up together."

There are two interesting points brought up from that quote. First, that the fear and panic of battle led many soldiers to be unaware that their rifle was somehow disabled, and so they continued to reload and attempt to fire, some of them several times before being shot themselves or discarding their firearm and picking up another from a fallen comrade. The second is the poor training and discipline of many in the infantry, and the general lack of knowledge of basic firearms use by the line officers. Many soldiers were allowed to load up their rifles with any quantity of bullets and buckshot, on the theory that more is better. This is all the more strange when one remembers that soldiers were issued pre-measured, pre-wrapped individual paper cartridges that had the powder, ball and wadding necessary for each shot.

Towards the end of the war, some new rifles were available that were practical breech loaders, but they were still single shot weapons using stiff paper cartridges. It wasn't until the mid-1870's that well engineered multishot rifles using brass cartridges were mass produced. In the USA, lever-action rifles were issued to the army, especially in the western states where the majority of the fighting was from cavalry troops fighting Native American tribes. Although lever-actions had limited range due to their short barrels, they were the perfect weapon for what were essentially battles between light cavalry forces.

European armies, not having to deal with patrolling a vast frontier, never adopted the lever-action in their armament, but rather moved more quickly to bolt-action rifles as soon as they became available in the 1880's. With better range and firing far more powerful ammunition, they better served the needs of the largely infantry units of Europe.

The Rise of the Machines

The fruits of the economic and technological growth of the nineteenth century leads to the mechanization of warfare, the blanketing of cities in concrete, and the replacement of agriculture to heavy industry as the center of economic power. Transportation and communication, almost unchanged since the time of Babylon, now shrink the world with terrifying speed.

The Naughty Nineties to Roaring Twenties

Time Frame – 1890 - 1929

Politics/Economics – By 1890, the United States felt that at least for the lower forty eight states, there was no area left that could be called a frontier. Rail service quickly connected almost every village to a metropolis, and the feeling of isolation between the civilized world and the more remote areas of the country slowly faded. Even oceans were no great barrier to movement, as what once was a two or three week perilous journey on a sailing ship from London to New York could now be done in six days in the comfort of a stateroom aboard a luxury steamship.

As the workplace becomes more machine oriented, effective production using machines requires that the flow of work accommodate them instead of the workers. Focus on the craftsman must be left behind as assembly-lines transform factories. Even social services follow this trend, with ever larger hospitals, prisons, orphanages thought to be the most efficient way of taking care of the less fortunate. The electrification of cities, automobiles, aeroplanes, subways - all of these incredible advancements were only in their first stages, but captured the public imagination immediately. They felt as the century drew to a close that they were witness to a grand beginning in the life of humanity. It was a heady time, full of optimism that human endeavour could conquer any problem.

Along with this confidence came a certain amount of decadence, with upper society allowing themselves a certain libertine license. The two decades that bracket this period have more dissimilarities than commonalities. During the Naughty Nineties, the sense was that Christian Man had finally conquered nature and the heathen, bringing the fruits of God's bounty to its rightful owners. The capitalists and industrialists who created this massive change saw themselves as the next aristocracy, the true leaders of the civilized world. A new century was about to usher in a future of promise. This was a male-centered world, with women providing a diverting background and taking care of some domestic concerns, but even in entertainment the men were catered to almost exclusively. It is at this time that men withdraw to smoke their cigars after dinner, or retire to private clubs after work, or visit burlesques where decent women were not allowed. Wherever men of power congregate, that is the center of the social world.

But by the time of the roaring twenties, many things had happened to shake that confidence. Disasters large and small - the flooding of Galveston, the sinking of the Titanic, the San Francisco earthquake - took the lives of both rich and poor, sinner and saint. A World War wiped out half a generation of young men in Europe, and the influenza pandemic of 1918 wiped out millions more. Yet at the same time, cities had become modern, no longer made of low wooden structures, but towered above the landscape in concrete and steel. As the postwar world began to regain its economic footing, people were ready to enjoy all that a bustling city life could offer. Light and heat came on with the flick of a switch, hot water came out of faucets in every floor of the house. It didn't matter that the United States had passed Prohibition. Speakeasies were open, nightclubs were available, jazz was playing and whiskey was flowing. People were ready to party.

<u>Fashion/Manners</u> – There was difficulty in adapting 19th century manners to 20th century realities. A bustling city requires practical manners, so the bow fades into disuse. A wave of the hand might be quite acceptable. The hat may be removed with the right hand so long as transferred to the left, leaving the right free for handshake. Removing the hat was expected in any private room, but not in a public place. But in a crowded city, this was often difficult to establish. By convention, an elevator was deemed a private room, so off came the hat. But you would put it back on in a building hallway or corridor, which was considered to be the equivalent of a public street. Tip the hat to a stranger; remove the hat to an acquaintance. But when tipping the hat to a lady, do not make eye contact, for that would require her to return eye-contact, and that would be a serious lack of propriety. Nor should a man smile to an unknown or only casually known male or female on the street, as it makes an assumption of familiarity.

In the 1920's, by contrast, there is a palpable feeling of people throwing out old ways by the shovelful. Informality is the rule of the day, with people greeting each other directly, male or female. Introductions are appreciated, but no longer necessary. A cosmopolitan flair was strived for, and an easygoing stride and a boyish enthusiasm for fun and nightlife and entertainment in all its forms. And while there was still a strong line between the upper class and the serving class, the stuffiness and gender isolation of the Edwardian period was tossed out in favor of elegant sophistication and thoroughly modern sensibility. Everyone had seen too much of death; dance now, was the theme, while the band is still playing.

For formal wear, men's fashion, as usual, mimics the military uniform of the time, even going so far as to put a satin tripe down the legs of Tuxedo pants, mimicking the parade dress uniform. That satin sash, black on black, is still the distinctive feature of men's formal trousers.

Civilian Conflict –

The great influx of both immigrants and of former agricultural workers into the largest cities also brought about the gangster era, made even more powerful by the wealth they were able to amass during Prohibition. So while the rest of society went about without so much as a penknife in pocket, city criminals begin to carry any manner of hidden weapons. Brass knuckles, switchblade knives, and small revolvers are all designed to kill someone from a very close distance. Even the Tommy gun was a close-in weapon, for in attacking in a city environment there is no need for accuracy or distance.

For urban dwellers, pistols are not only hidden when worn, but are also somewhat hidden when used. The elbow is kept close to the body as the forearm is extended, and the rest of the body keeps a normal stance without trying to brace for recoil. From across a crowded street or even in a large room no casual bystander would even notice that a gun was being held. Naturally aiming the gun by looking down the sights is impossible, but it is assumed that the victim is going to be no further than twenty feet away. For all of these reasons, pistols tend to be of shorter barrel length and of lower caliber.

Warfare – The beginning of this time finds us at the end of Victoria's reign in England, and most European armies are engaged against poorly armed and inadequately organized rebellions in their third-world colonies. A sense of complacency develops within the Western military, believing in their own invincibility. They were completely unprepared for the carnage that WWI inflicted.

In the decade before the war, all armies have discontinued colorful uniforms in favor of drab khaki, brown, or green clothing for service use. With radio communication and rifles now capable of accurate fire up to 300 yards, there is no longer any point in having lines and columns of soldiers exposed in the open. Better to try to blend into the background if possible, limiting the enemy's view of your position and numbers. But with trains and trucks able to transport millions of troops, armaments and supplies to the very edges of battle, a stalemate quickly developed during WWI. Both sides were outfitted with high-powered machine guns, semi-automatic pistols and fully automatic submachine guns, yet the standard response by the generals was to attempt direct charges at the line of the enemy. Each such charge ended in hundreds of deaths. So the infantry/cavalry dynamic is in a state of unequal stalemate. The foot soldier with his bolt-action rifle is still the heavy infantry, and he is pinned down by an extremely effective light infantry in the form of three-man machine guns. But there was no effective countermeasure, which was normally the job of light and heavy cavalry. Slowly the battle became that of trench warfare, with soldiers hiding in long ditches to escape the wall of machine gun bullets, and then chemical warfare, with poison gas lobed into the trenches. Neither side had an effective answer to the new style of war, and in the end it was the simple attrition of materials and men on both sides that made the parties sue for and accept terms of peace. After this, no war would ever be described in the romantic views of the past.

Relativism

Time Frame – 1930 - 1965

Politics/Economics – Rise of Fascism, Communism, Socialism. The rapid decline of colonialism.

The Great Depression did what Prohibition couldn't - sober up America. Interestingly, it also made entertainment more powerful. With the wide availability of radio and film, people were willing to spend a few of their hard-earned pennies on escapist entertainments without having to turn a blind eye to reality. The 1930's gave birth to modern jazz (with its darker tonalities always bubbling underneath even the happiest tunes), screwball comedies (where normal can become surreal in a second) and superheroes (because a normal guy is no match for the brave new world). Counterpoised to that is the underlying presumption, especially in the United States, that any problem can be overcome so long as we put our collective minds and muscle to it. Not just engineering challenges, but social ills, natural disasters, environmental concerns, finally even reaching the moon - all are bendable to the will of science and technology.

The two greatest effects of WWII was the catapulting of the US as the bona-fide world power, and the decline of the European countries, even the victors. Strict colonialism could no longer survive, and most colonies quickly gained independent nation status.

The United States largely won the Second World War on the strength of its industrial power. It was able to produce the tanks, planes, bullets, guns, and ships to outfit itself and its allies, as well as provide the petroleum to power them. American society took two lessons from this. First, that if industrial bureaucracy could crush fascism, it could be used to handle any task. Companies large and small copied military protocols and organization. But hospitals, schools, department stores, public housing, suburban residential developments - all became industrialized. Large works better than small.

The second lesson was that the war was won by the average Joe, not by the snooty aristocrats. America turned away from looking to France and England for its art and culture. So begins the era of the common man, and with it the dominance of American culture worldwide. Even as early as the 1920's, but certainly by the end of the 30's, upper class entertainments are viewed with ever more suspicion. Opera, ballets, symphonic music, poetry; these have little place in the new culture of the common man. Film is the main art form, the only one that reflects popular sentiment and is actually seen by most of the population. There is less production of what had fed aristocratic desires, and now a flood of lower luxuries fulfilling the American Dream.

Warning: big digression coming up: Here is where I start to part company with the many books on theatre history and period style. Too many of them take their cues from art criticism and art history. These tend not to follow popular art, but rather at this point delve into modernism and post modernism. But when trying to follow period style, it helps not a bit to focus on the "art for art's sake" schools, which unfortunately is most of visual art of the twentieth century. Those artists, geniuses to be sure, are interesting to only a small subset of the population at large. In effect, they become an aristocracy of art, looking down on the majority of people for whom cubism and deconstruction and ambiguity of theme have no meaning. It is not to the fringe that one must look when trying to find a period style.

Fashion/Manners –

Instead of proscribed manners, it becomes more important to act directly in a personal way to whatever is happening in the moment. A man was expected to stand straight and have a firm handshake in the business world, but was expected to relax and "loosen-up" when at home or with friends. The body begins to slouch into a comfortable chair, and the legs can cross in any way that is comfortable for the sitter. Formal introductions are completely gone, and most people feel completely at ease in simply introducing themselves to a stranger in any situation.

Civilian Conflict – Continuing unchanged from the prior period, most men are unarmed. At most, a hidden gun or knife might be worn, as most countries pass laws prohibiting the wearing of weapons.

Warfare – Armies replace bolt-action rifles with semiautomatics, and then finally fully automatic rifles. Aviation and tanks redefine the infantry/cavalry dynamic. The foot soldier can become both the heavy and light infantry, but now tanks can barrel past trenches, filling the role of heavy cavalry and airplanes being the light cavalry. Because the expense of war rises exponentially with each technological improvement in weapons, smaller armies or poorer ones use irregular fighting strategies, now called "guerrilla" warfare. The concept is ancient, and resorted to when facing a force superior in numbers and weaponry. In short, it involves attacking when the enemy is in retreat, disappearing when the enemy wants to attack, and disrupting the enemy when he is not prepared for engagement.

Youth Culture

Time Frame – 1965 - present

Politics/Economics – Power shifts from mere heavy industry to entities that can expedite and control all levels of production, from raw material to final consumption, with minimal restraints from geographic boundaries. Of the three descendants of the free market form - communism, fascism, and corporate capitalism, only the last proves to be a successful economic model. Global technologies allow for multinational corporations, entities which no longer are restricted to sharing in the successes or failures of an individual "home" country, but can move resources and production facilities quickly from one country to another as best befits the immediate need.

The availability of leisure time and the affordability of the tools of entertainment increase exponentially. The widespread use of air conditioning and central heating allows people to remain largely isolated from the effects of the natural world whether at home or at work, or for that matter even when commuting between the two.

The trend of commerce to emulate production line techniques leads to the creation first of supermarkets and then multiplex theatres, the "big box" warehouse stores and finally the "mega-stores". Large volume sales are aided by the introduction of prepackaged units of food and clothing, man-made materials including "disposable" plastic items. Nearly every type of vendor moves to incorporating self-service, in whole or in part, in order to expedite the movement of customers with minimal staff. This parallels the trend of consumers to limit the amount of "face time" they need to endure as they go through their daily schedule.

Fashion/Manners – With an unprecedented rise in living standards and the explosion of mass media, entertainment becomes not merely a diversion but the goal of living. Almost every home worldwide turns on a radio, a computer, or a television set - every day. The contemplative life, formality, articulate speech, intense scientific inquiry are all viewed with suspicion. A new concept - retirement - develops, and in western society becomes an assumed entitlement. By mid-century, business attire resembles the new architecture; big, bland and boxlike. By the end of the century, even business attire is no longer considered necessary in order to run a business.

In daily life, the increase in commercial consumerism allows two trends - perpetual infantilization and performance identity - to play out to every sector of the population. The backlash in American society to the Vietnam war accelerated the post WWII trends that were already in play. The male ideal slowly continues its devolution in age, from that of a successful 40 year old man-of-the-world, at ease in any social situation, to the archetypal wired 16 year old, in-your-face and disdainful of social manners. Body posture is, as we shall see, by contrast apologetic and fearful. The concept of the inherent nobility of the common man becomes twisted into the emulation of traits that are common. This combination of youth worship and disdain of formality has led to an elevation of the acceptability of childish behavior well beyond what had always been the loose cut-off point of adolescence. Notice the increase in crudity used in popular media. Although scatological humor has existed uninterrupted since ancient Greece, it was always used for its shock value, and those characters who demonstrated it were themselves objects of ridicule. The current trend uses it in order to sell products to the general population. Crudity is the status quo, the great equalizer, proof that you and I are equal because we can all sink to the lowest common denominator. In what other society would you sell fast food by showing people who are unable to put the food in their mouths or cannot eat with their mouths closed? Advertisers know that we will relate to hands and faces smeared with undigested food but not to someone who eats small portions neatly and without the need of a napkin.

The current adult has kept the same food stuffs with which he was familiar as a child. Instead of a simple cup of coffee or tea, highly sweetened lattes, mochas and chai's soothe the child/adult palette. The candy bar has been repackaged as an energy bar, milkshakes become smoothies, but these are mere changes in nomenclature so as to please the buying public. We still want our highly sugared pacifiers that we got as treats when we were four.

In clothing, leisure wear is accepted as standard wear for nearly all daily activities, and, with oversized pants, loose shirts and sneakers worn for nearly every occasion, young and old alike emulate the attire of toddlers, for the societal norm is to look in the mirror and see youth. With prices of clothing having dropped to unprecedented lows (relative to income), people can choose their "look" according to their mood. Yet it is interesting to point out that while a man's complete business suit can be purchased for $50, most adults see no need to own a suit. [Most will spend that much or more on running shows and will never run a mile in their adult lives.] For different occasions, people no longer simply dress in their best apparel, but instead costume themselves as the character they wish to portray. In some ways we are a performance society, going so far as to the wearing of slogans on T-shirts as a way of subtitling our lives for the benefit of the viewing audience. Lost in an impossibly complex and isolating world, we wear these articles not only to express ourselves to others, but more importantly to define ourselves to ourselves. Like good method actors, we then strive to take on the characteristics of the characters we have created. At the same time, by the end of the century rare is the person not branded by a corporate logo on at least one article of clothing every day. It's as though the character we create defines his meaning by the corporation he represents.

There is a continuing conflict being played out between our nineteenth century cultural heritage and our twentieth century desires (it'll take several decades before a new 21st century style develops). Most of our current forms were structured around a semi-agricultural life-style. We take summer vacations, our holidays set long ago by the down time between ripening and harvest. We put away our cars in a garage exactly as our forefathers put away their horses in barn. We bypass an unused dining room where at one time a large farm family would have sat down twice a day to eat. We sit in a family/living room laid out for genteel conversation, but have to turn the chairs and sofas to face the real central feature of the room - the television set.

It is easy to dwell on the changes to our society since the invention of television, beginning with reminding you that whereas all prior peoples would look for entertainment by either going out to see live performances or by enjoying the fellowship of neighbors and friends, we moderns relax in front of a box. Live performances, movie houses, neighborhood pubs, even informal activities such as the bridge party or sitting on a front porch and talking to neighbors are all losing their appeal. As the television became less expensive and a single family could afford more than one set, entertainment became personalized. No longer would the entire family sit and watch the Ed Sullivan Show. The universal spread of information and ideals that was the hope of television has mushroomed into a flood of fragmented and tightly focused programming to targeted market segments.

When the automobile was invented, it was treated as the natural successor to the horse, so we built garages that look like barns in which to house them, and the style we wanted to see for the vehicle itself was that of the elegant carriage. The automobile was the public representation of a family's position and aspiration, even built so as to parade the entire (nuclear) family in its journey to town and church.. In the current period, the car has become another of the entertainment devices which we purchase not to fill a need but to more tellingly enhance our childlike pleasure. Notice the shape and color of vehicles of the past twenty years: it is not an accident that Detroit has given them the unmistakable look of the old Matchbox cars and Tonka trucks of our childhood. Purchase for practicality here again has given way to fitting the products to a film in which we cast ourselves as the central star. Reality need not interfere with fantasy. Notice how car ads on TV show the driver doing 70 mph on winding country roads, even though we all know that the actual driver is going to be going about 7 mph in bumper-to-bumper traffic.

In the vehicle or out, at work or at play, we also keep a running sound track to fit the self-image we create. Stereos and mobile music players allow us to change the mood of our surroundings just as we costume ourselves to fit the scene we are living out at the moment. Especially in the United States, this dovetails with a rejection of communal ritual. Weddings, funerals, really all of the rites of passage, are individualized rather than conforming to tradition. Traditional elements may still be included, but the focus is on making every event a reflection of the individual rather than a recreation from an ancient template. So traditional elements are picked buffet style, so that no two weddings should ever look alike. Even as we value our anonymity, we strive to be different, just like everybody else.

A youth culture chooses to ignore the reality of aging and death, so even as retirees use plastic surgery in order to look twenty-nine, we move our cemeteries far away from neighborhood churchyards and isolate them into park-like "death-ghettos", away from view and away from our thoughts.

For a moment, think of how different we moderns are from any other people in history (then consider the subset which is the vast majority of actors; usually under thirty and middle class), and how that affects our world view. Whether born in city or country we have in reality been raised in a suburban life-style, not connected to the land in any real sense, have not seen a dead body outside of a hospital or funeral home (even there we often never see the body). We have access to information from around the world but cannot look at the night sky and tell what week of the year it is. We do not know what it's like to walk down a street and have most people recognize us by name and know most of our family history. Our supermarkets offer us every type of produce known without a thought as to seasonal availability. We have always assumed an unlimited and immediate supply of electricity and water and access to instant communication. Cut off those things from a modern person and you have the set up for a horror movie. And all of what is considered meaningful information either arrives or is confirmed by television and the internet.

Originally, this increase in the availability of resources and information was supposed to usher in a feeling of empowerment, but oddly, the opposite has occurred. Paranoia is the societal norm. Compared to other generations, we live in a nearly constant state of fear and anxiety. All public discourse centers on defining what we should fear most. Commercial products are sold to us based on eliminating what we should deem as constant threats. We live with the assumption that our streets are not safe, that our children are not safe, that our water, food, air, strangers, homes, germs, wildlife, odors, books, movies, insects, philosophies ... all of these and just about anything else with which we come in contact are sources of grave and immediate danger to us.

We stand and walk in such a way as to hide from the public eye, with slumped shoulders and arched back, eyes cast to the ground. As we walk, this feeling of collapse continues with each step, so much so that the torso drops into the hip. This, combined with the slumped shoulders, restricts our lung capacity and reduces our speed and placement of our body center. As a result, we tend to lead with the feet or with the forehead.

Of course, youths have been told from time immemorial to stand up straight and not slouch. But as they reach adolescence, they naturally look to the adult ideal of the time and begin to shape their mannerisms and postures to fit that model. It just happens that the current adult ideal comes from entertainment and sports, themselves eschewing the image of sober adulthood and taking on the persona of irresponsible children. Indeed, anything associated with the traditional image of responsible adult, sober in demeanor, is ridiculed as being uptight and repressed. This causes a great problem in business situations. For men, this often translates into a strange double life - dressing for the boardroom, but maintaining the frat-boy persona.

Our natural default facial expression is one of veiled hostility, the better to hide the latent fear. Except in business situations, the handshake greeting has been reduced to a very limited hand clasp or touch, with countless variations to establish social placement. Sitting in a chair involves a full collapse into the contours of the seat and back, one step away from reclining, as though attempting to disappear from the room.

Warfare – As potential battlefields expand into the air, and even above the atmosphere, soldiers become either operators of war technology or guerrilla fighters. The days of large numbers of individual infantry fighters taking a field en masse is over. The set-piece battles of WWII with clear battle lines have given way to rapid assaults by combined forces using primarily aircraft in both the light cavalry and heavy cavalry roles, with infantry being highly mechanized and shifting from being either light or heavy, or both, as situations warrant. Direct infantry fighting is now handled by small units of specialized regular forces trained in guerilla techniques, and the bulk of the army either providing logistic support or operating explosive weapons from a distance. The model used in the Vietnam War of using large numbers of lightly armed ground troops to do the bulk of the fighting is no longer seen as effective, although, as is common throughout history, generals are the last to learn those lessons.

Fully automatic firepower and high energy explosives are available now to even the poorest faction. Bladed weapons have no place in battle strategy, although combat knives and bayonets survive as weapons of last resort for ground forces. The oldest form of the sword, however, is still in use, although no longer for soldier to soldier fights. Machetes are used by combatants to massacre unarmed civilians in many parts of the world.

A worrisome trend has been the use among many insurgent armies to use children as soldiers. Although children have been used as drummers, tenders, and deck-hands for centuries, their numbers were limited and their application was in minor support positions and not in combat roles. What we are seeing now is something else entirely - entire armies in which only children are recruited [or stolen] as combatants. The reason for using children is obvious - they are far more susceptible to the brainwashing and character break-down during indoctrination and training that helps turn decent civilized people into killing machines. [That's why regular military forces don't like to take in recruits that are older than twentyfive.]

What is most troubling about this isn't that it is some diabolical aberration, but a horrifying realization that the historic barrier to using children has disappeared. Unfortunately, there has never existed a societal taboo on using children by itself to keep it from happening. The barrier was ultimately practical, not emotional. Young children simply don't have the endurance to be able to march nor the strength to handle the fighting. That is no longer the case now that soldiers can be trucked in to even the most remote areas. As far as the actual fighting, modern weapons such as the AK-47 variations are light enough for a child to carry and simple enough for a child of twelve to disassemble, clean, reassemble, load and fire 50 rounds into a village with only one hour's worth of instruction.

Civilian Conflict – Continuing the trend of the beginning of the century, most men are not armed when outside of the home, gang and drug-related tit-for-tat killings notwithstanding. Most weapons used in anger are pistols using high powered ammunition, and confrontations are usually one armed belligerent facing an unarmed one. The youth gangs of the last two decades of the late twentieth century differ from those in mid-century in that the drug trade provides a baseline income that can easily allow for the purchase of even high-priced modern weaponry. That, and the flood of cheap assault rifles coming in from former Soviet Union client nations, has made assault rifles such as the AK-47 available to even low-income teenagers in urban areas.

Also new, and especially seen in the United States, is the development of anonymous violence, made possible by the ubiquity of the automobile. And as is common in youth cultures throughout history, lack of self-control leads to a much faster resort to lethal violence.

The Future

Time Frame – ?

Civilian Conflict – Over the course of our 5,000 years of written history, it seems that violent conflict between individuals has consisted primarily of spontaneous attacks and corresponding self-defense or reprisal. There was one brief blip of about 300 years in which mutual combat in the form of duels of honor flourished in both Japan and in Western Europe (amazingly at roughly the same time), but then quickly reverted back to crimes of passion and of predation. Dueling could only exist in a society which valued the wearing of a sword, and that quickly died with the rise of practical pistols. A duel allows both parties to make the decision to enter into battle; refusal to fight is possible so long as you can at any time simply step away from the field, a choice not possible with firearms. There is no reason to expect any change in the near nor far future. The firearm cannot be uninvented, and laws prohibiting ownership will not dissuade people from having or even building those of their own. If the propensity to resort to violence does not change, the desire for weapons cannot.

Warfare – Warfare responds to technology slowly; warriors forever fight battles with the newest weapons while generals use the previous war's tactics.

There is a great divide in the ability of the world's combatants to wage war. Large armies like those of the United States, China, Russia and NATO can so overwhelm a less well-stocked opponent in a traditional war that achieving the standard objective [control of territory] is readily accomplished. That leaves smaller belligerents a limited choice when waging war: attack only those who are similarly or less-well armed, or, when fighting a larger force, change the rules. Of course I am not talking only about terrorism. Since traditional objectives are impossible to achieve, both terrorist groups and small armies simply strike at any weakness with no traditional "strategic" objective in mind. Any attack, successful or not, is a victory, for the only objective is to attack and cause disruption. Since no territory is gained, the attackers can melt away after each assault, therefore successful reprisals are difficult.

So the future of warfare will continue in three directions. Overwhelming technological superiority will be brought to bear wherever possible, with a specific focus on the use of high explosives and automated attack. A superpower such as the United States can wage this type of expensive war without bankrupting its citizenry or even putting large numbers of its soldiers at risk. This type of warfare will continue to rely on soldiers that can handle ever more sophisticated and remotely operated weapons. News stories will still be filled with accounts of individual soldiers involved in rifle firefights, but military planning focus is now all about delivering maximum damage while avoiding exposure to same. Since few other individual countries can sustain that kind of military cost for long, regional armies might be created to form "mini-superpowers" in Africa, Asia, or the Americas. China by itself stands at the brink of becoming the next unchecked superpower should it be able to combine a robust economy to its military advances and as of yet untapped resource wealth. In terms of pure military success, these large modern armies are nearly unbeatable once fully committed to battle. Only they can continue to wage decisive warfare.

In opposition to this technological superiority, we will see a continuation of terror attacks on exposed military positions and large civilian centers; in other words, provocative warfare. When performed by small nations or pre-national insurgency forces, those actions will exist side-by-side with guerilla tactics, but the lines will be increasingly blurred. One of the reasons that these forces rarely achieve military success is because of the nature of their goal. Since these groups are looking to achieve nationhood, they at some point need to expose themselves in number so as to obtain the standard objective of securing territory. Once done, their opponents can begin successful counterattacks using traditional military means. So these guerilla tactics at some point have to give way to political options.

No such problem exists for nontraditional groups who have only an ideological objective. Since these are transnational groups that need not exist in any one country, they can attack anywhere from anywhere. Counteraction is difficult. There is no identifiable central command headquarters, since the terrorist cell structure will not have a typical strict hierarchy. And since the objective is the attack itself, even ineffectual explosions are counted as successes. These TNI's (transnational ideologues) depend on wearing down their opponents' resources, commitment, and support from other political groups. As such, success strategies against TNI's usually involve reducing their popular support, thus cutting them off from money, safe harbor and recruits, rather than concentrating all resources in a purely military defeat. (By the way, there is no such thing as a war on terrorism. Terrorism is a tactic used by an enemy, not the enemy itself. One can no more have a war on terrorism than one can have a war on the flanking maneuver. Defeating the use of the flanking maneuver does not defeat the enemy.)

The last form of warfare will be resurgences of the Congolese model: large scale attacks on unarmed civilians using very low tech weaponry, the idea being to destroy enemy populations without bringing in reprisals from the major powers. Usually this takes the form of a relatively small military force using assault weapons backing-up a large ad-hoc army of non-uniformed homogenous partisans wielding simple impact weapons [machetes, knives, clubs], in other words annihilation/raiding warfare.

It is possible to imagine a successful defense against this kind of slaughter, one harkening back to ancient Europe. Should local populations begin to develop township fortifications, they might be able to withstand these attacks. One can imagine the equivalent of the medieval castled protectorates, with semiautonomous political organization, cropping up in Southeast Asia and sub-Saharan Africa. We have seen one form of this in the warlord-controlled regions of Afghanistan, both pre- and post- the Soviet and US invasions. However, as this always requires a concurrent collapse of the viability of the nation-state of the affected region, this outcome is best suited to geographically isolated regions and is unlikely to provide success in other areas.

Politics/Economics/Fashion/Manners – How far can the crystal ball see? One of the problems with looking to the future is that we can only look at the past and hope to follow the trends in a straight line to guess what is in store. But history is a bad predictor, for the very things that have marked changes in culture and society have come about as surprises. In male fashion, for example, if we were to see an unbroken continuation of the trend of the last eighty years to ever more youthful appearance, the next twenty years should see us wearing diapers as day wear. But history rarely takes a straight line; it runs up against something unprecedented and bounces off, sometimes in several directions before lumbering down a new and unsuspected path. Who could have anticipated all of the circumstances that pushed Europe from medievalism and into the Renaissance? Who could have predicted the rise of the middle class and the throwing-off of monarchy in the eighteenth and nineteenth centuries, actions unprecedented in history yet now viewed as inevitable? But there is nothing inevitable in history, only the reactions made by rulers and masses to a string of circumstances, circumstances that occur without regard to experts' sensibilities.

Some very long term trends bode well for us humans. We have given up slavery, infanticide, and human sacrifice, for instance. Oh, slavery still exists in many regions, but considering that it has been around from the first civilizations and was always defended by the countries in which it flourished, we have reached a point where it is universally condemned as a crime. There now exist no apologists for slavery, for even where it exists, the countries involved cannot admit to its existence. Even in that denial there is proof of its status as an obvious crime. Progress has been made. Will war go the same way? Unfortunately, the very long term trend has been to move over the course of 8,000 years to ever more destruction in each conflict, the only limit on casualties being an attempt to limit the duration of the battles by inflicting overwhelming damage in the shortest amount of time.

Some theorists have posited that the great trends are at their apogee, that we have exhausted the supply of new ideas, that we are at the "end of history". It's easy to take that view. Economic systems may still be debated in universities, but every country seems to have tied its boat onto some form of capitalism even if they continue to rail against its evils. Political systems, seemingly in mighty contrast throughout the world, are all moving steadily to republics (some democratic, some tyrannical) and away from monarchies.

But that stasis may be illusory. The passenger in a plane can be easily convinced that the jet has come to a complete stop even when traveling at 700 miles per hour. And even the most seemingly stable systems sooner or later begin to disintegrate. The great empires have had their moment in the sun, and then slowly faded from their place as the center of the universe. Following the western progression, Greece gave way to Rome, followed by France, then England, then the United States, and now ...

When empires reached their peak, they not only exerted military dominance over all others, but their cultures also spread, so that even those societies dominated by the empire tried to emulate the manners and art of the dominators. This is well known, but what is also true but easily forgotten is how each nascent empire borrowed the culture of the fallen, borrowing its glory and by extension its legitimacy. Just as the art and learning of the Greeks were co-opted by the Romans, the glory that was Rome was emulated by the French. The English, as they gained power of the world in the 19th century, aped the manners and refinement of the French, but then when America dominated the world in the 20th century we kept the culture of the English and still view it as superior to our own. Our American entertainment, our form of dress, our "culture", is now rapidly devoured by all the world. But our position as the industrial and agricultural might of the planet might soon be more a memory than reality. From whence shall we see the next empire rise?

There is one country that has all of the elements to overwhelm not only its region but also the current "superpower". China - converting successfully from an authoritarian socialist command economy to a nationally controlled capitalism with some free-market elements within a strict authoritarian structure - has established in essence the fascist system. But unlike the twentieth century Axis regimes, China is now realizing its ambitions primarily through economic dominance.

Both WWI and WWII (and the Cold War for that matter) were finally won because the United States was able to produce staggering numbers of tanks, ships, planes, munitions, and petroleum - not only for our own use but also for our allies. Those capabilities are no longer ours as our resources dwindle and our factory output drops. We prop ourselves up with borrowed money, but if China continues to take advantage of this trend, turning the United States into a net importer of goods, we will go the way of Europe, a large economic engine responding on the periphery of the true world power.

[Note to the gentle reader: I first wrote the above paragraphs in 1993, so it's not as though I'm merely riding on the coattails of current events. The continuing trends of the last decade and a half have confirmed my opinions, but I feel saddened rather than vindicated. Besides, many people have been forecasting this general scenario since the 1970's]

* * *

Western culture itself has really not developed any truly new ideas since the early part of the twentieth century. Clothing, architecture, visual and performance arts, all continue to take different elements of what has been done before and repackage it, deconstruct it, or simplify it so that it can be called new, but in reality are merely very minor variations on a reaction to the status quo. Until a new matrix takes hold, we will continue to use and reuse the elements solidified in the past century.

In art, we have completely embraced virtual realism over live presentation as our favored art form, so film, then TV and perhaps in the future interactive entertainment will have replaced all forms of live theatre as relevant performance art. By relevant I mean being an integral part of the fabric of our lives, rather than just responding to it from the edges.

Forgive yet another digression, but theatre is dead. Oh, there is certainly plenty of it out there and some of it earns some producers a ton of money. But whenever and wherever live performance art has had relevance it was when it served the needed value of ritual for that particular society. But during the past century we have excised ritual as an important element of activities large and small, largely because we associate it with being non-relevant, archaic, even repressive and antagonistic to personal freedom. Even the ritual of the nightly family dinner is fast becoming a quaint memory of a slower time.

Our society as a whole no longer believes that sitting with others in a darkened listening room and watching a live performance is a ritual worth preserving. Watching a movie still has some value, but even that has changed from a respectful communal experience to one that is more and more individualistic. The movie experience must now have comfy reclining chairs and allow the giant Tub-o-Nachos and 64oz ThirstBuster so that the viewer may believe he is really at home, and therefore can remain unconcerned about anyone else who might also be in attendance. It is noteworthy that 70% of cinema attendees - people who actually go and see movies - state that they prefer seeing movies at home. With every passing year, more and more are doing just that. Perhaps in the past, people put up with the discomforts associated with going out to see a live performance because there was no other alternative. That certainly is no longer the case, so people stay home.

Live theatre retains a limited role as a training ground for television and film actors. Granted, there are still blockbuster shows that pull in millions of dollars on Broadway, but these are the exceptions, not the rule, so for the most part live drama has gone the way of ballet and opera - unable to pay its own way due to lack of viewership, the patient stays on life support so long as there are wealthy donors willing to subsidize an archaic form of entertainment. For better or worse, art that can't travel through a cable no longer has an effect on our society.

I am not saying that is necessarily good or bad, merely pointing out that it is happening. Opera, ballet, live theatre, dance performance, modern visual art - all have their passionate advocates, and continue to produce wonderful works of art, but society no longer values this production and so it appeals only to a tiny audience of cognoscenti. This is no different than the disappearance of the family farm, the corner store, the brass band playing in the town square, or the doctor who makes house calls. The few extant specimens are exceptional because of their rarity. We enjoy hearing about them, and we even root for them to survive, yet we still shop at a supermarket and go to an HMO for our needs. People can be nostalgic for things and still contribute to their extinction.

The explosion of personal computer technology and the spread of the internet has led some to proclaim the birth of a brave new world, but it would seem merely to be a further development of the trends already established by the telegraph, telephone, and television. The grand hope of the computer was to usher in a new phase of development in human society, but mainly it just created a new version of the old Sears catalog, combined with the Encyclopedia Britannica and the world's largest party line. But at least a party line required civil interaction between strangers. Now, even as vast quantities of material are shipped by truck and by train, people spend more and more time isolated from actual human contact. The ubiquity of cell phones, PDA's, headset music players, internet - all are possible not only because the technology allows it, but because we currently would prefer not to have random interaction with actual humans. In gas stations, banks and in stores it is possible to go through entire transactions without having to acknowledge nor be acknowledged by another human being. Most automobiles still have four seats, and yet are occupied by only the driver. Even with family vehicles, there is a demand to include distractions (music, cup holders, video screens) that can keep the occupants isolated from each other. This is not forced on us by technological progress - we want this.

Is this a linear trend? I doubt it is, for it feels static. It seems unlikely that we can find a way to become even more informal, embrace even more public crudity, become more anonymous, demand even more entertainment values. All play and no work makes Jack a poor boy. Rome fell not only because the barbarians battered the gates but because the wealth of the empire finally all came from overseas while the local citizenry placated themselves with bread and circuses. All of the elements that together we can call the current period style have an uncomfortable similarity with other periods in which a series of primary trends merely feed on themselves until a dynamic redirection comes along. Many are the similarities to ancient Rome, but we seem to share many parallels with Europe of the Mannerist Renaissance, or even of the mid to late 1700's Rococo. No one then could have guessed how things were going to change in the future of their children. No one could have foreseen the collapse of the feudal system, nor the birth of the age of enlightenment.

No, when the next big shift comes, the one that will affect fashion, manners, public and private conduct, governance, art, music and society, few will have predicted it. It may come slowly, the result of a thousand minor shifts over time which only in retrospect will be viewed as one surge. It may happen almost overnight, some cataclysm that shakes all of our previously held beliefs to the core. It might be some new technology providing perhaps an unlimited supply of power and water to every person on the planet, or a devastating cataclysm which causes a massive continental migration. Whatever it is, it will probably cause a geographic shift in power, possibly add a new religion or two, and cause a reevaluation of the nature of the individual in society and in the universe.

That is, if history is any judge.

The Thin Blue Line

From *Much Ado About Nothing* to *Arsenic & Old Lace* to *Lobby Hero*, civilian police are a staple in theatre. But our common notion of a standing civilian police force is a relatively new concept, and the weapons available to them have evolved even as their duties and position in society have shifted.

It is interesting to reflect that the vast majority of peoples throughout history have conducted the business of regulating an ordered society without establishing a police force of any kind. An accused miscreant would be hauled before a representative officer of the ruling power, and acting in the name of that prince or king, guilt or innocence would be established, and punishment swiftly delivered. The only little drawback to this time-honored system is that the punishment could be arbitrary and cruel, guilt was often assigned without the benefit of evidence, and the people who did the arresting were more likely to administer their own brand of immediate justice, bothersome proof of innocence notwithstanding.

Even in tightly regulated bureaucratic powerhouses such as ancient Rome, an elaborate judicial system might exist without use of a police force per se. A civilian watch was organized that could alert the authorities to a crime. Should an arrest be required, soldiers were used on an ad hoc basis. An order would be given, an arrest made, the prisoner taken to a magistrate, afterwhich the soldier returned to his normal duties.

[A case has been made that ancient Egypt's marketplace guards were the first established police force, but this might be a case of extrapolating a wider theory than the evidence allows. The Nubian slaves that were posted throughout the market place could more accurately be compared to modern security guards. They could assist vendors in maintaining order and preventing thievery, but did not have true police powers.]

With the fall of Rome and the resulting segmentation of authority in medieval Europe, policing became an almost exclusively village-regulated system. As long as the village memory could identify each member to the ruling lord, laws could be established and order maintained. Punishment was limited, however, as confinement was too costly for most communities to afford. Although compelling restitution and inflicting torture or death are the first things that come to mind, there was also one punishment which to the medieval mind was even more terrifying. That of being declared "outlaw".

Laws were certainly not uniform throughout a kingdom, and even the few "citizen's rights" that did exist were only useful so long as there also existed someone with the power to enforce those rights. Straying a mere few miles from a nobleman's castle or populated township and one was far from anyone's protection or expectation of recourse to justice. To be declared outlaw would mean that even within the geographic limits of the lord's power one was stripped of any right or protection. Anyone could take from you, strike you, even kill you, and there would be no crime, for you were now "outside of the law". To be an outlaw meant that your life and livelihood were forfeit if you remained in the town, so to the un-populated woods you would go. Most perished, but some became even more dangerous, preying on those who traveled between villages. Any stranger entering a town without a letter from his own shire reeve was assumed to be an outlaw.

The reeve was a representative of the king and had two principal duties for which he received occasional payment. First and foremost, he had to collect the taxes due from every household, and second, in time of war had to muster the shire inhabitants for military duty if needed. With these two duties and in the name of the king, the shire reeve could also be called upon to arrest and imprison, but not punish. The term shire reeve over time became shortened to sheriff, and was perhaps the first non-military police officer.

Larger towns could hardly keep an institutional memory of all of its inhabitants, but did at least begin to develop a rudimentary policing system within the confines of the town limits. We get a little flavor of such a system in the opening act of Romeo & Juliet, where a general level of disorder rises to inflame the population enough so that they call for "bills - partisans". They are calling for the only police they know about, in other words, that fellow citizens should grab the pole weapons used for civil defense and separate and subdue these threats to social peace. Those pole weapons were often warehoused in populated areas as weapons to be used against foreign invasion. Their easy availability for civilian peacekeeping was a secondary benefit. There were no specific individuals assigned to take up such a task - the responsibility was assumed to be that of every hearty male in good standing once the alarum was sounded.

More ordered was the night watch, assembled on a rotating basis among the citizenry to patrol the streets for a full night. The watch was expected to detain suspected criminals, and for that purpose was given a polearm for the night. This was the perfect implement for an untrained guard, for it is very threatening and also keeps the holder at a safe distance from anyone wielding a knife or sword. As the watch received no pay for their service, and were more interested in maintaining a quiet vigil rather than meting out punishment, they tended to do a reasonably good job in keeping order and not succumbing to the bloodthirsty excesses of the daylight mobs.

Smaller villages usually did not require a watch of any kind, as crimes were rare and the miscreants well known. But without any facilities for imprisonment, punishment tended to be harsher than in the townships and was a financial burden to all. A good example are the early Massachusetts colonies, in which even the shackles to hold a prisoner, without a lock and merely riveted closed, had to be manufactured to order by the local blacksmith. Even if the accused during the Salem witch hunts had somehow been found innocent of all charges, they would not have been released until their families had paid for the cost of building and removing the shackles, as well as the cost of feeding the prisoner during his incarceration, and even the fee for the visiting judge to hold the trial.

The last segment of "proto-police" civilian control was not civilian at all but a standing military force used in a peace keeping function. From the 16th to the 19th centuries, it was common for European countries to keep small contingents of specialized warriors employed in extra-bellum service. To the extent that they could afford it, nations found it prudent to keep the nucleus of the harder to train units intact, thus simultaneously keeping them battle ready, providing a useful function as guards and patrol, and keeping them from being hired by potential enemies. We have many examples in theatre of such soldiers. The Cardinal's Guards as well as the title characters in *The Three Musketeers* are obvious examples, but don't forget the Hussars that shoot Bill Sykes in *Oliver!* and even Inspector Javert in *Les Miserables,* a man with exclusively police functions but paid by the military, not civilian, authorities. [We still use the French term *gendarme* to designate police forces that have grown from a military force.]

As military control gradually shifted to civilian oversight throughout Europe, police duties were officially reserved to newly created purely constabulary forces. In England, the first professional constables were known as "Peelers" or "Bobbies", from the name of the founder, Sir Robert Peel. Their uniform was designed to make them obviously distinct from the military - no helmets and no firearms. Instead, each constable was supplied with a pair of handcuffs, a wooden rattle (later replaced by a whistle in 1888) and a nightstick. The uniform itself was a variation of common civilian formal dress, and included a top hat and longcoat, although the tail of the coat did have a long pocket in which to carry the nightstick.

Last to join this trend was the United States, and when American cities developed police departments they armed them as did their European counterparts - with two foot nightsticks. Only after confronting large scale riots at the turn of the century did municipal officers begin to carry firearms, almost always the Colt New Service 32 caliber revolver, later replaced by the Smith & Wesson 38 revolver (long barrel for patrolmen, snub-nose for plainclothes). Most images we have of the beat cop strolling through a city street comes from this tradition, and is certainly the kind most often found in American theatre.

The increased demands of city policing came at the same time as the development of steel handcuffs. Their use allowed officers to quickly restrain prisoners for the difficult walk back to the local precinct. Unlike older iron manacles, steel handcuffs were easily portable and one size could fit almost any sized wrist. One set could even be used to restrain two prisoners by cuffing each of their right hands together, preventing them from easily using a weapon or even running away in the same direction.

During the mid 1960's, largely in response to the increase in firepower used by drug runners, most police departments added the pump-action shotgun to the patrol car, followed by the replacement of the revolver to the semi-automatic pistol - usually the Colt 45 caliber during the 1980's. That gun is now being replaced by the Glock semi-auto 9mm - matching the shift made by US armed forces, but as all three guns have their own peculiarities and drawbacks, it is not unusual to see uniformed members of the same large city police force wearing different guns. At the same time, the beat cop all but disappears as most officers find themselves in patrol cars rather than scuffing shoe leather.

The latest additions to the police armory are in the use of protective gear and the introduction of so-called non-lethal devices such as the taser and pepper spray, and no police department uses the old style truncheon. Instead, the side-bar nightstick, allowing a wide range of offensive and defensive actions and take-down restraint moves, is now standard issue throughout the US.

The first decade of the 21st century sees a proliferation in the use of AK-47 type submachine guns throughout urban and suburban high crime areas. After adjusting for inflation, they have become as easy to purchase as were the semi-auto pistols during the 1970's. City police departments are quickly adding M-16 type assault weapons in direct response to this domestic arms race.

Development of the sword in Europe
(when commonly used, not when invented)

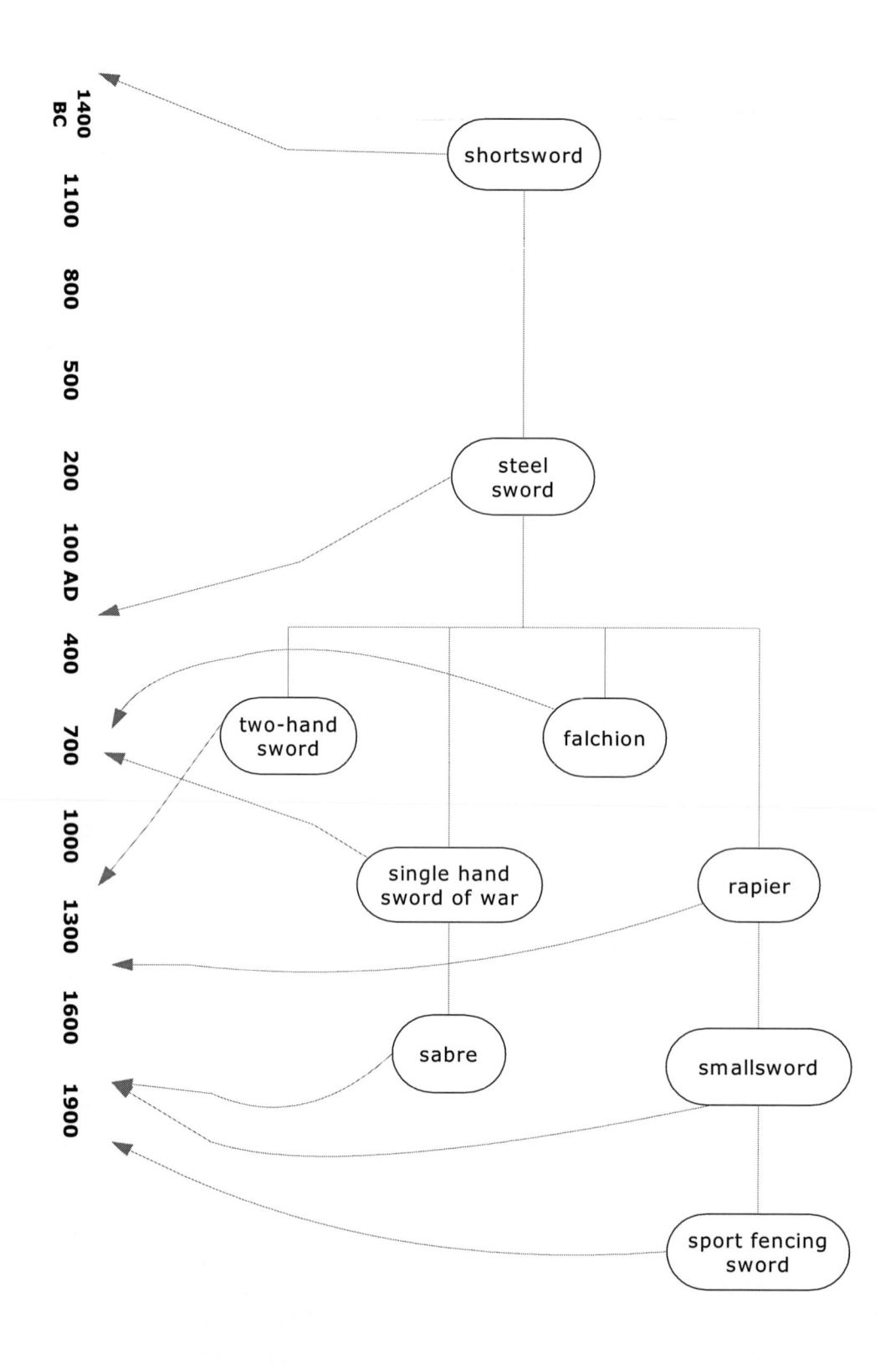

Time	Sword
1400 BC	shortsword
1100	
800	
500	
200	steel sword
100 AD	
400	
700	two-hand sword — falchion
1000	single hand sword of war — rapier
1300	
1600	sabre — smallsword
1900	sport fencing sword

Development of the long firearm in Europe
(when produced in large quantity, not when first introduced)

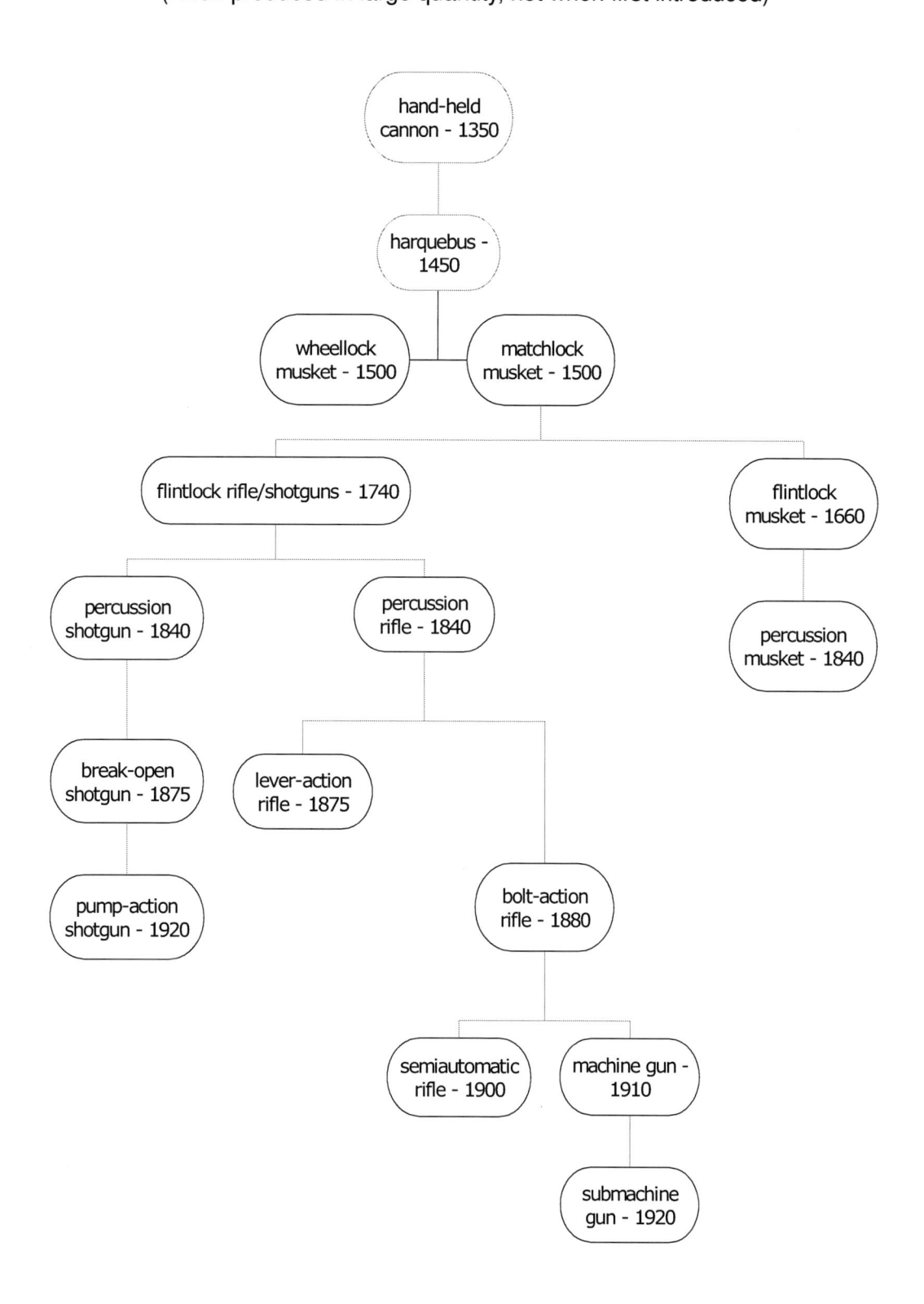

- hand-held cannon - 1350
  - harquebus - 1450
    - wheellock musket - 1500
    - matchlock musket - 1500
      - flintlock rifle/shotguns - 1740
        - percussion shotgun - 1840
          - break-open shotgun - 1875
            - pump-action shotgun - 1920
        - percussion rifle - 1840
          - lever-action rifle - 1875
          - bolt-action rifle - 1880
            - semiautomatic rifle - 1900
            - machine gun - 1910
              - submachine gun - 1920
      - flintlock musket - 1660
        - percussion musket - 1840

Development of the pistol in Europe
(when commonly used, not when invented)

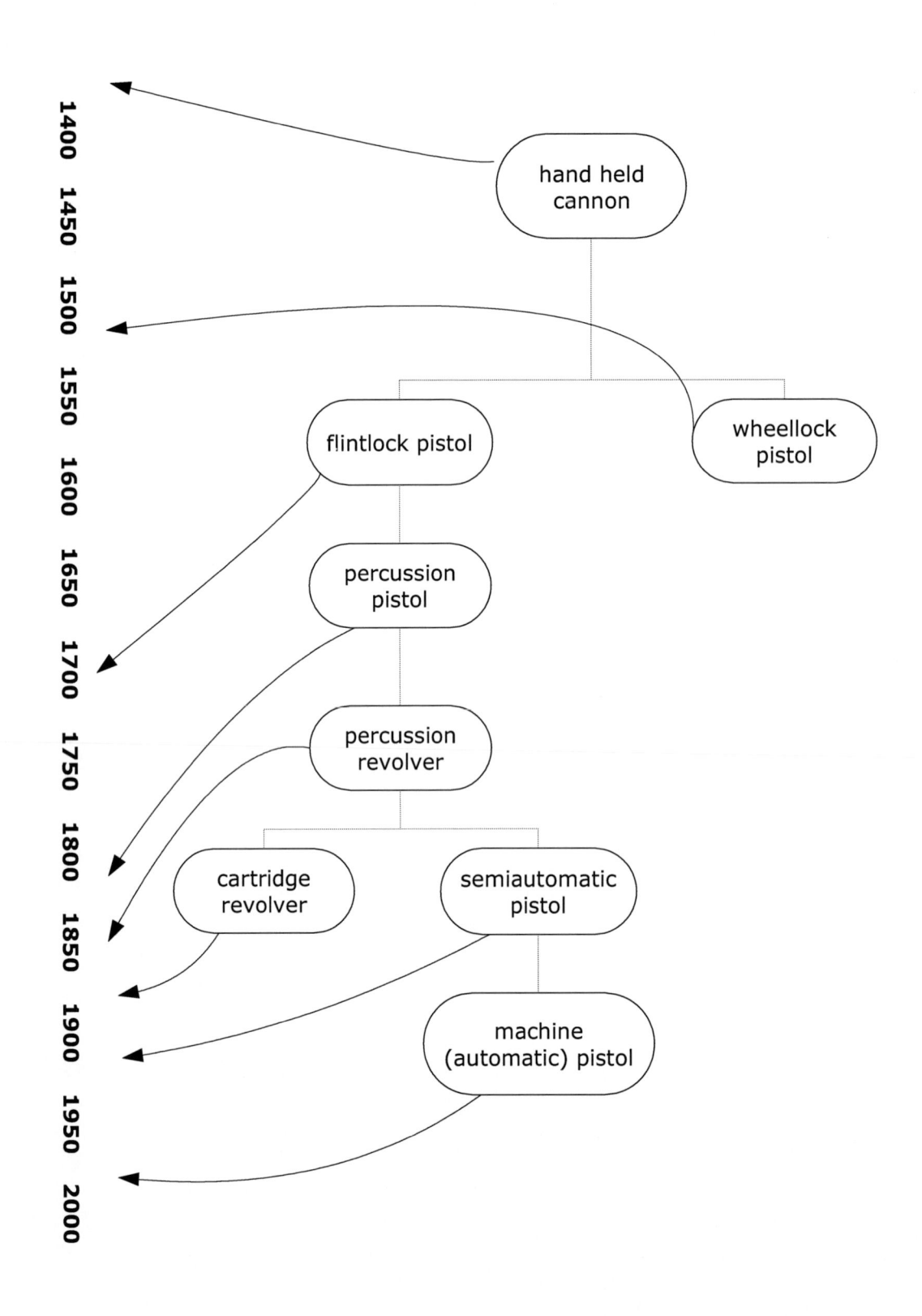

Year	
1400	← hand held cannon
1450	
1500	←
1550	flintlock pistol — wheellock pistol
1600	
1650	percussion pistol
1700	←
1750	percussion revolver
1800	
1850	cartridge revolver — semiautomatic pistol
1900	← machine (automatic) pistol
1950	
2000	←

Weapons Defined
A Specialized Dictionary

12 gauge -	One of the barrel sizes for shotguns, but also a modern and incorrect catch-all term for any large shotgun.

22 -	Modern nickname for a 22 caliber pistol, usually a very small frame revolver. Also sometimes used to mean a very small rifle.

30-06 - One variety of rifle cartridge, sometimes also used to describe a rifle (any style) that fires this size cartridge.

30-30 - Another variety of rifle cartridge, sometimes also used to describe a rifle (any style) which fires this size cartridge. Usually the reference is to a lever-action or bolt-action sporting rifle.

32 -	Modern nickname for a 32 caliber pistol, most often a snub-nose revolver.

35 mm revolver - An anti-aircraft gun mounted on warships. 35 mm ammunition is about 1 3/8 inches thick, so those rounds are the size of short fat carrots. The guns can fire aprox. 1,000 rounds per minute, at either a low flying plane or a fast moving ship. The assembled weapon usually stands between eight to fifteen feet high once it is secured onto the deck.

Obviously, a 35mm revolver is <u>not</u> a handgun. It's called a revolver because its central operating system revolves, but it is not a pistol because you certainly can't hold it in one hand. For some reason, some people are starting to use the term "35mm revolver" as though they are describing some sort of pistol. The only "pistols" that can be 35mm are those that fire emergency signal flares, but even those are single shot and not revolvers.

The key here is that they are saying millimeter (mm) instead of caliber (cal).

357 magnum -	Modern nickname for a .357 caliber pistol, usually a revolver, and especially for the long-barreled version from the 1960's, the Colt Python. The .357 cartridge was developed in the mid 1930's, and were used in any .38 caliber handgun, but the first revolvers specifically designed for the cartridge came out in 1955.

38 -	Modern nickname for a 38 caliber revolver, usually that with a four inch barrel, but sometimes used for the snub-nose style.

44 -	The most common reference is for the Remington six-shooter cowboy revolver of the late 19th century.

44 magnum -	Modern nickname for a 44 caliber pistol, either semiautomatic or revolver, of the 1960's.

45 -	Modern nickname for a 45 caliber semiautomatic pistol, although it used to be the common nickname for the western cowboy revolver made by Colt.

9 -	Modern nickname for a 9mm semiautomatic pistol.

Action - For firearms, it refers either to how the powder charge is ignited for single shot weapons, or for multi-shot firearms the mechanism by which rounds are brought to the firing position. Some actions include flintlock, wheellock, percussion, lever action, pump action, bolt action, and blow back.

Ahlspiess -	A two-handed thrusting spear used by medieval German armies. This was a foot soldier's polearm, not to be thrown, with a yard-long steel spike mounted on a wooden shaft of anywhere from four to six feet long. Between the wood and steel was a round hand guard, about 12 inches in diameter. Nothing fancy in its use, it was a down and dirty thrusting/impaling weapon stout enough to pierce armour.

AK-47 - Automatic-Kalashnikova army firearm, model number 47. The standard issue Soviet sub-machine gun since 1951. Subsequently produced by dozens of countries and distributed world wide, the Kalashnikov is the most successful automatic firearm ever designed.

Ankus - The single-hand hook used by elephant trainers in India. Also called an elephant hook or bullhook. An ancient tool, the older versions look very scary and are usually included in books describing the weapons of India, although there is no evidence that they were ever used in combat.

AR-15 - The original designation by Armalite Co. for what would be known as the M-16.

Arbalest - The medieval continental European term for the crossbow.

Arquebus - also Harquebus, Hackbutt. The earliest of the handheld firearms, first developed in the mid 15th century and commonly seen in European battlefields by the mid 1500's. They began as mere short cannons strapped onto a wooden stock, and usually had a metal ring from which the weapon could be hung from a hook to support the weight and diminish the recoil. In time a tripod was added to allow for maneuverability in the field and the weapon was lightened considerably. Fired just like a cannon, a lit match or fuse was manually applied to a touchhole in order to set off the powder inside the barrel. When a reliable trigger and matchlock was developed by the late 16th century, the term arquebus was dropped and the term musket became common. For some armies, both terms continued to be used simultaneously until the early 1600's. Firearms with shorter barrels but of larger caliber continued on for some time with the name arquebus, and musket became the name for the longer barreled weapons of slightly smaller caliber.

Arrow - The pointed shaft fired from a bow, but not from a crossbow. Arrows must flex during their flight.

Artillery - Originally meant all and any weapons and ammunition of war, then anything fired (arrows, bullets, shot) from a weapon, but for the last 200 years refers only to the larger firing weapons (guns which must be mounted from a fixed or heavy platform) and its ammunition.

Assault - A very recent term to describe pistols or rifles that fire in fully automatic mode, can be easily carried and operated by one person, and have a clip capacity of at least 20 rounds. Assault weapons have only one purpose - to kill as many humans as possible as quickly as possible.

Automatic - A gun that can fire continuously so long as the trigger is held. (As opposed to *semi-automatic,* in which the trigger must be pulled separately for each shot.) Soldiers trained to use automatics are taught to squeeze the trigger in short bursts, to allow re-aiming between firing, and so that not all of the ammunition is discharged within a few seconds. Most modern assault rifles often have a "short-burst" setting to aid the user in this.

The term is commonly but incorrectly used to describe a <u>semi</u>-automatic pistol. [Some insist that semi-automatic pistols are really automatics, for the gun automatically loads itself after each shot, but this only confuses the issue.]

Ax, Axe - A broad metal blade mounted on a shaft, used for cleaving. Decapitation by use of a large two-handed ax was the medieval punishment for traitors.

Backsword - During the 16th and 17th centuries, the same term described one of two different basket hilted weapons:

1) a single-edged straight blade, the precursor to the military sabre. With a single edge, the overall blade weight can be made lighter and easier to manage than a double edged broadsword and still be an effective cutting tool.

2) a blunted stick used as an alternative to a steel blade for use in [relatively] nonlethal duels. A "backswordsman" would be one who specialized in public prizefighting duels using the wooden backsword.

Back Edge - The unsharpened edge of a single edged weapon. Although a two-edged blade does not have a back-edge, the term is sometimes used in stage combat to refer to the "weak" edge when any weapon is held - the thumb side edge rather than the knuckle or cutting edge. Sometimes mistakenly called the false edge.

Baldric - The strap that holds a weapon or bugle onto a soldier by suspending it from the shoulder, as opposed to securing it on a waist belt.

Ball - The metal sphere fired from a smoothbore gun or crossbow. Balls, made of metal, were the precursors to bullets, which are conical shaped.

Ballock - A dagger with a wide long blade and very short grip, having no guard or hand protection. The term is descriptive of the shape of the handle, ballock being an old word for testicle.

Bardiche - A curved headed two-handed polearm of northeastern medieval Europe. An exotic looking military battle-ax, the blade is about two-feet long, most often mounted on a haft of between four to six feet.

Barlow - A maker of an early style of folding pocketknife popular in the United States during the early 1800's.

Barrel - The metal hollow tube from which is expelled a projectile. The barrels for the first cannons and then arquebuses were built by the same coopers who built regular wine casks, so these weapons really were metal barrels.

Baselard - A type of shortsword and dagger of the Middle Ages, having no true pommel and usually a minimal handguard. Most had just a small flair on both ends of the handle to provide a good grip, and a shortsword style blade. Primarily a Swiss weapon.

As a dagger, the same style was revived by Nazi Germany for military presentation items.

Basket Hilt - For rapiers and backswords, hilts made up of strips of metal in a symmetrical design half encircling the hand. Unlike standard rapiers, the basket has an integrated knuckleguard and no quillons. Called the *schiavonna* in Italy, or *mortuary sword* in England during Cromwell's inter-regium of the 1650's, basket hilt swords are held using a firm hammer grip rather than a looser rapier grip. They remained extremely popular in Scotland, replacing the Claymore as their national sword.

Bastard Sword - First developed in the 1400's, these were long bladed broadswords balanced for primarily single hand use, but fitted with a longer than normal handle so as to allow two-handed use for especially powerful blows. Also known as the "hand-and-a-half", but both such terms are modern.

Battle-ax - Take a standard wood-cutting ax, make the handle thinner and longer, make the metal head twice as broad but half as thick, and you have the military battle-ax. More devastating than the sword, two-handed varieties were used by foot soldiers, while knights on horseback used the single-hand styles.

Bayonet - A small knife or spike meant to be fixed onto the end of a musket or rifle, giving the firearm the properties of a thrusting spear. In the 1600's, the handle was simply jammed into the barrel, but thereafter the bayonet has been affixed underneath the barrel to allow for firing of the gun. Although there was some experimentation of making bayonet-swords, blade lengths of over 15" are impractical.

Bearing Sword - Large double-edged straight broadswords held and carried in front of royal processions. The practice began during the Renaissance. These swords were supposedly of some famous warrior, and were generally oversized.

Beretta - An Italian firearms manufacturer of many rifles and pistols. Their 92F semi-automatic pistol became the US standard issue in 1984. The Pentagon declined to use an American company, although this gun, designated by the Army as the M9, was known to suffer from many significant flaws. In the US, the term is also used to describe (incorrectly) any small frame semi-automatic pistol.

Bilbo - A cut and thrust sword from the Bilbao region of Spain. Developed first in the late 17th century, it featured a substantial rapier dish hilt and no other hand protection, but fitted with a wide broadsword blade. The term also includes any rapier hilted thick bladed straight swords found on battlefield throughout Europe and America until the early 1800's. They were meant for use on the battlefield only, but were not issued as official sidearms. Bilbos and cutlasses were often purchased individually by soldiers in underfunded units that were not issued swords.

Bilboes - A type of shackle, consisting of a long iron bar fitted with two limb constraints. By keeping the feet or hands at a fixed distance from each other, a miscreant could be inconvenienced and humiliated but still handle daily activities, even continuing to work.

Bilboes were especially used where space limitations precluded incarceration, for example on sailing ships from the 15th to 18th centuries.

Bill - A form of halberd or poleweapon in which the head is primarily a slightly concave large cleaver. [The word in Old English referred to a type of broadsword, and in Old Teutonic a large ax.] Bills were used by some infantry units in medieval warfare, and from the 14th through to the end of the 18th centuries were the common weapon for the civilian nightwatchmen, especially in England.

Billy Club - A small club. The term "billy" was a variation of "bully", which also referred to highwaymen.

Blackjack - A small leather pouch filled with lead shot. Used as a small concealable club for whacking a victim on the head. (Originally the blackjack was a large leather bag with an outer coating of tar, used as a poor man's bottle for carrying beer.)

Blackpowder - Historic gunpowder. A combination of nitrogen, carbon and sulfur which, when ignited, burns extremely rapidly, causing an even more rapid expansion of gas which is used to propel a projectile to a target. When blackpowder burns it causes a dense cloud of gray smoke to hang around the gun and a lot of fouling inside the barrel.

Blade - The essential part of a sword, as opposed to the hilt. The blade is the length of metal that actually does the cutting. Some people incorrectly refer to a complete sword as a "blade".

The blade of a sword has two parts - the blade proper is the part that is visible, but the steel continues inside the handle. That part is called the tang. For most blades, the tang is much narrower than the exposed blade, and the site of the abrupt narrowing is called the shoulder. The hilt rests on the shoulder of the blade.

The blade proper is itself loosely divided into three sections: forte, middle, and foible. Some blades have grooves running lengthwise which are called fullers. Some of the thinner sporting blades may have a tip that has been blunted with a wider flat "nailhead", referred to as the button, which may or may not be covered in rubber or leather for additional safety.

Blank - A firing cartridge which is complete except for the bullet itself. A powder charge made for firing a gun without discharging a hard projectile.

Blank-fire - A gun built or modified so that it can only fire a blank cartridge. It may or may not be block-barreled.

Block-barreled - A gun built or modified so that when firing a blank, no discharge travels out of the muzzle of the barrel. Designed solely to be a blank-fire gun.

Blow Back - The type of action used in all automatic and semi-automatic firearms. For semi-automatic guns, the explosion of the cartridge not only causes the bullet to fly out, but part of the discharge is directed back into the gun. The discharge pushes he workings of the gun so as to produce a cascade of mechanical actions: kick out the pent cartridge, bring up a new one into the barrel, and pull the hammer back to firing position. The operator need only press the trigger to fire again.

For fully automatic guns, all of the above takes place and the striker (hammer) is allowed to fire the next round without a pause. The gun will keep firing (cycling) so long as the trigger is held.

Blow back systems have been around from the 1890's.

Blunderbuss - A German term that means "thunder gun", a two-handed firearm of the mid 1600's to the late 1700's, with a short but very wide barrel, most often with a flared muzzle. Not designed for firing a single ball or bullet but rather a handful of pellets, gravel or broken glass. This was an "assault weapon" meant for defending corridors or suppressing insurrections, never for hunting. By the way, never used by the Pilgrims, greeting card illustrations notwithstanding.

Bolt- 1) The very short projectile fired from a crossbow. Whereas arrows must flex in flight, bolt must remain rigid.

2) The distinctive feature of the bolt-action rifle, the little lever on the right side that loads each round for firing.

Bolt-Action - The working mechanism of some clip and magazine fed rifles. Each fired cartridge is ejected from the gun when the user lifts and pulls the manual bolt on the right side of the gun, and then the next round is put into the barrel and secured for firing when the bolt is pushed and then lowered. Bolt-actions saw their apogee during WWI, saw somewhat less service during WWII, and then survived as a hunting rifle for the rest of the century. Some snipers in SWAT units still prefer bolt-action rifles due to their stability during firing.

Bow - A curved weapon used to fire arrows, the propulsion derived from the spring-like action of returning a string from a drawn to a resting position. Bows may be constructed of a single piece of wood (self-bow), several layers of wood or bone (composite bow), or one of several modern plastics.

Almost all self-bows are also known as simple bows, for when unstrung have almost no curve to them, and when strung form a simple arc. All others are called recurve, and are strung against the natural curve of the bow. This allows for much greater power to be delivered to the arrow, and gives the bow the classic triple curve shape when strung, with the bow tips curving away from the shooter.

Bowie - A fighting knife of the American South and Southwest of the mid 19th century. Bowie knives cover a wide range of looks, but most have the following in common: a single edged blade of between 10 to 15 inches, at least an inch and a half wide, with a slightly curved and tapered double-edged tip and a limited straight handguard. The guard has only one function - to prevent the user's hand from sliding forward during a stabbing and accidentally getting sliced on the blade.

Brass Knuckles - A hand-weapon that covers the striking surface of the fist, a single well-placed blow from which can shatter the skull. Brass knuckles [which can be made of any metal] actually have two properties. The most obvious is that the striking surface of a punch is hard metal instead of fragile fingers. The second is that the grip allows for a much stronger fist to be made, much as holding a roll of coins improves a punch.

Breach - For firearms, it refers to the end of the barrel closest to the shooter. As opposed to the muzzle. The gunpowder and bullet need to be at the breach end for firing. Most guns built after 1870 are referred to as breach loaders, for the bullet and powder are introduced directly into this end of the barrel rather than sliding it down from the muzzle.

Break Open - A type of shotgun with a hinged frame that can open just in front of the trigger, allowing the shooter to load the gun at the breach end and then close the gun again before firing. A very few pistol styles were also designed the same way.

Broadsword - This term has changed a few times over the millennia. At first, as far back as the time of Beowulf, it meant a single-hand wide-bladed sword. Then the term fell into disuse until it was resurrected in the 17th century to describe the straight-bladed basket hilt infantry sword which was the forerunner of the sabre, and distinguished from the backsword by being double edged. By the 1800's, it became again attached to the medieval sword of war, and that is pretty much where it has remained. In England, it still might refer to any of the above mentioned weapons, whereas in the US, we only use it to describe the single or doublehand medieval sword of at least three feet in length.

Broomhandle Mauser - The first practical and widely used semi-automatic pistol, saw extensive use on the German side of WWI, not merely by officers but also by the infantry as an effective weapon for close-quarter trench fighting. Mauser was the name of a manufacturer that produced dozens of firearm styles, and the "broomhandle" part of the name refers to the distinctive shape of the grip.

Brown Bess - The nickname given to the British military musket of the late 1700's. The barrel was often browned (as opposed to blued) to resist rust.

Browning - An American inventor and designer of several firearms. Many of his patents were used by Winchester, Remington and Colt in their most famous firearms. The majority of his semiauto pistols were and still are manufactured by a Belgium company.

At least one play ("The Physicist") makes reference to a "Browning revolver". Sorry, but there is no such firearm. All Browning pistols were and continue to be semiautomatics, not revolvers. The erroneous term has been common in England since the first semiautos were produced at the turn of the century. It is still relatively common in that country to call any multishot pistol a revolver, regardless of the firing mechanism.

Buckler - A small shield, usually less than 15" in diameter, used as a defensive support when fighting with the sword or rapier. A civilian, not military, shield, although many mercenary soldiers carried them into battle during the Renaissance for hand-to-hand fighting.

Buckshot - As opposed to birdshot, the relatively large pellets in certain shotgun cartridges. Buckshot would be used to bring down medium sized mammals and humans, but is too large for bird hunting and ironically too small to bring down larger game such as deer.

Bulldog - A snub nose British revolver with a smallish grip, usually of higher caliber, 38 and 45 being the most common. Popular during the 1910's and 20's as a pocket pistol for self-protection.

Another gun, built in the US in the 1970's and 80's, was also trademarked as the Bulldog, and had many of the same characteristics.

Bullet - a ball of metal, usually conical in shape, for use in a firearm with a rifled barrel. The conical shape allows the spinning bullet to fly straighter and longer, just like a thrown football.

All modern bullets come already attached to the proper *cartridge* and *primer*, making it ready to fire. When the gun is fired, only the bullet leaves the gun. The cartridge remains behind.

Bull Pup - Slang for a modern assault-rifle layout in which the clip is placed between the stock and the trigger instead of between the trigger and the barrel. This allows the rifle to have the best features of the long-barreled M-16 and the short and comfortable Uzi. Most military rifles of the future will apparently follow this design, as more encounters will be in crowded urban settings.

Butt - For rifles and shotguns, the end of the stock braced against the shoulder. For the quarterstaff, the end not pointed at the opponent. Since both ends of the quarterstaff can be used to strike, the designation of butt end can change with nearly every action.

Butterfly Knife - Same name, two different knives.

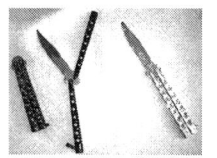

The Western butterfly is a relatively recent development, a way to circumvent the restrictions imposed on switchblade knives. The butterfly has no springs, but the blade is connected at one end to two sections of handle. The three parts are freely moving so that the handle sections can either close around the blade or swing back around toward each other, exposing the blade. With a little practice, it can be opened and closed with one hand, the movement of the knife vaguely giving an appearance of the flutter of butterfly wings.

The Chinese butterfly knife [Ba Jaan Dao] is far older, and is more accurately a hatchet with a knucklebow. In "traditional" (modern) wu-shu practice, it is fought with in pairs.

Cage Hilt - For rapiers and certain other swords, a guard style that is built of interconnected strands of metal. Differing from a swept hilt in that there is generally more protection to the hand and the strands are laid out in a relatively symmetrical pattern.

Caliber - The internal diameter of the barrel of a gun, measured in either hundreds of an inch or in millimeters. So a 38 caliber gun has a barrel opening (and therefore a bullet size) of 38/100's of an inch, or about a third of an inch wide.

Cannon - A <u>very</u> big smoothbore gun, but still just a gun, using the same firing system basics.

Cap - For percussion firearms, it is the tiny thimble-shaped item placed on the outside of the gun which actually sets off the powder charge inside the barrel. The percussion cap is single use only, and is coated on its inside with a quick igniting compound, which sparks when struck by the hammer.

For toy guns, it is the very small amount of gunpowder glued into a piece of plastic or paper that, when struck by the hammer, creates a small explosion.

Modern city slang also uses the term as a verb, "to cap" someone meaning to shoot them. It is not used as a noun to refer to the bullet.

Carbine - Originally a shortened musket designed to be fired from horseback, carbine now means a "shorter" rifle. Shorter than what? Whatever the manufacturer of the rifle decrees. There is no standardization of rifle lengths, so none for what constitutes a carbine. Most gun makers tend to make carbines at around six to nine inches smaller than whatever the rifle is. A carbine will be of course lighter than the rifle, at the expense of distance firing accuracy.

Cartridge - The cylindrical case, usually of brass or cardboard, which holds the powder charge and projectile (bullet or pellets) together as one unit.

Case of Rapiers - Two rapiers, built as a set, intended for fighting with one rapier in each hand.

Cat o' Nine Tails - The short flail used as an instrument of punishment. Especially popular for use on 16th and 17th century ships, the cat had a short stock and several thin strips of leather that would break the skin of the exposed back. The strips sometimes had small metal barbs on them in order to maximize skin damage.

As a form of punishment, it is the equivalent of the common whipping, but on a sailing vessel there is simply no room to wield a whip.

Centerfire - Type of cartridge ammunition in which the firing pin of the gun must strike the center of the primer so that ignition can occur. Also, a gun designed in this way.

Chamber - As a noun, that part of a firearm that holds the cartridge in place for its firing position. As a verb, it means to work the action of a gun so that a round is mechanically worked into the chamber.

Cinqueda - The very broad-bladed knife of the ancient Romans. Not a battlefield weapon, the cinqueda gets its name from the "five-fingers" width of the blade at the hilt. Wedge or "pie" shaped, some reached lengths of almost two feet. Worn across the small of the back in a sheath suspended from a belt. As a knife or a smallish sword, it gained a renewed popularity in Italy from 1470 to 1550.

Claymore - From the Gaelic words *claidheamh mor,* meaning "great sword", it is the two-handed sword of medieval Scotland, especially of the Highland clans. This massive five-foot sword was best used by foot warriors against English horsemen riding more slowly on the rocky terrain of the north, where the Scots could use the long reach of the heavy blade to cut through the legs of the horses and then dispatch the fallen knight.

The term is an ancient one, revived during the 1700's to also include the singlehand basket-hilt sword. This has led to a great deal of confusion and dispute amoung antiquarians as to which is the correct use. While the debate continues, it is helpful to refer only to the large two-handed weapon as being a Claymore, and for the sake of clarity to call the other simply a Scottish basket-hilt.

Clip - For automatic and semiautomatic firearms, the often removable magazine which both houses and feeds the bullets into the firing chamber. Within a clip, the ammunition is stacked like cord wood, pushed upward by a spring.

Clip-Fed - Any multi-shot firearm that receives each successive round from a spring loaded (and usually removable) stacked-ammunition container known as the clip.

Club - A heavy stick used with one hand, with the hitting-end usually thicker than the gripping end. Types include the stone head composite club, the baseball bat, the mace, the billy club, the Irish shillelagh, etc. This is of course an ancient weapon (even baboons have been known to pick up heavy tree limbs and defend themselves against attacking leopards) yet is still universally used by modern police forces in the form of the nightstick. Rarely less than one foot or more than three feet in length.

Colichemarde - A smallsword variant of the 18th century, with a distinctive blade, wide near the guard and then suddenly narrow about two thirds of the way down. The theory was that it was supposed to make the blade more resistant to breakage, but in practice the blades broke just as often as the thinner common smallsword, and usually right at the point of the narrowing.

Colt - An American firearms manufacturer that has been around since the early 1800's, and has provided a wide variety of guns for civilian use as well as for police and military contracts. Colts span all the way from the first practical percussion revolvers of 1835 to the modern M-16.

Corseca - Another name for either the runka or for the spontoon, two types of bladed polearms.

Cosh - A kind of nautical billy club. Short, with one and sometimes both ends knob-shaped with a thin handle or center. Most often made of wood, but some were made of carefully woven hemp rope. Nicknamed the "life preserver".

Courtsword - A sword worn in the presence of or presented by royalty. Richly engraved and gilded, they were purely for show and never intended to be useful weapons. Although the concept of wearing a non-practical sword this way began in the mid 1500's, fake ("dancing") rapiers looked like their practical counterparts, whereas true courtswords were developed as very elaborate variations of the smallswords of the eighteen and nineteenth centuries.

Crossbow - Technically it is a miniature version of the ancient Roman ballista, but in this case the mechanically-firing torsion bow is laid crosswise instead of vertically, and firing a sharpened rod rather than ball-shaped projectile. The rod is called a bolt rather than an arrow. Crossbows in Europe go back to the 12th century AD, but were used in China as far back as the second century BC.

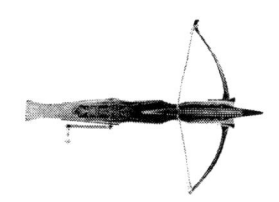

Cudgel - A short rustic club, usually less than two feet long.

Cup Hilt - For rapiers, a guard style which incorporates a solid concave metal hand protection. It can range in shape from a simple shallow lens to a half-sphere, known as a full cup.

Cutlass - Literally meaning "cut rope", it is a short sabre designed for shipboard use, where a standard length sword would only get in the way of the rigging. Cutlass blades were never over two feet long.

Cuttoe - Slang 18th century term for any single-edged short bladed sword, usually slightly curved, whether used as a cutlass or hunting sword.

Dag - The term given to short-gripped pistols when differentiating them from the large cavalry pistols of the 16th through 18th centuries. Dags were normally wheellock, not flintlock.

Dagger - A double edged knife with an acute angle at its point; primarily built for thrusting. Daggers are weapons, not utilitarian knives. Blade lengths of more than eighteen inches put the weapon in the realm of short sword rather than dagger. Daggers disappear from men's dress by about 1660.

Dancing Sword - In 16th century Europe, a sword worn as an indispensable part of elegant dress for a court appearance or formal dance. Most men of position purchased a rapier for this and no other reason, so the blade did not need to be of high quality. In order to save money, many "dancing swords" did not even have real blades. Men who would have only occasional need for such an item could rent them for the day, often from theatre companies.

Derringer - The name Derringer can mean either the manufacturer (which made several different styles of handguns), or one of three different blackpowder single shot pistols of the 1800's, or a completely different style of two-shot pistol of the 1900's (add to that the problem of three different manufacturers trying to use the Derringer name, and it gets really fun). To make matters worse, newspaper reporters of the 1800's often called any pocket pistol a derringer.

Dirk - A straight dagger with a long and thin blade. Dirk blades are by convention never more than an inch wide, and generally are the length of one's forearm.

Doglock - An early precursor to the flintlock mechanism. It incorporated a small hook that had to be manually engaged in order to hold the hammer in the half cock (loading) position. For any kind of machine, a "dog" is any simple device that keeps something else from moving.

Double Action - Describes the working of the hammer for a pistol. On double action guns, the hammer will pull back automatically before dropping forward whenever the trigger is squeezed. As opposed to single action. In other words, the hammer on a double action gun does two actions although your trigger finger does only one. The benefit of double action is that the user can fire the gun as quickly as he can pull the trigger, although it tends to jar the gun slightly and so can disturb the accuracy of the shooter's aim.

Most revolvers can fire in either single or double action. Shooters will use the double action when firing several shots quickly; single action when careful aim is necessary. Single action also reduces the power necessary from the shooter's finger, so is often used by those with weaker arm strength.

Dragoon - A corruption of the French word for dragon.

1) A short musket of the 1700's designed to be light enough to hang from a soldier's belt and also fire from horseback.

2) In the same period and beyond, a soldier in a military unit trained to fight either as infantry or cavalry.

3) Any of the weapons [sword, pistol, rifle] used by a dragoon.

Dry-Fire - To pull the trigger on an unloaded gun, causing the hammer to strike an empty chamber. Without the cushioning effect of the hammer landing on soft brass, dry-firing is extremely damaging to any gun, whether real, prop or toy.

Dueling Pistol - Not to be flippant, but it's any pistol used in a duel. It is not descriptive of any specific weapon type, but rather a marketing term. During the 18th and 19th centuries, pistols were sometimes sold in pairs and in a wooden case, catering to the upper class who were more likely to have to use them in a duel. But there was nothing distinctive about the pistols themselves, so the dueling pistol changes with each generation and concomitant improvement in pistol technology, from flintlock to percussion to revolver.

Dueling Sword - Again as with the dueling pistol, there is no standard look of the sword used for duels. Whatever is the civilian sword of the given period is the defacto dueling sword, although when the sword ceased to be worn (around 1800) it was obvious that those who purchased them were not doing so for self-defense nor to adorn their attire.

Enfield - The British military bolt-action rifle of the first half of the 20th century. From the city in Middlesex, England in which it, and all of the other firearms from the Royal Small Arms Factory, were manufactured.

Epee - is merely the French word for sword. In English, it's another word that has been saddled with more meanings than it can comfortably hold.

The epee proper is a sporting weapon based loosely on the European dueling smallsword of the early 19th century. The blade is triangular in cross section with a deep groove running down its center and a very blunted or even turned back tip. When the sport became popular enough to be an Olympic event, both the blade and simplified guard became standardized into their current forms. So just as with the word foil, epee can mean one of several things:

1) the entire weapon used in the Olympic sport of epee fencing

2) the large off-centered half-dome guard of the Olympic weapon

3) the blade used for the Olympic weapon, regardless of the guard

4) *[incorrectly]* any blunted light dueling or sport weapon

5) *[even more incorrectly]* any single-hand sword with a thin blade

Estoc - A type of medieval longsword with a thin blade, meant for thrusting but not cutting. In England called the *tuck*.

Estoque - The killing sword of the matador. Uniquely, it has a straight edged one-inch wide blade that is purposely bent about eight inches from the tip. This bend helps drive the sword into the bull, rather than risk its skimming off the back.

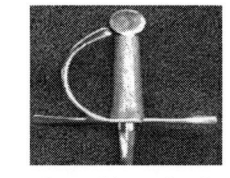

Eye Ax - A single-hand piercing axe of Bronze-aged Semitic peoples. Although introduced into Ancient Egypt, it never became an item of common use there. The name came from archeologists, and derives

from the two holes drilled into the back of the axe head, through which twine or leather could lash the bronze head onto the wooden shaft. The "eyes" are therefore only noticeable when the head is not connected to the shaft, as the first archeologists found them.

Falcata - A single-edged inward-curved short sword with a distinctive open knuckleguard. Found in the bronze aged cultures of the Mediterranean, especially Greece and Celtic Spain. The memory if not the shape of the falcata continued on to name the medieval falchion and the 19th century Argentine facón (dueling knife).

Falchion - A medieval single-edged heavy-bladed short sword. Used primarily by the untrained infantry as a chopping weapon, the blade is similar to the modern machete.

False Edge - on single edged sabre blades, the last few inches of the back edge have been filed down to a sharp edge, not with the idea of attempting a backhand cut but in order to reduce resistance in the event of a thrust. Part of, but not the same as, the back edge.

Flail - Although technically a flail is the agricultural tool which has a free swinging stick connected to another stick, for weapons it is anything that swings free at the end of a handle [chain, ball, leather strips, etc.].

Flick Knife - A nickname for the gravity knife. The name is appropriate, as the blades on these knives are not spring loaded, so a flick of the wrist is needed to pop-up the blade.

Flintlock - Firing system for longarms and pistols in which, as the hammer drops, a piece of flint is made to scrape against a steel plate sending a shower of sparks that in turn sets off the main powder charge. In common use from 1660 to 1850.

Foible - The weakest part of a sword blade; the third closest to the tip. Usually used in reference to the more "bendy" blades such as the foil or epee.

Foil - 1) in Shakespeare's time any blunted sword used for practice.

2) the specific sword used for the modern sport competition of foil fencing. The sword, reduced to its thrusting basics, is used for Olympic fencing, where cutting attacks are not counted and only thrusts to the torso are valid. Originally developed to increase mental quickness for epee dueling students.

3) the blade of the Olympic foil.

4) *incorrectly* - any stage sword, fight-worthy or not.

Forte - The strongest part of a sword blade; the third of the exposed blade closest to the handguard. The least flexible part and therefore the only part strong enough to use when blocking.

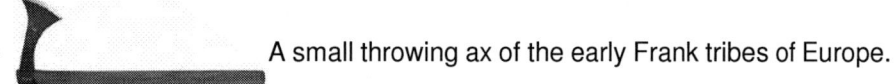

Francisca - A small throwing ax of the early Frank tribes of Europe.

Frog - An open leather pocket that can fit onto a belt or sash, into which can be secured a scabbard or a small axe. When pistols were finally small enough to be worn, scabbard frogs became the first holsters. The origin of the word is unknown, but dates back to the 18th century, and my guess is that it started as an English mispronunciation of a foreign, probably Dutch, term.

On stage, frogs are now often used by themselves as a substitute for the scabbard or sheath. In this way once the actor draws the sword, there is no worry about banging about or tripping over the dangling scabbard.

Fuller - On a sword or knife blade, the groove running through a portion or all of its length. Sometimes gruesomely called a blood groove, fullers are used to lighten the blade without loosing any of the strength. Indeed, often the blade is more rigid for having the groove cut into it than the plain flat steel would be.

Fusilier - A rifleman, a sharpshooter. Fusil is an archaic term for a blackpowder rifled musket.

Garand - The semi-automatic rifle invented by John C Garand that became the standard US military firearm during WWII and the Korean War. Also known by its military designation, the M-1.

Garrote - Originally a simple way of securing a load on a donkey's back, a couple of sticks connected with a string or wire are twisted, slowly tightening the string. Now used to describe any apparatus for strangulation using a thin wire, normally improvised from whatever is handy.

Gatling - A large machine gun of the late 1800's which used a series of semi-automatic firing barrels arranged on a cylinder and turned by a crank, automatically firing and reloading as long as the crank was turned.

Gauge - The measurement of the bore (barrel-width) of the shotgun. Instead of simply measuring the opening and stating the diameter, gauge is a convoluted way of describing that diameter without any benefit of clarity.

To determine the gauge of a shotgun barrel, a ball of lead of the same diameter as the internal measurement is cast, and then weighed. The number of these balls that it would take in order to weigh one pound is the gauge of that shotgun. So you can see that a 16 gauge shotgun has a smaller barrel opening that than of a 12 gauge, and a 20 gauge is smaller still. To restate: a larger gauge number is a smaller diameter.

If shotguns were measured by caliber rather than gauge, then a 12 gauge would be known as a 69 caliber gun.

Gewer - A German military designation of something built for military use.

Gladius - A short sword of the ancient Romans.

Glaive - A polearm with a simple but large single-edged cutting blade, sometimes augmented with a spike on the backedge. A sword blade on a pole.

Glock - An Austrian firearms manufacturer whose successful semi-automatic pistol has become the NATO and now US Armed Forces standard, as well as being the latest standard issue sidearm for most police departments. Distinctive because the exterior frame is made of a lightweight polymer plastic. Hollywood movies created a myth that Glocks are therefore invisible to X-rays, but actually the polymer is even more dense than steel and shows up quite clearly on airport scanners.

Gravity Knife - A hidden-bladed knife in which the blade resides inside the handle but is not spring loaded. A button holds the blade in place, and when pressed releases it, but the blade must then either be shaken out, flicked out, or pointed towards the ground and allowed to drop out into its fully exposed position. It is neither a switchblade nor a retractable knife. Also known as a flick knife.

Grenade - A small, usually fist-sized, bomb in which the primary destructive power comes not from the explosion but from the quantity of shrapnel produced by the fragmentation of its own casing. Grenades are either thrown or launched, sometimes from an adapted rifle, and have been around since the 1600's. A soldier who specializes in the use of this weapon was known as a grenadier.

Grip - The part of the sword onto which the hand actually makes contact. Formally, the grip should only refer to the leather or wire covering of the handle, so a wooden handled sword technically doesn't have a grip at all, only a handle. Most people use the terms interchangeably.

Guard - For edged weaponry, the part between the handle and the blade; the part that protects [guards] the hand.

Gun - A tube of metal from which a projectile is discharged by using expanding gases. Strict military use of the word is limited to cannon and other heavy fixed-mounted long-barreled weapons, whereas common usage refers to only pistols, shotguns and rifles.

Gunpowder - A dry chemical compound meant to burn extremely quickly, releasing rapidly expanding gases. The gaseous expansion is what propels a bullet to its target.

Gunpowder used in blanks will either be blackpowder or "smokeless". Blackpowder is ancient, used from the time of the very first cannons until just after the American Civil War, when it was largely supplanted by the modern "smokeless" powders. Those still produce smoke, but in much less quantity than does blackpowder, and the smoke that they do produce dissipates much faster, making it more difficult to locate the position of a shooter. Smokeless powders are much more explosive than blackpowder, however, so can only be used in guns in which the barrels are specifically designed for modern compounds.

Handcuffs - Developed in 1862, handcuffs differ from old style shackles in that, as they close, they adjust to fit almost any wrist size. Made of steel, they are also lighter and more easily portable than iron manacles.

Hackbutt - English term for the *arquebus*.

Halberd - A polearm whose head has all of the features of a spear, ax, and hook. In this fully developed form it is seen as early as the mid 1400's.

Hammer - One term, two very different weapon meanings.

In medieval and Renaissance warfare, it was literally a hammer used as a club, double-headed and heavy at first [think of Thor's hammer] but then gradually becoming lighter with each passing century. A hammer is useful in fighting against helmeted or armored opponents, for it won't pierce through the steel [which can cause an ax to get stuck in the armor], but the dent which it produces can act as a wedge, and that could be as deadly as any sword cut.

As crossbows became more numerous, the war hammer faded from the battlefield.

In firearms, the hammer is the part that swings around and actually strikes the firing pin, which in turn strikes against the cartridge or primer so as to ignite the gunpowder. Sometimes called the striker, the hammer is actually quite light. What really has the driving force is the strong mainspring that pushes it forward.

On flintlock guns, the part that holds the flint and then drives forward when the trigger is pulled should not really be called the hammer but rather the "flint jaws", but modern usage has nearly eliminated the term. Nowadays flintlock is used to describe the entire weapon, and that part on top is called the hammer by nearly everyone.

Hammerless - A term for some revolvers in which the hammer is not seen from the outside, but in truth a better term should be recessed hammer.

Handle - For edged weapons, the part with which one holds the sword. Sometimes called the grip, but grip is actually the name of any material wrapped around the handle.

The British, for some reason, when speaking only of swords use the term to describe the entire hilt, and many sword collectors on this side of the pond do the same. It makes for a great deal of confusion.

Hang-fire - A dangerous event in which the trigger is pulled on a firearm, the hammer strikes the cartridge, but there is a delay until the cartridge explodes. How to know whether the misfire was a dud or a hang-fire? How long do you wait until you find out? Many people have been injured and even killed by someone making the wrong choice.

Hanger - 1) any of the cheap curved sabres from the mid-1700 to the late 1800's, mass produced to quickly outfit the broad masses of infantry. Usually with a simple two dimensional knucklebow for hand protection.

2) an open-ended leather sword holder [see *frog*].

Hilt - Originally, the handle of a weapon, but now more correctly the entirety of the sword that is not the visible blade.

The British, for some reason, use the term to describe only the guard, and many sword collectors on this side of the pond do the same. It makes for a great deal of confusion.

Holster - The word corresponds to an ancient Dutch word for arrow quiver, but does not appear in English until the mid-1600's. The first holders for pistols were made to strap onto the saddle, as the pistols of the time were too large to be worn as one would a sword. It is not until the mid-1700's that the pistol becomes light enough so that holsters can be worn on a soldier's belt, yet not until the early 1800's do armies actually include it as part of a uniform and produce the first holsters to accommodate them.

Hunting Sword - Until the advent of reliable multishot firearms, hunters often carried a short, stout, simple sword as a weapon of last resort should the quarry become dangerous. Straight blades were preferred over curved.

Jackknife - A folding pocket knife meant as an all-purpose tool, as opposed to a penknife, for example, which has only one principle use. The term "Jack" originally meant a regular guy, an everyman, or a relatively poor man.

Kalashnikov - The last name of the designer of the rifle ultimately built as the standard Soviet issue submachine gun. Also can refer to the rifle itself, which is also known as the AK-47, and its close cousin, the AK-74.

Katana - In medieval Japan, one of the swords of the samurai class. The two-handed katana is perhaps the only sword ever designed that excelled as both a civilian and battlefield weapon. So well balanced is the three foot weapon that, even though it is a two handed sword, it is easier to use as a single hand sword than is the western single hand military sabre.

Kentucky Rifle - A misnomer for the Pennsylvania rifled musket of the 18th century. A hunting, not a military, firearm.

Knife - A short cutting blade, either single or double edged, set in a handle. The blade length may be any size, although once it gets to eighteen inches can start to look an awful lot like a sword. A knife is meant as a tool, not a weapon, as opposed to a dagger.

Kopesh - The unusual curved short hacking bronze sword of the ancient Egyptians. The shape provides a very strong cutting power of an ax with some of the slicing power of a curved sabre. When the English translation of the Bible speaks of the Egyptians using their "scimitars", this is the sword they mean, as the scimitar had not yet been developed when the Old Testament was written.

Kukri - The knife of the Gurkas of Nepal, a curved knife with the cutting edge on the inside rather than the outside of the curve. The shape is similar to the Ibero-Celtic falcata (falchion).

Kwaiken - In medieval Japan, the knife of a woman of samurai class. It had a short blade, only about 4 or 5 inches, either single or double edge but always straight, and meant as a self defense tool. If used for the ritual suicide known as sepuku, this knife would be used to open key veins, and the woman would pass out slowly to death.

Lochaber Axe - Any of the two-handed battle axes favored by Scottish warriors during the 17th and 18th centuries. The term is a catch-all for many sizes and shapes of war axe, so there is no single specific look for the Lochaber, although the majority will have most of the following features in common: a wooden pole of at least five feet and no more than eight feet in length, a broad, wide chopping surface of between eight inches to two feet in spread, and a spike or hook on the back edge. As such, many bardiches, halberds, bills, and glaives become rechristened "Lochaber" simply by having been used by a Scot.

Lance - a spear which is used only from horseback. Never thrown, the lance is used to impale opponents from a charge, and were generally over ten feet long.

Lever-Action - working action for certain rifles in which a pivoting lever underneath the rifle ejects the spent round and loads in the subsequent round into the firing chamber.

Lock - For firearms, the mechanism which sets-off the ammunition on a single-fire muzzle loaded gun. Some of the more common types of locks are the *matchlock, wheellock, doglock, flintlock,* and *percussion lock.* The lock (with its attached mechanical components) was one of the three main sections of a firearm, the other two being the wooden *stock* and the iron *barrel* [from which we get the phrase "lock, stock and barrel"].

Longarm - A firearm which must be held and operated with both hands, and generally longer than three feet.

Longbow - More correctly known as the Welsh bow, it is a single piece of wood, usually yew, about six feet tall, firing an arrow of nearly one yard in length. When fired by a trained soldier, it had an effective range of nearly a quarter of a mile.

Longsword - A broadsword. In *Romeo & Juliet*, Capulet calls for his longsword in the opening battle, and tradition usually has the two fathers flourishing very long two-handed swords, but the sword he is requesting is actually a single-hand weapon with a three-foot long and fairly wide blade. He's asking for his sword of war, used normally while mounted, as opposed to a rapier.

Lugar - German arms designer Georg Lugar developed the model P-08 semiautomatic pistol of WWII fame (although it was widely used in the first World War as well). The gun stayed in production from 1908 until 1943.

M - Using M and then a number is a common way for military arms manufacturers around the world to designate different models of weapons. Whether rifle, pistol, grenade, or tank, the "M" merely stands for "model number". The numbers that follow sometimes refer to the year that the item was developed, but at other times are completely arbitrary.

M-1 - The US Army designation for the semiautomatic rifle used during WWII and the Korean War. Also known as the Garand, for its designer, it was intended to be only a transitional stopgap piece as the arsenal moved from the bolt action rifle of WWI and on to a light machine gun. The M-1, however, proved to be a very successful design, being easy to operate, nearly indestructible, and cheap to mass produce. The rifle's formal name is the Springfield M-1, and there are over a dozen official variations on the basic layout, not counting the M-1 carbine, which has the same stock and firing system but uses pistol ammunition.

To make things a little more confusing, M-1 was also the Army designation for the Tommy Gun.

M-4 - The latest incarnation of the M-16, although mechanically the same, has so many integral additions (including nightvision scope, IT compatibility, and grenade launcher) that it deserved its own designation.

M-9 - When the US Army decided to have the Italian Beretta 92 become their standard issue pistol, they changed the designated model number to something that to them sounded more military.

M-16 - The American military standard issue infantry weapon from the Vietnam War until the Second Iraq War, and the first made with an all aluminum frame. It is a fully automatic rifle which has been in use, with modifications, since 1966. Many US allies have purchased M-16's for their own armed forces, although the gun is still plagued by some very serious reliability and jamming problems. Since 1982, the fully automatic feature was removed in favor of automatically firing in three-shot bursts, so cannot truly be called an assault rifle. The Colt AR-15 is the civilian version of the same gun.

Mac-10 - Also known as the Inghram, it is one of the smallest high-capacity assault pistols, first developed in 1970. Note that the bullet clip in the handgrip is very long, increasing its capacity to 30 rounds compared to a regular semi-automatic pistol.

Mace - A club with a metal head and metal shaft. (A weapon with a metal head and a wooden shaft is more accurately termed a composite club.) The head can be a solid or hollow sphere, or an array of flanges set in a circle. The wider use of maces in the 14th century came about as a direct reaction to larger number of warriors wearing plate armour. The impact from the rounded head could stave in the armour, causing more damage that one could with sword or axe. (Medieval clerics sometimes preferred the mace when fighting, for as a weapon which breaks bones but doesn't necessarily draw blood, it was justified as being more in tune with Christian ideals.)

Machete - A long bladed cleaver; a single-edged short sword of the West Indies first used as an agricultural tool to clear heavy brush and cultivate crops in the mid-1500's. Still used to cut vegetation, the machete is the last remaining sword that humans still use with which to kill each other.

Machine Gun - A mounted gun capable of automatic loading and continuous fire. Technically, a true machine gun is too large to be held while firing. The single-soldier models are known as submachine guns.

Magazine - In multi-shot breach-loaders that are not revolvers, the magazine is the springloaded container where the bullets are housed until introduced mechanically into the firing chamber. There are three types of magazines. Clips house the bullets stacked side-by-side directly underneath the chamber, tubes house the bullets end-to-end underneath the barrel, and drums can hold 50 or even 100 rounds side-by-side but in a spiral.

The word is derived from the Arabic "makhazin", meaning an ammunition storehouse.

Magnum - From the Latin meaning "great" and secondarily "large", this is an ammunition designation that plays a bit with the normal caliber numbering system. A 357 magnum or 44 magnum will have a slightly smaller diameter than a comparable 38 or 45, but carries far more gunpowder in a longer cartridge. More powder propelling a slightly smaller bullet can increase the muzzle velocity by over 50%, therefore more force can be transmitted for impact. It does not in any way have anything to do with the look or the size of the gun itself. 357 and 44 magnum ammunition was developed first, and used in standard 38 and 45 caliber guns. It was only later that some gun models were specifically built in the magnum calibers.

Main Gauche - From the French meaning "left hand", it is a dagger with a stout and long blade [from 12 to 20 inches in length], used only as a companion weapon when fighting with the rapier, not as a stand-alone dagger. There is nothing intrinsically left handed about the dagger besides the fact that the right hand of the fighter would be holding a rapier.

Mameluke - Hilt style distinctive of the sabres of the Mamluk cavalry of Egypt. These thin bladed curved swords featured a short cross-hilt, no knucklebow, and an off-centered swelling of the handle instead of a pommel. The style has become popular as a presentation sword among modern Western military forces, for example the US Marine Corps.

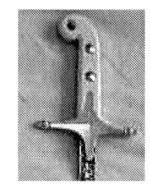

Manacles - Any metal (usually iron) non-adjustable restraint that secures the wrists. A type of shackle.

Matchlock - The type of firing mechanism used in early muskets. When the trigger latch was pulled, a slow burning fuse [*match*] would drop forward onto the touchhole and ignite the gunpowder. The lit fuse was a long rope-like coil, several feet in length, simply carried over the soldier's shoulder, the lit end clamped onto the hammer of the musket.

Mauser - A German firearms manufacturer most famous for its bolt-action rifle and semi-automatic pistol of WWI.

Morning Star - Another name for a spiked-headed mace. A translation of the German "morgenstern".

Mortuary Sword - This was a nineteenth century term describing a seventeenth century English basket hilt sword. These swords often had generic chiseled profiles of a man's head on the hilts, and to the Victorians resembled the martyred King Charles I. In truth, these swords were used by both sides of the English civil war.

Musket - The name for the infantry blackpowder longarm, whether matchlock, flintlock or percussion. In the 16th century, different sized firearms were named for different birds of prey, musket being a corruption of the French word for a breed of sparrowhawk. It quickly became the generic name for any longarm.

Muzzle - The end of a gun barrel from which the bullet exits. The "business end" of the gun. Until the

1870's the only practical and reliable firearms were muzzleloaders, meaning the gunpowder and ball were emptied into the barrel from the muzzle and then pushed down to the firing position at the breach end.

Navaja - A swing-out folding knife of the Andalusian region of Spain, featuring a slightly curved blade, and producing a distinctive ratcheting sound when opened. The knife can be partially flick-opened with one hand, but only after the first part of the swing-out is started with the other hand.

Night-Stick - Up until the 1910's, city police did not wear guns but did use the thin two-foot club known as a truncheon or nightstick. By the late 20th century, the nightstick added a sidebar, which converted it from a simple club to a versatile immobilization tool as well as a more powerful striking device. It got its name from the simple fact that it was first used by nightwatchmen patrolling private property after dark during the 19th century.

Over and Under - Of double barreled shotguns and rifles, those in which the barrels are stacked one above the other, rather than side-by-side.

Pappenheimer - A distinctive rapier guard style featuring two perforated round plates. There is no reason to suppose that these swords were any more popular than any other rapier style, and the tiny perforations did nothing to lighten the hilt.

Partisan - Poleweapon used by irregular units during the Renaissance. The styles varied enormously, but most have several blade points projecting symmetrically from the head.

Patch Cutter - Not a fighting weapon, but a small broad bladed knife with a curved integrated rod as a handle carried by percussion riflemen. Used to cut off the excess paper or cloth wad around the musket ball just as it's being loaded into the barrel.

Pavis - A giant shield, generally rectangular and usually from four to six feet in height, meant to protect medieval infantrymen from the shower of crossbow arrows. Many had small hinged poles connected to the back so they could be free standing when in use on the battlefield.

Pen Knife - A small folding knife with a narrow blade. The name comes from its primary function - periodically giving a fresh cut to a quill pen.

Pennsylvania Rifle - Developed by the German and Dutch immigrants to the American colonies, by 1740 was a rifled-barreled blackpowder longarm of exceptional accuracy (the distinctive angled butt appearing in the muskets after 1790).

Pepperbox - The nickname for the multibarrel percussion pistols in which a very heavy cylinder sported many complete barrel openings, each with its own percussion nipple. Technically not really a revolver, for the entire barrel assembly would have to be rotated by hand for each shot. Made by several manufacturers during the 1830's, none had good hammer action and the thick multibarrel cylinder made the entire gun very heavy and cumbersome. Pepperboxes were replaced almost overnight by the lighter revolving multi-chamber single-barrel system pistols, the true revolvers, of the late 1840's.

Percussion Lock - Firing system for longarms and pistols in which a percussion cap is struck by the hammer, sending sparks that in turn sets off the main powder charge. In common use from 1820 to 1880.

Pike - A long shaft with a pointed end, the primary weapon of the infantry until the development of the bayonet. Pikes are a form of spear, but are not used for throwing and only rarely for thrusting. Pikes range in size from eight to twenty feet in length, and were used to form a bristle hedge to hold back an attack or to advance and take ground on the battlefield.

Since the bulk of most armies were composed of minimally trained, part-time warriors, pikes were a cheap weapon to produce and simple to train a soldier in the basic uses.

As opposed to the more manageable spear or halberd, the pike has no use as an individual weapon, but when tightly massed in a formed infantry line or square, it is the best defense against a charge of cavalry, and an excellent tool for allowing a group of soldiers to take and control territory.

Pillow Sword - During the 18th century, several smallsword hilt styles were relatively flat and two dimensional, eliminating the dish or cup hand protection found in most other civilian swords. In the 19th century, these pieces collectively picked up the name pillow swords. The story goes that these were weapons that were laid by the bedside allowing a gentleman to have instant availability to a sword for self defense. I have a couple of problems with that etymology. First, it is always suspect when a term pops up a century after the weapon is in use, and the term is used primarily by collectors. Secondly, these swords make very poor self-defense weapons. The very thin blades and absent hand protection indicates an item of dress rather than use, a vanity piece rather than a dueling sword.

Pilum - The special spear of the Roman soldier with a short wooden shaft and then a long thin neck of iron topped with the spear head. This was a thrown spear, rather than a close-in thrusting spear.

One of the problems in using throwing spears is that the enemy can throw them back at you. The Roman pilum eliminated this drawback. If the pilum hit and stuck onto an enemy shield, the long neck would prevent the enemy from simply hacking off the shaft, thus leaving the shield too heavy and cumbersome for use. If the spear was deflected or missed entirely and struck the ground, the long neck would bend, making it useless for the enemy to throw back. After the battle, the Romans could recover the spears and hammer them straight again for future use.

Pinfire - An unusual type of cartridge ammunition of the late 1800's. Each cartridge had a small pin sticking out near the primer. The hammer would drive the pin into the primer, igniting the cartridge. Also, a gun designed in this way. The guns themselves were reliable enough, but the cartridges had to be handled with great care so as not to distort the pin, and the failure rate was high.

Pistol - Any firearm small enough to be held and fired with one hand. All revolvers are also pistols.

Polearm - A cutting or clubbing weapon with a metal head and a shaft of three feet or longer. Usually does not refer to a spear or pike. The "pole" part of the word is not a reference to the shaft, but is an Old English word meaning "head". Polearms fade from the battlefield at the beginning of the eighteenth century.

Plug Bayonet - A seventeenth century double-edged dagger with a cross hilt and a smooth tapered handle. Jamming the handle into the barrel of the Spanish musket would quickly convert the firearm to a practical pike, thus providing a temporary but effective defensive weapon against a cavalry charge. Plug bayonets lasted only a few decades until supplanted by the invention of the socket bayonet, which cleared the barrel and allowed the musket to fire.

Pommel - The "top end" of the sword, the counterweight at the end of the hilt. Some swords do without any pommel at all, and on some of the larger broadswords it may reach a weight of nearly a pound and a half. The term is French, meaning "little apple".

Poniard - A dagger with a very thin stabbing blade and almost no cutting edge. A forerunner to the stiletto, the poniard was not only popular as a trim self defense weapon, but also found good use on the medieval battlefield. For a final killing move, the poniard blade can thrust in between the scales of armor and even force open the links in chain mail.

Although poniard bladed daggers were not used historically for rapier and dagger fights, nowadays they are very commonly used on stage. When the theatrical sword is epee-bladed, a regular thick dagger blade can cut right through the sword, so the poniard offers a much better match.

Primer - From the Spanish meaning "first", the initial combustible material which sets off the powder charge in a cartridge. Primers do not cause an explosion, but only a brief spark.

Pugio - From the Latin root word for fist, the pugio was a short broad-bladed dagger meant for close-in killing thrusts.

Pump-Action - For rifles and shotguns, the working mechanism which ejects the spent round and loads in the next with each pull and push of an underhanging in-line sliding lever.

Punch Dagger - A short straight bladed knife with a handle constructed in such a way so that the blade is in line with a punching closed fist. Punch dagger handles are always set perpendicular to the blade. Western punch daggers usually have a single shaft connecting the blade to the center of the handle, the shaft protruding between the fingers of the closed fist. Those of India (called katars) connect the blade to both ends of the handle, traveling around the fist. Either way, the benefit is that a stab can be delivered without having to bend the wrist as one would need to on a regular knife. The driving force created by punching allows the blade to pierce through even chain mail and armor.

Quarrel - another name for the crossbow bolt (arrow).

Quarterstaff - A long, straight stick of wood, usually five to eight feet in length. A weapon of the lower class. At various times and countries, steel weaponry was outlawed for all but the nobility, so fighting styles developed from simple farm implements and even a common walking stick.

Why it is called the quarterstaff is not known. Some say it is because the staff is held "at the quarters", but that's not really true since most of the time it is actually held at the thirds. Another theory is that it refers to a quartered length of the ash tree, but this would lead to too much variation in length. My own belief is that it refers not to the length but to the best *width* of the staff, about a quarter of a palm's breath (for most people about one inch). This optimum width is mentioned throughout the world and throughout time wherever the staff is used as a fighting weapon.

Quillon - The name for either arm of the hilt of the sword that forms a vaguely cross-shaped guard. Also refers to any dagger that has a guard similar to that of a broadsword.

Quiver - The case that holds the arrows, and sometimes also the bow, for an archer.

Because of the various Robin Hood movies, the popular conception is that in Europe the quiver was slung over the shoulder and the arrows were drawn one by one by the right hand from behind the back, American Plains Indian style. But that is a Victorian era conceit, designed for sport archery. In medieval battles, the quiver was worn at the waist, and once an archer was in position the arrows were removed all at once in a bunch and stuck into the ground, allowing for much faster loading and firing.

Rabbit Pistol - As far as I can find, this term is only used in Tom Stoppard's *Arcadia*, and would seem to refer to a small caliber single-shot percussion pistol, which would be the most appropriate for shooting at small game such as rabbit. As such, the pistol would hardly be a valued piece, but a mere working tool used as an inefficient pest control device. These days we would call such a gun a "plinker".

Rapier - This word is a tough one to define because it has gone through so many countries and traditions. This means that the script may call for a rapier, the director wants a rapier, the props master provides a rapier, and all three are talking about different weapons and all three are somewhat correct.

Sometime around the mid-1500's, a sword was developed in Spain that, compared to the broadsword, was light enough to actually be worn around town for extended lengths of time. This was done by simply making the blade much narrower, only about an inch wide. There were thin-bladed battlefield swords already (the "estoc", or tuck), but this new sword was purely a single-hand weapon, designed to fight against an unarmored opponent. It could rest on the hip comfortably at an angle so as to allow easy movement while walking or sitting and engaged in daily activities. The Spanish referred to this sword as the "espada ropera", literally "dress sword", as opposed to the regular "espada" or sword for war, the broadsword. The term "ropera" went through France untranslated but given a linguistic twist as "ropierre", and then in England corrupted again into "rapier", pronounced *ray-peer'*. I include all of this because so many Americans try to give this word a French pronunciation [*rah-pee-ay'*, or some such] where one is not called for.

Something interesting about the rapier became evident almost immediately to the Spanish. The sword is light enough to simply hold for quite a while, pointed with an outstretched arm at someone's face to hold them off. If your opponent is holding a heavy broadsword, he is going to have to lift up his arm even higher in order to get momentum to deliver a cutting blow. All you have to do is step forward in that instant and you have run your partner through. All of a sudden, massive arm strength is no longer needed to win in a sword fight, which previously was a fearsome bashing contest. With only the right hand needed to wield the rapier, the left hand is free to punch or grab the opponent, or to use another weapon as a defensive tool. Anything could be used - a cloak, a club, a chain - but the most popular was a long-bladed dagger known by the French term "main gauche" (*men-goesh*) - literally "left hand". Rapier and dagger fights became the way in which most disputes of honor or drunkenness were settled.

The rapier in history only lasted a brief 140 years, when it was replaced by the smallsword of the late 1600's. Initially sporting simple cross hilts, the height of its development was circa 1620, when the full cup and swept hilts to protect the hand reached their largest dimensions. The popular image of the rapier is the sword used in the Three Musketeers or Cyrano de Bergerac, with the full hand protection exemplified by the Spanish guards of the period. Many people believe that only this type of hilt is a rapier, when actually rapiers came in a huge variety of styles, lengths, and hilt sizes.

The rapier was not a weapon of war. The use of a dueling weapon requires that you know who and where your opponent is, and that there won't be another 12,000 people nearby all trying to kill you. In addition, a blade thin enough to be light is also thin enough to snap in half when hit by a heavy sword, and it certainly can do nothing against someone wearing even the most basic armor. The rapier was purely a civilian weapon, never used in battle. Unfortunately, in later years, after the extinction of the weapon itself, the term remained and was used incorrectly to describe any dueling and then any sporting weapon. Some people still use the term this way, thinking they are talking about the swords used in modern Olympic competition and sport fencing.

Also, there are all of those theatre people who used the term to describe the only swords they have ever seen - those found in theatres. Many directors will ask for rapiers, when what they really want could be broadswords with blunted tips.

Finally, one last use of the word: describing the blade but not the hilt. As I mentioned, the actual rapier blade was about an inch wide and up to four feet long - simply too heavy for most actors to wield safely. For that reason many fights are performed using a German blade called the schlaeger (*shlay'-gger* or *shlah'-gger*), a bashing blade as was the true rapier, but only 1/4 of an inch wide and 35 inches long, therefore much more manageable. But the schlaeger is not used as often as the even lighter epee, which also gets named rapier by many.

There we have seven different uses for one term. So, when someone asks for a rapier, what does he want? ...

- the civilian European sword of between 1520 and 1660 ?
- the Spanish Cup Hilt (but not the blade) of the early 1600's ?
- any light dueling sword ?
- any sport fencing sword ?
- any blunted sword ?
- the 1" thick blade for stage combat or costume purposes ?
- the 1/4" thick blade for stage combat purposes ?

Be safe - ask the follow-up questions.

For now, let's go back to the historic rapier that Shakespeare wrote about. The rapier with which he was familiar had a handguard a little bit more ornate than that of a light broadsword, but still flat. The blade was approximately three feet long and an inch wide. I say approximately because there was little standardization in armaments of war in this period, and none whatsoever for civilian weapons. Blade lengths of 28" were rare, and three feet seemed to be most common, but many rapier blades were four feet in length and some even approached five feet. These monsters would literally drag behind the wearer and were considered inherently unfair, so much so that at one point the guard of London Bridge would stop entry of anyone entering the city with a sword of extended proportion. (The prospective entrant had a choice - leave the city, surrender the sword, or have the guard remove it from the scabbard, break it over his knee, and have it returned at a new, reduced length.)

Remington - An American firearms manufacturer of a long and varied line of shotguns, rifles, pistols and ammunition.

Revolver - A pistol which has a multi-shot revolving chamber, so that it can be fired in rapid succession before reloading.

Ricasso - On certain swords, a portion of the guard extends beyond the quillon, allowing the first finger to hook over the quillon for a better grip while protected by the extra guard. The section of blade between the guard and the quillon is called the ricasso, and is sometimes a little thinner than the blade proper and is always left unsharpened.

Rifle - A longarm with a rifled barrel [as opposed to a smoothbore], firing a bullet [not a ball]. The interior of a rifle barrel has grooves cut into the surface in a gentle spiral, which makes the bullet spin when fired for greater accuracy and distance. Rifling of barrels had been attempted since the early 1700's, and made for excellent hunting weapons, but because of the difficulty in loading, they were not practical for wartime use until the mid-19th century and the development of the Minie bullet.

Rimfire - Type of cartridge ammunition in which the firing pin of the gun must strike the edge of the primer so that ignition can occur. Also, a gun designed in this way.

Rimless - Said of ammunition in which the base of the cartridge is the same diameter as the case. Most ammunition has a base wider than the case, which keeps the cartridge from sliding too deeply into the chamber. Semi-automatic ammunition cannot have an exposed rim that would interfere with the loading mechanism, so rimless ammunition was designed for that use.

Rondel - A dagger with a handguard made of a simple metal disk.

Round - The individual fireable unit used in a firearm. Sometimes used synonymously with the terms bullet or cartridge.

Runka - A polearm with a symmetrical head composed of a central flat blade and two smaller blades on either side coming out at about 45 degrees. Probably first inspired by the trident or pitchfork, it is also known as the septum and corseca.

Sabre - Here is another word that has a couple of possible meanings.

Coming from the Arabic "say-fyr", the sabre was originally the single handed curved blade of the Middle East. Although Europeans were certainly familiar with the weapon, it wasn't until the early 1700's that high quality steel construction had improved in the West to allow for its mass production there.

The sabre was always a purely military weapon, and equally devastating when used from horseback or by an infantry soldier. Unlike the straight bladed broadsword, the sabre can inflict deep cuts even from off-placed blows, therefore requiring less training, and since the blade has only one striking edge, can be made much lighter than a broadsword of the same length.

With time, European armies experimented with the severity of the blade curvature, and in many cases sabres were constructed again with straight blades. The curved blades are perfect for cutting at the enemy, but straight blades were specifically designed for cavalry use to run-down and impale foot soldiers.

In the Olympic sport of sabre fencing, the blade is as narrow as a foil and has no cutting capability whatsoever. Thin, straight and whippy, the blade serves as a scoring device in a sport where both the tip and the edge can be used to strike at an opponent.

Saex (also Sax) - The single edged all-purpose dagger of several Germanic tribes of the Dark Ages, especially the Saxons of northern continental Europe and England. The blade length varied from 10 to 24 inches, with a distinctive off-centered tip that looks for all the world that the blade is broken.

Sam Brown - You'd think that something named for its designer [British Army officer General Sir Samuel J. Browne] would have just one meaning. Unfortunately, it has two.

1] A military belt combined with a sash, usually on the right shoulder, worn by officers and meant to better support the weight of a sword or pistol. [It is always fascinating to see police uniforms in which the sash attached to the belt at the hip *opposite* of where the gun is worn, thereby rendering the sash useless except as an interesting design choice.]

2] In the USA, it can also refer to the modern police belt (no sash) that holds nearly all of the apparatus [gun, cuffs, flashlight, nightstick, radio, etc.] that the modern cop requires.

Samurai - Specifically the fighting retainers of Japanese feudal lords, and, more generally, the warrior class of medieval Japan. It is sometimes used to refer to the swords used by the same. Although the sword [katana] was the most prized weapon of the samurai, he was expected to be proficient in combat with every battlefield weapon.

Sap - A blackjack. The etymology of the word is unknown, although some have posited that it is short for "sapling". [I rather doubt that, and am more inclined to believe that it came from another meaning of sap, which is to weaken or destroy by stealth.]

Sawed-Off - An aftermarket modification of a rifle or, especially, a shotgun in which the barrel is shortened to about one foot in length. Often the butt of the gun is shortened as well to pistol-grip size.

Scabbard - The protective carrying holder for a sword or knife that completely covers the blade. Distinguished from a sheath in that the scabbard is made of hard material such as wood or brass and therefore retains its shape even when empty.

Scattergun - Slang term for a shotgun.

Schiavonna - The Italian version of the basket hilt sword, and likely the first of the genre, pre-dating the Scottish variety by a couple of centuries. The word is a Florentine term for the Slavic people who drifted into Italy in the 15th century.

Schlaeger - Derived from the German word for blade, it is in fact a type of dueling sword blade.

Schmeisser - This is actually an inaccurate name for a series of submachine guns used by German paratroopers during WWII. The specific model numbers include the MP-38, MP-39, MP-40, and the MP-41. Captured weapons were preferred by American G.I.'s over US submachine guns due to their higher quality. The Schmeisser company produced only limited numbers of these submachine guns, but the name became the common nickname for the entire genre.

Scimitar - A single edged curved sword of Persia. A Western mispronunciation of the word *shamshir,* the scimitar was designed as a purely cutting, not thrusting weapon. To ease drawing the sword while at full gallop on horseback, the blade was often more curved than that of a standard sabre. The true scimitar has a blade of equal width throughout its length.

The thick wide blade with the even wider peaked backedge is a Western fantasy.

Scramasax - A single edge, short, straight sword/dagger of the Anglo-Saxons and Vikings. Usually of less than two feet in length and having no handguard. Similar in design to the Saex dagger.

Semi-Auto - A firing system for guns in which one shot is fired for each pull of the trigger without having to reload the gun. So why isn't a revolver called semi-auto? Well it really should be, but the term has stuck for those pistols and rifles in which the bullets are automatically fed from a magazine. Not to be confused with automatic firearms.

Septum - Another name for the Runka. A polearm.

Service pistol (or revolver) - Any handgun issued to military or law-enforcement personnel. Therefore there is no single look for a service pistol. It is whatever gun a particular agency issued in a particular year.

Shackles - Any metal fastening that secures or restrains any part of the body, usually the ankles or wrists.

Sheath - A close-fitting covering for a blade. Distinct from a scabbard in that a sheath is made of soft material and is relatively flexible.

Shell - 1. For certain rapiers, a type of cup guard.

2. A hollow tube to be filled or is already filled with explosive powder and some type of projectile. A hand grenade is a kind of shell, and any ammunition fired from a modern pistol, rifle, shotgun [all the way

up to those giant naval battleship guns] is a shell.

For modern ammunition, the shell is composed of four parts: bullet or shot, cartridge or casing, the explosive powder, and the igniting primer.

3. Incorrectly, the term is sometimes used for the ejected brass casing or cartridge found on the ground after a semi-automatic gun is fired.

Shield - A large solid piece of stiff material used to defend the warrior against impact weapons. Although most people have the idea that shields should be made of steel (the better to clank with!), metal shields were pretty rare and used mainly by knights in tournament fighting against swords or lances only. Early shields were made of hardened leather stretched over a light wood frame, and later shields were of wood. Arrows fly right through thin steel shields, but get stuck in wood shields of even less than a half inch thick. A shield hangs on the arm, exceptions being the smaller *buckler* and the much larger *pavis*.

Shillelagh - The simple and ancient club of Ireland, cut from the twisted limb of a blackthorn tree, most are just under two feet long. The best have a knot on the end for a heavier striking surface.

Shortsword - Of course a sword with a short blade, but now used to describe specifically the ancient swords of the Bronze and Iron Ages, with blades of two feet in length or less. Can also refer to the many two edged swords of medieval Europe that were built for relatively untrained infantry, crossbowmen and archers. Not to be confused with the smallsword.

Shot - most common usage is for the small lead pellets, fired from a shotgun, although through history could refer to any kind of projectile.

Shotgun - A longarm with smoothbore barrel in which shot is fired instead of a single bullet. Because the shot spreads as it leaves the barrel, shotguns are used for hunting small game, especially birds in flight, or against humans when there may be multiple attackers or whenever a maximum amount of damage is required in one shot and the target is relatively close.

The term "shotgun" actually precedes the invention of the gun itself. From 1775 it was used to describe any musket loaded with shot. By about 1850 some muskets were fitted with barrels better able to accommodate shot, and these should probably be considered to be the first true shotguns, although they were still muzzleloaders and could not break open.

Shotguns can be of four styles depending on how they load: ancient muzzleloaders (from 1775), break-open (starting in 1875), pump-action (1893), and semi-auto (1948).

Side-By-Side - A double-barreled shotgun in which the two barrels are set next to each other; as opposed to an over-and-under. Someone firing a side-by-side needs to slightly adjust their sighting from right to left between the two shots.

Side Sword - A very modern term, used to describe rapier hilts with wide blades, often used in combat rather than civilian duels. The term was used rarely in the 16th century, and only in Italy, but reenactors have enjoyed creating an invented fighting style to go with their invented term.

Sidearm - A military weapon worn on the side at waist level, such as a sword, bayonet or pistol.

Silencer - An apparatus, usually screwed onto the barrel of a gun, that can muffle part of the sound of gunshot. Silencers only work on real guns, where all of the blast is directed down the barrel; they cannot muffle any of the sound of a blank-fire gun.

Single Action - Describes the working of the hammer for a pistol. On single action guns, the hammer must be pulled back manually with the thumb before the trigger is squeezed. As opposed to double action.

Although single action takes longer than double action to fire, it does provide a benefit to the shooter. Once the hammer is pulled back, it takes very little muscular effort to depress the trigger, so the aim of the shooter tends to be more steady.

Skean Dhu (various spellings) - A very small knife tucked into the stocking of the Scottish Highlander. Usually no more than a three inch blade and five inches overall.

Sling - An open piece of leather connected to two strings. A rock is placed in the leather and the string ends are held in one hand. Using it is fairly simple: swing the sling overhead several times to build up speed and then let go of one of the strings, and the rock will travel a good distance with a lot of force. Although widely used in Biblical times, it had limited acceptance in most European battles even in the pre-medieval period. Occasionally seen now in street riots against police and lightly armored soldiers in the Middle East.

Small arm - A firearm that can be held and operated in one hand. A pistol.

This is another term that has changed with time. Originally meaning strictly the pistol, military usage by the twentieth century considered both pistols and rifles to be small arms, for they could be fired while held, as opposed to from a tripod. NATO currently defines small arm as a weapon firing nonexplosive rounds that can be carried by one or two persons or can be mounted on a "light" vehicle. Small arms apparently get larger with time.

Smallsword - Name for the civilian sword of the 18th century. Smallswords were the direct descendants of the rapiers, but the emphasis is exclusively on thrusting rather than cutting, and use of the blade itself for parrying rather than relying on a second weapon in the left hand for defense. The smallsword blade was lighter and shorter than the rapier, and the hand protection was greatly reduced. Overall, the weapon was not superior to the rapier, but was designed as an upper-class accoutrement and dueling sword, rather than a practical self-defense weapon. Not to be confused with a courtsword or a shortsword.

Smith & Wesson - An American firearms manufacturer of mostly revolvers. So varied has the output of this company been that there is no single look that is definitively "S & W". [For some reason, playwrights so love the sound of having actors say "Smith & Wesson 38" that it is uttered in dozens of twentieth century plays, but the phrase is as descriptive as saying "rubber-tired Toyota".]

Smoothbore - Said of gun barrels in which the interior is smooth, without grooves, or in other words not rifled. Most guns were smoothbores before the mid 1850's.

Snaphaunce - An early flintlock firing system in which the flint strike plate and the flash pan cover are two separate pieces.

Snub Nose - Any revolver with a barrel length of less than three inches. For some reason, the term is not used for single shot nor semi-automatics. Snub-nosed revolvers are used for very short distance firing, personal protection, or when concealing the weapon is necessary.

Society Sword - Similar to court swords, society swords are light presentation swords with decorated hilts and weak costume blades given to members or officers of such fraternal organizations such as the Knights of Columbus, the Masons, or the Ku Klux Klan. They may take many forms, but most are variations on smallsword hilt styles.

Solingen -   A city in Germany that was a center of extremely high quality military sabre blades during the 18th and 19th centuries. Several manufactures in Solingen still produce superb sport-fighting blades to this day, especially the schlaeger. Blade forging for fighting swords has continued uninterrupted in the area since before the Norman conquest.

Spanish Musket - The gun of the soldiers (Musketeers) of the 17th century. Difficult to load and dangerous to operate, it was heavy and inaccurate. But the matchlock firing mechanism it used made it more reliable than the crossbow in damp weather, so it quickly became the standard light infantry arm for all European armies. The nickname "Spanish" had to do with its purported country of invention, although there is no substantiation for that claim.

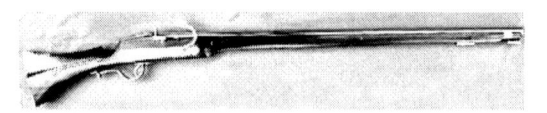

Spear -   A sharpened stick at least 2/3 the length of the person holding it. Most spears have a stone or metal tip, often much wider than the pole to which it is attached. The shape of the weapon is determined by its primary use; either thrust, thrown, or defensive placement.

Spears can be as short as the four foot thrusting weapon of the later Zulus, or up to 20 feet tall as in the case of some European infantry defensive placement weapons, although spears that are more than ten feet tall are more correctly termed pikes.

Spadroon -   Late 18th and early 19th century term for certain swords worn by military officers. Spadroons were in every way modeled after the smallswords of the civilian upper class, and showing the same wide variation in hilt styles, but where fitted with slightly heavier and wider blades. They were always single edged, so as to at least give the appearance of being a useful weapon for war.

Springfield -   Every country has a central armory where the bulk of its military weapons are produced, and in the USA it is the Springfield Arsenal in Massachusetts. Going back for over 220 years, nearly every rifle used in American warfare has technically been a Springfield rifle, but the Model 1903 bolt-action has been most strongly associated with the name.

Spontoon -   A short partisan, usually carried by infantry officers in the 1700's.

Squib - A low intensity explosive with electronic detonation; used for pyrotechnic special effects. Most commonly used in film to produce the effect of gunshots striking a wall or human. The explosive is preset on the set or underneath the costume of the actor and wired for detonation. It is then ignited on cue, most often remotely, by completing an electrical charge through the explosive compound.

Staff -   Varied meanings. It can be a walking stick, a shaft for a spear or polearm, or a long stick used as a weapon. See Quarterstaff.

Starter Pistol -   A pistol which was originally constructed to accept only blanks, used to start foot races. All modern starter pistols are block-barreled and cannot operate if loaded with real ammunition.

Stave - Another term for *staff*.

Sten -   A "cheap and dirty" submachine gun manufactured by **S**heppard and **T**urpin for **EN**gland during WWII. Easy to mass-produce, it was distributed to British soldiers and air-dropped to resistance fighters around the world.

Stiletto -   A very thin bladed Italian dagger of the 16th to 18th centuries. It has the reputation of being an assassin's weapon, although the extremely thin blade makes it a very poor single-thrust killing tool. With a very small puncture, even if made very deep, the victim dies rather slowly.

In the twentieth century, the term has also been used, incorrectly, for thin bladed folding knifes and for switchblade knives with blade lengths of five to eight inches.

Stock - The wood on a longarm. Most rifles and muskets have stocks made of one piece of wood running the length of the gun, although many rifles and almost all shotguns have a break in the center of the wood where the firing mechanism resides. In such guns, the wood under the barrel is referred to as the foregrip or forestock, and the part which goes against the shoulder is called the butt stock or simply the butt. In modern guns, the stock is now often made of plastic, but the term remains the same.

Striker - In firearms, the part that drives the firing pin. Sometimes used to refer to the hammer, but hammers pivot in an arc, whereas strikers move in a linear path.

Submachine Gun - An automatic rifle that can be carried and operated by one person. Usually made to fire pistol or light rifle ammunition instead of heavier rifle or machine gun rounds. All assault rifles are submachine guns.

Swept Hilt -   Refers to a rapier guard style built of strands of steel in an openwork style. Although similar to the cage hilt, the swept hilt is usually asymmetrical and designed to trap the opponent's blade in addition to protecting the hand.

Swiss Dagger -   A shortened version of the baselard sword, with a wide twelve inch blade. During the 16th century it was popular throughout Europe. The shape was later resurrected as a sidearm dagger in Nazi Germany. Sometimes now also called the Holbein dagger, as so many of that painter's 16th century portraits featured the subject wearing this style of dagger.

Unfortunately, a very different knife, also, very popular among the Elizabethan English nobility, is often incorrectly called a Swiss dagger in many antique listings and art history books. These dress poniards had thin stiletto blades and narrow curved quillons.

Switchblade -   Any knife with a spring-loaded blade hidden completely in the handle, and can be opened with one hand by pushing a release button. Switchblades are either swing-out [the blade pivots at one end of the handle and swings around to the locked position] or pop-up [the blade shoots straight out of the handle]. All switchblade knives are illegal for purchase or use in the United States. Not the same as a gravity-action or drop-action knife.

Switchblades were designed for covert use and were often carried by pilots and paratroopers in the 1940's in case they had to cut themselves out of a tangled parachute. They also became something of a cult weapon among the demimonde in Europe and a favorite with youth gangs in the 1950's in the USA. When the general population began to clamor for their political representatives to "do something" about the threat of gangs, laws were passed in the 60's and 70's making the availability of switchblades all but impossible. (A cynic might note that gangs simply moved from knives to guns, but that view is churlish. Obviously the laws were well thought out and have led to the complete elimination of gang violence.)

Sword - A bladed weapon for cutting and/or thrusting. But when is a weapon a sword and not a dagger or a spear or an axe? A good rule of thumb is that a sword has a blade at least four times as long as, and no wider than twice the width of, the handle. The length of the blade should be at least as long as a person's forearm or it is really a dagger.

Tang - The part of the blade which is not exposed, in other words hidden inside the handle.

Tanto - In medieval Japan, the knife of the samurai. Although it was used on occasion for the ritual suicide known as *sepuku* [by self-disemboweling], the tanto was a fighting weapon, a gently curving single-edged dagger with a blade length of around 15 inches, and an excellent companion to the wakizashi [Japanese shortsword] for close-in fighting.

A woman of the samurai class also wore a knife, but it was the smaller *kwaiken*, not the tanto.

Target - The round shield of the knight when fighting dismounted, often carried by his assistant, the squire. Opposing archers in the field would use the easily visible shields as a point of focus, leading to the term "target" as something to aim for. Also known as a "targe".

Tech 9 - Also known as the Inghram, it is one of the smallest high-capacity assault pistols, first developed in 1970. Note that the bullet clip in the handgrip is very long, increasing its capacity to 30 rounds compared to a regular semi-automatic pistol.

Thompson Submachine Gun - Also known as the Tommy gun, the first successful fully automatic rifle that could be carried, loaded and operated by one person. Used famously by gangsters and G-men in the 1920's and 30's, the butt stock was often removed for easier handling. The gun could be further disassembled for packing in a small suitcase (or, yes, in a violin case) but then it could take some time for reassembly.

Because the butt stock of this gun has a rather sharp down-angle towards the shoulder, and the recoil is so strong, the barrel of the gun jumps up with each shot. When firing in fully automatic mode, the bullets can easily start spraying up into the air. Even experienced shooters find that the pattern of fire veers strongly up and down as one tries to hang on to the rifle.

Little remembered now is that this gun remained a valuable instrument in the arsenal of the US Army through WWII.

Toledo - A city in Spain once known for building swords of superior quality. The term then came to mean any sword, and then any blade, made in that city.

Though there was a time when the mark of "Toledo" on a blade was a guarantee of high craftsmanship, the region has not had a true sword industry for over a century and a half. The only swords from Spain now are cheap touristy wall hangings. Many of these weapons can be found in most theatre props cabinets, but should never be fought with.

Tomahawk - In English, it means a small hatchet used in fighting. In the original languages of several east coast native communities, it literally means a cutting thing, a general tool for agriculture.

Tommy Gun - Nickname for the Thompson submachine gun.

Transitional Rapier - This is a modern term for the rapier hilt styles seen from roughly 1640 to 1720, during which the full burly rapier gradually morphed into the sleek and elegant smallsword. Therefore, there is no single look for a transitional rapier.

The first noticeable change was the shortening of the quillons until they extended no further than the cup, and then the cup itself slowly became smaller and flatter. The rest of the parts of the sword followed the shrinking process, with the blade being the last to follow. The one defining feature that differentiates between transitional rapiers and smallswords is that the rapier still offered a legitimate cutting threat, which would be completely lost in the smallsword.

Trident - A three-pronged fishing spear. Not used in war, but a popular weapon in the gladiatorial arena of ancient Rome.

Trigger Pull - The amount of resistance that the finger must work against in order to pull the trigger and fire a gun.

Triple Action - A fairly rare hammer action found on some of the early cartridge revolvers. Not only could the gun be operated in standard single and double action, but the hammer could be pulled back to the cocked single-action position without using the thumb. Instead, the trigger could be very carefully pulled back to almost the firing position, at which point the hammer could be heard to "cock" and lock at a now hair-trigger position. At that point it would take only a touch of the trigger to fire the gun.

As it turned out, this was a very impractical way to draw the hammer back, it being much easier to simply use the thumb. Accidental shootings as operators tried to cock the hammer by using the trigger were frequent and nearly unavoidable.

Truncheon - The short club used by police officers; the nightstick. Not used in warfare except as an occasional symbol of rank. The term goes back to the 9th century, and actually meant a length of stick from a broken spear shaft, used as an improvised weapon of desperation.

Tuck - The English term for the *estoc*, the long two-handed strictly thrusting sword of the medieval battlefield. The term was sometimes used incorrectly to refer to any single hand sword.

Uzi - The last name of the Israeli designer of the distinctive short and stocky assault rifle. The standard for Israeli armed forces for several decades until replaced by US manufactured M-16's.

Wakizashi - The secondary, shorter, sword of the samurai warrior, with a blade length of about two feet. Although most Japanese warriors used the katana as a two-handed weapon, many used the katana in the right and the wakizashi in the left. Although a samurai might remove his katana once inside the confines of his home, the wakizashi was his twenty-four hour companion.

Walther -   A German firearms manufacturer most famously known for its semiautomatic pistol of WWII.

Webley -   A British firearms manufacturer best known for its WWI era military revolvers.

Wheellock -   A firing mechanism for some pistols of the mid 1500's and early 1600's in which the powder charge was ignited by sparks flying away from a spring-loaded wheel rubbing against iron pyrite. It was created as a replacement for the dangerous matchlock system, but was costly to build and prone to constant disrepair, so was finally replaced by the flintlock system by the end of the century. [There is some legitimacy to the story that the first design of the wheellock came from Leonardo DaVinci.]

Whinyard -   An obscure [around 14th c.] term meaning shortsword.

Whip -   A short rod or stick with a long thin strap of flexible (usually braided) leather attached. A whip can only "crack" when the tip moves faster than the speed of sound.

Winchester -   An American firearms and ammunition manufacturer most famously known for its line of lever-action rifles of the late 1800's.

Yataghan -   An interesting Turkish shortsword with a distinctive double curve. Popular with the Janissary units of the Ottoman empire during the late 18th century, the style was supposed to provide all of the cutting force of the curved sabre with the thrusting ability of the straight sword. It actually did neither well.

The pattern was later incorporated into several bayonet styles, the most famous being that for the French Chassepot rifle of the late 19th century. It was an attempt to build a combination weapon, something that could be used as either a sword or bayonet. A curved blade is more useful for infantry units, but the same curve can get in the way of the bullet leaving the barrel when mounted as a standard bayonet. The double curve was an attempt to remedy that dilemma. Unfortunately, it proved to be a poor thrusting bayonet and less than satisfactory as a fighting sword.

Zip-Gun -   A homemade single-shot pistol. Usually very crudely made, using scraps found at building or demolition sites. Urban youths in the USA [and to much lesser extent in Ireland] made zip-guns from about the 1920's until the late 1950's. The firing pin was often a large nail, and the driving force was either a section of flat spring or even a rubber band. Because neither the materials used nor the construction of the weapon could contain the explosive power of the gunshot, these guns as often as not exploded in the user's hands. Zip-guns disappeared in the mid-1960's when very cheap handguns flooded the country.

Weapons Explained
The Nature of Violent Props

Before we get into a discussion of the props themselves, let's lay out the two most important rules, nay, commandments concerning stage weaponry:

First and foremost: NEVER allow any prop nor real weapon to be used or even seen outside of a controlled rehearsal or performance space. Why? Because actors have been <u>shot</u> by neighborhood "heroes" for rehearsing outdoors with rubber knives; they have been <u>arrested</u> for making violent gestures in public with rubber guns; they have been <u>killed</u> while holding very phony looking prop weapons. If there is even a sliver of a chance that someone from the general public will see an actor holding a weapon outside of a controlled space, you must a] notify the appropriate law enforcement officials, b] post notices explaining to passersby what you are doing, and c] seal off the entire area so that no one can enter without getting past one of your assistants.

It should go without saying that "street theatre" or "guerilla theatre" simply doesn't mix with prop weaponry. This includes doing a promotion of an upcoming show by staging a scene of violence to an unsuspecting audience. The following story is true, although no one ever believes me:

A university theatre in the Midwest was in rehearsal for a production of the musical *Assassins*. Ticket sales were low, so a few of the cast members decided to do a little impromptu publicity on campus. What better way to advertise than to do a number from the show? And where can you find a lot of students hanging around? Why, of course, at noon in the Student Union, where there are hundreds of students having lunch. The actors got hold of the prop guns used for the show, loaded them up and hit the Student Union in the middle of the lunch rush. In order to get everyone's attention, they decided to enter the cafeteria area with guns blazing. Then they were going to launch into one of the show tunes.

As you can guess, they never actually got to the show tune part of their plan. After the barrage of gunfire, the screaming exit of dozens of students, and the inrush of campus police, no one seemed in the mode for a peppy Sondheim number. Needless to say, all of the students were arrested (one night in jail), and the weapons were confiscated. Luckily the faculty was able to convince the university that it was not in any way part of the students' actions, but even then there was thought given to the immediate dismissal of the department head.

If this story seems outlandish, please take a moment to consider all of the foolish things you've seen students do, and especially student actors, over the many years that you have been in theatre. The inconceivably moronic is always just one inspired moment away from being committed. You think that your props cabinet is secure? I'll bet there are a couple of extra keys floating around that you don't know about. I can also almost guarantee that several students have learned how to get into the theatre afterhours, even though you think that it is safely locked up.

Second: NEVER improvise with prop weapons. Improvisation works only when the participants can work in complete trust and safety, and safety cannot be assured if waving a weapon around. Whether the scene is dramatic or comedic doesn't matter. If you're going to improvise, you must pantomime sans props.

In some of the more traditional forms of Japanese martial arts, the students are expected to bow not only to their opponents but even to the punching bags they use in training. It seems silly at first, but it is meant to remind the students that they can only improve so long as they have good materials in good working order with which to practice. Taking care of the equipment shows how much respect you have for your craft. Would that actors had the same attitude.

Unfortunately, we know that actors tend to treat prop weapons as though they are toys, there for their own enjoyment. So for their safety and your budget, let them in on the secret that someone had to design, construct, pay for and maintain every prop that they touch, and that a successful show is the accumulation of everyone's efforts, including the lowly props assistant.

Weapon props require even more care, for the danger level shoots through the roof, and not just because the items are often inherently dangerous, but because the actors themselves are dealing with violent emotions. And here is where we have to make a distinction between fight-worthy and costume props, for not all props are created equal.

Swords

What is a stage sword? A replica sword that is safe enough for the actor to use in accord with the demands made by the production. Right there you can tell that no one sword can fulfill all of your needs. Certain shows will require light swords, others heavy, and some for purely costume needs - swords that need not be made very strong at all, just enough so that the actor can wave it around but not touch anything with it. And then of course some will have to be fought with. But even what qualifies as fight worthy will depend on the requirements of the fight.

"Fight worthy" is not synonymous with "stage sword", and it also doesn't mean actor-proof and unbreakable. Fight worthy means that for a controlled fight using trained combatants, the weapons in use have been constructed of appropriate materials. Appropriate is the key word. The look of the sword has to match the style of the production design, but the blade has to match the needs of the fight choreography. I have seen swords in props cabinets each made of one solid piece of indestructible steel, but they were so heavy that no actor could ever safely control them during a fight. So the fight worthiness of a sword comes down to the construction of the blade based on its intended use. We'll get to that in a moment, but first ...

Care & Handling of the Sword

For both costume and combat swords, rust and stress are the main villains. Both are always present, and both must be looked to at every opportunity. Maintaining the temper and integrity of the steel is a vital long-term goal.

<u>Temper</u> - is that combination of strength, flexibility, and "springiness" that is built into the steel, and will vary from blade to blade, often on purpose. Temper is a balance: too stiff a blade is also too brittle and can shatter; too soft a blade will gouge easily. Temper is lost by stressing the blade and also by excessive heating and cooling of the blade, so for long-term care of the weapon, practice the following:

* Refrain from grabbing the blade with an ungloved hand. Not only will this prevent cuts and scrapes, but our hands have oils that contain many salts. Salts attract airborne water vapor; water creates rust.
* Oil from time to time with a light weight machine oil or WD-4O (or heavy grease or car wax for long term storage).
* Never leave weapons lying on grass; never stick the tip into the ground. Both actions are an invitation to rust.

* When rust is spotted, remove it. Use a piece of dull emery cloth or fine steel wool.
* If make-up or stage blood gets on the weapon, remove it as soon as possible. Most stage blood is quickly corrosive to steel.
* Avoid storing the sword with the tip resting on the floor. It could create a permanent bend in the blade.
* Between seasons, remove all weapons from their leather sheaths. Leather breathes out water vapor, and leaving the blades sheathed will corrode the steel and rot the leather.
* Keep weapons away from extremes of temperature.
* Never allow power machinery to build-up heat on the blade.
* Always disassemble a sword when repairs to any part are necessary.
* Unless you have experience in cutlery tempering, never attempt to weld a fight-grade sword blade.

Stress   All weapons can break. It is unfortunate but true. Even a broadsword can snap in half in the middle of a fight and it will give no warning before it happens. That is because swords are constantly under a great deal of stress, and sometimes adding just a little bit more can be the little bit that causes it to shatter. Where does stress come from? Either internally or externally.

Internal stress comes from over aggressive pommel tighteners who try to squeeze the pommel down as far as it will go in order to make the sword ring louder. [Some choreographers even go so far as to tighten the pommel using a pair of vise grips!] Ringing is just the aural manifestation of unrelieved stress - the more you hear, the more you have. Tighten the pommel using only your hands until you can turn it no further; then and only then use a wrench to give it one more turn to line it up with the blade if necessary.

Stress can cause the pommel to loosen during use. This is normal, so check for loose pommels before each rehearsal.

External stress is the banging of swords when in use. Naturally you need to use the swords, but always make sure that the actors are well grounded in good stage combat basics. All fights should be choreographed by an experienced stage combat instructor. [Not necessarily a fencing instructor. The techniques of competitive fencing are unsafe for both actors and swords.] No actor should ever be in the position of having to make a block in order to save her life. Discipline and control have no substitute.

> *If a sword must touch another sword, even if only once, or must be dropped at any time, only a fight-grade blade must be used. If the sword is merely going to be drawn and flourished, a costume grade blade may be used.*

Things that people tell me (that drive me crazy):
"I don't need real weapons, the actors are only faux fighting"
"The actors are just making ever-so-slight and light contact for comic effect"
"Oh, they aren't really fighting; they only have to hit them once or twice".
OK, I understand what you're thinking, but that's like saying that you don't really need brakes on your car because there is only one stop sign on your way to work. Even if you only need to touch the brakes once all day

- at that one time YOU REALLY NEED THEM. The same with swords. Even if the sword only has to touch another one time, or if it has to be dropped, it must be a fight worthy sword.

Everyone thinks that as long as the attacks are kept weak, the swords won't sustain damage. But strong attacks rarely break a sword. Strong defenses are what weaken the blade, especially near the hilt. In a non-choreographed fight, a hit one night might be 5% stronger than it was the previous night, or might land one inch further away than it did two nights before. The defender isn't going to be able to second-guess that, so each actor ends up making every block as strong as possible and makes sure that it swings out as far as possible, putting even more strain on the blades.

Another thing that actors tend to do in "fake" fight attacking motions is to keep the arms very relaxed and pull the cuts. Intuitively, it makes sense, and they think that they are being light with the swords. But to make the fight move along, they flick the blades quickly with their wrists, putting far more strain near the hilt than would ever be caused in a full-out "real" fight.

The only way to keep the weapons and actors safe is to have all fights, even the "faux" ones, carefully choreographed. For theatre, there is no difference between a real fight and a fake one, at least not to the sword. There is only appropriate technique used for appropriate weaponry. There should never be any contact between two swords that is not carefully choreographed and meticulously rehearsed. It must always be considered stage combat, for that's precisely what it is. And never assume that the actors are going to know how to do this. I've had to re-teach a lot of experienced actors and even fight directors on how to get back to drilling with correct technique.

Disassembling and Assembling a Sword

The best way to learn about any sword is to take it apart and put it back together again. For some swords this is simplicity itself, for others extremely difficult and unadvisable unless the condition of the item is so questionable that the only options available to you are to either attempt a repair or throw out the sword. In attempting to take apart an unfamiliar sword you always run the risk of breaking it, so your first step is to find out how the sword is staying together.

All swords have at the very least two parts - the blade and the hilt, the hilt being anything that isn't the blade. Carefully look at the hilt to see if it is of one cast piece or if it also is made of many parts. What you are looking for are any signs of imbedded rivets either at the very top of the hilt or along the handle. If you don't see any, it could be that the pommel [the very top end of the hilt area] simply screws off just like a jelly jar lid. If that is the case, you have a blade with a "rat-tail" tang. About half of costume swords and the vast majority of stage combat swords use blades with rat-tail tangs.

Things that can go wrong at this step:
- The pommel or pommel nut was tightened down so hard that it is going to take a table vise and channel lock wrench in order to loosen it.
- You misjudged the nature of the pommel and it turns out that it wasn't a separate piece after all, so that in trying to twist off the pommel you actually broke the hilt. I lost one sword this way, but what can you do?
- The threads that the pommel screws onto were filled with epoxy or a product like Lok-tite, which hardened like cement. It will take some WD-40® and even more strength to break that bond. If the adhesive is too strong, you might break off the tang at the pommel instead of loosening it from the threads, in which case you'll

have a broken, shortened tang and a useless pommel that has the rest of the tang stuck inside of it.

Actually, all may not be lost here. If you are patient, you should be able to drill a new hole right down into the pommel, following where the tang broke off, and tap it to let's say 1/4 20. Go at least an inch deep. The tang that is still left on the blade might still have some thread on it, but if it doesn't you can thread it 1/4 20 as well, and here go for about 3/4 of an inch. The handle will need to be shortened some, so slice off about 1/2 inch there. When you reassemble the sword it should be nearly as good as new.

Assuming you *were* able to unscrew the pommel, you now have access to all of the constituent parts of the sword, which we will evaluate in just a moment, but first we are going to take a look at those other swords which aren't as easy to take apart.

Top-Riveted Tang

Again, if you don't really need to, don't bother to take apart a sword that is held together with rivets. You'd be in for a lot of work and the sword might not fit together as well when you try to put it back again as it does right now. That said, let's get in there!

If at the very top of the sword you can see that a circle of steel seems to be flush with the brass, then you might be looking at the very top of the blade steel itself, the tang. If that's the case, the builders of the sword have used the very blade as a giant rivet, stacking all of the parts onto the shoulder of the blade, allowing the tang to poke through the top, and then simply hammering the top until the tang flattened out over the brass cap. This is still a rat-tail tang, but the makers figured that no one would ever take apart the sword, so they just hammered it shut. In other to reverse the process, you're going to have to weaken that rivet head. Simple: just grind down that section a tiny bit, or better yet drill straight down into the steel at a little less than that visible diameter, being careful to drill only the steel and leaving the brass alone. Either way the steel should now collapse when you hammer out the pommel cap.

Things that can go wrong at this step:
- You didn't know that there were additional rivets along the sides of the handle, so the hilt can't come off until those are drilled out as well. The rivets are always made of steel, and the handles are usually made of brass, so locating the rivet heads should be easy. [see below]
- You didn't know that there was a threaded nut underneath the riveted head, so the hilt can't come off until it is exposed and removed. This kind of sword is a combination of threaded and riveted tang, and it might require some gentle tapping of the pommel cap until it can come off, exposing the top of the tang and the threaded nut.

Side-Riveted Tang

Some of the finest swords ever made are held together with rivets going sideways through the grip and into the tang, namely the Japanese katanas. Those weapons are all beyond museum grade, articles of incredible value zealously coveted by collectors throughout the world. If the sword in your hand is side-riveted, I'm reasonable certain that it is not one of those exquisite weapons, but rather a cheap replica.

If the sword is *not* a katana replica, spotting the rivets is fairly easy once you've established that it is not in fact one of the other kinds of swords. You did carefully look for a pommel that is not part of the handle, right? And very carefully looked for any sign of a top rivet? I knew you did. Now just look for the one or two or three steel rivets that are showing themselves on the handle of the sword. Side rivets vary in size from about a quarter inch down to less than 1/32 of an inch, and those thinner ones are often compression springs rather than true rivets. You might need to drill through the thicker ones, but most of the thin ones can be hammered out with a finish nail. Then the blade should just slip right out of the handle. Unless the manufacturer also used epoxy to keep the handle secured. If that is the case you can very carefully try to tap the handle pieces off of the tang, but the likelihood is that the handle will break when you try.

If the sword *is* a replica katana, then you have even more work to do, for you'll have to remove that fabric wrapping around the handle. Don't even consider doing this unless you have no other way to make a repair. Memorize every twist and turn, for you will have to repeat it in reverse order to reassemble. The wrap usually ends up tying down the pommel cap and then the end is deftly tucked back into the wrap, unseen by all. After removing the wrap and the end cap, you'll see (just barely) the two compression springs that act as rivets through the scales of the handle and the tang. You'll need to use some thin tool which is a little less than the diameter of the rivet in order to punch them out of the handle. I've found that a good hardened but blunted finish nail being firmly tapped with a hammer works best.

Assuming you've come this far, no matter what sword it was it should be apparent now as to how to take the rest of the sword apart, if it hasn't already done so on its own. When you are ready to reassemble the sword, it should be a simple matter of reversing the process, unless it was a top riveted tang. If so, you have two choices - go back to a riveted tang, or change over to threaded. I prefer threaded for all swords, so that the nut may be adjusted according to different temperature conditions, but that's just me.

Either way, your overall tang length on the riveted rat-tail tang is right now just a little bit shorter than when you started, so you'll have to make up the difference somewhere. One way is to shave off about 1/8 of an inch of the bottom of the grip. Another is to lengthen the tang by welding on a small extension, and yet another way is to lengthen the tang by grinding down some of the blade shoulder. If you are going to do the latter, be careful not to build up heat on the blade, which can ruin its temper. Few people have the patience to do this without causing major damage to a fight-worthy piece, so this should be a last resort only.

If you are going to re-rivet, simply assemble the pieces, including that slightly shortened handle, which should leave a fat 1/16th of an inch of tang protruding at the top. Just hammer that puppy down until the tang end flattens against the pommel. Ta-da! You've made a rivet.

If you are going for a threaded tang, then you need more tang sticking out - at least 3/8ths of an inch, more if you can. Then of course you'll need to thread the tang. Just go for the closest size you can with the deepest grooves. By convention, most costume swords are threaded 1/4 20 English, and combat swords at 6mm metric, but use what works for your tang. Be sure to thread a little beyond what you think you need so that the threads continue down into the handle. Better to have over-threaded than to risk bottoming out the nut and leaving your hilt forever loose.

A cap nut should finish off the sword nicely, and be sure to add a washer so that the nut doesn't grind into the brass. Choose steel rather than brass for the nut for longevity's sake. I know that brass matches better, but the threads will strip a lot sooner. Cut off any excess tang poking through the nut and you are ready to rock.

Now lets talk about the individual parts of the sword.

The Pommel

The pommel is meant to act as a counter weight, so that the sword doesn't feel so heavy in the hand. In general, heavy blades are matched with heavy pommels, and light blades with light pommels or even no pommel at all, but this is not a hard and fast rule. Military sabres meant for broad slashing cuts often have no true pommel so that, like a hammer, the swinging force is all directed at the impact point, with no chance to take the motion back. Other swords, especially very light dueling swords, sometimes had relatively heavy pommels, allowing the tip of the sword to "jump-up" at the opponent's face without effort.

The "heaviness" of a sword isn't all about the weight. After all, even the biggest broadswords, those over five feet in length, only weigh about seven pounds. But if the weight distribution is such that the center of balance is right in the middle of your hand, the sword feels quite light and is easy to manoeuver. It takes a little bit of arm strength to hold seven pounds in your hand, but if it's resting on your palm it is manageable.

Compare that to a cavalry sabre at only two pounds. At first it seems light, but it has no counterweight at all, merely a cap nut that pokes out just beyond your fist. Since all of the weight is forward of your hand, your forearms, wrist and fingers need to constantly work to keep that weapon from dropping out of your hand. Attempting to cut with the sword, or worse yet to stop the sword that is in motion, puts even more strain on your arm. In a very short amount of time this sabre will appear far heavier than that giant broadsword. [So why don't sabres have big pommels? Sabres are specifically made to be very difficult to stop once they are in motion, and being blade heavy keeps the momentum traveling forward, much like a hammer or axe.]

Whatever the weight, the inside of the pommel is usually threaded - matching the threads of the blade. The pommel should be made of steel, as the threads inside a brass pommel will strip in a short amount of time. Stay away from aluminum, as those will strip in no time at all.

Pommels will loosen with use. The vibrations caused by banging swords together shake the pommel, which naturally wants to unwind in the direction away from stress. A lock-washer can help hold the pommel in place, as can a drop of Lok-Tite®, found at most hardware stores. Lok-Tite® fills in the gaps in the threads of the pommel and then hardens, keeping the pommel from moving. Once you do that, however, it also means that you won't be able to adjust the tension as the metal expands and contracts in different temperatures, so it's not the best choice.

Some pommels are drilled through and then a cap nut is used to hold the sword in place. Cap nuts actually loosen less frequently than threaded pommels, but the threads of the tang can strip more easily if over tightened. But even with that slight drawback, they are preferred over threaded pommels for the heavier broadswords. When heavy pommels are required, the point where the pommel touches the grip is an area of great stress on the blade, for the shear weight of the pommel puts lateral pressure on what is normally the thinnest part of the tang . The pommel literally wants to snap the tang in half. Sending the tang all the way through the pommel and then holding it down with a cap nut divides that strain in half, distributing it to both the top and bottom of the pommel instead of the bottom only.

Lastly, you may come across some pommels that are completely hollow, in essence false pommels that are only for looks. These can collapse with occasional tightening, so after some time they need to be replaced with a stronger, solid pommel.

The Handle

This is the part you hold. It is sometimes called the grip, but technically the grip refers only to the leather or wire wrapping found on some handles. The handle is hollow to allow the tang to run through it, and can be made of almost any material, the most common being wood, but plastic and steel are also used. Never drill sideways though the handle and into the flat of the tang in trying to hold a fight-quality sword together. Many a good weapon has been ruined in the attempt. Some swords, especially those of Japan and some European military sabres, were built using handle rivets, but stage swords should not be held together this way.

Wood handles were the standard throughout history, but today are used only in historical replicas. Wood feels good and looks good, but can split and even rot, and that rotting will encourage the tang to rust. Fine blades have been destroyed by the invisible rusting away of the tang inside a wooden grip.

Some woods are better than others for handles. Pine is just too soft and splits too easily along the grain. Maple, mahogany and walnut work reasonably well, having a nice even grain that resists splitting. Hickory, cherry and ironwood are superb, but their extreme toughness make them very difficult to work with. We have had some limited success with rattan, which resists rotting, but unless the handle ends are perfectly seated they have the same problems in splitting as does pine.

With time the compression of a tightly seated pommel will cause any wood handle to collapse. That failure is sometimes exacerbated by an incorrect facing of the ends of the handle to the pommel or to the guard. When this happens, the force of the pommel tightening down actually drills into the wood and acts as a wedge, causing the handle to split open. To prevent this, wood handles are often protected by shims (metal washers) which help disperse the pressure to the entire handle.

A lot of people hate shims, and I understand why. Shims can take away from the clean look of a sword [when viewed very close-up], and every additional item placed along the tang is one more joint where a sword can loosen. But there are excellent reasons as to why a sword may need one or more shims. We already mentioned the drilling into the wood caused by the rotational screwing in of the pommel. But shims can also add decades of life to the handle by preventing premature warping of the ends. Any piece of wood will have different pockets of hardness and softness, and the use of a shim at the top and bottom of the handle helps prevent uneven compression. Shims are also important when split-ring lockwashers are used, for it allows them to press up against the pommel instead of just digging into the grip. Without a shim, the rough edge of the split-ring gouges a groove into the wood during the final tightening of the pommel, thereby acting as a tiny wedge itself that can split the handle.

Shims can also help isolate the vibrations of the blade from dispersing into the guard, allowing the sword to ring instead of clunk. This isn't terribly good for the sword blade, for a ringing sword is more prone to develop microfractures in the blade than one in which the vibrations can quickly dissipate. But directors all love the sound of ringing steel, and sometimes one shim at the bottom of the handle is all you need to make the sword ring like a bell.

Where most people hate to see shims is when they are used to fill a gap between the handle and the pommel, a gap that should never exist. What sometimes happens is that for some reason the handle has become a little too short, and when the pommel is screwed down onto the tang the available threading runs out, causing the pommel to bottom out before it can even touch the handle. For a short-term fix, someone will stack

5 or 6 washers to make up the difference. Then the short term turns into long term when no-one wants to take the time to do a real repair job, and the sword goes back into the props cabinet with the half inch stack of washers. Instead, you should really do the proper repair, which is either get a new handle, extend the threaded length of the tang, or re-drill and re-tap the pommel deeper to cover the distance.

So, bottom line on shims: don't go crazy with them, but by all means use them when you need them.

Metal handles have longevity going for them, but since they have no compression, they tend to lead to pommel loosening substantially more than do swords with wooden handles. A metal handle will almost always require two shims sandwiching a lock washer to keep the pommel from loosening.

All modern swords and many historic replicas now use plastic handles. They have some of the compression characteristics of wood, but none of the grain problems, so they break less often and don't breathe water onto the tang, so hidden rust is less of a problem. The biggest drawback to plastic is, well, it's plastic, and some folks just don't want to have plastic on their sword. Some of the Ren-Faire crowd refuse swords made of modern materials. Another drawback with plastic is that it can bend when exposed to the combination of ambient heat and pommel pressure, and once bent will stay bent.

Any handle might be just the bare material or it might have a covering, known as the grip. The grip is either of wire or leather or sometimes both. Leather grips seldom need more than an occasional regluing to keep the edges down. On the minus side, if held with an ungloved hand it will absorb sweat and rot out over time. A wire grip lasts a long time, but if one strand breaks the whole thing unravels quickly and is a tough fix, so after playing with it a couple of times you may decide that taking it off and simply going with the bare handle is acceptable.

It really shouldn't matter what the covering of the handle is, for all combatants should wear gloves when using a sword. Many fighters prefer not to do so, for fear of loosing some of the feel of the sword, but actually that "feel" can get in the way of proper technique. The vibrations and occasional sudden pinching of the handle into the skin of the palm often leads the actors to loosening their grip right at the point where they need the most control. So unless it's simply inappropriate for the character to be wearing gloves, don't fight bare-handed.

<u>The Guard</u>

The guard is the metal part that protects the hand, and is sometimes also called the hilt. To be precise, hilt actually means anything that is not the blade, in other words all of the parts of the sword that stick out of the scabbard - guard, handle, grip and pommel. The guard proper is merely the piece between the handle and the blade, and can be as simple as a flat cross piece or as complex and ornate as the 17th century cage hilt rapiers. With very few exceptions, guards are made of metal, usually brass or steel.

Parts of the Guard

Naturally, not all sword guards will have all of the parts listed, and each part has a very specific function:
1	Knucklebow - When swinging a sword, the knuckles of the fist lead the action, so this large curve is there to protect what its name indicates. Knucklebows on rapier and smallswords are simple thin strands, while military and sport sabres have very wide bows, sometimes forming the entire guard.
2	Backguard - On some rapiers, there are additional strands supporting the knucklebow that sweep down the "back" of the hilt. In this case the back is considered that part of the hilt that rests against the body when the sword is worn, or, stated another way, the backguard protects the fingernails when holding the sword. (You'd think that it would be the part protecting the back of the hand, wouldn't you?)

3   Forward Quillon - Quillons are merely the crossguards of a sword. On broadswords, they form the entire guard. The forward quillon is the one on the leading edge of a sword swing, or the knuckle side. Quillons are the most common form of hand protection found on swords throughout history. Their main function is to keep incoming cuts from sliding down the defending blade and cutting the arm.

Parts of the Guard

Backguard, Knucklebow, Disc/Cup, Quillon, Loop Guard, Pas d'Ane, Side Ring

4   Rear Quillon - You've probably guessed that this quillon is the one on the trailing side of a sword swing. On true two-edged swords such as broadswords there is no designated forward or rear quillon.

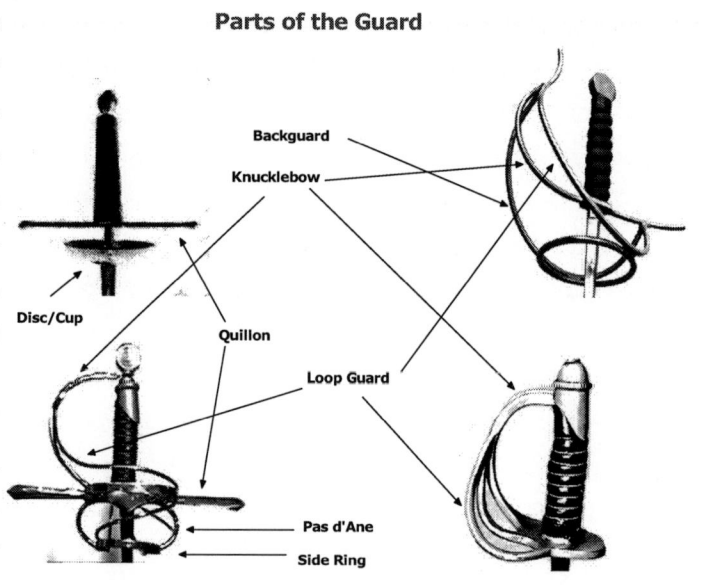

5   Cup/Disc - When rapiers were invented, fighters quickly realized that a simple thrust to the sword hand could finish a fight in one move. It took a little while, but sword makers learned that quillons are good protection against cuts, but very poor against thrusts. For that, a solid circle of metal is the best. The largest discs, called full cups, on 17th century rapiers were half spheres enveloping the entire fist. The smallest were simple flat circles barely covering the forefinger.

6   Loop Guard - On cage hilt or swept hilt rapiers, many strands form one or more loops so as to provide protection for the back of the hand against sword cuts. In other words, these are the protections for the back of the hand. The opposite of the backguard, we see the loop guards as the part of the hilt that faces out, away from the body when the sword is worn. Loops are both light weight and strong, but give little defense against a direct thrust

7   Ring Guard - If a loop comes out of the quillon center at 90º, it is called a ring, not a loop. Ring guards tend to be simple, with one ring on a dagger or two on a sword.

8   Forward Pas d'Ane - When trying to maintain control of a sword, it is really tempting to let the forefinger swing out over the forward quillon. It dramatically improves tip control but it leaves that finger exposed to a sudden slicing off by an incoming cut. A little half circle loop of steel coming down from the forward quillon and almost touching the blade keeps the finger shielded. First seen on some broadswords of the 14th century, pas d'anes became indispensable to rapier play of the 16th and 17th centuries.

9   Rear Pas d'Ane - As rapiers became more elaborate, the pas d'anes became a handy place from which to connect further expansions of the guard. By the late 1800's the forward and rear pas d'anes provided a secure place from which a new fencing grip was developed. The Italian grip uses the index and middle finger passing through the forward and rear pas d'anes respectively, putting the thrusting blade in line with the hand and forearm (but losing the ability to perform an effective cut).

The Blade

The terms blade and sword have sometimes been used interchangeably, which is unfortunate nowadays when someone tries to purchase a weapon. Many ask for a "blade" thinking that they are getting a complete weapon, when all they get is a strand of steel but no way to hold on to it. It's not all that dissimilar to what would happen if you tell a salesman at a Ford dealership that you need a "set of wheels". You'll get something very different from what you would get with the same request at a Goodyear tire store.

Parts of the Blade

- Tang - that part of the blade you don't see, the part inside the grip. In the strongest swords, the width of the tang is the same as the blade [called a full tang], and the two halves of the handle are simply riveted or pinned onto the tang. But it makes for more difficult construction, so usually the tang is trimmed a bit narrower than the rest of the exposed blade. On some the tang only extends a short distance into the handle. Called a push tang, it is usually held on by some epoxy, and makes for the weakest swords. Other tangs narrow to a rod that runs the length of the handle and beyond, called a rat-tail tang. Depending on how the sword is assembled, the rat-tail tang may be threaded or smooth.

- Shoulder - the sudden narrowing of visible blade to tang. The sword guard normally rests against the shoulder. This area of the blade is under great stress when used, and is always a potential breaking point.

- Ricasso - on those swords in which the index finger loops over the guard [rapiers, for example], that part of the blade the finger will touch. It is the final part of the blade before the shoulder and is always left unsharpened.

- Forte - the strongest part of the blade, considered approximately the first third of the blade beginning at the shoulder. This is the defensive part of the sword, the part on which one can absorb an incoming cut.

- The middle of the sword is simply that - the mid third of blade between the forte and foible. Ineffective for an attack and too weak for strong defense, it should rarely show signs of wear except when used by an inexperienced fighter.

- Foible - The furthest third of the blade, and generally the weakest. The blade usually becomes much thinner the closer it gets to the tip so as to reduce weight and therefore fatigue. It is also the striking portion of the sword edge, the impact point for a cut. With very thin blades, foibles are inherently weak. When striking another sword in an attempted cut, the forward momentum causes the foible to bend around the blocking blade, so naturally this is the most common fracture point for lighter blades.

- Edge - Simple, right? The part that you cut with, also called the leading edge or true edge. On two-edged straight blades, either side can be the cutting edge. On single edged swords, sabres for instance, the opposite of the leading edge is called the back edge, and is always unsharpened.

- False edge - on single edged sabre blades, the last few inches of the back edge has been filed down to a sharp edge, not with the idea of attempting a backhand cut but in order to reduce resistance in the event of a thrust. Part of but not the same as the back edge.

- Spine - The part of the length of the blade that has the greatest strength. On single edged blades, the back edge is thickened to become the spine, while on narrow double-edged blades the center has been similarly designed. On heavy broadswords that have a groove (fuller) down the center, the two ridges on either side of the groove could be considered to form a double spine.

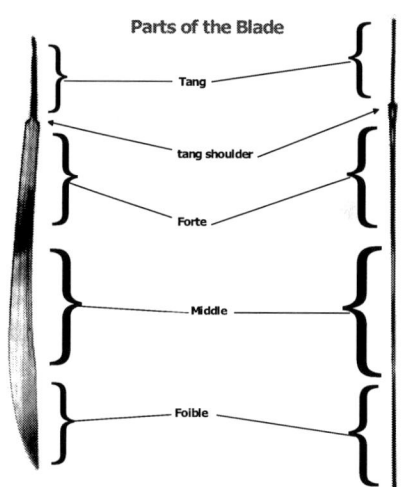

- Fuller - How do you make a blade that is both as light as possible but still retain its strength? One way is to build in one or more groves into the length of the blade. Called fullers, the dome shape that they create makes the blade much stiffer than it would be without having the metal removed. Sometimes gruesomely referred to as a "blood groove", there is a myth that they are added to the blade to keep the sword from getting stuck in the victim, or to make the wound impossible to close. Not true.

- Tip - the point of the blade. If the sword is meant as a practice weapon, the tip of a very thin blade will have a thickened button welded on as a safety aid. In modern sport fencing, this steel button is covered with a rubber button for additional safety. The rubber button is always removed for stage combat, for it gives the actors a false sense of safety. [I have noticed that actors trained with full mask and rubber tipped swords tend to develop poor and unsafe technique, putting their partners in danger.]

Checking a Blade for Fight-Worthiness.

Only two materials are appropriate for use in order to construct fight-worthy blades - high carbon tempered steel or the more costly but significantly lighter tempered ("aircraft") aluminum. Which is better? Fighting with a light aluminum blade makes life much easier for the actor, but great care must be made so that these costly pieces are only matched against other aluminum swords. Tempered aluminum is relatively soft, and can be easily gouged by even a costume grade cheap steel-bladed sword, rendering it useless after only a few rehearsals. But a serviceable steel broadsword can be used to fight nearly any weapon made of any material. As a choreographer, I prefer using steel.

Just because a sword blade is "carbon steel" doesn't necessarily mean that you can fight with it, so take some time to carefully examine any sword with which you are not familiar before giving it to your actors, remembering that "fight-worthy" refers both on how a sword is built and how you intend on using it.

To evaluate an unfamiliar sword, first take a look at the flat. Is there anything written on the blade? Most will have a manufacturer's logo stamped on the blade proper, usually near the shoulder. That's normal but not required. What is troublesome is if the blade has ornate engraving or has been acid etched - almost always a sign that the blade is non-tempered. Another red flag is if the blade has been marked with "India", "Spain", "Toledo", or "Mexico". These blades are probably just tourist wall hangings and cannot take any kind of stress. On the other hand, many blades from Pakistan, although not sold as fight-worthy, stand up to stage combat better than many French combat blades.

Now tap the blade and hear the sound. Does it ring like a bell? Then you can be sure of .... nothing. A blade that rings is no more fight worthy than a blade that clunks. People get very pleased when they hear a ringing blade, so here at Weapons of Choice we try to get every weapon to ring before it leaves the shop, but that is only to please the director.

Permit a tiny physics review. Ringing is the aural manifestation of unrelieved stress. When anything is struck, a pressure wave travels through the material. That wave has to go somewhere, and normally it dissipates into a substance, for example wood or skin, that absorbs the vibration. The pressure wave is transformed into a very small amount of heat.

When no release is possible, the vibration continues to circulate within the metal, often at a vibration rate that our ears can translate as that wonderful ringing sound. This is what happens in a tuning fork, a brass bell, and a sword blade. But that vibration, that running pressure wave, is always looking for somewhere to go. The vibration doesn't last forever; because after a while the vibrating steel molecules cause enough internal friction so that the vibration slowly dissipates into heat energy. In a perfect world, that dissipation would happen evenly throughout the blade. But steel is not perfect. There are microscopic defects that all metals have. Cheap steel is filled with them, but even the best steel blades will have tiny flaws in its structure. Those flaws are so small that they have no effect on the vibration rate, therefore the sound of the ringing. But the vibration does turn those flaws into micro fractures, which with time can become break points for your sword.

It is interesting to point out that the swords used for film work do not ring at all. The film swords are usually made to be sturdy and extremely light, with no thought given to "ringing steel". The wonderful sounds that you hear in a movie sword fight are all added in post production. As that option is not available for stage, directors insist that all swords ring like bells.

Any metal can ring so long as the vibration within the blade proper can be somehow isolated from the handle, which would normally be able to absorb the vibration. So what can you tell from the ring? Nothing in terms of fight worthiness, but there is one benefit during rehearsal. Once you become accustomed to the way a particular sword sounds, a subtle change in that ring could mean that the sword is beginning to loosen and needs to be retightened. You may get a sudden drop in tone, or perhaps a secondary rattle or low rumble as some part of the guard starts to shake. But that is it. Some really cheap worthless swords ring wonderfully, and some very high quality swords simply clunk when struck. In order to check for fight worthiness, you need to examine the blade more closely.

Does it bend? Even the heavier broadswords will show some spring in them, and you need to see if the sword will spring back to its original shape. Some of the thinner sport fencing blades will allow for a little change in the bend, but for the most part if you can take a sword, bend it over your knee, and it stays bent, then keep it as a costume piece but don't fight with it.

Assuming you have springy steel, now check the tang. You can only do this by removing the blade from the hilt [see the beginning of the chapter]. If you have a very wide blade, but a very narrow tang, the blade might crack at the shoulder. There is no hard and fast rule here, but a two-inch wide blade with a tang only 1/4 inch at the shoulder is not something I would trust in a fight scene. I feel more comfortable when the tang is at least one third the width of the shoulder on a light blade, and at least one half the width of the shoulder on a heavy blade, but that is just the minimum. Wider is always better.

Incidentally, a tang that stays bent (not springy) is not bad, for most fight grade blades are differentially tempered so as to leave the end of the tang soft even if the blade proper is stiff. That makes it easier to thread the tang and bend it to fit the handle. Also, many fencing blades have a tang that is not in a straight line with the blade but is actually at a slight angle to it. That's done on purpose, to allow a fencer to point the tip of the sword at the opponent without having to overly bend the wrist.

Now check the edge. Most blades for stage combat will have a beveled, though not sharp, edge, and if the angle is too acute the blade might gouge into other swords. Even if fight worthy, you may want to grind down the edge until there is more "meat" on the contact surface. This is one of the reasons that most Ren-Faire swords are not practical for stage combat. Most are strong and correctly tempered, but the edge is so thin that they deeply gouge, often to a depth of more than 1/2 inch, after just a few strikes from another sword.

The edges of any blade are not impervious to strike damage. Burrs should be removed and gouges reduced, as not only are they potential break points on a blade, but the burrs are sharp enough to slice through skin and costumes. When the combat is aggressive, it is quite common for the edge to nick and develop burrs, especially on new blades. But if the edges deeply gouge with nearly every strike, the steel is probably too soft for use in stage combat.

There are some people who are so concerned about hurting the temper of the blade that they will only remove the burrs by grabbing a good hand file and working away at them, but if the metal is hard they have to be at it for hours. Just as good is using a grinding wheel with a medium grit stone. You can avoid overheating the blade by making several light passes on the edge until you have removed the amount of the nick that bothers you. Take several breaks to allow the steel to cool down between a few passes. Flip the blade several times so you're not always grinding from one side, and keep the blade at a little bit less than 90 degrees to the face of the stone. Don't go directly at 90 degrees or the wheel might catch the blade and pull it out of your hand. When you are done with the edge, then round the tip, and here you don't have to worry about heat buildup.

The edge will now be a bit ragged to the touch, so use either a wire brush attachment on your grinding wheel, or just use a bit of fine grade steel wool or better yet some emery cloth (most hardware stores will carry it, usually near the copper pipes) and rub it up and down the edge until the steel is smooth to the touch. Although any nick on a blade (called a stress riser) is a natural susceptible break point, you have to balance how much steel you take off of an edge in order to smooth it down. You may end up reducing the life span of the blade by too much concern rather than from neglect. Everything is a trade-off.

By the way, the nicks and burrs should all be along the foible and forte of the blade. If the nicks are congregated primarily on the center of the blade, your actors are fighting with extremely poor technique. Either hire a fight instructor or get rid of the one you now have. Your fighters need some competent instruction immediately.]

Assuming that the blade has passed all of those inspection points, you still can't immediately assume that it is safe to stick into your fight. Stage combat is actually much harder on blades than a real battle would be, for theatrical fights are exaggerations and have all of the abuse taken on the sword instead of on a human. Also, different fights require different moves, so a "fight-worthy" fencing sword will disintegrate in a swashbuckling rapier fight. Your sword has to be able to handle the strongest move within your fight.

Many people will pick up a sword and try to determine fight-worthiness by determining three attributes: finding the center of balance, determining the center of percussion, and listening to the ringing of the blade. All of which are completely inconsequential and tell you nothing about fight worthiness.

Current Common Blade Varieties Used for Stage Combat

The first three blades come in both practice and competition forms. You'll want the practice variety always for stage use. Competition blades have a tiny groove in the length of both the visible blade and the tang to allow placement of an electrical wire. That's because competition blades need to be wired for connection to the point scoring apparatus. This groove weakens the blade somewhat for stage use as well as increasing the price.

As these first blades are made for competition fencing, and are very thin strands of metal, steel buttons are welded onto the tips as a safety measure. They are not necessary for the other blades, and indeed of not much help in stage combat in any case.

√ Foil - the lightest full length blade made, it starts off with a square cross-section of only 1/4 of an inch, and then tappers down to a springy and flexible flat band of steel, the blade proper being about 35 inches long. Used for competition in the Olympic sport of foil fencing where there is no cutting and the incoming thrusts are deflected, not blocked. Usually having a built-in slight "C" shaped bend overall so that in the event of a hit the blade will continue to bend rather than try and force its way into the opponent. It is not designed for nor can it tolerate any type of cutting motion. The foil blade and fencing style associated with it was developed originally as a practice tool for dueling students to increase reaction speed. Extremely "whippy", it should never be used for stage combat. Even a pulled cut can bend right around a block and smack the defending actor right in the face.

√ Olympic Sabre - also a flat band of steel, also 35 inches, it has a very slight narrow "V" cross-section giving it both a leading and a back edge if you study it closely, the bottom of the "V" being the leading, cutting edge. Although Olympic-style sabre fighting does use a cutting motion, it is all snap-cuts from the wrist with very little arm strength or body weight behind it. Just as with the foil, this blade is very whippy and not appropriate for stage combat.

√ Epee - the lightest and most popular blade for use on stage. A prominent flattened "V" shaped cross-section and a deep groove running down its 35 inch length provides excellent stiffening while keeping it as light as possible. Unlike the above Olympic sabre, the bottom of the "V" is the spine, allowing each arm of the "V" to be a leading edge, in theory making the epee a double edged blade. When mounted onto the hilt, general practice is to have the spine pointing out when wearing the sword. In other words, when holding the sword with the palm facing up (supine) you should be looking down into the groove. The blade can certainly be mounted the other way, but it does change the feel of the sword.

Over the length of the blade, the epee forms a gentle "C" shape, curving slightly toward the spine, that is, away from wide part of the "V". That curve is built in to the blade. With time, an "S" shape may develop, but this can weaken the steel during use, so the blade can and should be bent by hand back to its normal curve. It can survive that kind of re-bending hundreds of times, and that doesn't weaken the blade appreciably. The epee can, with time, also develop a bend along the edge. This is cause for concern, for it means that the actor has been completing his cutting motions with far too much force. See the stage combat section for correct technique.

Using the epee blade for stage combat allows for all of the lightening fast moves of competitive fencing while still having just enough strength to handle most of the controlled cutting and blocking of stage combat. Epees are very flexible and springy, accepting bends of over 90 degrees. It is still a fragile blade, however, and in a big show with, let's say, twenty fighters you can expect one or two blades to break in normal rehearsal and performance.

√ [Demi-Epee] - Not normally purchased from fencing supply companies, but at 28 inches is just the right length for a historically accurate smallsword blade. At Weapons of Choice, we started providing these blades for not only the smallsword replicas but for any lighter sword in which the distance between the combatants can be a problem. In theatre-in-the-round or 100 seat houses, for example, having two actors stand-off with full length blades sometimes means that one person ends up in the wings or on an audience member's lap. This cut-down version of the epee also happens to take a lot of stress off what is normally the most brittle part of the blade, so the blade once so shortened seems to last forever.

√ Double-Wide Epee - also known as the Musketeer blade. With twice the steel and a much deeper and dome-shaped groove, the idea is that it was supposed to be much stronger than the common epee. I've noticed that the foible seems to be even more brittle, and the failure rate to be twice that of its thinner cousin since the wide blade is still fitted with only a 1/4 inch tang. That extra weight puts a lot of stress on that little tang, and these blades often break off at the hilt. It is no longer widely manufactured, so on occasion is difficult to find, but some still pine for its [slightly] better visibility from the house. You can still find it in many props cabinets, and different European cutlers come out with one version or another every so often, usually at about three times the cost of a standard epee.

√ Schlaeger - The lightest of cutting permissible blades. It starts out the same width as the epee, but it maintains that same width throughout the 34 inch blade length and has no groove, having a lens shaped cross section. Designed for the Mansuer style of aggressive dueling of the Heidelberg University, it allows for stout cuts and blocks. The tang is also at least twice as thick as that of the epee, increasing its survivability. Finesse wrist moves and exact point work are still possible, but the slight addition of weight down at the foible means that all moves will have to be performed more slowly compared to the epee. At the time of this writing, lens shaped schlaeger are no longer being produced. [There is a longer version of the same blade, but stay away from it. At 39 inches but the same width, it has a horrible tendency to wave and wobble during fighting.]

√ Diamond Schlaeger - built the same as the standard schlaeger, but has a lozenge cross section. This shape reduces the amount of steel on the blade without sacrificing strength, so the sword is much more responsive in the hand [but still nowhere near as fast as the epee]. Some sword makers choose to weld a steel button on the tip, but for stage combat this is absolutely unnecessary.

√ Canelure - Definitely a cutting sword, and long at 39 inches and 7/8" wide. I've seen it used as a dueling rapier weapon with the fancier blade work, but it made the fight look slow and cumbersome. Easy to spot with its off-centered grooves running the length of both sides of the blade. Not meant for the trained back and forth of theatrical rapier play, but a fine bashing blade for a light broadsword or straight sabre or strict historical rapier play. This blade was actually very close in weight and size to the historic Elizabethan rapier blade. Unfortunately, replacement blades are no longer being made.

√ [Vorpal] - Another Weapons of Choice modification. Since the canelures were so long, we cut them down to about 28 inches, which puts more control back in the hand of the fighter. It's my favorite combat blade, but unfortunately no longer available.

√ Single hand - Now we're getting into the real broadsword weight blades. This one is meant for use in a singlehand sword, but we've sometimes put them on two-handed handles for fighters who may not have time to build-up the shoulder strength necessary for injury free two-handed broadsword fights. About 33 inches long.

√ Hand and a Half - sometimes called the bastard sword, at 35 inches it is the most common blade used for two-handed fights. Although only two inches longer than the above single-hand, because of extra width it is 50% heavier.

√ Double hand - this is a lot of blade, and there are very few who can both control the sword and not pull some tendons. Thirtyeight inches long and almost twice the weight of the hand-and-a-half.

√ Zweihander - This is really fun to see on-stage, but either leave it for the weight-lifters in the cast or for use in a comic fight. The exposed blade is 45 inches long, and although actually lighter than the two-hand, the extra length makes it very difficult to control.

√ Shortsword - Most swords for iron and bronze aged cultures were built with this kind of blade, as longer blades were simply not practical when using those weaker metals. In steel it is very light and responsive. Made by a variety of companies, most are about an inch wide and 18 to 24 inches long

√ [Leaf] - Trying to match the look of the distinctive shortsword variation in a fight worthy blade is difficult, but we build them and keep them as light as the standard shortsword, but between 2 to 3 inches wide. The only problem is that in making it light, it is also brittle, so has a tendency to crack more often than standard blades.

√ Sabre - An excellent and nearly indestructible recreation of the cavalry sabre, also used in oriental versions of two-handed swords. As a cavalry sabre it has a drawback in that the weight is very forward. It is very similar to the single-hand broadsword blade, even having the same 33 inch length, but on a military sabre hilt it lacks the necessary counterbalance to allow for easy control. With a short tang and no true pommel, it means that the sword is easy to swing but very difficult to stop. When built into a two handed weapon, the longer length of the handle and being able to balance the weight by use of a heavy pommel, the blade makes for a fine weapon. It is unfortunate that as of this writing they are disappearing from the market.

√ Cutlass - The cutlass is really merely a shortened sabre blade, and as with all shortened blades it makes a very user friendly sword. Balances well in the hand with almost any hilt.

√ [Fantasy Cutlass] - Just as with the leaf blade, Weapons of Choice built a wide flat blade using machete blades as a starting point. This way we could get a very wide blade at a very low weight. Due to the vagaries of the construction process, it is actually less brittle than the leaf blade.

√ Scimitar - Historic scimitars were simply what we would identify as standard sabre blades, but Western imagination gave it a much wider cutting head than it really ever had. Because of audience expectations, these fantasy blades are used for many "Middle Eastern" swords. Luckily, several Chinese firms make a durable and light blade usable for stage combat. But stay away from the ultra light wushu style weapons. Any blade that wobbles when you shake it is inappropriate for stage.

√ Machete - Very thin steel, but of great strength (which shouldn't come as a surprise considering what the tool is supposed to do in the field). The biggest concerns come in the wobbliness of the blade and that the edge tends to burr very quickly. Stage combat is possible with machetes so long as the moves are modified to deal with the realities of the weapon, and of course you have to grind down the tip and edge.

The Complete Weapon

Assuming that the sword is correctly assembled and suitable for stage combat, there remains the final attribute of the weapon - its "feel", the way it handles. And here is where the makers and purchasers of swords will start to throw out the terms center of percussion, sweet spot, center of balance, and blade harmonics. Let's start with the easy stuff.

The *center of balance* (CoB) of a sword is pretty self-explanatory, and easy to find. Simply balance a sword on your finger; there it is. Where is the optimum center of balance? That is a personal preference. The further the CoB (also called the center of mass) is from your hand, the more momentum, therefore power, can be delivered to a cut. But the drawback is that it becomes harder to stop the blade once it is in motion. The closer the CoB is to your own palm, the lighter the sword feels, but then you lose the benefit of gravity to aid in control of the tip. For stage combat, a balance point of between one to six inches beyond the hilt seems to be the average.

The *center of percussion* (CoP) is a little more complicated, especially since the term is used differently by different people. First, pure physics. Assuming that an item is suspended in air somehow, striking it at the CoB will cause the item to move away without spinning. But if it is struck off of that center, the item will also move away but in addition will spin around the CoB. Now suppose the item is suspended or held at some spot that isn't the CoB. If you strike the object at the CoB, the object is going to try to pivot around the hold point. Strike it somewhere else and there are two pivot points to calculate. Somewhere in between the hold point and the CoB is the center of percussion, and striking the item right here will cause the two pivoting forces to cancel out. The object won't try to spin; it will simply move straight back (if it weren't held down).

So the CoP is determined by a combination of the center of balance and where you happen to hold the weapon or tool. This center of percussion is useful to know for sword play, because it is the spot that you want to use to block an incoming attack. If the block is made too close to the hand, the blade will try to pivot forward. It the block is made too far away, the blade will be pushed back.

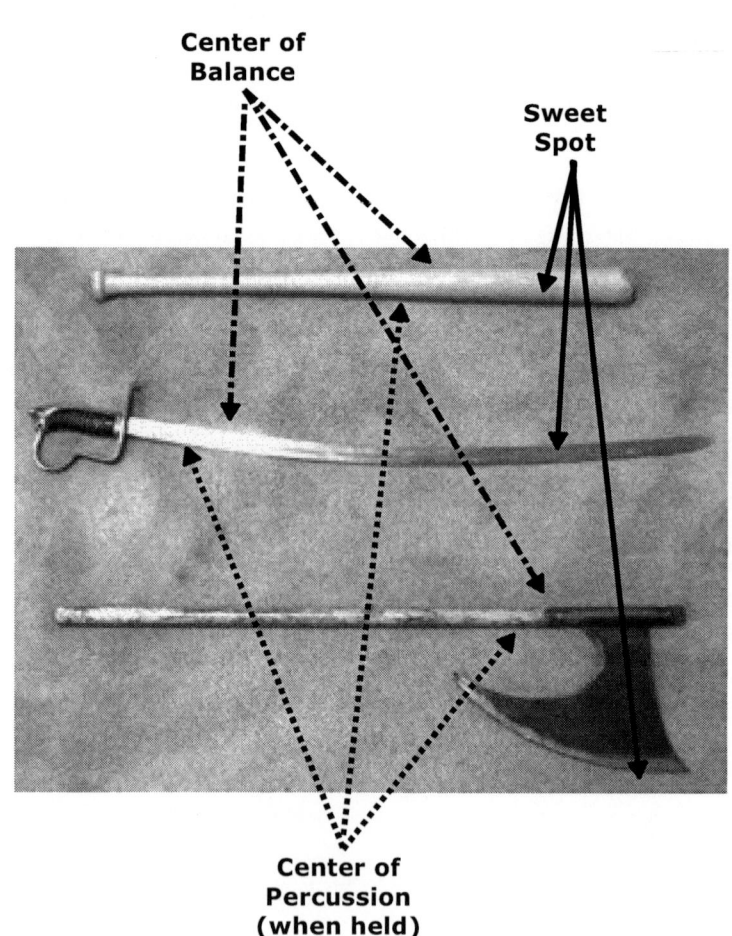

Then there is the other *center of percussion*, the term as it is used by sword people. They like the term percussion to mean where one should strike with a sword to do the most amount of damage. What they term the center of percussion is commonly referred to as the *sweet spot*. Striking or cutting something at the sweet spot feels the most comfortable, but the reason for this has nothing to do with the actual CoP. I hate improper use of perfectly good terminology, so even though other sword people call this spot on the blade the center of percussion, I'm just going to call it the sweet spot.

Determining the location of the sweet spot for any given sword is both objective and subjective, because more important than the amount of force that one can generate is the way a sword feels when it makes contact with the item to be struck. This is relatively easy to do with something like a baseball bat, for the CoB is way down at the end of bat, so the CoP and the sweet spot are going to be down there too. There are a lot of very good physics papers which eloquently explain the phenomenon for baseball bats and tennis racquets. But a sword is different. The CoB is very close to your hand, but you have to strike with the far end. This conundrum has let some to work out a theory based on *blade harmonics*.

The idea there is that everything vibrates when it is struck, and that certain "vibration nodes" naturally occur along the object. These nodes differ for each weapon, but in theory the vibration is less noticeable at those spots. If one holds the sword at one node, striking the sword at the other node will cause the least amount of vibration to be felt in the hand. This is a wonderfully constructed and utterly bogus hypothesis. I won't go through the physics, but the bottom line is that these nodes have not been established for swords, and that the vibration that does occur in a well constructed sword cannot be felt by the holder. The reason a sword or bat or racquet doesn't feel right when you miss the sweet spot is simple - the handle wants to pop out of your hand. You can feel this by gently pushing on the blade - no striking, no vibration, no harmonics. Instead, simple leverage.

Think of an axe as compared to a machete. An axe has a center of percussion very near the center of balance, so it puts the sweet spot right at the axe head. If you've ever chopped wood and missed the strike, hitting the handle instead, you've felt that horrible pull of the handle as it tries to pivot around the axe head. On a machete, if you miss and make contact with the middle of the blade, it doesn't sting the same way - it's just an ineffective cut. None of this has anything to do with harmonics.

So we're back to the sweet spot and the CoP. Again, those two are nearly the same for a baseball bat or an axe, but at opposite ends on a sword or machete. So what's happening with a sword? It has nothing to do with the CoP, and everything to do with the *swing arc*. This is a term common in golf, and refers to the path that the furthest end of whatever we swing takes. That furthest end is moving faster than the close end, and therefore has much more power. This can be measured in pounds per square inch, and it is well known that when you choke up on a bat you put less power to the ball because you have shortened your swing arc. The same thing happens when you hit the ball at the true center of percussion. You've neutralized the pivoting, but you fail to take advantage of the full power out of your swing arc.

"Wait a minute. Doesn't that mean that the most powerful part of the cut would be with the very tip of the sword?" Well, you're right, it would be. The only reason that it isn't practical is that it's really hard to keep the blade straight the closer the strike is to the tip. The blade starts to bend out of the way of the impact, scraping in front of the target rather than digging into it.. That's fine for a passing slice, but it's really hard to get good contact for a clean cut. Curved blades accentuate that problem, making contact with the last part of the blade, the foible, fairly ineffective as a strong cut. No, the best compromise between maximum power and maximum contact is that spot between the foible and the middle of the blade.

So, to summarize: The best spot to absorb a blow is at the <u>forte near the hilt</u>. The best spot with which to cut is at the <u>juncture of mid-blade and foible</u>.

<u>Converting a Costume Sword to Fight-Worthiness</u>

You might have a collection of costume swords in your props cabinet that you'd like to convert to fight quality by replacing the blade. Sometimes this is simplicity itself, especially if you are going to pop in a very light blade such as the epee. But there are a few things to take into consideration before you start.

It is almost a certainty that you will need not only a new blade but also a new pommel. The old pommel is probably made of brass, so will have to be replaced. Why? Because under the strain of swordplay, the pommel will loosen quickly, so naturally the pommel will have to be squeezed down harder and more often. Brass is soft, and the threads will strip very quickly. If you really want to keep the old pommel, there is one way to keep it so long as the new blade has a very long tang. Drill the hole all the way through and through, so that the blade tang can stick out of the top. Then tighten an appropriate steel cap nut on top, cut off the excess tang, and you are ready to go.

If the old pommel happens to be made of steel, you're still not off the hook. It has almost certainly been threaded 1/4 20 [English], while most fight-worthy blades are threaded 6mm [metric]. 6mm is smaller than 1/4 20, so you can't just retap the same hole. If you really want to keep the old pommel, drill a deeper hole and tap the entirety at 6mm. Of course this assumes that the tang of the new blade is long enough to allow for this.

Some swords have no pommels at all, or a hollow bulge called a false pommel. This is where the "center of balance" comes into play. Military sabres, especially, are designed to be swung without inhibition, so the center of balance is usually way down towards the middle of the blade. For a go for broke swing a weighted counterbalance is counterproductive. But stage combat sword work requires that you have control over your sword at all times. If you are going to put in an epee blade, you don't need a counter weight, but anything heavier and you'll need to get a weighted pommel on there somehow and bring that center of balance much closer to you hand. Does a big round ball on top of your sabre destroy the sleek look? Sorry, but you can't fight without it.

Moving down the sword, the handle and grip can cause their own difficulties. To properly seat the pommel, the handle should have a flat, solid top. Many grips on costume swords, again mainly sabres, have asymmetrical tapered shapes. If there is enough wood, you might be able to simply give the top a fresh cut. If not, you'll need a new handle. The asymmetrical handles will slowly collapse under the pressure of a tightened pommel, and even the tang can begin to bend inside the handle and crack.

You might also find that the old handle isn't wide enough to support the tang of the new blade. Even though it may look plenty big from the outside, the hollow inside may need to be drilled out in order to accommodate your new blade. This can cause its own set of problems, especially if the wood is already weak.

Wire wrapped grips, especially common on sabres but also seen on many other swords, have to be handled with great care if you plan on using them with different blades. The wire ends are anchored to the inside of the grip, so drilling through the center of the handle shears the wire ends. After that, the whole wrapping quickly unravels.

A seemingly stout guard may not be suitable for a fight worthy blade. The width of the guard opening may be too thin and narrow for the new blade, but carving out the slot may weaken the metal. Also, even assuming that everything comes together, you might find that in tightening the pommel the blade will punch right through the metal of the guard. To forestall this, place a good sized washer on the tang shoulder. This will not only spread out the pressure and protect your guard, but has the added benefit of isolating the blade from the hilt, creating that nice ringing sword that you wanted.

Finally, all of the parts may be good, but the assembly can leave the sword in poor condition. Here are some photos of a sword that was returned to us from a fight show. All of the parts are correct, but when someone reassembled the weapon they made two changes that diminished the sword's suitability for stage combat. Can you spot the errors?

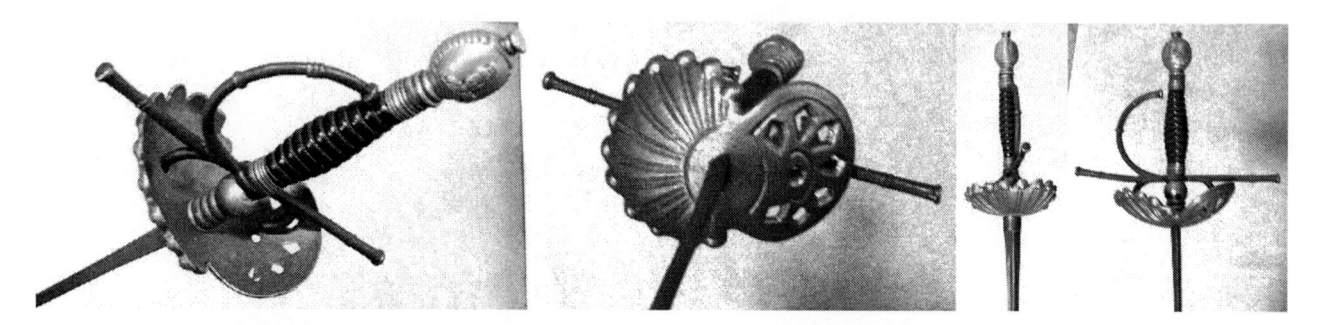

Ok, the first one I have to give to you, because you can't see the blade width easily here. The blade edge on a sword must always be in line with the knuckles of your hand, therefore in line with the knucklebow. Take a look at the blade on the last two pictures. This person mounted the blade 90 degrees off, which would force the actor to cut using the flat of the blade instead of the edge. That's like hitting a nail using the side of a hammer instead of the hammer head.

The second error is easier to spot. Notice the guard. It is asymmetrical, not uniformly round. A lot of people, including that props person, assume that the longer part of any guard should be aligned with the knucklebow. It looks prettier and is easier to wear since the sword then rests closer to the hip. Alas, it is not so. The longest part of the guard must be placed so that it runs crosswise to the knucklebow, thereby protecting the front and back of the hand. After all, the knuckles are already protected by ... the knucklebow.

Dagger Blades

Daggers in many ways are small swords, with many of the same components. Dagger blades differ from knife blades as they are double edged and symmetrical, meant primarily for stabbing another human. Some stage combat blade choices are listed here. Note that the blade lengths listed again refer only to the exposed portion of the blade, not the overall size of the complete weapon.

- Poniard - the lightest of fight worthy dagger blades, it is usually made from a cut-down epee blade. A mere 5/16 of an inch in width, it is commonly cut to between 12 to 15 inches in length. Designed for the quick fencing style of modern stage combat swordplay, it is just flexible and light enough to be the best match for the epee or schlaeger bladed sword.
- Dirk - At from 1/2 to a full inch in width, it is more stout than the poniard, and makes a legitimate visible threat in a larger house. The length by definition stays at between 10 to 15 inches.
- Wide Dagger - Also called the pie or wedge blade, it is the most common look for the fighting dagger. Usually one foot long, starting at about two inches wide and tapering in straight lines down to the point. Smaller lengths are available, but anything less than ten inches makes it very difficult for the actor to parry incoming attacks.
- Main Gauche - Literally "left hand". While the wide dagger blade above was also an all-purpose knife, the main gauche was developed purely for the rapier and dagger fights of the Elizabethan period. Since the sword blade at the time was nearly 40 inches long, the dagger had to be made long as well, and the current main gauche blade is a tapered wedge of 18 inches. Some of these modern blades have two holes drilled at the forte near the shoulder. These serve no purpose; they are merely stylistic flourishes made to give the impression of the "sword breaker" notches that were found on some historic main gauches.

Knives

Knife blades are usually single edged and are primarily cutting tools. Although knives are used as weapons, they usually have a primary utilitarian function unrelated to killing - as opposed to daggers.

Since most real knives, even the cheap ones, are so strong, you rarely have to worry about fight worthiness. If you are thinking of purchasing a knife for stage, you can't do any better than picking up what you need at a garage sale or thrift store for a couple of bucks and then grinding down the edge and tip until it isn't sharp. That makes it as safe as any other prop. As with the swords, remember to check for temper.

There are a number of replica knives and daggers, and those are made of non-tempered steel and have weak tangs. Careful: some of these won't bend if you test them but instead will simply snap in half. When in doubt, pass it up.

Blade lengths come large and small, thick and thin, but there are a few specialty styles that you might be asked to find:

Retractable knives - Also called collapsible knives. Here is a prop that can never be made safe. A retractable knife has a floating blade rather than a fixed blade. Inside the hollow grip, the shortened blade tang is surrounded by a compression spring. When the tip of the blade is pressed against something, the blade retracts into the handle, and then is pushed back out by the spring when the "stab" is over. Well, most of the time.

There are other times when the blade presses ever so slightly along the edge of the handle opening. When that happens, the blade does not retract and the actor gets impaled with a blunt "fake" blade. That is exactly what happened rather famously during a performance at an opera in New York. The singer was not only impaled, but she suffered a collapsed lung which could easily have proved fatal. When examined, the knife was found to be **in perfect working order**. Insurance companies began reviewing the injury rates related to these items and concluded that they are too dangerous to use. Most insurance carriers will not cover injury claims for a show in which a retractable is used, even if the injury had nothing to do with the knife, because they consider the use of retractables to be proof of an unsafe work environment. I consider them so dangerous that when I go to theatres to evaluate their weapons stock, I advise immediately destroying any retractables I find, metal or plastic. A retractable knife cannot be constructed, designed or retrofitted to be safe.

In case anyone is missing my point here, let me simplify. All retractables must be destroyed.

Gravity Knife - Also called a flick knife, the blade has no tang and again floats in the handle. Unlike the retractable, there is no spring inside to push the blade out. Instead, a small spring presses against the side of the blade, gently holding it in place. When an exterior button is pressed, the spring is lifted, allowing the blade to drop into any new position until the button is released. The blade can drop in or out according to gravity (hence the name), or with a little practice it can pop up with a flick of the wrist (hence the other name). Never use a flick knife as a retractable. It is just as deadly, possibly more so.

Paratrooper's Knife - Also called an OTF [out-the-front] switchblade. Just as in the gravity knife, the blade lives in the hollow handle until it pops out of one end, but this knife is double spring activated. A simple slide switch on the side of the handle can both open and close the knife with one hand. Pretty rare nowadays, but since you might run across one and someone suggests using it as a retractable, let me just say: illegal and extremely dangerous.

Switchblade - This kind of knife doesn't have a floating blade, but one that pivots like a folding knife. Unlike folders, switchblades are spring loaded, so the blade can pop open with a simple press of a button. The blade swings out sideways, then locks in place in the open position until a release tab is pressed, allowing the blade to be folded closed. So switchblades need two hands to close but only one hand to open.

The purchase, distribution and carrying of switchblades is illegal for civilians in every state of the union, exceptions being for police officers and military personnel. We civilians cannot legally purchase nor build one with a blade length longer than three inches. The closest thing you can find is the novelty switchblade comb. If you need the look for *West Side Story*, you can always buy the novelty, remove the plastic comb, and drop in a very lightweight piece of thin sheet aluminum to make it look like a knife. It won't last long, but it is the right look. Here's how:

1. Open several times and check the strength of spring. No need to waste your time if the comb starts out defective. Notice that the "safety" slides on its own, so you'll need to put a drop of glue or little piece of tape on it so that you can always open the knife.

2. Spread open the spine of the comb by sliding a strong knife blade in between the spine and the plastic comb. Gently wiggle the blade to pry up the spine. Continue along the length of the comb.

3. Separate the plastic comb from the spine.

4. Cut off the plastic comb just where the teeth begin. Do not remove the bottom piece of plastic.

5. With a pair of tin-snips, cut out a length of very thin aluminum for your blade. An aluminum soft drink can works out fine for this. Use the piece of comb that you cut out as a template for the width, but give the length an extra inch or two to make your life easier. [Some people try to use thin steel for the blade, but the spring mechanism of the comb simply can't take the extra weight, and the comb starts to fail in just a few rehearsals.]

6. Slip the "blade" into the spine, making sure that you are not covering the small hole on one side of the spine base.

7. Close down the spine so as to secure the blade in place. A couple of turns on a table vise work best, because you want a nice even flattened finish in order for the blade to operate easily.

8. Using the tin-snips again, trim the blade so that it has the shape you want.

That should be it. If the assembly went well, the knife should be working fine. If not, or if the knife starts to fail in the future, try the following fixes. Naturally, these things don't last forever, but before you throw it away, one of them just might prolong the life of your prop.

First, keep in mind that the black handle is where the blade lives, so is of necessity hollow. It is also made of soft aluminum, so each time that you press the release button, or even stick it in your pocket, it compresses slightly. Not enough so that you would notice, but every time it's used the handle gets just a little bit squished. It can also get squished as you try to build the thing.

The first clue that something is going wrong is that the blade won't pop out, or if it does, it seems that the spring seems weak. It's never the spring; the spring is fine. The very first thing to do is the easiest - add a drop of WD-40 on each side of the blade right where it pivots on the handle. It can't hurt, and every once in a while that's all there is to it, problem solved!

OK, so that didn't do, so you have to try the next step - opening up the handle. In order to do that, you need to have the knife open, so you may need to hold the release button down and give the blade a good strong pull to release it. Then stick a wide blade into the handle just above where the release button is. Twist it back and forth a couple of times until the handle opens a bit. This should do the trick.

It didn't? It could be that the blade itself is slightly twisted or bent and is rubbing against some part of the inside of the handle. The spine of the blade is made of soft aluminum too, so if you can spot the bend, you should be able to twist it back using a couple of pliers.

If you get it working, but the blade still seems sluggish, it could be that the pivot point is the problem. You've already tried the drop of WD-40, so now get your trusty knife and give a gentle press between the blade and both sides of the handle at the pivot area. Then be sure and use the vise again to squeeze the blade (not the handle) down at the same point.

After that, you're on your own. But seriously, most times these will get the prop working again in only a few minutes.

Butterfly Knife - Something like a folding knife, but the blade pivots on two pieces that combine to make a handle. By holding the closed knife by one part of the handle, the other part can be swung around in a full circle. Swing one way, the blade is exposed; swing the other way, the blade is back inside the handle.

There are a couple of drawbacks on using this knife. All three parts are free moving, so the blade never locks into place, making it inherently weak and giving it a perpetually loose feel. Also, the opening of the knife requires some dexterity, for you have to catch the spinning part of the handle when opening the knife in order to get the blade to stay open. More than a few knuckles have been soundly rapped during the learning process. In addition, its sale is being restricted in many states. Lastly, it has only limited theatrical use. The knife hasn't been around for too long, was never terribly popular, and only seen on the street from the late 1970's to the mid-1990's. Even then it was more of a novelty than a serious knife fighter's weapon.

Polearms

Not many shows use them, which is a shame because they add so much flair to a fight. But if the show calls for some, you might be pressed to quickly find some, or more likely, build some.

Some of the same rules that apply to fight-worthy swords still hold true here, but in a relaxed form. You want to make sure that the head of the weapon is made of a resilient metal such as steel, but it need not be tempered steel for it will not be under that constant blade-to-blade contact that you would find in a sword fight. As a matter of fact, in most polearm fights the ax blade will very rarely strike anything, with most attacks blocked at the neck of the weapon. Yes, some of the points will bend on occasion when you use soft steel, but a simple pounding with a hammer and they'll be as good as new in no time. And you certainly don't need heavy duty framing steel. I've seen quite a few weapons in theatre props cabinets made of steel so thick that the weapons were positively dangerous - to everyone's feet should one of these things be dropped. I'm not suggesting you use 20 gauge sheet metal. The last thing you want is a floppy halberd. But if you stay with 16 or better yet 18 gauge you'll have plenty of strength. No, the big concern with poleweapons is with the pole.

The steel head of the polearm picks up a lot of momentum every time it is swung, and naturally that spot between the steel and the wood gets a little weaker each time. Add to that the act of striking that very spot with another weapon during a fight, and sooner or later the wood is going to snap and the head is going to fly off. You can minimize the chance of that happening in both the type of pole you select and in the way you build the polearm.

You'll be lucky if you can find some choices in the wood. What you are looking for is nice round stock about an inch to an inch and a half thick and about five to six feet long without any weaknesses (knots, cavities). Ash wood, the kind used in baseball bats, is wonderful but very hard to find in round stock. You may have to settle for whatever you can find, but first ask around and see if you can find some martial arts oak quarterstaffs (also called *staffs, staves,* or the Japanese term *bo*). These are great because they can take a lot of abuse, even a certain amount of broadsword strikes, without causing deep fractures. Some might even have tapered ends, which will make fitting the heads onto them much easier.

The second choice is also a martial arts quarterstaff, but made of rattan. Rattan staffs are ideal for quarterstaff fights because it isn't really wood, but a fibrous grass. It is flexible and very light, so it's easy to handle and doesn't hurt as much as oak during accidental contact. And because its structure is continuous fibers rather than grained wood, it will show damage as the fibers begin to separate weeks before actually breaking. Wood poles don't give you any such warning; they just suddenly break one day. So why not always use rattan? The flexibility of the staff is greatly magnified once the polehead is attached, and since the staff is so light anyway the off-balanced completed weapon actually feels heavier. That makes it a bit temperamental to control, especially trying to stop the forward momentum during a full swing. Some people simply never get used to it.

Third on the short list is hickory. It's certainly strong, but is also pretty heavy and you'll be hard pressed to find a six foot length of it. You will, however, be able to find up to four foot lengths at just about any hardware store. Just ask for the tool replacement handles. (Pick up some extra drill bits and saw blades, because going through hickory builds up a lot of heat and quickly dulls the sharp edges of your tools. You'll need some replacements.) Your weapons may end up shorter than you wished, but they'll be stronger than any others.

OK, you've searched everywhere and can't find oak or rattan and you really need something longer than the available hickory. Then all you are left with is pine, specifically, closet rod. All lumber yards and most of the larger hardware stores will carry this in eight to twenty foot lengths. Just tell them what you want and they'll cut it to the length you need. This stuff is fairly inexpensive, and you can work it with basic tools and stain and varnish it to look great, but it is in no way as strong as any of the other choices. Pine grows very fast and leaves a lot of air gaps in its grain, so it can fracture pretty easily. Since it's meant for closet rods, it is also only available at an inch and a half diameter, which is right at the limit of comfort for a polearm fight. If you choose pine, you have to make up for its deficiencies by how you attach the head.

Which leads right into - constructing the polearm, and here again you have to make a choice, although it's pretty straight forward. Either socket or sandwich.

If you have oak, rattan or hickory, you can cut out the shape of the weapon head of your dreams from 16 or 18 gauge steel and have it welded onto a section of steel tubing as close to the diameter of the pole you have chosen. How long should the tube be? It doesn't really matter, for the stress point is always going to be at the point at which the wood slips into the steel. Once you have welded the polehead sheet onto the tubing, just drill the tube and pole through and through and pop in a nut and bolt to hold everything in place.

What's that you say? You can cut out the metal but you don't have a way of welding it onto a tube? Then you'll need to use the sandwich method, which is also what you'll need to do if you are using pine closet rod. Before you cut out the weapon head, add a long "tongue" or tang to the outline. This is the part of the blade that will live inside the pole. Once you have the head cut out, you'll need to run the wooden pole lengthwise through a table saw. Not the entire length, just enough so you can fit the tang into the slot. Fit it in, drill several holes (at least three) and bolt the assembly in place. This should be fairly strong, at least as strong as is possible with whatever wood you've found.

But wait, you say, *why can't I use a socket on the pine pole?* You actually can if you provide a way to dissipate the lateral stress from that one point at the bottom of the socket. The only way to do that is to weld some flat steel straps on either side of the socket that can travel about three feet down the length of the pole. Drill five or six holes through what is in effect a reverse sandwich and each bolt therein should alleviate some of the stress on that pole. But you've also added more weight to the overall weapon and made it pretty thick along half of its length, making it much harder to wield.

Found Objects

Simple props that are not normally recognized as weapons may find their way into the fight, and when that happens they are referred to as found objects. Sometimes in a brawl it's fun to have a nearby object used, or perhaps, as in *The Miracle Worker*, the object at hand is used to lash out at someone. Nothing against the props or the people who have provided or built them, but the odds are that at first it will not be up to the stress of being used in a fight, so must be reinforced for stage combat use. It is impossible to make an exhaustive list, but what follows are some examples of some found objects required for various productions.

The example from *The Miracle Worker* is a good one, for Helen strikes Ann with the doll with which she has been playing. The doll required for historical accuracy has a ceramic head sewn onto the fabric body. Well obviously you can't really hit someone with the ceramic head - you'll hurt someone that way. But even if the strike could be managed so that it doesn't knock out the actress playing Ann, the stitching holding the head on will break after a few rehearsals and the head will soon fly off. Better to use a doll with a hollow rubber head and reattach it to the body using much stronger material such as fishing line. For added strength, make sure that the fishing line runs through the body and all the way down through the legs and into the shoes. Now you have transformed a weak prop into a sturdy prop. [That still doesn't mean you can smack at someone with the doll. Check out the playlist section of the book for some tips on this scene.]

In several shows, a bedpost, picket from a fence, or a banister (balustrade) is "kicked" out and used in a sword fight. Always fun to see and play with, but we have to make sure that the wood is strong enough for the fight. If the wood is uniformly thick, there might be no need for further reinforcing, but most balustrades are thin and won't survive being hacked at by anything thicker than an epee-bladed sword. A few wood chips flying away might be acceptable, but to prevent the wood from shattering when struck by a broadsword or sabre, the entire length should be drilled through and a roughened steel rod or piece of re-bar needs to be epoxied inside. I like using epoxy rather than wood glue, for the epoxy makes a much deeper bond into the grain of the wood and adheres better to the steel.

Tools: crowbars, shovels, brooms, hammers, pickaxes, etc. Most of these items are by their nature very solid, so the safety issue comes in 1) making sure every day that the head is securely attached to the handle, and 2) making sure that the item is light enough so that the actor can control it. Fighting with something like a crowbar seems simple until you realize how even a tiny tap with the thing can snap someone's rib or leg like a matchstick. You might be better advised to try to find rubber or hollow substitutes for certain props. But rubber has its limitations: too soft and the audience can see it waggle during the fight, too stiff and it hurts like hell to be hit by it.

Some of the wooden-handled tools might need some reinforcement with a steel rod running through its length, or perhaps removing the wood completely and directly welding a hollow steel substitute handle.

West Side Story is a great show for found object fighting in general, and a few common sense pointers can keep it and similar shows fun and safe. Make sure that metal trash can lids (directors love them) have the center handle removed, because those things will hit your actor without dissipating the energy around the rest of the flat of the lid, and that really hurts.

Use light weight thin-wall aluminum instead of plumbing pipe, sand all wood to prevent splinters, use no glass bottles, but also no "break-away" bottles because, well, read on.

Break-away glass - Really expensive, but you know that already. Breakaway glass is made of either melted sugar or plastic resin, and is of course much safer than real glass. But what a lot of people don't know is that once it breaks, the shards can still cut you if you step or fall on them. Use with caution and treat with respect. Helpful hint: If you want to use a broken bottle for a fight, scour the local stores for plastic look-alikes [i.e.. shampoo bottles?, soft-drink bottles?], then cut out a ragged broken bottom, sand the edges, and finish by sealing the inside with a painting of rubber cement. The broken bottle is then "found" by a character from somewhere on the set. If he finds it in a trash can, you can always use an off-stage crash box to provide the illusion that the character has smashed the bottle while it is still inside the can, and can then pull out the "broken" bottle.

Guns

Guns can explode. You didn't know that, did you? Even people who deal with guns everyday can forget that, but it still remains true. Granted, it is extremely rare, but it is a fact that anything that fires an explosive can itself explode, including starter pistols firing a commercial blank. That shouldn't immediately put you off of using a firing gun on-stage, for after all we all know that tires and gas tanks and engines explode on passenger vehicles all the time and yet we still load up our families and drive them to the mall. Yet we must remember that although unlikely, it is one of the possibilities that may occur anytime a shot is fired. Risk is a factor in every decision, and it helps us little to ignore the possible.

Every once in a while we at Weapons of Choice get a call from someone looking for "a replica gun that can fire but doesn't use a blank", which I guess means something that can make a big noise but that doesn't actually fire anything. I wish that could be possible, but the few "non-guns" designed so far are very unreliable, difficult to maintain, costly and do in fact have explosives. For the time being, if it makes a sound, it comes from firing a blank, which produces rapidly expanding hot gases leaving the gun. And that is where the danger lies.

We'll get to how guns for stage work in a minute, but first let's get some terminology straight and other confusions cleared up.

What is caliber, or, How can a 38 be a 22?

"... the script specifically calls for a 38, but the technical director said we shouldn't fire anything louder than a 22, but the director doesn't want a small gun for that scene and would prefer a 45. What are they talking about !?! "

There is always a great deal of confusion concerning the choice of handguns in plays, often compounded by the description in the script. Part of the problem comes from the playwright perhaps not knowing much about guns, but much of it comes from the shorthand terms that police departments and armed forces use. Some of these terms have become part of our common usage through the sheer blanket force of movies and television, which ironically have so much power that they in turn affect newspaper and even gun-enthusiasts' terminology.

The result is that most people think they are talking about something specific when actually they are only describing the generic or incidental.

Suppose for a moment that you're helping a friend find his car in a large parking lot. He tells you that he owns a V-6. Then to be more helpful, mentions that it is a Ford V-6. He thinks he has told you a great deal, but he has only described the engine. You still don't know if you're looking for a sedan, a pick-up, a sports car, a van, what color it is, how many doors, etc. Ford Motor Co. used the V-6 in a lot of car and truck models, and right now you need to identify the car by look, not by what's under the hood.

The same problem happens when we talk about guns. If you tell me you need a Colt 45, you have told me the manufacturers name and the barrel interior diameter. I'll have a good idea that you are probably taking about one of two guns that at different times have been described that way, but since there are actually two dozen different gun models that could just as accurately be called Colt 45's, I'd much rather know in what year the play is set, who the character is, and where did he get the gun.

The biggest confusion begins when we try to identify a style of handgun by its caliber. We read "shot by a 38" or "was carrying a 357 magnum", and we attach a mental picture of what the gun must look like. Unfortunately, caliber numbers refer only to the internal diameter of the barrel, measured in hundredths of an inch, and so describes the width of the bullet it requires. The bigger the number, the bigger the bullet. It has nothing to do with the look of the gun or the barrel length. Most gun manufacturers make several different styles of guns, and then will make each style in several different calibers, both English and metric, to appeal to the widest possible market. Since the same basic gun layout might be outfitted with any one of a half dozen different sized chambers and barrels, it is impossible to look at a photograph of a gun and identify its caliber. So where do we get this "shot by a 38" business? Well the papers might be correct in saying that someone was shot by a .38 caliber bullet, and that it logically came out of a .38 caliber gun. The most common of .38 caliber handguns is the revolver that was for the better part of the 20th century the standard issue revolver of most police forces in the United States. So ubiquitous had this gun become for police officers that when they speak among themselves of a .38, they are referring to the gun frame style with which they are familiar rather than the bullet. But there are many completely different styles of guns that can just as correctly be described as a .38 caliber handgun.

The US army issues a side arm to its officers, and after the turn of the previous century had decided not on a revolver (the bullet chamber revolves before each bullet is fired] but on a semiautomatic pistol (the bullets are fed from a clip inside the grip]. The job was granted to Colt Firearm Company. Colt had already made successful pistols for the government since 1836. So which is the "Colt 45" mentioned in the script? The western cowboy gun, or the square frame modern looking semi-auto? Model 1870, 1873, 1878, 1894, 1898, 1902, 1911? They all look different, and are all "Colt 45's".

The .44 magnum is not a more powerful handgun than the .45 caliber revolver, but merely a caliber (slightly smaller that the .45] that was made famous by the Dirty Harry movies. In those films, the weapon of choice was a long barreled heavy frame revolver, so naturally this is the popular image of what a .44 magnum gun must look like. (Actually, .44 magnum ammunition *is* slightly more powerful that the larger .45 ammo at equal powder loads, but this has to do with weight/load/velocity calculations that are very boring, so let's skip that for now.]

Movies and television have also forced the idea on us that a larger gun is a more powerful gun, but again the size of the gun frame has nothing to do with the size of the bullet or how much gunpowder is behind it. A long barrel will make a bullet fly more accurately and further, so would be chosen for target practice or hunting, and a short barrel is going to be inaccurate at even mid-range distances. So it is not uncommon to see massive revolvers that are only .22 caliber, or tiny guns that can fit in your palm that are .45's.

European manufactures use metric measurements; they measure their bullet diameters in millimeters rather than in hundredths of an inch. In order for US armed forces to be able to use NATO stock in the event of a war, the Army has switched to metric guns. A lot of semiautomatic handguns are made for 9mm ammunition, so we hear of a "9" as being a semi-auto pistol. But English or metric, a bigger number means a bigger bullet. Below are some (very rough) equivalents:

$$.22 \text{ cal} = 6 \text{ mm}$$
$$.32 \text{ cal} = 8 \text{ mm}$$
$$.38 \text{ cal} = 9 \text{ mm}$$
$$.45 \text{ cal} = 12 \text{ mm}$$

Note: caliber refers to the inner diameter of the barrel. Well, sort of. Because the barrel has grooves in it, the bullet is made slightly larger than the inside of the barrel. That way the bullet can dig into the grooves and start the spin necessary to give the bullet a stable flight. All of this means that the listed caliber number is actually <u>not</u> the real measurement of the barrel <u>nor</u> the bullet. Take a set of calipers and you'll find some interesting numbers:

common name	barrel bore diameter	bullet diameter
.22 cal	.217"	.225"
.32 cal	.315"	.322"
.357 magnum	.348"	.357"
.38 cal	.373"	.375"

but even here there are differing manufacturers' variations, so that the .38 caliber bullet which fires perfectly in one gun might cause problems in another.

One other part of the confusion in identification is the name of the manufacturer. Popular styles beget popular clones (just ask the makers of Scotch tape or Xerox copiers], so when one company comes out with a popular gun, every other manufacturer follows suit. The common name would often be associated with the maker that made it first or sold the most, but for example an Iver-Johnson .25 might refer to one of several pistol or rifle styles that Iver-Johnson Co. made over the years, so you would need to know what the common terminology was in the year the show is set if you want to know what kind of gun the character is talking about. Wait, it gets worse. The name Derringer can mean either the manufacturer (which made several different styles of handguns), or one of three different percussion single-shot pistols of the 1800's, or a completely different style of two-shot cartridge pistol of the 1900's. Add to that the problem of three different manufacturers trying to use the Derringer name, and then newspaper reporters using the name to mean any pistol small enough to fit in a coat pocket, and it gets really fun.

What is a Gun?

All guns have the same basic layout in common - a hollow tube that has one end closed. If gases can be made to rapidly expand inside this tube, anything solid between the gases and the open end is going to fly out with force.

Anything that burns releases expanding gases, but how do get something to burn in a small area that has no outside oxygen? The most common way to create expanding gases is by burning gunpowder, which actually creates its own free oxygen as it burns. And the most common projectile is one made of lead. For a pistol or a rifle, the lead is in the form of a single bullet. For a shotgun, there are dozens of small projectiles called pellets or simply "shot". Modern ammunition combines the powder and projectile in one easy to load cartridge. Gunpowder is actually a bit difficult to set-off, so a quick igniting compound, called a primer, is set-off first, and that is what really ignites the gunpowder. The hammer of the gun strikes the primer to begin the ignition, and the trigger is what releases the hammer to start the whole chain reaction going. Got it? Finger pulls trigger, which releases hammer, which strikes primer, which ignites powder, which sends lead flying out of barrel.

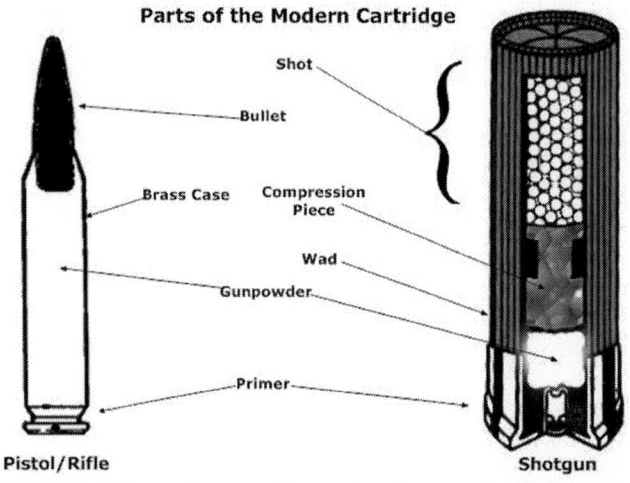

Parts of the Modern Cartridge

Pistol/Rifle: Bullet, Brass Case, Gunpowder, Primer

Shotgun: Shot, Compression Piece, Wad, Primer

Let's take a look at the cartridge, since we'll need to know what's in real ammunition before we can understand what a blank is. If you think about it, a loaded cartridge has all of the components of a hand grenade; it merely lacks a way of igniting itself.

Bullet - The conical shape of the modern bullet allows it to fly through the air with a great deal of stability, especially if it can be made to spin as it leaves the gun. The inside of gun barrels have gently twisting grooves (called rifling) that start that spin, and the bullet actually digs right into the grooves as it is forced out when shot. This helps get the spin going and also seals off the spaces from the grooves, preventing the expanding gases to leak around the bullet. That means that all of the force from the explosion can be transmitted directly to the bullet. So that the bullet can dig into the grooves, it is normally made of a soft metal, such as lead. The fact that the bullet gets carved by those grooves is what lets ballistic experts determine what gun fired what bullet. It also means that a thin layer of lead gets stuck inside the barrel after each shot, which has to be cleaned out periodically.

As I said, most bullets are made of lead, which is very cheap and malleable. Some modern bullets have tips or cases that are made of brass, steel, and even titanium, and some are made of layers in combination. The bullet diameter is the caliber designation, and bullets of one caliber can only be used in a gun of the same caliber. The length of the bullet, however, can vary widely, as can the shape and angle of the bullet nose. These different bullets have different penetration and flight capabilities.

After a bullet has been fired, it will usually be deformed on impact. The recovered deformed bullet is then called a slug. [I love those scenes in movies where the detective pulls out his penknife and digs out a slug imbedded in a door frame, peruses it for a moment and then declares it to be "a 32" or whatever. Priceless, and completely impossible. Slugs are usually so deformed that only intense microscopic examination and careful measurement can determine the caliber.]

Compression piece - For shotgun shells only. Usually plastic "snow" or a hefty piece of plastic with spring-like properties that helps keep all of the parts of the shotshell in place as it is being assembled. It flies out of the gun when fired but has nothing to do with the firing itself. It drops out of the way long before it can reach the target.

Pellets - Once fired from a shotgun, the pellets will all fly in the same general direction, but since their shape is spherical they each tumble in flight, which leads to a scattered pattern. That's just what the hunter wants, a fuzzy distribution so he has a much better chance of striking his quarry than he would if he were to depend on a single bullet hitting a target.

The pellets can be purchased in different sizes, depending on the size of the intended quarry, but the thickness of the cartridge must always be an exact diameter match for the shotgun in which it will be used.

Wad - a stiff piece of cardboard or cloth that compresses the powder and also keeps it separate from the pellets. It also drops to the wayside once the charge is fired. Although used in shotgun shells, wads are also used in some, but not all, commercial blanks. These wads can sometimes hold onto a burning ember for some time after firing.

Powder - The explosive charge. The amount and composition is carefully calibrated by the ammunition manufacturer to not simply explode all at once but to produce an ever expanding force so as to keep accelerating the bullet during its travel down the barrel. It is considered an explosive burn rather than a true explosion. Gunpowder can be set-off by high heat or by an electrical charge. It also requires no oxygen to burn (the chemical reaction actually produces its own free oxygen), making it ideal for the airtight confines of the loaded barrel. That's why a gun can even be fired underwater.

There are two basic types of powder that you will come across - blackpowder and smokeless. Blackpowder is the kind used for over a thousand years, and leaves a nice thick gray cloud of smoke around the gun and plenty of dirty residue inside. Smokeless powder gets its name by comparison only, for any gunpowder creates some smoke, although "smokeless" smoke dissipates very quickly. The residue from any burned powder (called "fowling") is corrosive to steel, which is why guns need to be cleaned after use.

Either style of powder needs to be confined somewhat in order to produce enough pressure to create a gunshot sound. Even a large quantity of gunpowder poured on the ground will not cause an explosion if ignited with a match. You'll get a lot of flame, heat, smoke, and a very strange hissing sound, but no bang. (Yes, it's true: you can outrun a trail of burning gunpowder.)

Primer - A very thin coating of a quick igniting compound is allowed to dry onto a thin piece of metal. When this is struck by or against another piece of metal, the friction causes a spark that in turn creates sufficient heat to ignite the gunpowder.

The hammer of a gun actually strikes the reverse side of the primer, the part that doesn't have the igniting compound. So what really ignites the primer? Cartridges are constructed so that there is a little bit of distance between the inside of the primer and another piece of metal. Dropping the hammer squashes the primer onto the other metal, and that friction is what causes the spark.

Shell - This term gets a bit mangled. It should refer only to the combination of the primer and the outer casing that holds the powder. Shells are made of brass for pistol and rifle rounds, and of plastic or cardboard for shotshells. When a gun has been fired, the spent rounds [minus the bullet] are often found near the gun, and these empty casings are correctly called shells. Because the shotgun shell looks the same before and after being fired, it is common to call the fully loaded cartridge a shell. Less excusably, the unfired rifle bullet/casing combo [live ammo] is also sometimes called a shell.

Down the road, the military designers are looking to eliminate the casing completely, simply fusing the primer and the bullet onto either end of a solid block of formed gunpowder.

So here's how a typical modern gun works:

A round is placed in the barrel, either manually or by the automatic or semi-automatic action of the gun. The hammer is pulled back and then locks in place but under a great deal of tension from the powerful main spring. When the trigger is squeezed, it releases the hammer, which, driven by the main spring, drops down onto the primer of the cartridge. The quick igniting compound is crushed between two pieces of metal and produces a modest spark which in turn sets off the main powder charge.

As the powder burns, the expanding gases dislodge the bullet from the casing and propel it down the barrel. It also causes the bottom of the bullet to expand, sealing the barrel and forcing the bullet into the interior barrel grooves. The grooves have about a 1/4 turn from start to finish in most pistols, but that is enough to have the bullet fly out spinning. The expanding gases also cause a pressure wave which, when it hits our ears, our brains translate into a "gunshot".

If we want the sound of "gunshot" without anyone getting shot by a bullet, we can use the same gun firing system, but instead of using a bullet, we use a blank cartridge. Let's take a look at what a blank looks like compared to the real ammo shown above:

Parts of the blank cartridge:

As you can see, a blank is a cartridge that is only missing the bullet, Sometimes a small cardboard or plastic wad is used to hold the gunpowder in, and sometimes the brass end is merely crimped closed without a wad, and sometimes a false wax "bullet" is used to seal the tip and also make the blank look and act more like a real cartridge.

Without a bullet, a blank is perfectly safe, right? Well, NO! A blank has all of the explosive force of a regular bullet, just without the projectile. That force can do a devastating amount of damage. Let's go through the list:

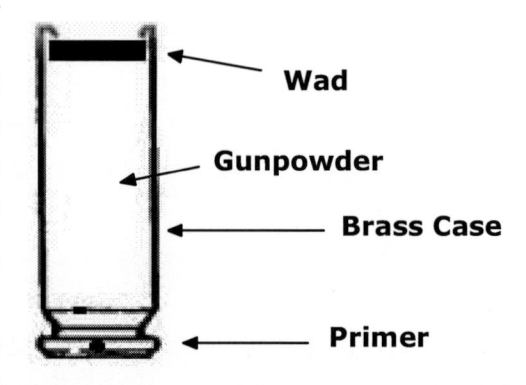

Ears - These things are loud, and there are only so many times that your ears can handle loud noises before permanent hearing loss sets in. And keep in mind that the loudness is comparable to a candle in the dark: from 30 feet away, it provides a comforting glow, but from two feet away can be blinding. Because of that intensity, always remember that firing even a "quiet" blank near someone's head puts them at great danger of permanent hearing loss.

Eyes - The expanding gases are hot, and the louder the blank, the further the gas travels. Not only can it damage the eye by burning, but tiny fragments of unburned powder can be imbedded into the lens. So find out where the gases go and keep the eyes out of the firing line.

Skin - The hot expanding gases don't travel in a straight line, but twirl in a chaos of turbulence. And many stage guns direct the blast "safely" to the floor. The hand that fires the gun can get scorched, and it isn't even in the firing line. The heat can cause second degree burns if the skin is close to the barrel or chamber.

Fire hazard - The burning gunpowder can set stuff on fire, like fabric... or paper ... or hairspray-treated hair. Make sure that nearby objects have been made fire resistant.

Static electricity - It is very hard to get a blank to fire. Something has to strike the primer just right and with a considerable amount of force in order to do so. Even external heat from a nearby fire won't set one off until the temperature gets extremely high - sitting around a regular campfire isn't hot enough to concern those gun-toting cowboys, although a building fire can cause ammunition stored inside to explode. Static electricity is another matter entirely. It can build in unexpected places and lead to some interesting results, as this anecdote will illustrate:

When we at Weapons of Choice buy blanks, we order only small quantities, about fifty thousand rounds at a time. One shipment several years ago of the 6mm variety (tiny .22's) came in the normal way - one cardboard box lined with bubble-wrap, filled with 50 cardboard cartons of plastic tins, 10 tins to a carton, 100 blanks inside each plastic tin. When we opened the large box, we noticed that one of the cartons was singed and blackened. Further inspection revealed that inside one of the tins, eight blanks had fired without being struck, causing a small fire that broke through and melted the plastic tin and began to char the carton. Somehow a static electric charge had built up at that spot and set off those blanks. If the rest of the plastic and cardboard had caught fire, it wouldn't have been hot enough to ignite any other blanks, but the burning plastic would have melted and quickly spread the fire to the rest of the cargo container. This is why blanks can never be shipped using any kind of air service. Although this kind of incident is rare, it can happen, and better it should happen in the back of a delivery truck on a highway rather than in the cargo hold of a jet at 25,000 feet. This is also why you should store your blanks in a fire proof container.

By the way, when real bullets are caught in a fire, the gunpowder will explode, and some of the brass can certainly fly off as fragments, but the lead bullet itself won't go very far - maybe an inch or so. Without being confined in a gunbarrel, the explosive force cannot be directed towards the bullet. The force will always move in the line of least resistance, and that is through the thin brass casing. The lead bullet has too much mass, therefore too much inertia, to be effected by the small amount of force directed its way. Those movie scenes of smallarms ammunition thrown on a fire and then the bullets flying everywhere are a complete fantasy.

Let me tell you a couple more stories concerning blanks. The first is about a successful young actor named Jon-Eric Hexum. In the early eighties he parlayed a solid career as a hunky print model into a starring role as a hunky TV spy in a show called "Cover-Up". His character used a .44 Magnum caliber snub-nosed revolver, which one evening was loaded with blanks. During a break in filming, he was killing time by just sitting and joking with the crew. In the middle of kidding around, he pulled the gun out and put it up to his temple, as though playing Russian roulette. Unfortunately, his finger did squeeze the trigger, and the gun went off. It was not a block barreled gun, so the expanding force traveled down the barrel and pushed against the thin soft tissue of the temple. The skin was not broken, but the force traveled like a wave into the skull. The pressure shattered a thin piece of bone and forced a fragment deep into the brain. There was no bullet in the gun, just expanding gases. He died almost instantly, and the body was taken off of life support a week later.

The mistakes committed, at a network studio no less, are unforgivable. The gun was supposed to have been taken from the actor during any break in filming. But more importantly, the actor had from the beginning been allowed to play with the prop guns as though they were toys. Instead of firing him at the first offense, the producers kept the actor, ignoring the many complaints from his co-star.

The second story is a little better known, but certainly bears repeating. Brandon Lee [son of martial arts superstar Bruce Lee] was in production for "The Crow", and one scene required that a pistol be fired at him. An earlier scene was a close-up of the same revolver being loaded. This is a common enough event in action films, but in this case a long chain of mistakes came together to cause a tragedy.

The producers of the film hired (mistake one) a not terribly experienced person as the weapons provider. He had brought in (mistake two) a real non-modified gun, and had ordered both some blanks for the shooting scene and some dummy bullets for the loading scene. The blanks arrived on time but the dummy bullets didn't. Instead of notifying the director (mistake three) so the scenes could be rescheduled, he purchased real bullet cartridges, removed the lead bullets, tapped out the powder, and then reattached the bullets to make his own - Ta Da! - dummy bullets (mistake four).

The loading-of-the-gun scene took several takes - taking the rounds, loading the chambers, closing the revolver, over and over again ad nauseam. At the end of the day the dummy bullets were tossed aside without a final count (mistake five) and the revolver was put away without inspection (mistake six). If either of these last two safety measures had taken place it might have been noticed that one of the dummy cartridges was missing the lead bullet. You see, the weapons guy didn't disable the primers on those "dummy" bullets he had made (mistake seven), and when some primers are fired they make barely any sound at all. That in fact is what happened - at least one time during the many takes the hammer was allowed to strike the dummy bullets. On one of those, the tiny little explosion of the primer was able to ignite the thin leftover gunpowder residue that sticks to the inside of the brass casing. The tiny puff that this created was just enough to break loose the lead bullet from the already once loosened casing and push the bullet an inch down the barrel. One of the technicians thought that he heard a little strange sound, but decided that, since he wasn't an expert, he shouldn't say anything (mistake eight). So there the bullet rested, like a ticking time bomb. The gun was put away without a complete cleaning (mistake nine), or even a basic safety check of inserting a pencil down the barrel to check for debris (mistake ten)

On the day of the shooting scene, the gun was brought in and without prior inspection (mistake eleven) was loaded with commercial blanks, perfectly appropriate powder charges with no bullet head or any other projectile on it, not even a paper wad. Since blanks can't hurt anybody, the actor was handed the gun without giving him a safety lecture nor performing a "chamber check" (mistake twelve). He was told to shoot directly at Brandon Lee (mistake thirteen). When the gun was fired, the expanding gases of the blank crashed into the lead bullet in the barrel. The bullet flew out of the gun and directly into Brandon Lee's heart.

If any one of the thirteen mistakes had been averted, Mr. Lee would be alive today.

Both of these tragedies happened from using commercial blanks in regular guns, meaning that the barrels were not blocked. But using a blocked barreled gun is still no guarantee of safety, for whatever force doesn't travel down the barrel has to go somewhere. A lot of accidents happen every year with blanks fired, and it always comes down to people forgetting that blanks are not designed to save people's lives. Blanks are designed to prevent holes from being blasted into walls. If you put a human near the blast, that person is going to lose.

Choosing a Blank

Heated words are exchanged ... a gun is pulled out of a jacket pocket ... a shot rings out! And then the audience can't hear the next five minutes of dialogue because of the ringing in their ears. How do you know what blank to use when you need an on- or offstage gunshot?

Although it may sound strange coming from a company that makes its money in part by selling blanks, the best sound effect for a gunshot comes not from a gun at all but from your soundboard. Of course, not your old reel-to-reel or cassette player. Taped sound is hard to cue-up and is unforgiving if there is any technical glitch. No, I'm talking about a good modern sound system that accepts an exact cue search from a CD or internal memory. Such a sound can be generated at the sound operator's touch whenever it is required. With the right equipment a good sound designer can make the gunshot appear to come from any point onstage or off.

If, however, the choice is made to use an actual or live gunshot for the effect, please remember that less is more. Some directors and fight choreographers want very loud gunshots for nearly every show, so please remind such people that audiences need the impression of gunfire, not the real thing. As a matter of fact, most audiences prefer not to be deafened in order to experience verisimilitude. So what caliber should you use?

A brief explanation of caliber: again, it is a number that describes the width of a casing or bullet. In the English or American system it is listed in the hundredths of an inch diameter measurement of the inside of the gun barrel. So .22 caliber is a little less than 1/4 of an inch wide, 38 caliber is a little more than 1/3 of an inch wide, etc. Metric measurement is the same except listed in millimeters.

Caliber describes the diameter of a circle, not the area, so all things being equal a .32 caliber blank is not 50% louder, but over 200% as loud as a 22 caliber blank of the same height. What the caliber also fails to tell you is how long the blank is, so it tells you nothing about the volume of powder inside the cartridge. Ammunition manufactures can make a blank as long as they wish, and filled with as much gunpowder as they wish. For this reason, 32 caliber blanks are actually over six times as loud as the 22 caliber blanks made by the same company.

Some blanks come in volumes reduced from standard, and are called either half-loads or quarter-loads, but there is no industry-wide standard here, so the volume of a "full" load changes with each manufacturer. You would have to know what the standard is for that particular company's brand of blank at that caliber before you can guess what the half load will sound like. A half tank of gas in a Hummer is going to be a lot more expensive than a half tank of gas in a Vespa. A half load .32 caliber blank from Winchester is about fifteen times as loud as a full load 22 blank from Pobjeda.

Notice that the term used is half-load, not half-loud. Having half of the powder doesn't mean that the noise produced is going to be half of the full load, for there are other variables that affect the actual sound that the audience will hear. If both full and half loads are packed into the same size cartridge without adding any filler, the extra air in the half-load acts as a kind of shock absorber to the explosion, reducing the sound level considerably. On the flip side, some blanks use primers that make quite a bit of noise themselves, so going from half to quarter load can end up being not very different at all.

For most theatres, .22 caliber blanks are all you are going to need. This is good because they are the least expensive, and can be found at most sporting goods stores. However, there are three commonly found 22 blanks available nationwide and they have very different sound characteristics, even though they are all considered full-load. Your local sporting goods or gun store will usually carry only one brand.

By the way, there exist both rimmed and rimless ammunition in several caliber designations. On rimless ammo the base of the cartridge is the same diameter as the case. Rimmed ammunition has a base wider than the case, which keeps the cartridge from sliding too deeply into the chamber. Semi-automatic ammunition cannot have an exposed rim that would interfere with the loading mechanism, so rimless ammunition was designed for that use.

Why do you need to know this? If you are looking for blank ammunition for your stage gun, you need to know that the two styles cannot be interchanged, even if they are exactly the same caliber. 9mm rimless can't work for your 9mm revolver.

Some common blanks:

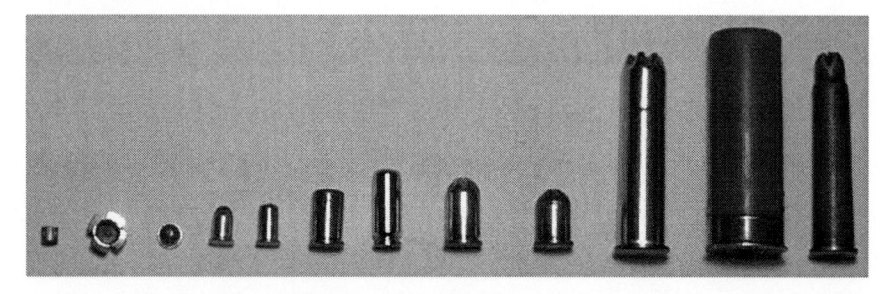

shown in increasing order of loudness: #11 percussion cap, musket cap, 6mm, .22 cal crimped, .22 cal blackpowder, .32 cal blackpowder, 8mm, 9mm half load, 9mm full load, .45-.70 quarter load, 12 gauge, .303 British. The first two are not really blanks, but are shown here for size comparison. Also notice that the full load 9mm is actually a little smaller than its half load equivalent.

Many gun rental suppliers make their own blanks for their own stock, and there are a lot of casual jobbers who hand-load bullets of every caliber for hunters, and can make blanks as well if asked, therefore blanks can be found for every style of gun ever made and virtually any level of sound. But, as you can imagine, hand-loaded blanks are going to cost you. So your first step should be to find out if there are mass-manufactured commercial blanks available. Line up your source early on, for even these will run out on occasion. Blanks that come from foreign manufacturers can experience export delays of several months. American manufacturers, such as Winchester, survive because of military contracts, not the civilian market. So when there is a hot war (for example the prolonged Iraq and Afghanistan actions), all production is focused on fulfilling government contracts. Making blanks for track meets, dog training and theatrical productions is low on their priority list.

Some of the more common varieties include:

• The 6mm Pobjeda and Flobert brands are crimped blanks from a variety of importers, and packaged in a variety of other brand names. They are manufactured in Bosnia Herzegovina and Germany respectively (yes, they will fit in a .22 handgun). At one time they were made by a company called Precise, and they are still commonly referred to by that name. They are only as tall as they are wide, come 100 to a canister, and look like tiny little acorns, which is also their common American nickname. They produce the least amount of sound you can get in a commercial blank because there just isn't room for much gunpowder. This is about as much sound as you can get away with in 50 to 150 seat houses, especially if the first row is close to the actors. The one drawback is the quality of the sound produced - it has only high register notes so tends to sound "tinny".

• The CCI brand short .22's come in boxes of 100, but are about twice as tall as the acorns. Since more powder can be packed inside, they produce a slightly deeper and louder sound. From 100 to 500 seats, this will give a reasonably effective gunshot.

• Remington makes a very similar blank, and availability is a little better than the CCI, but be careful. Remington also makes a full line of .22 caliber blanks made for construction nail guns, but these have much harder cartridge casings that can ruin the inside of a starter pistol or real gun. Avoid the nail-gun blanks at all costs.

• Winchester brand short .22 blanks come fifty to a box and use not modern gunpowder but old-fashioned blackpowder. This gives a wonderfully rich sound with deep resonance and leaves a nice cloud of smoke hanging around the gun for a few minutes. It is considerably louder than the CCI blank, and for houses of from 200 to 800 seats or more, this is an excellent effect. Blackpowder is much dirtier than modern gunpowder, and the residue is more corrosive than that of regular powder, so scrupulous cleaning after every performance is a must. Winchester periodically threatens to permanently discontinue production of these blanks, and one day they may actually do so.

All .22 blanks are rimfire, meaning that the gun has to strike the edge of the primer, not the center. If you have a .22 caliber centerfire revolver (which would be a real gun, not a starter pistol, so you shouldn't be using it in a theatre anyway), you'll need to find specialty .22 caliber centerfire short blanks (<u>very</u> expensive, since they have to be hand loaded and no one wants to handle these tiny things). You can always try to use the rimfire in your centerfire gun, but the misfire rate will be quite high.

Note that the .22's are designated "short". The reference is in regard to the length of the brass cartridge. There are .22 caliber long rifle blanks available, but these are too long to fit into the chambers of starter pistols.

• There is another style of .22 blank that is commonly available in hardware stores. "Power loads" are designed for use in some nail-driving guns and also for a machine called a "dog launcher" (used for training retrievers). These blanks come in different loads and are packaged in different colored boxes to help in distinguish between them. **They must never be used in firearms of any kind, real or theatrical.** These things are not built to make noise, they're built to propel an object with far more force than even a real bullet would. The machines that they go into have barrels with very thick walls to be able to withstand the explosion. Your starter pistol doesn't. The use of these blanks in a starter pistol or stage gun will destroy your gun, and it puts the user and bystanders in danger of being hit by fragments when the pistol finally explodes like a handgrenade. I know that it's tempting to use them, especially since finding proper blanks can be difficult and these power loads are cheap and right down the street. But don't do it. Not even once. I once had a beautiful Remington lever-action rifle that had its receiver destroyed by just one shot from one of these "power" loads. If you have some of these in your collection, throw them out.

- 9mm rimmed blanks are made for the Italian 9mm blank-fire revolvers, and are also accurately called .380 blanks, so these can be used in 38 caliber revolvers. [Revolver is the key word, for these blanks do not fit into 9mm semiautomatic pistols.] They come in full and in half load, but again half *load* does not mean half as *loud*. The half load cartridge is the same height as the full-load, so the powder is packed more loosely. This means that the powder burns more slowly, so ends up being equivalent in sound to the .22 blackpowder blank. The full load is ten times as loud, and in an indoor theatre it sounds like a cannon going off. It seems to work best for outdoor venues or if you really need to simulate a chest-shaking explosion. Make sure that the actor firing the gun doesn't have to hear anything you say for about five minutes after firing. Either that or give him full hearing protection.

- There are blanks made for .38 caliber revolvers, but as these are designed for real guns, the casings are too long to fit into theatre starter pistols. A lot of theatres accidently buy them, and then leave them in the props cabinet for some future props master to deal with. If you have nothing better to do with your time, you can always trim off the excess brass with a small diameter pipe cutter.

- .32 caliber is somewhere in between the loudnesses of .22 and .38 (9mm), and would be a good compromise sound if it weren't for the scarcity of .32 caliber blank-fire pistols. The blanks are made both by Winchester in a very loud blackpowder version, and in modern "smokeless" powder by Pobjeda/Precise.

- Blank-fire semi-automatic starter pistols are only available in 8mm. The great thing about the 8mm blanks is that they are only made for these pistols, and these pistols can only take these blanks, so no real gun ammunition can ever be accidentally loaded into one. The drawbacks are many: stovepiping, jamming, availability, and that the 8mm blank is extremely loud, almost as much as the 9mm - deafening. Half loads are not available, and would only cause more problems in your gun even if they were.

- Shotgun blanks are readily available in 12 gauge, and the sound is deafeningly loud. Because the casing is made of plastic, it is fairly easy to reduce the load. But an especial care should be taken with shotguns. Shotgun blanks are not made for stage, therefore usually have a lot of inert material that comes out of the barrel, which can be deadly if anyone gets in the way. And that inert material is flammable and can still smolder after landing on the ground, with a very real fire danger. Shotgun blanks have another drawback in that they are the same size and shape as real shotgun shells. It's only too easy for someone to inadvertently stick a real shotgun cartridge into the replica and end up causing an awful lot of damage.

When a very strong sound is required, obviously the higher calibers can provide enough noise to simulate cannon-fire even in a 2000 seat outdoor amphitheater. The basic equation doesn't change: more sound means more powder burning and creating more very hot gasses leaving the gun.

As I said, if a gun is chambered for let's say .45 caliber, it can use only .45 caliber, but can fire effectively with a half or quarter load (or even just the primer with no powder at all) of that same caliber - with one important exception. Semiautomatic pistols and their blank-fire stage equivalents (8mm) require the force of a full-load in order to kick out the spent cartridge and bring up the second round automatically. Reducing the amount of gunpowder in the blank by even a small amount will mean that the gun will fire only once and then have to be reloaded manually for each subsequent shot. For several shots from a semi-auto, it's full load or nothing. And full load from an 8mm in a small house is simply too much sound. [We'll talk about the other problems with semi-auto's in a later section.]

One way to get around that is to use a replica made to look like a semi-auto but really is just an empty casing with a .22-caliber starter pistol revolver inside. It looks close enough like a semi-auto, but since it is really a revolver, it can fire full, half or quarter loads without difficulty.

The quality of the sound produced by any particular blank will vary with each show, for the angles of the set will direct the sound in different directions, and the materials used in construction will either reflect or absorb sound as well. Test fire some blank choices once the set is in place to hear how it affects the house. [Always use ear and eye protection when firing blanks.]

What if the sound is too loud? Well, if you're not dealing with a semi-automatic (see above), you can try to remove some of the powder within the blank and it won't affect the performance of the gun. Don't try to remove the primer; your time is more valuable than that, and you run the risk of exploding the blank. Instead, simply dig into the other end of the blank with an awl or large nail to create a hole big enough to tap out the amount of powder you want to, then seal it up again. [Because the casing is brass and will not spark, I usually just bore right into the end of the blank using an electric drill, although this freaks everyone out. I consider this relatively safe, since at the very low speed of the drill the brass does not heat up anywhere near the point where it would need to set off the gunpowder, but then again I don't ask anyone else to do the job for me. I do make sure not to drill all the way down to the primer, which then could indeed ignite from the friction of the drill bit, and that in turn would ignite the powder]. NOTE: if you seal up the hole on your newly reduced blank with hot glue or rubber cement, expect to clean out the gun a little more aggressively than normal, for you'll need to clear out the melted plastic from the works.

Tapping out half of the powder will not necessarily mean that you'll get half of the sound, because the amount of gunpowder is only one variable that determines the amount of sound. For some blanks, the primer itself is so loud that you can tap all of the powder out and still have quite a pop. On others the primer is almost silent. On some blanks the sound volume can be reduced by simply stirring (loosening) the compacted powder and sealing it up again. Experimentation is required, but use safety goggles, ear protection and gloves.

How Loud is Too Loud?

[There is a lot of information below, but I don't want you to miss the main point. Protect your ears! If a sound causes pain, it is causing damage.]

Below are the results of readings we've taken on several of the commercial blanks we've provided. When possible, we tested the blanks in three ways:

First we fired the blanks with the decibel meter at a distance of only two feet from the gun. This way we can get an idea of what the shooter experiences when he or she fires the gun with arm outstretched.

Then the same type of blank was fired in a typical blackbox style theatre at a distance of ten feet from the meter. In smaller houses, we figured that this is what another actor sharing the stage, or even the first row of the audience, would hear. Blackbox theatres are not only small, but the sound is also contained - a lot of the sound is bouncing off of the walls and coming right back at the audience, heightening the perceived sound level.

Finally, we shot off some blanks in a 600 seat theatre with the sound meter fifty feet away from the pistol. We were going for "middle-of-the-house" perception. Thinking of it now, it's a completely arbitrary distance, but there you are. We wanted to demonstrate the effect of the inverse square relationship of sound (if the distance from the source is doubled then the intensity is quartered). But remember that a lot of things affect the sound that reaches the audience's ears, starting with the shape of the set.

As you can see, the further you are from the gun, the lower the decibel level.

Stage Gunshots:

Percussion cap only
- shooter - 2 ft   85 dB
- blackbox - 10 ft   83 dB
- proscenium - 50 ft   72 dB

Percussion w/ 1 tbsp powder
- shooter - 2 ft   92 dB
- blackbox - 10 ft   88 dB
- proscenium - 50 ft   75 dB

6mm (.22 cal) crimped
- shooter - 2 ft   88 dB
- blackbox - 10 ft   85 dB
- proscenium - 50 ft   75 dB

.22 cal crimped
- shooter - 2 ft   88 dB
- blackbox - 10 ft   87 dB
- proscenium - 50 ft   78 dB

.22 cal blackpowder
- shooter - 2 ft   95 dB
- blackbox - 10 ft   90 dB
- proscenium - 50 ft   85 dB

.32 cal blackpowder

- shooter - 2 ft	115 dB
- blackbox - 10 ft	113 dB
- proscenium - 50 ft	93 dB

9mm (.380 cal) crimped

- shooter - 2 ft	135 dB
- blackbox - 10 ft	128 dB
- proscenium - 50 ft	100 dB

9mm crimped half-load

- shooter - 2 ft	96 dB
- blackbox - 10 ft	93 dB
- proscenium - 50 ft	85 dB

9mm primer only

- shooter - 2 ft	86 dB
- blackbox - 10 ft	85 dB
- proscenium - 50 ft	72 dB

Keep in mind that the decibel system is a logarithmic scale, in this case in multiples of 10, much like the Richter scale for measuring earthquake intensity. Something at the lowest level of hearing perception is designated as 0db, something 10 times as loud as 10db, 100 times as loud is 20db, 1,000 times as loud is 30db, and so on. But that's not what we perceive. Compared to our other senses, we're really bad at measuring loudness. We can differentiate between loader and softer, but not in the amount of the difference.

Perceptions of Increases in Decibel Level

"Imperceptible Change"	1dB	about 50% louder
"Barely Perceptible Change"	3dB	about twice as loud
"Clearly Noticeable Change"	5dB	about three times as loud
"About Twice as Loud"	10dB	about ten times as loud
"About Four Times as Loud"	20dB	one hundred times as loud

Since decibel numbers mean nothing without putting them into some sort of context, here are some readings from other sources (measuring sound is notoriously difficult - the same examples from different sources vary by as much as 20 decibels).

Environmental Noise

Whisper (3-5')	20dB
Normal conversation (3-5')	60-70dB
Busy Street Traffic	75dB
Telephone dial tone	80dB
Level at which sustained exposure may result in hearing loss	90 - 95dB
Average television setting	75 - 95dB
Power mower	107dB
Power saw	110dB
Pain begins	125dB
Pneumatic riveter at 4'	125dB
Noisy squeaky toy at 2'	135dB
Jet engine at 100'	140dB
full-load 12 gauge shotgun at 2 ft	158 db
"real" pistol shot (.38 - .45 caliber)	154 - 165 db
Ear drum can perforate	160dB
Death of hearing tissue	180dB
Loudest perceived sound possible	194dB

And keep in mind that gunshots are sound spikes, not sustained sound levels. The longer you are exposed to a loud sound, the more damage it causes. The Occupational Safety and Health Administration has set limits on the level of sound that can be allowed in a workplace, based on loudness and duration.

OSHA Daily Permissible Noise Level Exposure
(hearing protection not required)

Hours per day	Sound level
8	90dB
6	92dB
4	95dB
3	97dB
2	100dB
1.5	102dB
1	105dB
30 minutes	110dB
15 minutes or less	115dB

What does this all mean? Wear ear protection. Ear plugs are pretty inexpensive, but be sure to read the information that's on the package before you buy. Different plugs and headphones reduce sound by different amounts, and they are listed as ER-5 to ER-25. The number after the ER- is the amount of decibels that will be reduced when you wear the device. Make sure that the plugs you hand out are enough to reduce the level of anticipated sound to a safe range.

Notice that OSHA does not allow 120db sound spikes at a work environment unless the workers are adequately protected. Beginning at 125db, a single sound spike can cause hearing damage. Most of the .22 caliber blanks fall below that threshold, but under the right circumstances can still be painful to the ears. How are you treating your actors?

Black-box theatres

Most theatre throughout the world takes place in spaces that hold fewer than 150 seats. These spaces are usually converted from other uses, but even when built specifically for live performance, they are by their nature intimate spaces with close proximity of the actors to the audience. Projection for the actors is usually not a problem, for every seat can hear every whisper. Imagine what a gunshot sounds like.

Obviously we need to keep the sound as quiet as possible, which means at most using .22 caliber, and the softest variety of those that you can find. Even then, the sound can be so "bright" or "sharp" as to be painful for some listeners. So get creative. Perhaps the sound can come from behind a flat, or from the wings, or piped in from the sound system.

Powerful vibrations caused when a gun is fired:

For every action there is an equal and opposite reaction. In a real gun it means that however much force is transmitted to the bullet, the gun and the shooter have to absorb it on the recoil. That recoil travels in a straight line in the opposite direction of the bullet. Now when you hold most guns, the barrel rides a little higher than your hand. When the shot is fired, the gun wants to move backwards, but the grip gets blocked by the skin between your forefinger and thumb. The barrel still wants to travel backwards, so the gun starts to pivot at your hand. If you have a firm grip on the gun, that's what makes your hand jump up a bit after the shot. If you don't have a good grip, the gun merely spins out of you hand and flies over your shoulder (or hits you in the face).

In a block-barreled stage gun, however, the force isn't even transferred to a bullet, so most of that force is slammed into the gun frame. That abuse causes stress fractures to build up in every part of the gun, far more than a real gun would ever have to endure. On very well built firearms [those costing over $450] the individual components are of sufficiently strong material to withstand the constant battering. The less expensive guns used for stage simply are not manufactured to such demanding standards, and can be expected to first loosen and then break down simply from normal use. Some of the cheapest barely survive even one production.

Did a blank not fire? Getting a dud:

You can test a gun, but you can't test the blank you are planning on firing. There are actually a lot of reasons on why you might get a misfire even if the hammer has struck the blank, one of them being that the blank itself was simply defective; another being that the hammer didn't strike with enough force.

If you do get a misfire, check the blanks that were in the gun after the performance. The business end of the fired blanks will usually [but not always] show the residue of burnt powder and the torn edges of metal resulting from the explosion. Then check the primers. If the hammer struck, it will leave a dimple either in the center or on the edge, depending on the gun. If those dimples all look the same, that means that the blank was possibly a dud, and you should throw it out.

But duds are very rare in modern cartridges. If you get more than one misfire during the run of a show, it usually points to one of four malfunctions in the gun, not the blanks. It could be that the mainspring that drives the hammer has finally lost some of its strength and simply can't drive the hammer hard enough anymore to set off the primer. If you look carefully with a magnifying glass you can actually see the difference in the depth of the dimple on the primer from the dud compared to the successfully fired blank. Most gunshops can replace this spring very easily, even from the exotic Italian and German guns.

It could also be that something is gently scraping against the hammer as is drops. A good cleaning and visual inspection for particles of grit should remedy the problem.

The more common cause of misfires is one that plagues revolvers, that of the cylinder not advancing [turning] correctly. Referred to as the "timing" of a revolver, even a slight loosening of the mechanism can lead to the hammer missing the primer. Not by much, but enough to lead to a misfire. On real guns or some of the better built starter pistols this is a somewhat costly repair usually to one of the ratchets responsible for turning and then setting the chamber. For stage guns manufactured outside of the country, the repair is going to cost more than the value of the gun.

A less common cause could be that some of the chambers of the revolver are not permitting the blank to set fully in the chamber holes. When the same blanks fail on first attempt, but then fire normally on the second try, this is almost certainly the cause. What's happening is that as the blanks are loaded into the cylinder, something is keeping them less than 1/64 of an inch from completely setting in. The push of the hammer drives the blank in on the first strike, and probably dimples the cartridge, but that little movement was enough to keep the primer from igniting. What is getting in the way of the blank properly seating in the chamber during loading? Almost always it is due to a tiny burr that has developed on the edge of the chamber hole. It will be very small, so you may need a magnifying glass to see it. How did it get there? Because over time too many actors have dry-fired the gun while playing *Shoot-out at the OK Corral* backstage, and these are rimfire guns. So the hammer has been slowly chipping away at the chamber edge. How to fix? By simply smoothing out the hole with a rat tail hand file (takes a long time) or re-drilling the chamber hole with a drill bit that is exactly 22/100's of an inch in diameter.

There is actually one other cause of misfiring that has nothing to do with mechanical malfunction nor dud blanks. Instead, it comes from purchasing blanks not appropriate for the gun you are using. This especially happens when someone brings in a real .22 caliber gun and tries to fire commercial ..22 caliber blanks. Real .22 caliber guns are usually centerfire, but all .22 caliber blanks are rimfire, as are theatrical blank-fire guns. As the blanks are very small, striking the center of the primer is still fairly close to the rim, so most of the blanks will fire anyway. But the misfire rate is high, often close to 30% failure. When the same blanks are fired from a rimfire gun in good condition, the misfire rate is barely 0.01% - that's right, less than one in ten thousand.

Old Blanks

You might have some half empty boxes of blanks in a drawer somewhere, leftovers from a previous show. How long can blanks last?

There is nothing in the blanks themselves that naturally decomposes. This isn't nitroglycerine, so it won't suddenly explode after a few years. Only two things can set-off a blank if it isn't in a pistol - extremely high heat (such as from an intense building fire) or an arc of static electricity. That is why most safety and fire regulations require that blanks be stored in a fireproof container. They don't want to have to worry about your desk drawer suddenly setting off a Fourth of July celebration when they come in trying to put out a trash can fire. [Actually, that probably wouldn't do it. It would take the entire desk itself to be on fire to create enough heat to ignite the ammunition.]

The bigger problem is moisture, the concern being that enough moisture will enter the cartridge and render the powder useless. Of course, air brings moisture, so for long-term storage, an airtight container with an air-moisture remover would be the best, but a zip-lock bag with a paper towel in it in a dry fire cabinet is not a bad alternative. Check the blanks themselves every once in a while - if they are corroding, you should be able to see the brass turn darker or even bluish brown right at the line where the primer is connected to the brass cylinder. Even then, you don't necessarily have a problem, but you have [slightly] increased the chances of an occasional misfire. If there is a problem with the blanks, that is the worst that will happen, and you'll know that there is a problem during the rehearsal process. When in doubt, fire off a few of the ugliest ones. Still in doubt? Throw 'em out and buy some new ones. Check your local waste disposal authority as to how they want you to handle disposal [they usually frown on incineration].

Don't load your own blanks, or reload spent blanks. Yes, it is possible to do it, and if you don't have anything else to do, you can save quite a bit of money [assuming you value your time at less than two dollars an hour]. But you have also added a tremendous liability on your head. If anything goes wrong, you can expect lawyers to come down hard on anything that smacks of cost-cutting over safety - even if the blank itself did not contribute to the accident. People who load blanks and ammo for a living don't ever want to use spent brass casings. Why in the world would you take on that risk?

Cleaning out the Firearm

Those of you who have real guns know that cleaning them is a long, boring, and essential part of owning one. For blank-fire guns, the cleaning process is a short, boring and essential part of using one. The difference is that real guns must have the barrels cleaned to nearly surgical levels if the gun is going to fire safely and accurately. Stage guns have false barrels, and usually the powder residue has no way of even getting into them, so eighty percent of the work of cleaning a real gun doesn't even apply.

Start by completely unloading the gun and looking for obvious signs of damage and powder residue. Some blanks are dirtier than others and leave quite a cruddy crust of carbon that needs to be brushed or chiseled off, but even the cleaneest blanks will leave a film of grey smoky residue on the gun. So scrape, brush and wipe every part that you can get to without disassembling the gun. WD-40 works great as a combination cleaner/lubricant. If the gun is a revolver, run a bit of cloth through the holes where the blanks sit - there's going to be some residue there as well. When you think you are done, get a clean cloth and some more WD-40 and wipe everything down one more time. If the cloth comes up dirty, you've missed a spot. Finally, squirt some WD-40 into those areas you can't see but that house the moving parts such as where the trigger and hammer pivot. Too much WD-40 is a good thing. Some will leak out overnight, so you might as well wrap it in some cloth or a paper towel to catch the overflow.

That's all there is to it. As I said, short, boring and essential. If the gun has been fired for rehearsal or performance, it must be cleaned before that gun is put away for the night. This is something that cannot wait until morning, for both modern gunpowder and blackpowder residue are extremely corrosive, and permanent damage starts to set in within a few hours if the gun is not cleaned.

Different Stage Firearms And Their Use

But First A Reminder - Firing blanks from real guns.

In this chapter we're going to limit the discussion to those guns either specifically designed and built for theatrical use or permanently modified so that they can neither chamber nor fire real ammunition. Most deadly stage gun accidents come from the use of unmodified real guns that have stupidly been brought to a theatre. Don't ever bring a real, live-fire gun on stage, even if unloaded.

There are many times when that rule is broken, usually when someone has found that Uncle Jim's deer rifle is the perfect prop for the show, but also sometimes when the director wants to see flame or flash coming out of the barrel of the gun. A stage gun can't do that, so the director will override that safety concern in favor of the flash. But a flash also means that some hot gases are moving in that same direction, and that means that it could propel a pebble or a nail if someone through neglect or malice should drop one into the barrel. And debris in the barrel can lead to an even more deadly outcome. I already described two famous deaths of actors using real guns loaded with blanks, both of which were caused by pointing the gun directly at a human. But that is certainly not the only danger. Having the barrel of a real gun plugged with mud or snow or a wad of tape or even Styrofoam can cause a tremendous forward compression of the air space in front of a fired bullet or blank. Before the gases even have a chance to leave the barrel, it can cause the barrel itself to explode like a hand grenade. Have I made it clear that under no circumstance should a real gun be fired on-stage?

Blank-fire stage firearms have different levels of safety, depending on how they are designed. The best will not only have a completely blocked barrel (absolutely no muzzle flash) but also a partially blocked chamber so that a full-length real bullet simply cannot fit into the gun.

What About "Non-Guns"?

There are replicas of firearms that can make a sound but do not use blanks. Known generally as non-guns, they were supposed to be the final savior for all performers needing to safely fire a weapon. For film use, they've been not great but pretty good. Unfortunately for theatre, the results are far less satisfying, and the hype has turned out to be greater than the reward.

Non-guns are battery operated devices that electronically ignite prepackaged squibs within the housing of the replica. Squibs are very small explosive charges used for a variety of pyrotechnic effects. In the case of a non-gun, an electric circuit is completed when the trigger of the replica is pulled, causing the squib hidden inside to explode. Depending on the manufacturer, there might be some flash visible from the barrel.

Because the squib can be packaged using a very small amount of explosive, non-guns are considerably more safe than what had been the film industry standard - using unmodified real guns loaded with blanks. Film makers want the muzzle flash, so have no use for block-barreled stage guns. But non-guns have five big drawbacks for stage:

Ö   They are not safer than using blanks in a block-barreled stage replica. The general rule always applies - if you can see a flash, you are exposed to hot expanding gases. Hot expanding gases push solid things out of their way, and if that is the skin of your hand or your partner's retina, that flesh is going to lose.

- Ö   Squibs are explosives, and most fire marshals require someone to have a pyrotechnic license in order to handle them. Squibs are also more dangerous than blanks when not inside the replica, and explode more easily when exposed to heat or static electricity.
- Ö   Non-guns are less expensive to rent than real guns, but far more than block-barreled stage guns. Non-guns are for the most part financially out of reach for most theatres.
- Ö   Electrically activated squibs are prone to failure at any time, and nowhere more so than in non-guns. All of the components need to be made smaller than for regular pyro effects, for the charges, the wiring, and the battery must all fit inside the replica. So the thin wiring can crack, the connections loosen, and the battery can lose its charge. The non-guns are temperamental enough that they are used only for the moment where the film actor actually has to fire the gun. For running around and general use, identical dummy guns are used.
- Ö   In the event that a non-fire from a non-gun takes place, the actor has no recourse. On a film set, it simply means that they can take a break, fix the problem, and do another take. Not possible on stage, of course, and the actor can't just pull the trigger to go to the next blank the way he could with a stage firing revolver.

Non-guns also have limitations for film. The outside of the gun replica is a solid shell with no moving parts, so there is no way to pretend to load the gun, no brass cases ejecting after each shot of a semi-auto or automatic weapons, no movement of the carriage of a semi-auto or turn of the chamber on a revolver, etc. After an initial excitement, the major studios are turning away from non-guns and going back to real guns. Younger directors will often go with completely inert replicas, feeling comfortable with CGI adding muzzle flash and sound in post-production.

What about firing caps from those replica guns?

We get this question a lot at Weapons of Choice, and I completely understand the temptation. You're working a show that needs a single gun shot, and you have these great looking non-firing props made in Spain. Maybe it's a musket or a revolver, and you know that it's just a prop but it does have a working trigger and hammer. You don't need a big sound for this show, so why can't you just stick a cap or small blank where the hammer is going to strike and turn the prop into a noise maker?

Two reasons. First, the mainspring for these replicas probably isn't strong enough to set off the cap or blank. Second, if by chance the charge should go off, the replica parts cannot handle even the very small blast that will occur. Those weak metals will fragment and fly all over the place. You risk shrapnel being fired into the user's eyes.

Operating Stage Firearms

You will find these next two paragraphs repeated many times in this book, so get used to it. After each performance or rehearsal, first inspect the weapon for any obvious signs of damage as you unload the weapon. "But I didn't load the gun for this rehearsal". **Always assume that somehow, someone has loaded the gun since the last time you held it**. After unloading, take an old stiff toothbrush and scrape away any powder you see. That's right, even an unused gun can suddenly show some corrosion from powder residue that was missed on a prior cleaning. If you spot any rust, sand it off with some worn emery cloth or fine steel wool.

I always advise never actually pointing any weapon at anyone at any time. This goes for real guns, blank guns, toy guns, swords, knives, rubber chickens, any weapon, any time, anywhere. The depth perception limits of the audience allow for a little upstage cheating, and I believe it's important for actors to receive consistent instruction (tongue-lashings) wherever they work so as to avoid Jon-Erik Hexum and Brandon Lee type fatalities.

Revolvers

For all revolvers, always load <u>all</u> chambers before each performance. Goofy ideas such as loading only for the number of shots required for the scene, or loading every other chamber for some unfathomable reason, is just asking for trouble. If the gun is fully loaded and something goes wrong, the actor can just pull the trigger again to get the gunshot.

There are many theatres that modify that advice just a little bit, and suggest loading every chamber slot except the one on which the hammer is resting. The concept is valid, for that slot is not supposed to be the first shot on a revolver. The chamber of a revolver turns to the *next* slot each time that the hammer cocks back, either in single or in double action. With the hammer resting on an empty slot while the actor is just wearing the gun, it can prevent an accidental shot if he should accidentally drop the gun. This is great in theory, but too many times the chamber finds a way to roll backwards before the time to fire, and then the actor fires the gun on an empty space. It shouldn't happen, but it does.

By extension, always unload <u>all</u> chambers after each performance, even if the gun wasn't fired. If some blanks were shot, you'll need to clean the gun. Remember that blanks have a soft metal casing, which expands when fired, so some of the spent blanks may stick in the chamber. Just pry them up with a knife or any strong flat edge.

Single Action/Peacemaker/Cowboy style

These come in 9mm and in .22 caliber, and are all single action guns, meaning that you can't just pull the trigger to get the hammer moving. On the plus side, it allowed gunslingers to twirl the guns, as the pressure on the trigger wouldn't cock the hammer. But don't let your actors twirl the guns. They will drop them and break them. They really will; they're actors.

√   Loading - These guns can be loaded in one of two ways:

The quickest is to simply locate the chamber door on the right side of the gun, behind the chamber and forward of the hammer, and swing it down to the open position. Pull the hammer back to the first "click" (half-cock), which allows the chamber to spin freely, and then simply insert a blank into each empty chamber slot. Unloading is the same, of course, but you'll notice that most of these guns have an ejection rod located beneath the barrel, allowing you to help push out the fired cartridges. These ejection rods are rather weak, and some of the spent blanks can get jammed in the chamber, so you may need to jimmy the blank up with a knife edge first.

The other method is to completely remove the chamber from the frame for loading and unloading. There is a small axis pin release button located on the left side of the frame, just in front of the chamber. Push this button and you'll be able to pull the central axis pin forward. Remove it completely from the frame. Open the side chamber door on the right side of the frame and swing it down. The chamber can then simply roll out of the right side of the gun. You might have to pull the hammer back just a touch so that the firing pin will clear the chamber, but don't pull back too far or it will block the release of the chamber and possibly damage the working of the gun. When the chamber is out, you can easily unload, clean and reload the gun.

√   Operating - As this is a single-action gun, the hammer must be pulled back manually to the second "click" (full cock) each time before you pull the trigger. It is the action of pulling the hammer back that rotates the chamber, so the trigger doesn't really "operate" the gun, it just releases the hammer. Always keep your finger outside of the trigger guard while pulling the hammer back.

Most people will be able to pull the hammer back using the thumb pad while maintaining a normal grip. Others, with weaker hands or shorter thumbs, will have to relax their grip and ease their thumb around, hooking it over the hammer in order to draw it back.

There is actually one other way to fire the gun - fanning the hammer. I'm sure you've seen this on westerns. The gunslinger holds the gun in the right hand and with the left palm slaps the hammer back as fast as he can, firing off six shots in a little over a second. Is this even possible?

Technically yes, but only on some types of single action Western guns. This is actually a technique that comes from the earlier style revolver - the percussion muzzle-loaded blackpowder style. Since the trigger doesn't do anything except release the hammer after it's cocked, fanning the hammer simply removes the trigger from the equation. The trigger is squeezed and held throughout, and so that each time the hammer is slapped back, the chamber turns, and then the hammer drops down to strike the bullet. As simple as that and as fast as the left hand can fly. Most revolvers built after 1870 could no longer be fanned this way, but some could, so if you see it done in a movie, it's still plausible. But you shouldn't do it with your blank-fire cowboy gun, for that replica just can't handle the stress.

This action is extremely abusive to the working parts of the gun. In order for the turning cylinder to lock in place for firing, the hammer must go all the way back to the full-cock position, but not any further. With the trigger held, you can't tell when that moment is reached. So to be on the safe side, the hammer really has to be slammed back as far as is possible with each slap by the left hand before releasing it so it can fall on the chamber. This stresses not only the hammer but also all of the parts associated with turning and locking the chamber. Within a couple of rehearsals parts will break. So don't fan the hammer unless you are rich and want to buy a lot of these guns.

This is also a good time to remind everyone not to twirl the gun unless it is part of the action of the show. Sooner or later, It will drop and break the hammer.

√   Troubleshooting - The revolving chamber is supposed to lock in place when the hammer is pulled back to full-cock, but as the hammer drops the chamber is released again. Sometimes the chamber moves slightly during that small fraction of a second, enough so that it causes a misfire. Unfortunately, nothing can be done about this.

The center axis rod can be inserted too far during loading. There is nothing to stop the axis rod on these guns from going all the way through to the base of the hammer, where it can interfere with the speed of the hammer dropping onto the blank. Even a slight pressure against the base of the hammer can cause a misfire. To keep this from happening, make sure that the center pin locks into its correct place when loading - when it does, the small release button on the side of the gun will pop back up to its normal position.

The hammer can get jammed in the half-cock position. Slightly depressing the trigger as you pull back on the hammer to full cock will normally free it, but on occasion you might need to rock the chamber slightly back and forth as you pull on the hammer.

Double Action Revolvers

NEF starter

Available in either .22 or .32 caliber, this solid starter pistol is quite simply the finest blank gun ever made. Manufactured by H & R, Inc., but still keeping the older name of New England Firearms, these are made using the same frame and components as their regular real pistols. The tolerances are tight, the parts are strong and easily available in the USA.

√   Loading - Depress the center pin catch (which is a button on the left side of the frame in front of and above the trigger) then pull the center pin (located under the barrel) forward and out of the frame. This allows the cylinder to roll out and drop into your hand. Insert the blanks into the chambers and return the cylinder to the frame. Although the frame is completely symmetrical, it's usually a little easier to move the cylinder in and out from the right side of the frame. The central axis pin should slide right back into place without having to depress the center pin catch. But make sure that the pin catch pops back up when the pin is in place.

√   Operating - This is a double action revolver, so all you have to do is squeeze the trigger once for each shot. Squeezing the trigger requires good hand strength, for the main spring is quite strong. Some of that tension can be lessened by firing in single action, that is to say, cocking the hammer back first with the thumb, and then squeezing the trigger. Most people will be able to pull the hammer using the thumb pad while maintaining a normal grip. Others, with weaker hands or shorter thumbs, will have to relax their grip and ease their thumb around, hooking it over the hammer in order to draw it back. Always keep your finger outside of the trigger guard while pulling the hammer to prevent an accidental firing.

√   Troubleshooting - Since the chamber locks into place for each shot, there's not much that goes wrong with these. However, sometimes the central axis pin is not inserted all the way in, and that can prevent reliable firing. Make sure that the center pin locks into place when returning the chamber to the frame - when it does, the small release button on the side of the gun will pop back up to its normal position.

Every once in a while I'll get a panicked call from a client saying that the gun was working fine, then they unloaded it, cleaned it, and now the gun is frozen and won't work at all. The cause is always the same - the chamber was placed backwards in the frame. It's easy to do, very embarrassing, and if you own one of these things you'll do it at least once in your life. Just make sure that the flat face of the chamber faces the barrel, and the recessed face with the ridge faces the hammer.

Snub Nose starter

This model, whether in .22 caliber, .32 caliber, or 9mm, does not lock the revolving chamber into place, so misfires can happen at any time. The 22 caliber style is made especially poorly, and breaks down very quickly. For piece of mind, have a back up sound ready.

[NOTE: There is a quantum difference between the two versions of the .22 caliber pistols made by the same company. These revolvers, the "Champion" model, cost between sixty to eighty bucks, and with scrupulous cleaning and not allowing actors to play with them can last quite a while. There is another .22 starter pistol, the "Olympic" model, made by the same company and costs less than $50, but is of such poor quality that it rarely lasts more than one production. While the regular snub noses are good for most theatres to keep in stock, the little ones are worth nothing.]

√ Loading - Directly underneath the barrel lays an ejector rod. Tug on this rod forward (in the direction of the barrel) and the cylinder will release and swing out to the left. Sometimes you may have to give it a little shove with the fingers of your right hand. Insert the blanks into the chambers, then close the cylinder by simply swinging it back closed. Don't "flip" the gun closed. You can do that with well built, real guns. This one is neither, and you'll just ruin the advancing sear.

NOTE: The ejector rod itself is double spring loaded and made of several parts, and while loading and unloading can accidentally become unscrewed and come apart, with the very small springs falling out and getting lost. It is a very common occurrence, for naturally one has to pinch the end of the rod in order to pull it out, but you don't have to touch it at all in order to close the gun. So with each opening, the rod can slowly unscrew a quarter turn each time, and then one day the entire assembly flies apart without warning. So take care while pulling the rod, and tighten the assembly every once in a while. If you lose the springs the gun cannot operate properly.

To unload: Pull the ejector rod and swing out the cylinder to the left. Now push the ejector rod toward the hammer to raise the blanks slightly out of the chambers. The brass of the cartridges will have expanded slightly on firing, so you might need to dig out the spent round with a knife edge.

√ Operating - At least this part is simple: just extend your arm and squeeze the trigger. This can be fired in either single or double action.

√ Troubleshooting - The mechanism for locking the chamber in place for firing is so weak that it wears down rapidly, but even when new it cannot prevent the chamber from rolling out of position, so misfires tend to be very high with either model of this gun. Sometimes the reliability of the first shot can be helped a bit by firing in single action rather than double. Very few gunsmiths bother trying to repair these things, especially since, as parts are not imported into the USA, the gunsmith would have to manufacture his own parts. That will cost more than buying a new gun.

Patrol

Although a few of these meaty police style revolvers with four inch barrels were made in .22 caliber, they broke down so quickly that normally you'll only find the stronger .380 caliber (9mm) models still in use, in 4" and 6" barrel lengths

√ Loading - To load the Patrol style revolver, you will need to swing out the revolving chamber. Look at the left side of the gun and you will see a trumpet shaped piece of metal on the frame between the chamber and the hammer (above the trigger.) This "trumpet" slides back (towards the hammer), which releases the revolving chamber. At the same time, push the chamber from the right side and it should drop over to the left. Now simply fill the open holes in the chamber. To unload, repeat the steps, and once the cylinder is out locate the ejector rod, which is an extension of the central axis pin. Push on the rod and it will lift the blanks slightly from the chamber.

√ Operating - Either pull the hammer back and then squeeze the trigger

or simply squeeze the trigger. Most people will be able to pull the hammer using the thumb pad while maintaining a normal grip. Others, with weaker hands or shorter thumbs, will have to relax their grip and ease their thumb around, hooking it over the hammer in order to draw it back. Always keep your finger outside of the trigger guard while pulling the hammer.

√ Troubleshooting - There is not much that goes wrong with these pistols until they physically break down, at which point you'll need to get someone to attempt a repair. Specific repair parts are not imported, but many of the parts are very similar to others that are available for real guns, so on occasion a fix can be done.

Semi-Automatic Pistols

Semi-auto's are by their nature <u>extremely</u> unreliable, even the very expensive ones. You should always have a back-up sound ready.

√ Loading - The blanks are housed in a clip that fits inside of the grip of the pistol, so you have to load the clip first, then load the gun. There is either a release catch at the base of the grip, or a release button near the left side of the trigger. Drop out the clip and feed in the blanks from the top. Look at the top of the clip and you'll see that the opening is tapered, and that there is a plate inside. Press down on that plate to feel how it is pushed up against the tapered opening by a rectangular spring that runs the length of the clip. You're going to fill the clip by taking one blank, laying it flat but offset slightly forward against the plate, pushing it down and then sliding it in until the thin part of the taper holds the blank on its own. Continue with each successive round: push then slide, push then slide, push then slide. As the clip fills and the spring compresses, it will get harder to do, but you should be able to get at least seven blanks in the clip, more on a larger pistol. Then return the clip into the gun by sliding this clip up into the grip.

√ Operating - As with any firearm, always keep your finger outside of the trigger guard until you are ready to fire. Although the clip is loaded, the first round needs to be "chambered-up", or actually entered into the chamber in the firing position. While holding the gun firmly in the right hand, grab the top part of the gun with the left and gently but firmly work it once toward you and then back to its normal position. Don't let go of the carriage and let it snap back into place as they do in the movies. As a matter of fact, never force the action on a semi-auto, but always gently and firmly guide the moving parts where they need to go. NOTE: the pistol is now cocked; if you squeeze the trigger now the gun will fire, unload the spent blank, load the next round and re-cock the gun, all automatically. On models where the hammer is exposed, you have the option of gently easing the hammer down if you don't need to fire immediately, but in order to do that you have to very gently and oh so slightly squeeze the trigger. On these models, remember to pull the hammer back again before you squeeze the trigger or the gun won't fire. Because all of this can lead to an accidental shot, practice this gentle lowering of the hammer many times first with the gun empty.

To unload: simply remove the clip, but remember that you may still have one live round in the chamber ready to fire. To remove this one, gently work the carriage of the pistol back and forth two or three times. The blank should pop out up and to the right of the gun.

The blanks are closed with crosshatched plastic ends. These ends normally just crack open when the blank is fired, but sometimes a little bit melts during the blast and is shot into the blocked barrel. Not enough to see, but over the course of several shows enough to build up inside the chamber and the barrel. It can be enough to cause the blanks to jam inside the firing chamber and not eject after the shot.

When cleaning, be sure to squirt some WD-40 into the chamber and work a bottle brush inside to loosen anything that might get in the way of where the blank has to travel.

√ Troubleshooting - Several things can go wrong, and unlike revolvers there isn't much that the actor can do about it while onstage. Semi-automatics, even the real ones that the police use, are notoriously prone to jamming. NOTE: Always remove the clip before inspecting or working on the pistol.

* Stovepiping - this is where the round being brought up from the clip gets tossed out of alignment and starts to move sideways into the chamber, quickly jamming the works. The carriage will remain partly open during a stovepipe. Very rarely the actor can gently move the carriage back and forth and the jammed blank will release and fall out of the gun, but this works best when the gun is held upside down, and that isn't very practical onstage. Most of the time the gun is simply not usable. It will have to be taken offstage where you can dig out the jammed round with a knife or screwdriver.

* Failure to eject prior round. When a blank is fired, the brass often expands slightly. If it expands too much, the cartridge stays jammed in the chamber. Unfortunately, the rest of the gun doesn't know that, and it busily brings in a new blank that it tries to force into the space occupied by the spent round, further jamming it in the barrel. The actor's reaction is to keep working the action back and forth, which does nothing but make the matter worse. The gun will have to be taken offstage and the rounds removed.

* Failure to seat fully in chamber. You'll know that this is happening when the round goes into the chamber, you squeeze the trigger, and nothing goes bang even though the hammer has dropped. Then, without working the action, you pull the hammer back and fire again, and this time the blank fires just fine. What is happening is that the blank is not seating fully into the chamber after it comes up from the clip. The first hammer drop pushes the blank all the way into the chamber, and the second drop of the hammer finally fires the blank. If this happens more than once, it means that the chamber probably has some debris that is slightly blocking the chamber. Clean it out thoroughly and you are ready to go.

Two Shot Derringer

√ Loading - Look at the right side of the gun and you will see a black latch lever just above the trigger. Turning this lever down and forward will release the barrels. The barrels pivot up near the hammer, so just swing them up and you will see the two holes into which you will place the blanks. Be sure to load both barrels so you won't have to worry about a misfire. I suggest using the smallest blank available, as the gun cannot handle the vibrations from repeated firings of heavier loads.

√ Operating - As this is a single-action pistol, you'll need to pull the hammer back and then squeeze the trigger. Note that the discharge on this pistol is vented to the top of the gun.

√ Troubleshooting - This replica is supposed to fire a second shot by automatically moving the firing plate to a new position after the first shot, but we've found that the reliability of the system on these replicas leaves much to be desired. Treat it as a single shot pistol, but <u>load both chambers</u> so you won't have to worry about a misfire. Sometimes that means that both chambers will fire at the same time, but the amount of sound is still low due to the very small blanks that are normally used in these props. And as the construction of these things tends to be a bit loose anyway, you might want to stick to the smallest blank you can find so as to reduce the pounding the gun gets from the blast.

Lever Action Rifles

√ Loading - The bullets are held in a long tube magazine, which is that long tube just underneath the barrel. Most models will have two ways of filling that. The easiest, if available, is to either unscrew or push the release tab at the muzzle end of the magazine, releasing a very long compression spring rod. Just pull it out and then slip in the blanks one at a time, primer end first. Most rifles can take at least a dozen, some can take over two dozen, especially since blanks are usually shorter than real bullets. Return the compression rod and you are ready to go.

The other way to load is to feed in the rounds, "head" end first, through a spring trap door that is on the right side of the frame. Each new round you put in pushes that last one the rest of the way in, so you might need to save one round as a tool to do the final push for you without actually trying to insert it all the way in. The metal door can snap at your skin if you try to do it with just your thumb.

√ Operating - Don't crank the thing as fast as you can the way they do in the movies. Gently work it down and up <u>before</u> you need to fire. Bringing the lever down kicks out the previous (spent) round and opens up the chamber, pulls the hammer back, and allows a part called the elevator to grab the next round in line. Bringing the lever up moves the blank up the elevator and into the chamber in its firing position. When ready, just aim (left elbow pointing to the floor, right arm parallel to the floor and elbow pointing off to the right) and squeeze the trigger. For the next shot, work the action calmly, make a mental note of where the discharged spent cartridge has gone, and wait for your cue to fire.

√ Troubleshooting - Several things can go wrong, and most are not fixable by the actor onstage. Lever-actions are complicated beasties, and any small deviation from normal can throw them off.

* Stovepiping - this is where the round being brought up from the magazine gets tossed out of alignment and starts to move sideways into the chamber, quickly jamming the works. It only happens during the upswing of the lever. Very rarely the actor can gently move the lever back down again and the jammed blank will release and fall out of the gun. Most of the time the gun will be simply not usable. It will have to be taken offstage and with any luck you can see the jammed round and dig it out with a knife or screwdriver.

* Failure to eject prior round. When a blank is fired, the brass often expands slightly. If it expands too much, the cartridge stays jammed in the barrel. Unfortunately, it's easy to miss the fact that the brass didn't eject and then the next upswing of the lever brings in a new blank that it tries to force into the space occupied by the spent round, further jamming it in the barrel. Again, take the gun offstage and hope you can reach the jam without disassembling the rifle.

* Ejected round drops into elevator. Normally the spent round gets thrown out of the gun, high and to the right. There are times where it gets removed from the chamber, but then gets deflected by the housing shroud and simply drops back into the elevator, jamming the gun with the lever in the fully open position. Trying to force the lever can often crush the brass casing of the spent round and jam it into the works. When this happens, you'll be lucky to even see the round, let alone successfully remove it. Turn the rifle upside-down, give it one last gentle try with the lever action, but be ready to take it to a gunsmith for disassembly.

FYI - Lever-actions were never worn over the shoulder from a strap the way military rifles and other sporting rifles are. It was assumed that someone would either carry it in a saddle holster, or simply hold it in one hand (they are certainly light enough). The center section is relatively weak, even on real guns, so straps must never be attached to these kind of rifles. You would be inviting permanent damage to the frame.

Bolt Action Rifles

√   Loading - The magazine is located right in front of the trigger, and sometimes simply drops out like a clip from a semi-auto pistol, but on other models, especially the WWI Mausers, it is fixed and cannot be easily removed. If it is a removable clip, then loading is simply a matter of finding the release button or lever that allows the clip to drop down (usually right in front of the trigger guard), stacking the rounds one after the other into the clip (they will naturally stagger slightly as they are pushed in) and then pushing the filled clip into the rifle. The gun will not yet fire because there is no round in the firing chamber, only in the magazine.

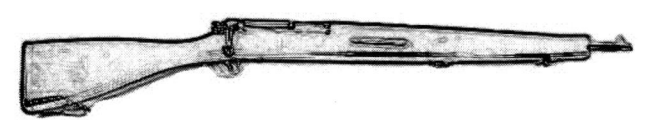

If the magazine is fixed, then the blanks will have to be loaded individually directly into the gun. [Originally, the soldiers had preloaded "stripper clips" that could drop in a stack of bullets right into the clip, but you will probably only have loose blanks.] Pull the bolt (the big lever on the right side of the gun) up and then back toward you. This exposes the magazine. Simply start pushing the blanks flat and straight down until you get usually five or six of them in there. Be careful here, because in order to close the gun you will push the bolt forward and down, and that action can also drive the first round right into the firing chamber. At this point the gun is fully loaded and ready to fire if you touch the trigger. If you want to close the bolt but without pushing a round into the chamber, simply push down the top blank as you slide the carriage forward, clearing the first round. As soon as it clears the primer, you can then remove your finger and continue to push the action forward to the closed position, with the first round resting underneath the chamber, still in the magazine.

√   Operating - Pulling the bolt up and back (towards you) kicks out the last (spent) round, and pushing the bolt forward and down brings the next (live) one into the chamber in its firing position, and automatically pulls the firing pin back. When ready, just aim (left elbow pointing to the floor, right elbow parallel to the floor and pointing off to the right) and pull the trigger. Note that this kind of firearm has no hammer, and that means that there is nothing you can do to "un-cock" the gun once you have worked the action. You can freeze it with a safety, but that really isn't safe. The only way to make the gun safe again is to both remove the magazine (if you can) and completely unload it by working the action several times until all of the blanks have been removed, then work it a few more times just to be sure. Pull the bolt up and back one last time and look in the magazine and the chamber to make sure that it is completely unloaded.

By the way, bolt-actions usually do have a safety switch, located at the very back of the carriage assembly. It's that toggle switch that's right near your nose as you aim. On some models, when the toggle is pointing to the left, the gun is ready to fire; when pointing up, the bolt will move but the trigger is safe; when pointing to the right, everything is locked down and cannot move. But on other models, it's the exact opposite. So you'll need to experiment a few times while the gun is unloaded.

√   Troubleshooting -

    *   Tip jamming. The blanks for bolt-action rifles tend to be long enough and tapered so that stove-

piping is usually not an issue, but they are still just a bit shorter than a comparable bullet should be, so the tip of the blank sometimes slides a little off track when the bolt is pushed forward. The weak brass can jam into the walls of the chamber, and you'll need to pull the bolt back again and dig out that jammed round with a screwdriver or knife.

   *   Failure to eject prior round. When a blank is fired, the brass often expands slightly. If it expands too much, the cartridge stays jammed in the barrel. Again, take the gun offstage and dig out the spent round.

   *   Bolt-action will not go forward. The usual cause is that the rifle has simply run out of bullets. When the last cartridge has been ejected, the spring-loaded plate in the magazine (that normally lifts up the rounds) rises up and gets pushed in the way of the bolt-action carriage. It is designed to do this. In the heat of battle it can be impossible to distinguish your own gunshots from those of others, and a gun that won't close is a good clue that you need to reload. In order to close the carriage when empty, push the plate down with the fingers of your left hand as you push the bolt forward.

Semi and Fully Automatic Rifles

  Semi-auto's are by their nature extremely unreliable, and fully automatic rifles are even worse. Always have a back-up sound ready. [Better yet, use taped sound.] No one in this country makes firing theatrical versions of assault weapons. Even with all of the legal hoops one has to jump through to convert the real ones to fire blanks, it is still far cheaper to re-work them for stage rather than try to build something from scratch. So if you want to fire an assault rifle for stage use, you need to rent real assault rifles. Not only is this still very expensive, but each type of automatic gun will have its own specific instructions and drawbacks, made worse by having been modified to handle blanks. The following is given as a short guide: you'll need to get specifics for the gun you are renting from the provider.

√ Loading - The blanks are housed in a large clip that fits into the frame of the rifle, in most cases forward of the trigger guard, so you have to load the clip first, then load the gun. There is either a release catch underneath the frame right behind the clip, or a release button near the left side of the trigger. Drop out the clip and feed in the blanks from the top. Look at the top of the clip and you'll see that the opening is tapered, and that there is a plate inside. Push on that plate to feel how it is pushed up against the tapered opening by a rectangular spring that runs the length of the clip. You're going to fill the clip by taking one blank, laying it flat but offset against the plate, pushing it down and then sliding it in until the thin part of the taper holds the blank on its own. Continue with each successive round: push then slide, push then slide, push then slide. As the clip fills and the spring compresses, it will get harder to do, but you should be able to get at least twelve blanks in the clip, more on larger banana clips. Then return the clip into the gun by sliding this clip up back into the frame.

√ Operating - Although the clip is loaded, the first round needs to be "chambered-up", or actually entered into the chamber in the firing position. There will be a knob or slide or bolt either on the top of the frame (on Tommy Guns and Uzi's, for example) or on the right side (M-16, Garands, etc.). Grab it and gently but firmly work it once toward you and then back to its normal position. Don't let the carriage simply snap back into place; they do that in the movies, but you can't afford the repair bill. The rifle is now cocked; if you squeeze the trigger now the gun will fire, unload the spent blank, load the next round and re-cock the gun, all automatically.

  Firing - If the weapon is semi-automatic, then each pull of the trigger will fire one round and automatically load the next. If it is an automatic, this process continues uninterrupted until the trigger is released (although almost all assault weapons also have a switch that converts the gun to semi-auto mode). In a Tommy Gun, it takes less than four seconds to empty the fifty round drum magazine. The twenty round clip of the AK-47 empties in only a second and a half. Since these blanks are nearly two dollars a piece, teach your actors to use *short* bursts, or they'll eat up your entire annual props budget in the first week. [M-16's are usually modified so that they will fire in 3 shot bursts with each trigger squeeze, but that's still five to eight bucks with each pull.]

Unloading - First remove the clip, but then remember that you may still have one live round in the chamber ready to fire. To remove this one, gently work the action of the rifle back and forth two or three times. The blank should pop out up and to the right of the gun.

√ Troubleshooting - The blanks for automatic weapons have wax false-bullet heads. They need the tapered shape so the blank will guide into the chamber, but problems can still occur. NOTE: Always remove the clip before inspecting or working on the rifle.

* Stovepiping - this is where the round being brought up from the clip gets tossed out of alignment and starts to move sideways into the chamber, quickly jamming the works. The actor can try to release the stuck cartridge by working the action, but he's just as likely to make matters even worse by forcing the jam. Most of the time the gun is simply not usable. It will have to be taken offstage where you can dig out the jammed round with a knife or screwdriver.

* Failure to eject prior round. When a blank is fired, the brass often expands slightly. If it expands too much, the cartridge stays jammed in the chamber. Unfortunately, the rest of the gun doesn't know that, and it busily brings in a new blank that it tries to force into the space occupied by the spent round, further jamming it in the barrel. The actor's reaction is to keep working the action back and forth, which does nothing but make the matter worse. The gun will have to be taken offstage and the rounds removed.

* Occasionally the first round can't be chambered up at all. Unless there is mechanical damage or some bit of debris getting in the way, it could be that the clip has simply not been inserted all the way into the frame. Make sure that it locks into place before working the action.

Shotguns

Anything that fires pellets instead of a bullet is a shotgun, and there are as many different styles in terms of look and operation as there are rifle styles. The two most common for stage are break-open and pump action.

The break-open is either a double-barreled or single-barreled shotgun in which the gun hinges open at the breach to allow the shotshell to be loaded. A lever or toggle is usually on top of the breach or along the left side, which releases the barrel and allows it to swivel down and expose the breach. The shells are then manually inserted into the barrel or barrels. It is not necessary to use the lever in order to close the gun, but on the other hand don't swing up the barrel while only holding the stock with one arm the way they do in the old westerns. The area of the stock near the breach and trigger is not only the thinnest part, but is also completely hollow, and therefore can crack and break if the gun is rudely treated. Use both hands to firmly but gently close the gun.

For the same reason, break-open shotguns must never be carried with a shoulder strap. It puts far too much stess on the center hinge and latch. Instead, shotguns are "cradle-carried", that is to say, barrel draped over the crook of the left arm and the right hand holding the butt stock.

Break-opens were for many years the bird hunter's preferred weapon, and they have a sport rather than a military look. Rarely manufactured or purchased now, there was a time when every farmhouse would have one as a general defense, hunting, and "varmint" gun. You don't have to be a marksman to do a lot of damage with a shotgun. Those who are proficient in hunting birds or skeet shooting learn that one "aims" a rifle, but you "sight" a shotgun. Aiming requires the shooter to visually line up the eye with the front sight, rear sight, and target. Sighting involves a looser focus, using the single bead at the end of the barrel as a targeting guide but focusing on an area just ahead of the moving target.

Pump action shotguns are the ones used by modern criminals and police, and now also by hunters. These modern single-action firearms can fire several rounds in quick succession. The mechanism is very similar to the lever-action rifle described earlier, but a sliding lever instead of a swinging lever is used, giving the back-and-forth pumping action between each shot. As with the lever-action, the spent shells are ejected out of the right side of the gun. Pulling the slide ejects the spent round; pushing the slide loads up the next.

Most shotguns for stage are not block-barreled, so safety is a concern since debris can come flying out of the muzzle. Break-opens are nearly foolproof to operate, while the pump-actions can jam and stovepipe just as lever-action rifles can. By the way, breakopen shotguns are never used with straps - it puts to much strain on the hinge and locking lever. There were some companies that actually built their shotguns with strap loops on them - a pity since using a strap does so much damage.

Actors tend to be more abusive than normal when handling shotguns, mainly because they want to mimic what they see in movies. With break-opens they want to swing the barrels closed one-handed; with pump action they work the slide as hard as they can. Both will break the guns.

Percussion Firearms

The percussion cap blackpowder gun was the most common form of firearm in the 19th century. The increased reliability compared to the earlier flintlock mechanism ensured its widespread use among both military and civilian shooters soon after its development in the early 1800's. They are still used onstage extensively for period pieces. The instructions and warnings that follow go on for several pages, and after a while you might start to wonder why anyone would go through all of the hassle of dealing with these dangerous props. Two reasons: availability and muzzle flash. Although these are real weapons, there are no federal or state restrictions on selling or shipping them [you're not going to rob a liquor store with something that takes two minutes to reload]. And having a line of soldiers fire off a volley with percussion muskets produces an astounding show of fire and fury.

The firing principle is very simple. When an explosive compound is ignited in a confined area with only one opening, anything between the explosion and the opening (normally a lead ball or bullet) is going to fly out with a heck of a lot of speed and force. So, you pour some blackpowder down the barrel of the gun, cover a ball with a patch of cloth or paper wadding, and slide the ball down the barrel with a rod until it fits snugly against the powder. The only problem is how to set off that explosive charge exactly when you want to.

The percussion cap is a relatively safe way of doing just that. The cap (usually made of copper or aluminum) is coated on its inside with a quick igniting detonating compound. This is placed over a hollow nipple on the outside of the gun, which is connected to a vent that leads right to the blackpowder in the barrel. On pressing the trigger, the hammer strikes the cap, crushing the compound against the end of the nipple. The resulting flash travels down the nipple to the vent to the blackpowder in the barrel. Then it goes boom.

Since the cap has a detonating charge, some theatres use only that for the sound of gunfire. Simply pull the hammer back to half-cock (one click), place the cap over the nipple, press it in snugly, and then pull the hammer back again as you depress the trigger, then gently lower the hammer down on the cap. To fire the gun, pull the hammer back to full-cock (two clicks), and then squeeze the trigger. Practice once or twice with just a cap until it makes sense. Caps have a low rate of misfire, but it is always prudent to have someone ready offstage with a backup sound.

Percussion caps are very thin, so they crush easily. They can be flattened simply by squeezing them with your fingers. In one way this is good because they can conform to the nipple as you load them. If the cap is too loose on the nipple, you can just give it a little squeeze on the sides to make it snug. The negative is that it also means that they are not very strong. Pieces of the cap can fly off in any direction when fired.

NOTE: With the hammer resting on the cap, any sudden pressure against the hammer can accidentally fire the cap, so the prudent thing to do is to leave the hammer at half cock as a safety. But then there is no pressure against the cap, so it can easily fall off while the actor moves about on stage. Which is worse: risking an accidental discharge or risking no shot at all? Your choice, I'm afraid. And remember that any "safety" is not foolproof, so the hammer can slip out of half-cock and accidentally fire anyway.

As I said, many theatres go only this far, using only the percussion cap in order to make the gunshot, But that little percussion cap makes a very tiny sound all by itself, something like a very loud snapping of fingers. It is even less sound then those old paper caps on toy cap guns. At least those had a pinch of gunpowder in them. Percussion caps have no powder at all, so the sound is soft, thin, and anemic. If you need more sound and fury, a small amount of blackpowder must be poured into the barrel. However, once you start down this road you are upping the safety concerns, so here is a new checklist:

- Check the barrel for obstructions or debris before loading or firing or storing. A loose pebble can become a bullet that goes through someone's head; a dirt clod can cause the barrel to explode like a hand grenade.
- Always have someone standing by with a fire extinguisher.
- Only load a barrel which is thoroughly clean and dry.
- Blackpowder is sensitive to static electricity, heat, flame and impact, Check your local fire marshal for storing and use restrictions.
- Even a gun with powder in the barrel but no percussion cap can still accidentally fire. The muzzle is always dangerous.
- Wear safety glasses and hearing protection
- Keep spectators behind the gun. Standing to the side of it isn't safe enough.

Only use blackpowder or Pyrodex, never any form of smokeless or modern gunpowder. These guns simply cannot take the stress of anything but blackpowder, which produces a comparatively low breech pressure. There are four gradations of blackpowder - Fg, FFg, FFFg and FFFFg, which correspond to ever finer granulations of the powder for differing uses. 1F is the most course and is used for very large caliber muskets, 2F is used for 50 caliber muskets, 3F for small muskets and most pistols, and the very fine 4F is used only as the pan primer in flintlock muskets. You don't have to worry about any of this, for you are using blackpowder to make noise and not to fire a bullet, so just buy the blackpowder you happen to find. The finer the grade the easier it is to ignite, so the preference is to use 3F or 4F for stage. Most sporting good stores will carry only 3F if they carry blackpowder at all.

Pyrodex is a brand name for a special formulation of blackpowder, and the only acceptable powder substitute that is allowable for blackpowder weapons. It is a cleaner powder, causing less fouling within the gun when fired, but by extension doesn't produce quite the same size cloud of lovely, smelly gray smoke that regular blackpowder will.

Before loading the firearm, pull the hammer back to half-cock and place a percussion cap on the nipple. Then pull the hammer all the way back to full-cock, aim the gun in a safe direction, and pull the trigger to fire the cap. This helps clear away any residual oil or grease which has been in the nipple vent from a prior cleaning. Be sure to clear out the now broken and spent percussion cap, and check the nipple to make sure that no debris from the cap is fouling the nipple opening. Now you are ready to begin loading the weapon with blackpowder. Leave the hammer down on the nipple when loading with powder. This will help restrict free air from entering the barrel and perhaps setting off the charge.

The rule is: powder first, then cap. Never pour powder into the barrel if there is a cap on the nipple.

How much powder do you need? Only enough to create the level of sound required for the scene. Gunpowder is normally measured by weight (specifically "grains"), not volume, since differing manufacturing techniques and even the sifting of the powder during transportation can affect the volume tremendously. So your 30 grains from the top of your new jar of FFg powder might form a pile twice as large as someone else's 30 grains from the bottom of his old jar of FFFg powder. But, since you probably won't have access to a grain scale, you'll have to experiment with volume until you get the sound you need. Start with measuring out one tablespoon and pouring that directly into the barrel. If the powder is left loose in the barrel, it will burn almost silently when ignited, so firmly pack the powder with a ramrod. The verb here is pack, not ram. Finally, slide in a small bit of wadding down the barrel to hold the charge in place.

The best choice for the wad material is magician's flash paper, for it will create a wonderful flame effect as it leaves the barrel, and then disappear completely. Another acceptable choice is gun cotton, but is harder to store and harder to find, whereas any magic shop and most novelty stores will carry flash paper. If there are no other alternatives, a crumpled sheet of toilet paper will do. But the paper will not burn completely as it leaves the gun, so you must have one person on hand whose one and only job is to track the wad and make sure to stamp out any burning embers before they burn down your theatre. Actually, let that person hold onto the fire extinguisher as well. Because not all of the wad may be visible, make sure that person has no other job for the next three minutes but to stare at the area where the wad went and look for any sign of smoke.

Again, do not "ram-pack" the wad. They do that in the movies, but that could cause an explosion instead of a very fast burn, which is what you want. Instead, push and tap the wad several times. The idea is to make sure that it is snug and to remove any air pockets around the powder. This is crucial, for an air pocket within the powder can actually cause the gun to explode. Scary, yes?

Here's how it happens. As I mentioned before, gunpowder doesn't really explode so much as burn really quickly. It happens way too fast for us to appreciate, but when the powder is ignited only the powder nearest the ignition spark begins its burn. This creates expanding hot gases that start to push the wad, and the unburned powder, forward. As the rest of the powder burns it keeps getting accelerated by the expanding gases behind it, until finally the last of the powder pushes the wad out of the gun. This works beautifully because all during this process there is no usable oxygen *behind* the burn, and the gunpowder itself produces more free oxygen *for* the burn *as* it burns.

Ah, but imagine an air bubble inside the powder. The ignition spark starts the burn as normal, and the powder that's in front of the burn starts to move forward. Then the burn hits the air pocket. The flame jumps the gap and starts burning the next section of powder, creating expanding gases both in front of and behind the air bubble. This double burn now compresses the bubble, putting it under tremendous pressure. Once the pressure reaches a critical level, it causes a true explosion, something like a tiny bomb. The explosion moves both ways down the barrel, sometimes blowing off the nipple, sometimes even bursting the barrel. Even if it only blows off the nipple, notice that it will fly off directly into the head of the shooter. So keep the barrel clean and make sure that you tap down that powder.

The last step is to put the cap on the nipple, give it a little squeeze with your thumb and then you're ready to go. Make sure that the area in front of and extending 30 degrees from the barrel is clear of all people, animals, and flammable material at all times before, during, and after the shot. Again, if you have used anything besides flash paper as a wad, you'll need to have someone visually track the trajectory to look for and extinguish any burning embers. All state, federal and local laws concerning the use of blackpowder and explosive devices must be observed, as should all the rules of common sense. Remember that people have died from being hit by "blank" loads.

Suppose you have the gun at full-cock and then change your mind and don't want to fire. Well, you can step back from the brink. Just point the gun in a safe direction and remove the percussion cap, then draw the hammer back with your thumb even as you pull the trigger. While squeezing the trigger, gently lower the hammer downward until it rests on the nipple, then release the trigger. This is an important skill and should be practiced on an unloaded gun until you can completely control the action with no danger of the hammer slipping. Remember, the live charge inside the barrel will need to be fully unloaded before the gun is put away.

In the event that blackpowder has been loaded, but upon firing there is no discharge, sometimes a second attempt at firing will do the trick. [Of course, on stage you don't have that option, which is why someone should be standing in wings with a back-up sound.] If the second shot didn't work, or there wasn't time to try one, remove the weapon from the stage, barrel pointing up, and leave it in a restricted area for at least three minutes. There exists a slim possibility that embers may still be smoldering within the barrel and can ignite the charge at any time. Only at the end of this cooling down period should the gun be unloaded. I used to suggest flushing the barrel with cold water for safety before attempting to unload, but so many people have fouled their guns this way that I no longer advise it. Instead, unload the gun in the reverse order that you loaded it. First remove the percussion cap. Then, using a patch puller, which is a twisted wire that can snag fabric or paper and fits onto your ramrod, remove the wad and then the blackpowder from the barrel. Don't have a patch puller? Not to worry, you can make your own just by getting a long stiff wire and twisting one end until it can serve as a hook and scraper to snag the wad and breakup the powder. Straightening an old wire coat hanger works perfectly. After the gun is completely unloaded, you'll need to troubleshoot to find out why the shot failed before attempting another shot.

Cleaning the percussion firearm

After each performance or rehearsal, first inspect the weapon for any obvious signs of damage as you unload the weapon. *"But I didn't load the gun for this rehearsal".* <u>Always assume that somehow, someone has loaded the gun since the last time you held it</u>. After unloading, take an old stiff toothbrush and scrape away any powder you see, especially around the nipple vent. If you spot any rust, sand it off with some worn emery cloth or fine steel wool.

If blackpowder has been fired, you will need to clean the barrel, which can be removed from the stock, but this is not mandatory and certainly gets you into a lot of disassembly and assembly that is more trouble than its worth. There are many gun cleaning solutions on the market, but soapy water works better than any of them. Use some cloth patches or a bit of sponge or old rag, connect it to a stiff wire or rod, and run it up and down the inside of the barrel with plenty of soapy water. Some water will squirt majestically out of the nipple, which is good because it means that the vent is not plugged and that it is getting cleaned as well. Keep checking the rags or sponge; when it comes out clean, you are ready to lube. If you feel mechanically inclined, remove the side plates and spray the mechanism with WD-40.

Change the wet rag to a dry one and spray it with plenty of WD-40 (or any light machine oil). Run it up and down just as you did with the soapy water. If you think there are any spots that still might have some water on it, go ahead and spray some more WD-40. Spray it everywhere - when in doubt, spray some more: too much is good! It will loosen rust, push away the residue, lubricate the moving parts, displace any hidden water, and generally make life more pleasant. Wipe down the outside, and you are ready for the next performance.

Well, almost. It is still frustratingly possible that the vent is plugged somehow, even if water was spurting from it during the cleaning. I know that it doesn't make any sense, but it happens. So you need to check the vent by blowing into the barrel. That's right, I'm asking you to do something ridiculously against all of the rules and put your lips right up to the muzzle of the gun and blow as hard as you can down the barrel. If everything is clear, you should be able to hear the air hissing out of the vent. If you hear nothing, or worse, you can't get any air flow at all, you've got to track down and fix the obstruction. You'll find information on this in a couple of pages.

Percussion revolvers - loading, firing and cleaning are about the same as they are for single shot pistols and muskets, except of course that the chamber turns 1/6th of a revolution each time that the hammer is pulled back. Also, the internal mechanics of the revolver are a lot more complicated, so that means also more prone to cause problems.

These are still considered muzzle-loaders, although one generally loads the muzzle of the chamber rather than down the barrel itself. When loading, pull the hammer back to half-cock, which will allow the chamber to spin freely. With the muzzle pointed straight up, pour the measured amount of blackpowder into one chamber [traditionally on the right side of the gun], and then rotate the chamber so you can line up the loaded chamber with the loading lever plunger (the integral ramrod underneath the barrel of the revolver) Use the plunger to seat the powder into the chamber, then add the wad or flash paper and repeat the plunging action. Finish by filling the remainder of the chamber with thick grease. Now go on to the next chamber.

"Wait a minute! Thick grease?!? What was that for?" Since they were first invented, one huge danger with blackpowder revolvers was and is that they can chain fire. That's when you fire one shot but the other chambers also ignite. How? When each chamber is loaded a very fine film of blackpowder gets over everything, especially the front, or muzzle end, of the chamber. When the gun is fired, the flame from the burning powder is supposed to travel down the barrel. Nothing should leak out in the juncture between the chamber and the barrel, but there is a very slight gap between the two. There has to be, or the chamber couldn't turn. As it turns out, that little gap is just enough to allow some of the flame to escape, which can ignite the powder in the next chamber, and then the next, and so on. It's very exciting when it happens onstage. Imagine what it was like in the Old West when the

gun was loaded with lead bullets flying out and hitting the gun frame. It was like holding a multi-step hand grenade when it explodes. So filling the muzzle of each chamber with thick grease after loading is an excellent countermeasure to the chance of chain firing.

"Wouldn't all of this loading and whatnot be a lot easier to do by just removing the entire cylinder from the gun frame?" Yes, you're right, but that means slightly disassembling the gun frame every time, and most people don't want to go through that much hassle. If you really want to, here's how:

There is a block wedge on the side of the frame of the revolver, sometimes on the left, sometimes on the right. Its purpose is to keep the frame together. Different manufacturers might build them with slight differences, but usually there will be a small locking tab on the thicker part of the exposed wedge. By either pressing or turning that tab, you should then be able to remove the wedge. That sounds straight forward, but it is usually in there pretty tight, so you'll have to tap it out with a hammer from the other side. With the wedge out, the barrel should slide forward slightly, enough so that the chamber can be easily removed sideways. Then just clean and load the chamber as per the above instructions, except of course that you won't be able to take advantage of the packing lever that is built into the gun frame. No worries; just make your own ramrod from a short dowel. When returning the chamber to the gun frame, obviously you just reverse the above instructions. But don't hammer in the wedge too tightly! Each tap on the wedge not only drives it in further, but also tightens up the entire gun frame. If it gets too tight, the chamber won't turn.

The revolvers share the same danger as the singleshot pistols in that, with the hammer resting on a percussion cap, any strike to the hammer can unintentionally ignite the charge. One way around that is to load every chamber except one, the one upon which the hammer is resting. Normally only five of the six chambers will be loaded, leaving one chamber empty. That way the gun can be carried with the hammer resting on an empty chamber, reducing the chance of an accidental fire.

Operating - As this is a single-action gun, the hammer must be pulled back manually to the second "click" (full cock) each time before you pull the trigger. It is the action of pulling the hammer back that rotates the chamber, so the trigger doesn't really "operate" the gun, it just releases the hammer. It's also a good safety habit to always keep your finger outside of the trigger guard while pulling the hammer back. Most people will be able to pull the hammer using the thumb pad while maintaining a normal grip. Others, with weaker hands or shorter thumbs, will have to relax their grip and ease their thumb around, hooking it over the hammer in order to draw it back.

There is actually one other way to fire the gun - fanning the hammer. I'm sure you've seen this on westerns. The gunslinger holds the gun in the right hand and with the left palm slaps the hammer back as fast as he can, firing off six shots in a little over a second. [It goes without saying that he kills six of his enemies - one with each bullet.] Is this even possible?

Technically yes. Since the trigger doesn't do anything except release the hammer after it's cocked, fanning the hammer simply removes the trigger from the equation. The trigger is squeezed and held throughout, and so that as the hammer is slapped back, the chamber turns, and then the hammer drops down to strike the bullet. As simple as that and as fast as the left hand can fly. But six targets hit with six shots? No, it's not likely that even one target will be hit, for in fanning the hammer the gun barrel is jumping around all over the place.

Also, this action is extremely abusive to the working parts of the gun. In order for the turning cylinder to lock in place for firing, the hammer has to go back to the full-cock position. But with the trigger held, you can't tell when that moment is reached. So to be on the safe side, the hammer really has to be slammed back as far as is possible with each slap by the left hand before releasing it so it can fall on the chamber. This stresses not only the hammer but also all of the parts associated with turning and locking the chamber, and those parts are very small and pretty weak. So don't fan the hammer unless you are rich and want to buy a lot of these guns.

The most common problem you'll come up against is the percussion caps scraping against the frame of the gun as the chamber turns, jamming the works. This can be obviated somewhat by pressing the caps down firmly against the nipples, but the shaking that happens when a gun is fired loosens the caps, so jamming is always going to be a concern. Then of course all of the other problems that occur with single shot percussion pistols can also occur with the revolvers.

Troubleshooting percussion firearms

There are times when a client calls to say that they have pulled the hammer back but now the gun is frozen and the trigger won't work. Most times there is nothing wrong with the gun. The client has simply misjudged how strong the mainspring is and has only taken the hammer back to half cock, not full cock. Some people may need to use both hands in order to cock the gun.

Misfires from a percussion firearm can happen at any time. Since these are usually single shot weapons, a good idea is to always have a backup sound ready, but on top of that you need to be able to identify the cause of each misfire.

Losing the cap is the most common mishap. The cap simply gets loose and falls off of the nipple. Pressing the side of the percussion cap when loading it onto the nipple can help it act as its own clamp.

Cap misfires - Duds are rare in percussion caps, so if the hammer is dropping but the cap is not firing, the problem is almost always elsewhere. Usually it is because the cap was not set firmly against the nipple. If there is even a slight gap, the force of the hammer will be only enough to move the cap down to its correct placement (often simply trying to fire again gives you a successful shot.). If it happens more than once, try the following:

a] After loading the cap onto the nipple, press it very firmly using your thumb. If you are leery of pressing down onto an explosive cap with your thumb, you can always gently lower the hammer onto the cap, and then even more gently press the hammer down with your thumb. This should set the cap nicely in place.

b] If you're still having a problem, check the top of the nipple before a cap is on it. With repeated use it might have flattened just enough so that the cap doesn't quite fit. The fix is simple. Just unscrew the nipple off [difficult] and use a hand file or even nail file to bring that little cylinder back to having straight sides, screw it back on [easy] and you're ready to go.

c] There are times when the cap and the nipple are fine but there are cap fragments from prior shots still stuck in the inside of the hollowed hammer well [the inside of the striking surface of the hammer]. These leftover copper fragments can act as a compression cushion preventing a clean strike. Just clean out the hammer well with a fine pick or finish nail.

d] Far more common is a hammer that has slightly bent out of alignment. The hammers are made of relatively soft metal and are only case hardened, and since the hammer is always exposed it can easily be bent during normal jostling and the occasional drop. Slowly lower the hammer onto the nipple and check to see if the nipple is sliding right into the hammer well. If you can see a misalignment, there is your problem. Luckily, it also means that you can fix this using simple shop tools. All you need is a mounted vise and some pliers. Place the entire gun on the vise, clamping right on the hammer screw. Grab the very top of the hammer with the pliers and using one slow, steady movement just pull or twist the hammer into alignment.

Now if the cap is firing but you are not getting any ignition inside the barrel, you have to look deeper. The causes are many, and not easily visible, if at all, so many times it means going through a series of trials until you happen upon a fix. The cause may be:

a] Damp or oiled powder. When a gun is cleaned it is also oiled, but any excess oil left in the barrel will soak into the powder you load and cause it to fail. If oil [which doesn't evaporate] instead of WD-40 [which mostly does] is used as the final lubricant, it can plug the vent and also saturate the blackpowder. You'll need to clean out the barrel completely. Next time, before loading, be sure to run several patches up and down the barrel until they come out clean and dry. Then run a patch lightly sprayed with WD-40 only and let it air-dry completely (several hours) before attempting to load.

b] Double loaded barrel. It sometimes happens when a gun had both failed to fire and was insufficiently cleaned out, leaving the powder and wad in the barrel. So the gun accidentally gets a second loading for the next performance, with the original powder still in there getting damp and corroding the barrel. This is extremely dangerous, for just because the first load didn't fire before doesn't mean that it can't dry out enough to fire in the future, and if it has a double load, the barrel can rupture with all of the lethality of a roadside bomb. One way to prevent this from happening is to have a stick or ramrod used as a "dry measure". Before loading, drop in the stick and mark the first part visible as it sticks out of the barrel. After firing but before cleaning, drop in the stick and see if it goes to the same level. If it sticks out further, you still have a loaded gun that must be completely cleared out before cleaning. Another way to prevent this from happening is by blowing through the barrel to check for blockage.

c] A plugged nipple vent can keep the spark created by the cap from making its way to the powder charge. Unscrew and remove the nipple and hold it up to the light. You should be able to see a pinpoint of light shining through. If you don't, you'll need to pick through the opening, and this is tough because the opening is thinner than that made by the average safety pin. Sometimes I find it easier to simply drill through it using a very fine drill bit, but be gentle. I've broken many a drill bit this way. On the plus side, it's a great opportunity to make that tiny opening two or three times the original size, which almost eradicates any future nipple fouling. [WARNING: drilling out the nipple must never be done on a gun that will later be used for firing a ball or bullet. When a barrel is loaded with a lead ball, the back pressure is tremendous and much of the flame can travel back up through the opened vent, towards the shooter's face. This in turn can cause the hammer to fly back or even fly off.]

d] Of course insufficient powder in the barrel can also cause a misfire. With not enough powder, the wad drops down to a level right at or below the vent, so the spark only strikes the wad but not the powder. Different guns have different barrel lengths, of course, but also different distances between the vent and the very bottom, or breech end. Using your dry measure stick (or ramrod) on the outside and inside should give you an idea of the distance that needs to be filled with powder so that the spark has a good chance to ignite it.

e] One last horrible spot that can give you a problem is the space in between the nipple and barrel, that sideways channel that connects the two. I've had guns where I've cleaned the barrel, drilled out the nipple, and then I can blow through easily, but when the cap fires the powder will still fail to ignite. Invariably there will be some crud inside that little side vent that lets air through easily enough but prevents the spark from reaching the powder. If your gun has a screw that permits direct access [it will be just below the vent], then no problem. Remove the screw and clean out the gunk. If there is no access, the only thing left to do is seal up the nipple and pour some

WD-40 or isopropyl alcohol down the barrel and let the gun stand overnight. If you're lucky, when you remove the nipple and blow through, the gunk should pop out.

Flintlock firearms

"No recruit is to be dismissed from the drill until he is so expert with his firelock, as to load and fire 15 times in 3 minutes and three quarters."

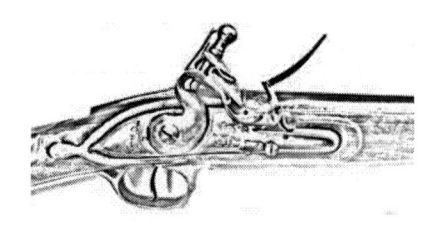

From an old military paper of the American Colonies dated 1768. If we work out the math, we can get an idea of just how quickly a soldier was expected to be able to reload his musket. This rapid rate of fire is one shot every 16 seconds. To be fair, this was for drill work, and probably impossible to replicate on the battlefield, but still helps us reflect that in those days they depended far more on the heavy volume of fire rather than accuracy. Thus a battle charge involving one regiment of 500 men on each side would mean that the attacking force would have to suffer the effects of 1000 bullets in two volleys in the 20 or 25 seconds that it would take them to charge less than 100 yards. The second volley would be at a range of about 30 yards. It must be remembered that the training was for firing in volleys at a compact and solid mass of men, a perfect target for rapid musket fire. Speed was everything!

On the other hand, a soldier might find it advantageous to learn how to load his rifle more carefully for shooting game to augment his rations, in which case a reload could take as long as three minutes. The basic method of flintlock musket fire (with variations for combat conditions in parenthesis) is as follows:

1) Wipe the bore clean of oil by putting a small quantity of primer powder in the pan and firing without loading anything in the barrel (skip this step).
2) Carefully turn the powder horn several times end over end to evenly mix the blackpowder (simply uncap powder horn with teeth and splash some powder into the pan; yes, you're right, if there are still some loose sparks in the barrel, the pan will now ignite in your face).
3) Place butt of musket on left foot and clean out barrel of possible sparks and fouling from previous shots by wiping the bore with a moist patch using the ramrod with a cleaning swab on the end (skip this step).
4) Place butt of musket on left foot and measure an exact quantity of blackpowder into measuring tin, recap powder horn, then pour powder down the barrel (pour an approximate amount of powder straight into barrel. Recap horn with your teeth).
5) Get a canvass patch and wipe it with a small amount of thick grease. Place musket ball in center and form a small sack shape (spit on a patch and wrap a ball with it).
6) Place patched ball in barrel so that ball is flush with barrel end and cut-off excess patch material with knife until patch is also flush with barrel end (skip this step).
7) Gently, with just two fingers and thumb, use the ramrod to slide the patched ball until it has reached the end of the barrel and is sitting against the blackpowder charge. NEVER pack the powder. (Ram the ball down the barrel)
8) Gently bring the musket to solar plexus level and pour a small amount of very fine grade (FFFFg) powder into the priming pan, then close the frizzen and then close the primer horn (skip this 'cause you don't bother with a separate priming horn and you already took care of the priming in step 2, providing you still have fingers and a face).

9) With musket pointed towards the target, pull the flintlock back to "full cock", or two "clicks" (the same except that the musket is held close to the body and pointing straight up).
10) Raise the musket to shoulder level and fire when ready (when ordered to and not a second before).

The most dangerous part of the rapid fire drill shown in parenthesis is that it violates the cardinal rule of muzzleloading - load the barrel first, then the primer. But it does reduce the number of positions that the musket must be held, and therefore speeds up re-firing considerably.

Most armies finally eliminated the need for several containers and powder horns by making pre-loaded charges. At first linen and later paper cartridges containing one ball and one load of blackpowder, the cartridge itself serving as the wadding. For those soldiers, they had no need for the powder horn or pouches for the lead balls and wadding, but would need either cartridge boxes on the belt or the individual cartridges hung bandoleer style on a sash.

With pre-loaded cartridges, the steps are reduced considerably:
1) Place butt of musket on left foot, hold barrel with left hand and remove one paper cartridge with the right.
2) The paper cartridge has the ball on one end and the powder in the rest. The end with the powder is tied-off. Tear that end off with your teeth and pour the powder down the muzzle.
3) Since the ball is already half-wrapped in the paper, stick the whole thing in the barrel. Because of the excess paper, it will stick just inside the muzzle opening.
4) Remove the ramrod and use it to shove the ball all the way down the barrel.
5) Return the ramrod to its place underneath the barrel.
6) Raise the musket with the right hand and have the muzzle pointed towards the target, as you pull the striker (hammer) back to "half cock", or one "click", and flick open the frizzen (strike plate).
7) With the left hand, pull out the primer flask and pour a small amount into the priming pan, then snap the frizzen closed. (The primer flask is filled only with very fine gunpowder and has a simple spring release spout, allowing for one-handed use.)
10) Raise the musket to shoulder level (ready), pull the striker all the way back to full-cock as you bring the musket up to eye level (aim), and then squeeze the trigger (fire).

This brings back the couple of previously eliminated musket positions, but made for faster loading overall.

As you can imagine, combat conditions led to many accidental firings and misfirings, and sometimes outright explosions of the men's powder horns or cartridges. With no time given to clean out the barrel between firings or even to allow the barrels to cool off, the muskets were close to ticking time bombs during a pitch battle. But generals usually assumed a 20% casualty rate on a victorious battle anyway, so they weren't too concerned with a few "technical losses" along the way.

Realistically, a lieutenant would give the order to fire every 20 seconds, but a soldier could only expect to hit an individual target at distances of less than 80 yards. (That's why, during the American Revolution, the early militia was told not to "fire until you see the whites of their eyes". The farmer-soldiers of the first battles had their own hunting rifle-barreled muskets, so could only fire about once every one or two minutes. They had an advantage in accuracy and distance, but could not expect to effectively fire in volley, nor to reload quickly. Each shot had to count, and then they had to run like hell for a couple hundred yards until they could stop again to reload and shoot. They weren't being crafty; they were making up for a lack of training and inappropriate weaponry.)

It would be most unlikely that a soldier would have his weapon loaded for an extended period of time when off of the battlefield, the exception being limited for the hour or two of guard duty. What with the powder becoming damp, the primer settling or seeping out, the ball dropping out of position, and the danger of unexpected fire, muskets and pistols were best left unloaded until the last possible moment.

As with any weapon, always assume that it is actually loaded at all times and never point it at or in the direction of a human or other animal. Never place your body or face over the barrel end of the musket and never place your finger inside the barrel, which not only is stupid but also deposits salts and oils, which will rust and foul the weapon.

If you must actually fire a weapon on stage, know that even without a bullet a blank charge is still a loaded gun. When the musket fires, a lot of force comes out of that barrel, enough to kill. Always treat a misfire as a potential time bomb. If a failure to fire should occur, point the barrel to the sky and get it in the hands of the stage manager as soon as possible. Allow at least three minutes to pass before attempting to unload a misfired weapon, and do so keeping the muzzle from pointing at anything you want to keep, including your fingers.

Blackpowder should be introduced with extreme caution to a weapon that has been fired within the last three minutes. (The barrel could still be hot enough to cause an explosion if there are any loose sparks from the previous fire.) Never hold the ramrod with a firm grip while sliding the wad down over the blackpowder charge. If the blackpowder goes off, that ramrod is going to fire into the sky like a Trident missile, and it's going to take the skin from your palm off with it, so hold the ramrod as loosely as you can with your thumb and two fingers. Always use protective eye covering when possible, and at the least, have the actors aim completely away from anyone or anything, and to close their eyes when pulling the trigger.

There are three ways of using blackpowder on-stage for flintlock firearms: pan-only, powder-and-wad, or flash cartridge.

Pan-Only - Often it is enough of an effect to simply put some powder in the pan and none in the barrel, and this is certainly the safest choice. The big drawback is that nothing comes out of the barrel and that the sound is more "poof" than "bang".

Powder-and-Wad - always measure the powder before pouring it into the barrel(start with 1/2 tablespoon and increase until you get the effect you desire), and then "set" the charge by pushing a patch or wad with the ramrod all the way down to the end. If the wad is just a tad oversized, it will hold the powder in place. You'll need enough powder to make a "crack" sound, but never a "boom" sound. The big drawback here is that the wad will either burn or fly or both, and it will certainly come out with a heck of a lot of force. Obviously a safety concern. Flash paper is best choice for the wad.

Flash Cartridge. - Using Zigzag (roll your own cigarette) paper, or better yet magician's flash paper, fill with powder and seal it as if making a stubby little cigar. If packed sideways down the barrel, it will stay in place until you fire. You may need a drop of glue here and there to keep the cartridge closed, and you may need to pack more than one at a time on some of the larger rifles. Crack open the cartridge as you load to let some loose powder spill around the cartridge within the barrel. Magician's flash paper is the better choice, for although it is more expensive and availability varies nationwide, it does burn completely as it leaves the barrel.

Go back to the percussion section for instruction on cleaning a muzzleloader, and for troubleshooting misfires. To those instructions we should add a couple of others that are specific to flintlocks. There is a considerable time lag between pulling the trigger, the pan flash occurring, and then the sparks actually igniting the main charge. Many times it can take a full five seconds, but that's just an average, so be ready for anything. The frizzen (strike plate) and the piece of flint in the hammer must be kept oil-free or you are not going to get any sparks. When you need to clean them, use isopropyl alcohol. And when you do get sparks and it ignites the powder in the pan, the "flash in the pan" can be unnerving to the shooter, for all he sees is a wall of flame erupting just inches in front of his face. I once saw an actor scream in terror and throw the musket out into the orchestra pit when he fired a flintlock for the first time.

Other Practical Weapon Props

Manacles

Old-style prisoner restraint devices rarely had advanced locks, even when the technology was available for other devices. Shackles were usually made by a local blacksmith instead of a locksmith, so the mechanisms were large, simple, and required several turns of a key to lock the devise and then more turns in the other direction to remove the key. The entire procedure was repeated in order to remove the manacles. Other shackles used the equivalent of a large solid rivet to close the restraints, which would need to be broken in order to release the victim.

For stage use, it is better to use a magician's trick-release replica, or even oversized manacles so that the actor can quickly free himself in case of an emergency.

Handcuffs

When possible, stick to using trick release "magic" handcuffs. They look and work like the real thing, but they have a tiny lever that the wearer can easily reach that instantly releases the lock. The key will also work. Most of these trick release models are not built as strongly as the real items, so the actors should be told not to struggle with all of their might.

Regular handcuffs on the other hand are very strong. Most real models can both single lock and double lock. The single lock happens automatically as the cuffs close. It's a simple one-way ratchet and a simple quarter turn of the key will release that. The only problem with the single lock is that the cuff can keep closing, with a chance of pinching the skin or even cutting off circulation to the hand, so the double lock can be used to freeze the cuff in place. An elongated slot on the cuff provides access to a tiny switch, which can be flipped towards the keyhole using the peg end of the cuff key. Once done, the cuff cannot be opened nor closed further. To unlock, insert the key in the keyhole and rotate in one direction to release the double lock and then in the other direction to release the cuff. The first move takes more force than the second.

Modern style leg cuffs are also available with much wider jaws and more space in the chain. Unfortunately, trick release versions are not readily available.

Bows and Crossbows

Although there is no explosive charge in a bow and arrow, please remember that ***this is as dangerous as a firearm***. Although an arrow travels more slowly than a bullet, because of the greater mass, it can cause far more damage. Someone hit with a rubber tipped arrow can **die**.

If you are planning to fire a bow and arrow (or crossbow and bolt) for a show, go back over all of the safety warnings concerning firearms, and then add one more. Arrows are hard to control. As a kid I once shot some arrows in my backyard, using the hanging fruit from a lemon tree as targets. One arrow glanced against a twig - not a branch, mind you, a twig - and the deflection sent it thirty degrees up and over an eight foot fence, landing in a yard two houses away. I don't know how you can really make a stage safe enough for firing an arrow, but I suggest that it begins with building a "safety" zone, a great big angled funnel with two kinds of stopping materials at the end. The arrow can be slowed by something like a mattress, hay bale, or thick Styrofoam, and then will need to be stopped by something like thick plank plywood (not pressboard). Using only one type of stopping material won't do.

Placing the arrow on the bowstring is called "nocking", and when nocking the arrow do so with the arrow pointed towards the ground. Only raise the bow and arrow up when ready to fire, and then only directly up to the "safety" zone, never towards a person. Only after you have sighted the target do you draw the arrow back. [If the show requires that someone threaten another with a bow and arrow, how about using a non-bending false bow with an elastic cord as the string? Even then, don't actually point it at anyone at anytime. You can always point upstage of where the human is and the audience will never know the difference. Why? Because the audience has no depth perception.]

There are three ways of pulling back on the bowstring. The *Mongolian draw*, in which the thumb hooks around the string and the forefinger gently keeps the arrow in place, is very strong but hard to control. The *Mediterranean draw* is the most common, and utilizes the first two or three fingers hooking around the string. I'm not thrilled with this method for stage, since we're usually trying to fire lightly, and the finger tips often scrape on the string during the release. This in turn can make the arrow fly significantly off to the side and too low. The best draw for stage is the *pinch draw*, which is the only one that grasps the arrow, not the string. It is a weaker draw, which is good because you don't want too much force anyway, and leads to a very clean release for superior accuracy from relatively novice archers.

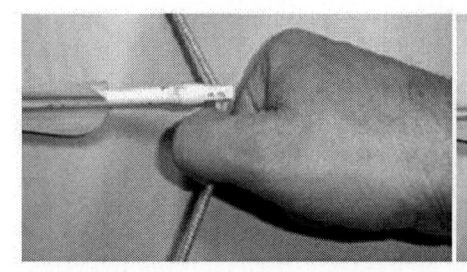

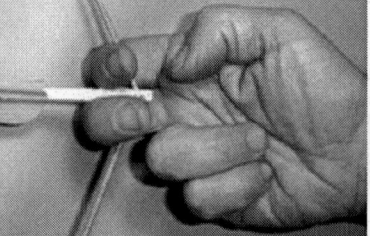

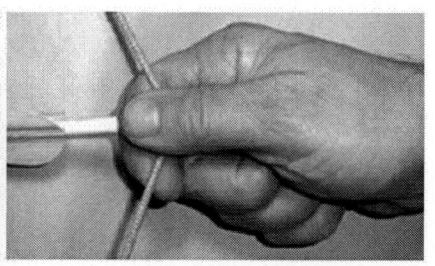

Mongolian draw - not very helpful   Mediterranean draw - much better   Pinch draw - best of all

Because you will be firing from a very short distance to the target, your arrow will probably not strike at the spot directly in line with the arrow when you aim. Why? Two things get in the way. First, an arrow will flex side to side as it leaves the bow. This oscillation evens out over normal target distances, but it doesn't have a chance in the short confines of even an outdoor theatre. Second, and more importantly, since you're drawing at much less than the maximum for the bow, the arrow shaft will be more affected by scraping against the bow as it leaves the string, pushing it off target by several inches. How to compensate? A lot of practice and absolute consistency of draw. I would go so far as to make a mark on your forearm and always draw the string to exactly that distance every time you practice. That way your draw is always the same.

♦	Even if you aren't planning to shoot with the bow, be careful of who has access to it. A simple stick fired from a bow can pass through the human body. Never leave this **lethal** item unattended or not in your direct control.

♦	If for some reason it is necessary to shoot the bow, get lessons from an experienced archer, especially if using a wood bow. Wood bow techniques are very different from those for modern or compound bows.

♦	Warm up the bow. Pull the string gently and slowly back about ¼ of full draw about ten times. This is a good idea for modern bows, and absolutely critical for wooden bows. There are very few things in life as exciting as having a bow break in your hands and near your face as you are about ready to shoot.

♦	Here is the order: First nock, then aim, then draw. Do not deviate from the order.

♦	Never pull the string back sharply or with a jerky motion.

♦	The string must never be pulled back to more than **24"** beyond its resting center.

♦	Never aim for longer than 2 seconds at a time. The stresses on a bow, especially wooden ones, are tremendous. Don't add to them.

♦	Insure that the path the arrow will travel is clear of all objects or living things. You should also take into account that arrows will ricochet, flying well off the intended course by glancing against even soft objects.

♦	Also, do not dry-fire the bow. Without the generated force being transferred to an arrow, the power from the released string can transmit enough stress to the bow to cause it to fracture.

Crossbows are merely bows laid down and connected to a wooden stock and some sort of trigger. Because it uses a trigger, and triggers are mechanical devices, and mechanical devices can fail at any time without warning, the crossbow on stage is the most dangerous item imaginable. Most crossbows use spring steel for the bow instead of wood, so even the smallest ones can generate a huge amount of force. Here in our shop we've made some large replicas with very weak plastic bows, so weak that the bolt can only travel about forty feet or so, but you still don't want to be on the receiving end of one of them. The crossbow must never be pointed at anyone at anytime.

Heed the one universal rule in operating crossbows - first draw, then aim, then load. You absolutely must not deviate from that sequence. So don't you think you should read that again? Because the crossbow could fire at any time, loading the bolt (arrow) must be done immediately before firing. Be sure that your actors understand this, for it is different than that for a regular bow and arrow.

There are three ways that a crossbow string might have to be drawn. With the weakest bows (those of a 10 to 20 lb draw strength) the string can simply be pulled by hand and hooked over the string catch, the little hook or nub that sticks up through the frame until the trigger pulls it down, releasing the string. For stronger bows, let's say 50 to 100 lbs, simple hand strength needs a bit more help, which it can get using an integrated pull. This is usually a straightforward rod attached to the stock. As it is pulled back, bends on the rod hook the string, which is then drawn back and hooked onto the string catch. The rod is then pushed forward so it doesn't get caught in the fired bowstring. Most novice users will at least once forget to do that last step, and then when they fire the crossbow not only does the bolt fly out but the rod is driven into the frame, doing quite a bit of damage.

The strongest bows will often require a mechanical drawing device, most commonly a crank that is either built onto the bow or is removed after the string is drawn. A stirrup is usually built in to the front of the stock to aid in spanning the bow.

Whether weak or strong, all crossbows fire a little differently than regular bows. Whereas normal arrows are notched so as to fit in to the bowstring for spanning and firing, bolts have flat ends that are placed near the string, but not actually touching it. When the crossbow string is fired, it jumps up slightly as it begins to move forward, and if the bolt is too close, the bowstring can skip right over the bolt end, missing it entirely and causing a crossbow misfire. So just remember to leave a little bit of space between the bolt and the string when you load the bolt.

Whips and Chains

And here we're going to include all impact weapons that have at least one moveable part, in other words, articulated weapons. These weapons all share two benefits over regular weapons. First, the articulation means that the ends can move at much greater speed than a solid weapon of the same length and weight, therefore can transmit more force. Second, they are more difficult to defend against, for stopping the movement of one part may not stop the movement of the rest of the weapon. The drawback is that the swinging end is very hard to control. If you miss your target it can swing back at you, and if you successfully hit the target it can bounce back at you. I advise not using an articulated weapon in a stage fight.

"cracking a whip"

It's so tempting for a director to try to add someone cracking a whip in some shows, especially big brawling scenes found in "Man of La Mancha" or some such. The problem is that whips are dangerous, and there are very few actors who are so experienced with a whip that they can guarantee the safety of everyone else on stage, or even themselves. Whips need room, not only to swing and crack, but for the bounce-back after the crack. Most of the time the end of the whip travels to the side of the operator, but not always. Anyone who has cracked whips for a while will be able to show you a couple of welts from a particularly nasty bounce-back. The face is in such obvious danger that anyone - anyone - who cracks a whip should wear eye protection.

Whips are made of long strands of braided leather wrapped around a stiff handle at one end and then gradually narrowing to one thin strand at the other. What makes a whip "crack" is getting the tip to go faster than the speed of sound. That creates a pressure wave that we hear as a mini sonic boom. The same thing happens when we snap a towel. Since getting the tip of thin leather to move that fast is difficult, usually a small length of fabric called a "cracker" is tied to the end of the leather.

There are many styles of whip-cracking, but all involve the same basics; first getting the whip to move in one direction, then suddenly getting it to come back on itself very quickly by flicking the handle in the opposite direction. If the flick is timed right, the end of the whip will make a 180 degree hairpin turn so sharp that it moves at over seven hundred miles an hour, an incredible speed that creates a temporary vacuum in space. The rush of air to fill the vacuum creates the "crack". But it also means that now the entire whip is moving pretty quickly in that second direction, which likely as not is back towards the operator. That's where things can get nasty.

If the director insists, there are a couple of things you can do to attempt to reduce the danger. First, get an expert to give instruction to the actor. Not someone who is pretty good but a true, experienced, expensive teaching expert. These are specialists, not garden variety fight choreographers. Next, consider using a carriage whip instead of a regular whip. Carriage whips were specifically designed to protect the user against bounce-back by making the handle very long. That way the whip will tend to bounce toward the far end of the handle rather than at the operator. It won't look cool at all, and it won't protect anyone else onstage, but at least the operator is somewhat more safe.

Here are some very basic notes on cracking a whip, or actually what to do if your whip cracking (having already been taught to you by an experienced instructor) starts to loose its reliability.

It is most likely that for the show you are working on, you have been given a six foot whip, due to the size constraints of the space in which you are to perform. And for safety's sake, I certainly wouldn't want you to use anything longer than that. But a shorter whip is harder to crack than a longer one, and certainly much harder to learn on. Why is that? The reason has a lot to do with how the whip itself moves through the air.

In order to make a whip crack you need to create a wave that travels from your hand all the way down to the end of the whip. In its simplest form, the wave looks like this as it travels down the leather: ∾ Now, obviously, you can't throw something at 700 miles per hour. Even the fastest baseball pitches max out at 100 mph, and that wave motion that you create at the handle of the whip is only traveling at an anemic 30 mph. But the construction of the whip, which includes a tapered shape and material that starts stiff but gets progressively softer as it reaches the end, allows the wave to flatten out as it travels, without losing any of the energy. As the wave gets tighter, it moves ever faster, finally going beyond 700 mph as the tip flicks around itself. If you put in a little more energy, let's say a 50 mph throw, the tip might loop around at over twice the speed of sound.

A long whip is rather forgiving, for you get more time and distance for that wave to increase its speed. You can even get a good crack from a "standing start", holding your arm by your side and then flicking it out in one short snap. So even if you are a little sloppy in your regular throw, you've still a good chance of getting a decent crack. On a short whip, your technique has to be nearly perfect and you have to start off with a fairly fast throw to begin with, with full arm extension behind and in front of the body. So if you are getting a lot of "almost crack", here are some things to look for:

1) Are you transmitting enough energy to the whip? When things go wrong, it is easy to get frustrated and try to increase the arm strength in an effort to muscle through the problem. But that just stiffens up your body, slows down your hand, and generally makes matters worse. The secret to speed is in relaxation. When you're relaxed, you can use your entire body to generate the wave, and then add a little more with your shoulder, more with your arm, more with your hand - all of it adding up to a smooth transfer of power and a much faster wave.

2. Is your whip moving in a straight line? If your hand is accidentally adding a tiny extra movement, it gets exaggerated by the whip, and then the wave never gets a chance to build up speed. You might also have begun

to "pendulum" your throw instead of moving your hand in a straight line. You'll know this if the tip starts jumping up to your face on the bounce back. Remember that you have to bend your elbow during the throw.

3) What's happening behind you? If you aren't allowing the whip to start off in a straight line behind you before you start the throw, you're making life much harder for yourself.

One last thing that you might want to try. Dip the cracker (the string on the end) in water before going on stage. It will help flatten out the tip and can increase the terminal speed of the loop. Not by a huge amount, but it can make the difference between a swish and a crack.

By the way, the fabric crackers at the end don't last too long. They fray considerably each time you crack the whip, so have to be replaced every so often. Instead of buying specially made "crackers, just tie on a shoelace. Much cheaper.

Flails

Different than whips in that the strands, either of leather (called a cat-o'-nine tales) or linked chain, are fairly short, about one or two feet long. Because of that, you can't "crack" a leather flail. There's just no way to generate that kind of speed with such a short length. Instead, the flail is used simply to beat someone with the strands, and certainly enough speed builds up that the leather strands will cut skin. So how do you pretend to flail someone onstage? I like using a flail with strips made of felt. They move wonderfully through the air, having the appearance of having weight while causing no danger to the actor being struck.

Flail Maces

A short pole, a length of chain and then a spiked ball on the end, and you have another articulated weapon. Medieval warriors found that these can do a huge amount of damage, capable of breaking bones with very little effort. Much like the Japanese nunchuk, the drawback is that the swinging end can easily come back and break the user's arm or ribs. Also, any link in the chain could break at any time, sending a solid object flying out (with your luck, out into the audience). Never use any kind of flail mace in a stage fight.

Staging Violence

The Acting of Angry Actions

Stage combat may extend to a full-cast medieval multi-weapon fight in a production of Henry IV or be as simple as a single slap. When done right it brings a level of excitement to the play unreachable by the use of words alone. When done poorly, the scene drags, it looks hokey, and the actors are in danger of getting injured.

"Stage combat is the simulation of violent actions specific to the production requirements of a play." Let's parse out my little definition.

Stage combat is the <u>simulation</u> ... for it is not real violence. It is also not stunt work nor martial arts nor fighting with pulled punches. We are creating an illusion, just as does a magician.

... of violent <u>actions</u> ... which is not the same as violent intent. An action with a violent consequence might come out of either anger or accident, so it could be found in a comedy as well as in a drama. Violent actions without violent intent are the hallmark of slapstick and the bread and butter of all of those home video TV shows].

... specific to the <u>production requirements</u> ... these will change from show to show, so the way a punch is performed in one show may need to be modified considerably for another, even if performed by the same actors portraying the same characters.

... of a <u>play</u>. The techniques are designed for use in a live theatrical scripted play. There are a different set of techniques for film, as there are another set for live-action stunt shows. Stage combat exists as a storytelling tool for theatre.

Physical violence on stage is most effectively used when the words alone are insufficient to contain the overflow of emotions that the character feels. But that doesn't mean that the actors can give themselves over to those feelings. Sometimes they want to, because they enjoy "feeling". But try to explain that what the character feels is one reality, one that must be transmitted to the audience. The actor, one the other hand, is the pilot of that character, modulating his own actions so that the audience can follow the story. Whether the actor feels anything is beside the point. Examples from theatre abound. I once watched a show in which a charming young couple were performing a love scene and it was absolutely true to life. The more and more intimate the conversation became, the quieter their voices dropped until they were barely murmuring to each other. Of course it was uncompromisingly real; lovers do create a miniature universe in which nothing else exits - *but the audience couldn't hear one blessed word they said*. The actors were performing selfishly, precisely because they were being so truthful.

In a good musical, characters speak until the emotions become so intense that mere words would normally fail, so the music becomes the vehicle by which these heightened and sometimes conflicting emotions can be shared. But the true physical response to intense emotion is usually to restrict the throat and to begin to hyperventilate, hardly actions conducive to producing dulcet tones. In the same way, a dance is usually a way of expressing a burst of emotion that normally exists only inside someone's heart. In order to fully express them, the dancer must have complete control of his body. So we know that acting/performing always has to provide the identifiable shape of a real human response, but expressed and controlled in such a way as to transmit it meaningfully to the audience.

That's what stage combat is. We are actors telling the story about some angry people without getting angry ourselves. We tell about a very traumatic episode while staying relaxed inside so that we can tell it.

In a very well written play, an instance of violence occurs because the emotional tension of the characters has reached a breaking point. Words alone no longer suffice in order to control these powerful emotions, and finally they explode into movement. Even a tiny attempt at a shove must have that reality behind it if we want the audience to believe it.

And now for a slight digression, I'd like to mention the one good reason why you should consider not doing stage combat. To be honest, most plays are not very well written. Too often, playwrights use a slap to the face or some-such in order to "cap" a particularly dramatic verbal confrontation. Where do all of these slaps come from? Certainly not from life. I've been in and seen hundreds of heated arguments, most of them fully abusive in tone and terminology and several far worse than anything I've read in a script. No one ever slapped the other in the face. Attempted choking, sure; scissors thrown, plates hurled, wild punches and flailing kicks galore, but no slaps. I'm sure it happens, and have heard of a couple of first-hand reports, but my point is that in film and on stage it has become like the poisons of Shakespeare - used to move the plot along but really a theatrical convention rather than something found in real life.

And yet we're stuck with the slap (or, if it's two men in a movie, the single punch to the face). Usually the pattern is -

    a] argument starts
    b] argument escalates
    c] slap or punch occurs
    d] argument stops or takes a new direction

- and it's pretty obvious that the violence is there because the playwright simply found it to be the easiest way to get from point "b" to point "d". We as actors are supposed to make it work, and we usually do, by committing fully to the give and take of the emotional buildup. But what if we find that we can take the plot to that new direction that the playwright wanted without having to resort to the slap? My guess is (and experience has been) that when we do, the moment resonates with the audience as being more truthful and therefore more affecting than by resorting to the cheap trick of a false action.

What I'm trying to say is that any bit of business or even any line of dialogue exists in service to the play. If it propels the plot forward, great. But if the same information can be presented without the action, why slow down the play by insisting on performing it? We cut lines from shows all the time for that very reason. We should be ready to do so with actions as well. Remember that a theatre audience doesn't pay to hear certain lines or to see a fight. They pay to see characters deal with issues and how that changes them.

Stage combat is similar to comedy in that they both require absolutely precise timing and subtle nuance. They also share the fact that actors want to do them by being big and frenetic. Most stage fights that I have seen performed for live theatre have been both badly executed and the participants have no idea how much real danger they are in. Too much stage combat is being choreographed by people not specifically trained in the discipline, or worse, the actors are allowed to simply improvise their way through the fight.

There is no way that anyone can learn stage combat by reading a book or watching a video, anymore than someone could learn how to drive a car by reading an instruction manual. Stage combat is only learned from the careful coaching of a competent instructor who is there to guide the student. The student does not learn from mimicking the instructor; real learning takes place when the instructor can correct the tiny mistakes and habits which the student can't help but make. The instructor makes every lesson more and more challenging, providing not only new information and new techniques but also those invaluable opportunities to learn from mistakes as ideas are translated into action. An experienced stage combat instructor will look at ten students performing the same technique and give ten different corrections. No book or video can possibly do that.

If you want to learn stage combat, get serious training directly from an experienced instructor, preferably one certified as such by the Society of American Fight Directors. I say this even though I know that there are hundreds of extremely capable, competent and brilliant instructors and choreographers out there who are not affiliated with the SAFD. And there are also just as many that have gone through all of the Society's training, test well enough to get their certification, but are simply bad when it comes to dealing with actors and directors. As with all professions, being associated with a large organization is still no guarantee of competence, and some of the best choreographers have never so much as taken one class from the SAFD. So why do I still suggest going through them? Because you are not likely to have much time to interview and test out a number of candidates, and the Society does expose their members to far more than the average person with an interest in fighting. And that is ultimately what you want to find - someone who can see the danger points well before anyone is actually in danger. When the actors know that they are not going to get hurt nor hurt anyone else, they feel free to continue to act during the fight, instead of clenching their teeth and bulging their eyes in terror.

The titles for this person are varied and are usually used interchangeably, which is why I prefer to be known as the "fight guy". But there are some subtle differences depending on what your requirements are. A fight instructor is someone who teaches the actors how to perform the techniques of the fight correctly, a fight choreographer creates the fight, a fight director takes the choreography and turns it into a fully developed performance, and a fight captain drills the actors in the mechanics of the fight. Most shows will have one person take on all of these responsibilities, but many will parse out the job according to the staff available.

Some things to look for in hiring a fight director. You are hiring another designer, someone whose input will have as much an effect on your show as the costume, set and lighting designers. The closest analogy would be to that of a dance choreographer for a musical, with one critical difference. Although some of the duties are similar, and in both cases the movements spring forth as pure expressions and elaborations of a moment of a heightened emotional state, dances in most musicals tend only to explore that moment without adding to the storyline. Fight scenes almost always are included so as to change the direction of the plot. Leaving these crucial moments in the show completely in someone else's hands can take too much away from the directorial intent. Make your vision crystal clear, and be specific. Let the fight director know what character traits you need to highlight, what the tone of the fight should be, even where the actors should end up on stage at the end of the conflict.

Primarily, your fight instructor is a theatre professional, not just someone who knows how to fight.. When the fight choreographer decides on the moves of the fight, he or she is in effect a playwright, for every move will tell part of the story of the play. She is also going to coach the actors on how to perform the movements, and what the emotional intent is of each action, so in effect also becomes the director. So test the skills of your presumptive choreographer. One possibility is to "test hire" your candidate. Invite her to teach a one or two hour session in some aspect of stage combat to your class or cast. Seeing someone in action with students is the best way to get a feel for their approach to the work.

Does the instructor clearly demonstrate the techniques so that your actors can pick them up quickly? Does he panic or show impatience when someone doesn't learn quickly? Does he leave anyone behind? Is safety not only stressed, but made understandable? Is there as much emphasis on how to act a fight as well as on how to do the techniques? Are "non-fighters" made to feel comfortable and confidant performing the actions?

Would you trust this person to lead these actors even in your absence? Would you let this person direct your show?

The specifics of stage combat are sometimes so subtle that they are lost on most beginning students, yet a slight change of the angle of someone's wrist can mean the difference between safety and injury. You will be hiring someone to not only teach some techniques, but also to see and solve the danger points long before anyone else would see them so that the actors can avoid a danger they never even knew existed.

So a word directly to all actors who may be asked to perform an act of stage combat. You have the inalienable right to walk away from any rehearsal, any scene, any show, any acting company in which you feel that your safety is being compromised in any way. Never fear any supposed damage to your career by sticking up for your safety. No show is worth a disability. If you think that your partner is out of control, refuse to continue working with him until he is stable once more. If something doesn't feel right but you have no idea why, but you were told that it is safe, still insist on finding a way to do it that makes you feel secure. Always challenge authority when your safety is at stake.

Stuntwork vs. Stage Combat

Movies and television use stunt professionals to do the bulk of violent actions when they film, mainly for very sound economic reasons. Well trained stunt artists are less likely to get injured than regular actors when doing a fall or swinging from a rope. They are also far less likely to injure someone else when throwing a punch or even just grabbing someone. They are very well paid to reduce risk to the production overall and especially to the featured actors, for even a minor injury to an actor can cause a delay of several days' filming, at a cost to the producers of tens of thousands of dollars. (A common saying for film producers is that there is nothing more expensive than a cheap stuntman.) For that same reason, stunt artists have to be replaceable. If one suffers an injury while filming, another can be plugged into his or her spot immediately.

In order to insure the highest level of safety, stunts are performed as individual units of action that can later be edited into the rest of the scene. All other action stops, the set can be specially rearranged, the stunt artists can wear special bracing and padding - in short the entire production comes to a halt until the single stunt is performed correctly. It might take a full day just to perform one sequence or even one fall, but the stunt itself is performed without any of the distractions of trying to maintain the flow of the emotional build or any other acting considerations.

Obviously in theatre we don't have that luxury. We're trying to tell a story and can't have the audience step out for a cup of coffee while we set-up all of the safety equipment needed for a stunt. Worse, the same person who does the acting is also the person who has to perform the violence, so we cannot risk any injury at all. Although we may take elements of stuntwork to help shape the illusions we perform, ultimately stage combat has its own very different set of techniques than is found on a film set.

Professional stuntmen are sometimes used as stage fight choreographers, but they learn a distinct set of skills (breaking falls, contact hits) which place the actors in more danger than is ever necessary on stage, and they usually have only a limited understanding of stagework. Having a stunt artist train the actors is only one step above having untrained actors work out the fight on their own, which is fine if you don't mind risking serious injuries. Stuntmen and untrained actors also share an enjoyment in performing contact techniques. It makes them feel manly, but of course the chance of injury is high. But there's another reason I and all good stage combat instructors try to avoid contact techniques.

When the receiver of, let's say, a slap to the face takes the hit, the pain he feels is his own, not the character's. So he can't help but take a fraction of a second to step out of character, evaluate the possible damage, and then find his way back into the life of the play. The slapper as well wonders how strong his slap was, how much damage he may have caused. In other words, both actors *stop acting,* and whenever they stop acting and drop out of character they fail to tell the story. So ultimately all contact techniques become a self-indulgent violation of the trust the audience gives us which allows them to suspend disbelief and accept the reality of the play.

Improvising and Stage Combat

Acting is a difficult craft. Not only does it require that the body and voice be strong enough and trained correctly to handle whatever the show requirements may demand, the craft also demands an open mind and spirit that can respond to subtle changes that come out in rehearsal and performance. There are many directors who, in order to nurture inspiration, will work almost exclusively using improvisation techniques. These can be invaluable in bringing out artistic responses both vast and deep, inspiration impossible to summon by cold calculation and rote rehearsal. They are also very dangerous when applied to stage combat.

Nothing in staged violence can be allowed to be improvised to any degree whatsoever. A simple shift in weight from one foot to the other can mean the difference between standing and falling. A change in trajectory of a moving arm by only a few degrees can mean the difference between safely missing someone and knocking him out.

The time for improvisation is during the early rehearsals, when the director and the actors need to explore the scene and the characters. By all means allow the actors to explore their impulses. Just don't let them touch each other until the moves can be carefully set, both for their safety and for believability.

Real Fighting vs. Stage Combat

Don't assume that a fencing instructor can choreograph a sword fight. The techniques of competitive fencing are dangerous to actors and very damaging to the weapons. The fencing instructor will not have the broad knowledge of all of the weapons choices that are now available for stage, and worse will tend to choreograph according to his or her own skills and experience. That experience is in moving quickly enough so that your opponent can't see the attack coming, which is competitive and not theatrical. For the same reason, most martial arts instructors make very poor stage combat instructors, even when choreographing martial arts scenes for theatre. Their focus is usually to make the moves look crisp, cool and fast, rather than in telling a story to the audience.

Fencers and martial artists learn to do things which are necessary for combat but dangerous for stage. For example, fighters learn not to look at an opponent's eyes, but rather keep a softer focus on the opponent's torso, the better to catch quick movements within the periphery. And they must never look at the punch or kick coming at them. In stage combat, both participants work together to create the fight and also to heighten the dramatic tension of the scene, so checking-in to your partner's face is crucial. And to help the audience follow the fight, we have to throw our focus to the incoming threat and also telegraph our attacks.

Where martial arts can instruct theatre arts:

I'm not against fencing or martial arts. I have studied both and I know that some aspects are excellent

training for stagework:
- body alignment - being able to move forward or backward and still maintain a pleasant balanced carriage that doesn't constrict breathing or movement is something I wish every actor could develop.
- relaxing the body even in moments of stress - allowing the limbs to move efficiently and fluidly without any extra body tension.
- allowing the limbs to move independently of the torso - actors sometimes find in difficult to step back when the arm is attacking, or to step forward while blocking.
- most importantly, looking like a fighter.

Where martial arts and theatre arts diverge:

After having taught and performed stage combat for some thirty years, I went back to competitive karate, something which I enjoyed in my youth but neglected completely in the intervening years as I concentrated on building my career. During the first year back I found that my stage combat work had forced my body into making some interesting choices, much to the detriment of my martial arts skills. My body simply refused to do the following:
- pointing objects at someone's face - I found that my punches were drifting off either to the left or right, or sometimes went flying above the person's head altogether. My opponents barely had to attempt to block any of my head level punches.
- closing distance - when moving into attack distance, my punches and kicks would land a couple of inches short of making contact.
- stepping and punching at one instant - I was telegraphing all of my aggressive moves, stepping in and landing my stance before generating the punch. My opponents simply stepped back long before my punches even started.
- combining hip movement with limb movement - even when I did land my punches or kicks, there was no power behind them, as my hips weren't generating extra force by turning into the aggressive act.

What a shame for my karate skills, but how wonderful for stage combat! I was performing in a way so as to cause the least amount of damage possible when fighting someone. These are the very techniques that are too often lacking when a fencing instructor or martial artist choreograph a fight, and that is why you should be very leery of hiring them for stage. Even more importantly, never allow members of the Society of Creative Anachronism or similar Renaissance Faire aficionados to lead your fights. They have no qualifications to handle a sword on stage, let alone teach other actors to do so. Stage combat is not stunt work, it is pantomimed acting using a prop. [As a fight director, I usually don't allow those actors who are SCA members to handle weapons. It's unfair of me and very prejudicial, I know, but I really don't care. In my experience they invariably end up hurting someone when they are involved in any way with the fights.]

So for all those reasons, stick with someone trained in the specific techniques of stage combat.

Hiring the Fight Choreographer

The fight director's actual job duties will be whatever you agree on. If the person you have in mind is a full-time professional, your budget may only allow for one day of his time. In that case he will only be able to talk to you by phone to get a feel for the show, choreograph a fight beforehand, and then take one of your rehearsal slots to teach the fight to your actors. The assumption here is that your actors already have basic fighting skills or that there is someone on staff or in the cast who is a competent fight instructor and can follow up with specific technique coaching after the fight master has gone.

At the other end of the spectrum, perhaps you have a huge budget or have found someone willing to work for much less. In that best of all possible worlds, the fight choreographer will provide input during design conferences and auditions, train all of the actors in the stage combat techniques, choreograph all of the fights and redesign them as needed during the rehearsal process, provide copies of all fight notation to the stage manager, procure and inspect all of the weapons, train the technicians and actors in their maintenance and use, review all matters that might affect the safety of the actors and audience as relates to the fight, hire outside specialists for any special effects outside his own capabilities, designate and train the fight captain, establish the fight call protocol or perhaps even run the fight call himself. In a word, be there for every rehearsal and performance to baby every possible contingency related to the fight.

I've worked at both extremes and every possible combination in the middle, and of course it's better to have the time to be able to really work with the actors than not. But just as in every other aspect of mounting a theatrical production, there is no right or wrong, merely compromises and realities that will affect who you can get and for how long.

I mentioned earlier that doing a test hire is a good way to evaluate a prospective combat director. It won't cost you much, perhaps a hundred bucks, and you'll learn more than any resume can tell you. I know that you may not have the chance to do that, so if you are stuck with going by someone's CV, at least call as many directors on that sheet and ask them how she was to work with. Your fight person not only has to be good, but also needs to be a good fit with your style of work.

There are some things that your fight person may not be qualified to handle. Most will not have much training in firearms, explosive effects, tumbling, lifts, fly rigging, falling from heights - all those really fun things that can get you in trouble in a hurry. Fight folk tend to be a bit cocky, and very few of the ones I've met like to say "I don't know how to do that". Make sure that the skills of your hire match your needs.

Once you've found someone, you'll need to set the ground rules before you can agree on a price. What exactly do you need from this hire? Which scenes do you need him to choreograph and which do you merely need her to observe? How many rehearsals will be required? How many tech and dress rehearsals do you want her to attend? How many design meetings are there going to be? Are all of the actors already trained, or will a separate schedule for skills training be required? Who is going to provide the weapons? Who pays for the damages?

When both you and she agree on those items, she'll be able to come back with a cost proposal. You should have a number ready as well.

Your theatre may never have hired a fight person before, so you may feel at a loss as to what you should offer. The best advice I can give is to compare the position to a dance choreographer for a musical. The skill level and the teaching capability should be the same for both, so the stipend should be about the same as well.

What your fight director will need before the first rehearsal:

Give your fight director as much information as early on as possible. This of course will include your vision of how the scene should progress, but also any specifics you have on nearly every aspect of the show as it can relate to the scene in question. Here are some things about which the choreographer will [or should] ask:

- the set- Do you have a complete ground plan and elevation plan, with all platforms and steps clearly marked? How much of a rake will there be? Are you expecting any "fancy" elements in the fight? Swinging from a rope, jumping up on a bench, climbing a wall? Are you including fog? Water or oil based? Are there stairs? Handrails?

- the lighting   - Mood lighting for a fight is wonderful, but will it have enough contrast so that the actors can safely see the weapons? Where are the dead spots in the lighting plan? Where are the spots on stage where the lights might be blinding them. How low will the fixtures hang? Any footlights?

- the costumes   - What will the footwear be? Rubber souls? Will there be gloves? hats? cloaks? jewelry? jackets? puffy sleeves? belts? sashes? tight fitting or loose? What about undergarments? Any item being borrowed or rented and must not be damaged?

- makeup   - wigged? prosthetics? oil or water based makeup?

- the props   - What weapons will be used? Are there any items not considered weapons which might be handled during the course of the fight? Are there any liquids in the scene?

- the sound   - Will the fight be underscored? If so, the fight director will need a copy of that music before the fight can be choreographed. Will any of the fighters have to wear body microphones? Will the set be mic'd? Where is the exact placement of each pick-up, especially floor mic's

- the director   - What kind of violence do you want to see? Some movements are comic-book, some are gruesome, some are graphic, some are emotion charged. Are you going for hyper-realism? Or do you want a "stylized" fight? What exactly does that mean to you? How much blood do you want the audience to see, if any. What do you want the characters to have learned by the end of the fight? Where do you want the audience emotionally to be at the end of the fight?

The most frustrating part of dealing with tech week is having the fighters have to deal with costume surprises. I know that most theatres don't have the luxury of having early access to the clothing, but there are some things which the actors need by the end of the first week of fight rehearsals. The actual footwear to be used for the show must be used in rehearsal. The rehearsal clothing needs to be as close a match as is humanly possible to the costume itself so that the actor can find out if the movement needs to be modified.

As for the set, carefully go over all of the extra strengthening that will be required for balustrades, stairs, wall units, etc. Keep in mind that the fight director should not be in charge of the design nor installation of any structural safety elements. That's the job of the technical director. Swinging from a rope might be very exciting, but choreographers don't have any special training in it, and certainly don't know how to do this kind of specialized rigging.

By the way, a set with many levels is not fight friendly, and even something as minor as the type of flooring planned may require certain moves to be avoided, so get the fight choreographer involved as early as possible in the design of the show.

It is unlikely that your fight choreographer is going to be available for every fight rehearsal and performance. Most of the time, a fight captain will have to be named. This is the person, usually an actor in the cast, who will run the fight rehearsals in the choreographer's absence, and then during the run of the show will check the weapons, run the nightly pre-show fight call, and report to the choreographer any problems with the fight and request modifications to it which may be necessary. Depending on the choreographer, he might also have to notate the fight choreography, provide the stage manager with updated copies, rehearsing the understudies, and training any replacements to the cast. Because of all of those duties, it should not be one of the principles, and ideally should be someone who is both well versed in stage combat but not actually part of most of the fights, for the simple reason that it's hard to look at the fight if you are in it. Don't be in a rush to name the fight captain too early. Most choreographers want to get to know all of the available personnel and make that judgment themselves. He's looking for someone who not only knows about stage combat, but can also meld well with the choreographer's style. A mismatch here can ruin the fights.

Of course, in a major fight show the choreographer may require an assistant well before the first rehearsal. When that happens, the fight captain will not be a member of the cast but rather act as an assistant stage manager, and assigned purely to the fight choreographer. In that case, the fight captain will take a much more active role in pre-production meetings, serving as liaison between choreographer, stage management and the rest of the design team. He will also need to learn all of the parts of all of the fights, assist in partnering the fight segment of the audition, run all warm-ups before each fight rehearsal, assist the props crew in assigning weapons transfer protocol, advise them of any damage, run all of the pre-show fight calls, and at strike assist with the final check-in of all weapons.

* * * * *

Now, I'm not so naive as to think that fights will only be choreographed by a professional fight director just because I wrote the previous pages. It's going to happen that either from budget constraints, scheduling difficulties, or just not being able to find anyone, a fight director is not used for a production. It is also reasonable to assume that just as there are novice directors, there have to be opportunities for nascent actor/combatants wanting to learn about choreography to actually have the opportunity to work on a show. It is only for the eventuality that actors are left exposed to harm that the following pages are offered. It is certainly not meant as a substitute for adequate supervision.

But please remember - less is more. Choreograph only the basic minimum needed to tell the story and then stop. Make sure your actors understand that only rehearsed and polished moves can be in the show. Every second of performed stage combat is another accident waiting to happen. Reduce your risks.

By the way, whether you hire an outside choreographer or not, know what you want to have happen within the fight. Not just who wins and who dies, but really examine why the plot requires the audience to see violence at that particular point in the play. Don't be afraid to work out a rough draft of the way you envision the fights. You don't have to know the names of the moves or even decide what specific moves need to be used in order to block out a fight. Even if you delegate the choreography to someone else, the finished fight is still your responsibility. Get an image of how the fight will "pulse", and by that I mean the changing flow of upper and lower hand, winning and losing, aggression and fear. The clearer your internal vision becomes of the fight the more easily you'll be able to translate that into some very specific actions. Storyboard it, just the way film directors do. Some choreographers may resent that much input and may even let you know that you are treading on their turf. Tell 'em to lump it. It's your show. A good choreographer will take everything you come up with and either mold it into something effective, or give you some very good and understandable reasons why it should be cut.

Why demonstrate the fight at all? The Greeks wrote powerful drama without showing any at all, and they certainly dealt with emotions as powerful as anything written since, so why does your show need visible violence? What do you need to transmit? What does your audience need to know by the end of the fight that they can only receive by witnessing violence?

What is the simplest, most straightforward way to transfer that knowledge? Is demonstrating the violent act the *best* way to do so? Is it the *only* way? If you have no alternative to demonstrating violence, how much *must* you show to get the point across. Can it be implied? Can it be shown stylistically or symbolically? Be honest - are you adding violence because it is fun for your audience? Because it is fun for you? I've had to choreograph fights that were added by a director's whim to give more actors a chance to participate in the "fun", and these fights have always detracted from the show.

Hiring the Fighter-Actors

Or, as the SAFD prefers to call them, the Actor-Combatants. And it's a good designation, for the performers do have to act the fight. It helps your production not at all to have technically proficient fights that add nothing to the story because the fighters don't have the acting chops to give meaning and nuance to the actions. For that reason, always follow the basic rule during casting as you would for straight play or a musical - hire the best actor you can for the role. All other considerations are secondary.

Secondary, but still important. Those other considerations include general physical health and flexibility, emotional stability, and a generally pleasant demeanor. Rehearsing stage combat can be stressful and frustrating, and having to work with a difficult partner can only make things worse. Trusting and respecting someone on stage is always desirable, but it becomes crucial once the swords start swinging.

The actors should know during the audition process what kind of activity the show will require from them, and should gently be made aware that they are volunteering for something that might place them in danger. Don't guarantee that they will be safe, only that you will try to make the environment as safe as you can.

In a musical you would of course have the audition process broken down into three segments - acting, singing, and dancing. For a fight show, you'll want to do something similar, but you don't actually have to have them perform a fight sequence. You'll get a lot more information by having a true modern dance audition, just without music. Seeing how well they can understand and replicate a series of even arbitrary movements requiring different body postures and limb positions will tell you volumes about their ability and training, and it can level the playing field somewhat for those who have natural talent but haven't yet picked up a sword.

If I have only limited time to have a movement audition, or if the show has already been cast but not yet choreographed, I like to do a quick test of the actor's general suitability. I lay a bunch of swords and daggers in the center of the room, then without comment or introduction allow the auditioners to enter about 10 minutes before the stated audition time. I sit in a corner, pretending to read a newspaper. There are always going to be a couple of actors who rush to the weapons, pick them up, wave them around, even start to play with them. These are the actors I won't cast, or if already cast I make sure to reduce their combat time to the bare minimum, because such a person is going to hurt others simply from lack of self-discipline. It's a snap-judgment of someone's character, I know, and not fair at all. It is also infallible.

The Fight Rehearsal

Please find a way to schedule plenty of time for supervised fight rehearsals, preferably with the fight choreographer present, but if that isn't possible then with the fight captain. If even that isn't possible, at the very least the rehearsals should be watched by someone respected enough to control the pace of the rehearsal, keep any bystanders out of harm's way, and act as the surrogate audience to make sure that the positioning of the actors is set for maximum believability.

I know that time is always at a premium, but see how much can be set aside for the actors to rehearse the fights without feeling rushed or having been squeezed into the general schedule as an afterthought.

Dressing for the fight rehearsal is a progressive affair. Certainly during the initial blocking rehearsals the combatants should wear soft soled shoes and comfortable workout clothes. The clothing should not hide the contour of the body, as the choreographer will need to see and correct body alignment and limb position. Many joint injuries can be prevented at this early stage. No dangling jewelry of course, and pocketed objects which might hurt if landed on must be removed as well.

As soon as the fighters have the choreography reasonably well-memorized, the substitution of the workout clothes can begin. Rehearsal clothing at this stage is necessary for the actors so they can learn to deal with capes, jackets, hats, gloves of course, but most especially shoes. Costumers are sometimes loathe to provide the actual costumes to the actors before the first dress rehearsal [indeed the costumes usually aren't even built yet], but an exception must be made for footwear. The safety factor is too important to allow any delay in getting the final shoe choice to the actors.

Layers of rehearsal focus

Just as one doesn't simply memorize lines and blocking and assume that one can act, the fight rehearsal is more than just repeating a bunch of set moves. Character development, pace, build, highlight of intention and reactions are all explored during rehearsal. Having said that, none of that work means anything if the lines aren't memorized, and the same thing applies to the stage fight. So let's get that out of the way first.

Write It Down! The fight choreographer should hand out a sheet with the fight written out, but if not, the actors as well as the assistant director should be writing down every move of the fight at each rehearsal. The actors should make sure to add any modifications to the fight immediately, for what you think will be remembered will be gone from memory at the next rehearsal. Don't count on one written version of the fight; disagreements will come up as to interpretation. Three versions are better than one, and two versions are almost useless.

Our natural instinct is to memorize the progression of moves in chronological order [1st move; 1st and 2nd moves; 1st 2nd and 3rd moves, etc.], but this has often led to the actors knowing the beginning of the fight cold, but as the fight progresses they feel less and less sure of it. I like to work with <u>reverse progression</u> when giving out the fight. I give them the last phrase, then the last two phrases, then the last three phrases, etc. By the time the blocking period is over they have the final phrases of the fight down pat, and any memorization glitches are going to occur at the start of the fight rather than at the exciting and stressful finish. Here are some other things to try during the fight rehearsals:

Footwork. The actors walk through the fight with the hands clasped behind the back. Offense and defense are shown through the eyes and with the shoulders. It really helps the actors work on the part of the fight which is usually the least convincing - intention and reaction.

Distance fighting. Have the actors stand three or four feet away from each other or more, completely outside of contact range, and go through the fight. A great way to make sure that they are working on the partnered pantomime aspects.

Getting into weapons fights, we do the above and add a few other exercises:

No weapons. No kidding, the best way to perfect a sword fight is to leave the swords in the props cabinet several times. Have the actors stand much closer than normal and go through the entire fight using just the hands. The fingers should actually reach out and try to touch the intended target [hip, shoulder, head] and the defensive hand merely deflects the attack only one inch away from reaching the target. Really try to touch the partner's body. Since the focus is on the finger tips, the intention of attack and defense becomes much clearer and the techniques improve dramatically. Really focus on the exact square inch that the fingers must strike. This is the best single way to take someone from novice to looking like an expert.

Speed Sit down. The opposite of *Footwork*. The actors sit facing each other and only work thru the hand movements of the fight, but just as in the above exercise holding no weapons. Keep working until the movements become fluid, fast, and second nature. Actors can rehearse this way anywhere and at anytime. Just like line speed-thrus, a great way to keep the fight crisp.

Dropped parries. This is scary but an excellent way to improve control. Go through the fight as normal, but one actor [without warning and in no discernible pattern] simply does not make the appropriate defensive move. If the attacker doesn't have excellent control, the partner gets hit.

How fast should the fight be?

The old answer is always the best. A fight can only go as fast as the audience can follow the story. *All* of the story. If the actors are moving too quickly, the audience can only see a blur of movement, but nothing that progresses the story. The story of the fight is told through precision, which is why the initial fight rehearsals must be conducted in painfully slow motion. Every movement during the critical initial sessions must be performed at an agonizingly slow pace so that all of the little mistakes can be corrected before they become part of muscle memory.

With each rehearsal, the pace can be allowed to increase slightly, but only as fast as the actors can demonstrate specificity of intent along with correct technique. By the time the show is ready to open, the fight should be ready to run at a little faster than full speed. And then the actors have to be convinced to actually *perform* it at only 80% of full speed. It's great to have an exciting fight, but the actors still have to have a little reserve left in order to act the fight, as well as be able to handle any unforeseen contingencies.

Who is in charge?

This can get a little complicated. The director always gets the final word on what stays in the fight, but the choreography itself is the intellectual property of the choreographer. No change to the fight must be allowed to occur unless authorized by the choreographer. A fight captain or assistant may provide correction, but the moves themselves are sacrosanct. This should be the prima facie rule, and anything beyond that is to be worked out between the director and choreographer. For example, if I have to be gone for the majority of rehearsals, I let the director know that if a bit isn't working and makes the show drag, it may be cut so long as I get a phone call the next day. Same thing goes if there are certain moves that cause anxiety to the actor. Sometimes I'll also explain which fight phrases cannot be modified in any way and which phrases may be cut completely if time or ability to memorize is a problem. But that's just me. Others may not be as comfortable with giving that much control to the director and others will give far more leeway. The main thing is to keep the choreographer in the loop when changes appear necessary. A change may have a hidden danger which the fight director may be able to spot, even through a phone call.

During performance, the stage manager takes over. It is her call as to whether or not a fight must be cancelled due to any safety concerns, including inclement weather. In addition, both she and the fighters themselves have the right and obligation to cancel the fight even in the midst of performing it should it appear that there is any condition which might cause an injury to either the actors or audience. As I've said before, there is no show that is worth an injury.

The Fight Call

A fight call is a short rehearsal of all of the fights in a show. It takes place just before every technical rehearsal and performance starting with first tech and continuing all the way through to closing night. If your show has a fight, you must run a nightly pre-show fight call. Of course it would be wonderful if this could happen starting well before first tech. I for one would love to see a fight call schedule for every single rehearsal starting the day after the fighters are first given the choreography, but I know that isn't realistic for most theatres. But certainly starting with first tech, the fight call must be incorporated into the call schedule. It doesn't matter if the fight is only a couple of punches, you can't short change this vital aspect of actor safety.

A fight call allows the actors an opportunity to get the moves of the fight back into muscle memory and to fix any of the little problems that may have cropped up during the prior performance. That's all there is to it. For my money, there is no point in running the fights at full speed nor in slow motion. A simple light and quick walk-through of the fight is usually all that is necessary. If a particular issue needs to be addressed, the specific action should be worked through and then the entire fight run one more time, but that's it. There is no benefit in exhausting the cast before the show. It's analogous to a line speed-thru. It only takes about twenty minutes and it awakens the brain so that the actor is ready for performance.

Actors resent the fight call. They hate showing up early, and I don't blame them. But since keeping the fight fresh can prevent serious injuries, all of the actors should know that anyone who fails to show up for fight call will be cut from the fights in that night's performance. For that reason the fight call is run by the fight captain, but is set and called by the stage manager. Showing up on time is the only requirement that must be set in stone. Bring this up at the first company meeting, for anyone who cannot make the fight call should not be cast in a fight.

Beyond that, be flexible. You may need to work out a split call if there are many cast members and some have different make-up and costume calls, or you may need all of the fighters to arrive twenty minutes before the rest of the cast, or you may need to set the fight call for twenty minutes before curtain. The specifics don't matter so long as a practical routine is set and then kept.

In some theatres the rigidity of fight call protocol can get a bit silly. Some places insist on the fight call taking place on the set, with all of the set dressing in place, and all of the actors in costume. Some also require every fight to be performed three times: once as a walk-through, then at half speed with lines, and finally at full performance speed. But why put everyone through all of that? The call can be performed nearly anywhere so long as there is enough room, and at some point you need to trust that the actors know what they are doing. They just need a quick chance to freshen up the fight and check the weapons for damage. Certainly there is no benefit to having them run the fights at performance speed.

* * * * *

Before we get to the combat itself, there are some other aspects of teaching staged combat that should be addressed - the first being actors playing with violence off-stage. Actors are given the liberty to play as children while exploring their characters, but a lot of them also want to play with the fight techniques they are learning. The impulse to play is understandable but really gets in the way of good rehearsing. For one thing, as soon as you start playing with stage combat, your body starts memorizing bad technique, so the super slow motions and mind numbing repetition of careful fight rehearsals is really the only thing that will lead to a believable fight - and a safe one.

That being said, slow motion rehearsing is a tool that helps us get to performance, but we can't confuse one for the other. In any art discipline we can't show the audience that we have learned correct technique. We have to provide a believable illusion, to hold the mirror up to nature. So at some point the actors are going to have to bring the fight up to speed and give each simulation a look of real danger. Whether director or actor, never be satisfied that you have "taken care of the fight stuff." Each simulation must be judged on safety _and_ believability. If it doesn't strike an audience as being true, it has no business being in your show.

A third concern is that some actors may simply not be comfortable around violent actions, and they can begin to lose the trust that they need to have in their partners. These actors are going to be very reticent about expressing their discomfort for fear of being seen as "wimps", so please keep a weather eye out for them. If they are given a chance to approach the material slowly and in a spirit of exploration and sharing, with a little patience you'll find that they can soon more than hold their own in even the most demanding fight scenes.

Another point that both directors and actors need to remember is that stage combat will <u>never</u> have the feel of action sequences in popular movies. I know that's sometimes a bitter pill to swallow, especially after seeing breathtaking fights in such films as _The Matrix, Braveheart, Gladiator_, or _The Lord of the Rings_. Stage actors want to re-create the cool moves they've seen, but we just can't speed up the film when the actor gets tired, or show something at three different angles, or perform something twenty times in front of the camera and then keep the best move for the final cut, or edit out every time a weapon breaks, or bring in a stunt double, or take ten hours to film an entire fight in segments of only four moves at a time, or delay finishing a scene waiting for an actor to recuperate from a bruised knee, or change out a heavy steel sword for a plastic duplicate that weighs only a tenth of the first one and use it in the middle of a fight sequence, or pretend to fire a gun and add the sound and the flash in post-production.

Stage combat is an illusion that works only because we can control the placement of the audience and they have suspended disbelief. Playing with these actions outside of rehearsal really looks goofy to passersby, and adds to the reputation of immaturity with which the acting profession is already burdened.

Finally, stage combat training does not mean that injuries will not occur. They will. Good training will lead to fewer injuries, but accidents will happen and actors will get hurt. If you are not comfortable with that, cut the fights from the show.

Unarmed Stage Combat

The basics of unarmed stage combat are simple movements combined so as to give the illusion of violent contact. It is not violence itself. When I began teaching I developed the anagrams of **VINO** and **SPAR** so that the actors can evaluate themselves and others even in my absence. These are easy to remember and contain the basics of correct technique. They are also helpful in evaluating the work of other fight choreographers as you see them working with actors.

In order to have a successful simulation of something, you must understand what the reality is. You are taking a three-dimensional reality of an event, compressing it into two dimensions to understand what the audience really sees, and then pulling it back into three dimensions with all of the safety measures built in. And what makes stage combat possible is that the audience has no depth perception.

The first anagram is a reminder of the essence of what makes stage combat different and, we hope, safer than stunt work. These are principles to keep in mind *before* attempting to choreograph the fight.

V - victim stays in control
I - interactive flow of energy
N - non-contact techniques
O - off-line targets

In stage combat, the **victim** is the person who at any specific moment is the one who is on the receiving end of any intended violent action. This is not a "good-guy, bad-guy" designation, as it will switch many times during the course of the fight. The rule of having the victim of any simulation stay in absolute control must never be compromised in any way. This means that, for starters, the person who is receiving the simulation of violence is the first and final arbiter of how fast a technique is performed, when it is to begin, and even if it is to be performed at all. The victim is never pushed, never thrown, never pulled, never tripped, never slapped. The audience may think that it is seeing these things happen to a character, but the actors both know that the reality is something else entirely. And if during any performance the victim feels that the next simulation has any level of danger or even uncertainty, the technique is simply not performed.

Instead of merely trading techniques back and forth ("first I push you and then you punch me"), both actors must work together on each simulation to establish an **interactive** flow of energy which gives the audience the illusion of real action given and received during the fight. To accomplish this, each actor must be acutely observant of the minute movements which his or her partner brings to the simulation. Respecting the laws of physics and constantly adjusting the reactions are part of establishing a flow of energy, and in stage combat this flow is transferred in an intensely specific way from one character to another. This energy is first motivated by one character, translated into an aggressive intent, demonstrated through physical action, and then has a logical result for the intended recipient.

Whenever possible, try to find a **non-contact** technique for your simulation. Exhaust the possibilities. Even if you are working on a thrust stage or in the round, it is always possible to create the illusion of striking someone without actually having to make contact. Don't give up; you will reduce the injury rate dramatically if you simply find a way to eliminate contact.

Always have the aggressive movement aimed to a target which is **off-line** of the victim. For example, instead of aiming for a person's face for a face punch, the fist is directed to a spot just above the shoulder. Instead of running directly towards someone to grab him, run in a parallel path slightly upstage or downstage of your partner. Remember: audiences have no depth perception.

The other anagram comes in when it is time to actually work out and perform the simulation. SPAR helps us break down every simulation into its core elements. When a fight looks phony or fuzzy, it's usually because one of these elements has been rushed or forgotten.

S - safety set-up
P - picture
A - action
R - reaction

Any simulation begins with a **set-up**. This is the moment in which both actors establish the safe distance and position they require, as well as the moment they make eye-contact with each other to make sure that they are both ready for the simulation. The feet are placed in position, and must not move until the action is complete. They might also establish physical contact as well, but that contact is not part of the illusion of the violent action. The audience is not aware of a violent action at this point, so if either actor feels that something isn't right, he or she can simply step back and either wait for the danger to pass or move on to the next safe bit of business. Inhale during the set-up

The **picture** is what we show to the audience so that they know what it is they are supposed to believe they are about to see. They must have a clear moment where, for a split second, they make a mental note that someone is about to be hit or kicked or whatever. Without the picture, they will not understand the simulation.

The **action** is the movement which the audience believes to be violent, often accompanied by a slapping or striking sound but *always* accompanied be the exhalation of breath and sound from both actors. Ironically, the audience can rarely focus on this movement, so it is here where, magician-like, we can fool the audience into believing what we want them to believe. The action includes the theoretical point of impact between the participants, and this impact point is always hidden from the audience's view. Exhale during the action.

After the movement is executed, an appropriate **reaction** from both participants is necessary for the audience to believe the action. The reaction is both physical and emotional. It includes a final split-second "pose" from the aggressor in order to show the audience what they are supposed to have witnessed. It also must be filled with all of the physiological responses that occur when violent actions happen, as well as be truthful to the inevitable relationship change between the characters.

Stage Directions

I'll be using the common stage terminology in order to explain relative actor positions for these moves. Most of you know all of this, but I just want to make sure that we're all on the same page here, so I'll very briefly run through the ones I'll use.

Stage Right - relative to the actor when on stage looking out towards the audience, the right side of the performance area. (Also known as house left)

Stage Left - relative to the actor when on stage looking out towards the audience, the left side of the performance area. (Also known as house right)

Up Stage - towards the back of the performance area, away from the audience.

Down Stage - towards the audience, approaching the front of the performance area.

Those are the terms that describe where the actor should be or move to, but there also exist terms used to describe which way the actor should turn his/her body. *Full front* is the actor standing with his/her body placement completely open to the audience, whereas *full back* of course is the opposite. When the actor turns 90 degrees toward stage right it is called *profile right* or *half right*, (which is ironic because the audience is then looking at the actor's left profile), and the mid-positions between those are called *quarter right* and *three-quarter right*. And then of course all of these have corresponding positions when facing stage left.

I'll also be using some anatomical terms that have a colloquial meaning but are not technically correct, such as *solar plexus* and *stomach*. For the sake of simplicity, I'll continue to use the common meanings.

Unarmed Simulations

Stage fights that do not involve weapons are more dangerous than sword fights if for no other reason than that the actors are standing very close together. So make sure that you understand how the descriptions below have built-in safety measures, but always feel free to change any aspect of them if you can make it even safer.

I'll repeat this many times: actors learn movement the same way they learn their lines - one at a time. But actors must perform movement the same way they perform their lines - in natural varied rhythms. You can stretch out or speed up your timing, or even overlap some of the lines, but you can't eliminate some words just to get to the end of the sentence faster. The same holds true for the individual moves that make up a simulation.

All of unarmed stage combat works because of four deficiencies of human perception:

1] We make very poor eyewitnesses. The police and court lawyers all know this, as do researchers of paranormal phenomena. Invariably our memory tells us that we saw more than what was really there to see. When we see shapes that we can't identify, our brain quickly tries to fill in the gaps so as to make sense of the incoming information. So what appeared to be a child standing near a curb at second glance was obviously a mailbox on a post.

2] We have trouble tracking movement. We are both distracted by it and are bad at focusing on it. We tend to think we've seen longer motions than whatever actually occurred.

3] We have very poor depth perception. Even though we live in a three dimensional world and have binocular vision, our view of things is pretty much flat. We rely more on cues based on visual comparison to other known objects to tell us which items are closer. The relative size of recognized objects and their overlap as they move are our main criteria, rather than actually being able to judge exact distance purely from focusing our eyes.

4] We demand a story. When we see a movement pattern, even random actions, our brains will weave it into a narrative, an explanation of what is happening, and in that process we stick in motivation and outcome. Not only do we see a tree fall, we try to figure out <u>why</u> the tree fell.

All of these deficiencies normally don't bother us during the course of our daily lives. As a matter of fact, in the real world they are probably crucial to our survival. It is better to "see" six false lions than to miss one real one. But on stage, we take advantage of each of these attributes so as to convince an audience that they have witnessed something that did not happen.

Now is a good time to repeat - the only way to safely learn stage combat is by direct lessons from a competent and experienced stage combat instructor. As a young man I tried to learn judo from a book. And even though I picked-up a lot of interesting fine points on technique, I didn't really learn how much I didn't know until some competent instructors threw me around a few hundred times.

Anyone can pretend to punch or kick someone. That is the part of the simulation that requires the least amount of rehearsal, but is the one on which new actors wish to focus because they feel that they are doing something. But just as repeating memorized lines in front of an audience doesn't make you an actor, performing the action without the set-up, picture and reaction isn't a stage fight. Oh, I grant that it is very exciting for the actors, but it is very boring theatre for the paying customers.

Let's use a single basic face punch simulation - a right cross - to see how we take a moment of real violence and take advantage of human perception and add in the elements of both **VINO** and **SPAR** to make the violence safe. The characters of our play for some reason are in a dispute which escalates in anger and tension until one of them takes it beyond words and crosses over into the physical. For our purposes we're going to make it a big looping right hand punch to the face.

First, we need to look at the reality before we can design a simulation. There are many ways that a punch to the face can happen, so for now we're going to pick one - a big looping right cross. Usually the aggressor will start to lean back a bit on the right foot while the right hand moves straight back, folding into a fist. The left arm comes in front of the body as the torso turns slightly to the right. As the fist swings around forward in a big looping arc towards the victim's face, the body turns to the left as the weight shifts onto the left foot. After contact, the right hand ends up forward and to the left, past the plane of the victim, or could continue in the same looping arc and end up over the aggressor's left shoulder. That reality is one that we need to simulate, removing the danger but maintaining the illusion. How do we do that?

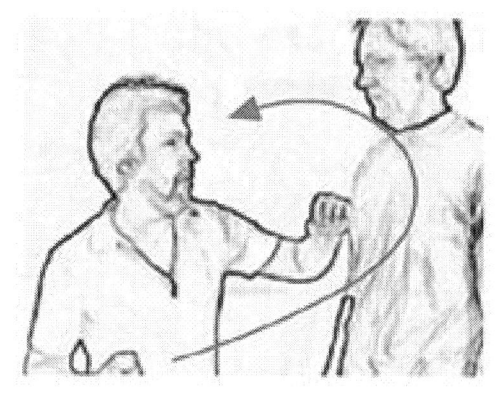

There is a three dimensional reality to the real punch, but we remember that the audience has no depth perception, so we only need to replicate the two dimensional image that they perceive. As long as we don't violate that flattened view, the movements of our simulation can incorporate all of the safety features we need. This is the basic formulae for all of stage and film violence.

Before they do anything else, our actors have to move into position for the simulation. They have probably moved quite a bit during the argument, and little shifts in blocking can be expected from performance to performance, but the fight itself can brook no variations. The actors have to find their way to the exact spot onstage on which the fight will begin. This usually happens three or four lines before the punch so that the audience doesn't notice the set-up.

Don't let the actors slide through the set-up. They are usually really antsy to get right to the action, but the set-up serves two vital functions. First, if the actors do not find their exact positions, the mechanics of the simulation will be visible to the audience and the illusion will fail. Second, and more importantly, the quick visual contact between the two actors provides the last chance to back away from each other before the action begins. And even though it is only for a split second, that brief eye-contact can prevent a serious injury. Two examples to illustrate what I mean:

I once watched a performance in which one actor had to run up a flight of stairs and throw open a door, behind which was a surprise character that punched the first actor in the face, sending the victim down the flight of stairs. They were supposed to perform the very simulation I am about to describe. On the night that I saw the show, when the door flew open the actor on the other side (the aggressor) had a look on his face that can only be described as "a deer in the headlights". It struck me that something seemed odd, and in the next moment I saw him swing his arm, heard a resounding crack, and then saw the victim fall down the stairs as the look on the aggressor changed to that of shock. It was obvious that something had gone horribly wrong. After the show I made my way backstage and asked the actor what happened. He told me that in that instant when the door flew open, he somehow forgot how to do the simulation. The two actors of course had rehearsed and performed the punch many times, but at that moment the mechanics of the illusion simply left his brain. Instead of not doing anything, the compulsion to do something led the actor to simply punch the other in the face. That's right: he had actually cold-cocked the victim - stuck him full on the chin. Stupid? To be sure. Avoidable? Perhaps, if the victim had taken a split second to look at the aggressor when he opened the door. That "deer in the headlights" look boded only ill, and when he saw that he should have stepped away from the aggressor until they could establish the same eye-contact that they were used to seeing in rehearsal.

The second story is quite similar, and again I was a witness to an unfortunate choice made by a panicky actor. This time it was one actor on the ground and the aggressor simulating a kick to the victim's head. A dicey illusion, but when well rehearsed very effective. It was a costume drama, and in this evening's performance the victim's cape somehow flipped over his head as he went to the ground. The victim had a little bit of trouble in trying to flip the cape back. The aggressor should have simply waited, but instead choose to do something (never a good idea). He, in his panicked brain, went through all of the possible choices and settled on the one he thought was the best. He simply kicked the victim in the head. Actually kicked him. The lesson to learn is obvious: don't try any action until you can establish eye-contact, which is part of the set-up. It doesn't have to be noticeable to the audience, and it only needs to take a fraction of a second, but it is as vital a part of the simulation as any other part of the movement.

Directors usually like to have actors facing each other in quarter right and quarter left stances. However, for this particular face punch we are going to have the actors placed so that the aggressor is full-back and the victim is full-front and directly upstage of the aggressor. This means that just before the punch, the aggressor's face and body front will not be seen by the audience, and most of the victim will be blocked from view as well.

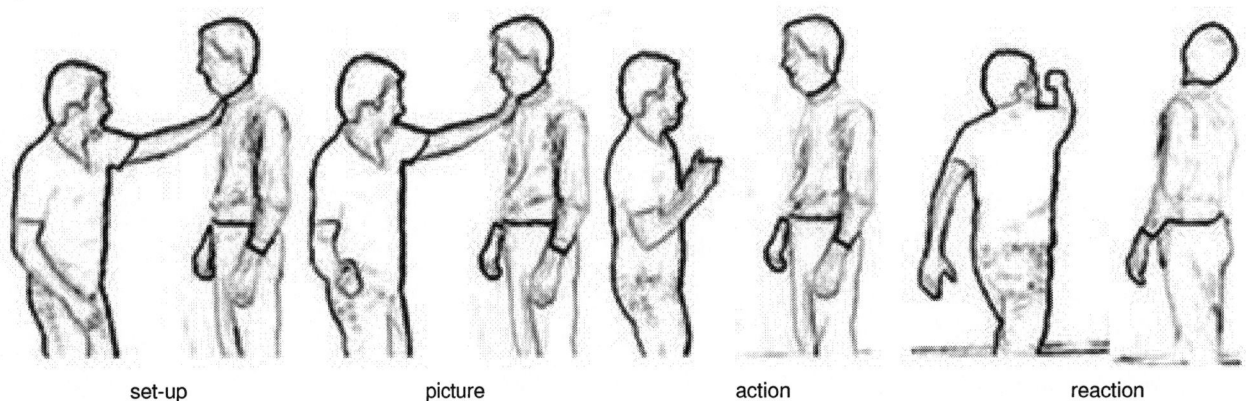

Right Cross: Side View

set-up   picture   action   reaction

We need not only the verbal cue for the violent action, but also a physical one, perhaps noticed by the audience but not necessarily part of the violent act itself. For this punch we are going to have the aggressor put his left [non-punching] hand on the victim's shoulder [*the set-up*]. The reaching arm should be almost fully straight, creating as much distance as possible between the two actors. This can be justified as, let's say, preventing the victim from turning away or grabbing at the victim's lapel, whatever, so long as it flows from the character choices and the scene. Once this touch occurs, the actors are not allowed to move their feet. Eye-contact is established between the actors - not the characters. If the victim dislikes anything about the body placements, or if eye-contact is not established, he or she merely steps back away from the aggressor [*victim stays in control*].

Right Cross: Audience View

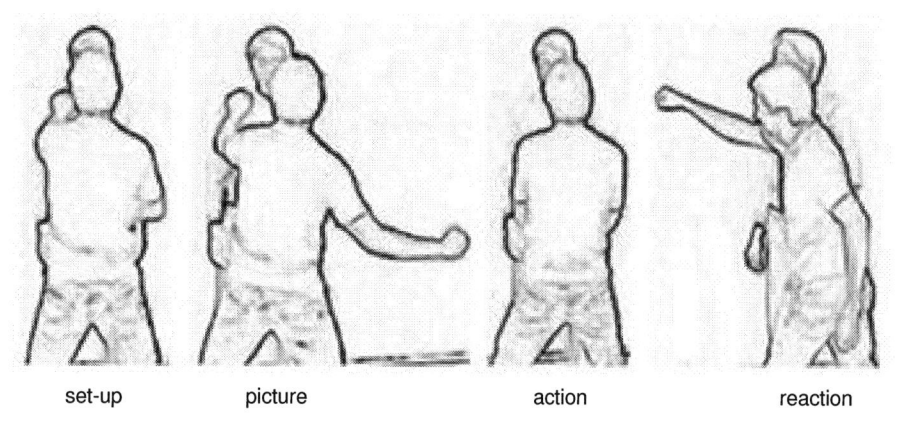

set-up   picture   action   reaction

Keeping the hips and shoulders square to the victim, the aggressor places his right fist out to his right side, showing the audience that a punch is about to occur [*the picture*]. The aggressor must not move his feet nor twist away from the victim; he merely presents a two-dimensional view of the preparation for a punch to the face. The picture does not have to take more than an instant, but it does have to be clear.

Now the aggressor gently brings both hands together, making a clapping sound so as to give the sound of fist striking face [*the action*]. Don't punch the right fist into the left hand: that merely hurts the hand and makes a poor sound. Once the fist disappears from the audience's view, simply create an openhanded clap, and then make sure to create the fist again as soon as you hear the sound. This is called a slip hand knap for only one hand is moving, the other merely being a static target, although it did have to move to get into position.

The fist will never approach the victim's face in this simulation. Make sure that the aggressor understands that the right fist doesn't actually loop around toward the victim's face, but rather that both hands make a beeline directly to a spot three inches away from the aggressor's chest. Clapping the hands by the aggressor takes place in a prayer position, never near the victim's face. The audience has no depth perception, so there is no reason to move the fist towards the victim, but instead it travels across the front of the victim well below the level of his chin [*aim off-line*]. We perform a two-dimensional straight line reality, and allow the audience to imagine a three dimensional looping fiction. The feet of the aggressor stay planted on the ground, and the torso doesn't lean into the punch, but merely pivots like the agitator in a washing machine.

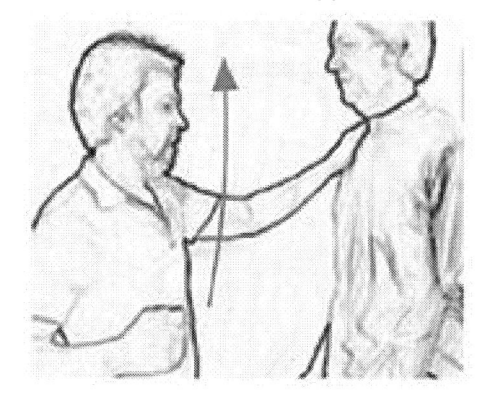

The knap, however performed, provides the percussive sound of the impact, but it is not the only sound that the audience needs to hear. Far more important is the natural forced exhalation that comes from *both* participants in a violent action. That exhalation may or may not be vocalized, but in one degree or another must accompany every move in the fight. That's why I had you inhale during the set-up. To ignore the exhalations in a fight is to rob the audience of their most critical cues to believing your simulation.

Only after the sound has been heard should the actors respond to the punch [*the reaction*]. Sound travels, so in a large house the victim must not react until he consciously hears the clapping sound, or else the back third of the audience will see the physical response before the sound of the punch has reached them. Also, actors tend to jump the gun when it comes to reacting, so making them wait until they hear the sound helps clean-up the action. The victim will move the face and right shoulder back and to his right, following the impetus of the imaginary traveling fist. In a larger reaction, the body might travel one or more steps, after the head reaction, but again back and to the right, increasing the distance between the actors. This reaction must match exactly the amount of impact which has been transferred by the punch from the aggressor to the victim, so all of the laws of physics must be obeyed [*interactive flow of energy*] The aggressor will finish his reaction not by sending the fist over the victim's shoulder, but simply continuing the straight line started during the action, in other words, moving harmlessly in a safe line parallel and between the two participants.

The reaction is largely overlooked or given short shrift by the actors, but it is the only part that can impart realism to the simulation. The set-up, picture and action can be learned in a matter of minutes, but the reaction can take every bit of rehearsal time that can be spared. For the aggressor on this simulation, he should know that in all likelihood his character is experiencing an extraordinary adrenaline rush. The heart is pounding, the breath rate is increased, the muscles have tensed. The increased bloodflow includes that to the eyes, so much in some cases that the belligerent literally "sees red". Pain may not be noticed in such circumstances, but quite a bit of damage can be caused to the punching hand, especially a number of fractures in the finger bones and knuckles, often a sprained or even broken wrist. This may not matter to the character immediately, but at some point the actor should incorporate the pain and stiffness when we see the character in other scenes.

The victim has just as much work to do. The simulation must include a realistic depiction of the transmission on energy that travels in a straight line through the victim, for as it travels it will affect each body part in turn. Let's say that one of the moves is a face punch. If so, the victim must carefully decide exactly where on the face the fist has landed. If on the left side of the jaw, for instance, the lower jaw will be shunted violently to the right, the force of which will spin the head also to the right, but with the top of the head slightly trailing the jaw. The ligaments of the left side of the neck will begin to pull, stretch and tear, but also finally to draw the left shoulder around to the front. At this point the momentum will cause the top of the head to tilt suddenly to the right. Combined with the left shoulder turn, it will move the victim's center of balance off of the left foot and back over the heel of the right foot, causing the body to move to the right and back. And that is merely one possibility.

Physiological changes for the victim include perhaps watery eyes and runny nose at least, perhaps slight shock as well. The extent of damage can include a broken lip, broken teeth, dislocated or broken jaw, certainly some tendon and ligament damage to the left side of the neck.

How much damage has been inflicted and how far the body will travel depends on how much force was behind the punch. Both actors must work together on every rehearsal to pay close attention to this, for not only must the victim modify the reaction so that it matches the apparent force delivered, the aggressor must make adjustments in body placement so that the path the victim takes after the punch makes sense. [Look to the section on punches for more tips on performing this illusion.]

All of this is of course rehearsed by the numbers and in extremely slow motion during the early rehearsals, and only after much practice slowly increased in speed until the individual parts of the simulation appear to blend together. For performance, all of the parts will be there, but the bodies never come completely at rest, so the audience is unaware of the components of the simulation. What you're going for is a sequence of clear fluid movements. It remains axiomatic, however, that the closer the two actors are to each other, the more that time must be stretched so that the audience can refocus their attention to a smaller sphere of action and be able to follow the story that even the simplest action describes. Whether timid or aggressive, actors always want to do stage combat too quickly, and too quickly translates as muddy for the audience, which greatly resents not being able to follow a story.

Actors learn fight moves the same way they learn their lines - one at a time. But actors must *perform* movement the same way they *perform* their lines - in natural varied rhythms. You can stretch out or speed up your timing, or even overlap some of the lines, but you can't eliminate some words just to get to the end of the sentence faster. The same goes with the individual moves that make up a simulation. The goal is to perform all of the actions of each simulation and letting them appear natural.

Once the moves are perfected the actor's challenge is to let the body flow so that the audience sees a fully developed natural impulse, not a staccato series of still images. A good exercise is to have the actors go through the fight, but standing several feet apart. If the fight looks convincing at that distance, then it will look great and still be safe when they move back together.

Stance

Although balance is absolutely essential in swordplay, it is perhaps even more important here in unarmed fighting, though a little less obvious to the audience. Foot placement should appear normal, but at all times provide a solid base from which to move. That means that both heels should stay planted whenever possible, and the weight of the body should rest comfortably on the hips, not leaning forward. Knees need to be slightly bent and relaxed to further aid in maintaining balance. As you can guess, since in unarmed stage combat the actors are so close together, one actor losing his balance means that two actors fall down. So keep the balance off of the toes and back down on the heels. It might be a common reaction for the aggressor to throw his body weight forward along with the momentum of a punch, but if we include that in the simulation, it must be under complete control.

And, although it sounds impossible at first, both actors have to be as physically relaxed as possible. Tension leads to injury

Pantomimed Impulses

All of stage combat is a pantomime, of course, but some simple illusions are not overtly violent yet still fall within the parameters of controlled movement. Mastering these techniques will make the impact simulations even more realistic. We'll start with the basic moves, which is not to say the easiest. Indeed, these pantomimed impulse moves are more difficult to do because of their subtlety.

grab

I start all actors out with the grab, for it is the simplest of stage combat actions, and one that need not have a violent intent at all. Stated another way, it reminds us that stage combat is about actions, not anger. Actors learn something instantly practical and it begins to prep them in the concept of stage combat being a shared art form.

Any character might want to stop another simply out of excitement (*"You've go to see this - it's the most incredible thing!"*), - and the hand grabs the friend's wrist. Even in such a friendly situation, we have to obey the cardinal on-stage rule: the victim must stay in control. You may ask, where's the victim? Well, we're concerned with this single action, and at that moment of contact the friendly aggressor is restricting the movement of her partner, therefore the partner becomes the victim. No matter how friendly the motivation, the act of grabbing establishes the roles for an instant.

"All of that is a fascinating philosophical discussion, but why are we wasting time on something so simple as grabbing?" Because doing so too brusquely can hurt the victim's shoulder, bruise the forearm, or even cause one or both actors to fall. Also, if the victim resists, the aggressor has no way of knowing if the character is trying to get away or if the actor really does need to get away.

In this as in any other static illusion, always find a way to give the victim an escape route. In this case, the aggressor first steps into position, and then reaches out and makes contact with the victim's arm using only an open hand. The thumb is pressed against the index finger creating a bear-paw look - not a primate opposable thumb grip. The force of this connection is provided by the victim - as long as the victim chooses to press his arm into the aggressor's "bear-hand", the illusion is maintained.

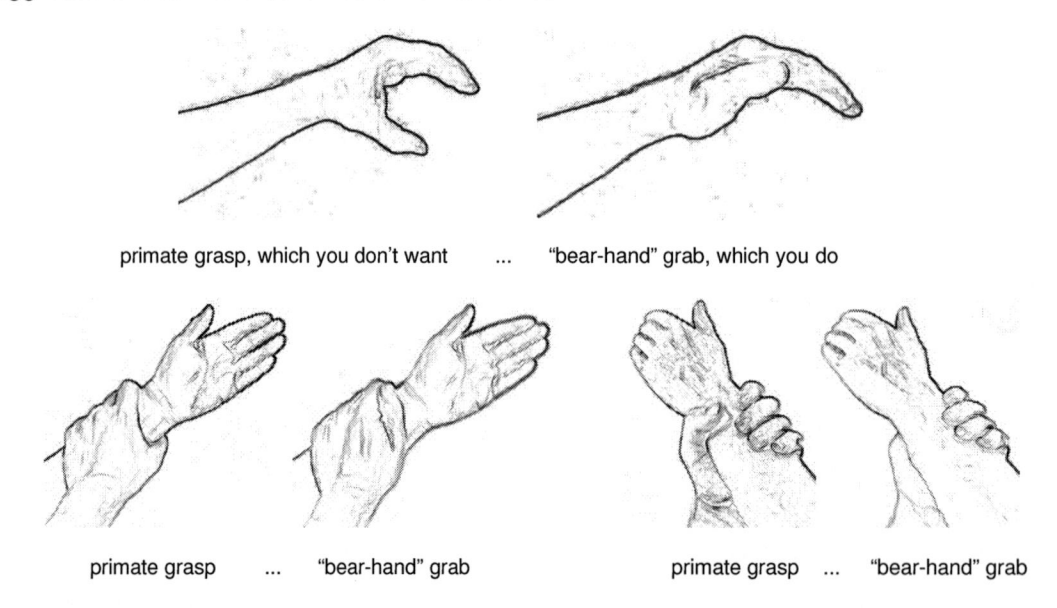

primate grasp, which you don't want   ...   "bear-hand" grab, which you do

primate grasp   ...   "bear-hand" grab   primate grasp   ...   "bear-hand" grab

If for any reason the victim has to get out of the way, he simply releases his arm from contact and steps back. Easy. That's all there is to it! Our primate grasp with the opposable thumb make a great clamp, but you don't need that on-stage. Simply have the aggressor keep the thumb and fingers pressed together in the bear paw position and grab the victim with the cupped fingers. No more bruised arms or wrists, and the victim can always slip out of the grasp if absolutely necessary. Just roll the arm towards the fingers for an automatic release.

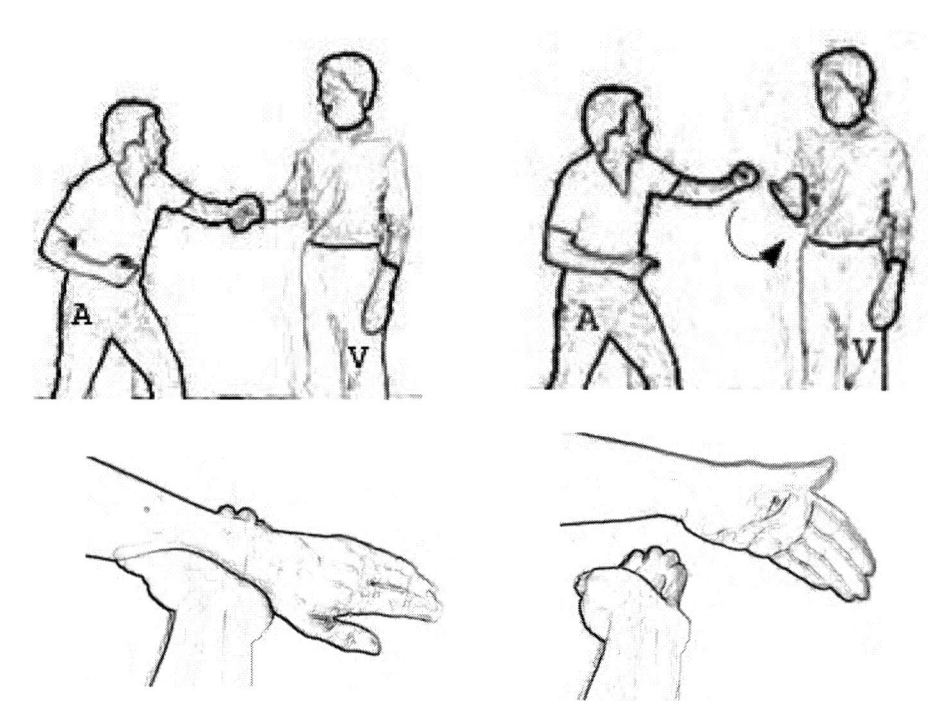

"But the audience will see that I'm not really grabbing him." No they won't, not if the rest of what you're doing is interesting. Anyway, if the audience is looking at your thumb position during the middle of a scene, it means that you lost their attention a long time ago.

push

So simple, and yet so much can go into it.

Actors at first put too much energy into being pushed, but people don't fly away from each other at the merest touch. Neither should one actor have to fling the other across the room. After all it's still a pantomime. Certain physical rules have to be followed in the order in which they occur naturally. Try pushing a wall, and then try pushing a pair of pants hung in your closet. Without conscious thought, your body will go through the same biomechanics both times, the only difference being in the response to the amount of resistance anticipated or encountered.

First the fingertips touch and assess the weight and composition of the object. Then the legs, torso and shoulder readjust in order to make a better bracing angle against the floor, and as the elbows bend and the body leans forward. Then the arms straighten as the object is moved away. If the object is heavy, the legs will also bend and then straighten, providing even more power. All of this happens in direct proportion to the resistance encountered, and it happens in a split second without conscious design.

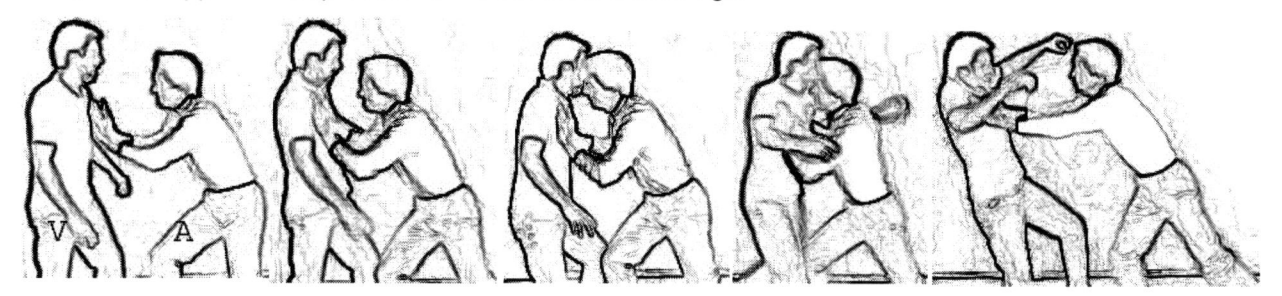

We do exactly the same movements in a staged push, with slight changes. As the fingertips touch the body of the victim, the victim gently and almost imperceptibly leans into the aggressor, who in tern bends the elbows so as to get closer to the victim. This nearly invisible pre-movement, in opposition to the action to come, is what gives these impulse simulations their believability. Now the aggressor must wait for the victim to initiate and complete the illusion of being pushed. The aggressor merely follows the movement of the victim. Make sure to establish an exact correspondence between the amount of body English of the "push" and how far the victim travels.

The aggressor should take care not to make contact with and accidently push at the shoulders of the victim, for the ligaments there can easily tear with repeated stress. Better to make contact at the superior portion of the chest muscles, away from any joints.

pull

Much like the push, but the direction is different. As we mentioned before, the aggressor will not use his thumbs to grab the victim but use a loose "bear paw" to make contact. A very slight movement in opposition from the victim forms the picture of the opposing force. The action starts as a continuation of the opposition move, with the aggressor slightly pulsing into the victim, as if to gear up the force necessary to pull the victim forward. The true action is in the victim deciding to go forward. The reaction of both participants form that interactive flow of energy which sells the illusion to the audience, a flow that must sequentially travel through the body of the aggressor and then transfer to the victim before the victim's feet begin to move. The aggressor must appear to lead the action, although the victim is never truly "pulled" at all.

trip

It's the simple things that can do the most damage. I saw one actor nail another in the shin trying to do a trip. If you've ever taken a hit on the shin, you know that the pain is temporary but excruciating. It naturally stopped the scene.

For this bit, all the actors have to do is remember that the audience has no depth perception, and that less is more. We'll assume here that the aggressor is stationary and that the victim is in motion. The set-up in this case happens before the victim starts to close in, a quick glance for eye contact and to insure that the aggressor is just upstage relative to the victim. The picture is the victim moving across the stage up to the point where he is directly downstage of the aggressor, and the aggressor sharply stabbing the ground with the ball of the foot. This is a very small movement, and it lands upstage of the victim's planted lead foot. The action is completely non-contact on the aggressor's part, while the victim taps the top of his trailing foot against the heel of the planted lead foot, giving the slight "stutter step" look, as well as just a little bit of impact sound. That's right, this is a self trip, and although in direct view of the audience it is invisible to them because of their limited perception of objects in motion. The physical reaction is passive on the aggressor's part. Normally he just looks on and gloats, but if the character's intent needs to be more violent, a pantomimed push on the victim's shoulder can be added. But it must be pantomimed, no more than a modest touch, for even a slight real shove could knock the victim off-balance.

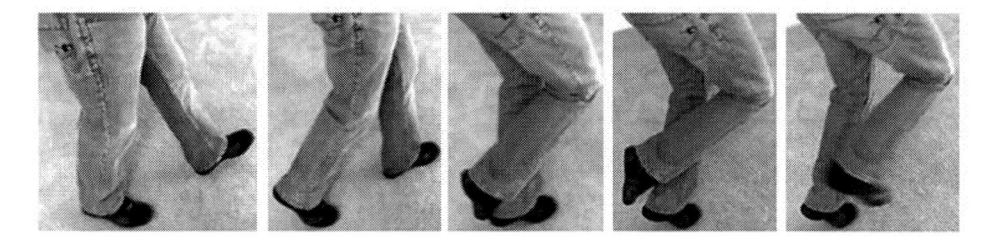

In order to sell this illusion even in tight quarters, the reaction from the victim should lead the audience to look up instead of down at the feet. A slight "whiplash" reaction of the head and letting the arms fly up will help in the distraction.

pull hair/ear/nose

An elegant simulation that I love teaching, and one in which the victim does almost all of the work. The initial danger point is actually as the aggressor moves in to make the grab, so just make sure that the hand doesn't move in towards the eyes, but rather goes up along the side of the head and then to the hair. In a real hair grab, the fingers dig into the hair and then the wrist slightly twists. It is the twisting motion that actually causes the pain, not the lifting. For stage, the aggressor's fingers curl in, making a half fist, which then gently lands on the head of the victim without grabbing any hair at all. At this point, the aggressor is just along for the ride, while the victim acts the pain.

Keep in mind throughout this illusion that in real hair pulling, there is very little pain from simply pulling the hair straight up. It is the slight twist of the wrist that causes the hundred little pinpoints of pain that shoot through the scalp. That is what the victim needs to sell if the illusion is going to work.

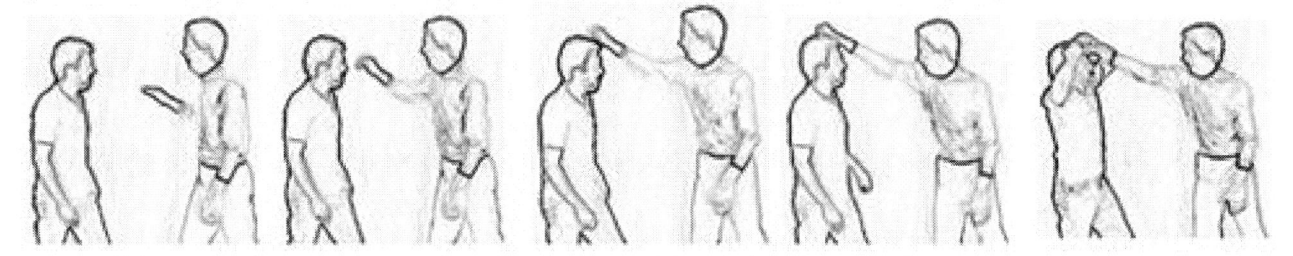

If the action is going to move from here, we need the victim's hands to fly up to the hair, as though to pull away the offending hand. What actually happens is twofold. One hand will land on top of the aggressor's, thus insuring that the hand will stay in contact with the head and not ruin the illusion. The other hand if at all possible will cover the aggressor's wrist and act as a brace - for the aggressor's safety. During the rehearsal, a very carefully choreographed stepping pattern will be worked out, with only the victim actually setting the movement and the aggressor trying to make it look as though he is the one initiating the movement. The aggressor's wrist is in danger if the victim does any sudden movement, so not one muscle twitch must be left to improvisation on a moving hair pull.

If pulling the nose or ear is what you need, the set-up and actions are the same, just a different target. As always the danger is in moving the fingers in the direction of the eyes, so have the hand come in sideways in front of the face and then allow the victim to gently lean into the hand.

side view

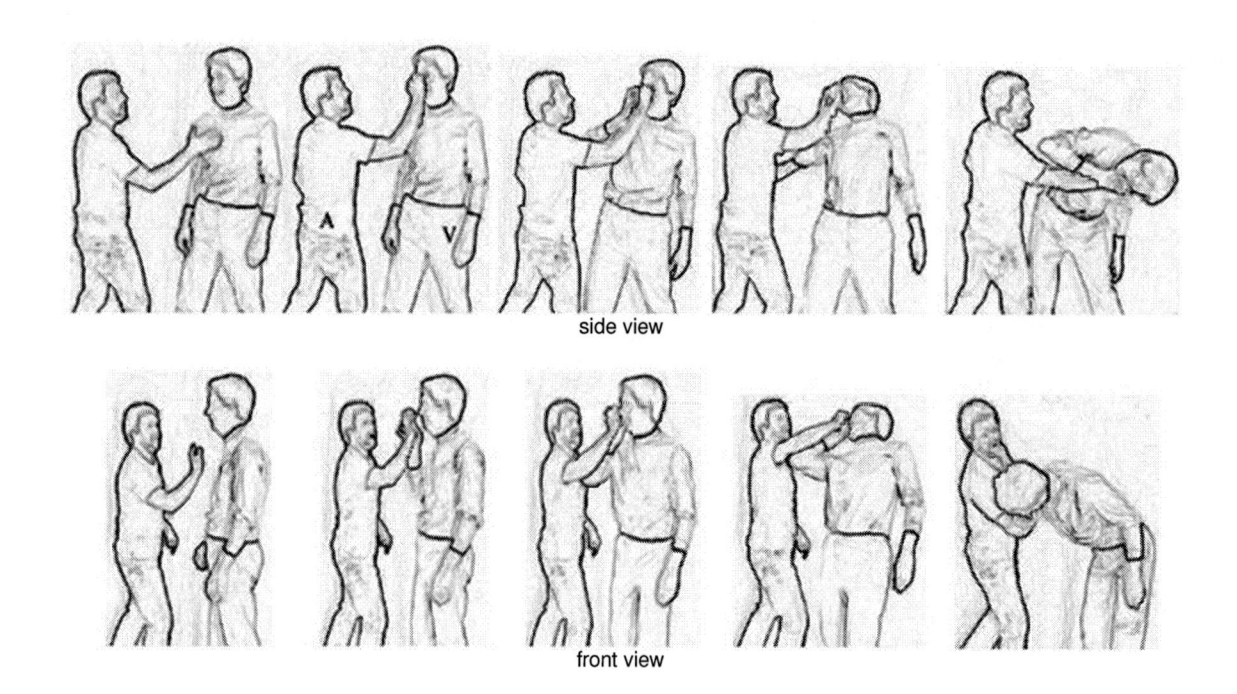

front view

In pulling someone by the nose or by the ear, think push, not pull. Have the victim push her head into the aggressor's hand, and he gently pushes back to maintain contact. Both will walk together to the choreographed location, with the victim providing more force than the aggressor.

smothering

Smothering Desdemona with a pillow while she lies in bed is the obvious example, but also included here is anytime that someone covers someone else's month, if only to shut them up. We always want the victim to be able to breathe, and we don't want to damage the nose either, so the focus is to take away any pressure going towards the face.

If it is an open hand smother, the aggressor slides the palm up, parallel to the face instead of swinging-in in a slapping motion. Let the hand hover away from the face, and let the victim close the gap by pressing forward into the open palm. The aggressor merely keeps the palm curved so that the contact to the face is limited to the finger tips and the palm heel. The key is that contact is maintained by the victim pressing into the aggressor's hand.

The pillow smother is dicier, but can be just as safe. We can't do the side slide as above, for the audience is going to need to see the pillow come down straight onto the victim's face. Assuming that the aggressor is straddling the victim and holding onto the pillow at both ends, start by letting the pillow come down with apparent force, but allow the pillow to release from the hands as soon as contact is made. The victim will very quickly wake and try to pull the pillow away, right? So here is where we reverse the energy. We have the victim grab the aggressor's arms and pull them *towards* her face, with the aggressor trying to maintain distance by pulling *up*. It is a static moment, but physically engages the participants, so we see a fully engaged struggle between the two characters. Most importantly, if anything goes wrong the momentum is going to go away from the victim.

choke - hands on neck

The obvious danger here is that the victim can actually get choked, but also that the forward momentum of the aggressor might accidentally push his hands forward, accidentally punching the victim in the throat. Here is one illusion in which we cannot use the "bear paw", for the audience must see the aggressor's thumbs on the victim if they are to believe the choke. We also need to see some activity in the aggressor, so we will redirect the physical energy to the victim's shoulders instead of the neck.

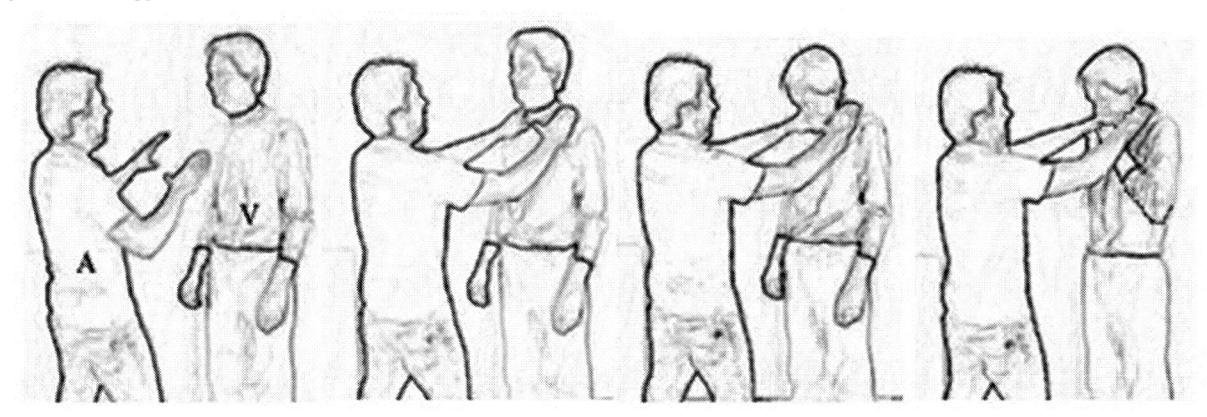

On the set-up, the aggressor plants his feet and extends the open hands towards the throat. Make sure that the heads are not directly in line with each other. For the picture, the aggressor rests the palms onto the victim's trapezius muscles (the ones going from the shoulders to the neck), and the thumbs search for the victim's collar bones. Because the audience can see the aggressor's hands so clearly, we can't get away with doing the "bear hand" bit - the audience needs to see the aggressor's thumbs. But the thumbs can be safely placed below the collar bone, away from the neck. The nice thing about this placement is that these bones are easy to feel through even the thickest costume. Since the thumbs are so far away from the throat, the victim must help close the picture by immediately tucking his chin to his chest. Keep that chin tucked or the illusion is lost.

For the action, the aggressor starts pushing down towards the floor, away from the throat. This wonderfully engages the fine muscles of the hands and forearms. Be sure and keep the arms straight but don't lock the elbows. The victim uses his own hands to cover those of the aggressor, giving the impression that he is trying to remove the hands but actually making sure that the hands don't slip away. (To add another element of safety, the victim can surreptitiously and gently hook onto the aggressor's thumbs. Just in case the aggressor gets too violent, a quick pull back on his thumbs can bring him back in focus.)

The reaction usually involves some sort of shaking or pulling on both parts, and this must be carefully choreographed and set in stone - no improvising. It is also recommended that the partners not shake forward and back but rather side to side, so as to avoid an accidental head butt or broken nose. This is why it is so important that the heads not be in line with each other.

choke release

The universal release from actually being choked is to bring both hands and elbows together in front of your stomach and then drive them straight up into the sky while keeping your elbows touching. This will break even the strongest grip. If your hands should lean forward a little and break the attacker's nose, well, so much the better. A simple movement which requires very little modification. But it is crucial that for stage the arms and hands are kept close to the body and that the choker (who is now the victim, by the way) stay as far away as possible during the release. Otherwise, that upthrust can knock out the choker/victim with either the aggressor's fists or elbows striking the chin. That's why the choker should keep the arms as straight as possible during the entire illusion.

single arm choke from behind

I think you can already guess how this works. The arm comes around from behind and lands on the collar bones, not the neck, and you don't actually choke the victim. Again, the victim should pull his chin to his chest so we don't see the gap. If the arms of the victim are going to go up to the attacker's arms as though to pull the arm away, don't actually pull. That will only cause the attacker to tighten the grip in towards the neck - not smart. Instead have the <u>victim</u> push the aggressor's arm towards his own neck. The attacker will naturally respond by pulling the arm away, and there is your safety.

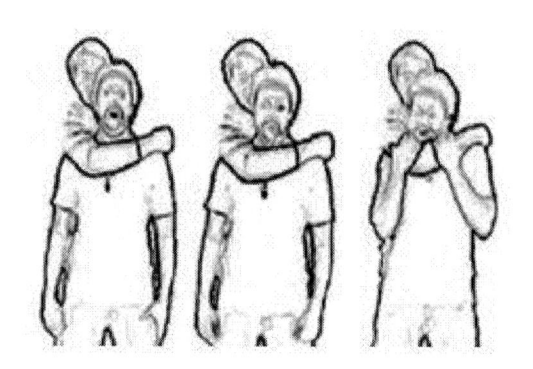

choke with garrote

Anytime that any rope or cord or wire is used to choke someone, it is called a garrote. The mechanics of doing so for stage combat are exactly the same as the above one-armed choke from behind. Simply have the aggressor loosely wrap the cord around the victim, and it's a good idea to mark the cord in such a way that the aggressor knows that he is giving plenty of slack. Then the aggressor simply rests his hands against the victim's back. It is the victim's responsibility to raise his shoulders and push gently into the cord. All of the activity of being choke must come from the victim; the aggressor should stand still as a post.

Strikes

These actions are the ones in which we need the audience to believe that hard physical contact has been made, with a recognizable moment of impact. That moment must always be accompanied by sound - sometimes a percussive sound, but always an exhalation of breath from both participants. Whether vocalized or not, the sound of breath is necessary for the illusion to be effective. There is no exception to that rule: every strike must have a sound.

No matter what the strike, the aggressor need not do the simulation quickly. It is the victim that must sell the violent impact in the reaction. Be sure that the victim understands to not begin the reaction until he can hear the impact sound - the "knap". Sound travels more slowly than light, if the victim moves at the same instant of the strike, the audience is going to see the victim react before they hear the sound and it will get a laugh. Remember: aggressive move, then sound, then reaction.

foot stomp

This is one of those illusions that actors think they know how to do without instruction, but they often leave out one or two points that can add a lot of realism. First, make sure that the foot doing the stomping is directly downstage of the intended victim's foot. If you stomp upstage the audience simply won't believe it. Secondly, but more importantly, make sure that you bounce your foot high off of the floor after doing the stomp. If you leave it stuck on the ground, it proves that you missed the victim.

Go back and practice the trip a few times and you'll see that the two illusions are mechanically similar, just with a different set of pictures and reactions. From one thing learn ten thousand.

face punch

These come in two broad varieties, either the cross or the jab. The cross starts from as close to the body of the aggressor as possible, travels to the impact point and beyond. It gets its name because the natural trajectory of the fist will cross from one side of the body to the other. (If the punch doesn't cross to the other side but merely moves through the victim but on the same side that it started, it is called a straight punch). As the body weight is usually moving along with the punch, the cross usually has a lot of force behind it. The jab, on the other hand, usually causes less damage. It travels just from the shoulder straight to the target and then back again without committing the body. Therefore the jab is much faster that a cross, but also does less damage. In either case, this fist must form a straight line with the forearm: don't let the actors curl in at the wrist unless you are trying to show that the character has no experience in fighting.

That's the reality. Now let's look at the illusions.

cross

This is the punch we explored in the beginning of this section, so we'll briefly go over the basics. [Go back and read the full explanation on pages 237-239.] Actors feel that they already know how to do a fake punch, so the most difficult aspect of this is in having them perform the illusion rather than the reality of a real punch.

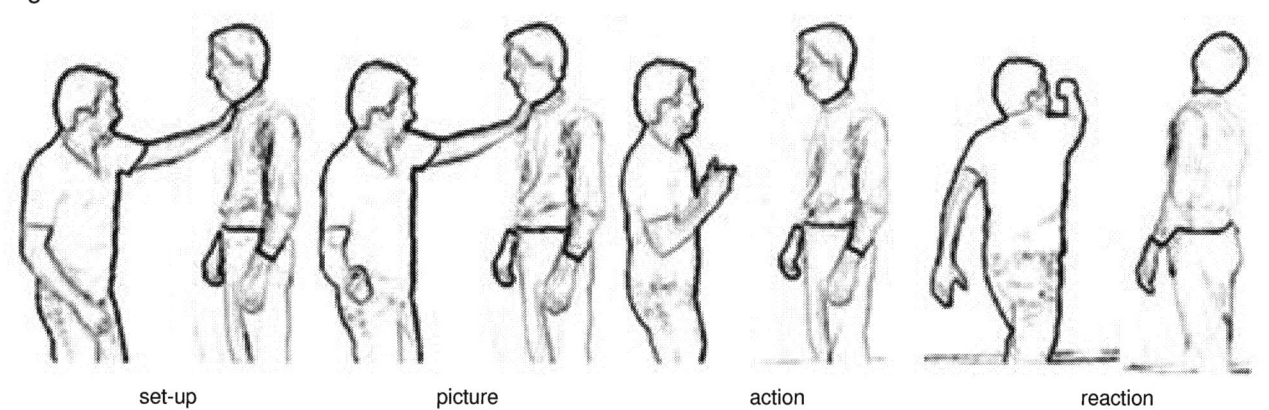

Right Cross: Side View

set-up   picture   action   reaction

Set-up: the aggressor is full-back and the victim is full-front and directly upstage of the aggressor. Aggressor puts his left [non-punching] hand on the victim's right shoulder.

Picture: Keeping the hips and shoulders square to the victim, aggressor places his right fist out to his right side, far enough away so that the audience can see it.

Action: Aggressor gently brings both hands together one inch away from his own chest at solar plexus level to make the knap - the impact sound. [be sure to use open palms for the knap] The punching hand travels in a straight line to the knap point - it does not swing out to the face of the victim. The fist will never approach the victim's face in this simulation, nor will any part of the action travel at face level.

Reaction: The aggressor's hand re-forms a fist and continues its straight line travel, finishing at face height but parallel to the proscenium, between the two participants. The victim will turn head and shoulders in the direction of and proportional to the pantomimed force.

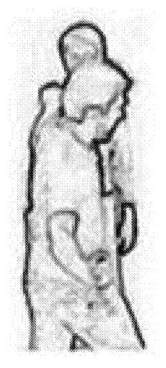

Things NOT to do: over-rotate   the fly-away   the morphing punch/slap

There are some things to make sure that the actors NOT do when performing the aggressor role. These are bad little habits that can ruin the illusion. First, most actors will want to rotate their bodies for the picture portion, instead of keeping their shoulders square to their partner. By over-rotating and pulling the punching hand behind them instead of off to the side, it can expose the handclap moment to the audience's view.

Second, actors tend to let both hands fly off in the direction of the punch during the reaction. Unless they force the knap hand to go down and low, the audience can easily figure out how the punch was faked.

Lastly, some actors will get the picture right with a closed fist, do the action correctly with an open handed clap, but then forget to close the hand into a fist again for the reaction.

jab

I love the jab, for it looks so real to the audience, even when they are right on top of the action. But it can only be performed in a proscenium stage, because it depends on a very narrow visual field. A jab is a straight quick punch, usually to the head, delivered from the leading hand We are going to assume a jab coming from the aggressor's non-dominant hand, and that both actors have assumed a boxing stance. For most people, that means left foot forward and left hand forward. The jab is a set-up punch, causing pain but probably not enough to stop an opponent. It is usually used with the left hand to wear down an opponent's defenses before a knock-out punch with the right hand.

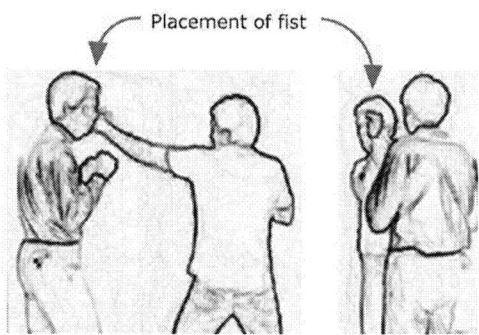

Set up: actors stand facing each other, arms bent. Left fists are extended slightly from the body and held at shoulder or face height. The right fists are held close to the body at solar-plexus level. Both actors are leading with the left foot, and the shoulders and hips are turned sharply to the right to give the thinnest target to the opponent. In this combat stance the actor stage right will be half profile left, and the actor on stage left will be in three-quarter right. As opposed to many of the other simulations, that are performed just out of contact distance, the actors here must be in-distance, close enough for the wrist to reach the other's shoulder.

Placement of fist

Picture: In this case, there is no other picture needed or desired, for the movement must come as a surprise to the audience.

Action: There are two possible actions here depending on the position of the aggressor.

If he is standing stage left that means that the front of his body, therefore his right hand, is not visible to the audience. The left hand shoots out to a spot directly upstage of the victim's upstage ear (disappearing for a split second behind the victim's head) and immediately snaps back. At the same time, the right hand opens and makes a nice popping knap against the chest.

If the aggressor is stage right, than of course that right hand is visible, but the victim's is hidden. In that case, it is the victim who needs to make the knap. In other words, the hand the audience can't see at any particular moment is the one you use to slap. Either way, be sure not to twitch at the elbow when slapping the chest, or the audience will know how you made the sound.

Reaction: The victim's head snaps up and down once in a slight whiplash reaction. A lot of actors want to follow the direction of the aggressor's hand and turn the face slightly up-stage, but the simulation here is of being hit flush on the nose, so the face must not turn sideways at all or the illusion is ruined. The aggressor needs no reaction, as the jab causes minimal damage to the tight fist.

By the way, the same basic mechanics can be used to simulate a punch using the trailing hand. In that case it is called a straight punch, not a jab, and we do have to make one slight modification. Instead of having the actors stand with their shoulders square to each other, we have to off-set the actors, with one of them standing slightly more upstage than the other. That way the straight punch can travel upstage of the victim's head without the aggressor having to twist the torso. Otherwise the simulation looks like a right cross, not a straight punch.

So remember: three hands are visible, so the one that isn't does the sound. And no matter which hand you use, the punch always goes upstage of the victim's head.

upper cut

Side view

A simple illusion. Full-back to the audience for the aggressor, full left arm safety distance touch to the victim's shoulder, and then the left open palm dropping back to the solar plexus as the target for the knap. Keep the torso straight, but bend the knees so as to give strength to the coming punch. The right hand goes down as a fist to as low as comfortable to the right side, then drives up in a straight line to the target [left] hand. As in the right cross, open the fist so as to clap hands, then close into a fist again as it drives up to forehead level or higher, finishing the simulation. Naturally, if the actors are standing in reverse position, the victim can provide the knap. Either way, never let the aggressor's fist move in a curve toward the victim's face.

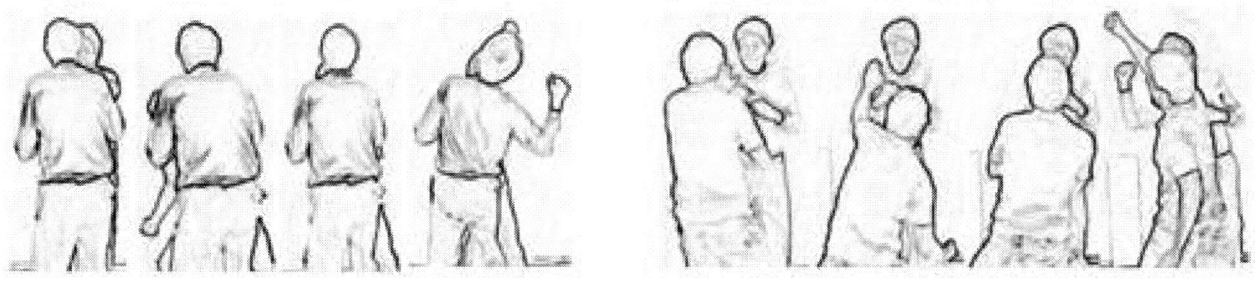

Victim full-back to the audience .... or ..... aggressor full-back to the audience

Remember that an upper cut delivers terrific damage, and boxers know that even with gloved hands if it connects it can be a one-punch knockout move. Save this move for the end f a fight, or at least for a point where the victim is going to remain severely disabled or disoriented. A broken jaw, severed tongue, double concussion (the brain slamming against first the front of the skull and then against the back), even a broken neck are all real possible consequences of this punch.

hook punch - face level

The upper cut just described travels from low to high, of course, perpendicular to the ground. If we shift the angle of this so that it travels in a tight semicircle parallel to the ground, we've created the look of a hook punch. The hook punch is used when then opponent is successfully covering his face with his hands, making the cross or jab difficult. The hook loops tightly around the opponents defenses, and does not follow through but must appear to "bounce off" the opponent's head. As with the jab, the easiest way to provide the knap is to have the aggressor smack his own chest with his left hand. The victim's reaction will be to tilt the head viciously to the right or left, the body following. Care must be taken not to have the victim twist at the neck, for that implies a different punch. Of course the trajectory of the actual movement will go to a safe spot between the two combatants. For this reason, this simulation can only work when the actors are stacked, never when in profile. But because the distance of the victim's head and the aggressor's moving fist are so close, this should be considered an advanced technique.

pile driver

Although this looks as powerful as the above upper cut, the damage is actually less, since the top of the head is a very hard object to strike. The simulation, on the other hand, is much the same except for the direction. If the victim has his back to the audience, with the hands hidden from view he can make the loudest clap possible without moving the elbows. If the aggressor has his back to the audience, then he will make the knap as he did for the right cross face punch. The aggressor's arm starts high, and simply drives the hand in a straight line to the ground, of course going nowhere near the victim's face. The victim matches the action with a clap, being careful not to move the elbows. If possible, have the victim get lower than a natural full upright stance, for we need to see the aggressor rise up on his toes and then "lower the boom", the body dropping into the punch.

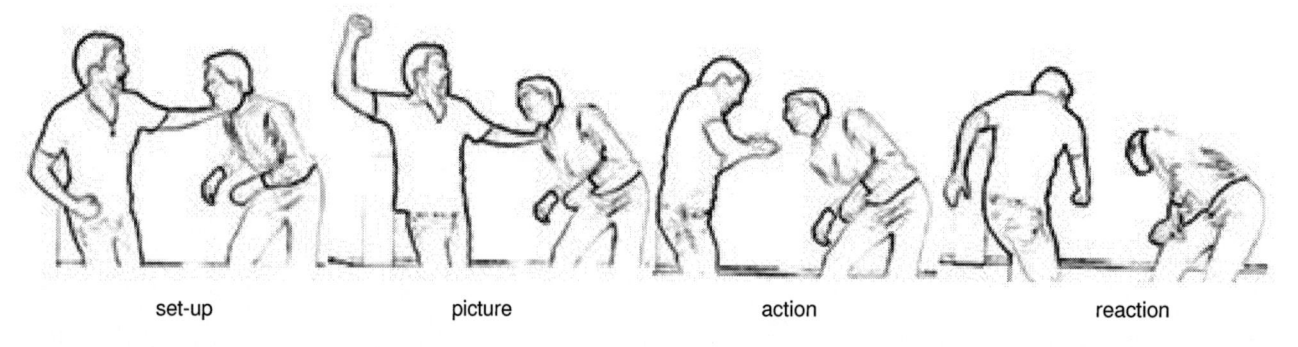

Pile Driver: Side View

set-up   picture   action   reaction

The reaction for the victim is a little counter intuitive, so you'll have to trust me on this. The path of the pile driver naturally has a slight angle to it, and contact is usually around the near eye socket. So instead of following the path of the fist, the face will twist not only down but also sharply to the side. Think of it as an angled billiard shot.

Pile Driver: Victim's Back to the Audience

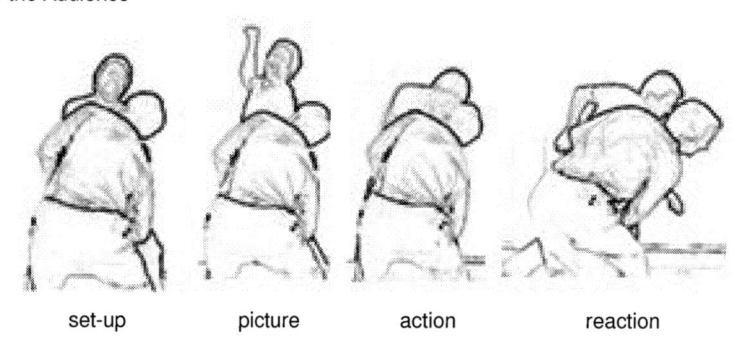

set-up   picture   action   reaction

The reaction for the aggressor is pretty straight forward. Many of the bones of the hand will be broken. If it is necessary that the character not sustain that damage, consider simulating the punch using a hammer punch, that is to say a strike using the bottom of the fist, the little finger side.

<u>slap, in distance and out</u>

Ok, I'm going to get off of neutral ground here and say that for this simulation - DON'T WAIT FOR PROFESSIONAL INSTRUCTION. Oh, you should still get an instructor to show the correct technique and prevent injury if at all possible, but I know that the reality is that actors are actually slapping each other every day on stage and I what to put a stop to it. Today.

There are some stage combat "experts" who insist that an actual contact slap to the face is perfectly safe as long as it is modified slightly. I have seen videos sold by these same professionals showing actor/students facing each other and trading slaps back and forth to prove the safety. Those experts are wrong. The contact slap is inherently unsafe. The slap to the face sends more actors to hospital emergency rooms every year than all of the other techniques of stage combat *combined*. Did you get that? This includes knife fights, broadsword fights, swinging from ropes, gunshots ... all of the other techniques of stage combat **combined**.

Actors are often taught that all one needs to do to safely slap someone in the face is to cup the hand slightly, keep the fingers and wrist very relaxed, and go for the fleshy part of the cheek. It is true that most of the time it causes no injury, which is why those "experts" assume that it is safe. But when this contact technique goes wrong, the results are devastating.

In a perfect world, the slapping hand will strike at exactly the same spot every single time, but that is simply unrealistic. When a hand is relaxed, the palm forms a slightly shallow cup shape. When that cup strikes the cheek, the air inside becomes pressurized and searches for release in the line of least resistance, which makes that satisfying popping sound as it slips by the fleshy skin of the cheek. However, if the hand drifts a mere inch closer to the victim, the ear is now inside the coverage of the hand. The pressurized air is still looking for a means of escape, and it's found it - right down the ear canal. At the bottom of the canal is the tympanic membrane - the ear drum - which easily bursts. If the membrane doesn't heal properly [all too common even with immediate medical attention] or if an infection develops [which is highly probable] the actor can expect temporary or permanent, partial or complete, hearing loss in the affected ear.

If this were the only bad thing that can happen to the actor, it would be reason enough to ban this practice, but there are other injuries which also occur - every year. If the hand is flexed a little, the face is hit with not a cushion of air but with the outer edge of the hand, or the hard ridge where the fingers meet the palm, or worse, the heel of the palm. In other words, bone strikes face. This can and does lead to dislocated jaws, broken cheek bones, broken hands, broken cartilage of the external ear, broken teeth, split lips - nasty stuff.

The damage need not occur only on the first contact of the slap itself. Many have escaped injury on the initial slap only to have the trailing fingers scrape across the near eye or break the nose. Some have been taught that, in order to avoid all of these potential dangers, the slap can be delivered lower, to the side of the neck. Very poor advice, as this can lead to a bruised trachea, and in one instance a slap collapsed the carotid artery and the victim died from lack of oxygen to the brain. Died.

No one should have to risk deafness, blindness, broken bones or death because of a play. But even if we could make the contact slap completely risk free, there is still another reason not to do it. It leads to bad acting for both the aggressor and the victim. The aggressor has to stop acting for a moment while she worries if the slap has really done any damage, which is the opposite of the feeling she is trying to convey to the audience. As for the victim, he usually ends up with a look of stoic resistance just before the slap - not exactly helpful in trying to sell the idea that the slap has come as a surprise. The timing can suffer, because most actors tend to get a bit "slap-shy" after being struck in the face a few times in rehearsal, and then start to react to the slap before the hand has started moving. Also, the pain received is real pain, therefore the reaction is the actor's, not the character's. It might be similar to the character's, but at that moment the actor has removed himself from the world of the play and lives completely within himself as his body deals with the pain. All of the work of trying to create a world specific to the playwright's intention is thrown out the window, and the audience has to wait for the actors to regroup and find the characters again. This isn't acting; it's the opposite of acting. It's the equivalent of rubbing onion juice on your cheek in order to bring up tears.

Directors tell me that they would rather that the actors hit each other because it is very difficult to make the simulation look real. Yes, that's true. It is hard work, harder than any other simulation you will ever ask your actors to do. But since it can save them from permanent injury, just suck it up and add the extra rehearsal time and work it ad nauseam until you can fake out five observers looking at the slap from five different vantage points.

I have more than once heard an actor tell his partner to "just go ahead and slap me - it'll keep me in the moment and it will look better". I've noticed that the offer is never made if he is supposed to be struck on the head with a baseball bat. Well, if they can make a simulation of being clubbed work to the audience's satisfaction, they can do the same with a simulation of a slap. I obviously feel strongly about this, so strongly that I will not work for a director who insists on having the actors perform an actual contact face slap. You shouldn't either.

Now, let's get to the simulation. A real slap to the face, especially as written in most Western plays, comes as much of a surprise to the aggressor as it does to the victim, so in the simulation we need to remove any hint of premeditation. So there isn't going to be much of a wind-up nor follow through. If anything, the body and even the rest of the arm will stay neutral and the slapping hand will look as though it had a life of its own from the wrist outward. Let's try a difficult slap first, and that's with the aggressor's back to the audience.

Slap: Side View

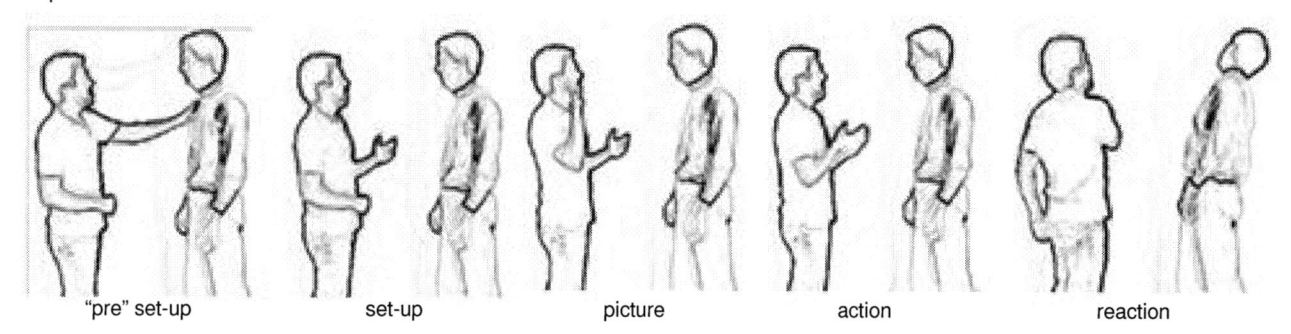

"pre" set-up   set-up   picture   action   reaction

Set-up: As the victim crosses slightly upstage, the aggressor uses the fingers of the left hand to touch the shoulder, stopping the victim from continuing, by happenstance stopping directly upstage of the aggressor. This is a small movement that can happen several lines before the slap, for it merely establishes distance. We can call this the "pre" set-up. Once the left hand is no longer seen by the audience, it can move to its target position - right in front of and against the solar plexus, palm turned up at about 45 degrees.

Picture: On the cue for the slap, the right elbow stays tucked against the body as the right hand flies up almost to ear height. Don't short change this step, because there is no body English that goes along with this simulation. You must give the audience a brief look at the back of the hand or they won't register the slap that is to come. But the elbow must not move.

Action: The hand, and only the hand, moves quickly here from right ear to left ear. Along the way, as it disappears from view, it scoops down to the target hand, makes contact with a light slapping sound, and then continues to its final position. Think of slapping water out of a bowl being held by the left hand, and throwing the water over your left shoulder. Do not move either elbow, don't move your body, and you don't need to move the target hand either. This is a tiny little movement; not an action that has the force to drive someone through a wall, but just enough to turn the face slightly.

Reaction: The aggressor must show the audience the fingertips of the right hand over the left shoulder for just a brief second, and the left hand must simply appear down by the left side. We want the audience to think that it was there the whole time, that way they won't think that it was part of the action. Again, eliminate all movement except for that of the slapping hand. The victim must wait until he hears the slap sound before moving the face.

Slap: Audience View

"pre" set-up   set-up   picture   action   reaction

No matter what the relationship was between the two characters, once a slap has occurred it means that the world of these people has changed forever. One person has decided that words alone cannot express emotion, and that violence - the specific intent to cause physical pain - was the only remedy. There is no ignoring the transgression. The characters may make up afterwards, but the damage to the relationship will be there forever.

Both characters know it, the audience knows it, and that is why the damage is far greater than the act. The audience now needs to know what will happen next - where will the relationship go? - and so they will look at the victim's eyes for help. That is where your focus should be as well. The slap is over in a second; the emotional scar may last a lifetime.

I said that this simulation is the most difficult, so if you master it, everything else is a piece of cake. An easier version is to reverse positions, having the victim step slightly downstage and then turn his back to the audience. Now he can clap his own hands together, or even just use one hand to slap his chest, although the chest slap is a deader sound, so I prefer that the victim simply clap his hands. This one must be a slip hand knap, with one hand held stationary as a target and the other traveling in a straight line from down by the hip to the target hand to the "struck" cheek as part of the reaction.. The aggressor can stand a little further back and his hand need not dip so low, although I still like the fingertips to scoop underneath chin level so that the victim knows he has nothing to fear. In any case, the slapping hand need never get any closer to the victim than halfway between the two actors.

As both actors feel more secure in the knowledge that they can't hurt each other, the director can keep making adjustments to make sure that the audience is fooled by this illusion. As everyone masters these techniques, slowly turn out the relative placement of the actors. Instead of one being full back to the audience, try moving them so one is three quarters front and the other is one quarter front. The body placement will have to change slightly, and the path which the arm takes may need to change as well, but it is possible to open this simulation up quite a bit, especially if the actors are in motion slightly just before the set-up.

Slap: Audience view, Victim establishes set-up, Actors off-set

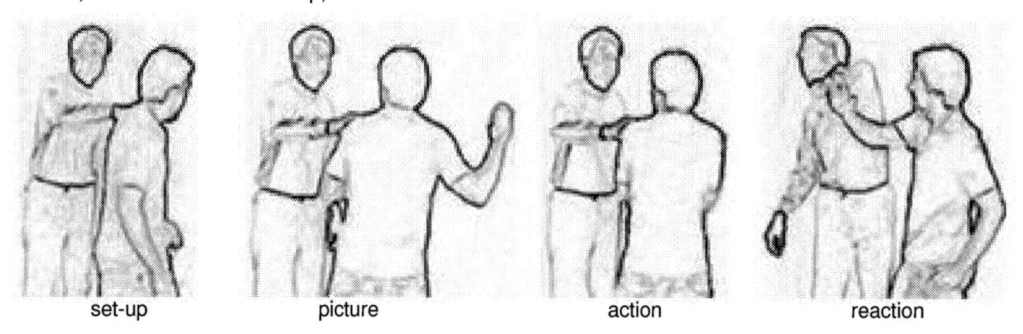

set-up   picture   action   reaction

This kind of simulation can be a pain to work through, but it is definitely worth the effort. I have yet to find a circumstance in which there was no alternative to actual contact. To give you an idea, I once choreographed the fight scenes for a theatre-in-the-round production of Macbeth, and in this production for some reason a general slapped a soldier in the face. The actors were surrounded by the audience so there was no hand that could disappear from view, and we couldn't provide the usual cheat of doing an off-stage noise. We finally worked it so that when the soldier finished his line the general stood for a moment in livid silence and then turned slightly away, as if the soldier was off the hook. Just as the soldier relaxed with a sigh of relief, the general suddenly turned back and savagely struck him. The soldier instantly raised his hand to the side of the face, and the general let his own hand hang in the air at face level. The audience heard the slap, and they were sure that they had seen the soldier's face brutally struck, but the actor had merely been slapped on the *shoulder*. So long as the actors believed the illusion, the audience did as well, because they were given the right picture before and after the sound.

backhand slap

Set up: Both actors parallel to the proscenium. This one works rather well no matter which actor is upstage, so long as one is standing full front and the other is facing him full back. The distance between the two should be slightly more than the length of the aggressor's arm. For our example we have the victim attempting a stab with a knife in the right hand, which the aggressor has blocked with his own left hand.

Picture: Although it's called a slap, this kind of strike packs a heck of a wallop, so the stance has to be much wider and deeper than for that of a regular slap. The aggressor should make a slight step to the left as his open right hand reaches low and to the left, making it clearly visible to the audience. The victim raises his left hand to solar plexus level, about six inches away from the body, leaving it loose and parallel to the ground.

Action: The aggressor sweeps his right hand in a gentle arc from low left to high right, connecting with the victim's contact hand to provide a shared knap, and then continues to a point above the right shoulder at face height.

Reaction: The backhand is one that can spin someone's head around, so the victim should gauge the severity of the reaction according to how much apparent force the aggressor is pantomiming. The victim must make sure that the contact hand not fly up with the force of the slap, but instead drop down and away. If the contact hand goes anywhere but down, it destroys the illusion.

spanking

Just a brief word here, because I have seen this done so poorly. Many actors, wanting to do a series of spanking slaps, pause at the bottom of the spank. It just doesn't look real. Instead, concentrate on bouncing the hand away from the target. If there is any pause or slow down, it should be when the hand is up, not down. And have someone provide sound out of view with a slapstick. The audience needs to hear this sound if they are to have any chance of believing what you are selling.

backhanded punch

Not to be confused with the backhand slap, this has more in common with the jab in that the strike is quick and has no body weight behind it. But because of the arc of the striking hand, it is much more dangerous. With the fist traveling directly toward the victim's face, we've broken the rule about making sure that all energy is directly off-line. Attempt this simulation only under the guidance of a trained instructor.

Set up: both actors on the same plane and parallel to the proscenium, both full back, victim stage right, aggressor on the left, although this simulation can work in almost any angle. A pre-touch should establish a one arm length's distance.

just the picture: downstage (audience) view   sideways view   upstage view

Picture: The aggressor's left elbow rises up and points four inches downstage of the victim's nose, as the right fist, slightly curled in, rests in front of his own right shoulder. The right arm gently crosses in front of the chest in a ready position, with the fingers of the open right hand near the let fist.

just the action: downstage (audience) view   sideways view   upstage view

Action: Making sure that the aggressor's elbow doesn't drift upstage, the upper arm remains immobile as the fist travels in a horizontal arch until almost fully extended and then immediately returns to the original position. The fist must go no further than that spot directly upstage of the victim's upstage shoulder (it's hard to see, but note the arrow on the illustration above. That's as close as the fist ever gets to the victim's head). The fist snaps out and back like a whip at the fullest point of the extension, and the act of pointing the elbow will keep the fist away from the victim. Be very careful not to hyperextend the elbow when performing this action.

By the way, the back of the hand is not the striking surface in a backhand punch. Just like any regular punch, contact would be made with the front of the fist, so we have to include that reality in this illusion. That means the wrist must curl out at the last part of the swing so the audience can believe that this was a punch, not a closed fisted slap.

The knap for this is similar to that for the jab, in that the palm of the right hand quickly slaps the space between the right shoulder and pectoral muscle. This works even in full view of the audience so long as the left hand moves as one unit with the arm - no separate movement at the wrist, and certainly no flapping at the elbow. And this isn't a big move - you should be able to get a decent knap with the arm traveling only an inch or two. The toughest part is to not bounce the slapping hand off the chest after making the sound (the extra movement will give away the illusion) The punching hand can't "stick" in the air - it has to bounce right back to the ready position.

Reaction: Only the victim need react here, and it is a relatively small "whiplash" reaction with perhaps the subsequent realization that the nose has been bloodied. The simulation will not work if there is even a hint of reacting too soon, so it is absolutely critical to hold the reaction until you hear the knap.

stomach punch

(I know, I know, a hit to the belly misses the stomach entirely, but no one uses the phrase "small intestine punch" and neither will I.)

Every cast seems to have some young idiot, usually a young male, who insists on showing everyone how to do a contact stomach punch by getting someone to punch him in the belly with full force, at which point he clenches his stomach muscles and takes the hit. In my youth, I was the young idiot. There is actually a way to do a relatively safe contact stomach punch, but it's neither as easy nor as dangerous as the one our young actor would have us perform. A *stage* contact punch doesn't require any stomach clenching on the part of the victim, and feels like a light tap, but only let an experienced fight person teach it.

We're going to learn a non-contact technique. I love this one because once you get the hang of it, it can be performed at almost any angle.

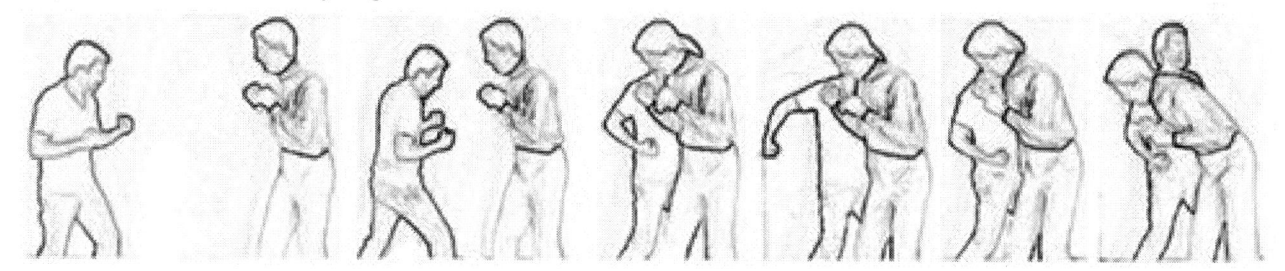

From a safe distance ... right foot crosses to right foot ... then left foot to behind victim ... then do the punch.

Set-up: The victim stands stage right, profile left, the aggressor stands stage left and profile right but slightly downstage of the victim. The right feet of both are almost touching. The aggressor takes a big step forward with the left foot, actually past the victim, and the hips have turned slightly closed. The aggressor should be able to see the victim's back. When the actors are this close, the victim's stomach is hidden from the audience's view. At the same time, the aggressor's left hand touches the victim's right shoulder. At this point there is still no movement of the punching arm.

Picture: The aggressor slightly bends at the knees, closes his hand into a fist as the right arm arches back into the view of the audience.

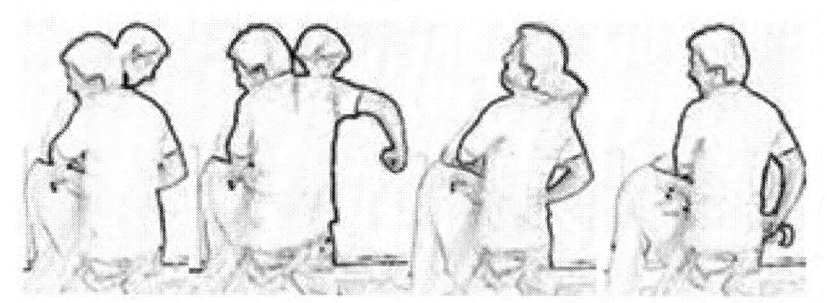

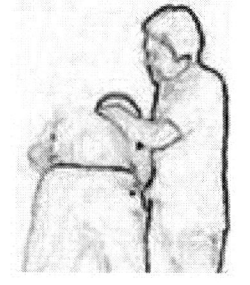

Audience view   Side view

Action: The punching arm quickly moves into the target, which is a spot downstage of the stomach, right into that clear gap between the two actors. Since the aggressor can't see the target, I like to have him aim for his own right hip - easy to find and it keeps the victim safe. To make clear, I repeat: the target is not the victim's stomach. Don't let the hand stick in place. In order to sell the illusion of hitting the stomach, the fist must appear to bounce off of the target, so this is a quick out-and-back punch.

The percussive sound of contact is not necessary so long as both actors exhale with a slight vocalization. An actual punch doesn't sound like much, so there is no reason to create a hidden clap.

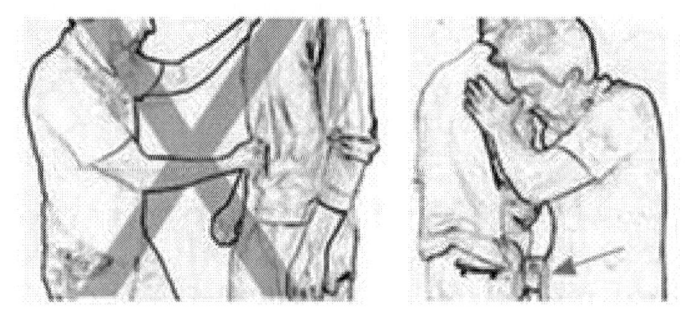

No need to aim for the stomach. The fist is aimed <u>between</u> the two actors.

Reaction: The victim simply bends forward at the waist. But don't lead with the head; that's not natural. The bend happens as a wave, with the stomach contracting first, then rolling the shoulders in as the butt moves back slightly, and only at the very end will the head look down. The aggressor should do the opposite, that is to say stand up even more straight. (For some reason, sometimes the aggressor doing the punch wants to bend at the waist too. Strange.)

<u>elbow to stomach from behind</u>

Warning: this is a more dangerous illusion, in that we are aiming force directly at the victim. This should be taught under direct supervision of a trained instructor.

This is the typical escape from a one-arm choke hold from behind, and is a simple variation of the above stomach punch. From one thing learn ten thousand. (I obviously enjoy that phrase. I've borrowed it from The Book of Five Rings, and serves as a reminder that each technique can be modified to create countless variations and alternatives.). Since this technique is an elbow strike, the roles of aggressor and victim are reversed: the choker/aggressor suddenly becomes the victim, while the person being choked becomes the aggressor. For this example, we are assuming that the choke is being performed with the right arm.

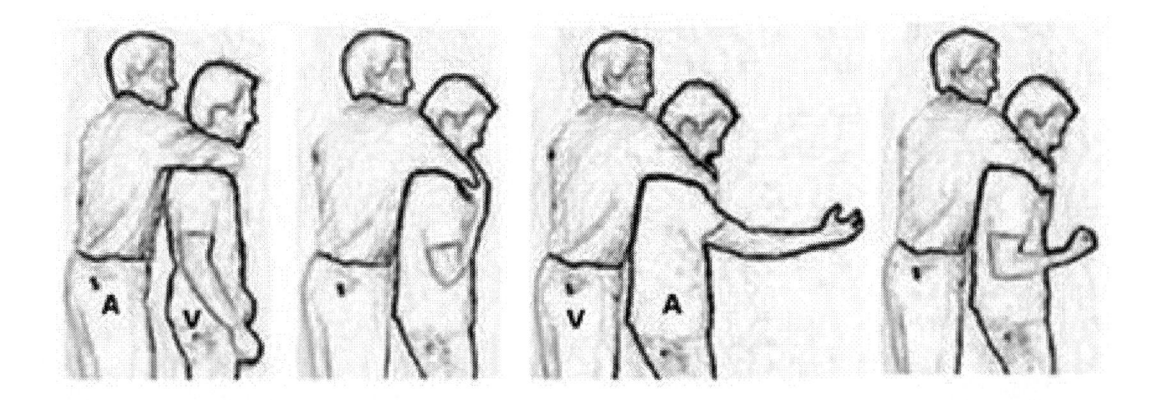

Set-up: The victim and aggressor stand full front to the audience, the aggressor slightly to the left and in front of the victim. The right heel of the aggressor is almost touching the left toe of the victim. The victim has his right arm loosely round the aggressor's neck, and the pressure of the arm is pressing lightly down and forward. The aggressor, pretending to try to remove the choking arm, is actually pushing the victim's arm towards his own chest, so that if he relaxes his push, the choking arm would naturally drop away. The aggressor's chin should be tucked into the chest so we can't see that he is not really being choked. The head of the victim must be safely looking over the right shoulder of the aggressor.

Picture: The aggressor's left arm stays on the victim's choking arm, while the right straightens out forward.

Action: Be careful here, because an elbow to the solar plexus can do a lot more damage than a punch to the stomach. The elbow smoothly moves into the target, which is the aggressor's own right hip, and must not be allowed to drift further back than his own hip level. The elbow doesn't stick there, but bounces off rather quickly. Again, the only sound of contact needed is a vocalization from both actors.

Reaction: The victim simply bends forward at the waist, but this time the chin should lift up so that the audience can see the reaction. The aggressor simply holds position.

elbow to spine

We're getting into some dangerous territory here, but I include it because I see a lot of high school students play around with their own simulations. They see this stuff on professional wrestling on TV and then try to recreate it. Ironically, they know that what they see is fake, so they assume that the simulations can't hurt anyone. Unfortunately, it can if done improperly, and an elbow strike more than others even if done lightly. So here are some guidelines on turning a very dangerous simulation into something tolerably safe:

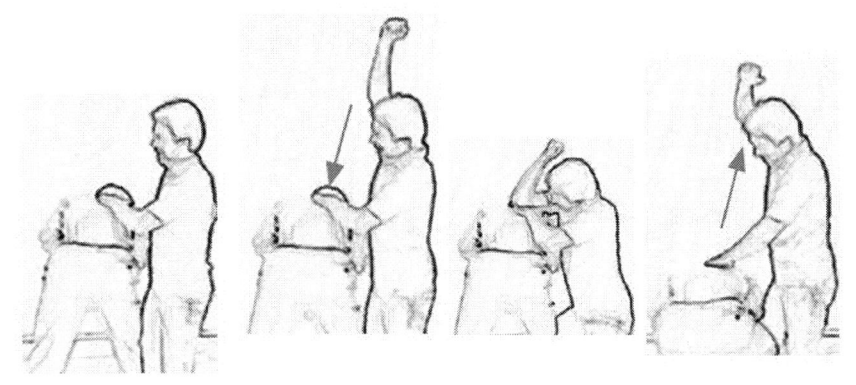

Set up: Usually, this simulation comes directly after a regular stomach punch, so the set-up is already implied from the final reaction - the doubling over of the victim, with the aggressor's left hand still touching the victim's right shoulder. The aggressor is standing very close and squared-off to the victim.

Picture: Let the left hand slide from the shoulder to a spot to the right of the victim's spine. You're looking for a large muscle group a little above the floating ribs but below the scapula. Let the heel o the palm rest there as the fingers lift up. The right hand shoots straight up into the air and forms a fist.

Action: The aggressor merely bends from the knees, keeping the back straight, as the right arm bends. The contact is made obviously NOT with the elbow, but with the back of the upper arm, the triceps. To add further safety, contact is not made with the victim's back at all, but with the back of the aggressor's left hand, just below the wrist. So that the victim can time the reaction, the aggressor uses the slightly curled fingertips of the left hand to tap the victim's back at the moment that "strike" has occurred.

Reaction: The aggressor straightens his legs and lifts his arm slightly, giving a "bounce-off" look to the simulation. The victim should arch the back and lift the head slightly, curving into the strike, and then of course dropping to the ground is expected. This action is a fight-ender.

bite

It surprises me that people think that a lot of work has to go into this. Start with a phony grab and then the body part to be "bitten" is merely brought up in front of the mouth so that the aggressor's teeth are blocked from audience view. The bite needs almost no movement by the aggressor besides a little facial mugging. The victim just has to sell the pain reaction. No contact, no worries.

My favorite: biting someone's finger (especially popular in *Taming of the Shrew*).. If you are the aggressor, use both hands to loosely grab the victim's hand. Of the three hands involved, two should be pointing in the same direction, let's say his right and your right. Let your hand slide underneath his, and some of your fingers slip up between some of his. Your left hand will act as a visual distraction. Then bite one of your *own* fingers as the victim lets out a bloodcurdling scream. There is no way that the audience is going to figure out how you did it (unless the victim is wearing nail polish and you are not).

face scratch

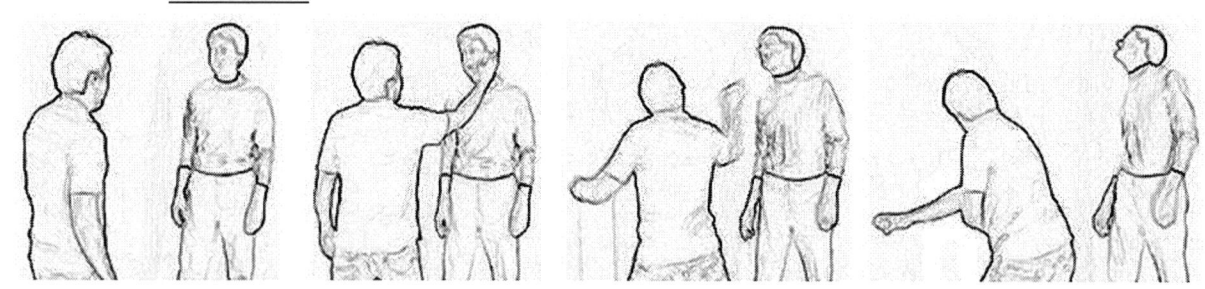

This s a simple pantomime that relies more on the victim's reaction than on the simulation, but we still want to make sure that no one gets hurt. A real scratch to the face brings the fingers directly across and into the skin, so on stage we redirect that energy *away* from the victim's face. Having the actors stagger their positions on stage helps to disrupt the audience's focus. The right hand, say, curls in a half-fist and reaches up to the level of the victim's left ear. A simple quick pull down and left but towards the aggressor's left hip makes for a convincing scratch. So the energy of the "scratch" actually moves away from the victim, not across the victim's face. As with most of these small moves, it's the victim's reaction that creates the believability to the action.

head butt

Too dangerous to use for most theatre companies. I tend to stick this one into *The Three Musketeers* as a comedic payoff, but it is a close-in simulation that can cause a lot of damage. Include it only if you have a very trusted choreographer working for you. There are two ways of doing this, depending on the placement of the actors, but I'm not going to go into specifics. It's simple and quick, and if I'm there to guide the actor's head with my hands, I teach it. But otherwise, stay away from it. This is not only extremely dangerous but also looks amateurish if done poorly and detracts from the show.

Blocking Punches

Obviously we're trying to give the illusion here of deflecting a punch by using the forearm, and if our partner is considerate enough to aim slightly away from us, we should have no difficulty in simply meeting his punching arm at a prearranged point in space with our forearm. We don't really want to block a real punch because that can leave bruises on both actors, but even our simulation can hurt if done improperly.

In a real fight, blocks are performed by striking the incoming punch using the sharp outside edge of the forearm. That means that the forearm is turned so that either the little finger or the thumb is leading. In stage fighting, we modify that by using the fleshy part of the forearm, either top or bottom. So that means that we have to turn the arm so that we lead with either the palm side or the back of the hand. The hand need not open. It will actually look a little better if the defender keeps the fist closed. Helpful hint: for all blocks, the attacker is wise to turn his punching arm a bit also, so that contact with his punch is made to the fleshy part of the forearm rather than the boney edge. Real bruises only lead to tentative fights.

There are four common blocks seen in Western style fighting:

Outside - For this block the arm [with fist pointing up] moves horizontally across the body from the same side to the opposite side. The body should twist slightly in the same direction as the block, very slightly evading the punch. The feeling is more of turning the torso like the agitator on a washing machine; the blocking arm is just along for the ride. For safety, let the palm-side of the arm lead the movement. In martial arts this is actually called an outside-inside block, and in fencing the same action is called an inside block.

Inside - Here the arm is vertical, just like in the outside block, but it moves very slightly to the center of the body and then back to the same side that it started from, the look of it being that it caught the punch and pulled it to that same side. It is a tiny movement, so don't overdo it. There is no way that the arm can turn enough so that the inside of the forearm, the palm side, can make the contact of the block, so this block will have to lead with the back side of the arm. There is a little muscle cushion there but not much, so go gently.

This kind of block is difficult to perform in its fullest form, so usually is only performed if the arm is already held at the center of the body in a defensive posture so that the block is just a quick flick rather than a complicated scoop and pull. Unlike with the outside block, the body in this case will twist slightly away from the block. In martial arts this is actually called an inside-outside block, and in fencing is called an outside block.

You might reasonably ask why in the world the same action is called by polar opposite terms in different fighting disciplines. The answer is simple and a little frustrating: tradition. The fencing terminology describes where the arm is going to end up at the end of the block. Martial arts describe where the arm needs to be before beginning the block.

Down - The down block is pretty rare in Western fighting, but it does have its uses when defending against kicks or low punches. From the normal defensive stance, the arm swings down, pivoting at the elbow. Again, try to make contact with the inside of the forearm rather than the boney edge.

Unlike the other blocks, the body doesn't turn on this one. Why? A down block assumes that the blow was coming in pretty low, low enough so that you would clench your stomach to absorb any hit as it glances off the block.

Rising - This is used only for deflecting a punch to the head. The arm first drops horizontally in front of the chest and rises up as a unit, because you're trying to lift up his punch, right? Try to keep the palm side of the fist pointing down so as to reduce bruises to your partner's arm. If you twist the fist forward, you'll be striking with the bony ridge of your forearm, and that hurts.

On any block, don't just "reach" for the incoming arm. That disrupts the illusion and confuses the audience - they can't tell who is throwing the punch. We have to believe that if the punch hadn't been blocked it would have actually hit the victim. So every block must cross the plane of the intended target first, as though the incoming punch was pushed away at the last moment. Again, the aggressor doesn't really aim for the victim, so the victim is never in danger of getting struck, but both *characters* must focus on where the "real" punch would land if not blocked.

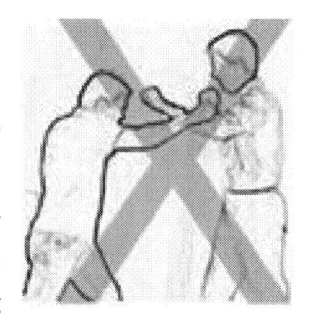

The aggressor may need to modify the look of the punch. Normally, a closed fist is thrown with the palm facing down, but when such a punch is blocked, it exposes the bones on the side of the arm, and this can be painful if the contact is strong. A slight turning of the wrist so that the thumb is pointing up means that the contact is made on less sensitive muscle tissue. The audience won't notice the difference and it can save some bruising. And of course there is no need to aim any of these punches or kicks directly at the defender. If the blocked punch is going to be "deflected" to a spot to the left of the victim's shoulder, simply aim the punch there to begin with.

Be flexible enough to adjust the overall timing of the actions. For example, a successfully blocked jab may happen too quickly for the audience to appreciate what has just happened, so the aggressor might have to hold the punch out there for a nanosecond before snapping the hand back to a ready position.

Kicks

Kicks are mere variations of punches and slaps, but the potential force behind them is much greater. Add to that the fact that most people have no idea how far their foot really can travel on a kick, and you'll see how we've moved a step up on the danger ladder. To reduce that risk, we have to be even more attentive to relative body positioning at every point in the kicking simulations.

fan kick

In reality it's a big looping slap to the face using a foot instead of a hand.

Fan kick viewed from the side (and would have been more impressive if I could have kept my back and legs straight, but the dancer that I was is a distant memory).

Set up: Victim stands full back, and the aggressor is upstage and full front, facing the victim. The distance between the two needs to be twice the distance of the aggressor's arm. To make sure, initial contact can be made by, let's say, one actor touching the other on the shoulder, and then taking a big step back with the non-kicking foot.

Picture: The aggressor keeps the non-kicking foot planted, and ten takes another step back with the kicking foot. But be sure and keep the body weight over the non-kicking foot.

Action: For a right-footed actor, an inside fan kick will travel right to left, and an outside fan kick from left to right. Either way the leg is kept straight as it swings in as big a circle as is comfortably possible, landing at the same spot that it started. Try it very gently a few times and you'll realize that this requires great hip flexibility and strong thigh muscles. (Most actors won't be able to perform this kick unless the victim is on hands and knees.) As the victim's back is to the audience, he can provide the knap by simply clapping his hands.

Reaction: The aggressor's reaction is static, ready for the next move. The victim is going to move the head and body in the direction of the kick (although in a broad comedy such as *The Three Musketeers* the reaction turns into a cartwheel!)

groin kick

DO NOT suggest to the actors that it is safe to do a contact groin kick so long as the victim wears an athletic cup. Athletic cups are meant to protect against incidental contact. On a full contact kick, the edges of the cup can rupture the lymph nodes on either side of the groin, leading to systemic toxic shock within an hour. People have died this way.

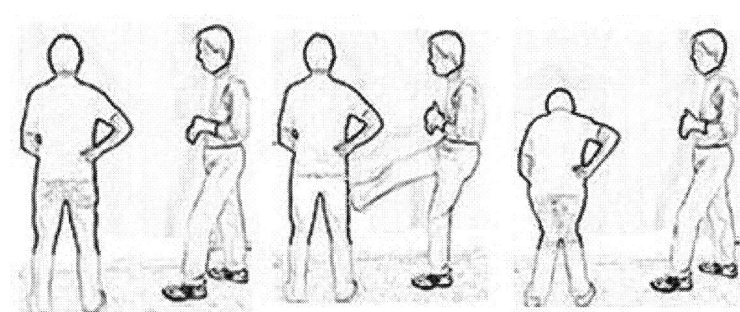

DO NOT suggest to the actors that it is safe to do a contact kick by simply aiming for the victim's inside thigh. A slight miscalculation can lead to getting nailed in the groin anyway or, worse, the strike hitting low and breaking the leg. It only takes about 45 lbs. of pressure sideways to break the knee. So DO NOT have any movement going toward the victim. Instead:

Set up: have the victim stand full-back to the audience. Without turning the head towards the aggressor, cheat some eye contact before continuing. The aggressor stands in profile but slightly up-stage of the victim, and about one and a half arm's distance away. The body of the aggressor must not face toward the victim, but rather at the empty space directly upstage of the victim. The toes of the downstage foot point at the victim's left and right toes. At this point on, that downstage foot remains planted; it is the upstage foot, the foot furthest from the victim, which performs the action.

Picture: Much like the slap, the groin kick works best when it comes as a surprise to the audience. And yet there still has to be a tiny moment that the audience can identify as a precursor to the action we want them to believe. In this case, it is a very small bit of preparatory body movement in opposition. It can be as simple as a little lift of the foot off the ground, or a momentary shift of weight to the rear foot.

Action: The upstage knee rises and points towards the spot upstage of the victim, and then the foot swings out and back quickly, parallel to and upstage of the toes of the victim. Don't allow the foot to arc towards the victim. The foot must immediately go back to its starting position. Any hang time at all on this and the audience will not believe the illusion.

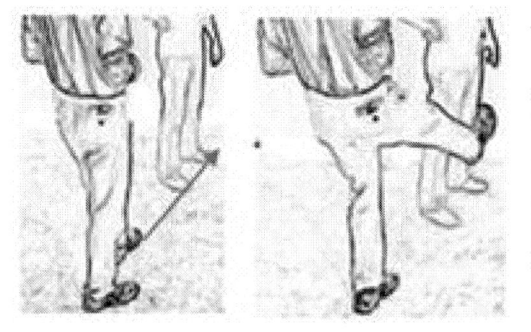

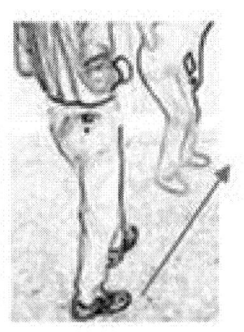

Reaction: The victim performs the universally understood reaction - bending the knees, sticking the butt out and lifting the chin. Don't collapse the head down nor bend over at the waist - that only confuses the illusion. The reaction is funnier if the vocalization of the victim can be high pitched, if the knees can touch (knock-kneed) and if there is a slow continuing collapse after the initial shock of the impact. The aggressor should not bend over at all (so many male actors want to in unconscious sympathy), but maintain a victorious posture.

The kick is more of a flick kick than one that is capable of doing any serious damage, so the aggressor's action must be as quick as possible, especially coming away from the target. There is also a truism at work here in that if the aggressor's foot actually rises to the height of the victim's groin, the audience thinks that it has seen a kick to the stomach, because the viewer's mind always adds a little more movement to what he actually sees. So stop the foot a little lower than groin level. Be sure to include the look of the foot bouncing back from the groin, like a ball bouncing off a wall, to give the illusion of contact. In order to sell this, it might be necessary for the foot to swing up for the kick a little slower than it will move on the bounce back.

If you want to simulate a groin kick with the knee rather than the foot, the basics will be the same, but look ahead to the knee to stomach explanation.

front kick to stomach - victim standing

There are two ways of simulating a front kick, but I'm only going to tell you how to do one kind - the safer one. This one is really the same as the groin kick, with some obvious exceptions. So look at the groin kick pictures on the previous page. All we have to do is change some very minor points:

Set up: have the victim stand full-back to the audience. The aggressor stands in profile but slightly upstage of the victim, and about one and a half arm's distance away. The body of the aggressor must not face toward the victim, but rather at the empty space directly upstage of the victim. The toes of the downstage foot point at the victim's left and right toes. At this point on, that downstage foot remains planted; it is the upstage foot, the foot furthest from the victim, which performs the action. Get eye contact.

Picture: For the picture, we can have the aggressor step back with the kicking foot, bending the knee of the supporting leg, as if gearing up the energy for the kick.

Action: The kick is going to be a bit different as well, with the foot allowed to drift just a little higher (but still lower than stomach level), and the entire kick rising up in a full arc from the ground up to the target level, swinging from the hip, as opposed to the quick flick of the groin kick. Always keep in mind that there is no reason to hook the kick toward the victim, for the audience has no depth perception. The victim can use a free hand to pat the stomach to produce the sound of impact, but the most important noise to make is a huge exhalation of breath.

Reaction: And of course the reaction of the victim is going to be very different than that of the groin kick, most especially in that the head can be allowed to look down. The body of the victim can move slightly downstage as with a stomach punch, but also can almost hop even as the victim doubles over, for the direction of the impact has come up from the ground.

front kick to stomach - victim on the floor

This is where the victim is already on the floor for some reason on all fours, and the aggressor simulates a full kick to the stomach. When this was taught to me, back in the day, I learned it as a full contact kick. I was expected to clench my stomach muscles and simply absorb the blow. This worked well almost every night.. But there was one performance where it didn't work well, where just before the kick I ran out of air and needed to take a quick breath. I tried to wave off my partner, but it all happened so fast that he didn't have time to notice my change of expression, and his foot landed on my stomach just as it was relaxed enough to suck in a gulp of air. That little bit of air was immediately pushed out of my lungs, and the force of the kick lifted me up off the ground. I was left in a crumpled mass on stage with no way to continue the scene. My partner simply had to stand and wait for what seemed like an eternity until I could manage to say my next line and get the scene going again.

If you really must do this simulation, here is one way to do it which is marginally safer than what I was taught. Have the victim on all fours placed so that he is heading 45 degrees from either profile or straight. The aggressor moves in sideways but upstage of the victim, so that no matter which way the victim is pointed the aggressor is facing 1/4 out, with hips and shoulders square to the victim's stomach. The non-kicking foot is planted about six inches away from the victim. That is your set-up.

For the picture, the kicking foot steps back and the front leg bends slightly at the knee, so as to aid in maintaining balance. The action is the part that can get actors in trouble, for the tendency is to swing in too close and accidentally make contact with the victim. That is precisely what we do not want. Instead, slowly bring the kicking foot to a spot parallel to the planted non-kicking foot, and at the moment of "impact" pull the foot away again as quickly as you can. To repeat: slow in, fast out. And no closer than your own planted foot.

The reaction is pretty obvious, and you might even be able to sneak a little self knap if you can hide one of the victim's hands from the audience's view. But don't ever let the aggressor try to make the sound by jabbing his kicking foot into the floor. It just sounds horribly *not* like any kind of kick to the body.

front kick to head

Once again, we follow the mechanics of the above groin and stomach level kicks, but in this case we have to lower the victim since most actors won't have the flexibility to kick at higher than waist level without pulling a hamstring. For our purposes we're going to try the easiest form of the kick to the head - one performed with the victim's head only a couple feet off of the round.

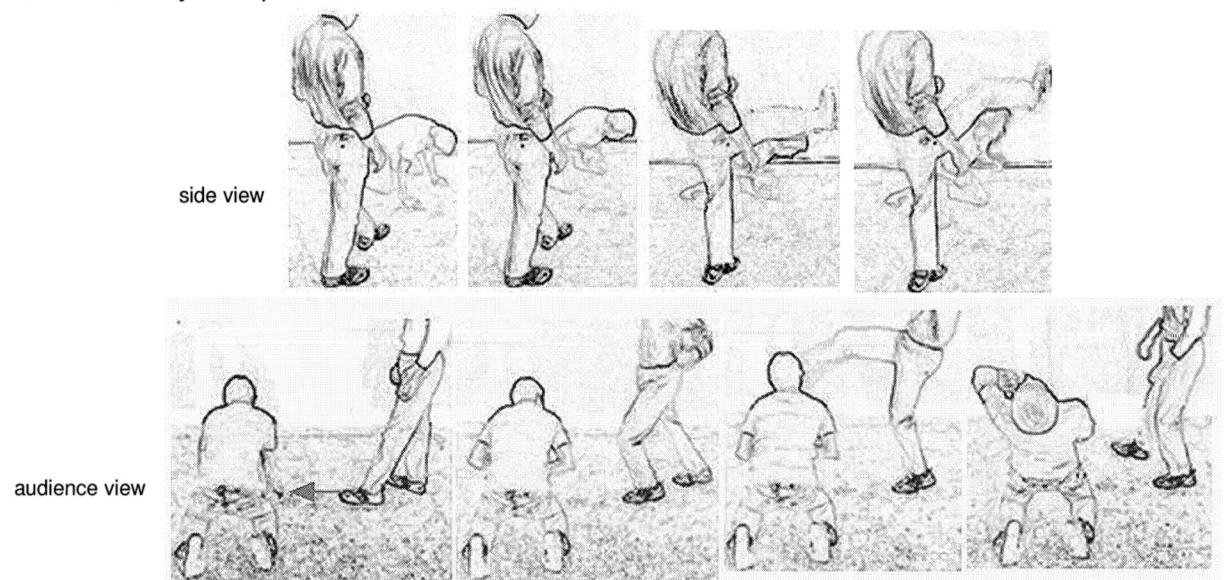

side view

audience view

Set up: The victim is already on the ground for some reason, on his hands and knees and full back. The head must be held back some, so that the hands are further upstage than the head is. The aggressor, standing stage left, profile right , lines up his left foot so the toes point in a straight line to the victim's finger tips. Once the aggressor is in position, then the victim can rock back slightly so as to shift weight off of the hands, freeing them to provide the knap for this simulation. The hand nearest the aggressor should be directly beneath the other, ready to clap. Care must be taken during this shift that all of the movement be hidden from the audiences view. The victim then establishes eye contact only when ready. Be patient. Don't rush into the picture unless every part of the set-up is comfortably in place.

Picture: As with most kicks, we can have the aggressor step back with the kicking foot, bending the knee of the supporting leg, as if gearing up the energy for the kick.

Action: The aggressor's foot swings in an arc parallel to the proscenium, following the path of where the victim's fingertips *were*. As opposed to the other kicks, this one does not bounce back, but continues past the level of the head. Keep the heel of the standing foot securely planted for balance. The victim provides the sound of contact by driving the bottom hand into the top (target) hand, and then continues to the face. Careful not to let the elbow "flap", for the audience can see the tiny move and figure out how you made the sound. If the victim wishes to add a vocalization (and he should), keep the sound higher in pitch than that for a stomach punch.

This simulation is most often taught with a different kind of knap - a "cage knap". It's a shared knap requiring both actors to make the sound. The victim cups his hands, one overlapping the other a bit. With the palms facing the floor, it creates a dome shape. The aggressor then kicks the open "cage" with the top part of his foot. I've been leery of this ever since I saw the victim's hands kicked right into his own face, breaking his nose.

Reaction: The aggressor should not quickly return the foot to the ground, as she would for the other front kicks. On this one, we like to see a little hang time before the foot naturally drifts down. The victim will arch his back and let the head snap up and very slightly away from the aggressor.

roundhouse

This kind of kick is not a street fighter's act, but comes from eastern martial arts. The rear heel and knee lift up to waist height, and then are swung around in a big looping motion parallel to the ground until it strikes the opponent's waist, ribs, knee or face. The strike itself is something similar to that of a snap-kick. The danger level on this kick is so high, and the kick itself so rare, that there is to need to include it in a show without having an expert on site, so I'm not going to include a description of how to do it here.

rear kick

This would be a simulation of kicking someone who is standing behind you, and is actually very similar to the front kick in execution. But it is a difficult kick for most actors to perform with consistent accuracy (they usually have difficulty maintaining their balance and keeping control of the direction of the kick), so I suggest leaving it out of your fight unless learned under the direct tutelage of an experienced instructor.

knee to stomach

Go back and re-read the section on the groin kick and the stomach punch. You should be able to see how many of those elements are modified to make this kick easy and effective. This is an excellent close-in simulation that can work in almost any direction.

Set-up: No matter where the victim is, the aggressor moves directly in-line and faces the victim's right side. The victim is turned out, showing his right profile to the aggressor, either or both of whose hands may lightly land on the victim's right shoulder. The aggressor's left foot is placed behind the victim's right heel, so that the aggressor is almost straddling the victim's right leg. Establish eye-contact.

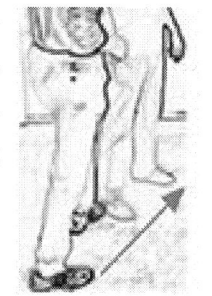

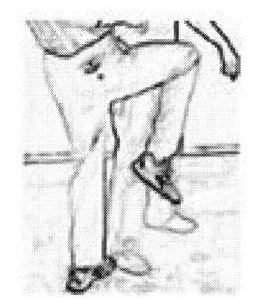

Picture: We don't get to see any leg prep on this, so it all rests with the aggressor's body English, who needs to bend the knees a bit and really sell that he is about to drive the knee into the stomach. If the actor believes it, we'll believe it.

Action: The knee glides along the front of the victim's right leg and stops when it is at stomach level. On this illusion, the leg will "stick" there for a moment, allowing the victim to double over around the attacking leg, closing off the distance between the leg and stomach. Full breath exhalation - no need for a knap.

Reaction: The victim has the wind completely knocked out of him, and probably has a broken rib or two, so this is a fight ender. Staying doubled over, with head down, is the most you can expect. The aggressor allows the kicking leg to drift down to the ground.

head to wall

This is usually performed as a compound series of separate actions: the aggressor grabs the victim by the hair, drags him over to a wall, and slams his head into it. Three distinct actions that combined look very scary but can actually be done very safely.

The hair pull has already been discussed, as has the concept of the aggressor making it appear that she is dragging the victim across the stage, when actually the victim is leading all of the action. The aggressor is merely pantomiming the pulling while moving ahead of the victim. As the ending location is going to be a wall, let the audience see the aggressor do the hair pull first and *then* make the decision to go to the wall. Here is where actors start to muddy this simulation.

Actors want to run into the wall nonstop. That cannot be done safely, so don't let them try. Instead, they have to cross to the wall first and then do the head to the wall bit. First complete one, then do the other. Once they have finished the drag/cross, only then can they perform the following:

Set-up: Assuming for now hat the aggressor has been pulling on the victim's hair with his right hand, it means that he will be to the left of the victim as he stops in front of the wall. The victim can stand square to the wall, but for additional balance and control, one foot might actually be pushed against it. The aggressor could turn to face the victim, who is facing the wall with legs bent and a bit bent at the waist (coming naturally from having been pulled by the hair). It will be difficult to make eye contact, so the aggressor has to be completely relaxed and apply no pressure whatsoever to the victim.

Picture: The victim keeps the knees bent, and arches back to the point where the head has fully raised up. Completely let go of the aggressor's hand.

Action: The victim pivots the head quickly down to where it was at the set-up, and then immediately snaps it back up as though it has bounced off of the wall. As he does so, his own hands will slightly lead the way, and with one open palm smartly rap the wall for the impact sound. The hands must then drift down, away from head level. As the hands are leading the movement, and the smack to the wall is done at head level, there is no worry that the victim will hit the wall with his own head, for his hands will get in the way. *Important note*: don't ever let an actor kick a wall in order to make the sound of impact. The audience can see that a mile away and it just looks horrible.

The aggressor's hand does not follow the head as it arcs down, but moves in a straight line towards the wall and parallel to the floor. At the moment of impact, the hand can flair up a bit. The aggressor's hand should not get too close to the wall or the audience will think that she had something to do with making the contact noise.

Reaction: The victim should keep the knees bent but the rest of the body should be fairly upright, with the hands continuing to drift down instead to going back to the head. We want the audience to forget that the hands were involved in any of this.

knee to head

Here's a simulation that is even more dangerous than it looks. It shouldn't be, and if done correctly is very safe indeed. But there is no way under heaven that this should be attempted unless under the direct supervision of a very competent stage combat instructor.

When I include this in a show, I first demonstrate it a few times to the actor, then have him do the motions several times without a partner, and then bring in the victim to have him try it in super-slow motion. Even with all that, believe it or not there have been many times that the actor will bring his knee up directly into the victim's face. I was always standing right there to stop it, and they were working at extremely slow speed, so no one has ever been hurt, but you can see my trepidation at having actors try this without an expert standing by.

Going to Ground

This next section is fraught with danger, because the stage floor is very unforgiving and has no qualms about damaging actors. I'm starting with the easy stuff and moving to the more complex, but just because I am describing it doesn't mean that it is safe. It isn't. I have seen similar techniques taught with painful results, sometimes because of a moment of inattention of the instructor, sometimes because of a minor misunderstanding by the actor, and sometimes because a human body is not designed to be hit by a hardwood floor. The first simulations should be studied by every actor, the latter ones should only be attempted by those who already have a lot of experience and control. And complete control is the most important thing here - if you can't do the movement in slow-motion, you can't do the movement. Unless you have the physical control to freeze your body in space at any and every point along the way, you haven't mastered the action and must not perform it.

knees to floor

How I hate the sound of an actor's knees hammering the boars as he kneels to the floor, especially when his character is a prisoner being "forced" to the ground. No matter how gentle the guards are, the prisoner himself drives his knees to the floor as though they were nails into plywood.

To get the knees gently to the ground, keep your back and head nice and straight as you gently bend your knees until you are almost sitting on your heels. The knees are a few inches off the ground right now, but we've taken your body weight out of the equation. Now just lean *back*, and the knees will gently and automatically lower to the floor, completely under your control without the rest of your body forcing the knees into the boards. To give it a little bit more of a natural look, I let one knee land slightly ahead of the other, and then allow the upper body to bend forward to finish the pantomime.

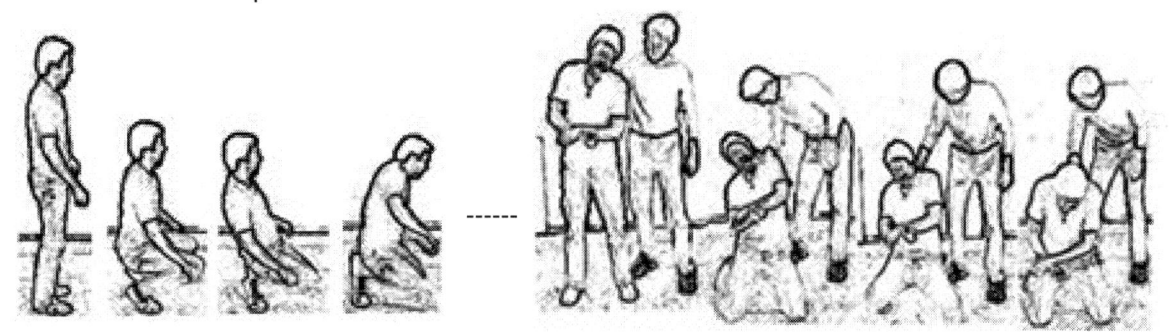

If the moment to be portrayed is in fact a prisoner being forced to the ground by a guard, let the victim perfect the drop before adding the aggressor, who merely has to match his pantomime to match the drop. The same applies to converting any of the following drops into a throw.

back/sit fall

This is called a back fall by some because that's what it looks like, and a sit fall by others because that's what you actually do. Falling backwards usually comes after a push, and actors sometimes respond to the push by leaning backwards and letting gravity take over. What a great way to damage the arms, spine and head.

The main thing we want to protect is the head, so we're going to break down this simulation, each step designed to reduce every possible inch of distance between head and floor before we ever lean the head back. First, take a giant step backwards with the upstage leg and slowly sit on that heal. The bigger that first step is, the easier the rest of the simulation is. (Taking a step back with the upstage leg makes it look as though the fall came from being pushed back. By kicking out the downstage foot forward and sitting on the stationary leg, it looks more like being pushed down. Some people like to call the first a back fall and the second one a sit fall. I don't much care what you call it so long as you don't hurt yourself.)

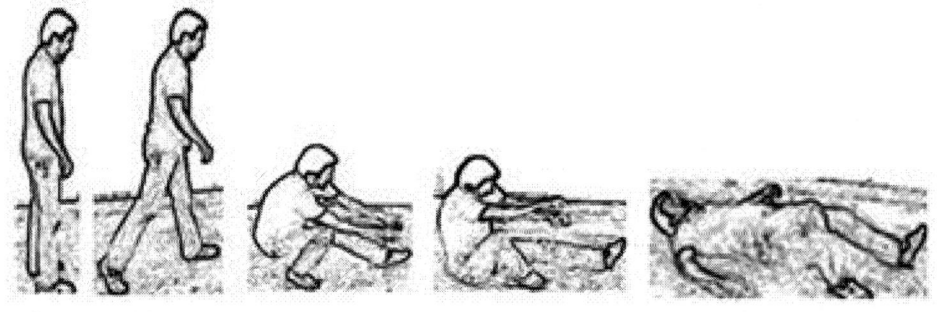

Back all as viewed from behind. Note that the upstage hand is used to hit the ground for the sound of impact.

The upper body should still be straight with the head facing forward. Gently roll back off of your heel until you are sitting on the floor. Now, tuck your chin to your chest and roll back onto the floor. At the very last moment release the chin, lifting your gaze up but still keeping the back of your head an inch off the floor. Smack the ground with your upstage arm to add the sound of the head bouncing on the floor to complete the illusion. This is a simulation using controlled and fluid motion. Challenge yourself to not use your hands to stop your momentum. If you use your legs and work your balance, you shouldn't need to ever use your hands, which is a great skill to develop should you need to be holding props when you fall.

With time, the movements will naturally blend until it looks more like one drop instead of five segments, but don't rush. Make sure that each part feels comfortable before moving on to the next. Remember that your goal is to have enough control so that you can stop the simulation at any point of the fall should you need to.

side fall

You've guessed it! A side fall is nothing more than a back fall going sideways. Just a couple of modifications are needed to make it work. Of course you'll need to step deeply out to the side instead of backwards, but you'll also need to let your hips roll out a bit so you can sit on the floor before continuing to roll on your side as you finish the fall. Your upstage hand is not seen by the audience, so it can smack the ground to give the sound of impact. Just as in all falling simulations, challenge yourself to stay in control. You should be able to stop and reverse movement at any point of the fall. Challenge yourself to not use your hands to stop your momentum.

forward fall

More difficult than the other falls, but very necessary to learn. Just like the side and back falls, a bigger initial step makes it easier to control your center of gravity. Unlike the other falls, this illusion has to take a detour halfway through.

First step deep in one direction .... then melt into the other

Let's say you are going to fall straight forward. If you step directly forward trying to get low, your knee is soon going to get in your way. Instead, keep your eyes on that spot on the ground where you should end up, but take that first step out about 45 degrees from that center-line. Make that step as long and deep as you can, but don't lean forward from the waist yet or you'll lose control. Now you are going to very gently use your fingers, then palms, then forearms to help melt into the floor as you slide back to that original center-line. As you melt into the ground, keep your head up as you arch your back. Your belly should make contact with the ground before your chest does, and turn your head to the side (you don't want to stop your fall with your nose). Add an appropriate body impact reaction to give the illusion of a sudden stop.

Never use your hands to stop your momentum. I keep harping on that for three reasons. First, it doesn't look like a fall, it looks like a push-up. Secondly, because you can't trust your wrists to actually stop your body without starting to damage some very delicate ligaments. Lastly, you might be holding a prop. Learning to fall without using your hands means you can safely handle the prop as well.

forward roll

A forward roll is not a somersault. In a somersault both hands are placed on the ground and the head and body go directly over in a straight line and into a roll. Too many things can and do go wrong with somersaults, especially neck and wrist injuries, so for stage we use the forward roll.

I'm going to describe the mechanics of the forward roll, but the danger level is so high that it absolutely requires the supervision of someone with excellent teaching capability in tumbling skills. If an actor insists that he or she can safely perform a forward roll on a hard surface, challenge that by having him or her do the roll in <u>super-slow motion</u> as well as at 3/4 speed. Then have them do the same thing in reverse. Someone who is truly in control should be able to go backwards or forwards, and freeze the motion at any point of the roll while in slow motion. If they get that far, then close your eyes and listen to the roll when performed at 3/4 speed. They must be able to do so in near silence. Any thumping on the floor means that an injury could and probably will happen in the future. By the way, the head need never, and must never, touch the ground.

Unlike the somersault, the forward roll is asymmetrical, and you should learn how to perform it both left and right. Start by kneeling on the ground, right knee close and left knee further back, and put your left hand down as well, making a comfortable 3-point stance. Your right hand is free and I want you to look at it. Keep staring at it as at touches the ground between your left hand and right knee and then travels along the ground all the way back to your left foot. Yes, all the way back. At some point you will find this to be impossible, but you will also have placed you right shoulder completely on the ground and your face is practically under your left arm. Reach some more and gently push off with your right knee, and your upper back will begin to roll with your legs following gracefully along. OK, maybe not so gracefully, but you've just performed your first forward roll and you didn't hurt yourself.

You must tuck your chin to your chest and not ever have your head touch the ground, but you will do that automatically if you concentrate on reaching for that trailing leg and you really look at that reaching hand. Just stick with this baby roll until it feels second nature, and then try the same thing but switching to the left side. At first it might turn into a side roll, but for now that's fine. As you gain confidence, you'll be able to focus more on improving the look by forcing your feet to actually go over your head instead of falling out to the side. Each time you finish a roll, make sure that you're in control of your legs as well. At the end of the roll at least one foot should land flat on the ground, and that one can take the force away from the other leg. You don't want your leg to simply crash into the floor or you'll hurt that exposed ankle bone. Don't try to do too many of these at one time. A dozen or so each day is fine: more than that will just make you dizzy.

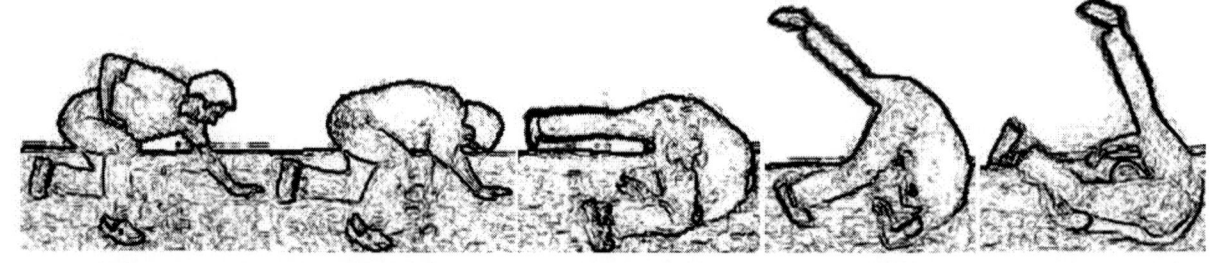

Ready for more? Then with time slowly increase the height. First, try going into the 3-point stance but with the right foot on the ground instead of the right knee. Now you'll have to push off a little bit more in order to start the roll, and you'll have to tuck in you chin even more. When that works for you, we increase the height a bit more by lifting that left knee off the ground as well. That's right, the 3-point stance is now both feet and the left hand, but the reach and tuck remain the same. And remember to try both left and right rolls.

Feels good? Excellent - now do the rolls in reverse. If you can't go forward *and* backward, stop here and do not continue until you can.

*   *   *　　　　　*   *   *

Well, I congratulate you on mastering the backward roll! As difficult as that was to do, you'll find that it will give you the control you'll need when you have to change directions in the middle of a roll, as you may need to during performance. Crazy things happen: the scissors that were safely on the mantle are now on the ground, right in your path. You'll just catch a glimpse of it as you begin the roll - can you stop in mid-roll, alter your direction while your tush is in the air, and roll out of harm's way? Of course you can, because you have developed the skills in rehearsal that can protect you in performance! Aren't you glad you put in the extra sessions to practice something you thought at the time was unnecessary?

As your body gets higher and higher, it will get more difficult to lower that shoulder to the ground, so you'll find that you'll need to support the drop with that reaching arm, using it as part of the roll before your shoulder even gets there. Start thinking of your body as a giant steel hoop starting from your pinky finger tip, and continuing in one unbroken curve past your wrist, elbow, shoulder, crossing your back to the opposite hip then the side of your knee and the opposite foot. Those are the body parts that will touch the ground during the roll and no others. As you get momentum going be sure and keep your ankle from smacking the ground. (I broke my ankle that way in performance once - really dumb. That's one reason why regular judo techniques don't work onstage - no padded mat.)

As you steadily improve you'll find that you can begin to step into the roll instead of rigidly forming the stance first. In other words, you'll step forward with your right foot and start your reach with the right hand *before* your left hand has touched the ground. Instead of reaching so dramatically back to your trailing foot, you'll find that you can push off a bit more with your feet and still have control of the roll. Finish this move by rolling onto the hip - not by banging it to the ground. You'll find that you can even roll right onto your feet and then stand right up without even slowing down the roll.

One more thing - some very highly placed fight choreographers, the tops in the field, teach this with a flat-backed landing, using both feet slamming to the floor to take the impact. While attending one of their workshops, I witnessed an actor seriously hurt doing this - *while under the direct supervision of one of these famous experts*. I knew it was unsafe before I saw the injury occur, but foolishly said nothing. These same fight masters still insist on continuing to teach the forward roll this way. An unsafe move is unsafe no matter who teaches it.

tackle

This is a partnered illusion that increases the danger level, so I am hesitant to include it. But given the number of shows in which actors have to grapple with each other, I feel compelled to at least offer a suggestion as to how it can be made safer.

The tackle from the front is a combination of a back fall by the victim and a forward fall by the aggressor. As you'll recall, the back fall travels in one direction, while the forward fall makes a detour on its way forward. Since the person being tackled can only go back, the tackler should plan on moving first away from the victim as the "tackle" begins, and then finish by moving back toward him once he is safely seated on the ground. For the victim the sequence is get hit, then step back, then sit. Have the actors practice this at least four feet apart from each other, then slowly inch them closer together until it looks as though one has caused the other to fall.

throw from choke from behind

Again we are in a high danger level here, but a brief description. This is a forward roll from the victim along with a simple kneel to the ground for the aggressor. (A reminder here that once we begin the simulation of the throw, the roles of victim and aggressor are reversed; the victim is now the one who was doing the choking and the aggressor is the one who was being choked.)

The first part is an elbow strike to the victim, which "releases" the choke hold. The aggressor lightly touches the victim's arm. When the victim is ready to begin the forward roll, he leans back a little bit to let the aggressor know when to begin the simulation of the throw.

With the outside leg, the victim steps just in front of the aggressor before starting the roll. The aggressor helps the illusion by pointing to the ground in the direction of the victim's roll to seal the illusion of actually having thrown someone. The lower the aggressor can kneel to the ground, the easier for the victim to do the forward roll. The aggressor does NOT lift up the victim at any point. The aggressor's only job is to provide an illusion of throwing while the victim performs a standard forward roll. If the victim wants to jump up in the air first, that's his business. Don't let the victim tell the aggressor to "help him out" by lifting him up.

traps and locks

There a whole raft of illusions designed to look as though one actor has immobilized another by either twisting a limb and painfully applying pressure to a joint. Most of these are taken from aikido and its parent discipline jujitsu. Although simple to perform, the margin for error is very small and so the possibility of doing real damage to the victim is very large. For that reason they are to be considered advanced techniques, and we must relegate them to the list of those that must only be taught under the direct tutelage of an on-sight instructor. With one exception.

Twisting someone's arm behind their back is probably the best known of the immobilization techniques, and actors are apt to do this one on their own. For that reason only I am going to provide some instruction for the aggressor. In performing this technique he must do ... nothing. Just let the victim twist his own arm behind his back. The aggressor does absolutely nothing except act his little heart out. [Which is basically the same instruction for all traps and locks.]

fall down a flight of stairs

Now we're really into the bruises and broken bones area, but too many shows have this in it for me to ignore here, so let me give you some pointers, though you still need to get someone with experience to help with this. By the way, this is way beyond the training of most fight directors, so make sure that the person you get knows his or her stuff.

Just to make sure that you have the skills to do this, first practice doing slow-motion continuous forward rolls, no standing up in between.. Begin on a flat surface with a gentle decline. If you have the space, put two chairs about three feet apart and do continuous rolls in a figure eight around them. Then roll down some equally gentle steps, preferably carpeted ones. Try rolling uphill as well - it's a great workout for the abdominals. As the mood strikes you, try twisting in different directions as you roll. As you start to feel some of the bumps and bruises, feel free to pad those areas of your body that always seem to find the hardest part of the floor. Very thin foam pads can be sewn right into your costume that can protect you and will not be noticed by the audience.

From the top of a staircase the biggest danger is in the initial loss of control, gravity and momentum being what they are. Instead of attempting a forward roll from a standing position right down the stairs, try beginning with a "slip" into a sit-fall first. This at least gets you sitting down on the first step, from which you can slowly tuck into a front/side roll. In order to keep your speed under control, allow your limbs to make contact with the wall and rails. This not only gives you the opportunity to continue to practice the fall in slow motion, but it also gives a better random look to the fall for better believability. It's funnier and safer if you work in the idea that you are not just falling but are desperately trying to *stop* from falling. Trying to grab at the railing, bouncing off of the banister, getting a foot hooked in a rail that can spin your body into a belly slide - all of these things can be incorporated into your fall and can help control the tumble. But remember: if you can't do it slow, you can't do it at all.

Don't try to do too much at once. A dozen or so rolls during each session is plenty. Anything beyond that and you risk getting too dizzy and bruised for any useful rehearsal.

fall from a height

It's very exciting of course to see someone leaping out from a high point on a set and have them disappear into the void. Please, please call in an expert stunt artist. You need someone who can not only teach the technique but also evaluate the performance area. By the way, this is way beyond the training of the vast majority of stage combat instructors, so don't ask your local fight guy to work it out for you. People will only get hurt.

Obviously the higher you go it becomes more dangerous for the actor. Building a fall protection system (a "drop box") is mandatory for heights above nine feet, and it must be built by a professional company. Don't do it yourself. The legal liability is huge if anything goes wrong. And even small drops of less than six feet put tremendous strain on the ankles, and there is always the risk of someone striking his head after the fall and killing himself. I'm serious.

stomach throw

An exceptional tumbler can make this simulation work, but it is also exceptionally dangerous. The stomach throw (*tomoe nage* in Japanese) is the Judo technique of pulling your opponent down on top of you while you do a back-fall, simultaneously thrusting your foot into his stomach, and them kicking straight up, his momentum taking him over your head and behind you. In a perfect world, it can be simulated by a variation of the sit fall combined with a leaping forward roll, but don't let your actors convince you that they can do this safely. There is no way that something like this should be included in a show unless you have the best fight director in the area teaching it and a very talented tumbler for the victim. When this goes wrong, it goes horribly wrong and can lead to a broken neck.

Asian Unarmed Combat
[i.e.; Martial Arts, Karate, Kung Fu, etc.]

Finally, a brief mention of Asian martial arts. Because martial arts moves are designed to allow for maximum impact using the least amount of movement, even the simulations carry with them a lot of power. These should be considered advanced techniques, as the margin for error has shrunk considerably.

There are many styles, usually based on regional differences. Karate developed in Japan and tends toward linear movement, Kung Fu from China has more circular and animal inspired motions, Tae-Kwon-Do from Korea centers on kicking, Capoeira of Brazil hides circular kicks and strikes within a distracting dance pattern, etc. While each system teaches hundreds of moves, each also has a distinctive look based on variations of stances, blocks, and attack preferences. The study of any one style can take a lifetime to master, and it might be beyond the rehearsal schedule to try and train actors to get enough flexibility to perform even simulated martial arts with any degree of believability. If this is the look you need for your show, cast it many months early and get some serious daily training for your actors.

On the other hand, if you merely want to give some of the flavor of martial arts, there are some things you can do that can dress up the already described moves.

1] Get low and stay low. The stances in martial arts are designed to keep a solid connection to the ground even when moving, and this means dropping down low in a fairly wide stance and not bobbing up and down when moving. The pressure on the knees and thighs is tremendous, but this is what separates East from West.

2] Don't bend at the waist. Martial artists learn to perform head-high kicks without changing their torso position. We can mimic that look of complete control, even if it means not kicking so high, if we keep the torso looking neutral and relaxed.

3] Add more blocks. Among trained fighters, more of the attacks are going to be aimed correctly, so will have to be blocked effectively. Read the section on swordplay, and use the arms the way a sword would be used for blocks and attacks.

4] Think linear. There is more precision of all attack and defense techniques in martial arts. Whereas a brawling fighter might loop a punch out and then let it fade away after it reaches or misses its target, a martial artist will whip out a fist a straight line and then immediately back to the original starting position, ready to fire again. For a stomach kick the foot will not simply sweep up from the floor like a pendulum in Western fashion, but first is driven straight up by lifting the knee to the chest, heel almost touching crotch, and then the foot is fired out like a punch, returns back to its ready position, and then is lowered to the ground.

There are exceptions to these rules, of course, but the exceptions should always be chosen because of what they can deliver, rather than resorted to because the body lacks flexibility and strength. On the other hand, the conceit in all martial arts films is that any strike can send someone flying and yet everyone can take a lot of physical abuse and keep coming back for more. Audiences seem to go along with it, so it seams that you can throw out realism without repercussion.

* * * * *

Ok, so you still want to add the cool kung-fu moves. Below are the basic strikes, kicks, and blocks for staged martial arts. Just as past stage combat instructors have taken the incredibly varied and complex movements of swordplay and reduced them to a tiny handful of easily repeatable moves, so have I taken the basic techniques of one martial arts style and distilled them to a small set of simple actions. Just as in stage sword combat, it is better to have both actors completely understand the mechanics of a couple dozen moves rather than confuse them with the couple thousand possibilities that each real art form contains.

For a better understanding of how the moves can be polished, be sure and read the entire section that follows this one concerning fighting with edged weapons. Much of martial arts gets its inspiration from swordplay, and an understanding of one greatly benefits the other.

In describing the moves below I am assuming that each strike and kick is blocked, that is to say, that we are not simulating contact. If you want to make it seem as though a strike has connected, go back and re-read the first part of this chapter. I'm sure you'll find a simulation there that will fit the bill, and all the actors need to do is provide a different "picture" from the list below and substitute it for the Western style described earlier.

chambering

Chambering refers to the placement of the hand (and sometimes the foot) before it strikes or blocks. The position itself is very simple. With the hand closed in a fist, the fist rests very tight against the hip bone, palm facing up, and the elbow pulled in, expanding the chest. More importantly, it is a critical component of the look of what the non-striking hand is doing during the strike or block by the active hand. Unlike Western boxing, where both hands are kept in front of the body, in classical Japanese karate every strike or block is counter balanced by a sharp pull back of the other hand into its chambered position. In this way, even as the striking hand is shooting out to make the hit, the other hand is drawing back, ready for the next move. It is not a passive move. So aggressive is this pull-back that the elbow could easily crack someone's ribs if someone was to stand behind the fighter.

The arm that does the chambering (non-striking) is most often called the draw arm, for the feeling is like that of drawing back the string on a bow, loading it up with energy before releasing it for the attack.

For most kicks, the foot must also chamber-up to its most effective striking launch position before striking. In this way, the kick is better targeted as well as keeping the rest of the body from failing off balance.

stances

Martial artists train for years so that they can stand and move in ways that the average Joe would find difficult to perform for even a few minutes, but this above all is what gives karate and the like their special look. Just as with staged swordplay, the realism of the fight rests with the stance.

basic (fighting) stance

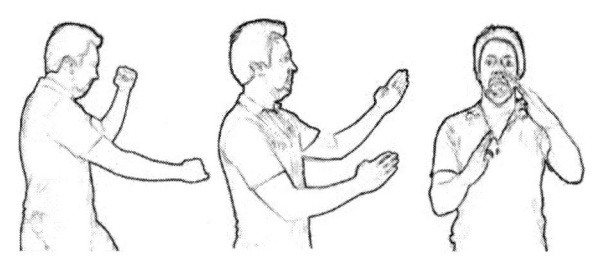

Just as in swordplay, most stances are very temporary positions used at the moment that a technique is delivered. In between these moves, the body might drop into a neutral position, committed to nothing but ready for anything. The weight shifts gently when moving, trying to keep no more than 60% of the weight on either foot. (Of course, that's impossible, but if you think about doing it that way, it will really improve the look of balance and control.) The knees are bent, the feet shoulder-width apart and not overly extended. The hands, either closed in fists or in tight flat palms (*Charlie's Angels* style) are in front of the body, usually in a center line with the forearms gently sloping down. The hands may shift in position, but generally one hand is at face level, the other at stomach level. One arm is often extended to about 80% of full distance with a slight bend at the elbow, while the other arm is closer, with a 90 degree bend at the elbow. With this combination of positions, the face is always protected by one hand, the stomach by the other, and attacks coming from the side protected by the elbows. As always, the shoulders must be relaxed and down. The head rests directly over the torso, which is erect and not leaning or bending at the waist.

front stance

This aggressive stance is usually seen as an attack is launched or a very strong block is delivered as the body is moving forward. The lead knee bent and the back leg straight. The lead knee should be directly over the heel, bearing 70% of the body's weight. The torso should be erect and relaxed. Feet are about one and a half shoulder widths apart. The lead foot must point directly at the opponent. It's nice if the rear foot can do so as well, but usually a slight turnout is more practical.

Just as in fencing, moving either forward or backward can be done by either bringing the back foot up to the front foot and then launching the front foot forward again, or by a simple passing (walking) step. However, in classical forms, the body does not bob up and down, so the actors will need to learn how to move while keeping their heads on one low plane. How to do this? The feet and the knees come together for each step, the legs both squeezing together and bending even more before the foot goes out to its new position. That means that the torso is moving gracefully forward (not up and down or side to side), with shoulders relaxed, while the traveling foot is drawing a half-moon shape on the ground with each step. Both feet have the toes pointing directly at the opponent, not turned-out. This is really hard to do, and requires considerable abdominal control as well as strong thighs and good ankle flexibility.

Stepping backwards is the same as going forwards, but don't let your actors cheat in shifting their weight by sticking their tailbones out and leading with their butts. The lead foot will always be carrying 70% of the body weight, so the tailbone must always be tucked in. This way the torso can move as one unit in any direction, always in control, always ready to strike even in retreat.

back stance

Different styles have different back stances, but I have chosen one that is easiest to perform as well as being the most visually interesting. This back stance is nice to use during blocking and evasions, as well as a solid platform from which to perform a rear thrust kick.

With the face forward, looking at the opponent, the torso turns and shifts the weight balance from lead foot to back foot. At the same time, the feet will turn (on the heels, not the balls) so that the rear foot, the one bearing most of the weight, is pointing away from the opponent and the lead foot is pointing off at 90 degrees (more if possible). The lead leg straightens and the rear leg bends, again so that the knee is directly over the heel.

If accompanied by a block, it's nice to lean the body away from the opponent so that the torso and lead leg have the same long, elegant line.

horse stance

The most stable of the stances, a variation of it is found in every martial arts form. I've chosen one the least damaging to the knees.

The weight distribution is 50-50, with the feet about double shoulder apart, toes turned out to about 45 degrees, and again the knees directly over the heels. In this position with the tailbone tucked in tightly, the knees and hips should all be at a straight line, again probably not possible for actors, but that is what you're aiming for. This is not all that different from a ballet plié in second position, except that the feet should not be turned out so severely. From here the torso is free face to forward or turn to either side, flexibility permitting.

Some karate styles have the feet stay parallel to each other, but that puts a huge strain on the knees and ankles. I would rather you concentrate on the pelvis, because as soon as a little fatigue sets in, the butt starts to swing out. It looks horrible. As with all of the stances, tuck it in and keep it tucked.

cat stance

All of the previous stances are called "outside" stances, for the feeling is that of the knees pulling out, away from each other. There are many "inside" stances, where the thighs squeeze together, but I have included only this one for our purposes. The cat stance works especially well as a strong platform from which to deliver kicks from the lead foot. The leading knee also automatically protects the lower torso from attacks.

Facing the opponent, the back leg turned out to 45 degrees, both knees bending and the lead foot pointing at the opponent. As the thighs squeeze together, the lead foot is drawn in close to the rear foot, but with heel off the ground and the toes supporting only 10% of the body weight, purely for balance. The weight shifts back to 90% on the back leg. The lead knee is pointed directly at the opponent and the tailbone is tightly tucked. The torso is relaxed and erect. Squeezing the thighs together provides stability, while shifting the weight off of the lead foot allows to quickly snap out a kick if necessary.

Strikes

Strikes encompass any attack made with the upper limbs and can be aimed at any joint or vulnerable spot on the human body. For training purposes the attacks are mainly thought of as either high (face) medium (solar plexus) or low (belly or even crotch). We are going to modify this to three levels and five targets - the same ones we use in broadsword fighting. As in stage swordplay, left and right refer to the attacker's view of the targets. These targets are:

√ Head level is going to be dead center but slightly above the forehead
√ Shoulder level right is slightly outside and below the victim's left shoulder
√ Shoulder level left is slightly outside and below victim's right shoulder
√ Mid level right drifts to the victim's left flank but on the same plane as the navel
√ Mid level left shifts to the victim's right but on the same plane as the victim's navel

As you can see, we're staying away from any attacks to joints, and we are trying to send the real energy of these attacks slightly away from the body of our partner.

straight punch

Every strike is supposed to be performed incorporating the concept of chambering, and nowhere is this more easily seen than in the straight punch. This punch travels in a line from the chambered position directly to the target, the fist turning from palm up to palm down just as the arm reaches its full extension. The strike goes in a straight line to the target, "sticking" there for a fraction of a second before moving to the next position (usually chambered). There must be no curling of the wrist, so the striking surface of the punch is the "flat" of the first two fingers. But again, what really give this punch an Eastern look is the fact that the other fist is simultaneously pulled back to its chambered position at the hip, palm up. Try several punches in a row until the "pushme-pullyou" feel becomes comfortable. Remember - just as much energy is committed to the pull-back as to the punch itself.

The twisting of the striking hand from palm up in the chambered position to palm down when completing the strike is crucial to the look of Eastern punches. Don't twist the torso away with each punch - you want to "lock" the chest forward at the completion of each strike for a much more powerful and confident look.

spear hand

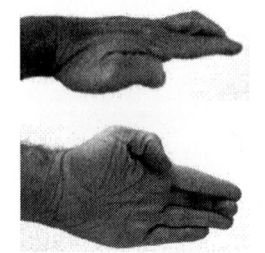

A variation of the straight punch, except the fist opens to form a flat hand, fingers tightly together and thumb side pointing up. In actual martial arts, the middle finger is pulled back slightly so the center three fingers form an even striking surface. The audience is never going to see that, so it is not necessary to try to simulate it. The strike goes in a straight line to the target, "sticking" there for a fraction of a second before moving to the next position (usually chambered).

Sometimes the other arm, instead of pulling back to the chambered position, stays forward to support the spear hand at the elbow. In this augmented strike the non-striking fist also opens up and, palm down, slides under the striking elbow, the entire forearm ending up parallel to the chest. The look is very angular. Be sure to push the shoulders down - don't let them start rising up out of tension.

palm heel

The bottom of the palm is a very effective striking surface, so long as the fingers don't get in the way. To get the look, stick your right hand out as though you are checking for rain. Keeping the palm flat, fold the fingers at the second joint (and the thumb at the first joint) so that the fingertips are touching the palm at the knuckle joint. Now bend the hand at the wrist so that the palm heel pushes forward, facing the target as you pull the elbow back to chamber the hand. Kind of uncomfortable, isn't it. The strike goes in a straight line to the target, "sticking" there for a fraction of a second before moving to the next position (usually chambered).

For stage, this strike looks best used to attack to the side, combined with a nice side stance, where you get the most visual length of the arm.

knife edge

Commonly called the "karate chop", it actually has only a limited use in true martial arts. It is designed to attack vulnerable points that are hard to get to by using a closed fist, the neck and temple being the more obvious targets. But of course for stage we can use it for anything we want to.

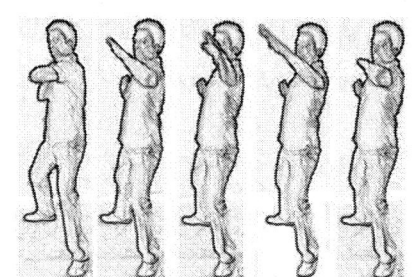

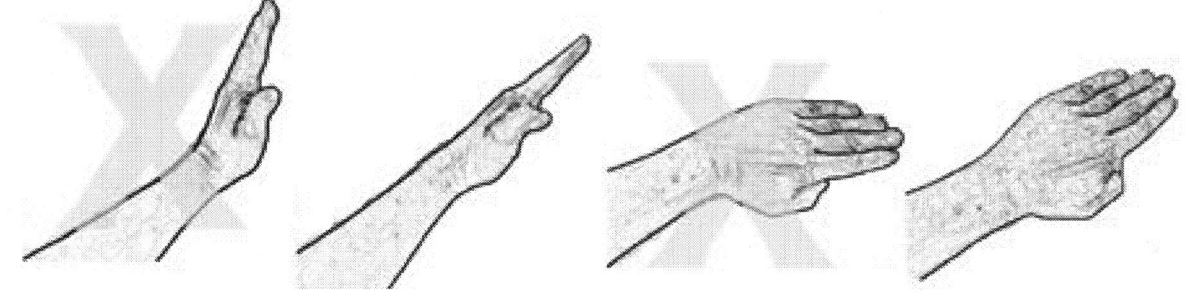

We all know how to hold the hand (palm open and fingers tight, thumb bent so it is not exposed), but too many films show the wrist bent for some reason. That doesn't make any sense at all. From tip of middle finger to elbow must be an absolutely straight line.

To execute the strike, we again borrow from the cutting moves of staged swordplay. The striking hand chambers by touching the finger tips to your own opposite ear, elbow pointing at the target (off-line of your partner). The elbow does not move as the hand swings out and back in one quick snappy motion. The emphasis is on the return, not so much on the extension. Careful not to hyperextend the elbow (and keep your shoulders down!).

back hand

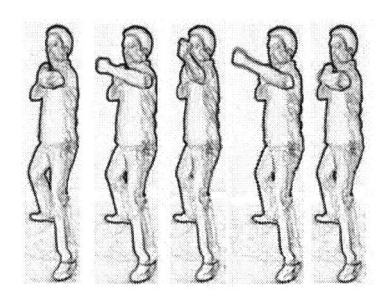

This is actually very similar in construction to the knife edge strike. It again is a snappy move instead of a "sticking" move, the elbow pointing right at the target. All we have to do is give it a different look, and that we do by keeping the fist closed and chambering it, not at the opposite ear but right at the near armpit. In order to do that, you'll need to turn your other shoulder away from the target, but that's fine because it improves the look. The fist, thumb side up, swings out parallel to the ground, and then back.

The other hand can chamber to the hip as usual, but a nice variation is to have it provide a "home" for the striking hand. For this, both hands meet at the chambered position at the armpit, the non-striking hand palm open, fingertips up as if to stay "stop", thumb pressed against the chest, the palm almost touching the closed fist of the attacking hand.

blocks

Real blocks in martial arts come in two flavors, deflections and power. Deflections allow the incoming strike to skip off the blocking surface and then continue on harmlessly out of the way. Power blocks meet force with force, usually using the bony outside edge of the forearm or other very strong striking surface. Such blocks can develop so much force that they can break bones. We, of course, don't want to do anything so dangerous, so the following, all of them power blocks, are modified. The blocking surface is turned wherever possible so that soft tissue rather than bone is used, and each block then merely meets the incoming "attack" at a predetermined point in space, with very little actual contact at all.

Just as with the strikes, both arms are active when performing most of the power blocks. When one arm performs the action, the other arm pulls back just as powerfully to the chamber position. This dramatically expands the chest, making the block, and by extension the attack, appear much more powerful. For each block, there should always be an initial contraction where the arms cross at the elbows, and then one arm performs the block as the other pulls back to the chambered (hip) position. The look and feel is something like sharpening two very large knives. But no matter what, all blocks should have the look of taking a threat aimed toward your center and moving it harmlessly away.

As with the strikes, the non-blocking arm is active, moving forcefully back to the chambered position. And again, this arm is referred to as the draw arm. If the blocking arm has to do two or more actions in a row, the draw arm usually stays where it is, although we still have to see some sort of expansion (however small) with each move, even if only in the chest. This additional pulse helps lend a bit more believability to each block.

down block

The contraction brings the blocking fist up to the opposite shoulder; the draw arm crosses in front of the body, elbow straight, elbow touching elbow. For the block, the blocking arm slides down and across the draw arm until it points downward, even as the draw arm moves to its chambered position at the hip.

To reduce damage to your partner, turn the fist thumb-side down slightly so as to strike with the fleshy part of the forearm.

inside down block

In this block, the arms do not cross and there is no contraction. The draw hand, from wherever it has been, moves directly to the chambered position. The blocking arm moves forward to what would normally be the final position of the down block (but this time with the fist up) and then sweeps in front of the body to the opposite side, with the fist turned so that the palm-side leads the movement and the block is made with the inside of the forearm rather than the edge. For this block, the look of power comes not from chest expansion, but from the quick twisting of the torso.

rising block

The contraction brings the draw arm across the body, at an angle in front of the torso, with the fist in front of and at the same height as the opposite shoulder. The fist of the blocking arm slips underneath the draw arm so that the wrist joint rests underneath the elbow. For the block, the lead arm slides up across the draw arm until the forearm forms a straight line parallel to the ground at about forehead level, even as the draw arm moves to its chambered position at the hip.

To reduce damage to your partner, don't allow the fist to twist as it moves up. You'll want to make contact with the softer back part of the forearm instead of the boney edge.

inside block

The contraction brings the blocking fist up to the opposite arm pit, underneath the draw arm; the draw arm crosses in front of the body, elbow bent, elbow touching elbow, fist about shoulder height. For the block, the blocking arm slips under the draw arm and then slides along it. It will stop at the blocked position, forming a 45 degree angle upward, fist in front of the same shoulder and elbow about a fist distance away from the same side hip. As expected, the draw arm has simultaneously moved to its chambered position at the hip.

To give the block its best look, hyper-twist the fist so that the inside of the forearm makes contact with the incoming attack. Difficult to do, but not impossible.

outside block

In this block, the arms do not cross and there is no contraction. Instead, it is the twisting of the hip and torso that provide the strength for the block. The draw hand, from wherever it has been, moves loosely to any area in front of the body; at the same time the blocking arm moves up to the same side ear, thumb side pointing down, forearm now parallel to the ground. For the block, the blocking arm swings across the body, ending with the fist directly above the elbow, forearm perpendicular to the ground. At the same time, the draw arm moves to its chambered position.

If blocking an attack to the torso, the blocking fist will end at shoulder level. If the attack was to the face, the block of course will be higher, with the fist at forehead level. This block can carry a lot of accidental momentum, so be sure that the point of contact is the inside of the forearm by finishing the block with the fist thumb side pointing towards you.

knife hand block

This is a nice variation of the inside block, all the more interesting because both hands are kept in the "karate chop" open palm shape. The contraction brings the blocking hand up to the opposite shoulder, over the draw arm; the draw arm crosses in front of the body, elbow slightly bent, elbow touching elbow, and the hand out in front almost making the universal signal for "stop". For the block, the blocking arm slides across the draw arm until it forms a 45 degree angle upward, open palm in front of the same shoulder and elbow about a fist distance away from the same side hip. Really scrape the forearms as you do this move for the best look.

In this simulation, the draw hand doesn't go all the way to the hip. Instead, as the block is executed, the draw hand comes to rest right at solar plexus level, palm up. The torso turns slightly, so that the shoulder of the draw hand moves somewhat away from the action.

double block

Combine two blocks and you get a new animal. For example, an inside forearm block with the right arm and an inside down block with the left, if performed as one action, and you have a cross block protecting the right flank. Simultaneous rising blocks with a slightly exaggerated angle and you have a nice cross block protecting the head. Have fun and experiment. Double blocks in stage combat give the illusion that the incoming attack was especially forceful.

open hand deflection

Looks especially nice when defending against strikes to the face, the look here is not meeting force with force but in merely deflecting an incoming straight line strike so that it just misses its intended target. Strange as it may seem, these are very effective defensive moves and very simple to perform. We just need to make them dramatically understandable and not painful.

We want to move the open hand along with the incoming strike a bit, rather than arriving at a predetermined point in space (that is of course what we're doing; we just don't want it to look that way). So the defensive hand is going to describe a small half circle in air as it moves up, first moving out a bit to meet the threat and then guiding it half way to its finish position. For the aggressor's part, he won't actually throw a punch that is truly a threat and needs to be moved, but rather launches his strike already going to that point where the successfully deflected punch is going to end up anyway.

Generally, the hand making the block will first make contact with the incoming fist, and then allow it to slide past a bit, so that the finishing contact is at about mid-forearm. Either side of the hand can be used for these deflections, but if using the back of the hand, make sure that your partner is being kind when punching. If not, the back of your hand can get some very nasty bruises.

Kicks

Just as with a strike, the path of the kick must always be directed to a spot away from the victim. If the actors are parallel to the proscenium, then the kick that misses or is blocked is aimed just up or down stage of the victim. If the actors are stacked and the simulation is that of a kick that actually makes contact, then the kick can be aimed toward the victim but only if the distance has been extended to one-and-a-half the length of the aggressor's leg.

With all except the fan kick, the higher you can lift the knee during the first part of the move, the better the kick will look. The attempt should always be to have the kick "live from the waist down". In other words, in a perfect world the kicker's posture from the waist up will remain unchanged during the entire kick.

front snap kick

Western-style kicks are simple - the foot swings up in an arc, and then either swings back or just flops down. By contrast, this front snap kick is a four part-er, as are most Asian-style kicks.

First: raise the knee until it is pointing at the intended target (remembering that the "target" is a spot usually upstage or downstage of your partner). If your target is high, you have to point the knee high. At this point, the foot itself has not yet swung out, but is right next to the non-kicking leg, usually at about knee level, but higher if you can manage it. Second: the foot swings out to the target, ball of the foot reaching out but the toes curled back. (I understand that when wearing shoes, this is all but Impossible) The strike point is the ball of the foot, not the toes. To help with balance, the hip might thrust forward a bit, but the torso should not lean back. Third: since this is a snap kick, not a thrust kick, the foot immediately comes back to its place high up next to the non-kicking knee, ready for another kick if necessary. Lastly, the foot drops down to the floor in a straight line. This is a very quick and smooth kick, but each of the segments have to be executed.

You're only supposed to kick as high as your knee can point, so for most people that's going to be a waist high kick. Yes, if you swing your hip into it and arch your back, you can snap off a head level kick, but it's not really in control, is it. Also, I've noticed that in most TV shows and movies the kick is delivered with the toes pointed, not arched back. In reality, you'd break your toes if you were to actually make contact that way. But the look is a little cleaner, so if you want to, go for it.

rear thrust kick

With the body turned away from the target, the knee first rises up as in the front snap kick. This keeps the foot close to the supporting leg, but of course there is no attempt to point the knee to the target. Second, the foot travels backward in a straight line to the target, leading with the heel, moving parallel to the ground. The body is much less flexible in this direction, so the torso will need to lean forward somewhat. As this is a thrust kick, not a snap, the foot will "stick" in the air for a half second. Third, the foot pulls back in to its chambered location as the torso straightens. Fourth, the foot is brought down to the ground.

This kick is not always aimed at someone who is standing behind you. With an opponent standing directly in front of you, a rear thrust kick can be delivered simply by turning the body away during the first move. Why would someone do this? The rear thrust kick is the most powerful kick possible, and one that also protects the kicker from being hit himself. The opposite arm will still rise up to protect the face, just in case.

side snap kick

Even experienced martial artists sometimes fudge this move, performing what is really just a front kick to the side. But this is a kick meant to swing freely from the knee rather than "punching" in a straight line.

First, the foot rises up to the chambered position near the knee of the supporting leg. The body, especially the hips, turns slightly so that the kicking leg is closer to the opponent, but the knee must point directly at the target. Try to get the knee as high up as possible, with the arch of the foot trying to curl around the supporting leg. Second, keeping the knee high and stable, it becomes a pivot from which the foot will swing out in an arc to the target. The toes are pointed down so that the striking surface is the outside edge of the foot. The torso does not lean back during this kick, although the hips might swing along with the movement for extra height. Third: since this is a snap kick, not a thrust kick, the foot immediately comes back to its place high up next to the non-kicking knee. Fourth, the foot is lowered to the floor.

This is not an easy kick, as it can put quite a strain on the knee, but it gives a nice flavor to a fight, so use it if you can. Flexible martial artists can use it as an upper cut to an opponent's chin.

roundhouse kick

This kick is a bit more risky to make safe, in that it requires the actor to generate a lot of force but also be able to stop it before making contact with his partner, much like swinging a broadsword. This kick is meant to come in sideways, parallel to the ground. It's much easier for an actor to stop a broadsword than to stop his own leg, and I am hesitant to include this simulation in this book. But the roundhouse kick is so common in martial arts that it is difficult to imagine not using it in a staged fight, so I include it here in the interest of safety.

First, the chambering position itself is a bit awkward. With the supporting leg forward, the kicking leg is lifted up away from the opponent, foot and knee rising to hip height. Everyone calls this the "dog peeing on a fire hydrant" pose.

Second, the leg will swing around the body as the foot extends to the target, the striking surface for stage purposes being the upper plane of the foot rather than the toes or ball. Try to lean forward - into the kick - rather than laying down away from it. For this kick to look good, the leg must travel parallel to the ground, as though you are kicking over a table in order to reach your target. The body can't help but want to turn along with the kick, so we have to find a way to control that momentum and stop the kick before it hurts anyone. So we use the upper body to stop the lower body. Let's say you're kicking with the left foot, so the leg is swinging around to the right. As the leg comes across, sharply twist your shoulders to the left, aiming your right shoulder to the target. The feeling is like that of wringing a towel. With a little practice you'll find that this will suddenly stop your kick just where you want it.

Third, this is a snap kick, so the foot and leg immediately "bounce" away. The trajectory of the leg follows the same path going back as it did to get there, which means that it has to clear that imaginary table again as it travels behind you. Finally, from this hydrant position, the foot is lowered to the floor. Of course, if you are stepping forward after the kick, you don't have to return the foot all they back to your original position, which was behind you. But you shouldn't just flop the foot down, either. After the kick, the bounce-back of the foot should still have it travel parallel to the floor until it is back near your butt, and only then lowered to take your forward step.

roundhouse variation: the laying down front snap kick.

Also called the mini-round. Do the set-up for a front snap-kick as described earlier, but as the kick starts to move forward, let your body twist 90 degrees in that same direction, and lift up the foot sideways, so that the foot and knee form a line parallel to the floor. It's called "laying down the leg", and it will change the trajectory of the kick so now it can come in sideways instead of straight in. The recovery has to be very fast, with the body quickly twisting back in the other direction. This will provide the momentum needed to snap that kicking foot back to center. But don't resort to the mini-round just because the actor is having trouble with the regular roundhouse kick described above. The full roundhouse is much more showy and well worth the extra rehearsal time.

The mini-round is a fun little kick to add when you want to break up the look of a series of kicks, especially multiple kicks to different targets from the same leg. Choreographically, it allows for a kick from the front leg to be directed sideways to an opponent, rather than straight into him.

fan kick

The fan kick requires a lot of flexibility, and is generated with a lot of hip movement, so most people can't stop it once begun. Because of the momentum needed, this is not a move which is blocked - the actor needs the full space to follow through and complete the swing. Few actors will be able to make it look good, but it does have some good visual flair.

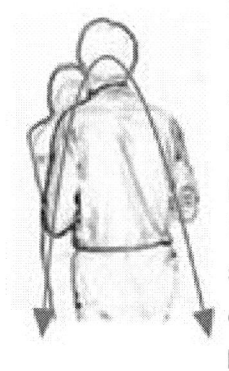

This simulation works best when the actors are "stacked", aggressor facing full front and the victim full back. First, establish a one-arm's distance between the two, then one or the other needs to take another (large) step away, clearing room for the leg to swing. The aggressor's supporting leg will be in front and the kicking leg behind. Second, the fan kick can travel either left to right or right to left, either "outside" or "inside", the important part being to not kick out toward the victim but rather swing the straight leg out in a giant circle in front of him. Think of the leg as a pendulum with the hip as the pivot point. The circle of travel (actually, it's more of a teardrop shape) is on a parallel plane between the two participants, the highest point being at face level. Third, again, there is no stopping this kick, so for the aggressor the simulation finishes almost as soon as it starts, just making sure that the torso has not gone out of plumb and that the foot ends up on the ground at roughly the same point from whence it started (only because it looks better than having it land somewhere else). If the simulation is a hit and not a miss, then the victim has a chance to add the sound and complete the illusion of being struck. Luckily, the audience can't see the victim's hands, so he can easily clap his hands together for the sound and the audience will be none the wiser. Just make sure not to move the elbows - those are visible and can blow the illusion if we see a flapping motion.

jump kick

Although any kick can be performed while in the air, we are only going to try a basic front snap kick. Make sure you are fully warmed up before starting - you don't want to blow out your hamstring here.

Let's say you are kicking with the right foot. Go over the basic mechanics of the kick described earlier, and try the kick several times until you feel comfortable with it. It's a four-parter, remember? Now, to mess with your brain some, get into a nice solid front stance with the *right* leg forward. Right knee bent, left knee straight, right? Try the kick with the right foot from this position several times - feels different, doesn't it? Kicking from the front leg is difficult because you don't want to simply rock back on your back leg. You've got to bend that back leg for support, really tighten the stomach muscles, and drive your kick forward. Be sure to continue to use correct technique and that you are not just flapping your leg out.

Now we're going to work on the left leg. Forget about kicking for a bit, we're going to go just for some hang time. Keep the same right foot forward stance (right knee bent, of course). Like a sprinter coming out of the blocks, try to touch your own chest with your left knee as you stand up straight with your right. You'll soon find that you get quite a bit upward thrust without trying too hard. Now go ahead and go for some height, letting your right leg add to the momentum by doing a little hop. The higher you can drive that left knee and combine it with a good hop, the more hang time you'll get. If you are a basketball player, this is the move you need in order to do a lay-up (if you get a lot of height, even a dunk!)

Ready for a higher jump? As soon as the left knee pumps up to the chest, add to the momentum by driving the right knee up to the chest also. By driving both knees up hard and fast in a quick one-two, your little hop gets transformed into quite a nice vertical leap.

Now you're ready to combine the two moves for one dramatic kick. The left knee pumps up, beginning the drive skyward, and then the right knee does the same but adds the snap kick when you are at the top of your jump. I'm not saying that this is easy for everyone to do - athletes and dancers will get it and perfect it in one day while others may struggle for weeks. [Heck, some dancers will get so much air time that they'll be able to throw in a kick with that left foot as well, and probably get them both at head level.] But it is possible for anyone to do a single jump kick, so long as you don't give up on the essential mechanics. Don't go for height, go for fluidity. With practice, everyone should be able to execute a front snap kick in the air before that left foot lands on the ground.

These are some very basic moves that demonstrate a little bit of the look of trained martial artists. Just as in all of stage combat, we are not trying to scrupulously recreate what an actual fight would look like, but rather we use a specialized physical language to tell a story. So just as sport fencing is different than staged rapier and dagger fights, a true karate tournament match will be very different from staged martial arts fighting, and all would be very different indeed from a real life-or-death struggle. Read the upcoming section on edged weaponry to get more ideas, for remember that all martial arts ultimately comes from the sword techniques of ancient Asia. All of the safety points in terms of distancing and targeting with swords are applicable here and critical to actor safety.

Let's look at a few attack and defense combinations, performed in sequence as a single fight:

Actor A	Actor B
face punch	rising block
open hand deflections	three face punches
stomach punch	outside block
inside block, cat stance	augmented spear hand thrust
front snap kick	reverse down block
down block	side kick
chop to throat	[take reaction]

Again, if you think of using swords instead of just limbs it will clean up the transitions. As always, be sure and get solid training from an experienced instructor of stage combat, not just a martial artist. It's not enough to perform the moves; it must be modified for performance on stage.

In Summary ...

Unarmed Fighting Styles

Most real fights occur between people who have reached a point of rage in which they no longer are acting rationally, so any training they may have had goes out the window. I've seen this happen to otherwise skilled fighters who get caught up in either fear or anger. For these combatants, the moves tend to be circular, wild, uncontrolled both in execution and in balance, the tendency being to throw the combatant off-balance whether or not he actually makes contact. There is very little effective defense, and what little there is is simply the instinctive curling up of the body as both forearms come up to protect the face. Untrained fighters also tend to use the same one or two moves over and over again regardless of effectiveness. The person who falls down first invariably ends up as the loser.

Among trained fighters who are able to keep their wits about them, there is a greater variation of moves both offensive and defensive, with an attempt to bring into play combination moves designed to establish distinct lines of attack and take advantage of perceived weaknesses. However, what the audience will notice most of all is the "on-guard" position which trained fighters will drop into when a threat is identified. Invariably the dominant foot and hand step back, providing a slightly reduced target to the opponent. The elbows both tuck in slightly to be ready to protect the stomach and flanks. The dominant (right) hand goes to shoulder level and stays fairly close to the body, while the left fist rides higher, just under eye level, and extends further towards the opponent. This allows both hands to protect the face. The ribs are protected by the elbows.

We know from art on excavated pottery that boxing goes back at least to the ancient Greeks, and it seems that the stances and guard positions would be instantly recognizable at any gym today. There is, however, a very distinct boxing style that developed during the mid-nineteenth century and flourished though to the 1930's. You have probably seen photographs of prize fighters with handlebar mustaches, with the fists tightly curled in and the head held stiffly back. The opponent would see the back of the fighter's hands instead of the little finger side of the fist. This is the era of bareknuckle prize fighting, the Marquise of Queensbury rules, the birth of the "sweet science". The seemingly unnatural stance is actually quite practical for the style of fighting performed. No grabbing or kicking was allowed, winner was declared by knockout only, and up through the turn of the century a round was counted not by the clock but with each instance that someone was knocked down. This was brutal exhibition fighting, and with no timed rounds or points given, the only strategy was to survive the punishment and inflict as much damage as possible.

In this style of fisticuffs, some moves needed to be modified. Punches that land with the flat face of the fist can deliver great force, but the delicate bones of the fingers can easily break, so constant jabs with the left can quickly ruin the hand. A better jab for bareknuckle fighting is to turn the fists in so that the back of the hand faces the opponent, the knuckles all pointing toward the opponent's face and the hand held directly above the elbow. From this position the fist can be quickly snapped out and down onto the bridge of the nose of the opponent. The knuckles might fracture but the hand was still capable of attacking. Either hand could jab, and to hide the attack the hands could roll in a vertical circle, providing an ever shifting presentation of fists. Alternately, the lower fist could quickly rise up, thrusting in for an upper cut to the chin or to the stomach. A fist could always attempt a quick looping roundhouse to break the cartilage of the ear, a hook punch to the ribs, and if the opportunity finally arose, go for the straight right cross for a knock-out punch to the chin or nose. My point here is that just because something looks funny to our modern eyes doesn't mean that it wasn't extremely effective.

The defense matched the offense. The forearms could slightly extend to either side to deflect the attacks to the face, but it was more important to keep the head leaning back and away from the extension of the attacking fists. The stomach and ribs were protected by the elbows. Because the punches had to cause damage in order to win the fight, dancing around in the modern boxing style was unknown and the feet were more firmly planted on the floor, always providing a solid foundation for the knock-out punch. Throw a punch while you're on your toes and you've dissipated all of its power.

As you know, boxers no longer fight that way. Why? Modern boxing is a much more controlled sport than it was a hundred years ago, and in order to try to reduce the damage to the fighters three changes in the sport changed every technique: 1] Winner by knockout was replaced with a point system. 2] rest periods only after knock-downs were replaced by timed rounds 3] and bareknuckle was replaced by padded gloves. Since modern boxers no longer need to knockout the opponent but rather can win by points scored, the number of jabs as opposed to solid punches has gone up dramatically. The moves are lighter and faster, with more emphasis in landing a greater number of points and a greater willingness to stay close in, since receiving the jab from a padded glove, though painful, usually cannot end the fight. Now the head can drop in closer to the hands, the center of balance shifts higher up into the torso instead of the hips, the weight shifts from the heels to the ball of the foot, and the fist strikes with the metatarsals rather than from the knuckles.

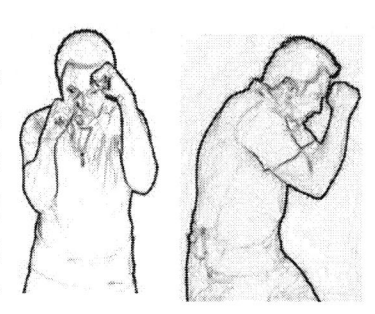

All of this means that the look of a stage fight will be very different if set in 1895 compared to 1995, but what never changes is the way that a stage combat technique is performed. A jab is a jab, a stomach punch is a stomach punch. The set-up and the picture might change due to the period specifics and the character choices, but the careful calculation of the action must conform to the safety needs of each simulation.

This is especially true for staged martial arts. Since many of your actors may have had some training in one style or another, each will have a certain preference on how a punch or block should be performed. Some will be adamant that their way is the correct way (often because they have never been taught another way), and certainly you may wish to incorporate interesting variations that actors may bring, or those from visiting martial artists, or even from the latest movie. Just remember that these variations can be incorporated into the look of the set-up and picture, but must never interfere with the mechanics of the action. Have doubts? Look at how each technique is performed and imagine the worst thing that can go wrong. It will happen. Not might; will. It's merely a matter of time. Are you comfortable with that risk? Are your actors informed about those risks? As long as everyone is ok with the occasional broken nose or cracked vertebrae, than who am I to stop you? But if that gives anyone pause, cut the fight. Want a happy middle-ground? Re-block the moves so that energy is never directed towards another human being.

Putting together the moves.

No reason to go into choreography here (I'll get to some basics at the very end of the chapter), but there is a certain natural progression in the types of moves that might be developed in a fight that shouldn't be ignored. Mainly it comes down to damage sustained and adrenaline produced. A fight progresses only so long as the combatants can continue to sustain damage. When someone connects with a strong punch, it's usually a fight ender. A connected punch to the stomach at best will knock the wind out of you, at worst cause broken ribs and a ruptured spleen. A punch to the face will leave you at best with a runny nose and inflamed eyes, at worst with broken bones, a concussion, shattered eye, even death. To extend a fight into a barroom brawl where every punch continues to connect but doesn't break a bone insults the audience. They will go along with a longer fight so long as the consequence of each action is not forgotten. Which in turn means that many strikes and kicks are going to have to miss or be effectively evaded or blocked on a longer fist fight.

As the movements are memorized, the actors must also add the character's intention and reaction to each of the moves. Any fight scene is also an acting scene, so just as one can only say the lines as fast as the audience can understand them, the fight moves can be only as fast as the audience can follow the story that goes along with the moves. And just as we also nuance the delivery of our lines so as to add layers of interest in our characters, so must we go far beyond the mere performance of the fight in technical terms. So forget the idea of too fast or too slow. Think instead in terms of clarity, believability of intent, and emotional connection.

There are many instances in which your show will be better off by hiring someone as fight instructor rather than as choreographer. I mentioned before that the fights should be rehearsed as early as possible, but for many shows we have to amend that slightly to make sure that they are rehearsing the right thing.

For many modern shows, I don't like to stick my nose in too early. I've found that as soon as I mention anything to the actors in terms of specific moves, even if only as a suggestion, they immediately latch onto it as though it were scripture. If on the other hand, the actors work their way into the scene and find out where their own impulses take them, the "fights" become more organically tied to the story that they are presenting.

I usually like to step in after the director and actors feel good about the nature of the emotional responses that are drawn out in their playing of the scene. That way I can take their impulses ("now I want to throw him to the ground"), and show them how to do it safely. But if I tell them that someone should be tossed to the ground before they themselves come up with that idea, that moment becomes a technical one for the actors instead of part of their creation. So for at least the first blocking, I prefer to let the actors rush to each other and even gently lay hands on each other, and then grunt or squeal or yell what they want to do. If nothing comes up on the first rehearsal, then maybe they'll need more time to understand their characters. But I don't like to have them or the director feel that we need to rush to get the fight blocking down too early.

Edged Weaponry

I know that many high school teachers are always leery of the fight scenes in Shakespeare plays, but we all know that you can get a lot more guys to audition if they know there's a chance to sling some steel. Interestingly, sword fights are usually safer than unarmed scuffles. The actors are further apart, and the weapons themselves generate a certain level of fear and respect that just isn't there when two actors tussle hand-to-hand. Nonetheless, accidents with swords occur, and when they do the injuries can be severe. And I hear way too many horror stories about well-meaning amateurs without experience telling the actors to really go after each other in order to make the fight look more exciting, The stories always end with broken blades and damaged actors.

The good news? The techniques used to make the fights safer are the same ones used to make the fight more believable, so art never needs to trump safety. These techniques form a solid basis for choreographed fights with the broadsword or rapier, and we can also use them for all kinds of weapons combat. [There are other forms of stage combat that specifically replicate the civilian fighting style of the 18th and 19th centuries, that of the dueling smallsword. Because smallsword techniques include thrusts directly aimed at the torso, and parries that keep the point on-line as a continuing threat to the opponent, they are by their nature more dangerous than the standard combat moves, so they will not be discussed in this volume. They should only be used under the direct training and supervision of a <u>very</u> experienced fight instructor.]

Before we get to specifics, let's go over the nine commandments of stage combat with swords :

1. There must never be even a fraction of a second in which any weapon is pointed at or crosses in front of anyone's face under any circumstance - before, during or after the fight.

2. Don't force your partner to block your weapon on your attack. If he is supposed to block your incoming thrust to just outside of his left hip, then simply make sure that your target is two inches outside of his left hip when you begin the attack. Always thrust and cut "off-line".

3. Conversely, don't force the block, pushing your partner's sword away. Simply meet the incoming sword at the prearranged point in space. Blades "kiss" on contact; they must never bash.

4. Always parry (block) with the <u>edge</u> of the blade, never with the flat.

5. Use gloves. It can mean the difference between a bruised finger or an infected and broken finger. Make sure everyone's tetanus vaccination is up-to-date.

6. Finish your attacks with a straight arm. Don't pull your cuts - push them.

7. Look at what you want to hit. We are built to do that automatically. DO NOT STARE AT YOUR PARTNER'S EYES! You will only end up losing track of your own sword. Follow the sword tips if you want to develop control of your sword.

8. A rule of thumb: actors should have _one hour_ of fight rehearsal time for each _five seconds_ of finished fight. Any techniques not polished _before_ going into tech week must be cut from the fight.

9. Only stage combat fight-grade weaponry must be used for the fight.

I want to explain all of those commandments, so I'm going to repeat them and expand on them (it won't kill you to re-read them).

1. *There must never be even a fraction of a second in which any weapon is pointed at or crosses in front of anyone's face under any circumstance - before, during or after the fight.*

Many years ago at the American Conservatory Theatre in San Francisco, they were working on their original mounting of *Cyrano De Bergerac*, starring Peter Donat, with the brilliant J. Steven White not only providing the choreography but also playing the role of Valvert. The fight was very exciting, and with such an experienced choreographer was also very safe. As you may know, just before the duel is a bit of back-and-forth insulting between the two. For this production Cyrano menaced Valvert physically, at one point slowly walking forward and twirling the tip of the sword in front of Valvert's face, but with that tip at a still safe distance of three feet away from Valvert.

During either the first or second dress rehearsal the heel of Cyrano's right boot broke off right during that little twirl. Since it happened just as he was putting his weight on the foot, it naturally threw him off balance, pitching him forward. He instinctively extended his arms as we all do when we feel that we are going to fall. Unfortunately, this also pitched his sword forward along with his body, and the tip of the epee blade struck Valvert directly beneath the right eye, under the ridge of the cheek bone, piercing the skin, bending the sword and pushing Valvert's head back. One inch higher and that sword tip would have entered the eye socket. Steven would have lost an eye and very likely his life had the blade entered the brain. I'll repeat: this was *before the stage fight had begun* and the actors were *far apart* from each other.

After that incident, Mr. White incorporated a new rule: Never point or allow a weapon to cross in front of anyone's face at any time. Anywhere. For any reason. You should implement this policy as well, starting today. It costs you nothing, takes nothing away, and will prevent injuries and save lives.

2. *Don't force your partner to block your weapon on your attack. If he is supposed to block your incoming thrust to just outside of his left hip, then simply make sure that your target is two inches outside of his left hip when you begin the attack. Always thrust and cut "off-line".*

We're trying to create the illusion that a strike was intended to be deadly, but was deftly parried out of the way at the very last second. On the other hand, there is no reason to actually put your partner in danger. So always send the energy of the attack to that spot in space where a successful defense would end up redirecting the attacking tip. Should your partner forget what the next move of the fight is (it happens) no one will be hurt.

3. *Conversely, don't force the block, pushing your partner's sword away. Simply meet the incoming sword at the prearranged point in space. Blades "kiss" on contact; they must never bash.*

There are three really good reasons why actors and directors should heed this point. First: straight-arming the block puts too much pressure on the blades and leads to early breakage. Second: it is confusing to the audience, which sees any straight arm as an attack, not a defense. Third: pushing the attacking sword away from the body further than is necessary leads the partner to start attacking far away from the defender, which soon leads to a non-threatening and boring fight.

4. *Always parry (block) with the <u>edge</u> of the blade, never with the flat.*

Those who say otherwise are wrong. Swords are built so as to handle great stress when leading with the edge, but not at all for lateral stress. Think for a moment on how you would try to break a blade without using any tools. You'd more than likely try to bend it over your knee, right? And you would bend it along the flat because it is impossible to bend any other way. Well, blocking with the flat of the blade is doing much the same thing. The slight bending that the blade goes through with every block stresses the steel every time, leading to more and more microfractures until it finally breaks completely. Blocking with the edge doesn't mean that a sword won't break - it'll just take years longer.

5. *Use gloves. It can mean the difference between a bruised finger or an infected and broken finger. Make sure everyone's tetanus vaccination is up-to-date.*

Little scratches can lead to big infections. That's a good enough reason to use gloves, but another is simple sword control. During a fight, the handle can slightly pinch the skin of your palm on occasion. It's not much, but it can be a distraction at a critical moment, even leading to an unintended disarm.

6. *Finish your attacks with a straight arm. Don't "pull" your cuts - push them.*

Every attack should be obvious to the audience, so show them that you really intend to strike your opponent. Don't just hack at the air in front of your partner- fully reach for your target. After all, if you are truly engaged in the struggle, you will naturally try to get as much distance as you can, so the arm will be perfectly straight as you attack, with the sword being an extension of your arm. Push the tip, even on cutting motions, all the way to your target.

By the way, the actor/combatant's job in targeting is difficult and a little schizophrenic. The "actor" has to sell his character's intended target as being some lethal spot on his opponent's body. Meanwhile, the "combatant" has to guide his sword to the true target, which is that safe point away from his partner.

7. *Look at what you want to hit. We are built to do that automatically. DO NOT STARE AT YOUR PARTNER'S EYES! You will only end up losing track of your own sword. Follow the sword tips if you want to develop control of your sword.*

Audiences have a tough time following a sword fight, so you need to help them . Indicate the meaning of each move by following the tips of the swords with your focus and body English. If you believe that the tip of the sword is deadly, the audience will believe it. And it helps the fight not a bit if your intention is to strike a generic target such as "the upper torso" or "left hip". Really focus on the exact square inch that is your planned target. Sloppy targeting leads to sloppy swordplay.

8. *A rule of thumb: actors should have <u>one hour</u> of fight rehearsal time for each <u>five seconds</u> of finished fight. Any techniques not polished <u>before</u> going into tech week must be cut from the fight.*

Rehearsing a fight is not just memorizing moves. The fight has to be so ingrained in the body that it becomes second nature. When the body performs the fight from muscle memory, the moves come out automatically, and only then is the brain free to concentrate on the acting. We know that the same is true for learning your lines: you're not really acting if you are trying to perform while at the same time consciously working on coming up with your next line. The difference with stage combat is that an unpolished fight not only detracts from the show, but is also unsafe.

9. *Only stage combat fight-grade weaponry must be used for the fight.*

"If weapons can be so dangerous, shouldn't we stay away from steel? What about plastic swords, or wood or rubber?"

Tempered steel is safer than any alternative. Think about it. The reason you want tempered steel is because it is less likely to break when someone is bashing away at you. Plastic and wood break more easily than steel, but they are stiff materials nonetheless, so when they break they leave the actor with a very sharp and unforgiving instrument in hand, quite capable of going through the human body.

Rubber is impractical for a sword fight. If made too floppy it just looks ridiculous, and to make it stiff it has to be as thick as a club. Only tempered steel or the more rare and costly tempered aluminum should be used for stage combat, keeping in mind that they can break as well. If that makes you uneasy, cut the fight scenes.

"Oh, but in this show, the actors aren't really fighting: they only strike the swords once or twice."

Ok, but that's kind of like saying that brakes on a car aren't important when you drive because you plan on going forward 99% of the time. However true that may be, when you need the brakes, *YOU REALLY NEED THEM.* Well, striking with costume swords is like driving a car without brakes - yes, you can do it, but it's really dangerous. If a sword must strike another or must be dropped to the ground, you need it be as sturdy as possible, and that means both fight-grade construction and tempered steel.

Whether fight worthy or not, there are also some very basic safety issues that have to be brought to the attention of actors whenever they are handed a sword. These are things which seem so obvious as to be unnecessary to even mention, and yet that is exactly why you must. There will always be one actor who will do the unthinkable, and it is an innocent who will get injured.

1] Don't touch the blade of the sword with an ungloved hand unless told to do so. Skin has oils that contain natural salts. Those salts attract water vapor, and that water leads to rust.

2] Don't walk around with the sword resting on your shoulder. One little turn in the wrong direction and the tip will go into someone's face.

3] When walking on level ground, keep the sword tip in sight as you move, especially backstage. The safest way to walk with the sword is to hold it in front of you in an underhand grip, tip pointing towards the floor.

4] When going up a flight of stairs, let the tip drag behind you so it doesn't get jammed on the next step.

5] When going down a flight of stairs, try to turn the sword so that the blade crosses behind you. You want to avoid the tip pointing behind you and at someone closing in on you.

6] Don't play with the swords. They are props used to aid a theatrical production, not to help you pretend to be Robin Hood backstage.

7] For outdoor theatres, don't stick the tip into the ground and don't lay the sword on grass. Rust happens.

8) In indoor theatres, be careful of where you leave the sword between use. A sword laid on a chair will be sat on, and left on the floor will be kicked.

* * * * *

Stage combat sword play is best defined as exaggerated "double-time" fencing. No, it doesn't mean fighting twice as fast. Double-time in swordwork means that every attack is first fully defended against in some way before a return attack is launched. Completely block before you attack. This is the way most people have fought throughout history, with a couple of exceptions. Both traditional Japanese swordplay and Western dueling from the 1700's through to today's Olympic style fencing is largely single-time. In defending against an attack, not only is the incoming sword deflected away but a return attack is initiated in almost the same motion. One motion - single time. This much faster style, instead of block and then attack, is sometimes described from the French as parry and riposte. But parry-riposte puts the actors in more danger, and is very hard for the audience to follow. For almost all stage and film purposes double-time fencing rather than single-time is used.

I'll repeat the following many times in this book: actors learn fight moves the same way they learn their lines - one at a time. But actors must *perform* movement the same way they *perform* their lines - in natural varied rhythms. You can stretch out or speed up your timing, or even overlap some of the lines, but you can't eliminate some words just to get to the end of the sentence faster. The same goes with the individual moves that make up a simulation.

A great analogy for swordwork is tap dancing. At first you have to learn how to do the steps, then practice so that the body performs without consciously thinking about every little movement. But it's not dancing until you have enough control to bring out all of the music inherent in the dance. If you are just tap, tap, tapping away you are monotonously beating out a rhythm without drawing out all of the tension, excitement and beauty that lives within the dance. Ten different dancers will perform the same routine in ten different ways, each in accord with his or her artistry, expertise, and personality. *But each dancer must perform all of the moves correctly.* You can never dump some of the moves because they get in the way of your emotional response.

One more analogy, and then we'll get to work. Point and click. Everyone now knows that in order to work a computer mouse you need to drag the cursor to the correct spot and then left or right click. Unless you have moved the cursor to exactly the right spot on the screen it doesn't matter how well or how fast you can click the mouse. Some people seem to fly across the screen and are able to jump from page to page and can cut, copy and paste with dramatic speed, but that speed comes only as fast as they can first precisely hit the mark and *then* click.

Sword play is exactly the same, except that it takes two people working together to make each move. Every attack must visibly develop *before* the defense can begin. Point, then click. Fights can go fast or slow, but the sequence of point then click, attack then defense, must be maintained. More complicated timing moves, such as counter attacks, simultaneous attacks, etc., will not be covered here, if for no other reason than it is confusing to the audience. So no matter how real such occurrences may be in an actual fight, if they cannot be clearly conveyed to the audience they only serve to interrupt the story you are trying to tell. (I'm overstating the case here just a bit - I have included both actions in a few of my fights, but only with actors who already had a good amount of experience with stage fighting and were excellent actors, able to convey a physical intention before even moving their weapon. A very rare trait.)

*   *   *   *   *

The same anagrams we learned for unarmed fighting can be used for weapon combat:

V - The **victim** (in swordplay we'll call him the defender) establishes control by making eye contact before the aggressor begins the simulation, and also by simply stepping back or away from the fight if something doesn't feel right.

I - The **interactive** flow of energy must follow reality. The force of the block must match the force of the attack. The defender *responds* to the aggressor's attack, not simply sticks up a parry at the same time as the attack. This timing of attack then defense must be established from the earliest rehearsal. Otherwise you get that all too common look of "E.S.P. fighting" the attack and defense occurring at the same moment. Remember - point, then click.

N - Only **non-contact** techniques must be used. Believe it or not, even with broadswords in their hands some actors have to be reminded of this.

O - The swords can give the illusion of being aimed at the opponent while never actually putting the other actor in any danger. When the energy of the sword moves **off-line**, a defender who forgets a move still won't get hurt.

The other anagram works just as well:

S - The **set-up** happens before any attack. Eye-contact is established to make sure that both actors are ready and at the correct distance.

P - The **picture** is what we want the audience to believe is about to happen. Show that little bit of prep which indicates that a thrust or a cut is about to come in, and look at the intended target. Let the audience see the danger first so they have a chance to emotionally respond to it.

A - The **action** is the thrust or cut itself, and must be performed smoothly. Actions unfold so that the audience can see the danger threatening the defender.

R - Finally, the part that nails the simulation is the **reaction** by the defender, usually a block or parry or evasion. By contrast to the action, this is a sudden movement, performed when the action is 95% developed. If the block is executed too early there is no dramatic tension, no chance for the audience to feel afraid for the character. Point and click. The aggressive attacking action is the "point"; the defensive blocking reaction is the "click".

For swordplay we add one more anagram - **BLED** - borrowed and modified from the London School of Drama.

B - **balance** includes keeping your heels on the ground and not leaning over as you attack. A wide and deep stance is preferred. The head rests on the torso, free of tension, and the torso rests on the hips. No need to lean forward nor stick the buttocks out.

Take a look at this series of moves. I didn't plan these - the fighter was merely blowing off some steam during our photo shoot and started to spar with me for real:

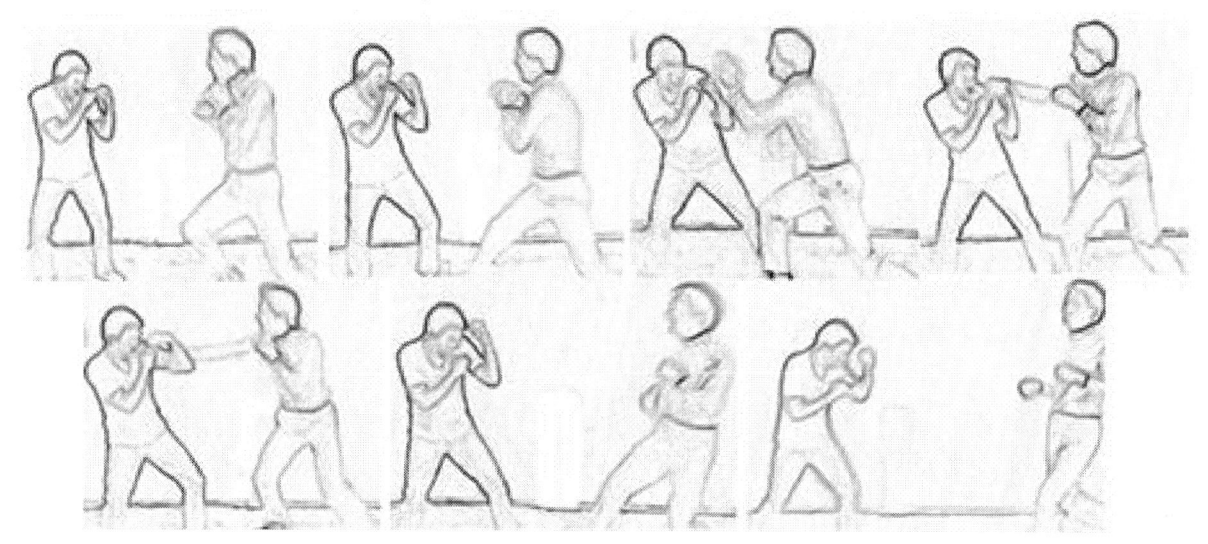

Notice how he moves in close, launches his attack (it was actually a blazing flurry of punches) and then moves out of distance - all without losing his balance. His head, chest and hips were never moved beyond the level of his knees, so his center of balance was always under his control. Whether advancing or retreating, the feet move first and then the upper body moves as a unit to the new secure spot.

If you want to make a fighter appear untrained, such as in Twelfth Night, think of doing the opposite - lean the torso out over the knees, stick the rear end out when retreating, that sort of thing. But naturally you must excise those postures from your actors if you want the audience to believe that they are real fighters.

L - The audience has a great deal of difficulty in focusing on the sword. It usually disappears from their view as soon as the fight starts, so they follow the fight by watching the changes in body **line** as it shifts throughout the fight. Line expresses intention - long and straight when attacking, short and bent when in defense. And not just with the arms, but with the legs and torso as well.

E - The **eyes** are busy in a fight - looking at your partner's tip when he is attacking - looking at your intended target when you attack - and always checking the room and your partner for safety.

D - Crucial to the audience's willingness to accept the reality of your fight is the **distance** between the combatants. The *closer* the combatants are the *less* dangerous the fight appears. Maintain distance so that the thrust sword tip is at least four inches away from the defender. Actor combatants are invariably too close to each other as they fight. If you are watching any fight rehearsal at any level of experience, you can yell out "too close" at any arbitrary moment, and you will always be right.

I've repeated this before in this book, and here it is again: actors learn movement the same way they learn their lines - one at a time. But actors must perform movement the same way they perform their lines - in natural varieted rhythms. You can stretch out or speed up your timing, or even overlap some of the lines, but you can't eliminate some words just to get to the end of the sentence faster. The same goes with the individual moves that make up a simulation.

Now let's get to work, starting with the basics.

Drawing and Sheathing the Weapon

Often, sheaths and scabbards slightly press against the blade, so you may need to hold onto the sheath with the left hand when you draw with the right. Easy, right? Just make sure to keep your shoulder down. Lifting up with the shoulder as you draw makes the subsequent movement ungainly.

What really gives a lot of actors a problem is sheathing the weapon. The action stops while the actor stares down at the scabbard opening and tries to poke at it with the sword tip until it finally finds its mark. Sometimes they slowly chase the scabbard opening, turning in a counterclockwise circle much like a puppy chasing its tail. There is an easier way.

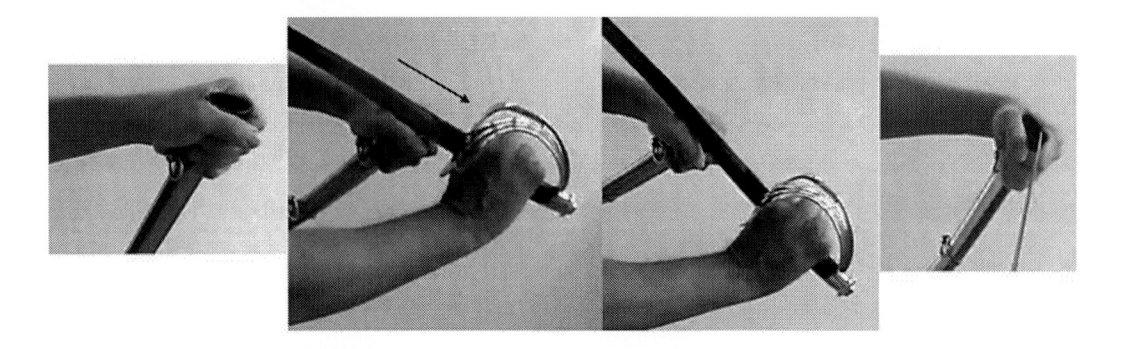

Grab the top of the scabbard with the left hand and let the web of the hand [the part between the thumb and index finger] ride high, just above the opening. Lay the flat of the blade against the thumb and draw the sword up and across the body until the tip simply pops right into the scabbard opening. If the blade is curved, you'll need to then give the sword a half twist so that it aligns with the curve of the scabbard. From there simply allow the sword to slide all the way in. With very little practice actors can sheath their swords without even looking at what they are doing, which not only maintains the flow of the scene but also looks really cool.

[Practitioners of *iaido*, the Japanese art of drawing and attacking with the samurai sword, practice this sheathing endlessly. As they work with "live" fully sharpened blades, and do not use gloves, most have sliced their thumbs or fingers at least once. Be glad that all stage weapons are dull.]

Holding the weapon

I'm going to remind you again here to use gloves, and not only to prevent injury. There are times during a sword fight when part of the hilt can pinch the flesh of the palm. Not enough to cause damage or even appreciable pain, but just enough to cause the perfectly normal reaction of instantly releasing your grip. Dropping your sword in the middle of a fight is embarrassing, and the simple use of gloves completely prevents that eventuality. The accompanying photographs show the hands ungloved, but only so that you can easily see the finger placement. For stage combat, use gloves.

There are several basic grips in stage combat, depending on what kind of sword is held. The weapon dictates the grip, the grip dictates the fight. But no matter which grip is used, one must keep the hand relaxed. There is an old saying regarding holding the sword that compares it to grasping a small bird. You want enough strength in the grasp so that the bird cannot escape, but not enough so that the bird is harmed. And the hand is always kept as close to the guard as possible.

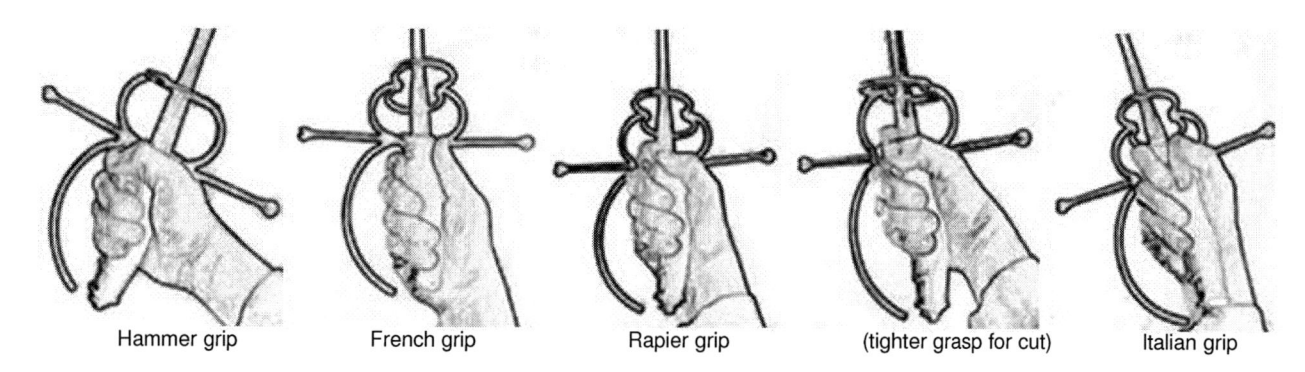

| Hammer grip | French grip | Rapier grip | (tighter grasp for cut) | Italian grip |

The simplest grip is the hammer grip, obviously used for the heavier weapons such as the broadsword or heavy sabre. But even this is not a death grip, for the hand must constantly grasp and release, tighten and relax, allowing the handle to move slightly in the palm as you fight. If you don't, the sword will unrealistically always stay at 90 degrees to the forearm, which limits your reach.

For longer weapons, a two-handed grip is necessary. It is helpful to give each hand a separate function: the left hand actually lifting and lowering the sword, and the right hand primarily guiding it to its target. [Note: Unlike the European broadsword, the Japanese katana was held with the pommel secured inside the grip of the pinky finger of the trailing hand].

The French grip is the one used for light dueling swords as well as for Olympic sport fencing. The handle rests diagonally across the palm as the fingers gently close around handle. [When you grab a small flag that's on a stick and wave it, or when you grab and flair a small fan, you are using a French grip.] Most of the tension to hold the sword is in the thumb and first finger, the others supporting the weight and directing the point as needed. When the sword is pointed at the opponent and the hand is in supination (palm up) tightening the little finger will make the tip jump up to the high line of attack. Relaxing the little finger allows the tip to point to a low line of attack. Neither forearm not wrist movement is necessary to raise and lower the tip if that hand is kept active.

The most common grasp for stage is the rapier grip, which is very similar to the French grip except that the first finger hooks around the quillon. This allows the hand to get much closer to the center of balance of the sword, and the first finger can control the movement of the blade far better than with either the French or hammer grips. (Even broadswords were sometimes wielded with the rapier grip (long before the rapier was invented, although it certainly put the hooked forefinger at a great risk of being lopped off!) Because of the variety of motions required for rapier fighting, the grasp cannot be locked into one position but must be very lively and constantly shifting.

Almost unseen these days is a variant of a sport fencing grasp called the Italian grip. In this grip, not just the forefinger but the middle finger as well hook over the cross guard. In this style, the blade passes between the first and middle finger. It is not nearly as strong as the rapier grip, but it does put the handle in-line with the forearm, giving greater tip accuracy during thrusts and more control during difficult pronated parries. Not a useful grip at all for stage combat, since cutting motions with this grasp are very weak.

No matter what the sword, cutting motions and strong blocks will feel more comfortable with the hammer grip, while finesse tip-work, thrusts, and deflective parries require the French or Rapier. Always relax the hand so that the sword can move freely between the various grasps as you need to employ them.

Stances - En Guard

When the fighter is not actively engaged in attacking or defending, he normally takes a position of "readiness", usually beginning out of distance, and then closing in to allow the blades to touch and slightly cross. These stances should never be stiff but rather still have a feeling of fluidity, even when the body is still. It represents a readiness to either attack or defend, without having committed to either action.

All stances will have the same basics in common - a slight bend in the knees, weight shifted slightly forward towards the balls of the feet, the torso erect and resting directly above the hips, not bending forward at the waist, shoulders relaxed. The head is held back - an observer of the fight in which the body is engaged.

Put a sword in an actor's hand and he immediately goes into the standard Olympic fencer's stance - left foot turned out and directly behind the right foot, left shoulder turned away from the opponent, and the left arm held up behind the head, elbow at shoulder level, with the left hand dangling down loose at the wrist. The sword is held at solar plexus level throughout the fight, the hand merely moving from right to left, parallel to the ground. This is fine for competitive fencing where the target is only the front of the torso and the fencing area is limited to a long and narrow *piste*, or runway, which does not allow for any sideways action. It doesn't make any sense for a duel or fight, where side stepping and use of the left hand is assumed. (To be honest, it has been many decades that they even take this stance in the Olympics.) So, instead of this severely linear stance, the stance for a sword fighter becomes more and more open as we move backward in time.

The smallsword of the 18th and 19th centuries is very close to the above competition stance, but the left hand, often gloved, is often held in front of the body near the face to protect the face or grab the opponent's blade, so the left shoulder is turned in a bit. By all accounts, the fighters stood much more upright than have fighters in other periods of history. This would seem to indicate that the emphasis was in using the sword to deflect attacks rather than relying exclusively on the legs. The left foot is turned out but is not directly in-line with the right foot. This gives better sideways stability and allows for quick evasions and attacks to the left and right. Since the face is unprotected, a common variation to the solar plexus on-guard is to hold the sword with a straight arm pointing at the opponent's face, but of course for stage this is modified to pointing no higher than armpit level.

Military sabre fighting in a duel is similar, which we would expect since it comes out of the same time period. But the weapon is completely different in weight and size and balance, therefore in the way it is used. The left hand, useless against the heavy hacking blade, is simply held behind the back to keep it out of the way. Generally the weapon hand and lead foot would be the same (although it is not shown that way in these images). Because the sword is heavier, the arm tires easily trying to maintain a dueling position, so the weapon is held either low at hip level with the tip pointing up, or above head level with the tip aiming down. Simply moving the sword from side to side can affect the fighter's balance, so the legs need to be bent and about a yard apart to provide a more stable base than is used in smallsword dueling.

The rapier of the 15th through to the 17th century is a brawling weapon, so the strict formalities of the duel of this period have more to do with the etiquette of issuing, accepting or avoiding getting a challenge to fight rather than how the fight itself should progress. Since both hands are expected to be engaged in fighting, the stance opens up tremendously to at least shoulder width apart, often more. The shoulders and the hips stay square with the opponent, so the feet cannot be in line with but rather will be set wide, wide enough so that at any time your opponent should be able to roll a bowling ball between your legs. There are many variations to the *en guarde* stance, but most fighters tended to hold the left arm out straight while holding a dagger, and the right arm kept more closely to the body and holding the sword. The height of the hands will move from waist to shoulder level as the needs of the fight require, and most importantly the *left* foot rather than the right, will lead. The idea was to keep the tips of both weapons at an equal distance to the opponent, not showing a weakness to or preference for either side. Movement patterns were circular, with the look of modern boxers trying to find an opening to attack. Most fighters were trained to bat-away an incoming attack with the left hand and almost simultaneously thrust the sword at the opponent's face.

The medieval broadsword was a battlefield weapon, so even in a knightly tournament the look here is of battering the opponent into submission rather than a show of elegant swordplay. The stance should be proportionate to the weight of the weapons, so that with the two-handed swords or with sword and shield we should see the legs in a full horse-riding stance, legs very far apart, the sword held at hip level. There is no preference for right or left foot leading. Indeed, leading strongly with either foot reduces the ability of the fighter to swing the sword from both directions.

For the earlier shortsword of bronze and iron-aged cultures, there is no studied posture to copy. The sword is light enough not to affect the stance, so the fight will have the look of brutal accepting and giving punishment until one person falls. If two fighters face each other, it is possible that one might take a defensive wide stance much like a boxer, left foot forward, with most of the weight on the right [back] foot.

Samurai warriors of Japan were the only group of fighters that developed a fighting style designed not only for war but also for dueling. The stance might at first be confused with that of the broadsword, but since the sword is so much lighter, there is no need for the deep stance of medieval European warriors. In single sword confrontations, the basic stance was the everyday normal stance, with either foot leading, and the sword held at a relaxed stomach height and slightly extended from the body. If two swords or sword and dagger were used, the stance looked more like that of the rapier. With elbows bent and the tip aiming up and toward the opponent's face, the samurai was trained to look for the decisive moment to attack, and then to kill with one blow. Just as in European rapier fighting, most duels were over in two or three moves. A successful attack would need no further action, and a failed attack would lead to a usually successful counter attack by the opponent.

Distance

With the actors facing each other, have the taller of the two slowly thrust with the sword and take a half lunge with the lead foot. Adjust the foot placement so that the tip of the sword is about three or four inches away from his partner. Keeping the back foot where it is, recover back from the lunge, and this is the correct distance for stage combat. Memorize this distance and go back to it at every opportunity, for actors invariably shorten it as soon as they start moving.

Distance of course will change. A vertical head cut must start from much closer than a thrust to the torso, so adjusting for the demands of the fight is constant. But actors will always tend to end up too close rather than too far apart, for we all take shorter steps when walking backwards than we do when going forward.

The main concerns are not only safety for the actors but also for the believability of the fight. When the fighters are too close it sends a message to the audience that completely undermines the tension you are trying to create, namely that it is a battle of life or death. What the audience instead sees is that the swords must not be dangerous at all if the characters are so comfortable being within striking distance. The actors have to sell the concept of the tip of a blade being white-hot and instantly deadly to the touch in order to create an exciting fight.

Attacking

There are at most only two things you can do with a sword in order to hurt someone: hack at him with the edge or stick him with the tip. [Yes, I know you can hit someone with the pommel or the guard, but those are really augmented unarmed techniques.] Whether cut or thrust, stage attacks are slower than real fighting. Stage attacks unfold; they do not strike, but rather develop.

All of swordplay is one person doing one of the above and another person preventing success. We can create swordfights on stage because, unlike real fighting, we can make sure that most of the attacks actually fail.

Audiences have no depth perception. You must trust in this for it is the one thing that makes all of stage combat possible. It's also what can make a sword fight confusing to the audience. From their point of view, an attack to the left looks the same as an attack to the right, and a sword tip that has disappeared upstage of an actor has gone through the character. Remember that you are creating a two-dimensional picture, so what looks right to the actors may not look right from the house.

The Five Basic Attack Targets

Of course in a real sword fight, any contact anywhere on the body has the potential of causing damage, so attacks are only limited by opportunity and creativity. For stage, we reduce all of these possibilities to only five spots. Why? Specificity and safety. It's hard for the audience to follow a sword fight as is it, and adding too many targets can confuse them. [There are choreographers who teach up to twelve attack points, but even they use the basic five for the majority of moves in the fights they choreograph and use the others sparingly.] Too many targets can also confuse the actors, making them miss their defenses and muddying up the fight.

The five attack points are
1) left hip
2) right hip
3) right shoulder
4) left shoulder
5) head

These are just nicknames that everyone uses for the five points in space where the two swords are going to meet, not really the part of the body that someone in a fight would actually try to attack.

For the first four positions, we want the audience to believe that the target for the attacker was always the same: dead center of the defender's torso, the solar plexus. But of course the actor isn't really going to aim for the solar plexus, because if the defender fails to make the block, you end up with a damaged actor. So the actor/aggressor aims his weapon tip for the point in space where the progression of the attack is going to be successfully thwarted.

We have to be extremely specific as to what the attack points are, and not allow the sword tip to wander. The difference between a high line attack and a low line attack is only a matter of a few inches. For the five attack points the aggressor's sword tip will land exactly at the following: 1) left hip - the point in space at belly button height, natural waist level, the top of the hip bone, two inches to the left of the outside plane of the body and four inches in front of the body. 2) right hip - the point in space at belly button height, natural waist level, the top of the hip bone, two inches to the right of the outside plane of the body and four inches in front of the body. 3) left shoulder - the point in space at nipple level, armpit height, solar plexus level, two inches to the left of the outside plane of the body and four inches in front of the body. 4) left shoulder - the point in space at nipple level, armpit height, solar plexus level, two inches to the left of the outside plane of the body and four inches in front of the body. 5) head - the point in space no higher than seven inches above the head, aimed top dead center.

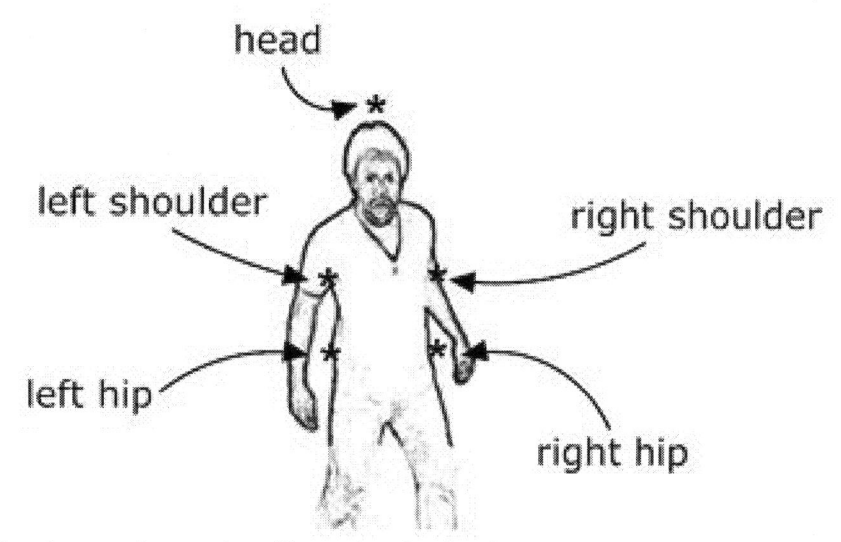

Try locating these points and you'll see that the first four attacks, the ones to the body, all end up slightly in front of the defender. The audience must always see some daylight between the attacking tip and the defender's body. This allows the tip to appear to be more dangerous and it also gives us somewhere to go when we need to do the kill shot. On the other hand, for the head cut we have to allow the tip to get past the frontal plane of the defender, for we what to have good solid contact between the two swords for safety's sake, and in this case (and only this case) it means we have to close distance a bit.

To be honest with you, I really dislike the terms "hip" and "shoulder" for stage combat, as it makes the attacking sword drift far too high on the "shoulder" attacks and far too low on the "hip" attacks. But the terms are almost universally used by choreographers, so we're stuck with them. What I want the audience to see is an attack always parallel to the ground, with only the tip pointing slightly up or down, just above or below the defender's hand. (When I teach, I simply refer to high and low attacks, and not shoulder and hip.)

We should also discuss the concept of inside and outside, which always refers to the defender. In fencing it is considered best to keep the sword held at the center of the body. That way any attack to any quadrant is equally covered, but the reality is that the hand tends to drift a little bit in the direction of the shoulder to which it is connected. So if you are looking at a right handed fencer, the left side of the body is going to be left a little bit more open to attack than the right. That left side is his inside (think of the inside of his forearm). His right side is his outside (think of the outside of his forearm. But if he switches hands and starts fighting with his left hand, his inside and outside are reversed.

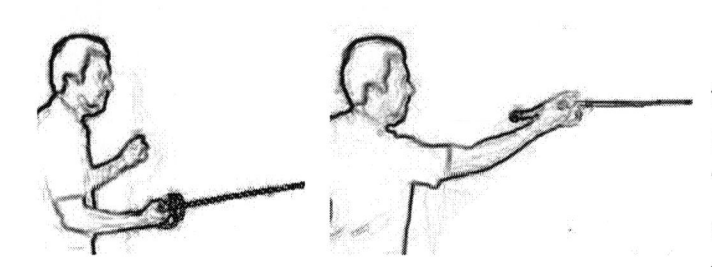

Thrusting

The thrust is an arm movement that attempts to stab someone with the point of a sword or knife. It is not a lunge, which is a lower body movement. The thrust refers only to the arm extension that makes the point of the sword more dangerous to the opponent. The thrust begins with the arm bent, with the tip of the sword aimed at a specific target on the opponent, and the hilt held close to the body. A line drawn from target to blade tip to attacking hand should form a perfectly straight line. The sword tip then moves in that straight line to the target as the arm is straightened. The thrust may be executed while lunging, or while stepping forward, or standing still, or even stepping backward. Again it only refers to the arm movement. There is no need to lean into the attack by bending at the waist. Keep the head up and the torso balanced on the hips.

There are such things as "diving" and "scooping" thrusts, which begin with the tip pointing up or down respectively, but these are advanced techniques best left to experienced combatants. On the other hand, there is no reason to assume that the hand must be returned to the center solar plexus position before beginning the thrust. If the hand happens to be, say, down by the left knee because of a previous move, the thrust can start directly from this position so long as hand, blade tip and target form a straight line.

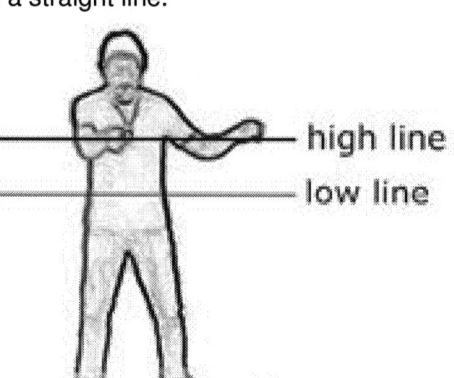

On stage, since the audience has no depth perception, we don't actually thrust at the other actor, but instead thrust very slightly away from the actor, to just outside of the plane of the body. This would be a point in space where the sword tip would end up if effectively blocked. So even though a real thrust would always be aimed at the center of the torso, directly at the solar plexus, the thrust targets for stage combat are four: Left high, right high, left low, and right low. Again, high is called "shoulder" by instructors for simplicity, and low is called "hip", but these are misnomers, for the sword tip should never be higher than your partner's arm pit [nipple level] nor lower than your partner's natural waist [navel level]. Think about that for a minute and you'll see that the difference between an attack to the high line and one to the low line is only about six or eight inches. Also, the tip should end up a couple of inches in front of the actor so that the audience can see that the attack failed. But remember that the actor's job is to sell an illusion, the conceit that the middle of the body was the intended target and that the defender deflected it away at the last nanosecond.

Notice that for thrusts, we left out the fifth target, namely the head. We never, NEVER, thrust to the face. The margin for error is simply too great, and the possible injuries are too frightening to risk. So for the thrust, we have only four attack points.

So as not to confuse the actors, I prefer to use the terms left and right according only to the point of view of the person actually doing the particular action. So you thrust relative to your own left or right, or you block to your own left or right. Don't worry about what your partner is supposed to do.

Lunge

As I said before, the lunge is what the legs do, not what the arm does. Real competitive swordplay involves a lot of attacks that may not all have the intent of actually striking, but are part of a constant probing and testing of the opponent. The bodies dance around and the swords are thrust and parried, but there will come one moment where a thrust is made and the opponent has left himself just a little too open. This fraction of a second is the opportunity that must be seized, so even as the thrust is beginning its extension, the body lunges forward to suddenly close the distance and hit the target. *Touché!*

Thrusts without the lunge are usually made just outside of striking distance. Adding the lunge is an act of great self-confidence, because if it fails the attacker is left hung out there vulnerable to counterattack.

The lunge provides the maximum extension of the sword to the target, so if the fighter is right-handed it is always performed with the right leg. The left foot is anchored to the floor, turned out to 90 degrees. The right leg steps forward into the deep lunge while the left leg straightens completely. Fencers will actually lock that knee joint for maximum stretch, describing the feeling as punching the ground with the left heel. That popping extension might even propel the fencer another half meter or so in the direction of the lunge. In order to avoid excess strain on the right knee, don't allow the leg to lunge too deeply. At the full lunge, the right knee should be right above the heel. To protect the left leg, straighten it but don't hyperextend it.

To get out of the lunge, fencers simply push off with the right leg, giving them really powerful right thighs. It's also exhausting, so a much easier way is to bend the left knee first and then just evenly "squat-walk" out of the lunge. Of course, one can also recover by bringing the back foot up to meet the lunging foot and then standing up, but naturally that drives the actor forward rather than back, so is usually used if the defender has retreated a considerable distance.

Riposte

This is a fencing term that is used often in stage combat, although the actual technique itself has no use on stage unless the actors have been intensely trained by an excellent choreographer. The riposte is an immediate attack following a successful parry, but so immediate that it becomes one movement with the parry. This is known as single-time fencing, the basis of all modern sport fencing. When the riposte is done effectively it becomes a true counterattack, one that strikes even before the opponent has finished his intended initial attack. Fencers are trained to riposte automatically, even instinctively, but the blending of movements is impossible for the audience to discern, therefore they cannot see the character's intention. All they can see are a series of simultaneous attacks, and this takes them away from following the story of the fight. For stage combat it is preferable to have the actors use only double-time actions: completely finish one move (the parry) before attempting another (the thrust). There are enough choreographers out there who use the term riposte, so you should know that they simply mean an attack that immediately follows a successful parry.

Cutting

For stage combat purposes, a cut is not just an attack using the edge of the blade, but an attack that has been successfully blocked.

Just as with the thrust, the target to aim for is where the sword would stop in air when a cut is successfully blocked. This is a mere two inches away from your partner, and again the terms high and low are nipple and navel respectively. The tip should end up a couple of inches in front of the actor so that the audience can see that the attack failed. So when all is said and done the tip of the sword is going to end up at the same precise point in space whether the attack was a cut or thrust.

What changes is the look of the attack as it unfolds toward the defender. Just as with the thrust, we want to start by forming a straight line to the target. But this time, the order is elbow, hand, then blade tip. That's right; the blade tip will be behind you before you start the attack. The movement of the hand will be the same - in a straight line to the target. The tip will make a gentle half circle, with the pivot point being the attacking hand, not the shoulder.

To the previously explained four body targets, we add one more - a vertical head cut. This one is scary at first but it can be made very safe so long as one key point is carefully practiced. As the sword blade drops down to make the cut, simply never allow your hand to drop below the level of your partner's eyes. So long as you don't lose sight of your partner's eyes, your sword blade cannot possibly touch him, and you cannot possibly hurt him. For this cut we allow the sword tip to extend past the front plane of the defender, which is far closer than we do for any other attack. The sword tip will stop directly over the center of the defender's head, not in front of the defender. This way the defender is certain to have enough incoming blade to make solid contact with the block, avoiding the straight-arm "reaching" block. The final image must have the defender keeping his arm bent when blade contact is made. If the defender has to reach forward to make the block, then there really wasn't a threat that is going to be obvious to the audience.

Cutting motions with the sword should not be confused with tree chopping, which unfortunately is what you'll usually see performed on stage. The problem is that the natural tendency of the actor is to execute the cut using a bent arm, like a baseball swing, and that's fine if we don't want the swing to stop. But if the cut stops in midair before reaching the victim (as it will in 99% of the choreographed fight) we have to believe that it was the block that did it, and that can't happen with an attacking arm that is bent. Why?

When the arm is bent at the elbow, the elbow leads the motion of the swing followed by the hand and then the blade trailing behind. This is what happens when you slash with a sabre - by the time the blade actually makes contact with anything, all of the body momentum and even most of the weight of the sword has already passed by the target point. There is nothing that is going to stop the progress of the slash. If the defender holds up his sword for protection, the attacking sword will glance off of the defending blade, but the path from one side to the other will not be impeded.

But what we get onstage (and in most action movies) is a sword coming in with that full bent-arm swing, and then inexplicably freezing in midair just because the other blade touched it as though it were some sort of powerful electromagnet. With both actors keeping their elbows bent, it also becomes harder to figure out who is attacking whom. After a while it merely looks as though both are hacking away at an invisible cabbage floating halfway between them as they prepare coleslaw.

We need to get the same clear attack vs. defense that we get with the thrust, and we do that by allowing the cut to develop as it is performed, rather than simply hacking. How?

- Ø Make sure that your arm, hand, and sword form a straight line at the very moment that your cut is blocked. If the elbow or wrist is bent, the impact point of the sword looks weak, the hilt has all of the momentum, and the blade cannot logically be stopped. It looks as though you just wanted to slice the opponent, not cleave into him. To the audience it looks as though the aggressor simply gave up. But if the arm and sword are straight (just like a thrust) then it gives the appearance of having tried to reach the opponent in order to cut into him with the far third of the blade, a point on the cutting blade known as the center of percussion. If the intention was to cut and not slash, then that far third, not the hilt, is going to be "loaded-up" with energy. If the blade is then blocked right at that center of percussion, the momentum to the sword is going to cause the blade to try to continue, not in front of the block, but by wrapping around behind the block, straightening the arm even more, even hyperextending it. This is a cut and block simulation that now obeys the laws of physics.

- Ø Remember the three P's of cutting motions: *point, push, point*. When you start your cut, the blade tip is going to be slightly behind you, so to begin you first **_point_** your elbow toward the target. This is important so that the audience and your partner can get a good visual cue as to what part of the body is being threatened. (If you're right-handed, the cut coming from the left is going to be easier than from the right. You won't actually be able to point with the elbow from that right side, but you should still try to get the feeling of leading with the elbow first.) Relax the shoulder - tension there isn't necessary for a cut. If anything push your shoulder down; then **_push_** the pommel toward the target as you straighten the elbow. This makes the hilt of the weapons travel in a straight line from your body to the target point. Once your arm is straight, then and only then engage the **_point_** of the sword to the target using only your wrist. It is during this last motion that the blade of the sword will swing around in an arc, but notice that the hilt went only in a straight line. This will both look far more real than the traditional "hack", but it also has the added benefit of completely dissipating the energy of the cut before it reaches your partner. As you get better, this three part break down will smooth out and look very convincing.

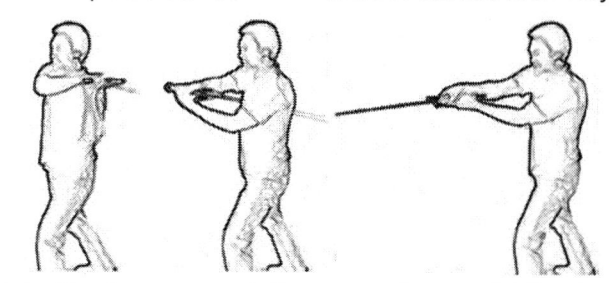

| point with elbow | push the pommel | point the tip | point elbow | push pommel | point tip |

- Ø Lastly, you'll need the slightest hint of a bounce-off after contact has been made. Keep the mental image of striking a crystal bell with your sword: if you come in chopping, you'll shatter the bell; if you don't flick your hand at the moment of impact, your strike will not resonate. (If it helps, imagine trying to reach behind your partner with your sword tip.)

The character's intent is to cut.
The actor's intent is to send the energy out <u>to</u> his partner, not <u>through</u> his partner.

To recap: each cut is an attack that unfolds as it develops, with the hand (hilt) moving in a straight line while the blade tip swings in an arc. Contact is made with the first third of the blade, not the midpoint.

To get the stage cut to look clean, aggressive, and still be safe, here are a couple of great exercises:

√ Get a plastic bottle of any size, fill it with water, and stand it on a tall stool. Try several full speed cuts to both sides of the bottle. How close can you get while not knocking it off of the stool? Make sure that from the blade tip to your shoulder is a straight line at the end of each cut. Until you can touch the bottle but not knock it over, you really don't have control of the sword.

√ Is the above exercise easy? Great! Now try it with an <u>empty</u> bottle.

√ Play catch. No, really. Just stand about two or three yards apart and use a soft rubber ball or tennis ball or bean bag. Catch and toss with the same hand, and try to have the ball only go to the five attack points discussed earlier. No fake outs here, really indicate your intended target. Don't make your partner reach for the ball - your job is make the ball land exactly where his target hand is waiting. If you swing your arm around in an arc as you throw, that ball will go everywhere. If your hand travels in a straight line, the ball will reach the exact target every time.

Short-Snap Cut

A slight variation to the full sabre cut is the short-snap cut, which is also the only kind of cutting seen in the Olympic sport of sabre fencing. The short-snap is performed with the arm already fully extended or nearly so, the sword is worked using only the wrist, allowing for a much faster series of attacks. As such attacks would not have any true cutting power behind them, they are usually added in fights as feints or set-ups for the real, more powerful attack. They are also often used for combination attacks, the first part of the attack being a regular full cut, and then the second part as a short-snap going immediately to a new target without having to waste time in pulling the sword back. It allows for more variation in timing, for the short-snap takes only a third of the time to perform than the full cut. Naturally, most combatants can only perform this action when the sword has a relatively light blade. In order to do a snap cut with a true military sabre blade, one would have to have Popeye forearms.

Long Sword Two-Handed Cut

Two-handed broadsword cuts are not dramatically different than cuts from any other weapon, except that we need to endow the prop with more weight. I say endow because military sabres actually feel heavier than broadswords, and so tend to move more slowly in air. But part of our job as actors is to not break the illusion of the broadsword being a weighty beast, so we generally pantomime a bit more prep and pretend to absorb a lot more crashing force.

The work of cutting with the longsword is divided into two distinct jobs - one for each hand. The dominant hand (for most people, the right hand) guides the tip, the non-dominant carries the weight and guides the hilt. In other words, the left hand does most of the heavy work, carrying the weight from side-to-side and forward-and-back, keeping the muscles of the right arm rested and fresh, ready to carefully guide the tip to exactly where the fighter wants it to go.

Defending

Just as there are two ways of using a sword to hurt someone, there are two ways of using a sword to defend yourself. <u>Blocking</u> refers to *stopping* the incoming motion of a cut, while <u>parrying</u> is a *deflection* of a thrust. It gets a little confusing because most people end up using the terms interchangeably. I'm just as guilty as anyone else, but we should always try to keep a distinction between the two. For both types of defenses the incoming attack is kept as close to the body as possible. But although the sword movement may look the same, the body response must be different. Your job is to understand your intention so that the meaning behind the move can have clarity.

Parrying is a finesse move, one that diverts the incoming energy and allows it to skip harmlessly away. Parries require very little effort and have more of a look of guiding the offending sword tip away from its target. Because a mere deflection is needed, either the strong (true-edge) or the weak (back-edge) parry may be used. A strong parry leads with the knuckles; a weak parry leads with the thumb side. Don't push the attacking sword away, for your partner is supposed to be thrusting just outside of the plane of your body already. All you have to do is gently meet the blade at a prearranged point in space.

Blocking, on the other hand, meets force with force, so we need to see that impact accepted by the blocking arm. Every movement has a specific consequence, so match the effect of your block on your own body to the amount of force your partner is pantomiming. Big cut, big reaction; light cut, light reaction. But it is, of course, a pantomime, for the blades will in reality only kiss on contact, not bash. The hand stays light - the effort is in the acting, not the sword. Blocks by definition need to be strong, so blocking with the weak or back-edge just isn't done unless you are showing a desperation move. Again, don't push the cutting sword away, merely meet it. The closer that the meeting point can be to the defender, the more exciting the fight will appear to the audience

Whether strong or weak, always block with the edge of the blade, never with the flat. Using the flat is slapping, not blocking. I know that there are several people who teach the opposite, but this is not a polite disagreement between differing stage combat philosophies. The others are WRONG. The only way to ever block is with the edge of the blade. Yes, the edge to edge contact will cause burrs and nicks along the edge, but those are easy to file off. You can't glue a sword blade back together if it snaps in half. Blocking with the flat is a great way to break a sword. [To those who think that blocking with the flat is a good idea, try breaking a blade. You can only do it by forcing it along the flat, not along the edge.]

Whether block or parry, the broad mechanics are the same. Audiences don't know from swordplay, so you have to help them understand what they are supposed to be seeing. They get the idea of attacking pretty quickly, but defense is harder to see. The more clues as we can give to them, the easier for us to tell the story. Since the attacking arm is straight, make sure that the defending arm is bent, especially at the elbow. Since the attacking blade is roughly parallel to the floor, the defending blade should have the tip pointing up or down, in other words, obviously not a threat during the moment of the block. The reaction of the defender must be proportionate to the amount of force coming in, so blocking a cut from a fencing sword will require very little arm strength, while absorbing the force of a broadsword cut will shake the entire body.

In order to sell the idea that the attack has come in on the low line, our defense will usually have the tip pointing toward the floor. If we are matching an attack to the high line, we generally show a defense with the tip pointing up. (There is something called a "hanging parry", in which the tip is pointing down even though defending against a high line attack. Used sparingly, it makes a nice choreographic statement and benefits some combinations.)

Try as much as possible to have the swords form a good right-angled cross at each move. Real fencers don't do this, of course. They try to keep the angle during the parry extremely shallow so that the tip is ready to thrust right back at the opponent even during the parry. This is excellent fighting technique, but very difficult for an audience to follow [one reason why competitive fencing is so hard to watch and requires that the combatants be rigged with wires connected to a panel of scoring lights].

We are trying to create the illusion that all of the thrusts and cuts are aimed for the center line of the opponent, but we can't actually attack center, so it becomes the defender's job to sell the illusion. The only way to do this is for the defending sword blade to cross in front of [protect] the center of the body before reaching the attacking sword. That sounds easy until you try it. As we will later see, many times the shortest distance when moving from one block to another doesn't go past that center point, therefore we must take a long route to get there so that it can.

While the attacker looks at the target, the defender's eyes should stay glued to the incoming tip, as this helps the audience follow the flow of the action. When contact is made, it must always be with the forte (the area of the blade close to hilt) of the defender against the foible (the area near the tip) of the attacker.

The timing of the defense should be different from the attack so as to increase the dramatic tension of the fight. An all too common outcome of rehearsing the fight is that the attack and defense happen simultaneously, but this looks like "ESP" fighting. ["How did the defender know exactly where the attack was going to go?"]. Instead, let the attack be 90% developed before allowing the defense to even begin, then quickly bring the sword in for the block at the very last possible second. During rehearsals, this is also a great way for the partners to help with targeting, for as the attack is just about to finish, the defender should not begin his block if the tip has drifted too high or too low. Instead, he just grabs the tip, places it where it should be, and then begins his defense.

* * * * *

Here's the part I hate: the French fencing numbering terminology of the parries. You may need to know it because it is so often used, but it doesn't help you become a better combatant. These terms refer only to the defense, not the attack, and are hand specific, so if I attack you to your left shoulder and you block with your sword hand palm up it is called parry *quarte*, but if you use your dagger hand it is parry *quinte*. Unless, of course, you are left handed, in which case they are both reversed.

Way too much time is spent trying to teach the fighters the names of the moves when they should really be rehearsing the moves. After all, in an entire acting career a performer may be involved in only one or two sword fights. If an attack is coming to a certain target, you need to know how to respond to that attack, and learning the fancy French terms won't help you memorize it any faster. And yet, we're stuck with it, so for what it's worth, here goes:

First the concept of inside, outside, high and low. There are entire glossaries out on the internet right now that get this wrong, which really makes it confusing, so we need to get this clear. *Outside* means a movement which brings the attacking tip to the side of the body near the sword arm of the defender. *Inside* means a movement which brings the attacking tip to the side of the body away from the sword arm of the defender. (When in doubt, just stick out your arm as if to shake someone's hand. Your palm will be facing "inside"; the back of your hand will be facing "outside".) So outside is generally the right-handed defender's right side, and inside is the defender's left [this is fencing terminology: martial arts nomenclature is exactly reversed]. *High* means a movement which brings the attacking tip to solar plexus height, or arm pit level, so the defending tip points up. *Low* means a movement which brings the attacking tip to just above hip bone height, or belly button level, so the defending tip points down. Low is at waist level, not lower than waist level. [Calling low and high hip and shoulder respectively is great shorthand, but tends to cause the actors to aim too high and too low with their attacks.]

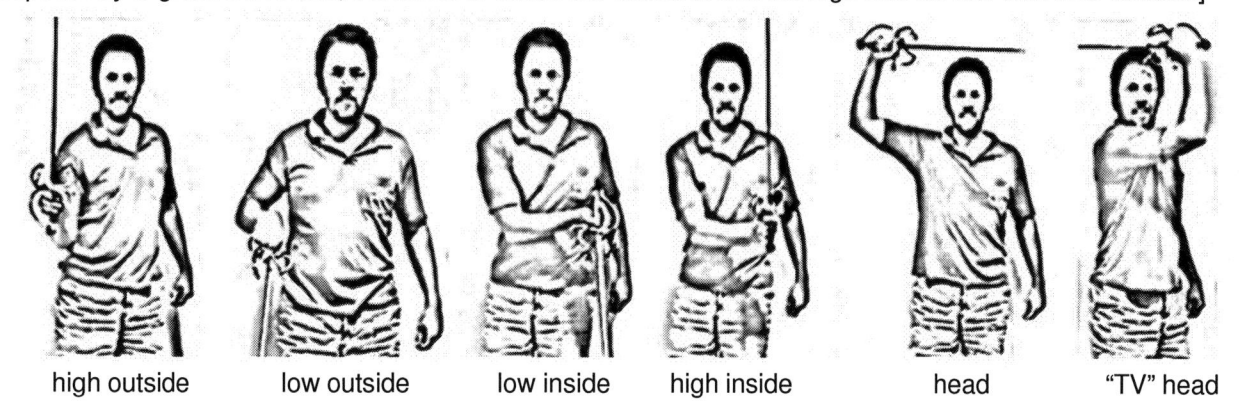

| high outside | low outside | low inside | high inside | head | "TV" head |

High Outside. With the hand palm up (supine, back-edge) it is called parry *siste* [6]. But it is sometimes called parry 5-A. With the hand palm down (prone, true-edge) it is called parry *tierce* [3].

Low Outside. With the hand in supination (back-edge) it is called parry *octave* [8]. With the hand in pronation (true-edge) it is called parry *second* [2].

Low Inside. With the hand palm down (prone, back-edge) it is called parry *septime* [7], but only for Olympic foil and epee fencing. With the hand palm up (supine, true-edge) it is called parry *prime* [1]. But in stage combat, those terms are reversed. A variation of parry [1] still leads with the knuckles but the wrist is turned around almost completely and the thumb pointing to the ground (true-edge). Meant for a very strong block, it is called the actor's parry or better yet the "look-at-your watch" parry.

High Inside. With the hand palm up (true-edge) it is called parry *quarte* [4]. With the hand palm down (back-edge) it is considered parry *quinte* in epee and foil fencing, but stage combat tradition does not recognize this parry, so they do not name it.

Blocking a Head Cut - With the elbow rising normally, it is parry *quinte* [5]. But it's also sometimes called parry 6. When the elbow swung across the body before lifting the sword, it is called 5-A, or the "TV" parry, because it frames the face so nicely. True-edge is used either way.

Why is the numbering so difficult? Because it comes from many sources, none of them specifically meant for stage combat. If you practice the first five numbered parries in order (especially starting with the actor's parry of *prime*) you'll see that they are all very strong block, all leading with the knuckles, meant for stopping strong cuts. That makes sense when swords were heavy bashing tools. The other three [6,7,8] can only be used as true parries since they use the weaker edge, the thumb side, to deflect a thrust. They developed as rapier play emphasized the easier to deflect thrust. As I mentioned before, the action called parry *quinte* [5] in competitive

315

fencing is unnamed in stage combat. Interestingly, the action is actually used quite a bit, but there you are.

I should also mention something about the hand position. We call it prone or supine because, again, the terminology is a legacy of real fencing. When they do a parry, the blade is pointing only slightly up or down, so the hand really *is* either prone or supine, that is palm down or palm up. But in stage combat we try to pull the tip either straight up or straight down, so really the hand should be described as either palm towards the opponent or towards yourself. But there you are - another legacy that adds confusion rather than clarity.

There is real value in knowing when to use *tierce* instead of *siste*, or *second* instead of *octave*, but the benefit is in the movement, not the naming. A combination such as 2,6,2 is faster and easier on the wrist than 8,6,8, even though both sets of moves protect against the same combination attack. Choreographers will work out those details when designing the fight, so the value is huge for them, but I just hate seeing actors trying to rehearse a fight and calling out to each other the order of the parries. Inevitably it ends up confusing to both.

"8, 3, 5, 7, 6, 1, 3, 6, 4, 3..."
"Wait, I thought it was 7, 6, 5, 3 ..."
"From the 1 or from the tierce?"
"Is tierce 3? Which one? The first 3 or the second 3?"
"The 3 after the 1"
"That's an 8 before the 3..."

There is a better way, and we'll get to that a little later in this chapter.

Moving

It seems obvious to say that you can't have two actors simply stand and trade blows for a while and call it a fight scene. The intent of the character is more apparent when the body moves across the stage, but what is easily forgotten is that the legs don't have to mimic what the arms are doing. Just because the sword is blocking doesn't mean that the legs can't be stepping forward. Likewise, attacking with the sword can occur while the character is stepping backwards. Feel free to move sideways as well, for it is far more natural and interesting to have the actors not rigidly maintain a profile view during the entire fight. It's fun on some of the finesse fights to include a phrase where one combatant is full-back to the house so that the audience gets to see what its like to have someone directly attacking them.

When stepping, keep that nice wide stance for a solid base. And unless you are replicating a modern fencing style, be sure to keep your hips and shoulders square to your partner. This will open up the body for left and right hand techniques as well as make evasions and sidesteps more stable. It may help to think of both actors' feet on railroad tracks as they fight so that the feet don't go linear.

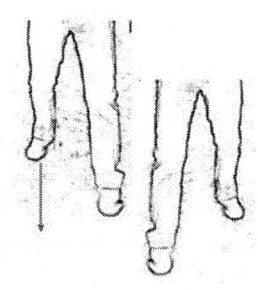

Two basic types of stepping are described for swordwork. When the combatant simply moves one foot in front of the other, it is called a passing step, and the movement itself is directionally referred to as passing forward or passing back. Taking one passing step means that whatever is considered the "lead foot" will of course change with each step. This is also known as "walking". (I realize that seems absurdly basic, and yet it's good to have everyone start on the same page. Also note that the lead foot always points directly at the opponent, while the rear foot is allowed to turn out slightly if needs be.)

The more "fencing" style of movement has the lead foot stepping forward and then the rear foot catching up, called an advance. A retreat is the opposite, with the rear foot first stepping back and then the lead foot catching up. Advancing and retreating move the body a shorter distance than will a passing step, but the lead foot is maintained and overall it is a more stable and balanced movement.

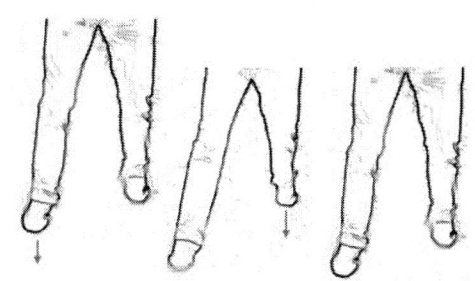

Remember that no matter which stepping style is used, we naturally walk backwards using shorter steps than when we walk forward. So exaggerate your retreating steps, really reach with your feet, or you will soon have your partner on top of you. Don't lead with your head when stepping forward, but let the hips initiate the movement even as you push off with the balls of your feet. It's the torso that moves in and out of the fight, the legs merely catch up and keep the hips underneath your center. The same applies when moving back, but actors often translate that into sticking the buttocks back in the direction of the step. Tuck your hips *forward* and keep the torso straight when stepping backward or you'll get that horrible and all-to-common look that stage fighters get. Oh, you've seen it. When they start going backwards it looks as though a rope has been attached to their butt and they are being pulled off stage. Very undignified. Not only does this throw them off balance, but it sticks the head closer to the opponent's sword. The same feeling of pushing the hips forward is used even in a backwards step. How do you do that? By squeezing the buttocks.

In general we try to keep the feet from crossing each other when moving sideways, for as the feet cross we are unstable and likely to fall. Crossing steps also make us more vulnerable to attack without providing any advantage. An exception is when trying to quickly get around an opponent's dominant side so as to thrust into the side of the opponent behind their arm (known as the *punto reverso*). For almost all the rest of stage combat, we move to the side by letting that nearest foot move first and then bringing the trailing foot to close the gap. Crossing steps are commonly seen in the fencing manuals of early rapier play, especially in the mid 1500's, but seem to have died out in popularity as the century wore on.

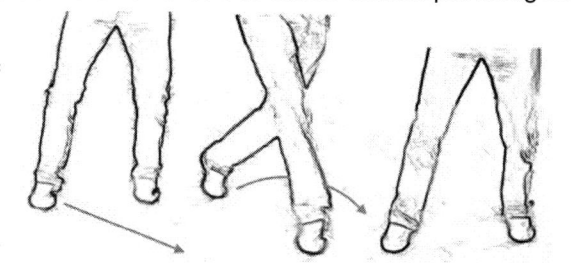

Balestra

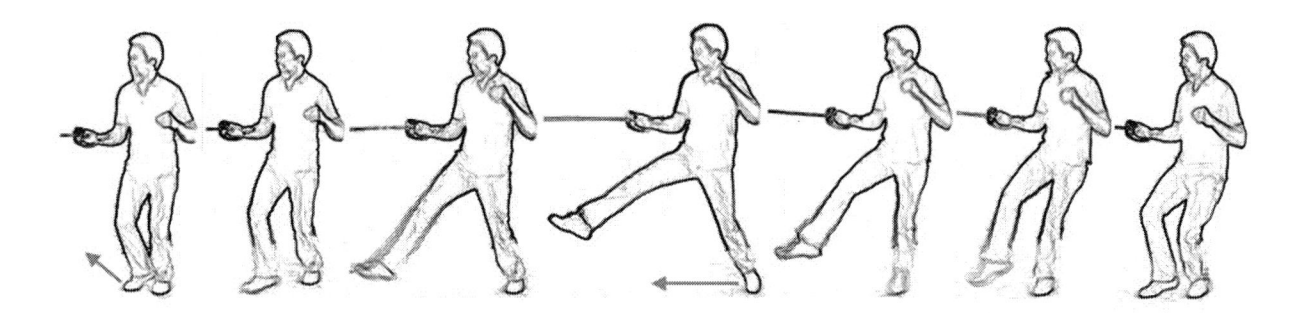

This is a very quick leap forward that dramatically closes distance. It is not a jump, but a hop executed from the back foot. In order to generate enough momentum to shoot the body forward, the lead foot kicks forward and the back foot slides very close to the ground. (The common instruction is to pretend that there is a coin under the ball of your lead foot and you need to scoot it across the room.) A reasonable balestra should move the body forward by a good four feet. As a hop, you must land on both feet, but in this case with the weight remaining on the back foot. The balestra can be performed with or without a corresponding thrust.

The balestra is often followed by a lunge, so often so that many choreographers believe that the term balestra always includes the leap and the lunge. Not so. The balestra does set up the lunge nicely, but they are two separate actions, and one can be performed without the other.

Slashing

For our purposes, a slash is a cutting motion that goes past the intended target without being stopped by a block (or a body). This is different than a cut. Cuts are blocked before the weapon can cross in front of your partner. Slashes move from one side to the other. I should point out that one of the founders of the SAFD (Society of American Fight Directors) detested using different terms, insisting that a cut is a cut, so the society still identifies slashes as cuts. But to be honest the techniques for the cut and slash are completely different for both attacker and defender, so using the same term is not only unnecessarily confusing to the actors, but also just flat out wrong.

With only a couple of exceptions, every slash in stage combat is accompanied by an evasion, which we'll get to below, and because of that, slashes are more dangerous than cuts. As already mentioned in an earlier section, in our version of a correctly performed cut, the defender is never in danger of getting hit even if the defender should forget to block. The slash is dicier, for without an evasion, the defender could get seriously hurt. So we need to change the mechanics of this simulation to add several safety valves.

There are three basic slashes - head [horizontal], diagonal, and stomach.

- Head Slash - This is a big sweep from side to side meant to look as though it could decapitate. Start by pulling the sword hand all the way back to your own neck level with the sword tip pointing behind you. Focus on your partner's forehead because that is the level that the blade tip is going to travel. Point your elbow there. Now wait. At some point your partner's eyes will widen, and the knees will bend as the body begins its drop. Then, and only then, you can begin your slash. The blade must travel on a flat plane parallel to the ground from beginning to end.

Never let your partner make you begin your slash before he has started his drop. Idiot actors want to do that, but it is foolish and unnecessary. And don't misunderstand: I don't want the audience to notice that little timing shift. If you rehearse it enough it will be a very subtle sign just between the two of you, and no outside observer will notice any break in the timing. But it is vital that you establish this critical safety check.

Your aim is that point in space where your partner's forehead *was* - not where it is now and certainly never the throat.

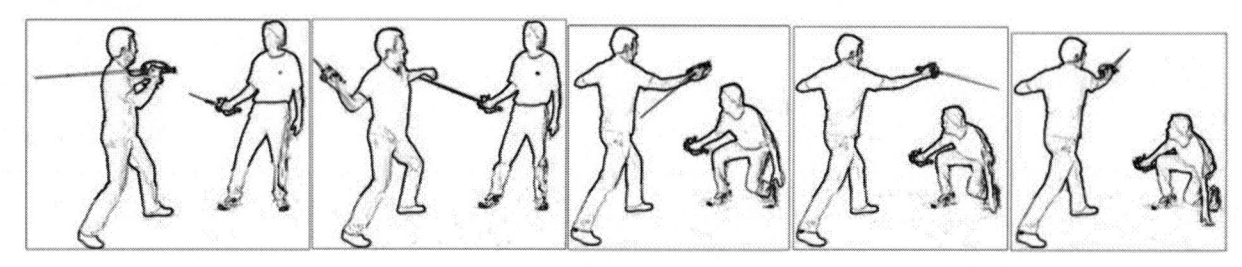

If the actors are parallel to the proscenium, the blade should pass over the defender's body, for if the blade is in front of the defender there was no reason to duck, was there. But if they are staggered a bit, the attacker can keep the wrist bent during the slash so that the blade never gets any closer to the defender than about a foot away. In that situation we can keep the blade further from the defender by taking advantage of the audience's lack of depth perception.

- Stomach Slash - For the attacker this is just like the head slash, except you have a different set-up and cue. Start with your sword at your own belly level with the blade tip pointing behind you. Stare at your partner's belly, point your elbow there, and wait. Your cue to begin the slash is when your partner raises his arms and sucks in his stomach.

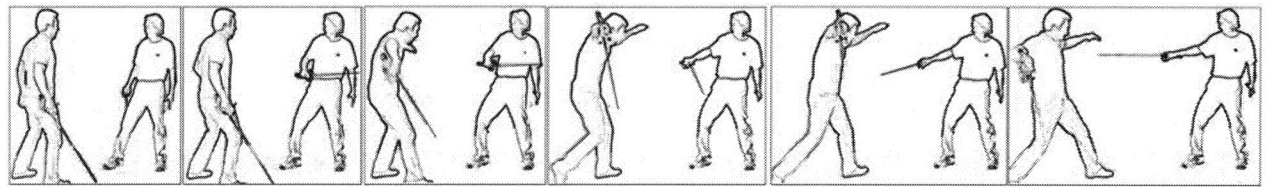

This is one that requires the slasher to keep his wrist bent for safety. That way the tip will trail the hand and is kept away from the victim. The aggressor can always lengthen the arm and straighten the wrist after the blade has past his partner, and still be able to get a good "swish" sound.

- Diagonal Slash - This looks really cool, and is much more believable than the other slashes. The look is that of trying to chop off someone's head or limb with a powerful sweep from either high-to-low or low-to-high from one side to the other. Because it moves diagonally it is harder for the audience to discern how close the blade was to the opponent.

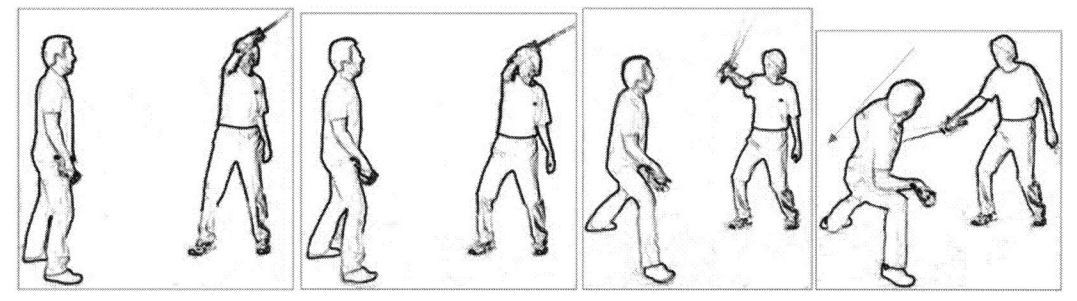

Aggressor creates the picture ... the victim begins to react ... aggressor begins the action ... and both complete the illusion.

It's also a bit harder to give a clear set-up for the diagonal going from low to high. Usually the hand is held low near the hip with the tip almost toughing the ground. Some body English is needed here - a look of starting a baseball pitcher's wind-up - or either rising up while straightening the knees for high-to-low or bending the knees even more for a low-to-high can help. Wait for your partner to begin the lean to step to the side, and then begin your slash. The focus, as with the head slash, is a point just outside where his head was, not exactly where he was, and certainly not where he's going.

- Slashing to the feet - leaping over the blade. This is just like the stomach slash, but done much closer and really extending the blade during the sweep. The look of it is improved if the attacker's body can already be fairly low and he really is reaching with full extension. But, no matter what, this bit usually looks dorky. So unless your partner is Gene Kelly and can clear his feet to a height of forty inches with a barely visible prep, don't bother with this move. [I once was fight director for a production of *The Three Musketeers* in which our D'artagnon was able to do a standing one-legged back flip. For him, I added the slash to the feet.]

Evasions

One way of not getting killed in a sword fight is to not be there when the sword comes at you. Evasions are only limited by the imagination, but the timing will always be the same. Recognition, reaction, action. See the threat, respond to the threat, and then the threat becomes an attack. If you don't allow the audience to read the fear in your face before you make your evasion, they get cheated out of being able to enjoy the moment. But you will have to move when your partner preps - don't wait for the actual attack. This of course is the opposite of what you would do in a real sword fight, but it will also insure that you won't get hit on stage. Don't get me wrong. I'm not asking that the aggressor come to a full stop and then wait for the victim to make his move. That just looks silly. *"Now, this overdone, or come tardy off ... cannot but make the judicious grieve"*. Lets take a look at a few possible evasions, all the while repeating the mantra - recognition, reaction, action (images are on the previous page):

- Ducking a head slash - Actors always want to do this one, but too many times you'll hear the victim tell the aggressor to "go ahead and swing; I'll duck in time". Very dramatic, but very dumb. Instead, the aggressor preps by pulling the sword back to his own shoulder level and waits. Once the victim begins to squat down, only then does the aggressor begin the slash. The slash should be aimed at that spot in space where the forehead was *before* the victim began the drop. You think it looks hokey? Too bad; it's safer.

- Evading a stomach slash - Just as with the head slash, the aggressor preps first and then waits for the victim to begin the move back before beginning the slash. The victim should "suck-in" his stomach to help the illusion, and it can be exaggerated by letting the arm reach out towards the opponent, but make sure that you aren't throwing your arms into the path of the blade.

- Diagonal evasions - Just as with the stomach slash, the aggressor preps first and then waits for the victim to begin the move back before beginning the slash. The evasion is really just stepping sideways away from the course of the blade, but it can look a lot more stylish and dramatic by having the defender's body match the line of the attack. The evasion is either to the left or to right, depending on the direction of the slash. Let's say the attacker is swinging from his high right to low left. From the defender's point of view, this is coming from high left to low right, so at the attacker's prep the defender steps deeply to the left, keeping the right foot planted. The entire body from right heel to the top of the head should have the same line that the attacking blade will mark in space about 12 inches away. (Again, look at the pictures on the previous page.)

The diagonal evasion of an attack coming from high to low can also be augmented with a hanging parry, one in which the hilt is held higher than the tip. In addition to the step to the side, the defender lifts up the sword as though blocking a vertical head cut. The attacker's blade will skip off the sword when the slash is performed. Since the defender has stepped to the side, the contact point on his blade will be on the mid to weak section rather than at the forte, so it makes sense that the blade will yield a bit, and end up matching the angle of the attacking follow-through. Naturally, you will need to have the sword tip pointing away from where the attack began. So if the slash is coming from your high right, you start with the hilt up to the right. If it comes from the high left, then your hilt goes up to left. Either way, you want the audience to see a head block that is parallel to the ground until contact is made, then allow the tip to dip to match the line of the attack.

For slashes coming low to high, the defender can use the sword in much the same manner, but of course the hilt is held low with the tip going straight up. Again, after contact is made he'll want to angle the blade to match the angle of the attack, but careful not to have him hit himself in the face (it happens).

- Limb avoidance - of course, it means pulling a hand or foot quickly out of the way in response to a corresponding attack. As with the other avoidances, it is simply a matter of recognition, reaction, action. The tough part is in giving a good motivation for the attack that the audience can appreciate.
- Passata Soto: One way to avoid a thrust is to duck underneath it. An elegant way of doing that is to drop into a deep reverse lunge (shooting one leg straight back while squatting deeply with the other). Think of it as a deep lunge that goes straight down to the floor rather than forward. The passata soto is performed so deeply, that usually the left palm has to press on the ground for balance.
- Volte: A method of pivoting the body, removing it from the line of attack by shooting the rear foot behind the other and then straight out to the front, so that the trunk is violently turned 180 degrees to the line of attack. Since the pivoting foot stays where it is, the body has shifted over the width of one stance during the spin. Also called the "bum in the face" move, it is sometimes combined with the passata soto technique of dropping down so low that the left hand touches the ground for support. 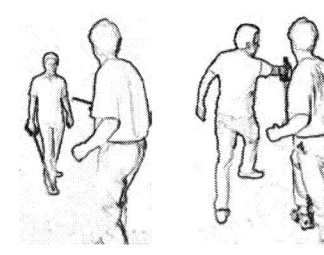
- Demi-volte - You can probably guess this one already. A far easier method of removing the body from the line of attack by swinging the rear foot behind and straight out to the side, so that the trunk is turned 90 degrees to the line of attack. A lunge is not necessarily added to this move.

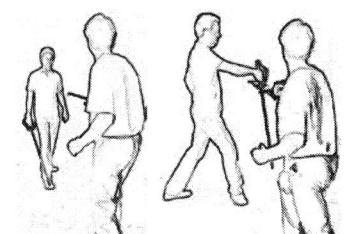

Combination attacks

We have spoken so far about simple attacks and basic parries. These of course can be combined in an infinite number of ways, just as the 26 letters of the alphabet can be combined to form all of the words in the dictionary, and then those words can be combined to form sentences and paragraphs. String the paragraphs together and you have a story. Good choreography will tell an interesting story through the expression of the strategy and tactics used by both combatants. This story is told through the expressive use of combination attacks. Settling for less than that is simply bashing away until someone loses.

When the same fighter performs two or more consecutive attacks, that is a combination. The idea is that perhaps only the last attack was the real intention, the others were feints or attempts to open up a poorly defended part of the opponent's body or simply taking advantage of a sudden opening. One form of a combination attack is a compound attack. A compound attack is an even more skilled combination, where the blade may attack more than one target but the arm has made only one thrusting motion forward. Compound attacks are fencing techniques, always done with a straight elbow, and should be learned under the guidance of an on-site instructor. These are wonderful finesse moves, but if learned incorrectly will look very sloppy. I'm going to go ahead and describe the four safest ones here if only because they are so often used onstage. You should have at least a passing familiarity with them before the fight director arrives. The fancier versions must only be practiced under direct supervision or they will detract from the show.

- same-side shifting-heights - let's try thrusting to high right (that's your own right side; your partner's left). Since your partner has responded by blocking with the tip up, he's left the lower part of the body open, so a follow-up would be to pull your arm back and then thrust low. That's a fine *combination*, but we're going to turn it into a *compound* attack by not pulling the arm back.

If you are a right-handed actor, perform that high right thrust with the palm down (prone). At the moment your attack is parried, keep your arm perfectly straight and roll your arm from the shoulder until the palm is up (supine). Your blade tip will almost magically spin around and end up directly underneath your partner's hand. Wait for the parry low, then roll your arm again so your palm turns down (prone) and your blade tip is now attacking the high line again. There you are: a triple compound attack high-low-high, with only one thrust but the hand turning prone-supine-prone. The defender is going to have to move awfully fast to pick-off all three threats.

Now try the other side of the body (your left, your partner's right). You also want to try a compound high-low-high attack, but now you will thrust with the hand supine, then turn it prone, then supine again. We've arbitrarily stopped at three, but it could continue on as long as you wish. And if you wanted to start with the low attack on the left, then you would simply start with the hand prone, etc. No matter what, these same-side compound attacks work because the arm is kept straight and the forearm rotates to automatically change the attack targets for the blade tip.

- degagé [Fr. = disengage]   This one goes from high line to opposite high line. Let's try that thrust again to the high right, and this time the hand is going to stay supine. As the defender starts to make contact, relax the grip. As the tip of the sword dips slightly, going under the defender's hand, draw your arm slightly across to the left. Then re-grasp the sword with strength and the tip will pop back up to the high target level. The arm stays straight throughout, merely moving straight across from side to side. Only the wrist will move slightly to help guide the tip around. The degagé only works when the parries have the tip pointing up.

- coupé   [Fr. = cut]   Also called the cutover, for this is similar to the degagé except that the tip goes over the defender's hand rather than under. How? With a tiny wrist flick, a little salute, a lifting up of the fingers just as the parry connects. This one works whether the parries are high or low, but of course if the parries are high the cutover must be more exaggerated so as to clear the defender's blade. Again, the arm stays straight on this, merely moving straight across from side to side.

- doublé [Fr. = doubled] This compound attack always goes right back to the same target, merely by making a small circle around the defender's hand as he attempts to make the parry. (For some inexplicable reason, the Society of American Fight Directors only considers it a doublé if two circles are made. They are alone in this.)

The obvious defense is to chase that sword around in a full circle, in what's known as the counterparry, circular parry or universal parry.

Combination Defenses

I mentioned earlier that when doing combination attacks, one doesn't need to bring the sword back to the en guard position between each move. The same holds true for defenses. Obviously, if someone is attacking you four times in a row, you're not going to waste time moving your hand back to en guard in between each move. I also said that even as an attack develops, you want to hold your last position until the very last possible second. You must wait until the attack is 90% developed, and then make a lightening fast move to pick off the incoming threat. However ...

... when moving from one block to another you still have to make sure that the center of the body is covered before you land at the next position or you might accidentally find your block outside of the attack. Here's an example: you are attacked with a vertical head cut followed by a thrust to your right shoulder. Naturally on the first block your arm will rise straight up, elbow pointing right. Now, for the second block, if you just drop your elbow down in an arc to the next block position, you have only a 50-50 chance of being on the correct side of the incoming blade. So what you need to do from the vertical head block is drop your hand to the center of your body first before you swing it out to the right, picking off the second attack.

You have to carefully look to this every time you have two or more consecutive defensive moves. We'll come back to this in a few pages, but I want you to ruminate about it first.

Attacks on the blade

There are times when a fighter finds it necessary to use his own blade to move the opponent's sword out of the way in order to expose a target for attack. They are mainly used in fights where the blades are light enough to quickly respond to wrist movements (they tend to look clunky when performed with heavy swords), and are especially used during the initial moments of a duel when the participants are testing each other. Small or large, these attacks work best when the opponent has already extended his arm on a prior attack. Just as with the unarmed fighting techniques, the opponent does the real work of moving his own blade, the attacker merely following the movement and both working together to sell the illusion.

Attacks on the blade should be kept to a minimum, and when used, performed with great precision, as actors tend to overdo them and ruin the believability. Some attacks on the blade are listed below, in ascending order of force required. Remember, on none of these moves should either blade tip ever cross in front of someone's face.

- Prise de Fer: [French term meaning "taking the iron"] From a successful parry, the attacker moves the opponent's blade to a new position while both blades maintain contact. The opponent must keep the arm and blade straight if the audience is going to have any hope of understanding what is going on. It also helps if the attacker can use the forte against the opponent's foible. It is neither an attack nor a defense, merely a preparatory move from which one intends to initiate a successful attack. There are three kinds of prise de fer, namely;

    1   Croisé: [pronounced - *k(r)wa-say*] from the French, meaning "crosed" the blade is moved from high to low or low to high, but on the same side of the body, not diagonally across like a bind. (You would think that something called a "cross" would have a cross shape, but there you are.)

    2   Bind: the blade is moved only in a half circle, ending diagonally opposite from where is started - for example high-left to low-right.

    3   Envelopment: the blade is moved in a complete circle right back to where it started. If large, the opponent's tip is directed around the body; if small then only around the hand - never across the face. Why is this not a counterparry (or circular parry)? Because the envelopment is controlling the movement.

- Beat Attack: a sharp tap with the forte or middle part of one's blade against the middle or weak part (foible) of the opponent's blade - to remove a threat, open a line for attack, or to provoke a reaction.

- Glissade: also "glide". A flowing attack on the sword that displaces the opposing blade by gently sliding down the weapon, foible to forte, pushing the sword out of the way. It can be combined with an attack if, at the same time as the glide, the tip is pointed at a thrusting target. The corresponding move to the *glissade* is the *yield parry,* (also called the *ceding* or *yielding parry*). The glissade is normally a thrust, but can also be used as a cutting attack, the important thing being that the sword blades stay in contact during the entire move. If the glissade is supposed to be especially forceful, it is called a pressure glide.

♦ Throw-off. Immediately following a block, the incoming sword is pushed even further away. The throw-off is always under the control of the person whose sword is being thrown off.

♦ Disarm. The ultimate attack on the blade, in that it removes it from the actor's possession. There are hundreds of variations on disarms, and some of them even have some relation to actual moves. I am only going to describe one that is both simple and believable to the audience:

Let's assume that Actor A has thrust to Actor B, and that the attack landed low and to the right of B. B parries with tip down and sword to the right. Actor A simply remains in place, and points his sword backward and to his left. Actor B merely follows the movement, pushing his parry in a glissade along A's blade, his own sword moving as one unit. B's hand can even lead a little bit. When the glissade reaches the end, A allows his sword to drop from his hand, gently landing on the ground.

No matter what the specific disarm is, don't violate some basic rules. 1) the person being disarmed is the person who controls the movement from start to finish. 2) Have the energy slow down. 3) Have the energy move upstage. That last thing you want is a weapon freely traveling toward the audience.

Pommel Attacks

I'm a little leery of including mention of pommel attacks, but I also know that they are popular, so first let me again strongly suggest that you get someone with experience to teach these to your actors. These are attacks delivered with the pommel of a weapon, and that means that the actors are going to have to move in close to each other. So we have the danger of unarmed techniques augmented by the danger of unforgiving contact with a ball of steel. If you get hit with a blunt blade tip it can smart: if you get hit with the pommel it can knock you out.

Because of the heightened danger, the most important aspect of a pommel attack is to make sure that every element of the simulation keeps the victim out of danger. Let's go through the most common one, the blocked pommel attack to the face.

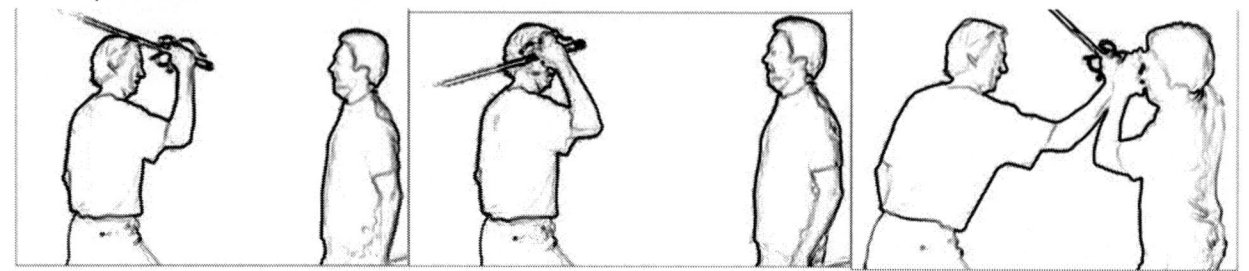

Set up: both actors on the same plane and lined up parallel to the proscenium, facing each other. Since this is a blocked attack, it doesn't matter who is on what side, left or right. The victim (let's say) steps in to close the distance between the actors.

Picture: The aggressor's right hand moves up to his own right ear, allowing the sword tip to move safely behind him. The pommel is now aimed at a spot to one side or the other of the victim's head.

Action: The pommel is pushed in a straight line to that spot either up or downstage of the victim's head.

Reaction: Only the victim has a reaction here, and that is to have an open palm rise up and meet the aggressor's hand, providing the illusion that the pommel attack was successfully blocked. Do not ever try to block the pommel itself or you risk some nasty damage to the blocking hand. To add a little more realism, slightly shift the head away from the attack at the moment of the block. In a larger house, you may need to add a body lean so that the audience can follow the action.

From here you can probably imagine many variations, but the concept is always the same.

Feint Attack

When an attack is begun but not completed, the intention being to provoke a response by the opponent, it is referred to as a feint. Most often it is an attempt to have the opponent begin to block in a certain direction, with the hope that in so doing he'll leave a part of the body open and unprotected. During that moment an attack to that newly exposed spot might be all but impossible to defend against. Most of sport fencing has a lot of feint attacks, but it is difficult for the audience to see the difference between a feint and a simple combination attack (as it is very difficult for fencers as well). For stage we have to exaggerate the feint slightly, but by all means we need to read the expression of panic on the defender's face when he realizes that in making a block for an attack that isn't real he has made a grave mistake. For the same reason, use of the feint must be kept to an absolute minimum.

Punto Reverso

In historical as in modern fencing, most thrusts were aimed to the center of the body. But especially in rapier fighting, since the defending hand was not held in front of the center of the body but was a little bit closer to the outside (for most people, their right side) most thrusts by default were inside thrusts. Thrusts to the outside were considered risky because they usually either were easily blocked or merely nicked the forearm. The Italians gave outside thrusts their own name - *punto reverso* - literally "reverse point"

Of course, in stage combat we thrust both inside and outside with equal frequency, so *punto reverso* has taken on a slightly different meaning. It is still a thrust to the outside, but exaggeratedly so, so that the thrust is almost delivered sideways into the victim's flank. In order to do that, the aggressor makes a deep crossing step to the left and forward with the right foot, practically a lunge. This is really an all-or-nothing move; if unsuccessful, the aggressor is left very vulnerable to counterattack.

The defender usually blocks the attack while taking a step forward and to the left with his left foot. This will move both participants in a slight clockwise turn. If they continue, trading punto's back and forth, they will naturally move in a large circular pattern.

Stabbing/ Thrust-kills with the Sword

Have I mentioned before that less is more? Nowhere more so than in finally finishing the fight and killing off a character. Always remember that the sword or knife is just a prop, and the audience gets its information from the actor's eyes and body language.

Keep it a firm rule never to have the audience see the sword go "through and through" the victim. It has been used in so many movies that it is now merely a cliché, and often provokes laughter rather than an honest gasp.

Where a character has been wounded is shown by the reaction of the victim more than the placement of the blade. If the actor can perform a movement isolation, pushing that part of the body slightly in line with where the force supposedly penetrated, the actual sword can be safely placed upstage of the actor. The audience has no depth perception, so they'll never know the difference.

The simplest thrust kill effect is a perfection of the old sword under the arm bit. The aggressor should initiate a slightly angled thrust to upstage of the midsection. The hand is aimed towards the stomach, but the tip is moved to outside of the body outline. When the tip of the sword has just passed the front of the victim's stomach, then the aggressor's blade can strongly slap the side of the victim, then press forward with the rest of the thrust. Only two or three inches of the blade should disappear upstage of the victim. Never allow the blade tip to appear on the other side of the victim: it destroys the illusion - and gets a laugh. As long as the victim doesn't turn in the direction of the actual blade going upstage, but stays focused and reacts to the imaginary blade hitting him dead center, the illusion will be effective. A slight contraction of the stomach muscles adds realism. When the blade is removed, the victim can perform a reverse of the prior stomach movement, as a real sword would find a good deal of resistance in both going into and coming out of the body.

If the audience is close to or surrounding the action (and the blade is flexible enough), the victim can bend the blade with his forearms to make it appear that the blade has gone right into the center of the belly. The downstage hand reaches out towards the opponent, hiding the upstage forearm which presses against the blade. Opening the fingers (not grabbing the blade) helps sell the illusion. It is amazing how realistic this simple technique can appear.

Other kill-thrusts involving placing the tip directly on-line with the victim must only be attempted under the direction of an extremely competent and experienced professional fight master.

Slicing/Cutting kills with the sword

There are two kinds - contact and distance. Believe it or not I am actually going to suggest that you stay away from the distance kills and use the contact variety. Contact slicing is a simple matter of placing the middle of the (dull) blade along the intended body part to be cut and then pulling the sword across the body. This must not be rushed, for not only is it safer to go slow, but the audience needs a little change of timing here so they can be prepared for an important change in the storyline.

At the end of the cutting motion, the sword is carefully placed with the flat of the blade right on the body part, preferably the stomach or a large muscle and not on a joint. Whether the sword is then pulled directly out [a side cut] or across the body [a drawing cut] the aggressor pulls the sword hand back to his own body center, removing the energy away from the victim. As always, keep the sword away from the head at all times. In fact, add in a slightly downward course for the blade instead of rising or even strictly horizontal. If anything goes wrong, the tip has a better chance of dipping towards the floor than popping up to someone's face.

There are times when a joint is the intended target, especially behind the knee. This bit is often used where one character has to deal with multiple attackers. A quick cut to tendons of the leg and one attacker is immobilized. Be especially careful if you do this bit that you don't smack the joint but instead very carefully lay the blade against it without any pressure, or better yet lay the sword just above the joint. By the way, here is some information which you might find interesting but won't be able to use. Normally, the above bit is done and the reaction of the victim is to bend the "cut" leg and kneel to the floor. This is exactly what the audience expects so you shouldn't stray from that. It's just that you should know that that isn't what really happens.

Our limbs move because of the opposing action of complementary muscles. A muscle can only contract and then relax; that means it can only pull a bone, not push it. So in the leg, for example, the quadriceps in the front of the thigh straighten the leg at the knee and the hamstring behind the thigh bends the leg at the knee. If the tendons are cut behind the knee, that muscle behind the leg contracts immediately but isn't connected, so no bending. The quads on the front of the leg aren't damaged, so the leg straightens and stays straight. But that looks really odd and the audience thinks that the actor got it wrong, so don't do that reaction. (Just another example of how reality can get in the way of telling a story.)

Cutting kills in which the actors are out of distance from each other and the sword is swung in an arc that simulates the slash must not be performed without expert supervision. It is different than the common slashing described in prior pages and very dangerous for it requires precise placement of both actors on the set. It's great for film work, but they have the time to take a half hour to set up the shot and do several takes to get it right. They also have better liability coverage than you do.

Corps à Corps

From the French, literally "body to body". This is when the two actors close distance so that literally the bodies are practically touching, chest to chest and face to face. This is usually the moment in a movie fight where one character will say something to the other along the lines of *"You've come to Nottingham once too often."*

In order to keep this safe, we just have to make sure that the sword hilts are kept away from the participants faces. The easiest way of doing that is to have the weapons go hilt to hilt and keeping the arms straight, low, and off to one side. You would think that something so simple wouldn't require actual actor instruction. You would be wrong.

Throwing and Catching the Sword

Here is a safe way to toss a sword to another actor - safe so long as you practice. Grab the sword by the blade with a gloved hand and then lower your hand to your side. Point the hilt towards the floor so that the blade rests against the back of your arm. Then gently point to the spot that you want the sword to go as you relax your grip. Your gloved hand will guide the blade as it is tossed, and with just a little practice the sword will gently arc to your partner without tumbling, hilt first for an easy catch. But this is critical: toss the sword *upstage* of your target. That way, if you partner misses the grab and bats the sword instead, it will fly upstage rather than out into the house.

Catching the sword should be fairly easy, so long as the sword is moving slightly upstage of where you are standing. If it starts to drift downstage, then move quickly to keep it to your upstage side. Why is this so important? Because again, more dangerous than missing the catch is to bobble the catch. If the sword drifts downstage of you and it bounces off of your catching hand, it could be accidentally swatted out into the audience. Better instead that your energy be turning towards an upstage toss when your hand makes contact with the sword.

Choosing the right swords

Unfortunately this often comes down to a never completely resolved conflict of what the director wants vs. what the choreographer wants vs. what the actors want vs. what the props master can squeeze out of the budget.

There is no right or wrong here; you can justify just about any blade choice so long as the hilt matches the production design and everyone is on the same page as to the requirements of the fight. The fight is the key, so ultimately the fight choreographer has to make the final call. Certain moves are mandated by the specific blade strength, so it doesn't make sense for the director to ask for big slashing movements and still want to use a very light thin blade. The weight of the blade will determine the speed of the fight and even what moves are possible. Compromises will have to be made.

Go back to the **Weapons for Stage** section and read the descriptions of the various blades that are out there for stage combat. Also keep in mind that if the actors have been trained correctly and have good control, even the lighter blades can be used to give the impression of very strong cuts. I've even used different blades within the same fight [*The Three Musketeers* is great for this] and not had any more weapon breakage than in other shows. Different blade widths and lengths can be more interesting for the choreographer and the audience. But ultimately, the blade choice will need to be made by the choreographer.

Once the fight choreographer has picked the blades, then the director needs to choose the hilts, or at least provide enough guidance on what the look should be for the show and each character. The hilt is the look of the sword, and often a wide choice of blades can be mounted onto a staggering variety of hilt styles. The blade determines the action: the hilt determines the look.

Now is the time for the props master to take the information provided from the director and choreographer and perhaps the costumer, look at all of the options available and the budget allowed for the show, and to narrow down the choices to something realistic for the production. All of this has to be decided well before the show goes into rehearsal; indeed, before the choreographer begins to write out the fights. Nobody needs the frustration of having to throw out prior work and start creating new choreography from scratch simply because the weapon availability changed during rehearsal.

The last input will come from the actors. They only get to have one moment of input, and that relates to any injuries or physical limitations they have that would preclude the use of certain moves, and by extension, certain weapons. That's it. They are not allowed to complain about a hilt being ugly or a sword being too long. Their job is to deal with it.

Ok, ok, maybe I was being too harsh there. Actors should always be allowed the opportunity at any point in the rehearsal process or even during the performance schedule to bring notice concerning a valid safety concern, and that includes their opinion on their props, their partner, their choreographer, or even their director. After all, it is usually an actor who will first notice a small problem on its way to becoming a major issue. But I must say that nine times out of ten an actor will complain about a prop for the same reason he complains about some aspect of his costume - he isn't used to it, and is too lazy to try to work with the object first. Far easier to have it changed rather than do his job as an actor.

As long as we mentioned blade lengths, let's not get too hung up on precise equality for every combatant. It certainly didn't happen in Shakespeare's time, and it provides very little benefit on stage. Many will insist that equal blades mean better control of distance between the actors as they move across the stage, therefore insures a safer fight, but that can only be true if the fighters happen to have the same arm, leg, and torso length. (I actually would like to see shorter actors have the benefit of using a longer blade, but the look is comical so will never happen.)

How to memorize and rehearse a sword fight.

Here is a repeat of other exercises mentioned earlier, but they are invaluable so I can't stress them enough:

- *Find the Intentions.* Usually a fight is composed of small groupings of a handful of moves, called a "phrase", each expressing a certain plan that the fighter had in order to make a successful attack. If it's not obvious from the choreography, make it up. It's much easier to remember a connected series of 8 clear emotional impulses than 153 random individual attacks and parries.

- *Progressing in Reverse.* I have my actors memorize their lines this way too. Start with the last phrase, practicing it until comfortable and memorized. Then add the next-to-last phrase, working it carefully, but always adding the other, already memorized phrase. Then tack on the third-to-the-last phrase, and so on until you have the fight down. So in a fight that has, let's say, 15 phrases, you will have worked number 15, then 14-15, then 13-14-15, then 12-13-14-15, and on and on until the fight is polished. Why this way? The part that they have practiced most will be to them the easiest, and after a while the fight will seem as effortless as rolling down a hill.

- *No Weapons/Finger Fight.* No kidding, the best way to perfect a sword fight is to leave the swords in the props cabinet several times. The actors stand much closer than normal and go through the entire fight using just the hands. Fingers should actually reach out and try to touch the intended target [hip, shoulder, head] and the defensive hand merely makes contact with the incoming fingers. Don't let them be sloppy on this. Attacks must be focused to the exact square inch, and defenders are not allowed to push the attacks away unless it is part of the choreography. Since the focus is on the finger tips, the intention of attack and defense becomes much clearer and the techniques improve dramatically. This is the best single way to take someone from novice to expert. Have the actors do this at least once a week and all of the attacks and defenses will stay sharp.

- *Sit-Down* - This is also a perfect way to rehearse when swords aren't available or when space and time are limited. The hand-work of a sword fight must become second nature to the performers, for it is simply not permissible to have the actors struggle to remember their next moves. It is the above *No Weapons* rehearsal, but without using the footwork, and done as quickly as humanly possible. After a while the actors will feel the flow of the pattern, rather than beat out each move like a metronome. The two combatants can always steal 30 seconds here or there, grab two chairs and sit facing each other, and "speed-through" the fight the same way we often do "speed-throughs" for our lines.

- *Look, Ma', No Hands* - Here is the flip side of the *Finger Fight*. Go through the fight using all of the footwork but with the arms doing nothing. They can keep them dangling at their side, or crossed in front of their chests, or clasped behind their backs, whatever, because for this exercise they are useless appendages. Let them call out the attacks so both know where they are in the fight, but the focus here is showing attack and response with the eyes, torso and hips. They must keep distance, but also "push" their opponent using the force of their intention. This should be done on the actual set if at all possible.

- *Dropped Parries* - This is scary but an excellent way to improve arm control and mental discipline. Go through the fight as normal, with weapons, but one actor [without warning and in no discernible pattern] simply does not make the appropriate defensive move. If the attacker doesn't have excellent control, the partner gets hit.

This exercise is good to use when you see that the actors are getting too aggressive with their moves, or if they start breaking blades.

- *Water Bottle* - Without question the best way to develop controlled cuts that look real. Get a plastic bottle (water, juice, milk) fill it with water and put it on a stool. Have the actors practice full speed horizontal cuts both right and left. Remind them to snap the cuts (like snapping a towel) with a fully extended arm. The game is to see how fast they can snap the cut and still touch the bottle - without knocking it off the stool. When that gets easy, have them try it with an *empty* plastic bottle.

- *Slide & Steal* - Not an all-around exercise for an entire fight, but it helps when working on sharing the energy of the fight using the blades, especially with the lighter rapier swords. The actors should imagine that there is a fiery ball of energy that is generated by the character's intent, which flows down the attacking arm and continues to move down the blade. With each attack, the defender's sword meets the incoming blade at the foible as normal. Then the defender takes that aggressive intent, "catching the fire" with his blocking sword. The defender slides his own forte along the aggressor's blade until it slips off of the tip, as if "stealing" the incoming energy. The defender slides the sword towards his own body, so no pushing away of the opponent's blade is allowed. This drill also helps establish correct distancing, as it is harder to do the slide if the attacker is allowed to stand too close. As you slip off the tip, you must still have your hand slightly in front of you (except after blocking a vertical head attack).

- *Rope Fight* - This is a good exercise (along with *Slide & Steal*) to use when one of the actors starts "pushing" his defenses, extending the arm toward the attacker or way off to the side as he is blocking. Correcting this has to be done at the earliest fight rehearsals before it becomes an unbreakable habit. Have the actors put aside the weapons and give them a three foot length of rope. Each actor holds onto one end, and then they run the entire fight. The only rule is that the rope has to be taut at the end of each move. Of course, the only way to do that is to pull the defending arm back towards the defender. After just a few runs, the "pushing" blocks disappear. Remind the actors as the defender should let the rope go slack during the beginning of each corresponding attack, even let the center touch the ground, so long as it is tight at the completion of the block.

- *Chase 'em Down* - There are times when the fight seems memorized and understood, but has no heart, no passion. Often this is because one actor feels disconnected to the idea of sword fighting. Find an open area without any obstacles [I like a good-sized grassy field at least three times the size of the performance stage] and let the actors reach for the other during the attacks - not just with the sword, but with the entire body. For each defense, have them run backward to get away. Except in making sure that the sword tips are safely kept away from each other, don't worry at all about correcting technique here. Encourage them to take huge leaps or even four or five steps for every attack, with the feeling of blasting their opponent across the field and then running like hell backwards in order to avoid getting hit. This is an aerobic workout that is also a lot of fun.

True Stage Weapon Story: I once had the joy of playing Macbeth as well as choreographing the fights. For the fight against Young Siward, he had a two-handed broadsword and I used a two-handed axe. Young Siward was played by Johnny Moreno, an accomplished actor and fighter who was my fight captain for this show. He rehearsed all of the other fighters (it was a very physical show) and had even memorized all of the fights. When he and I fought, it was my time to relax, for I had absolute trust in him as a performer and as a combatant. Our fight had a nice sequence of moves which ended with my swinging the axe to his downstage side, which he would block and then bind overhead into a sweet disarm, pulling the axe out of my hands and sending it deep upstage. Then just as he delivers what he thinks is going to be a killing thrust, Macbeth simultaneously deflects the blade with his arms, grabs the sword, does a 180º spin, and reverse-thrusts to kill Young Siward. Extremely cool.

Well, in one performance, Johnny came rushing out to the stage and as he was about to start his first move, his eyes went wide and he slightly but vigorously shook his head as his body stayed still. I knew what it meant instantly - he had forgotten how the fight started. This is perfectly normal and can happen to any actor at any time, no different than going up on your lines. Instead of trying to fake the choreography, I figured that we should just dump the full fight that night and go right to the final sequence. I jumped towards him and got into a corps-a-corps and hissed into his ear *"disarm"*, then jumped back. His eyes stayed wide; he didn't understand. So I jumped in again into a corps-a-corps and hissed once more into his ear *"disarm"*, then jumped back. Then it clicked. The relief washed over his face as he relaxed and slightly smiled. I stepped in and delivered the downstage swing, which he parried and then bound overhead to upstage. I let go of my axe to see it go safely deep upstage ... *along with his sword.* He had disarmed himself! The look of panic was now on both of our faces as we stood downstage facing each other without any weapons in our hands. Having not planned for a double disarm and knowing that Young Siward had to die, I ran up to him and did a stomach punch simulation. He instantly dropped to the ground as I ran upstage, grabbed his sword, ran back down, hurriedly stabbed a few times at the floor upstage of his prone body, and then ran back upstage to get my axe as I made my exit.

I mention this as a reminder that even the finest actors will find that strange things occur sometimes. The brain is a funny instrument, and it just happens that on certain nights the moves or the lines are simply not there for a moment. There has never been a show in which at least one actor didn't go up on his lines, even if only for a second, and the audience never noticed. In the same way, there has never been a stage fight in which at least one combatant didn't forget at least one of his moves for at least one performance. The important thing to remember is that the audience will never notice - unless you go out of your way to show them that you messed up. Did your attack go to the wrong target? The audience will just assume that it was part of the fight. As long as no one got hurt, who cares? You'll fix it tomorrow.

The other lesson from the story is that neither of us panicked and tried to force something unilaterally. When Johnny knew that the fight wasn't in his brain that night, he did the right thing, which was not to fight. But he was so well prepared as an actor and as a fighter that I knew that we could work out an unarmed simulation on the fly and that it would look good and neither of us would be in danger. This would have been unthinkable if we had not put in hundreds of hours of practice time together. I wouldn't have attempted it with anyone else.

In moments of stress,
we do not rise to the level of our expectations;
we drop to the level of our training.

Choreographic Notation

As promised, I'm going to show you a much easier way of notating a fight than using the French parry numbers. I have seen that this is also the best way to memorize a fight. The following system isn't mine, but I have made some modifications to it over the years. It uses numbers at their most efficient - showing the sequence of moves using regular counting numbers, because everyone knows how to count.

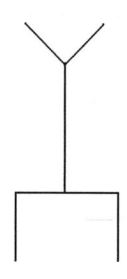

This little stick figure is not poor representation of the human form but instead a way to show the division of the five common target points for attacks and defenses. This is always going to be used to diagram your view *of your partner*. But the numbers are to indicate what *you* are going to do. Anything written in the upper V portion refers to an attack or defense for the head. Anything on either side of the center line is an attack or defense to the high line, and anything on either side of the lower box refers to moves on the low line. [Remember that high line means exactly armpit level; low line means belly button level, not an inch or two above]. The inside of the box is left for those things not part of regular swordplay, such as attack to the foot, throwing a punch, etc. When there is a "+", you are attacking; when there is a "-", you are defending.

The following is a completely arbitrary sequence of attacks and defenses:

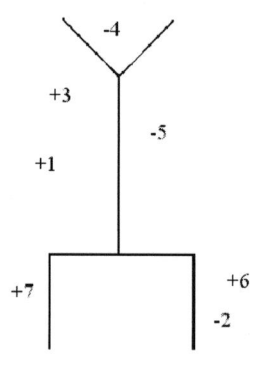

The numbers in this case refer only to the order of the moves. It doesn't matter that the "3" is higher than the "1"; they both go to the same target, namely, to the left (your partner's right shoulder). If there is a "+" in front of the number, it means that it is an attack. If there is a "-" in front of the number, it means it is a defense. Slowly go through the motions shown in the above filled-in figure. If you still aren't sure about the mechanics of sword work, don't worry. If the number has a "+" just stick your arm straight out and point at the target. If it has a "-", bend your elbow and bring your hand all the way to your own body.

So looking at the above figure, we would describe your seven moves like this:

1) attack to the left high line (your partner's right)
2) parry an attack to your right low line
3) attack to the left high line (your partner's right)
4) block a vertical cut to your head
5) parry an attack to your right high line
6) attack to the right low line (your partner's left)
7) attack to the left low line (your partner's right)

Now let's see your opponent's view of the same fight sequence:

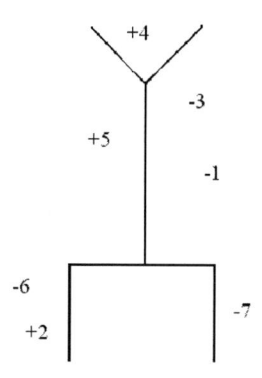

```
        \ +4 /
         \  /
          Y
           \ -3
     +5     \
             \ -1
              \
               |
               |
     -6        |    -7
    ┌──────────┴──────────┐
    │
    +2
```

As you can see, your partner's choreography is the mirror image of yours, which makes sense because each attack will have a matching defense and one person's left is the other person's right. And while your parter is doing the above choreography, he sees *you* doing this:

See: that's you doing the first set of moves, but from your partner's vantage point.

What's really great about this is that two actors can practice the hand movements without their partner being present, even without swords in their hands, and still memorize what is the hardest part of the fight - the sequence of attacks. I usually provide my actors with the written transcription of the fight on the first rehearsal, and even with complete novices they are able to read, understand, and replicate the entire fight within 30 minutes of instruction.

But what about the foot movement? What about the palm being prone or supine? What about cuts vs thrusts? There are some fight directors who need to have every body movement transcribed, but the actors don't need that. They'll pick-up the foot movement and the fine tuning of the sword movements very quickly in the course of teaching them the choreography, just as they pick up intention and emotional response in the course of rehearsing their acting. If the actor needs a reminder here and there that a certain move must be a thrust rather than a cut, then he will make his own notation of a "t" rather than a "c" next to the number.

When I hand out the printed choreography to the actors, I'll usually add a written description of each move next to the diagram as a record of what the moves are supposed to be. That way if there is a question and I'm not there they can simply go to the master instruction list. But I try to keep the diagram itself as clear and simple as possible. The actors need to memorize the fight first before they can feel comfortable enough to add anything approaching finesse. From what I've seen, using this diagrammatic notation is the easiest way to do so.

Getting from Move to Move

Let's try an even simpler pattern and see how to link some of these attacks and defenses. There is very little absolute right and wrong in this except that we must never violate the two cardinal rules of sword play: 1) protect the center and 2) stay away from the face. Protecting the center is all about maintaining the illusion that your opponent is actually trying to kill you, so the defenses must always radiate out from the center of what is being protected. And staying away from the face is about the very real danger that these even blunted weapons can cause. The tip of the sword must never point at or cross in front of anyone's face at any time for any reason.

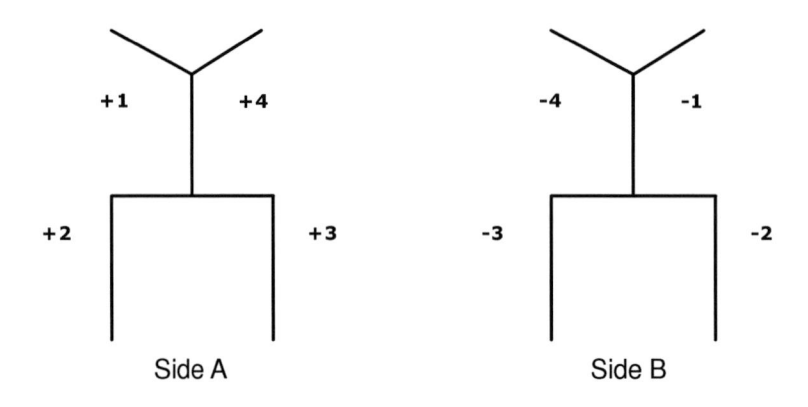

```
         +1    +4                    -4    -1


   +2            +3            -3            -2




         Side A                       Side B
```

As you can see, we have side A doing a series of four consecutive attacks. But right now, we're going to focus on side B, the defenses. Let's assume that B starts with the hand at center in a standard en guarde. The first parry is therefore going to be a very simple drift of the hand to the right and lifting the tip up. Moving to the second parry is really just a wrist movement. The hand can stay where it is as the blade makes a counterclockwise half circle in front of the body until the tip is pointing down. That half circle has to be big enough to go around the level of A's head.

The third parry is as simple as the first, simply moving the hand from right to left and leaving the tip pointing down. The fourth attack continues the circle, and here is where some actors get into trouble. They will often try to follow the attack in a clockwise half circle. What they don't anticipate is that once that chase catches up with the attack, their own blade will push the attacking tip right into their own body. What went wrong? They forgot the first commandment of blocking - clear the center. To get from the third to the fourth parry, the hand stays where it is as the wrist makes the blade do a counterclockwise half circle. Again, it has to be pretty big to both cover the center and stay away from your partner's face.

Let's go back to the arbitrary choreography that I laid out before.

```
        \ -4 /
         Y
    +3   |
         | -5
    +1   |
         |
         |
     ___ | ___
    |         |
+7  |     +6  |
    |     -2  |
```

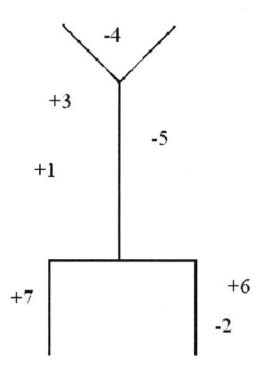

There is a standard back-and-forth on the first three moves, and then if you are right handed the head block on move four leaves your elbow pointing to the right. If from there you go to number 5 by just dropping your elbow, there is a good chance that the incoming thrust is going to get inside your block, putting you in real danger. Instead, from 4 your hand should drop down to the center of your torso while lifting the tip, and then move the sword to the right.

Now, for fun, try making move number five a hanging parry, that is the hand held high but the tip pointing down. From the head block on four, you can almost leave the elbow where it is and let the blade swing down to protect the high line, and then continue nonstop to the attack on six. Which way is right? Whichever serves the storyline better.

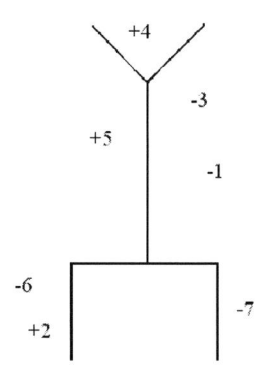

```
        \ +4 /
         Y
         | -3
    +5   |
         | -1
         |
         |
     ___ | ___
    |         |
-6  |      -7 |
+2  |         |
```

Looking at the complementary moves, again the first three moves are simple back-and-forth, and the attacks of four and five are likewise fairly intuitive. But the natural reaction of continuing straight down on the left side for the parry (#6) can get you into trouble if you don't clear the center. From five you'll need to pull the tip back and to the left, parallel to the floor, and then make the blade travel in a 270 degree clockwise circle between the two of you until it make the block on the lower left.

To get to the last move, one of course would normally slide the hand from left to right. But what if instead, you make a full counterclockwise circle? Added to the previous move it makes for quite a flashy combination. What does it suggest to you, compared to the simpler version? Arrogance? Panic? Think of variations whenever you work through choreography and see how a slight change can affect the emotional tone of the pattern. Don't change the moves, just the way they are presented.

Adding the Dagger

"what is his weapon?"

"Rapier and dagger."

"Well, that's two of his weapons, but no matter."

A little joke from Hamlet.

Fighting with the dagger uses the same techniques as those for the rapier. All of the cuts, thrusts, and blocks for one can be used for the other, and with two weapons we have a few other options as well. Simultaneous attacks are possible, as well as using both weapons to block a single powerful cut, either as a parallel block [both weapons pointing either up or down] or a cross block [the weapons forming an "X" in the air and catching the incoming cut in the formed "v" shape of the crossed blades]. The sword is the primary attacking weapon and the dagger is the primary blocking tool, but in a staged fight both weapons are used in both capacities for added visual excitement. For example, the sword might be used to parry an attack, but then the dagger is brought up to replace the sword, "holding" that attacking blade in place (called a transfer parry), which frees the defending sword to initiate its own attack.

When two weapons are used, the stances of the fighters usually change. You'll recall that in single rapier fighting the lead foot and the sword hand are on the same side, usually the right. In rapier and dagger, with the rapier held in the right hand, by standing with the left foot and left shoulder forward both weapon tips are equally distant to the opponent, and therefore equally dangerous. Which hand is held high and which is held low is up to the fighter, and would change constantly during a fight anyway in order to confuse the opponent.

Let's go beck to the previous fight phrase that we worked out to see a little rapier and dagger fighting. In notating the moves, we'll add "R" and "L" to each number so as so designate which hand is to be used, right or left.

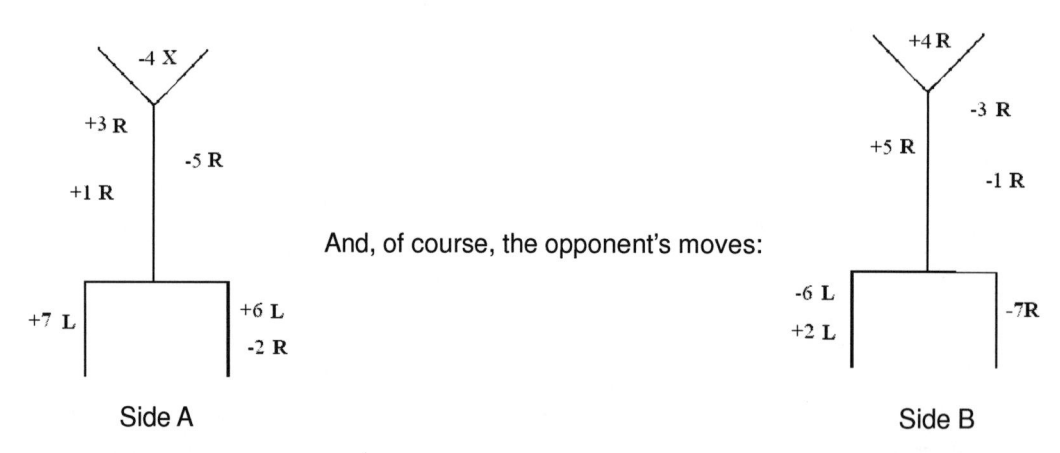

```
         -4 X                                              +4 R
    +3 R                                                         -3 R
              -5 R                                    +5 R
    +1 R                                                         -1 R
                    And, of course, the opponent's moves:
                                                      -6 L
         +7 L      +6 L                               +2 L            -7R
                   -2 R

         Side A                                              Side B
```

If we try to extrapolate a little story from side A, we might say that he starts off by confidently using only his dominant weapon for the first three moves (the sword), then has to use a *cross block* with both weapons on move 4 in order to protect his head, immediately uses the sword to protect his right flank, and then aggressively uses the dagger to push his opponent back in move 6.

For side B, he is playing it conservatively, rather predicatively using his right hand on the right side, left hand on the left. However, he does take advantage of an apparent opening when, after the vertical head shot on 4, he goes right to a high line attack on move 5 with the same weapon, probably as a compound attack.

Just for fun, let's try different hands doing the same sequence.

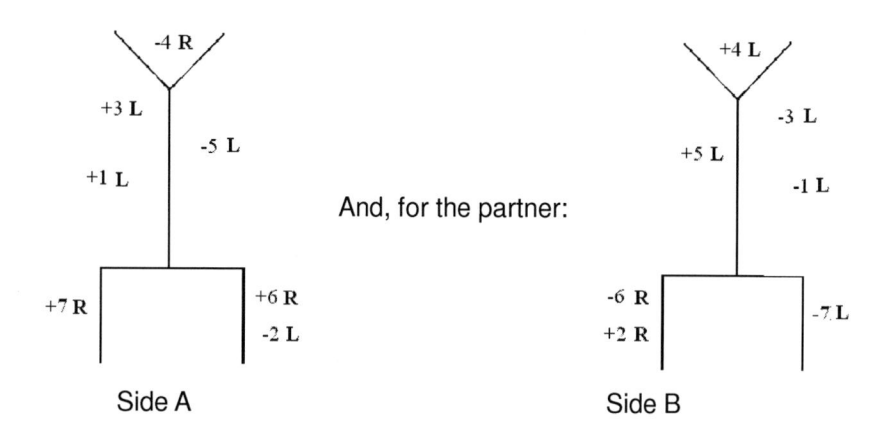

```
        -4 R                              +4 L
   +3 L                               -3 L
         -5 L                     +5 L
   +1 L                                    -1 L
                 And, for the partner:
   +7 R    +6 R                   -6 R    -7 L
           -2 L                   +2 R

      Side A                            Side B
```

So the pattern of attacks and defenses hasn't changed, but the phrase now has a very different feel. For side A, there is a strong feeling that he's holding his sword in reserve, waiting for the right moment to strike, which he finally does in the last two moves.

Side B has what at first seem to be ungainly combinations, but this can be used to the actor's advantage. Taken one way, the character could be in dire straights, desperately attempting to survive the fight without being able to construct a viable strategy. On the other hand, get creative with all of these moves that make the arms cross in front of the body. They open up great opportunities for elaborate circular arm moves or even spinning the body from move to move.

Shortsword/Broadsword

For our limited purposes I have made no distinction between broadsword and rapier techniques. The careful application of the same actions can be used for both weapons, and I make the assumption that the director and actors will endow the weapons with the weight and speed that would be appropriate for each weapon. Naturally, within the choreography there will be fewer thrusts and parries in a broadsword fight, mainly because the very width of the battle blades make them very ineffective thrusting tools. [To be blunt, a thick, wide blade gets held up by the victim's bone and connective tissue.] And of course all of the fancy compound attacks are only meant for fencing weight weapons and are completely inappropriate for heavy battle weapons. But a cut is a cut, a thrust is a thrust, and the blocks are performed in the same way as the rapier.

The shortsword fight, on the other hand, will have a very different feel to it altogether. Here we're talking about using the swords of ancient Greece or Rome [or perhaps combatants of WWI fighting with their long bayonets?], pirate cutlasses and machetes. For all of these the blade length will be between 18 inches to 24 inches long. With such short blades, the actors are going to be right on top of each other, so it'll look strange to have them fight in a prolonged cut and thrust of a rapier or even broadsword fight. Some major modifications have to be made in the fight.

First, many more unarmed techniques should be included, since punches, kicks, grabs and throws will be easily possible and even obvious at such short distances. Secondly, the regular thrust coming from solar plexus level now makes no sense at all. These short blades of the bronze and early iron ages were very thick, and it is unlikely that sufficient force could be generated by a standard fencer's thrust to do much more than knock back an opponent. Instead, it seems clear from archeological evidence that the successful thrust was performed with a straight arm, usually as an upthrust into the belly. We can approximate this by holding the sword down by our side with an arm held straight at the elbow, and then pointing the blade tip to either the left or right flank of our opponent.

Arcing thrusts were also performed with a straight arm held high and off to the side, thrusting parallel to the ground at the flank. This simple move should be considered an advanced technique for stage combat. This move brings the arc of the weapon from outside to inside, and the attacker cannot follow the track of the tip with enough certainty to keep his partner safe. This type of move should only be performed under the direct supervision of a competent instructor.

Machete blades make fine weapons for a theatrical fight, but they are more wobbly than standard stage combat weapons. A lighter hand during cuts is crucial, and augmenting the blocks with the second hand supporting the backedge near the foible helps considerably.

Military Sabre

Whereas the civilian weapon of the 18th and nineteenth centuries was extremely light and exquisitely balanced to rest as easily as a feather in one's hand, the military sword was heavy, brutal and cumbersome. With a heavy cutting blade and no counterbalancing pommel, the sword once in motion is very difficult to stop or redirect. These are purely practical design elements, for the weapon is designed for use in the maelstrom of battle, where there is no stand off between two equally matched opponents in an honorable duel. The sabre is built for maximum damage on the first swing, with absolutely no thought given as to trying to use the weapon for defense.

And yet, it was used at times for "fights of honor" between military officers. And in many Shakespeare plays that have been set in more modern periods, fighting with the military sabre is going to be the only option. But the sword simply will not handle the way that does, say, a rapier. Instead, it should be treated as a single hand broadsword, with allowances made for its special characteristics.

First, the sword does not rest easily in the hand. With all of the weight on the blade and no counterweight, the blade pulls down strongly, requiring more hand strength throughout the fight simply to keep the weapon from dropping. So the first change will be in the en guard. Instead of a fully extended arm, the fighter will find it easier to drop the arm somewhat, letting the hand remain at about waist height. The blade tip should lift up so that it is at shoulder level. This allows the hand to rest in a natural position while keeping the entire blade length ready to defend the full torso.

An alternate en guard is to raise the sword arm completely overhead, elbow pointed back and sword tip pointing towards the opponent. This position threatens a thrust while still providing some protection to the body by simply allowing the blade to drop down if needs be.

Assuming that the sabres you are working with have curved blades, you'll soon find that thrusts with the tip are somewhat impractical, as the tip will not strictly align with the path of the hand. One can still thrust, but great care must be taken to track that tip, for it can easily get away from you and pop up to a spot much higher than intended. Turning the hand slightly so that the blade comes in a flat path parallel to the floor can help, but that puts the fighter at a higher risk of having the tip arc in towards the opponent's body or foolishly away from the opponent.

The stance for the sabre needs to be rather wide, in an effort to stay underneath the momentum of the cut and not get thrown forward.

Most of the defensive moves will be hard absorption blocks rather than deflections. Because of the inertia of the sword, moving the weapon for multiple blocks may prove difficult to control. Some little shortcuts may prove useful. For example, when blocking high line attacks from one side of the body to the other, you might find it easier to leave the tip of the sword hanging in space about six inches above head level on the center line, and let the hand swing back and forth. The sword will look like a giant suspended pendulum, and the hand will be able to move much more quickly than if you had to shove the whole weapon from side to side. The unfortunate trade-off is that it weakens your block. I would say to get good instruction from a choreographer who has a lot of experience working with military sabres, but there are very few out there.

Moulinet

A strong cutting attack is difficult from either opening stance, so a move particularly suited for the sabre was developed, known as the *moulinet* (French), *molinello* (Italian), or *windmill* (English). With the sword held out in front, and gravity tugging strongly on the blade, the hand is allowed to relax its grasp for an instant. The blade tip will immediately drop toward the ground. Even as this happens the hand will begin a tight outside turn and then quickly regrasp the handle, so that the tip of the sword swings closely by the knee and then continues a grand circle past the right ear and then forward toward the opponent, building up momentum on the way. By strongly pushing the hand forward at the end of this circle, the sabre can deliver a cut as powerful as any from a broadsword, without having to pull the arm back in a big prep. No need to move the elbow. As a matter of fact, if the elbow drops during the execution of the moulinet, your really doing just a big cut and not a moulinet at all. And no matter what, the blade has to stay very close to the body and your head as it rises behind you.

The moulinet can be delivered from the left or the right side, and choreographers love to link these in a series for some very flashy filler moves, either multiple circles staying on one side of the body or back and forth circles. I myself like adding moulinets when the character is going to fight with a sword in each hand, fighting multiple attackers. By having him do chasing moulinets or parallel moulinets, it gives the audience a chance to anticipate the fun fighting to come.

Of course, choreographers throw in moulinets not only with sabres but more commonly with rapiers and broadswords. This has led to a minor controversy amoung fight directors. Many insist that the move is only appropriate for the sabre for it is only in the nineteenth century that it is first described. Others point out that it cannot be proved that it was *not* performed before that time, and that there exists at least some (extremely weak) evidence that it plausibly occurred in medieval times. I for one would like to have both sides remember that all of stage combat exists to please the audience, not to create a documentary on military practice. Do what works for the play.

Samurai-style sword fighting

Many of the movements of swordfighting throughout history remain the same, and therefore it is no surprise that the basic cuts and blocks of stage combat broadsword work will be used for fighting with the Japanese katana. What we need to add is the ritual and sense of control that was part of samurai life.

On the other hand, many of the techniques described below are somewhat difficult to master, and you simply might not have the rehearsal time necessary to really polish them, or even gracefully perform them by opening night. And it is certainly the case that although the style is popular, there are very few stage choreographers that have any training in it themselves. And you certainly don't want a martial artist without stage combat experience to work out a fight for your show.

So read the section below, but feel free to go back to regular broadsword techniques. If you can add some of the flavor of the Japanese style, great. Safety first, believability of acting second, and historical accuracy last.

Wearing the Sword

Traditionally the sword is not only tucked into the obi (the wide fabric belt) but also secured with the use of the scabbard cord. That is a bit much for our purposes, so we're just going to tuck it into the obi. Even this will require a certain protocol. Hold the scabbard in the right hand with the blade edge (outside curve) pointing forward. Make sure your right thumb clamps onto the guard to prevent the sword from falling out. With the thumb of the left hand, pull the obi slightly away from your clothing at a point just two inches left of your midline. Gracefully bring the right hand slightly up and with a clockwise swing bring the bottom of the scabbard to the opening you have made at the obi, sword edge now pointing up. Push the scabbard in about three quarters of the way with the right hand, then smoothly continue the movement with the left, remembering to cover the sword guard now with the left thumb. The fingers of the right hand can still gently touch the handle until this movement is complete, ready to draw the sword if need be. The sword guard (the *tsuba*) should rest directly on your midline.

The placement of any second weapon, the shorter wakizashi or the dagger known as the tanto, was not as strictly proscribed, and could end up almost anywhere on the obi, although just as with the katana always with the cutting edge of the weapon pointing up. The singular exception is the katana-like sword known as the tachi. This was a sword worn when on horseback, so was hung edge down in a ringed scabbard, much like the western cavalry sabre. Another sword, the nodachi, was an extra long sword that was normally worn across the back. Just as with European fighters, the sword would be unslung and then unsheathed just before battle, the scabbard left behind before engaging with the enemy.

When bowing, be sure to grasp the top of the scabbard with the left hand and hold the guard with the thumb. Nothing is more embarrassing than to have the sword slide out and hit the ground while in the middle of your bow.

Drawing and Sheathing the Sword

Grab the top of the scabbard with the left hand, the left thumb gently pushing the guard up by a quarter of an inch to raise the sword a bit out of the scabbard. As you draw the sword with the right hand, push the scabbard slightly down and to the left with your left hand. This will make the sword pommel point forward. You might even add a little clockwise quarter turn of the scabbard, so that the blade moves out parallel to the floor.. In this way the energy of the draw is directed towards your opponent instead of harmlessly up and to the right. Once the sword is drawn, bring the pommel back to your center and complete the grasp with the left hand.

In order to return the sword to the scabbard, grab the top of the scabbard with the left hand, making sure that the "eye" (top) of your fist is just a little bit higher than the rim of the scabbard. At the same time, the right hand gently swings the sword blade around in front of you and to the left until the back edge drops gracefully onto the left hand. The back edge (the unsharpened inner curve) of the blade is now pointing down and the true edge is pointing up, and the forte of the blade is touching the web of the left hand, left thumb almost touching the guard, the entire blade parallel to the floor. With the left hand gently pull up the scabbard and give it a quarter turn to the left (counter-clockwise). Push the right hand a little to the left at the same time, so that the pommel points at your opponent. The blade is now pointing behind you and to the left. Now push the right hand forward with a very slight rising motion, and the backedge of the blade will ride along the web of your left hand. As soon as the tip passes your web, the tip will drop magically into the opening of the scabbard. Immediately push the scabbard opening down with the left hand, so that you can slide the sword in with the right, still aiming the hilt at your opponent. Once the sword is in, let the left hand move the sword back to a comfortable wearing position, the fingers of the right hand still gently touching the hilt.

As you can gather from all of this, the essential meaning behind all of these moves is that the fighter was always ready to launch an attack or respond to a threat.

Holding the Sword and Basic Stance

The concept behind fighting with the katana is to take advantage of the one crucial instance where it is possible to strike before your opponent can react. In order to move from a completely motionless en guard to a lighting fast cutting attack, the body must be completely relaxed. Any muscle tension will slow down the reaction time for attack or defense. For actors to approximate this look, we must constantly work at relaxing our neck, hands and shoulders, dead giveaways to the audience of an untrained fighter.

The sword is grasped with the right hand lightly but firmly with the fifth and fourth fingers. The middle finger should hold with less pressure. The index finger will be relatively straight, almost touching the guard. The thumb will gently curve around the grip and rest lightly on top of the third finger. This is not a tight hammer grip, but a more relaxed and slightly angled grip, so that with the last joint of the index finger touching the guard, the web of the thumb will be about an inch away from the guard. With this placement, the handle will lay diagonally across the palm of the hand. The fingers of the left hand will be much the same, and if possible riding fairly high on the handle, preferably with the pommel of the sword cradled in the heel of the left hand and the little finger. If this feels very uncomfortable, go ahead and slide the left hand down so that it rests against the right hand, European broadsword style. For some actors, I've suggested that in order to keep a better grip on the weapon they use a modified golfing putter's grasp, with the left index finger interlocking with the right fifth finger. But as soon as the sword feels more natural, it is better to switch to a grasp in which there is a good two inch distance between the hands.

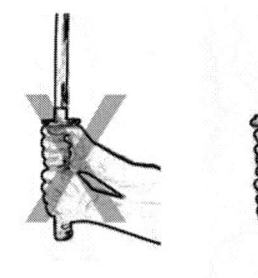

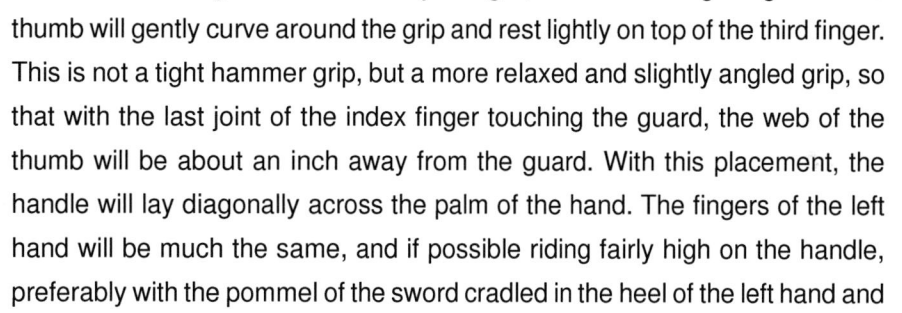

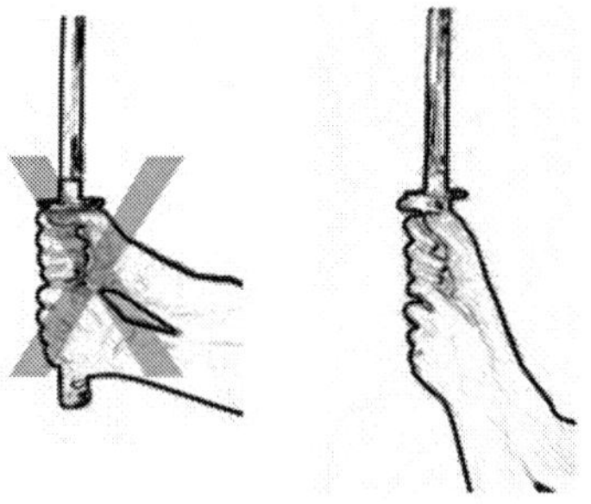

The wrists, elbows, and knees should be slightly bent so as to relieve any tension. One foot (either one) will be slightly in front of the other in a natural stance, usually with the toes of the lead foot pointing directly at the opponent and the trailing foot slightly turned out, but no more than 45 degrees from center. The balance on the feet should be about a 50-50 distribution. Hold the sword so that the pommel is about six inches away from the body and the blade is pointed forward with the tip at roughly shoulder height and to either side of your partner, not directly in line. The upper body must be completely relaxed, shoulders back, and the head must seem to float on the neck, but with the chin slightly tucked in to give better peripheral vision of the opponent's feet.

Moving with the sword.

Whether standing or moving, there must always be a straight line from the top of head to the center of hips. Never lean forward from the waist, but instead initiate forward movement from the center (the "tanden") and then let the feet catch up. This way you land at the same time that your attack arrives, and are perfectly balanced as you complete the move.

Attacking with the sword

As the katana was not built as a bashing weapon, the fighting style is lighter, quicker, and more subtle than medieval broadsword work. This is a concept difficult for American actors to grasp, made even more difficult if they have watched Japanese sword movies made during the last forty years. The "chop-saki" B grade movies have the actors flail away at each other as though they are holding aluminum bats, which in a way they were. If we are trying for a more realistic look to the fight, we'll want to remember that the true Japanese sword had a very strong cutting edge but also a fairly brittle spine, so blocking with the sword was to be avoided if at all possible.

The attacks themselves had to come in quickly with a minimum of preparation, so we won't do the broadsword big prep a' la "Casey at the Bat", pulling the sword all the way back to the shoulder before each strike. Instead, the cut will come directly from the en guard position. The left hand begins the forward movement, pushing the hilt toward the target. At the same time, the right hand gently pulls the handle, which sharply pulls the tip of the sword back. Almost immediately, the right hand changes direction, pushing the hilt towards the target, overtaking the left hand. This second part of the movement is what quickly brings the tip of the sword to the cut position. Both arms will be almost fully extended at the end of the attack.

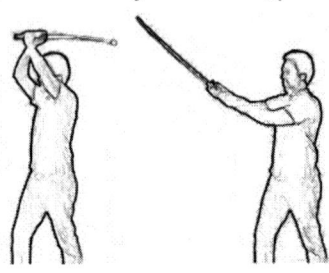

It is interesting to note that real fighting with the katana has many of the same elements that are found in stage combat. The samurai were taught to deliver the energy of the cut using mainly the momentum generated by the hips and torso but very little arm, shoulder, or upper body power. Never grip too tightly when attacking, and allow the hands to remain supple during the swinging movement. Only at the last second should there be a sudden tight grasping of the weapon at the very moment that the attack is blocked or we risk dropping the sword. Although both hands are involved, they each have slightly different functions. It is the left hand that actually delivers the cut, the right hand that guides the tip to the target. In order to do so, we have to allow the left hand to take up 60% of the weight of the sword, instead of a 50/50 distribution.

In order to maintain control of the sword, and to allow our partner to easily see the incoming attack, the blade is going to move back during its preparation for attack much slower than the actual forward motion of the attack itself. So practice with the sword until you can get the left moving forward at one speed, and the right hand doing its two motions at two different speeds. Back slowly, forward faster. At the final moment of the cut, the right hand squeezes a bit, with the thumb "pushing" slightly "into" the tsuba, giving the blade a snappy finish to its action.

Cuts, thrusts and blocks are all performed to the same five basic target points as in broadsword or rapier stage combat. [It is interesting to note that horizontal cuts to the flanks are a modern fabrication for samurai style swordplay, but they are now accepted as normal even in the most tradition-bound Japanese schools, so we can certainly feel free to add them to our choreography.] What we can also add are some of the deflections of attack which is seen in true swordwork with katanas. Naturally, we don't want to have the actors deflect and cut in one terrifying motion - far too dangerous. But we can angle many of the cuts so that instead of meeting the opposing blade at 90 degrees, the blade will come in at only 45 degrees, glance off, and then move safely away from his partner by the same number of degrees. The attack of course stays on the same side of the defender, but continues its path from high to low or vice versa. This will require a great deal of wrist control. These kinds of attacks are also more difficult to see for the defender, for they will look initially the same as a simple diagonal attack.

If we want to add one more level of authenticity to the fight, we'll have our actors turn the wrists when they block, so that they meet the incoming force with the back edge of the blade, not the true edge nor with the flat. The samurai would never choose to risk damage to the razor sharp edge by allowing another weapon to chip at it, and he would be only too aware that a strike along the flat could snap the blade in half. The back edge, on the other hand, has plenty of meat on it, and can absorb a lot of punishment. [A direct overhead vertical cut is difficult to block in this manner, but a trained samurai would find it wiser to avoid such an attack rather than block it in any case.]

Knife Fights

The use of a knife in a stage fight is supposed to increase the level of suspense for the audience, but unfortunately it rarely does. I just never get the feeling that the actors portray the real feeling of lethality that a knife fight creates.

The three scenes often seen are from *West Side Story*, *A View From the Bridge*, and *Rebel Without a Cause*. But for a look at an exciting knife fight, take a look at the film *From Here to Eternity*.

Here's an exercise you might find useful. When I'm having trouble having young actors develop a sense of fear within the fight, I pass out black felt-tip markers instead of the prop knives. Sometimes it helps increase a level of real tension.

By the way, here's a good spot to repeat my warning on using retractable knives - DON'T. It is not possible to use a retractable knife and keep your actors safe from harm. The blades sometimes don't retract - even on knives that are superbly built and in excellent working condition. If the blade presses even slightly against the inner shaft of the grip, the blade will not retract, and you get one actor impaled with a blunt stick. If I could I would outlaw these things.

There are two ways of grabbing a knife or dagger. The one we see in most knife fights is the overhand grip, that it to say holding the knife as we do a screwdriver, with the blade controlled by the thumb and forefinger. This makes sense because it gives the fighter the greatest amount of distance under his control. The only drawback to this grasp is that it is a little weak at the wrist, so for an especially strong thrust the grasp may need to shift to something that looks like a hammer grip. This overhand grip is the one used by most people who consider themselves dangerous with a knife, those who expect to face their opponents.

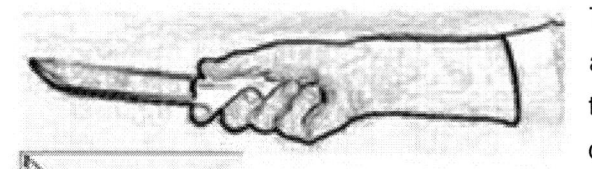

As that opponent is probably also holding a knife, the torso tends to round out somewhat so as to keep as far away from danger as possible. The legs of course will be slightly bent for better balance and ease of movement. Less obvious, but more important, is that the knife arm will be slightly bent, allowing for a quick thrust. The non-knife hand is actively engaged, ready to punch, grab, or block the opponent.

The underhand grip has the blade coming out of the bottom of the fist. This grip is used by the two extremes of knife users - either the opportunistic novice or the highly trained warrior. The novice usually has grabbed the knife with the intention of raising the knife up and then bringing it down in a severe stabbing arc, almost always against an unarmed or distracted victim. As such, there is no need to worry about distance, and the body often moves in very close indeed (think of the movie "Psycho").

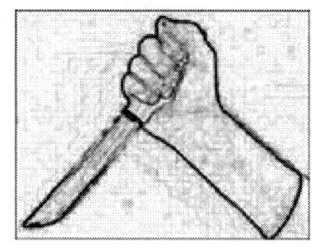

The highly trained fighter by contrast has grabbed the knife with a looser grasp, more like a reverse French foil grip so as to stab or thrust or cut or even let the blade rest against the forearm to use as a parrying surface. From this basic grasp he can shift back and forth from a tight reverse hammer grip for thrusting, to a tight reverse French grip for blocking and slashing. This is a very modern style of fighting taught first to special forces units, "commandos", during the post Vietnam era, and has the look and feel of Chinese martial arts, but stripped down to its most utilitarian. While the novice will have the knife in the dominant hand, the warrior will hold it in the other hand, leaving the dominant free to punch or grab the opponent. This style of fighting is very advanced, and for stage must only be attempted under the direct supervision of a very experienced instructor.

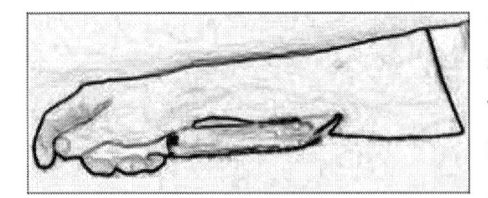

For cutting and slashing attacks, go back to the section on sword fighting, which is really much the same as knife fighting except for the distance between the actors. But because of the nature of a knife fight, there isn't going to be the same feeling of a back-and-forth command of weapons. Indeed, trying to pick off a knife attack with another knife as one would in a sword fight strains believability to the breaking point. In a typical stage knife fight, there will be very few actual cuts and thrusts, most of the action being evasions of slashes and feint attacks, with the intent of trying to keep the opponent off-balance mentally while setting up a kill shot. Many choreographers will use the closeness of the fight to introduce unarmed techniques - strikes, kicks, and throws - to help draw out the fight and provide more storytelling opportunities. Other techniques, such as traps and binds, should not be attempted unless taught by an experienced instructor. These are advanced techniques, and not because they are difficult. As a matter of fact, they are very simple to perform and very believable. But the margin of error in performing them is exceptionally small. A slight variation in arm placement can easily dislocate a shoulder or hyperextend an elbow.

The knife fight itself should have a "jittery" look, as though the knife blades could bring fiery death if it should even happen to touch someone. I mentioned earlier that I once had a heck of a time doing the choreography for a high school production of *West Side Story*. Try as they might, they just couldn't convey that sense of danger required for the rumble. So I finally made sure that they all arrived to one rehearsal wearing their regular good clothes. Then I passed out black felt-tip markers instead of the prop weapons and had them go through the fight. Finally, I got the panicky look of terror that we needed as the dancers tried to protect their clothes from permanent damage.

Here are some elements that can add a little bit of safety to knife fight techniques:

•	Show & Go. Because the actors are going to be standing much closer together than they would in a sword fight, it is imperative that they learn the concept of show & go when thrusting and slashing or cutting.

The idea is to give your partner a strong enough visual cue before the knife gets within touching range. As with sword work, people will forget a move now and then, so these extra cues can be enough to clue-in the actor as to what the next move is. They also actually help the audience, so that they get a split-second glimpse of what the danger is before the attack either fails or succeeds. Granted, it's a slight exaggeration of normal movement, but one that helps the show, so we keep it.

- Naturally there will be many times that the aggressor will need to close distance when attempting a slash, so to our "show & go" we add a "step & prep". The aggressor takes a step in towards the victim, *then* preps for the cut by extending the arm fully to the side (letting the audience in on what is about to happen). Be sure to make eye contact on the step in. The next part is crucial. The aggressor's cue for *initiating* the swing is when the victim begins his *reaction*. None of this "go ahead and swing; I'll duck in time." That's how actors get smacked in the head.

- Thrust out of distance. This one is easy. A simple one-two movement - show the knife by merely extending the arm and pointing to the intended target, and *then* take the step forward to close the distance and finish the attack. Sound familiar? Right, it's the Show & Go

- Thrust in-distance. Of course, when the actors are already within reach of each other and stepping in is not appropriate, we need to have a different prep. The "show" in this case is pulling the knife hand back to the hip with a little bit of a twist of that shoulder and hip, away from your partner. Then the hip and shoulder turn again towards the victim, leading the arm as it is extended.

- Blocking the knife. Some actors take the swordplay analogy too literally and think that they can engage the weapons blade to blade, blocking knife attacks with their own knife. Nice thought, but the look is hopelessly unrealistic. When a knife attack is blocked, it is either lightly batted away with the free hand or firmly blocked with either forearm. But it is not the knife itself which is engaged, only the knife hand or arm.

- For the bat-away, merely touch the attacking knife hand with the back or the palm of your free hand. The knife hand is not slapped away; this is a deflection only. Even though the look is to really slap the knife away, we only need to make minimal contact and then let the aggressor continue the pantomime of having his arm knocked off target.

- For the forearm block, again look back at the swordplay section. The arms will take the part of the sword, using obvious perpendicular blocks forearm to forearm.

When the time comes to do some virtual damage with the knife, I've already made it clear that a retractable knife should never be used. So what to do? Getting help from a fight instructor would be the first choice, because he or she will be able to set up a very realistic stabbing in less than a quarter of an hour. If you need to attempt any of the following without assistance, go very slowly and try a hundred variations from every conceivable angle until you get something consistently safe and believable.

- The upstage stab.

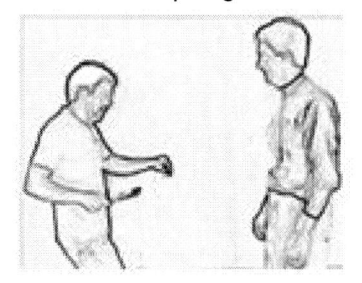

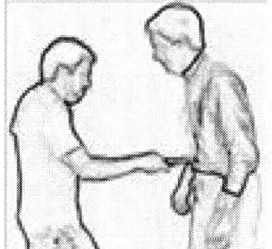

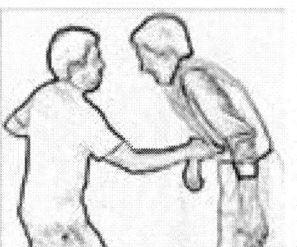

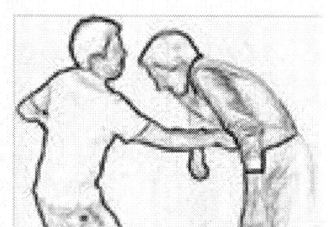

This is a variation of the old sword under the arm that has been parodied to death, but if done correctly is still very effective, especially if you have a bit of distance from the audience. The actors stand in profile to the audience and the aggressor merely stabs at the area of the victim slightly upstage of the victim's body. The hand can still be aimed at the body, so long as the tip is pointing just upstage. If the victim can reach out slightly with his downstage arm, it will help mask the knife. Don't let the blade go beyond the back of the victim; that will only get a laugh from the audience.

The reaction of the victim is what makes or breaks this illusion, for the reaction to both the stab and the pull out of the blade must be made to look as though the stab is to the center of the body, not upstage. Too often the victim turns slightly upstage, into the real arm movement, instead to selling the illusion. And notice how, even though the illustration above is from the upstage side, the knife still disappears from view blocked by the victim's upstage arm.

- Accepting the blade.

This is the most difficult illusion to pull off, but also the safest, because only the victim has control of the action. This is used for a direct stab to the stomach and is especially useful when the knife blade is relatively long and difficult to hide. This stab would begin at a bit of distance, requiring the attacker to show, go, and then step in. During the go, which is a thrust, the victim can reach out as though to stop the attack. In reality, he is locking wrist to wrist so as to guide the attacking knife into the intended target. The aggressor can use the victim's distracting hand to hide the fact that he has turned his own hand sideways, turning the blade safely away. Sounds hard to do? It is, which is why an experienced fight instructor is needed..

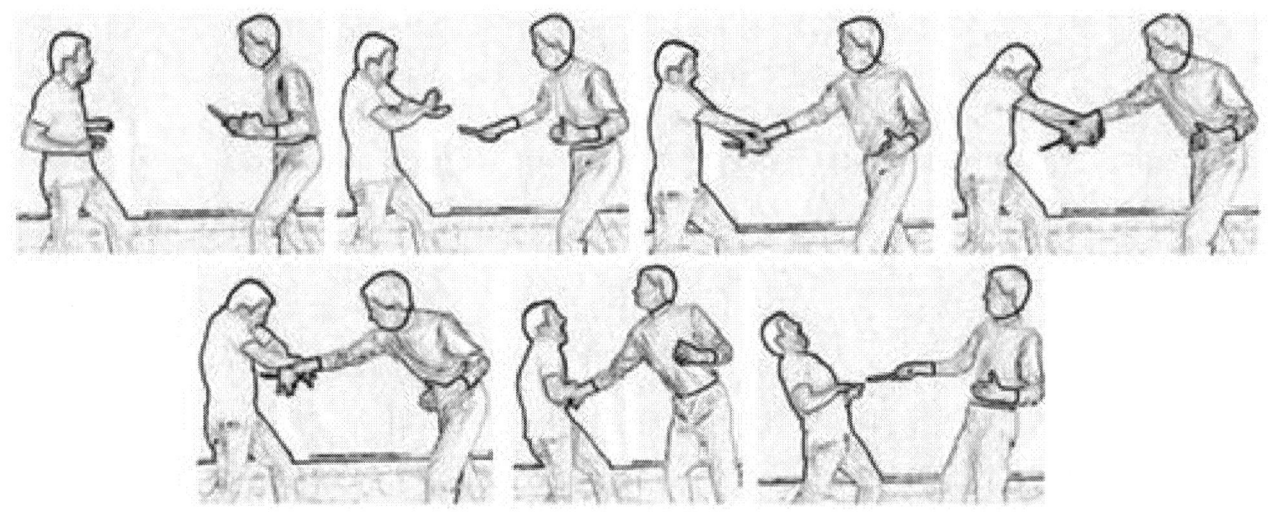

- In-distance punch stab. This is the one which is most commonly used. It's fast and easy so long as you have a lot of spotters to check for audience sight lines. Go back to the unarmed section for the techniques used for the stomach punch. The punch stab is done the same way, except that at the moment the knife has disappeared from the audience's view, the aggressor turns his wrist so the knife blade can be pressed sidewise along the stomach, the tip pointing safely away. It almost doesn't mater where the actors are facing or standing so long as the entire knife hand disappears from audience view during the stab.

- "Retracting" knife. While working on a production of *No Exit*, I had to have the actor do multiple stabs with the victim being only feet away from the first row. Since I wouldn't allow the use of a retractable knife, we needed to mix up the look of the staged stabs so that the audience wouldn't be able to see how any one stab was performed. The "retracting" knife bit requires a knife which has a very small guard and an extremely blunt blade. The actors stand very close together, as in the punch stab above, but in this case they align themselves so that the stabbing takes place in full view of the audience. The stabbing arm must have the palm facing upstage and the back of the hand facing downstage, in effect hiding the handle. The blade is pointed at the victim, and the blade tip might even be touching the victim just before the stab. The handle is gripped very loosely. For the stab, the knife stays in the same place in space while the hand travels forward into the stomach, grasping the blade. After the appropriate victim reaction, the hand releases the blade and pulls back and grabs the handle.

upstage view

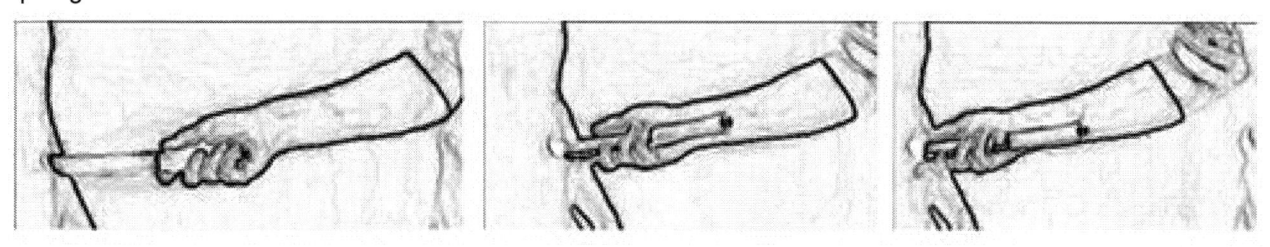

All of this has to be done without the audience seeing the fingers grip, release, and re-grip, with great attention to making sure that the handle is blocked from view by the aggressor's forearm. (It's also nice if the attacker doesn't drop the knife.) When done correctly, the audience is completely convinced that they have seen a blade actually stab someone.

This simulation obviously violates my own cardinal rule about never pointing any weapon at any person at any time for any reason. And, just as obviously, it carries its own dangers. I include this here, with apologies, to show that is always a way around a seemingly intractable problem, and sometimes the choice is between the lesser of two evils. But in this case it is both safer and more effective than an actual retractable knife.

- Back stab.

A lot of murder mysteries have this, and it is remarkably simple to do, being a slight variation on the punch stab. Usually the victim is full front and the aggressor comes up from behind, raising the knife nice and high so the audience can see it.

When the knife is brought down for the stab, it is aimed straight down with the tip pointing to the ground, instead of arcing towards the victim. So that the victim knows when to react, the aggressor merely touches the victim using a slightly extended thumb or finger of the stabbing hand, the knife blade angled away from the victim. But since the aggressor's left hand can provide the tap instead, the path of the knife blade need never be any closer than 12" away from the victim, for, as always, the audience has no depth perception. For his part, the victim needs to think carefully about the reaction, and not just collapse down. Rather, there has to be included a push out of the chest, keeping in line with the imagined path of the stab.

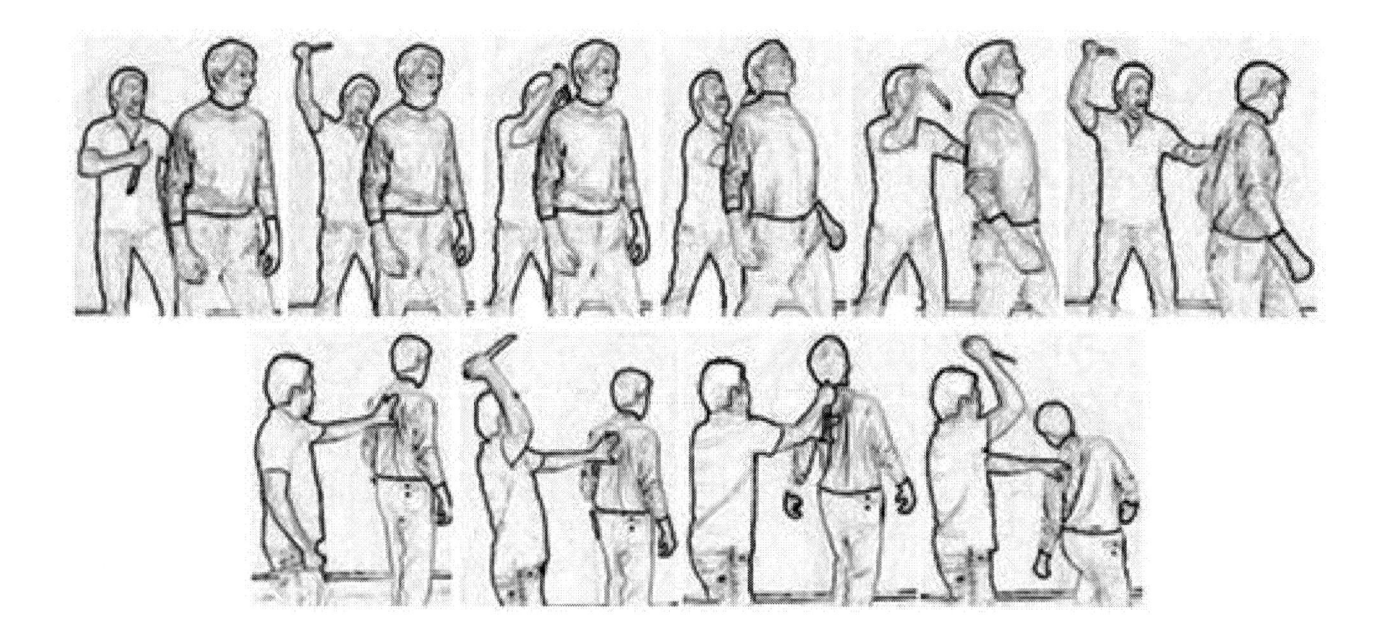

- Self stab. Especially made for Juliet's death scene, but of course can be used for any show which requires a suicide by stabbing to the stomach. The easy way to go is for her to use the upstage stab as described above, but in this case the audience is staring too intently at Juliet to be fooled by that. When they have this much time to focus, they gain back a lot of the depth perception they normally lose. So the following variation can be far more believable and dramatic.

The actor faces the audience and gives them a good look at the knife. Grabbing the handle with both hands, the blade is slapped against the forearm at the moment of the thrust. The hand higher up on the hilt covers the turning motion of the nearer hand, blocking the twist of the wrist. For more specifics on this illusion read the *Romeo & Juliet* entry in the **Violence on Stage** section towards the end of this book.

- Cutting.

Again, I refer you back to the earlier sword fighting section for the details, but the basics again include first laying the flat of the blade along the part of the victim to be "cut" and then drawing the knife's [dull] edge across or better yet back towards the aggressor, of course using the lightest, weakest grasp possible so as to remove any real pressure on the victim.

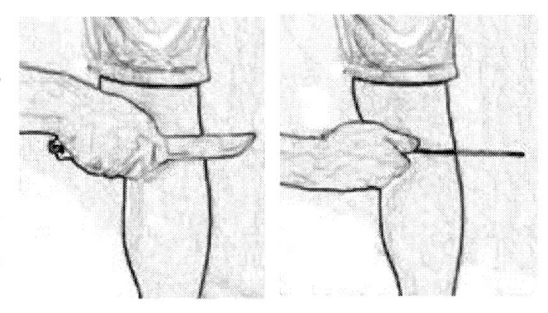

- Throat Slash. This is where most directors want to see blood. But blood FX knives are notoriously unreliable, and often drip before the slash. So I prefer using a regular (dulled) knife, and keeping the blood in the aggressor's control. Since this is a close-in moment, the action itself needs to be performed *slowly*. This makes it both more horrifying and safer.

For most throat slashes, both actors are full front, with the aggressor standing behind the victim. The arm holding the knife goes all the way across the victim first, and the aggressor's thumb gently lands at the throat just under the base of the victim's jawbone. The slow slash is done with only the aggressor's thumb making contact with the throat. Blood may not be necessary, but if the director insists on it, it can be applied by the aggressor. How? Somewhere on the set hide a small open jar of a sticky, viscous blood mixture (for this, often just a little lipstick mixed with baby oil is all you need). At some point before the slash, the aggressor merely scoops some blood out with thumbnail. For the slash, he merely paints the victim's throat as the action is simulated. With a little practice, he can even get some of the blood from her neck onto the knife blade during the slash. The knife will then act as a secondary paintbrush, leaving a wonderfully straight line that the audience will believe is a knife cut. The very slowness of the movement only adds to the realism.

Traps & Locks

There is a whole raft of illusion designed to look as though one actor has immobilized another by either twisting a limb and painfully applying pressure to a joint. Sometimes they are included in a knife fight to allow the actors to get in close for a strike, throw or disarm. Most of these are taken from aikido and its parent discipline jujitsu. Although simple to perform, the margin for error is very small and so the possibility of doing real damage to the victim is very large. It only takes an accidental extra inch of force against an elbow or wrist to lead to some nasty ligament tears. For that reason they are to be considered advanced techniques, and we must relegate them to the list of those that must only be aught under the direct tutelage of an on-sight instructor.

If it should come to pass that for some reason your actors insist that they need to have one in their fight and that they know what they are doing, offer this challenge. Have the victim stand alone and get himself into the lock/trap. The aggressor must do nothing; standing three feet away, he only demonstrates his portion of the simulation for his only job is to provide the pantomimed justification for the illusion. If you like what you see, let them come within touching distance. But even then, it is ridiculously easy for the aggressor to accidently twist a tendon beyond it's capability, so be very leery of including these simulations without expert instruction.

The Butterfly Knife

It's very rare when a show will have one or more of the fighters use a butterfly knife, and the only reason to do so is get that moment when the character pulls out the knife and goes through a flashy show of opening it. In the right hands, it's quite impressive, for the parts of the knife flicker and flutter as the actor waves it about. It's a special skill, not terribly difficult to learn but it has no practical application in a fight. It's just there for show, kind of like baton twirling or those silly nunchuck moves. It not really a part of stage combat, or a real knife fight for that matter, but if for some reason you want this in your show, here are some tips.

Keep in mind that there are really only four moves you can do with a butterfly knife: while holding one of the handles, you can swing it open, swing it closed, twirl the free handle left, and twirl it right. That's it. If you can do that, you've already mastered the basics. The rest of the time is going to be spent combining those moves into as many variations as possible so that it appears that the knife is doing a lot more than that. But that's all just illusion, for you can only open, close, twirl left, and twirl right.

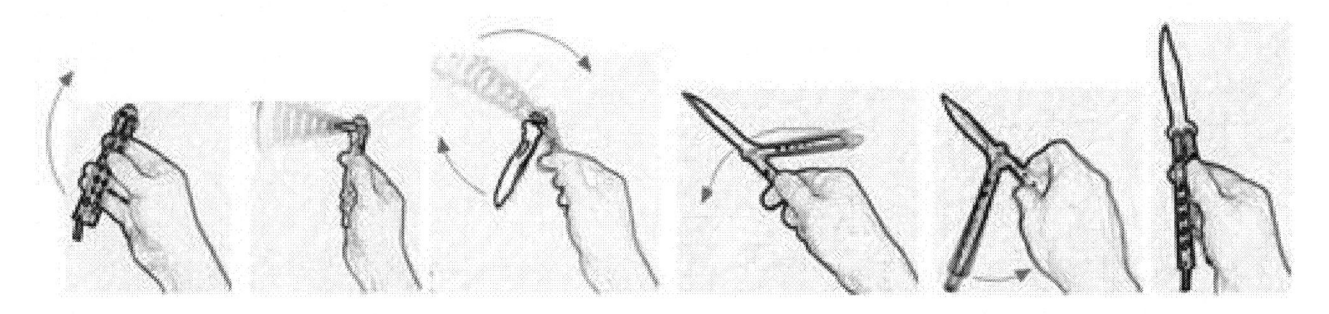

Of course, the artistry comes in the way you combine the moves while not rapping your knuckles. Opening and closing the knife as it spins in a half-circle twirl (shown above) has one look. Starting in one direction as you open and then reversing as you close has another. So does opening and closing as the hand turns upside down. So does opening and closing left to right compared to forward and back. I enjoy working in a few moves that borrow from cape techniques of bull fighting, and naturally each person will find his or her own style. But no matter what the finished routine looks like, the one constant is that the weapon always remains in motion, never completely closing or opening until the final pose. By working all of the geometric planes, you can really disrupt the audience's ability to focus on the movement and identify which is the blade and which is the free handle.

Quarterstaff

Truly the most versatile of weapons, and the one least seen on stage because there aren't many shows that require them. But remember that quarterstaff techniques are directly applicable to halberd and other hafted weapon fighting, so apart from the obvious Robin Hood / Little John fight there are many other period and even modern setting plays that can use the same moves. For example, assuming you can find props sturdy enough, these moves are the same a soldier would use when fighting with a long musket or rifle with a fixed bayonet.

If you find yourself winging it here, putting together a fight without the benefit of expert help, keep the moves as simple as possible. Getting knocked with one of these things hurts a lot more than getting struck with a broadsword. [And of course, always disarm a weapon *away* from the camera or audience!]

Shortform/Longform

There are two ways of holding, and therefore using, the staff. In shortform, grab the staff so as to divide it into thirds. Push with the right hand and pull with the left, and there you have a right handed attack. Push with the left and pull with the right, and there's a left handed attack. Compare this push and pull motion to the concept of chambering discussed in martial arts unarmed fighting.

Longform uses more distance, and you grab the staff in the center and then at the quarter [by the way, that's *not* the origin of the name quarterstaff - see pg. 130]. Whereas in shortform the hands stay relatively static on their positions, in longform the hands are in constant movement. Shortform is simple and intuitive; longform requires a lot of training until it feels comfortable. Mixing the two styles within a fight provides for exciting changes in distance and rhythm.

It is normally taught that the right hand holds onto the staff with the palm up and the left hand is palm down, but obviously that's just a starting point: make whatever changes you need to make when working out the fight. There is no right or wrong, just what works and feels secure and comfortable.

There is no consistent front and back to the staff, so whichever end is closest to the victim is called the fore end, and whichever is away is the butt end, and this of course will change with nearly every move. One thing that never changes is the distance you need around other actors. There is always a lot of weapon traveling around, above and behind you each time you make an attack.

Attack points

Just as with the sword, the staff can thrust or cut, although the cutting is really more bashing than slicing, but the idea is the same. The attack points are a bit different, and we have a lot more of them. The cuts are head, crotch, right and left flank, and all four diagonals. The intended target for all eight cuts is the exact center of the body, between the navel and the solar plexus. The job of the actor is to convince the audience that that is what he is intending to strike, although the energy is actually going safely outside the place of the defender's body.

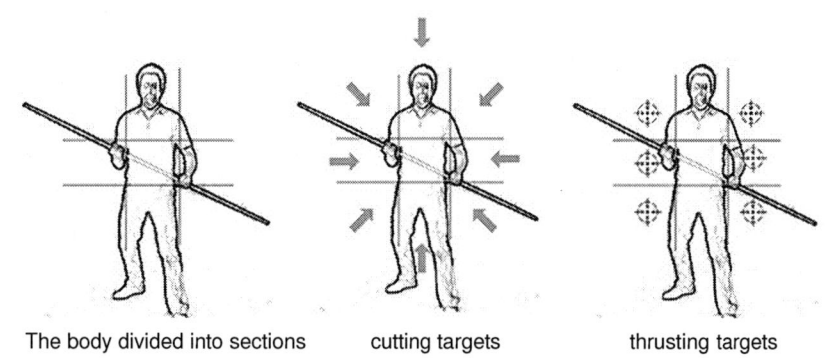

The body divided into sections | cutting targets | thrusting targets

The thrusts are expanded to both flanks, shoulders, and both thighs. Never to the head, never to the knee. As with the sword, the attacks are meant to match the un-exaggerated moves of the defense, meaning that they should land one inch away from the outside plane of the body.

Cutting Attacks in Shortform

These are nearly intuitive moves, but let's go through them anyway. Holding the staff in front of you, parallel to the ground. Keep your hips and chest square to your partner. Push your right hand straight out and your left hand in, all the way to your ribs. That's a right flank cut. [Just as with the swords I'm using right and left from the aggressor's perspective.] And the beauty is that the fore end stops before it can actually hit your partner because the butt end is stopped by your own body. Isn't that wonderful? The sweeping attacks can look very powerful when the slam to a halt by hitting your own body, and the audience thinks that it was stopped by a very powerful block!

Left flank cut? I'm sure you're there already - keeping the staff parallel to the floor, left arm straight out, right hand goes back to your ribs.

Right high diagonal - Right hand pushes out to shoulder level, left hand pulls in to the left hip.

Left high diagonal - Left hand pushes out to shoulder level, right hand pulls in to the right hip.

Right low diagonal - Right hand pushes out to thigh level, left hand pulls in to left shoulder.

Left low diagonal - Left hand pushes out to thigh level, right hand pulls in to right shoulder.

Crotch - Either hand pushes straight out toward the crotch, scooping up, while the other hand brings the butt end right next to the same side ear. (You'd be amazed how many actors have to be specifically told to do this or they will hit themselves in the head.)

Vertical Head - This is a little different than the others, so pay attention. Either hand pushes out to a spot just above the forehead of your partner and the other hand pulls up tight into the armpit. You see, we need to get a strong look of a real attack on this one, or else it looks more like a punch to the face instead of a big dropping cut from above. So we lift up the back end a bit so that the front end comes in high. So how do we keep our partner safe? By keeping the lead (attacking) hand no lower than eye level and the draw hand no higher than armpit level. That way, it is impossible to strike your partner on the head.

Defenses

Since the attacks all are supposed to look as though they are trying to reach the center of the body, the blocks will start from the center and radiate out. The center of the staff, the part between the hands, will pick off the head, crotch, and flank attacks; The further ends will block the diagonal cuts. These are not hard and fast rules, just really good simple starting points. But no matter what, we always try to have the blocking staff make contact at ninety degrees to the attacking staff.

When using the center of the staff, both arms will extend in the direction of the attack. Now these attacks are coming in sideways, right? So that's where you are going to push, not toward the attacker. Imagine your staff as being a great big sliding door, pointing straight up and moving side to side for the flank cuts, parallel to the floor and lifting or lowering for those head and crotch shots.

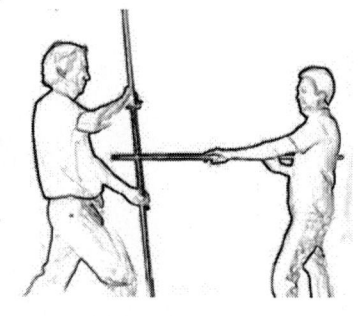

When using the ends, again mainly for the diagonal cuts, the hand on the side of where the attack is coming from will pull in close to the body while the far hand extends and crosses in front. This swings that end around easily to pick-off the attack. If the attack is coming in high, the near hand goes low and in - at hip level. If the attack comes in low, the nearest hand goes high and in - at shoulder level. The far hand is the one that crosses in front of the body and gently points to the incoming attack. Try these a few times and you'll see that the mechanics of the diagonal defense are very similar to that of the diagonal attack. The only difference is that the leading hand, instead of straightening and pushing forward, bends at the elbow and the hand crosses in front of the body. This does two wonderful things. First it keeps the defense close to the defender, which increases the look of danger. Secondly, it maintains the important look of the defender trying to protect the center of his body and absorbing the energy of the incoming threat, adding to the believability of the attack.

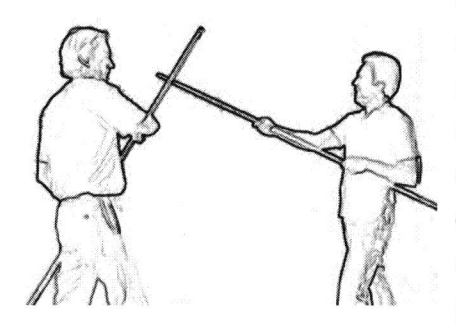

Notation

The diagram that we used for sword fighting doesn't work too well with the staff fight. Since there are more attack points, we need a slightly more involved diagram. So we can use the same tic-tac-toe drawing that we used earlier to divide the body into attack segments.

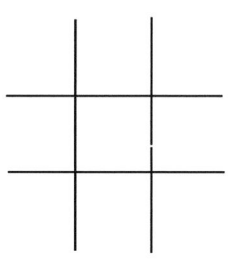

The center square is any shot directly to the body, and this should be rare or nonexistent. So instead, we use the center square to note any "pay-off" moves - trips, punches, kicks, what have you. Just like before, attacks are shown with a plus (+) and defenses with a minus (-), but now we have to also include the L and R designations for which ever hand performs the attack or block. The left and right open square are for flank attacks, the high and low squares are head and crotch shots, and of course the corner squares are all of the diagonal attacks. Here is a very simple phrase, and I'm showing both partners' movements. Try it out.

	+2L	+4R -7R
-5		+1R
-6R		-3L

Side A

	-4R +7	-2
-1L(h)		+5L
+3L		-6R

Side B

As you can tell by trying it out, the first four moves of side A are very straight forward moves using alternating hands. For move 5 there is no indication of which hand to use, for since the staff is pointing straight up

353

and down for defense against a flank attack, and I didn't care which hand is high or low. Note how moving from 6 to 7, making both blocks in sequence with the right hand, it makes a natural circle. It's always nice to smooth out such moves that naturally link together and perform them as one continuous motion.

Side B starts off with a defense against a flank attack, but here I specifically want the left hand high, so the notation has that reminder. Why so specific here? Well, it makes the swing up to the second move a little less jerky than if the right hand had started high on the first move. Moves 3 and 4 are natural enough, but for 5 the left hand is attacking. But when you do that move to the right with the left hand, you have to pull your right hand in to your left, leaving the arms crossed uncomfortably - and on purpose. The hands uncross for the defense on 6, and can lead in a nice big sweeping circle into move 7.

Adding Longform

Longform technique is all draw and slide. As you do the moves, just keep repeating, draw and slide, draw and slide.

Just to start, hold onto the staff with the right hand at the half way point, and the left hand at a quarter of the way down. For now simply hold the staff parallel to the ground. Pull the left hand in to your left hip and extend the right arm out, just as in short form, and you have executed an attack to the flank, right? And at quite a distance, since now you can strike a target about four feet away. But for the next attack you just can't pull the right hand back and push with the left, because your left hand is holding on to the stubby end of the quarterstaff. So if you want to strike to the other flank, you're going to have to ... draw and slide.

Leave your right hand where it is, out in front of you, and loosen the grip. With your left hand draw the staff back until your right hand can grab the far quarter. Grasp tight with the right hand and pull it in to your right hip. At the same time, relax the left grip while you push your left hand forward, allowing it to slide down the staff until it reaches the center, and you've executed a left hand longform attack to the opposite flank! Now keep your left hand out there and try for another flank attack back to the first side. Right hand draws the staff back, left hand graps the far quarter, and then as it pulls in to the left hip, the right hand pushes forward as it slides to the center. Voila! a longform attack to the right. Practice several times, draw and slide, draw and slide, quarter and center, quarter and center.

Try going to the other targets. You'll find that the attacks to the lower diagonals might bounce off the ground at first, and that the crotch shot is nearly impossible to perform in a direct line, but you get the idea here.

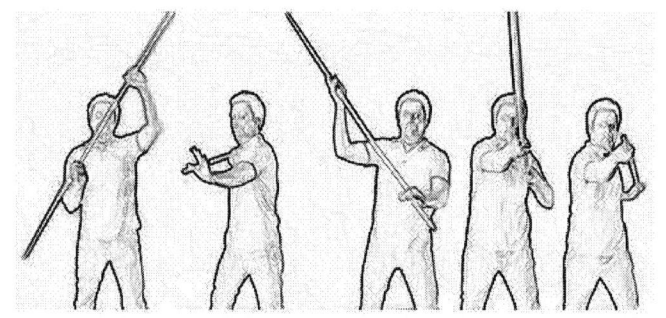

Starting with hands at the "thirds"... left hand slides forward...right slides to center ...left pulls staff back...

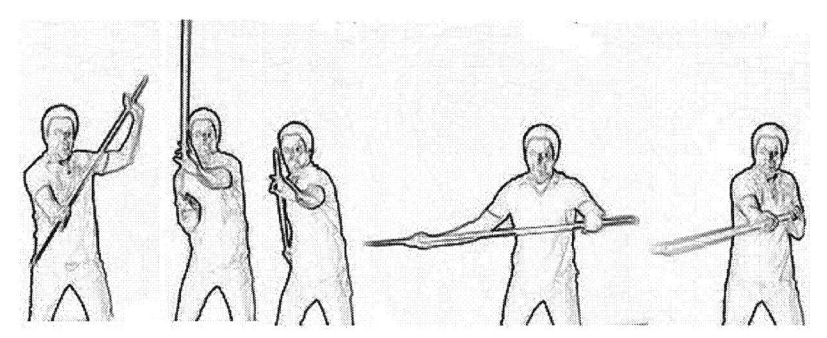

left hand attacks, pushes forward ...sliding to center ...right hand pulls staff back, then attacks forward...sliding to center.

Defenses in Longform

Technically, you can use the longform attack techniques to perform long distance blocks. Just as in short form, the defense is merely the attack move but extended so that it crosses in front of the body, "protecting" the center and then making the block. I have seen many fights choreographed this way, with longform block defending against longform attacks, for this is the way that the Society of American Fight Directors teaches it ... but why? I mean, think about it, who is the defender defending if the contact point of the staffs is four feet in front of him? If he is using a longform style block it means that he really had to reach forward with his weapon just to make contact with the attack, which makes no sense. Whether the block is made or not didn't matter because the attack could never have reached the defender in the first place. If someone is that far out of distance when attacking, there is no threat, therefore no need to block. If the longform attack can actually reach the defender, the appropriate shortform defense is the one to use. You always want to keep the incoming attack as close to you as possible when using any weapon if you want the audience to believe in your fight.

Other Impact Weapons

Shields/Bucklers

The use of defensive shields in real sword fights usually turned into literally "trading blows". First one person would strike, then the other, back and forth until someone would not block correctly. That missed block would translate into a pretty severe injury, and then quickly followed by the winner bashing the loser into submission or death. Men of taller stature and of greater arm strength won over shorter and slighter warriors. Always.

That kind of fighting is pretty boring for stage, so we allow for combination attacks which, although not historically based, are a lot more exciting. Linking together two or three attacks and blocking not only with the shield but also the sword can open up the look of the fight until it can approach the dynamics of the theatrical rapier fight. With that in mind, the fight can show all of the strategy and character development that we need for theatre.

The best way to learn how to use the shield is by first not using one. Think of blocking an incoming cut using only your forearm and you'll quickly appreciate that the best way to do so is to meet the sword with the arm perpendicular to the sword's approach. If the sword is being swung parallel to the floor, you naturally would point your hand either straight up or straight down. If a vertical head cut is coming down at you, then your arm will protect your head best by forming a barrier across where the sword would travel.

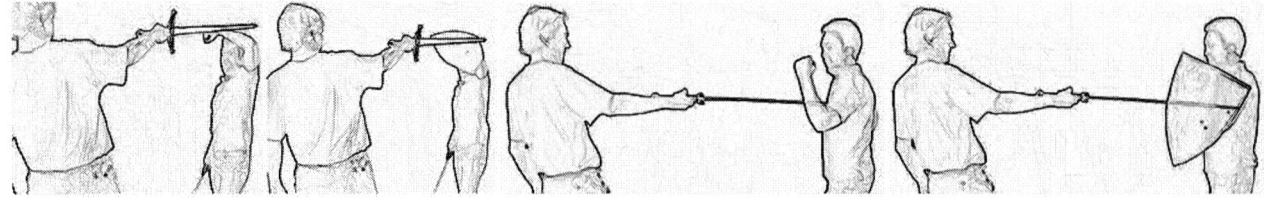

I realize this sounds ridiculously simple. After all, who would try to block a sword by lining up the arm parallel to it? The chances of lining the two up correctly is almost nil, and to block perpendicular to the sword makes perfect instinctual sense. The reason I mention the obvious here is that so many people forget all of this once the shield is strapped on.

Most shields have a strap that holds onto the forearm near the elbow and then a handle onto which the left hand can grasp. The shield looks so imposing that at first it seems that it doesn't matter if the arm is up or down or sideways, but after being struck a few times one learns that it matters an awful lot. If the forearm is parallel to the incoming blade and that sword does not hit the very center of the shield, the sword will push on the shield, spinning it around your arm. At best, the shield will bounce into your leg or chest. At worst, the sword can skip off of the shield and slice into your face. Arm position matters.

The shield can also be used as a weapon, both with the flat and with the edge. But although the techniques are very simple to execute, it would be best if they are only taught under the direct supervision of a competent instructor. Unlike the sword, the shield is a close-in weapon and the force of the impact can knock someone out, break a limb, or shatter a rib. Actors are always in more danger the closer they are to each other.

Bucklers are different beasties all together. A buckler is a very small shield, usually only about one foot in diameter, held from its center by a small handle. It is not a passive defense weapon as is the common shield, but an aggressive weapon used to attack the opponent's sword and thereby providing an opening for an attack with your own sword or dagger. One punches with the buckler instead of simply absorbing an attack. Indeed, with the buckler being so small, a traditional block would be pretty lucky and most times ineffective. In sword and buckler fights, the sword is often used in conjunction with the buckler to make the block, and then the buckler used to push down the opponent's sword as you follow up with your own attack using the sword.

Found Objects

In so many shows, a prop on the set is picked up and used as an impromptu weapon. Usually these fights have very few moves; most commonly a single swinging motion that either connects, misses, or is blocked by the victim.

There are two important aspects to keep in mind. First, the aggressor must be in complete control of the prop and how it moves from beginning to end. Go back to the sword section to learn how to swing a prop safely, for the victim must be absolutely safe for every second of every action. If the swing is going to be blocked, the attacker needs to learn how to perform a sword "cut". If the swing misses, then you are looking for the section of "slashes". Secondly, the construction standards for that item must be much higher than they are for most props. A prop that can break is also one that can cut an actor.

The term "found objects" is a catch-all phrase which includes items that aren't normally considered weapons, but that the character is compelled to use in the heat of action. Some of these were mentioned in the earlier section, so I'll assume that the items you are dealing with have been specifically built for the fight or have been thoroughly checked out and made secure for the safety of the actors. If you have any doubts, don't use the item.

When dealing with a found object in a fight, first spend some time getting to know the item. Find its strengths and weaknesses, find its center of gravity, learn how it can be safely grasped, how it can be thrust or swung. If it begins to slip from your hand, how is it going to turn or tumble? A stuffed doll seems harmless enough, but loose hair can act as a hundred little whips and could lash at someone's eyes. A piece of wood or a bar of steel might be plenty strong for itself, but too strong for the weapons it is going against, so moves might have to be modified. Here are some props I've encountered. From one thing learn ten thousand.

- Fan - There are some very sturdy steel-ribbed folding fans that can be purchased through most martial arts supply houses, and your costumer might be able to re-cover one or even paint it so as to fit the design of the show. Used as a substitute for a dagger in a rapier fight, it adds great visual flair once you get used to snapping it open for key moments and twirling it as an attack or defense. Keep in mind that strong blocks against even a light fencing sword will need to be done with the fan closed.
- Bottle - It has become almost a cliché to have Barrymore use a Champagne bottle in *I Hate Hamlet* or Athos use a bottle of Bordeaux in *The Three Musketeers* as a secondary weapon during at least one of his rapier fights. I like using empty Champagne bottles rather than regular wine or even beer bottles, for the sparkling wine containers are thicker and designed to withstand the much greater pressure that the fizzy wines create.

A bottle works best when the opposing blade is the forgiving and flexible epee blade, and definitely when used primarily as a parrying tool to deflect thrusts, rather than to block cuts. Even if you can have the attacker reduce the power of the cut enough to keep from breaking the glass, your audience will never believe the action. And don't hold the bottle as you would a serious weapon, but rather grab it by the neck as though you are going to pour yourself a glass. Let the base of the bottle simply hang down and swing your arm from side to side to make the parries. This also leaves your character in position to take a swig out of the bottle during the fight for a small comic bit.

If you are using the bottle as a club, read the section a little further below. If you are using a "broken bottle" prop, go back to the knife section. Same actions, different prop.

- Chair - Cane back chairs are the easiest to use due to the light weight and relatively sturdy construction, but be sure and check the item carefully every day to made sure that the wood isn't developing stress fractures. You may also need to reinforce all of the joints as well as the seat.

These things have a strange center of gravity, so work out with the chair for several weeks before incorporating it into the choreography. Swing it, toss it, catch it, lift it, push it, pull it - fully explore how the chair moves through space when you hold onto each leg or by the back, with two hands and then with one.

- Hats - Nice comic bits flow naturally when someone's hat is used in a rapier and dagger fight, but let the costumer and the make-up designer in on your ideas at the very first opportunity. Obviously the costumer is going to have to come up with some sturdy alternatives to what she may have had in mind (she's just going to love you) but why the make-up designer? Hats sometimes need to be secured to hair or wigs for a good fit, and using it for a fight might affect the hair choices. Talk it out early so there are no tech week surprises.

- Trash can lid - I've used it for *West Side Story* and for modern versions of Shakespeare plays. I know it's a bit obvious when the curtain rises and you see a trash can on the set that it's going to find its way into the combat, but it's just too useful in a fight to not include it. It can be used in two ways - grabbed by the edge or by the center handle. If you've been lucky enough to find a steel trash can (they're becoming an endangered species) you'll have to do something about the handle.

That handle on a steel lid is usually free floating or pivoting so it can lay down flat when not in use. So if the lid is to be grabbed from the center and used as a shield, you'll need to replace the grip with a rigid handle, otherwise the shield will be uncontrollable. When you do so, be sure to give yourself a little extra clearance than a normal handle would have so that you don't bruise your knuckles during the fight. Because of the light weight, the movement choices can be a combination of those for the buckler, the shield, and even the dagger by swinging the lid with the edge as the attacking point.

If you grab the lid by the edge, you are limited to swinging the thing either flat or edgewise, which in a real fight are probably the only instinctual moves. Someone will always want to hit someone on the back with the lid, and there is a safe way to do it, *but first get rid of that central handle*. If someone gets hit by it, it's going to hurt mightily. The lid is slightly concave, which is good because it keeps that nasty edge away from the victim. Hold the lid close to your own body and push - not swing - it toward the upstage plane of your partner (assuming he is facing downstage). The lid will swing around of its own accord and make sufficient percussion contact with the victim's back (or better yet, back and upper arm) to sell the illusion. The main point is not to swing your arms around baseball style; you don't need to and that makes the move dangerous.

- Club - Here I'm including any non-articulated, blunt, relatively straight object which is usually at least three times as long as it is wide and can be grasped comfortably with one hand, even if used with two. So this would include clubs, flashlights, walking sticks, baseball bats, musical instruments ... you get the idea. It also includes bottles grabbed in a much more threatening manner than described above in the bottle section. Read the section about using the broadsword and the entire unarmed section to get a thorough grounding on safe technique, and with the club we add one more bit - the strike to the head.

There are two ways to do it, neither of which sends any energy whatsoever towards the victim's head at any time. Both require that the movement of the club travel along a plane safely upstage of the victim. The first is the parallel stance strike, which is very similar to the unarmed jab illusion. Actors are parallel to the proscenium, the aggressor raises and then lowers the club, simulating a strike to the head, but the movement travels along an arc purely upstage of the victim. If this illusion is to work, the club must disappear for only an instant behind the victim's head and then must "bounce" back up into view. Don't leave the club hanging behind the victim for even a nanosecond or the audience will be able to figure out how you did it. This is just like the jab and groin kick simulations in the unarmed section isn't it? Be sure to include the appropriate sound of the strike.

The second strike is the staggered swing, with the aggressor fully upstage of the victim. For this bit, the club travels in a sweeping arc along a plane between the two combatants. The club is not swung in any way toward the victim (that's right, just like the fan kick of the looping face punch simulations). If the club were not in hand, the move would look more as though the aggressor had merely waved to the victim, not swung at him.

The audience will believe both of these illusions because they have no depth perception. We can put the finishing touch by including a contact sound, but this should be done by an off-stage assistant with a couple of blocks of wood. The bit works so well in fact that for one production of T*aming of the Shrew* we had the musician/sound effects guy completely visible to the house, yet they still winced and cried out in commiseration with what they thought they saw. Sound always makes it real.

- Side-Handle Baton - Modern police are well trained in the use of this successor to the old billy club. The addition of the side bar not only adds the possibility of a number of take down and restraining holds, but also converts it from a simple club to a powerful impact weapon.

The side bar baton can either be held by the standard grip and used as a traditional club, or held by the side bar, with the club coming out of the bottom of the fist. In this case the grip is slightly relaxed, allowing the weapon to freely spin in the hand. When the arm is swung side to side, the club swings around at twice that speed, and can easily break someone's ribs or arms. Actors should never use the club this way unless they are safely out of distance. But they can take advantage of this grip by pressing the baton up against the forearm and using it as a very effective blocking tool. From that same position, it can also be used as a punching and elbow striking tool.

- Cloak, Net - The fisherman's net was sometimes used in Roman gladiatorial games as a secondary weapon held in the left hand with a trident held in the right. The intent would have been to snag the opponent's weapon or helmet and then run him through with the trident. For stage, most of the moves are going to be big sweeps that are evaded by the victim and smaller circular sweeps used as defense against thrusts. Keep the moves simple and few, for the actor always runs the risk of tangling himself with his own net.

Cloaks were sometimes used as defensive tools in rapier fights, and are good replacements for using the dagger in a staged rapier and dagger fight. Usually, the bottom of the clock will need to be slightly weighted so that the fabric doesn't float too long between moves. Just as with hats, talk to the costumer before including this in a fight.

To use a cloak, grab it by the collar and give it an inside flip (coming up towards your face) and let it wrap around your wrist once. You want the fabric to fall away outside of your arm rather than inside so as to reduce snagging the incoming attacks. The cloak can then move back and forth in front of the body, hiding the rapier or dagger from your opponent's view until you are ready to strike. The cloak can also be used to make a distracting attack, to bat a sword out of the way, or to parry incoming thrusts. It strains credibility to use it as a block for an

aggressive cut, unless the cloak moves with the cut as the body evades the danger.
- Chains, Flails, Flail-Maces - all are dangerous, and have a nasty habit of reaching around blocks and lashing at defenders' faces, or bouncing back from blocks and striking the attacker. Leave this to the professionals.
- Food - Only three concerns to worry about - cost, slipping, and cleanup. Cover those issues and bringing in food to a comedic fight can be delightful. For safety, the actors will have to have strict protocols in place so that they can move the fight to a new location on the set if something slippery hits the floor in the middle of the fight.

Rubber knives, floppy knives, rubber clubs, foam props.

The impulse to use rubber props as a safety measure is very tempting, but ultimately self-defeating. For if the rubber is flexible enough to bend should it strike someone, it will wobble as it's being handled and looks phony. If the rubber is made stiff enough to approach realism, then you have something that's going to hurt just as much as a wooden or steel prop.

Styrofoam dressed to look like wood also hurts and can actually cause considerable damage, so under no circumstance should anyone's head be struck with any "soft prop". Minor cerebral contusions can occur from seemingly insignificant hits, and even slight bleeding in the brain can cause long-term brain damage.

Breakaway glass and other breakaway objects

Breakaway bottles, glasses and windowpanes are very well made these days and when used carefully are relatively safe for actors to use. Just keep a few things in mind. First, they are fragile, and you can expect to lose a few simply from shipping and general handling backstage. So you'd better budget and order twice whatever you had planned. Second, the bottoms of the bottles and glasses are thicker than the sides, so care must be taken not to strike someone with that firmer edge. Third, the pieces of broken "glass" can be quite sharp, so falling on the shards or grabbing them by hand could cut the skin. Lastly, and most importantly, never swing the bottle towards someone's face. If you absolutely must break a bottle over someone's head, have the victim face away from the bottle.

Knife throwing

Believe it or not, this is one of the easiest bits to perform. It is featured in the new version of *Annie Get Your Gun*, becomes a dramatic high point in *Tom Sawyer*, and I've had Kate do it in *Taming of the Shrew,* and Aramis take out a guard this way in *The Three Musketeers*.

The illusion itself is older than vaudeville. The knife is prominently held by the blade using the downstage arm. Go ahead and make a big deal about drawing the arm back and above the head. The throw should be done with great brio, the arm swinging all the way down and around to the upstage side of the body, with the eyes focusing fiercely on the intended target. The knife is quickly and invisibly passed to the upstage hand, which then drops it into a pocket when convenient. In one continuous motion the throwing hand comes back around to downstage so the audience can believe that the blade has been thrown. The second half of the bit requires a dummy knife already imbedded in a book or other prop or actor, hidden from view until the moment of the throw. As the actor lifts the embedded knife prop, he can also thump it with his finger, making the little contact sound that completes the illusion.

In multiple knife throwing, such as in *Annie Get Your Gun*, the real knife is not transferred to the upstage hand. Instead, that hand is already holding a half dozen or more knives (by the handles, not the blades) as a distraction. The thrower takes one knife, pretends to throw but this time allows the knife to pivot until the handle is resting against the forearm, hidden from audience view. He immediately pretends to pull out another knife from his collection, but it is of course the same knife that he swings back around, ready to "throw" again. The other side of this bit is an elaborately decorated target, made even more effective by having someone stand in the center of it. The face of the target is fabric, and the back of it has all of the dummy knives mounted on simple wood slats, and those slats fitted onto a small railing. An unseen assistant simply pushes the knives through the pre-cut fabric on the verbal cue [a grunt works fine] at each "throw. That's why the face of the target has to be highly decorated - to disguise the slits in the fabric.

An elaboration of the same is to have balloons mounted as targets on the target wall. In this illusion, the dummy knife handles will have very sharp pins affixed to the ends. As the dummy knives are pushed out they pop the balloons. So simple, so convincing.

Guns On-Stage

Non-Firing Replicas

Number one rule: NEVER allow any prop or real firearm to be used or even seen outside of a controlled rehearsal or performance space.

Do not use any prop weapon for "improvs".

Do not use any prop weapon for "promotional events".

Do not use any prop weapon within sight of the general public.

Actors have been shot by neighborhood "heroes" for rehearsing outdoors with rubber knives; they have been arrested for making violent gestures in public with rubber guns; they have been killed while holding very phony looking prop weapons.

Prop Firearm Protocols

When actors are given responsibility for a prop pistol or rifle for use in rehearsal and performance of a theatrical production, they need to be made aware of the limits that we have to place on them. Actors try to mimic the moves that they see in the movies, but they forget that guns constantly break down while on a film set. Film studios can afford to have several duplicates and a gunsmith on standby; theatres cannot.

While by all means we want the actor to feel comfortable working with the prop on stage, these cautionary points are prudent for them to keep in mind. Have them read a copy and sign it.

- First and foremost - <u>Never point it at anyone at any time.</u> I cannot more strongly stress the importance of developing sound firearms safety practice among this nation's actors. Always treat every prop gun as though it were a true and loaded gun, and if necessary to give the illusion of pointing the weapon, aim upstage of the other actor. The audience will never know the difference, and perhaps slowly we can all work together to prevent more senseless tragedies from occurring. This can only start with each and every person who sees any weapon, real or fake, to simply assume that it is loaded, white-hot, and ready to kill.

- Second - <u>Do not "dry-fire",</u> which is pulling the trigger when there is no blank in the chamber. Most guns break in rehearsal from actors dry-firing (playing) backstage. No gun, prop or real, is designed to be handled in this fashion. If it is necessary to the play that the gun dry-fire, then by all means rehearse as needed. But otherwise, why risk costly damage?

- Third - <u>Don't take it out of the theatre.</u> Police respond with extreme seriousness to any possible incident involving firearms, and merely displaying a replica outside of a theatre can be charged as a **felony** in most states. Any use outside of a theatre (including any film-work) requires prior notification and consent of the local police.

- Fourth - <u>The prop is not part of your costume.</u> Your holster is, but not the gun. It is to be picked up from the stage manager just before your entrance, and returned immediately on your exit.

♦   Fifth - <u>Perform a "chamber-check" with every hand-off.</u> The person handing over the weapon to the actor opens the gun to show that there is no bullet or blank in the chamber or magazine, o some other proof that the prop is harmless. When the actor returns the gun, the chamber check is repeated.

♦   Sixth - <u>Don't drop it.</u> Real or replica, these are delicate props, and simply can't survive aggressive action. If the gun must be tossed or dropped, we suggest that you purchase several for the run of the show, for they will break. For the same reason, don't "twirl" the gun or force the working parts.

Holding a firearm

For every action there is an equal and opposite reaction. For firearms, that means that if a bullet is coming out of the barrel in one direction, the gun is kicking back at you from the other. That reverse force from the gun, called recoil, has to be absorbed in some part of the body or the gun will simply fly in that reverse direction. So most of the techniques of holding a firearm have more to do with preparing for the recoil rather than aiming the shot.

The force of the recoil is in a straight line coming backwards from the path of the bullet. If the center of your hand could be in-line with the barrel, most of the force of a pistol shot could be easily captured by the forearm, so long as your arm is in line with the barrel when the gun is fired. Ah, there's the rub, for most guns have barrels that ride higher than the hand, parallel to but usually a few inches above the forearm. When the gun is fired, the pistol jumps back, the force actually causing the grip to pivot in the palm, spinning the barrel up.

The earliest muskets and arquebuses caused such tremendous recoil that it could dislocate the arm if the gun was braced against the shoulder. From the early 1500's to the late 1600's, the correct stance had the shooter standing with the left leg forward, knee slightly bent. The right leg was back and completely straight, ready to take the force of the recoil, but the weight distribution before firing was 70% left leg and only 30% right. The butt of the musket was braced against the chest just slightly off-center, specifically against the right pectoral muscle, and both shoulders faced the target. Both arms were needed to support the weight of the gun, with the elbows angled slightly down at about 45 decrees from vertical. (By the late 1500's and especially during the early 1600's as the musket grew considerably, a four foot pole, the musket rest, was used to support most of the weight of the gun.) Once the gun was fired, the soldier attempted to have the recoil transfer down to the straight right leg and into the ground. Often the force would lift the left leg off the ground.

Muskets and rifles of the 18th through 20th centuries are so much lighter than their predecessors that musket rests and bracing against the chest is not necessary. All are held with the left hand holding the bulk of the weight and the right hand free to stay relaxed for an easy trigger pull. The left elbow rides directly underneath the gun, pointing straight down [left arm perpendicular to the floor]. This placement also keeps the left arm at the best position to pull the gun straight down against the recoil. The right hand presses the stock against the right cheek and the right elbow points straight out to the right [right arm parallel to the floor]. Novices tend to hold rifles loosely and with the elbows both pointing roughly 45 degrees down.

The butt of the gun rests against the shoulder. The left foot points to the target, right foot turned out slightly (about 45 degrees) and the weight is now slightly to the rear foot instead of the lead foot, about 60-40. But the larger military rifles could still pack quite a wallop, so much of the initial training of the soldier is in having him press the gun as tightly as possible against the body. If the rifle and the body can absorb the recoil at the same time, the effect is greatly dissipated. If the gun is held loosely, it will move a fraction before the body does, and the feeling is like getting whacked with a baseball bat.

The basics of holding a shotgun are much the same, although there is a subtle difference in the nature of the shooter's focus. Rifles and pistols are "aimed", which is to say that one looks down the barrel of the gun and lines up the target with the front sight and the rear sight. The shooter focuses back and forth quickly down the sights and to the target. Shotguns by contrast are "sighted"; there is no front sight and only a small bead on the end of the barrel used as a reference point, which visually is kept just ahead of the flying or running target. The shooter's focus stays on the target, with the bead leading and staying in the visual periphery.

I should mention a little something about simply carrying a prop rifle or shotgun, even completely false ones. Many actors will hold them any which way, sometimes even absent mindedly allowing the barrel to point out into the house. It's not a safety concern, but it really freaks the audience out. So do what hunters are supposed to do - always treat the barrel of the gun as though it could fire flaming death in that direction at any time. So if there is a line of three people holding shotguns, everyone points the barrel in a different direction, each away from the others in the group. If walking in a line, the person in front doesn't let the barrel point back, the person in the back doesn't let his point forward, and the person in the middle points it off to the side. Treat the gun as though it were an infinitely long spear, one that must never cross in front of another actor and never in front of the audience.

One other little thing that happens is when an actor has a rifle or shotgun onstage for a while and absentmindedly starts to use it as a cane. No one who owns a real gun would ever do that. If the barrel rests against the ground and should fire, the barrel could explode. If the butt of the gun rests against the ground and the barrel is pointing up, an accidental discharge would take the shooter's head off. The safest carry is the "cradle carry", where let's say the right hand controls the butt of the gun (finger <u>not</u> on the trigger) and the barrel of the gun rest on the left forearm. This keeps the gun in front of you, barrel pointing off to the side but slightly forward, well within your peripheral vision. Switch it to the other side if someone walks into that danger zone.

Naturally, if the rifle has a strap it can usually be slung over the shoulder, and this keeps the barrel pointing safely up. But not all weapons should be slung. The old matchlock musket of the 16th and 17th centuries were far too heavy to use with a strap. They were also too long to carry in the modern style. Musketeers would throw the musket on the shoulder, butt end towards the back and barrel facing forward. They would then drape their arm over the barrel and gently pull the barrel down to roughly parallel to the ground. This way all of the weight would press down on one's trapezius muscle instead of straining the arm muscles.

Other firearms should also not be slung, even if the manufacturer has put strap loops on the gun. Straps put far too much pressure on the center of a gun, so lever-action rifles and breakopen shotguns soon break down if slung over the shoulder. These items are only meant to be carried in one's arms.

The earliest flintlock pistols had grips with a very shallow-angled drop. This helped align the gun with the forearm but left the wrist in a very uncomfortable position. The complete preferred stance for a pistol duel has the right leg forward, toes pointed at the opponent, and the left leg directly behind with the foot turned out at 90 degrees. The weight is distributed 50-50, for the pistol of the time has relatively little recoil. The arm is extended fully straight from the shoulder, and the torso is turned as is the left foot, 90 degrees away from the opponent, providing the smallest possible target. As the guns were of limited power and the bullet flight was erratic, the chance of actually getting struck with a pistol ball in a duel was very small.

Wherever both sword and pistol were used in battle, the sword was the primary attack weapon, therefore used with the right hand. Military pistols, even the six-shot revolvers, were secondary and defensive weapons, used with the left hand and only at targets within a range of twenty yards.

Keep in mind that all pistols up until the 1870's were muzzleloaders. For single shot pistols or poorly loaded six-shooters, there was always the chance that a loaded gun taken from a holster or from being stuck in a belt would fail to fire even if the cap ignited. I'm sure you've seen enough movies with duels in them to notice that the pistols, once loaded are held pointing straight up until the moment that the duelist fires. Why? For the same reason that these early flintlock guns were not worn in holsters. The general light movement of walking about would cause the ball to move slowly down the barrel, and the powder could always move down with it, making it harder for the sparks from the percussion cap to actually ignite the charge. A small chance, granted, but still possible, which is one reason why the pistols are held pointing straight up at the beginning of a duel - the other being good safety practice, for the hammer could always accidentally drop and fire the gun even if the trigger wasn't touched.

When practical revolvers become available starting in the 1850's, the stance and grip change dramatically, for the grip has to drop down considerably so as to provide more room for the larger gun frame. This lower grip means that the elbow can now bend slightly, taking pressure off the wrist but increasing the pivoting action during recoil, already increased by raising the relative barrel position to accommodate the chamber. To make matters worse, the recoil is made even stronger once revolvers move from being muzzleloaders to the far more powerful cartridge breech loaders. These breach loaded revolvers (starting in the 1870's) have a kick unknown in prior periods, and the only recourse was to develop enough arm strength to be able to hang onto the gun after each shot.

Civilian gunfights with the revolver then drop the sideways stance used by the earlier single shot duelists. Forming a smaller target isn't as crucial when six bullets are flying at you - you stand a big chance of getting shot by even a poor marksman. So the concern for the gunfighter is to maximize the effectiveness of all of his shots, especially the initial ones. That means squaring off the shoulders to the target, holding the arm in a position to both aim effectively and handle the recoil quickly enough so as to re-aim immediately for the next shot. The gun might be raised as before for careful aiming, although shooting from the hip was far more common. (It is no coincidence that the phasers on the original *Star Trek* series were also fired the same way. The show was described to producers as "Wagon Train in space", hence the look of the hand weapon and the way it is fired fit the cowboy feel. Compare with the "pc" Next Generation series, where the look of the phasers are as threatening as cell phones.)

During the 1920's, demand diminished for pistols with long-barrels. The accuracy that they provide is simply not a requirement for city dwellers, where the threat is more likely to be someone standing less than ten feet away. Not only is the gun fired without regard to careful aim, the gun is held close to the body so that any passing witness would barely notice that a gun is being held at all. This is the stance you see on all of those film-noir and gangster films of the 30's and 40's - fully erect body, gun held at waist level with the elbow tight against the hip.

Mid-twentieth century police officers are taught a stance somewhat similar to that of the earlier gunslinger. But a two-handed grasp is used, often with the left hand underneath the right hand, bracing the butt and providing a base from which to fire and to assist in stabilizing the gun after recoil. Also, modern police officers are taught to keep the barrel pointing safely up until a threat is directly in sight. The knees are bent, and the torso is slightly leaning forward. This stance remained the same even after the switch from revolvers to semiauto pistols, which, since the barrel can be lowered to a mere inch above the hand, has a more controllable kick. Since the gun, as always, has the grip pointing down and the recoil pushes the barrel up, several shots fired quickly in a row will show a typical up-and-down pattern.

A very different position is seen from inner-city gang members. Also using semiautomatic pistols because of the larger ammunition capacity, the gun is often held "flat", lying down, with the palm of the hand pointing down. This firing position means that the firing pattern will be side-to-side. This has a practical if coldhearted purpose: the recoil will push the barrel around along a horizontal plane, with most of the bullets staying at a lethal height and a far greater chance of someone getting killed, though not always the intended victim. The police, on the other hand, with the vertical grip and the up-and-down firing pattern, tend to shoot high and low, but at least put innocent by-standards at a lower risk of getting hit.

Gun Twirling

Unless the stage directions call for it, don't let the actors twirl the guns. Especially backstage, they like to play at being a gunslinger, but a twirled gun is a soon to be dropped gun, which then becomes a broken gun.

By the way, twirling should only be done, and would only have been done, with the single-action cartridge revolvers with six inch barrels, in other words the cowboy guns of the last quarter of the 19th century. No one would ever twirl the earlier blackpowder guns, even revolvers, because the powder would shift away from position and no longer fire. Anyway, the triggers on these percussion guns are rather thin with sharp ends, and can really cut up the finger during a twirl. Lastly, the weight of the chamber and length of the barrel makes the revolvers very unbalanced.

With the invention of cartridge revolvers, and especially the mass enthusiasm for the 1873 Colt 45 Peacemaker, all worries about shifting powder loads vanished, but other factors also abetted gunslingers to start twirling for showboating. The trigger was fatter, with smooth edges and a rounded tip, and the center of balance of the gun was closer to the trigger, so the gun was much easier to manage and not nearly so barrel-heavy as were the percussion revolvers.

During the first quarter of the 20th century, public taste shifted to a gun more appropriate for closer range. The long barrel of the Peacemaker was no longer as necessary, and this led to guns now being either grip-heavy or top heavy, so no longer as easy to twirl. Also, single-action guns lose favor to double-action, but this means that the natural safety inherent in the Peacemakers (the trigger won't work until you pull the hammer back) is gone, making twirling a modern revolver positively foolhardy (the trigger can be accidentally pulled in the middle of the twirl, thereby firing the gun).

Firing

In an earlier section we described some different kinds of blanks, so here I want to go over some protocols on how to use them, both backstage and on stage.

In addition to the warnings for non-fire weapons, firing guns need special treatment. I always advise keeping firing guns in a locked cabinet inside a locked room which has restricted access. These items are just too tempting, and theft is unfortunately too common. They are delicate props as well, so try not to have them used when a non-firing gun will do just as well.

Set a specific protocol for who handles the gun during the course of rehearsal and performance. Here is one example: the gun is made the responsibility of one person, who loads, cleans and keeps track of the weapons each night. This person, perhaps an assistant stage manager, checks out the guns and blanks from the technical director or props master, loads the gun and then keeps it at a spot where it is under direct view - not at the general props table. The gun is not handed to the actor until just before the actor's entrance. A chamber check is performed, and the actor then takes possession of the gun. As soon as the actor exits the stage, the gun is returned immediately to the ASM.

When the performance is over, the ASM unloads the gun, checks for damage, and then thoroughly cleans and oils the gun before returning it to whoever is going to lock it up for the night. Remember - if the gun was fired it must be cleaned immediately after the show; it can't wait until tomorrow.

It should be the props master who lays down the law concerning how the actors should treat the weapons. The following rules are to be added to the general rules concerning non-firing replicas. Be sure and go over these rules with the director early in the rehearsal process so that there are no surprises during tech week. The rules are:

1   Don't trust a safety to keep the gun from firing

Safeties are very small mechanical devices within a gun that either keep the hammer from dropping or the trigger from moving. Mechanical devices can fail, and some of them can be overridden by a small amount of force. They are not fail-safe.

2   Don't put your finger on the trigger until you are ready to shoot

Leave your index finger outside of the trigger guard unless you are in the act of firing the gun. In case the gun should slip slightly out of your grasp, the weight of most guns can cause it to fall forward, barrel end going down. If your finger is already within the trigger guard, this pivoting can quickly put the weight of the gun onto the finger. The weight of the gun can be enough to pull the trigger, firing the gun, and certainly trying to catch the gun before is slips out of your hand can do the same thing (this is how a lot of idiots shoot themselves in the leg with their own loaded pistol).

3   Don't ever struggle with a loaded gun.

I shouldn't have to point out that the gun can fall or that during the struggle the trigger might be accidentally pulled, but it's the more obvious things that people overlook.

4   Never allow a loaded gun to strike the floor or another object.

Any loaded gun can accidentally go off if jarred from being struck or dropped, even if the hammer isn't cocked. So you can never throw or drop a gun.

5   Never put a loaded gun near someone's head

And of course never fire a gun near someone's head. There are shows in which a character is shot in the head in close proximity, but the discharge from the gun is simply too loud and too dangerous from even the softest blanks. Use an offstage sound.

6   Never fire the gun near flammable material.

That includes clothing. The discharge is so hot that it can ignite someone's clothing. I've seen it happen - it's terrifying.

7   Handle a loaded gun only from the grip, never from the barrel or frame.

Again, a loaded gun can go off at any time, and if your hand is anywhere but on the grip when that happens, you're going to get some deeply penetrating and highly infectious wounds.

"Maintain a safe distance from other actors when firing a blank." How far is a safe distance? It doesn't exist. If you want to fire a gun <u>safely</u>, you'll need to wear a face shield and ear protection, clear the room of all other persons, and remove all flammable material. Even with that, there is always a chance that the gun can explode and send shrapnel out in any direction. Blank fire safety is a shifting compromise of different factors. If you are willing to accept more risk, you will have more choices in using blanks, but you will never be able to guarantee perfect safety. Some choices you can make might include, but not be limited to, the following:

It is safer to have the arm fully extended rather than having the elbow bent. The user will be that much further from the sound and the blast.

Find out where the discharge is going to go for the particular gun you are using and keep that area completely clear of all humans, animals and flammable materials. You're not looking for a minimum diameter around the gun but rather a danger alley extending from the gun and all the way back to a stone wall, no matter how far away, which must be kept completely clear. Is that always possible to provide? No. In fact it is almost impossible to provide. But you should exhaust yourself in the attempt.

Have everyone in the space use ear protection. Unfortunately, you can't hand out ear plugs along with the programs to your audience, and most of your actors will need to hear their cues. So at the very least, consider plugging the "near ear" of the shooter. Regular ear plugs are usually too visible, but you might find some in flesh tone. If that isn't possible, a little dab of petroleum jelly might be enough to block the worst of the sound, though the stuff will get in the ear canal and can get messy and uncomfortable.

Have everyone in the space use high impact eye protection. Well, of course that is flat-out impossible. I mention it because eyes are vulnerable to the hot gases expelled by blanks, and it does us no good to ignore the danger.

Don't shoot directly at someone. Now here is something that you actually *can* do. The audience's depth perception is very limited. You can point a gun (or knife, or sword) slightly upstage of where the victim is standing and the audience will never know the difference. This is one suggestion that every theatre can implement immediately. Simply never point a gun at someone. Never. Any where, any time, for any reason. Onstage or off, real gun or toy. There are dozens of people who died prematurely because actors failed to learn this basic rule. Pointing a prop gun at someone should be cause for the immediate dismissal of that actor or stagehand from the company. You want to save lives? Implement this policy today.

"But what about scenes where a character has to commit suicide?" I was afraid you would ask that. All I can offer are some suggestions in making that action safer, but not completely safe. There are two considerations here: the discharge and the sound. Most blank fire guns for stage are block-barreled, so there will be no discharge traveling down the barrel, but the discharge has to go somewhere, and that is usually off to either side of the gun and slightly forward. But when a gun is held that close to someone, there really is no safe area - the burning gunpowder can hurt you at almost any angle. But even more important is the level of sound that hits the actor at that distance. If the ears are unprotected, each shot is causing hearing loss, even from low-level caps. The actor is at ground zero, and no ear plug is going to reduce the sound enough to bring it to a safe level.

Can you go to black-out just as the shot is supposed to occur? Then and only then do you have a chance to reduce the danger. As soon as the lights die down enough, have the actor point the gun directly upstage. The audience will see a flash, but it will appear from behind the actor's head, and the look is very eerie. Can't go to black-out? Then tape the sound or have someone fire a starter pistol from off or upstage.

Remove flammable materials from near the blank-fire gun. A blank fired inside a purse can ignite the purse. A handkerchief wrapped around a gun can ignite when the gun is shot. Remember that a gun can fire if the hammer is struck even if the trigger is not pulled, so a gun in a pocket is still dangerous. The pocket should be made fireproof. Is that always practical? No, but it is one more risk reduced.

If the gun is a semi-automatic pistol or a multishot rifle, the spent rounds will be ejected onto the set. For most guns, those empty cartridges will fly up and to the right of the gun, and they can be hot for about a minute. Keep that area clear when blocking the scene. Have a plan that covers dealing with the spent rounds and collecting them from the set. As long as they are on the floor, they act like free bearings, and anyone who steps on one can easily slip and fall.

Easy Blood Effects

The easiest blood effect is to not use any at all. No, really. If the actors convincingly "see" blood, so will the audience. They know that any blood they see isn't real anyway, so they are perfectly content not seeing any at all. I realize that this is very unsatisfying for the actors and many directors, but for all that it remains true - audiences will believe what the actor believes.

Next on the short list of easy blood effects is pre-set blood. The fake blood is left in a small container hidden somewhere on the set, ready for the actor to dip his fingers in or scoop up with the back of the thumb and apply to the "cut". When doing a throat slitting or especially in the course of a very physical scene, this is the best way of controlling the blood effect, for it removes the worry of dealing with a messy liquid until just before it is really needed. The blood might be in an open container or in a blood pack.

Blood packs are a reasonably reliable way of getting larger amounts of blood on the actor, but the risk is that the pack may not open on cue, or worse still, open too early, especially when taped onto the actor's body. That's why I prefer to have the packs preset on the stage. The actors simply scoops one up just before the blood is needed, and pops it in his hand or on the body part as needed.

Blood packs are easy enough to make - all you need are some plastic sandwich bags, your fake blood, scissors and some thread. You are making tiny little water balloons. Just pour the blood into one of the corners of the plastic bag, twist it around a few times, tie off the balloon that you've made and cut off the excess plastic. Don't use tape to close the bag or it will leak. Remember that air compresses but liquids can't, so leave a little bit of air in the balloon. As you twist the bag you put the contents under pressure - it'll make it much easier to pop the blood pack when the time comes.

Note: you can use plastic wrap instead of sandwich bags of course, but plastic wrap stretches a bit, so you need to get the contents under a lot more pressure to make sure it will pop when the actor needs it to.

Blood FX weapons

Oozing knives, bleeding razors - I know that these things exist and that some of them are wonderful, but in my experience with them they have proved to raise the anxiety level for the actors without much benefit to the story. Most have a hidden latex bladder in the handle of the weapon, not seen by the audience but reached by the fingers of the actor. As the actor presses the bladder, the blood can squirt out with as much force as the actor chooses. The biggest problem with these blood knives is that they are too unreliable, often starting to bleed long before contact is made with the victim.

If the effect is needed, but you are leery of the bladder variety, a sponged blade can sometimes work just as well if not better. Instead of a bladder in the handle, a thin strip of sponge is glued onto one side of the edge of a regular knife, and the sponge is saturated with blood. When the sponge is pressed against the victim, the blood will drip nicely on the skin or clothing, and is a beautifully convincing illusion so long as the sponged side is hidden from the audience's view.

Squibs

There are many who work in theatre that ache for the day when they can replicate the bloody effects they see in movies. These people seem to be especially enamored of squibs. These are small explosives that are rigged with wires, preset on the actor's body and covered with blood packs. Complete the electrical circuit and the squib explodes, bursting the blood pack and sending a gory red spray just like in a Sam Peckinpaw movie. Here are a few reasons why you should not allow these people to convince you that squibs are a good idea for your show:

- Squibs are explosives. When handled by experts they are relatively safe. When handled by almost experts, they can cause deep dirty burns at best, blast wounds into the chest cavity or up into the face at worst.

- Squibs can and do fail. Connections can loosen, batteries discharge, the explosive can dampen from actor sweat.

- Squibs can ignite spontaneously. Actor sweat is salty water, and under the wrong conditions can cause an electric charge to arc past the switch, completing the circuit and igniting the squib. So can static electricity. And if the system is based on wireless remote, a random cell phone call can accidentally trigger a false "fire" signal. And I don't know if you've noticed that cell phones are more common now than they were twenty years ago.

• Squibs are expensive, at least the good ones. The show budget can be eaten through by setting up a special effect that the audience really doesn't need to see in order to enjoy a show.

Blood mixtures

It wasn't that long ago that theatres would simply order some fresh cow's or pig's blood from a butcher shop so that real blood was actually used for performance. It is still sometimes done in Europe, but the use is fast disappearing. Real blood, even if not already contaminated with viruses or bacteria, is a growth medium par excellence for a host of random and deadly pathogens.

Fake blood mixtures can be purchased from theatre supply houses, but considering the expense, you are usually better off making your own. For the look of fresh blood, start with good old corn syrup and add food coloring (I like the look of 2 drops blue to every 5 drops red), and then start adding water until you get the viscosity you need. If blood needs to go in or near the mouth or nose, this is a safe mixture.

If you are in an outdoor venue and don't want to attract flies with corn syrup, try thickening some hot water with powdered arrowroot. If you need blood that looks a little older, add chocolate syrup to darken it. For battlefield wounds, adding some crumbled Shredded Wheat gives the mixture a wonderful texture.

If the blood does not need to be on the face, you can add in some materials to help in clean-up after the show. Liquid dishwashing detergent instead of or along with the corn syrup makes a great base.

If the stage blood might get on costumes and you're worried about stains, you might consider adding a few drops of Photo-Flow® into the blood mix. This is a film developing component and can be purchased at most photography supply stores. It works like magic in getting the fake blood stain to lift right out of the fabric during washing, even white silk. But be careful because it is a toxic material. Under no circumstances should it be used if there is even a slight chance that the mixture might go near the face.

Cleaning real blood from costumes.

If someone cuts himself and real blood gets on a costume, and you can't start to remove the blood immediately, at least wet the garment as soon as possible so that the stain doesn't set. Then when there is time to work on the fabric, the best cleaning material to use is hydrogen peroxide. Pour a little and rub, pour a little and rub, just keep doing that until the blood has disappeared. And disappear it will, for the hydrogen peroxide reacts with and explodes the red blood cells. It also is color safe for most fabrics and completely non-toxic.

Blood on anything else should be wiped off with a solution of 20% bleach in water. If you want to sterilize anything that has blood on it, leave the item in a 5% bleach solution for one hour, but for no more than two hours, for even that light dilution of bleach will deeply corrode many metals.

Choreography Basics and Acting the Fight

You might find it odd that I have combined those two thoughts into one section, but the more I think about it the more I realize that the two cannot be separated. The actor will rarely be the choreographer, of course, but he cannot hope to be able to act the fight without understanding how the story of the fight develops. Just as actors break down the script in order to understand and then transmit the playwright's intent, they also need to break down the fight in order to bring meaning to the movements.

Human communication begins and ends with the face. The raw emotion plays on the face before the brain has time to transform the thought into speech or gesture. That's why we look at the face in order to judge the real meaning of what someone is saying - words can lie easily; but faces hide little.

Combining moves to form an interesting and believable fight is a skill far beyond what is taught in even intensive stage combat instruction, but there are some basic principles to keep in mind. First, don't try too much. A few carefully chosen and well rehearsed moves will add to your production whereas larger sequences tend to fatigue the audience. In my first years as a choreographer I often overtaxed my fighters' endurance and my audiences' patience.

It seems obvious, but match the move to the intention of the character. Let the emotional impulse of the character inform what kind of attack or response seems most natural.

Each move will come from an impulse and each in turn will have a consequence. Imagine a force slowly growing in strength, weight and size composed of anger and manifesting as a ball of fire welling up from one of the characters. It is restrained by use of words for a while, but at some point reaches such an intolerable level that it must be released by physical action. It flies to the other character, who must dodge it, absorb it, or command it to return to its owner. Sometimes that ball of fire is controlled so that the aggressor might have two or three moves before committing to the one which is supposed to actually do the damage. Sometimes the fire is so overwhelming that the aggressor can only lash out in a simple direct attack. But however it manifests, the release of energy affects and changes both the aggressor and the defender. Both are burned by this fire; both have to adjust to a new world.

Then it's the defender's turn to deal with that fire. Even If he chooses to evade the attack, he still hasn't evaded the reality of the anger. If he absorbs the attack, the physical damage changes his emotional response. If he commands or takes control of it by blocking the attack, he also has to evaluate the situation and see if the fire has dissipated. He may choose to send it back as a new attack, changing his role from defender to aggressor. He might add his own anger to the fire, increasing its strength and changing the dynamics of the fight. Two actors could spend hours just breaking down all of the ramifications of these actions - how it affects their breathing, their stances, their movement, balance and focus. Where does the fire come from - specifically? From where in the body does it spring and how does it travel down the arm, through the sword and exactly where (to the square inch) is the intended spot on the defender's body that the aggressor wants to burn with that ball of flame. Did the action work? How are the characters changed by the results of the action. And we've only been talking about the first two moves of the fight.

And of course, all actions must be accompanied by sound. Grunts, groans, yells, moans, even loud breathing - from the moment the fight starts until it is over, the vocal cords must be engaged. I know that it seems really embarrassing to just blurt out something, but there must be sound, for if not the fight becomes an aural black-hole, and that is deadly for any show.

Sometimes actors will be told to slow down the fight. It may be that the fight has become unsafe, but perhaps something else is happening. You see, many times it's not that the fight is too fast, but rather that it looks rushed, and there is a big difference. It isn't the speed that makes it look out of control - it's the dropping of the storyline. For instance, there are times where I'll watch a rehearsal and see so indication of intention - something that could be described as ...

"I'm going to attack her!" followed by moves 1,2,3.
Where what I would rather see is ...

"I'm going to attack her here!" - move 1; "That didn't work, so I'll strike her here" - move 2: "OK, then, she's left herself open on that side so I'll cut there" - move 3.

So the fight will go only as fast as your thoughts can take you from each move to the next. You may end up doing the fight just as fast as you were doing it before, but what we'll see is that each move is finished cleanly before moving to the next because each move had a purpose that either succeeded or failed. Each phrase of fight is as much a dialogue as anything else in the script, and the outcome of each move leads the character to choose the next action.

So no matter how long the fight, you have a little homework to do, and you can do much of this on your own. Go through all of your moves, attacks and defenses. Decide why you make that particular move. Does it succeed or fail? Because of that, why do you choose the next? This may take about a half hour. Then do it again until you can follow all of your moves based on what you want, how you're going to get it, evaluating if it worked, and then trying something else. (does this sound familiar? you're right, it's the same work you do with spoken lines.). Understanding the emotional inner monologue of the fight makes it easier to remember the moves. And if you forget a move? It doesn't matter: you will go to the character's next *intention.* And keep in mind that the audience doesn't know the choreography, so whatever you do is "right" as long as you stay committed to the intentions.

The outcome is that the fight will look even <u>more</u> dangerous, but actually be <u>safer</u>, for the fight won't roll away from you out of control. You'll be communicating directly with your partner, and by extension to the audience. And you will have a kick-ass fight!

If the choreographer has approached building the fight with this level of care and precision, the actors will find it easy to find the emotional flow and really be able to tell an interesting story through the fight. If the choreography is weak, perhaps visually striking but lacking in clearly defined emotional intent for every action, the actors and director will have to provide it. Luckily we are trained to do exactly that - make even poor writing seem real and interesting. So we might have to do the same with choreography.

If it falls into your lap to create the fight, then think in simple terms. You could begin with establishing in your own mind the essential story points that must be transmitted to the audience 1) overall, 2) for each scene, and 3) for each fight or confrontation. So read the play a couple more times and jot down some of the critical things that absolutely must happen within each fight. These are the barebones basics, not whatever is written in the stage directions.

As a matter of fact, black out all of the stage directions with a heavy felt-tip pen. Really. Block them out, all of them, even the ones not related to the fight. The ones that describe the blocking, the gestures, even and especially the horrible ones that give line readings. You know, the ones that supposedly help the actor by adding *angrily* or *knowingly* or *brightly* or whatever in parenthesis after or before the line. These aids are fine for reading a play, but they are the worst thing you can show to an actor preparing to act in a play. Slavish observance of stage directions only leads to lifeless directing and uninspired acting. An actor should be exploring all of the ways to say a line. And although we can't allow the same freedom when it comes to a staged fight, you, the choreographer, have to allow yourself the freedom to work out a fight that is specific to your actors, your set, your concept of what the play is trying to say. And don't worry about being true to the original version of the show. The original choreographer set the fight based on the director and actors he had to deal with. In a different production, he would be the first to change the fight to fit the new circumstances. You must do the same.

So in a production of, let's say, *Man of La Mancha* there is a big fight that pits Quixote, Sancho and Dulcinea against the muleteers that you have to choreograph. The stage directions are detailed and have the actors performing some very difficult moves with a lot of props. Well, there is no harm in reading the stage directions once if you need to get an idea of what is required from the fight, but then simplify. Write down what really needs to happen. That's pretty simple, really. The muleteers must be defeated and sustain some non life-threatening injuries, and each of our three principles must have at least one moment within the fight in which he or she contributes to the victory. Everything else is negotiable. However long or short the fight is, whether it is to be serious or comedic, whether props are going to be used and how, all of that is up to you.

Start with a basic outline of how the fight should progress in order to tell the audience what they need to know. I like to daydream the scene first in a fully imagined "real" space with the characters as vague out-of-focus shadows. Then I allow them in my imagination to approach and retreat from each other as the conflict progresses without seeing what their arms or weapons are doing. At this point I'm just trying to get a feel for the way their personalities make choices. In a short amount of time the basic blocking of the fight becomes clear. I write these down in outline form, and then keep playing the mental movie over and over, allowing the characters to become a little more sharply focused each time. Each time, a bit more of the characters and then the specific attacks and defenses almost manifest themselves. Before long the fight is complete, and I can fill in my outline with all of the specific choreography.

Since memorization is never as interesting as motivation, I like to keep the number of routines that each actor has to memorize down to a minimum, and I strongly suggest that you do the same. But that doesn't mean that the fight has to be boring and repetitive. Let's resurrect that little bit of fight notation we used before and build a small fight. Each actor will only have to know seven moves, but we can build a very long fight if we want to and the audience will never see a pattern.

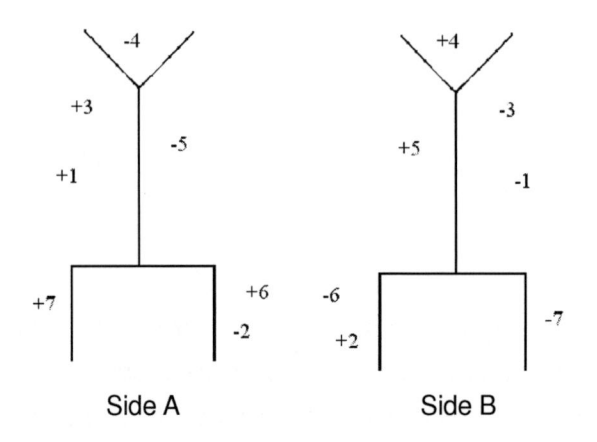

Side A   Side B

Side A did seven moves, and Side B performed a complementary set of moves. If these moves are performed at a steady pace, one beat per move, the fight has a certain feel. If the actors break up the rhythm, let's say by freezing for a split second after every third move, it looks like a completely different fight. Why? Because good actors can't help but fit in a bit of emotional response to even the slightest pause, and we as the audience pick up on that and read in motivation. If we stick to that fractional pausing after each three moves, we can perform the fight as an endless loop and the audience won't notice a pattern until the third time we run the basic routine, if then.

Want more? Each actor already knows what the other actor is going to do, so in a short time he really knows fourteen moves without having memorized anything new. So now loop the two routines together. The first actor will perform all of Side A and then continue right into Side B, then A then B, ad nauseam. The second actor starts with Side B, and then continues to A, then B, then A, etc.

Now lets add the legs. Try a full movement pattern across the stage. Have the first actor only going forward, one step with every move. The other actor only retreats - one or two steps back whether the arm is attacking or not. You'll notice that the "intention" of the attacks changes dramatically when the body is in retreat.

Right now is a good time to have them do what they really want to do - step forward any time they attack, step back every time they block. Just let them run through it a couple of times to get it out of their systems. As you go through the full routine notice how some attacks seem stronger than others now, some are more important and some are almost incidental.

Now for a real brain teaser. Have them step forward with each block; step backward with each attack. Even if you don't use it in the fight, it's a great exercise. By stepping forward while parrying, it can show a character in complete command of the fight, whereas backing up while cutting or thrusting gives a look of desperation.

To see how to change the look of the fight even more, try having all attacks be tightly controlled thrusts and all parries be extremely small deflections. Now try the same combinations but using all full arm swinging cuts. The matching blocks will have to appear as though they have to absorb so much incoming energy that it would shake the entire body. For another exercise, when an attack is followed by a parry, try maintaining blade contact during the entire movement (called a yield or ceding parry). How would you describe the different moods that each style creates? By carefully mixing parts of each of these variations, you can create a wonderfully nuanced fight full of character development and an interesting storyline. And we haven't had to add any fancy moves or augmented the fight beyond the original pattern.

I have only touched on some of the more obvious variants that can add a different look to what are essentially the same moves. But isn't that what we are already trained to do as actors? We take the same lines that hundreds of other actors have spoken but then filter them through our own interpretation to create something unique. We can also say the same line in any of a hundred different ways, depending on our intention. Those same skills apply to movement, so we can take a seemingly simple fight and fill it with passion, tension, ad excitement.

If you have been a director for any length of time at all, I'm sure that the following has happened to you. You're in the middle of a rehearsal, trying to work out a bit of business or a tight piece of blocking, and one of your actors stops any bit of forward progress with the phrase "but my character wouldn't do that". It just takes the wind out of your sail, doesn't it? You of course don't want to stifle the actor's efforts to make the character his own, and yet at the same time you are desperately stifling your own impulse to strangle him.

In stage combat, this problem is magnified, for the actor may be required to perform a fight and yet the interpretation of the character is of one who is weak. How do you justify a strong action from a weak character? But more importantly, how do you get an actor to break away from his first choice on playing a scene, which is usually facile and shallow?

I have had some luck with variations on movement exercises designed to break the actor away from preconceptions. First, have them pick an animal that they believe most closely matches the attributes of their character and play the scene that leads to the violence and the violence itself as that animal. Let them go to extremes, really exaggerate the animal attributes. It doesn't take long for actors to realize that any animal, no matter how weak, will defend and even attack a much larger animal if it feels threatened.

There is one particular Laban exercise that I love putting into my advanced stage combat classes. Laban normally has the actors explore taking on the qualities of light/heavy, fast/slow, straight/circuitous. In a series of exercises, the actors take each quality to its extreme and then combine one from each pair, and finally include them into the playing of a scene. For stage combat I change the last pair to strong/weak, since I can't have the actors change a movement direction. Naturally, the actors will first choose a combination with which they are most comfortable, and this is the one that they tend to choose 95% of the time whenever they act. Often it is something like fast-strong-light, so then after they have worked out the scene that way, I challenge them to explore the polar opposite choice, for example slow-weak-heavy. This brings out some wonderful acting, and if they can't actually use it in performance it often gives them a tool through which their character becomes a complete three dimensional person. For every "strong" person has periods of weakness, and every "weak" person has moments where they find tremendous strength. While one attribute might be predominant, it is never one hundred percent of that person's life.

I hope you can see by what I've said so far that I place the highest priority on a plot and emotion driven fight. That doesn't mean that I won't throw in some "fancy" moves or even cliché bits in order to add more pizzazz to the fight, so long as it fits the tenor of the show and doesn't violate the production's limit of propriety. That means that, depending on what the director is trying to create, for some productions of *The Three Musketeers* I'll put in every cheap bit in the book, and in others I stay true to a more "realistic melodramatic" form.

The one thing that I can't do too much with is when I'm faced with the director who wants to add a fight for a very different reason: making actors happy. It comes up in a lot of college and high school productions trying to do a big show. The director and producer get worried before auditions that not enough men/boys will show up. So they let out the word that there's a good chance that if you get in the show, you're going to get to swashbuckle. Well, there aren't that many shows where you can actually do that, so when the show is finally cast the director feels obligated to add some fights that aren't required for the show.

Most of the time, these fights drag down the pace of the show, and often add confusion, not clarity, for the audience. Staged fights, just like characters' emotions, are supposed to come up as the consequence of what has happened in the plot. When the emotions are too large and aren't supported by the actions, it becomes melodramatic. When a fight in part or in whole is not tightly connected to all of the production values and plot, it becomes a disappointment.

So do less. And what you do end up with, do perfectly.

Violence on Stage
Specific Scenes in Some Common Plays

Shakespeare

We won't worry in this section about the challenges of changing the weaponry requirements when a Shakespeare play is reset in a nontraditional time or place. That is part of the fun of mounting a production and there is a brief set of suggestions at the end. But we do need to be very sure of what the references are within the text so we can make an appropriate substitution for a different weapon or fighting style.

For example, in the film version of *Romeo & Juliet* with Leonardo DiCaprio, seeing all of the changes made when they modernized the design elements was great fun, but of course compromises had to be made. When Tybalt referred to his rapier, the production team had that changed from a sword to a handgun of a fictitious *"Rapier"* brand. That's fine, but it does mean that all of the references to Tybalt's fighting style (and therefore a reflection of his personality) take on a different tone. Shooting with a gun is just not the same as challenging someone with a sword. And certainly if someone draws a sword or a knife on you, you always have the option of running away. That option is always there, so getting involved in a fight is always a choice by both participants. But you can't run away from a bullet - and when that option is gone the character's motivations for that scene have changed. Pointing a gun takes command of distance; drawing a sword is an invitation to close in on distance. So although we should feel free to stray from the original intent if it helps our production, we should do it knowingly. I've seen too many shows where things were changed simply from ignorance, and the absence of thought showed.

Shakespeare always wrote about the people of his own time, even when the story takes place in other historic periods. When he needed a clock to chime in *Julius Caesar* to mark the hour, then a clock simply chimes. That the mechanical clock didn't exist in ancient Rome was not a concern. The same goes for weaponry. He knew about rapiers and broadswords, and he makes free use of them with complete disregard to historical or regional accuracy. So when we try to do one of his plays "in period," we have to be careful that in trying to stick to historical accuracy we don't gut the author's intent.

I am going to make a huge digression here [you shouldn't be surprised by now] and take some time to talk about ...

Acting in Period Plays

Many of the actors reading this book are trying to find an edge, something that can set them apart from other actors as they compete for the same parts, or something that can help them get a handle on tackling plays that seem so foreign. So in addition to explaining some elements of period style and stage combat and prop weaponry, it certainly hasn't escaped my notice that most actors can use some help in simply acting the plays written before the twentieth century, especially those of Shakespeare. I've worked with a lot of actors over the years, and the same hindrances keep popping up, so read through this section even if you feel that it may not apply to you. You never know; you may find a little nugget that can help you or someone else out of an acting dead-end. As Shakespeare's works are the most commonly performed plays of any playwright, the likelihood is that every actor is going to perform in one of his plays at least once in his or her career.

Please don't let another actor tell you that Shakespeare wrote in a foreign language. It is most definitely English, just one that we are not accustomed to hearing. Only a few generations ago that wasn't the case. When hardscrabble 49er's climbed down from the Sierras to take a break at the nearest one-horse town during the California Gold Rush, viewing a traveling acting troupe performing "King Lear" was a treat few would miss. Even the least educated could follow the play, feeling completely comfortable with the elevated language, vocabulary and convoluted sentence structure. For today's audiences, that is no longer the case. We just don't routinely use words of more than one or two syllables anymore, and certainly don't follow complicated syntax or poetic imagery. So the modern actor's job is to parse out the thoughts within the language so that the audience can follow what you're saying. In order to do that, *you* have to know what you are saying. Naturally, this may take some homework because not all of the words will be familiar to you. It's not as though you're reciting "Little Miss Muffet".

Actually, let's take a look at Little Miss Muffet.

Little Miss Muffet
Sat on a tuffet
Eating her curds and whey.
Along came a spider
That sat down beside her,
And frightened Miss Muffet away.

Pretty straight forward, right? We don't have to break that down the way we would Shakespeare's poetry because this is just regular language. Everything is easily understandable to anyone. Little Miss Muffet sat on a tuffet - what could be simpler? Little Miss Muffet. Little Miss. Little. But, by the way, what does it mean to be "little"? Is it short? Thin? Young? Can one be tall and young and still be little? Short and old? How about "miss". An unmarried female, right? A child? A spinster? And why the name "Muffet"? Just to rhyme with "tuffet"? So we go to the dictionary and find that the "et" ending is a common diminutive form, so Muffet might have something to do with muff. We check the dictionary again and find that the muff is that fur tube that people use to keep their hands warm when they are outside in cold weather. When does one wear a muff? Certainly not while eating curds and whey, I'll warrant. So is Muffet a descriptive nickname, perhaps? If it is, it's pointing out that this is not someone who is accustomed to doing manual labor. [Take a breath, we've only done the first three words.]

"sat on a tuffet". How do you do that? Do you perch on the edge? Lean way back? What is a "tuffet", anyway? Is it cushioned or hard? Is it low or high? We have to go back to our Webster's Collegiate dictionary to find that it is a three legged milking stool. But we note that the Oxford English Dictionary (OED) includes information that the word has that definition only because of a rather famous painting from the eighteenth century. It captured the moment that Little Miss Muffet is startled by seeing the spider. It is from that painting that people got the idea that a tuffet is a three-legged milking stool. Obviously, we can't settle for this circular derivation, so we dig deeper. It turns out that tuffet is a variation of "tuft", which means not only a small bulge of grass, but also a low rise of earth, a very small hill, much like the term "grassy knoll". So she isn't sitting on a piece of furniture at all!

Let's move a little faster through the third line. After digging a bit, we find that curds and whey is something like cottage cheese before they drain out all of the liquid, and that it was often prepared as a special treat when there was plenty of fresh milk available. The milk would be left to curdle overnight and then strained out in cheese cloth, separating the curds from the fluid (the whey), and would be served at breakfast, before it could spoil. This is not a worker's meal. So who is this person out on a hill eating a meal prepared for her in the early morning?

It seems that this bit of doggerel goes back to the 16th century and may very well refer to Mary, Queen of Scots. The scenario is that of Mary, on campaign with her army, making camp overnight on some unnamed highground, which makes perfect tactical sense. In the early morning, just as the camp was stirring, they were attacked by an opposing force (one led by a commander hairy enough to warrant the sobriquet of "spider"). Mary's forces probably fled the hillock before any combat was engaged, but at least one member of the attacking force was so pleased with the results of the attack that he composed this little soldier's poem, one that the other soldiers would repeat as they marched to the next engagement. They surely would have taken the story, with its catchy singsong rhyme, back home with them, and like all good nursery rhymes it slowly lost all of it's original meaning as it was repeated by generations of toddlers.

Is it necessary for the audience to know all of that information? No, but it is important to you, for your ability to transmit meaning to them starts with you having a crystal clear idea of what it is you are saying. The more sparklingly exact is your image, the easier it is for your audience to capture.

Ok, let's move from a nursery rhyme to something a little more performance based. Most of you have heard the song "My Favorite Things" from *The Sound of Music*. Maria very quickly goes through a quaint little list:

> Raindrops on roses and whiskers on kittens
> Bright copper kettles and warm woolen mittens
> Brown paper packages tied up with strings ...
> Cream colored ponies and crisp apple strudels
> Doorbells and sleigh bells and schnitzel with noodles
> Wild geese that fly with the moon on their wings ...
> Girls in white dresses with blue satin sashes
> Snowflakes that stay on my nose and eyelashes
> Silver white winters that melt into springs ...

In the stage version, this song is presented as merely an old county song, shared between the Reverend Mother and Maria. This is unfortunate, for it destroys any sense of discovery within the song. They both end up merely singing a quaint little song from their childhood, but have no emotional commitment to creating the images. It can be a nice moment that the two can share, but there is nothing special about the song itself.

Now consider that same song as it is introduced in the film version. There, Maria invents this little ditty while comforting the children, trying to get them to think happy thoughts instead of focusing on the thunder and lightening. What separates the average performance from one that soars is the attention to detail. Each image that Maria conjures comes from her own experiences and desires. Notice how pedestrian are the examples she gives. Doorbells? To a girl raised in a poor country village, electric doorbells were an unheard of luxury, the sound of which was proof of wealth beyond her imaginings. But to the Von Trapp children such a thing is commonplace. The image resonates with her but not with them. Sleigh bells? She obviously loves the memories that they bring, and perhaps some of the children share some happy thoughts, but it is also likely that they summon darker responses for some of the others. Have you ever ridden in the snow during a light storm in an open sleigh? It's cold and damp, and can be miserable. So perhaps Maria senses that she isn't doing too well with these "favorite" things, so she jumps to something that all Austrians enjoy - schnitzel with noodles.

And then, something remarkable. She somehow lands on an image of lyrical beauty. Imagine walking alone on a country road during a fall twilight, that magical moment when the last rays of the sun still glow in a dusty umber low on the western sky, but directly above the first stars are blinking on in the indigo expanse. The moon, almost full, has risen on the east, but is still low on the horizon. Suddenly, the flutter of wings as a flock of geese lifts from the dirt of a gleaned wheat field, and as they climb in front of you, the reflection of moonglow outlines the wings closest to you, the rest of their bodies black silhouette.

She makes a point of calling them wild geese. Does she rejoice in their freedom? Does she envy them? Does she compare them to the geese raised in her village? Does she long for a time and place where she can finally lift off and free herself from the drudgery of the farm?

"Wild geese that fly with the moon on their wings" can be simply a little bit of filler that the songwriter needed to fill out the phrase, but if the singer is intelligent she can turn it into an intensely personal image that will resonate with her, with her fellow actors, and with all of the audience. It doesn't matter that no one else will understand what that image is. It only matters that it is meaningful to the actor.

The song must be sung at the speed of the music, so the images must be produced by the singer quickly and fully formed. This is excellent training for the actor as well. All too often, novice actors will pause between each image, laboriously conjuring each mental picture while putting their mouths on hold. People don't do that in real life, and it is very boring for the audience to watch an actor contort his brow in silence while searching for the next descriptive word or phrase. If the image arrives clear and fully formed, the words will instantly tumble out, but this can only happen by doing a lot of scriptwork.

If this kind of digging can bring out so much from a simple nursery rhyme or standard musical number, imagine what some concentrated homework can do for Shakespeare? Now on the one hand you might find part of that work a little easier than it was for Little Miss Muffet, because most good editions of the Shakespeare plays will have lots of footnotes to describe and define the more obtuse references and obsolete words. But different editions will have different words defined, and sometimes defined differently. And none of them will have a word explained if the editor thinks that you should know it already.

For example: "thou". A fancy way of saying "you"; everybody knows that. Why two words for the same thought? It comes from the Romance language tradition of having both a formal and an informal way of speaking to people. It is similar to the "usted" and "tu" forms found in Spanish. But what most people don't know is that in English, "you" is the formal version, "thou" is the informal. So in general one would address someone younger or of lower social class or a relative in the "thou" form, and use "you" to address a stranger, a social superior, or someone older. So we can learn a lot about the relationship between two characters by what pronoun they choose to use. And note that when talking to God, the intimate and familiar "thou" form is used, not the more respectful and distancing "you".

How about words that are still commonly used today? Consider these two images of the moon. Which one is the crescent moon?

Only the one with the curve on the right (the one on the right side of the page) is really a crescent. The one with the curve on the left is the waning moon. Not many people in the United States would know that crescent comes from the Latin word that means "growing", and fewer still will have ever heard the phrase "curve on the right, moon grows each night." When you see the moon that has the curve on the right, it means that each night from then on it will appear bigger and bigger until it is the full moon. If the curve is on the left, it means that it will be getting smaller until it disappears completely into the new moon. When we still lived a primarily agricultural lifestyle we used to know that too, but the night sky is now alien to us. What we miss in a Shakespeare play is that when he casually makes a reference to the crescent moon, he is also inviting a comparison to other things that grow, things full of promise and anticipation. How much we miss from Shakespeare often has more to do with how distant we are from the world around us than any lack of clarity on his part.

Then again, he does use a lot of words. Why couldn't he just say what he meant without gussying it up? Sometimes what seems like extra filigree is actually some crucial information, depth that the actor can use to help us better understand the character and the moment. Consider in Romeo & Juliet, the moment that Romeo kills Tybalt. In that one moment he has destroyed his own life, killing the cousin of his newlywed bride and incurring the wrath of the Prince. When he realizes the enormity of what he has done, he cries out *"Oh, I am fortune's fool!"*. But he's not castigating himself for being an idiot, which unfortunately is the way most actors play it. If you do your homework you'll see that, to paraphrase, he's saying that he is Destiny's plaything, "fool" being used in the sense of a court jester, someone that can be abused for the pleasure of someone more powerful. He utterly fails to see any culpability on his part to any of the tragedy, and instead blames blind Fate for once again making his life miserable, instead of seeing that his impetuosity in anger is just as prone to create tragedy as his impetuosity in love. A casual reading of this one line changes the way you approach the character, and indeed can affect the entire message of the play.

Shakespeare could have used any words he wanted at that moment, but chose these. Why? Wouldn't he have been better served if he had made this crucial line more clear? Perhaps, but say the phrase slowly and out loud, and really listen to the sounds. Say it again, even more slowly. Hear how there are almost no hard stops or voiceless consonants to get in the way of one continuously voiced exhalation. The first three words become a plaintive vowel-only moan of a trapped animal, and allow the audience to feel at a deeper level the pure emotional agony that Romeo feels.

The choice of words illuminates not only the character's state of mind but his or her larger persona as well. When Caliban voices his hatred of Prospero in *Twelfth Night,* he curses him using the only imagery available to him. *"All the infections that the sun sucks up from bogs, fens, flats on Prosper fall and make him by inchmeal a disease."* Caliban is a demi-being, half way between animal and human. He cannot call on "angels and ministers of grace" from the ethereal plane, because he has no true awareness of them. He lives on the earthly plane only. And speaking of the profane, say his line out loud and listen to the series of consonants and vowels. How similar to good old-fashion Anglo-Saxon profanity! Shakespeare lets his character spout off a full line of invectives without actually using a single curse word, but the audience still can get the full effect as though they had heard every filthy word in a sailor's oratory.

By carefully choosing combinations of words, Shakespeare provides several levels of understanding of a character's feelings. This is not limited to consonants and vowels, and is most especially explored in the rhythm that springs from the flow of stressed and unstressed syllables within a phrase or sentence. I'm not going to get into an explanation of iambic pentameter, for you should all be aware by now of the "heroic meter" that was Shakespeare's favored form of laying out blank verse. And if you know that that rhythm [de-Dum, de-Dum, de-

Dum, de-Dum, de-Dum] is going to be the base line, look for those places where he breaks away from it. When Juliet, waiting for Romeo, cries out *"Gallop apace, you fiery footed steeds!"*, you can hear in those first four syllables the beat of horses hooves clattering on cobblestone roads, running to bring her love closer. When King Lear stammers out *"Never, never, never, never, never"*, we get a glimpse of his madness not only from the numb repetition of the word but also from the harsh break with the iambic meter. The more you explore how Shakespeare plays with meter, the more you'll see that he can stick to it religiously or dramatically break from it the same way a brilliant jazz musician will play with a melody line to give a deeper insight into the music.

You should be ready to break the meter as well. It is sometimes painful to hear an actor stuck in the drone of the meter, sounding more like a coffeehouse poetry reading than a real person talking to another. We are also often taught that we can figure out how to pronounce certain words in a metered line by counting the number of syllables. In Macbeth, when Young Siward says *"No; though thou callest thyself a hotter name ..."* that line works in ten syllables only if the two-syllable word "callest" is pronounced as a one-syllable "call'st". That works up to a point, but there are times when this can be hard on the audience. The same character a few lines later says *"Thou liest, abhorred tyrant; with my sword..."* and that can be forced into ten syllables by truncating either "liest" or "abhorred", but I would argue that for the sake of the audience, "liest" should be left as two-syllables and "abhorred" at three. If not, it can sound to modern audiences like some sort of insect/nautical insult: *"Thou liced-aboard tyrant;"*

So rather than using too many words, Shakespeare packs a tremendous amount of information with every line. And, indeed, especially for the male characters, the very ability and facility in commanding elaborate speech is often a sign of his intelligence, even of his virility. Only in this post-cinema age have we accepted the stereotype of the strong and silent hero. Certainly when approaching Shakespeare we have to toss out that idea. In these plays, every single character is the finest proponent of his or her particular viewpoint. There is no room for an inarticulate spokesman. If a character is muddleheaded, out the words come in a jumble, as with Dogberry in *Much Ado About Nothing*, but he is not shy about uttering them. So when in the same play Don John speaks his very first line, *"I thank you. I am of few words, but I thank you"*, we the audience already know that there is something untrustworthy about him.

Let the meter clue you in as to who and what is of importance. Many scenes will start in simple speech, and then shift into blank verse. Why? What changed? If you take note of the changes you'll see that the relative importance of either the characters or the situation is supported by the rise in poetic intricacy. So you can follow the progression from simple writing, which is just the basic idea, then the author adds force through the using of logic, in other words rhetoric. When the author then adds beauty it becomes poetry, and then gets heightened by the addition of rhythm, and in Shakespeare's time was specifically blank verse - iambic pentameter. At certain stages of the play, even this is insufficient, and then he adds rhymed couplets, and then finally goes away from iambic pentameter and into true rhymed verse in trochaic quatrameter, ending up with music.

The increasing level of complexity as the emotional stakes rise is the polar opposite of what we have now, where the character is not thought to be telling the truth unless he has dropped down to only monosyllabic words - with plenty of curse words to show how "real" the dialogue is.

You also have to be ready to play the opposites. Find the comedy in the drama, the love in the hate. A great example is *Richard III*. The role of Anne during the "wooing" scene is usually played as simple revulsion slowly turning into acquiescence. That's a bit boring, really. Much more interesting is to have her actually be guiltily attracted to Richard on some level right from the start, so that her revulsion is as much with herself as it is with Richard.

Lastly, don't get lost in the parentheticals, but let them take you to your final image. By parentheticals I am referring to all of the little subordinate sections within a sentence that add nuance to the main idea, but could be encased in parenthesis or even cut from the sentence entirely without losing the central idea. The best example of this is actually from the preamble of the United States Constitution:

> We the People of the United States, in Order to form a more perfect Union, establish Justice, insure domestic Tranquility, provide for the common defense, promote the general Welfare, and secure the Blessings of Liberty to ourselves and our Posterity, do ordain and establish this Constitution for the United States of America.

This is a run-on sentence where the essence of it is really "we ordain this constitution", everything else being filler. But what filler! All of those parentheticals describe who we are and what our dreams, fears, aspirations and challenges are, and that somehow we're going to try to meet them head-on. But none of that is going to be clear by just reading the laundry list that it seems to be. Instead, even as we visualize each possibility of those challenges we enumerate (what is the visible proof of having established justice?) our force is leading to the audacious pronouncement to the world that we have ordained and established a written reason for being.

See that last sentence? It had two parentheticals in it. The second one (with actual parenthesis) was subordinate to the first (the "even as we visualize" part). If you read it out loud, you'll probably hear yourself dropping in pitch when you read those sections, because you don't want to lose the hearer in trying to get from "Instead" all the way to "our force", and then we need to carry them all the way to the end of the sentence. The modern American speech patterns make it difficult for us to do this naturally. We tend to speak loudly and in higher pitch at the beginning of each sentence, and then trail off in both pitch and volume by the time we reach the end. Some of us exacerbate this by speeding up during the end, as if we've run out of air. Unfortunately, most of the important information is usually at the end of sentences. In modern speech, the listener makes allowances for this and can fill in the gaps. But we can't ask audiences to do the same when watching Hamlet - they won't make it through the first five minutes. Instead, we have to be generous with our speech, lifting the pitch as we deliver the character's thoughts, using up-endings throughout instead of allowing the energy to drop to the ground as we finish each phrase.

I should try to explain a little about this "up-ending" business. Listen to some of the shows on BBC America if you get the chance. Unlike Americans, the English are much more likely to use up-endings for their phrasing. At first, it almost sounds as if they are turning every phrase into a question. But what happens is that the slight lift at the end of each sentence invites the listener to subtly participate in the conversation without actually requiring a response. It is a way of checking in, making sure that the listener is still along for the ride. American down-ending speech, on the other hand, makes every statement a final pronouncement, unassailable and not open to further discussion.

And through all of this, we have to feel the emotions that are appropriate to the moment. But what does it mean for an actor to feel? Not to wallow in facile emotion, which is the all-too-common default mode for American actors. In order to FEEL a moment, the character must *find* it, *experience* it, *express* it, and then *learn* from it. (Thank you, Ada Brown Mather.) All in a split second - no "dramatic pause" because people don't pause dramatically in real life. And if the scene is well-written there may be hundreds such moments in each page or even paragraph. You have a lot of work to do, which is why actors love Shakespeare compared to standard television fare. There is always more to learn from and explore in even his silliest plays.

In addition to the danger of being blinded by our own modern perspectives, we can also have some incorrect preconceptions of what life was like "back then". This brings us to something that just drives me crazy. I often hear some variation of the following: "You know, people only lived to fifty years old back then - someone at thirty-five was already considered an old man." This is an interesting and common misunderstanding of actuarial statistics.

People live longer now. That is not in dispute. Human longevity has steadily increased since as far back as we can get data. But what is really being measured is life expectancy, literally how long one can expect a person to live once that person is born. It is an average from the entire population, not a measure of physical aging. If a country has a very high infant mortality rate, the life expectancy overall is going to be a low number, because the mathematical average age at death is pushed lower with all of those infants dying before their first birthday. Likewise, poor sanitation and lack of antibiotics killed large number of young people, so the life expectancy of Ancient Rome for the population *as a whole* was about thirty years old. But that doesn't mean that someone at twenty nine was considered an old man. Then, as now, someone who survived into his fifties was hardly a withered relic. An "old man" was generally considered to be someone in his late sixties or seventies. The body aged then just as it does now. Wrinkles and creaking bones happened on their own schedule, having nothing to do with life expectancy.

* * *

Ok, now let's get down to...

Specific Scenes from Specific Shakespeare Plays

All's Well That Ends Well

Act II, sc1 - Bertrand: *"... and no sword worn but one to dance with!"* In other words, not a sword of war or even a street brawler's rapier, but a "dancing sword" something worn for formal occasions only, never meant to be drawn.

Act IV, sc1 - Parolles makes mention of his Spanish sword. We cannot tell from this anything about what kind of sword this is, except that it is not inexpensive. Whether rapier or broadsword, the Spaniards made blades of excellent strength and durability, the hilts were highly ornamented, and the swords commanded a higher price than swords made in other countries.

Coriolanus

It's easy to think that this play would have all of the trappings of Rome during the height of its power, but if Caius Marcius Coriolanus did exist (there is some dispute among historians), it was during the fifth century B.C., a time in which the Greeks were far more powerful and Rome was only beginning to establish itself as something more than an ambitious Italian tribe. The bureaucracy and wealth that we associate with Rome were centuries away.

The Volsci whom Coriolanus had fought and finally conquered were fellow Latins, just south of Rome but from the same part of the Italian peninsula known then as Latium. The battles between the tribes were hardly the organized set pieces of massed soldiers, but more like the war parties of the Vikings - all of the available men raiding the unsuspecting enemy. The weapons used would have been the same as used by all of the Mediterranean tribes: small spears, long daggers, and axes.

Would Shakespeare have known all of this? No. So he would have had the actor/soldiers use standard late Medieval broadswords. But then again, the "costumes" would have been standard Elizabethan daywear with a short "toga" thrown on.

Hamlet

Act II, sc2 - After Rosencrantz and Guildenstern leave, Hamlet berates himself in the "rogue and peasant slave" speech, going through a litany of insults. *"Am I a coward? Who call me villain? breaks my pate across? Plucks off my beard, and blows it in my face? Tweaks me by the nose? gives me the lie i' the throat...?"* All of these were standard insults of the period designed to provoke someone into a duel, indeed, were sufficient cause to justify a fight. ["Giving the lie" means that you accuse the other person of lying, and the "lie in the throat" specifically is an ancient Italian expression meaning roughly that the lie was so heinous that it stuck in the throat of the liar and was never uttered. The delightful meaning there is that the offender didn't actually say a lie, but that it was obvious that he meant to say it, so is just as guilty.]

Act V, sc2 - Again, a rapier fight is called for in a play which takes place long before the rapier was invented. In this play, the fencing bout between Hamlet and Laertes specifically calls for both rapier and dagger, but a slight cut of two lines of reference [Osric's and then Hamlet's response] and you can use any weapons you wish.

The wager discussed before the fight has been a source of dispute among Shakespeare scholars for centuries, but I'll give you my understanding of it and you can take it for what it's worth. [It won't change the outcome of the fight, so you are pretty safe no matter what.]

"The king, sir, hath laid, that in a dozen passes between you and him, he shall not exceed you three hits; he hath laid on twelve for nine;" I read that as meaning that this is a best of twelve match. We are familiar with the concept, since that is how the World Series is played, except that the baseball championship is a best of seven series, or stated more simply, whoever gets four wins first is the champion. That doesn't necessarily mean that they play all seven games. Once one team wins four games, the show is over. It might happen on the seventh game, the fourth, the sixth, whatever. The important thing is that four is the magic number.

Same thing here, except that in a best of twelve, it takes seven points to win outright. So seven is the magic number. If the opponents are equally matched, you could expect an outcome of six points each, or 5 and 7, or 4 and 8, and so on. But of course all twelve points don't have to be played out, because whoever gets 7 points first wins since the other guy has then no chance of even tying. Big celebration, everyone goes out for pizza and beer.

Laertes is known to be quite the fencer, so instead of even odds (and an embarrassingly short match) the King has given uneven odds. Oh, he still thinks that Laertes will win, but that Hamlet's score will be no more than three points fewer than Laertes. Put another way, the difference between Laertes' score and that of Hamlet must be more than three for Laertes to win the match. Laertes now can lose even if he has a score of 7 points to 5. As a matter of fact, he has to get at least 8 points to Hamlet's no more than 4. Hamlet wins outright with only 5 points. Let's look at the different outcomes to see how this works:

Laertes	Hamlet		
12	0	=	Laertes wins
11	1	=	Laertes wins
10	2	=	Laertes wins
9	3	=	Laertes wins
8	4	=	<u>Laertes wins</u>
7	5	=	Hamlet wins
6	6	=	Hamlet wins
5	7	=	Hamlet wins
4	8	=	Hamlet wins
3	9	=	Hamlet wins
2	10	=	Hamlet wins
1	11	=	Hamlet wins
0	12	=	Hamlet wins

The magic number of points for Laertes is 8; for Hamlet only 5. Not all of the passes will be played, of course, since when the magic number is reached, the match is over. Whosoever reaches his own magic number first, wins. We'll see how this plays out later.

Hamlet - *"Give us the foils"* Well, are they rapiers or are they foils? Foil in this case means that the tip is not sharp, that it has been blunted, as in the phrase - "curses, foiled again."

Laertes - *"This is too heavy, let me see another."* Obviously Laertes has to make sure that he pulls the poisoned and sharpened rapier from the selection brought out, and it seems he pulled out or was handed the wrong one first and has to make an excuse in order to exchange it.

Hamlet -*"These foils have all a length?"* Or, paraphrased, *Are all of the blades the same length?* In Shakespeare's time, there was no standardization of blade length, and rapiers could range from 30 to 50 inches in length. Hamlet, hearing Laertes complain that one sword at least was substantially heavier than another, asks a perfectly appropriate question. The answer (possibly just a nod from Osric) should have given him pause, and if he had been more suspicious would have then examined all of the swords, but the moment quickly passes.

"A hit, a very palpable hit" The first point goes to Hamlet, as does the second, *"A touch, a touch, I do confess"*. Things aren't going smoothly for Laertes, but no reason to panic since there are still ten more passes to play out. Laertes still needs eight points to win and Hamlet needs three more, but Laertes is in reality just looking for one good strike to kill Hamlet. He doesn't care about winning the match.

Then an unfortunate situation on the next pass. Some move or another occurs that apparently looks like a strike by someone, but Osric the referee calls out *"nothing, neither way"*. That pass is done, but no points were awarded. This changes the calculations immediately. The total number of possible points is now down to 11, not 12, and Hamlet has 2 of them. Remember, Laertes still has to win by <u>more</u> than three points, so he still needs 8 points. But Hamlet's magic number is now 4. e now only needs **two** more points, or even two more draws, and the match is over, for then Laertes cannot win "at the odds".

A new look at the "what if" score board shows:

Laertes	Hamlet			
11	0	=	~~Laertes wins~~	*can't happen*
10	1	=	~~Laertes wins~~	*can't happen*
9	2	=	Laertes wins	
8	3	=	<u>Laertes wins</u>	
7	4	=	Hamlet wins	
6	5	=	Hamlet wins	
5	6	=	Hamlet wins	
4	7	=	Hamlet wins	
3	8	=	Hamlet wins	
2	9	=	Hamlet wins	
1	10	=	Hamlet wins	
0	11	=	Hamlet wins	

Laertes must hit Hamlet during one of the next two passes, for if Hamlet gets them or even ties them (that *"nothing neither way"* thing), Hamlet wins by the odds and Laertes loses the chance to strike with the poisoned sword.

The rest of the fight is described only in a very brief stage direction - *[Laertes wounds Hamlet; then in scuffling, they change rapiers, and Hamlet wounds Laertes].* That means that how they get to the end of the fight is completely up to you. Some versions of the fight take no more than 20 seconds from start to finish: some last up to six minutes. Some have Laertes sneak in an attack; some have it as a regular pass which happens to finally land.

Most versions have Hamlet realize that he has been stabbed with a sharpened point, but that is not necessarily the case. These swords wouldn't have had rubber tips on them, and after a few passes could easily have become nicked and have sharp burrs along the edge. A scratch or even a quick prick would be almost unnoticed in the adrenaline rush of being in the fight.

On a purely practical level, although a "broken blade" rehearsal is important for any show with a sword fight in it, it is absolutely crucial for this show. Think out the fight carefully with an eye as to who must die with the poison-tipped sword, and what the actors will have to do if either sword breaks at any particular point in the fight. Don't follow the swords - follow the poisoned tip. If Laertes' sword breaks early on, he is going to have to find a justification for picking up the tip and stabbing Hamlet with it.

About the poison: all of the poisons in Shakespeare plays are poisons of theatrical convention - fantasies that can do whatever the playwright needs them to do for the particular scene. They have no correlation to any real compounds, extinct or extant.

Random art notes: Keep in mind that there was an earlier version of this story, before Shakespeare's time. It was far bloodier, with Hamlet being the perfect revenge tragedy hero (acting quite a bit more like Laertes). Shakespeare did quite a bit to humanize his characters, but we still have a play that appealed to the bulk of the audience because they knew there was going to be a lot of action and that a lot of "bad" people were going to die (not unlike the early Clint Eastwood movies).

To be or not to be. I know that the popular conception is that this demonstrates how suicidal and melancholic is Hamlet, but a careful reading of this speech shows quite the opposite. The speech is a classic example of Roman rhetoric, in which the position is stated in pro and con, and then the ramifications and reasons are posited for closer analysis in the body of the speech. Therefore, "to be" [to live] is equated with suffering [allowing] things to be the way they are, and "not to be" [to die] is the result of taking arms [action]. Hamlet is not contemplating suicide itself, but rather a suicide mission - take action against the king and therefore surely die in the process. It is fear of death (which makes cowards of us all) that prevents Hamlet from acting, not indecision. While it is true that in Act I, Scene 2 we do hear Hamlet cry out "Oh, that this too, too solid flesh should melt", etc., this is more the equivalent of an adolescent "Oh I wish I were dead". He certainly is galvanized, even transformed, when he finally sees the ghost. From that point on he faces a brutal choice: ignore the ghost and live, or obey the ghost and die.

But merely wanting to live is not Hamlet's only concern. He also doesn't trust the ghost. The problem is that in the classic theology ["philosophy"] of the period, which Hamlet, Horatio, and Laertes have studied, ghosts cannot exist. The spirit of the dead resides with the body; and does not go to purgatory nor heaven immediately after death. Instead, all souls must stay in the body and await the final judgment, which occurs only after Armageddon. This according to his learning at Wittenburg, and so it follows that the apparition can only be a spirit damned, nonhuman, and manifests itself falsely as his father in order to trick Hamlet into committing a sin, and thereby losing his soul. That the general population believes in ghosts should not dissuade him from his learning, and yet he cannot ignore the possibility that the ghost is indeed his father's spirit. If that is true, he must do his duty as son and heir. His doubts as to the correctness of his actions are profound, as are the potential consequences of his decision.

Henry (et al)

An interesting note on the character of Pistol. Pistols (the firearms) in Shakespeare's time were large and ungainly objects, never used off of the battlefield, horrendously inaccurate and had only a limited military use. Quickly the term *pistol* became synonymous with *cowardly*, both the firearm and by extension the person carrying one described as something that makes a loud noise but is of little danger to the bystander.

Julius Caesar

There are only two scenes of violence that we actually need to see, the first being the more famous. The assassination with knives is a bit drawn out, as each conspirator takes his turn to do the deed. Some doubling up of attacks can be choreographed in order to shorten the time it takes to get to Brutus, but the fight director still has to find a variety of ways to kill someone. The easiest is to work ever changing angles of attack so each has some variation (check the stage combat section), with each character showing a different reaction to the act. Blood seems to be what every director wants, and my strong suggestion is to have the blood packs taped to the handles of the knives instead of on Julius' body (with the very real risk of a blood pack leaking before he gets stabbed). If you keep the blades short then it's easy enough to transfer the blood from the stabber's hand to the victim's clothing. The benefits are two: you don't have to worry about controlling unreliable "blood knives", and you have the conspirators get bloody hands.

The killing of Senna the poet is a far more difficult scene. You're obviously not going to show someone literally torn apart (at least I hope you're not). But much can be suggested by having poor Senna being slowly swallowed by the crowd, his screams doing more to transmit the horror of a bloodthirsty mob than actually showing the blood.

Several productions try to show something of the battles inferred in Act V. While I completely understand the desire to include some action in these very talky scenes, it might be more effective to at most only symbolically show some fighting (slow-motion?, showing only one side of the battle?) unless you actually have two or three hundred extras on hand.

King Lear

The story of Lear comes from the ancient Arthurian or even pre-Roman legends, so if set in that early Celtic period all swords would be of the short and stout variety, but as in most of the Shakespeare plays there is no attempt at historical setting. It is very likely that rapiers are intended as the weapon worn by all of the male characters until they prepare for war in Act V, at which point they would be put away in favor of the Gothic broadswords. But of course you can only use rapiers if you are setting it in the late Renaissance, rather than the Middle Ages or before.

When Kent confronts Oswald in Act II, sc 2, he is using the standard language for provoking a rapier duel. His insults provide the legal base for both men to legally engage their weapons. Kent insists that Oswald draw his weapon so that they may fight. Since Oswald refuses, Kent can only strike him, that is to say, hit him with an open hand or closed fist, but cannot use a weapon. *"Draw, you rogue, or I'll so carbonado your shanks!"* Carbonado is a Spanish term for roasting over coals, like a barbecue. Larger roasts were sometimes deeply cut so that the meat would cook more evenly. It is a vain threat only, for Kent will not use his sword until his opponent draws.

Edmond rushes in and from the stage direction seems to part the other two, although Oswald hardly needs much inducement to run away from the beating. There is no specific reference to Edmond and Kent fighting, but Cornwall's line is *"He dies that strikes again"*, so there has been at least one clash of steel. But if strike meant hitting with an open hand, why does it mean swordplay here? Because it is unlikely that Cornwall would threaten death if the two hadn't drawn swords.

Random art note: It is likely that the same actor in Shakespeare's company played both Oswald in this show and Osric in Hamlet. Both share similarities in being courtiers and not soldiers. The actor was undoubtedly a crowd favorite for his portrayal of this stock character, and would have been recognized as a source of ridicule from almost the moment he stepped foot on stage. The abuse that he suffers from Kent and Hamlet would have been savored by the Elizabethan audience.

Act III, sc 4 - This is the only instance in all of the plays of Shakespeare in which a member of the lower class challenges, let alone fights, a noble. The very idea of a servant raising a sword against his master, no matter how justified, would have made many in the Elizabethan audience very nervous. Regan - *"Give me thy sword ..."* - she's talking to one of the others in the scene, not to either of the combatants. It is not mentioned in the script, but Cornwall seems to have been wounded by the servant during the fight, spurring Regan to take matters into her own hands.

When Edgar and Edmond fight in Act V, they would use broadswords, not rapiers, for this is judicial combat, not a duel of honor or passion.

Love's Labour's Lost

Act I, sc 2 - Don Adriano de Armado, speaking of trying to fight against Cupid; *"The first and second cause will not serve my turn; the passado he respects not, the duello he regards not:"*. Not that the audience really needs to know what he is saying here, but the actor must. The first and second causes refer to some of the legal (well, at least socially acceptable) justifications for entering into a duel, establishing who is the aggrieved party. The passado is a calculated forward passing step of the trained fighter. The duello is shorthand for the Code Duello, the protocol of formalities governing all aspects of the duel. Don Adriano is saying that Cupid does not fight like a gentleman, so his own prowess with a rapier will serve him not.

The English of Shakespeare's time tended to regard Spaniards as being braggarts. Don Adraino would have been stereotypically armed (literally - armado) with a too ornate and too large rapier, and much like Aguecheek in the *Twelfth Night*, not likely to actually use it. (It is likely that the same actor in Shakespeare's company played the same stock character.)

Macbeth

A lot of productions enjoy sticking in a large fight just before the play opens. The play doesn't need it, but if you do decide to add one, take advantage of the opportunity by using it as a way of showing Macbeth as a heroic figure, brave and daring, one worthy of the honors that will be bestowed upon him. You might also have the tone of the fight look very different from the fights at the end of the play. No matter what, less is more, and get to the witches as fast as you can.

There are only two fights that are actually in the script, although many directors like to extend this by including full-out running battles in and around the two Macbeth set pieces. "Before my body I throw my warlike shield". Obviously a broadsword and shield fight is called for, but a slight trim of the above reference and you can use whatever weapons you wish.

If more soldiers are fighting, a variety of weapons might be used even in a traditional production, and use of spears makes for great 2-on-1 match-ups. The actual period of the historic Macbeth would mean that axes and spears would be the predominant weapons, supplemented with swords of less than two feet long. But most productions use longer swords. It should be noted that full two-handed broadswords sometimes requested are a much later development in Scottish warfare, but if the costuming matches the Elizabethan time frame, it is certainly acceptable.

The decapitation of Macbeth occurs offstage in the script, but many directors seem to like to have it happen in the audience's view during the on-stage fight. My opinion is that it destroys the tension of the following scene if we already know the outcome of the fight.

Whenever Macbeth fights, we do need to see that he is a superb warrior who is justifiably confidant of his skills. Just be careful not to make him superhuman. A staged production shown on PBS a few decades ago had their Macbeth fighting with a light staff in a completely upright posture, using as much effort in combat as one might use in folding laundry. The result was laughable because the physics of the fight was simply unbelievable. If a body is to be thrown back six feet, we need to see that same amount of force generated by the thrower. The aggressor can still appear relaxed, but the body placement for each move must be based in real-time physics. Even the animated superhero cartoons understand this basic premise.

On a personal note, I always feel sorry for our poor Macbeth, who by all contemporary accounts succeeded to the throne by accepted and legal means. He ruled wisely and well, led his country through seventeen years of prosperity. He was then overthrown by an usurper, who allowed the English to dominate the Scots by influence within the court, which they never would have been able to do by force of arms alone.

Macbeth's Timeline:

1040 Macbeth kills Duncan on the battlefield; named king of Scotland by legal vote of thanes

1042 Edward the Confessor becomes king of England

1054 Macbeth defeated by Malcolm and Siward at Dunsinane

1057 Macbeth is murdered by Malcolm, but Macbeth's stepson Lulach is voted by thanes as king of Scotland

1058 Malcolm murders Lulach and becomes king of Scotland; all thanes re-titled as earls, no longer have any vote in rights of succession.

Random art notes: There is a huge treasure of superstitions revolving around even uttering the name of Macbeth in a theatre, but having worked in over two dozen productions (and saying the name out load at every opportunity), I can state with confidence that the bad luck associated with the show has more to do with having the most violent and physically taxing fight scenes occur at the very end of an emotionally exhausting play. And keep in mind that it is also very bad luck to be superstitious.

A Midsummer Night's Dream

This show doesn't really have any fight problems in it, just some tussling amoung the lovers. But the following has always bothered me:

Random art notes: I love reading all of the graduate theses and critical commentary in literature journals concerning the title. The authors are usually trying to parse out the meaning, juxtaposing the midsummer reference in the title with the internal references to it taking place on the day of or surrounding the first of May. Do the lovers somehow dream that they are in summer rather than spring? Do the fairies alter time and the seasons with their presence?

Elizabethan plays were performed in summertime. It is the audience that is having the dream. *THE AUDIENCE!*

Much Ado About Nothing

There is no fighting in this show, but there is an interesting reference made by Leonato's brother Antonio in Act V, sc 1. During the tirade, the insults are based on the generation gap noted in so many of the Shakespeare plays. The references revolve around the disdain that the older generation had for the younger, especially their use of the unmanly rapier.

Random art note: Don't gloss over the title too quickly, for everything you need to know about this show is right there. To have the playwright say that this is all much ado about nothing seems callous considering the trauma that Hero suffers, until we reflect on how the word "nothing" in Elizabethan times was pronounced with a long "o", and therefore "nothing" rhymed with "noting". Throughout the play there are examples of people seeing things, looking right at them, but not really taking note of what it is they see. All of the plot twists happen when someone looks at something and takes it at face value, yet fails to note its true nature. Neither wealth nor power nor position provides this insight. Indeed it is the humble and ignorant watch who, while not understanding all of what they see, note that something is not right and bravely take action. The priest also carefully notes Hero's reaction and is able to discern truth from confusion.

Note as well the arc of the basic story line. A perfect world, then a flawed noble breaks away, sending the world into turmoil. A messenger of God steps in to set the world back on track, which must go through the steps of seeming death, atonement of sins, which leads to a rebirth, and a final confrontation between good and evil yet to come. Anyone from Shakespeare's time would have instantly seen the biblical comparison, yet modern audiences lose this added depth to the story.

Othello

Although it has long been tradition to play the character of Othello as an African, the "Moors" described by Elizabethan-era Europeans were not Africans nor even ethnic Arabs but rather what we would describe as Turks. The term was used to describe any follower of Islam from Muslim Spain, India, Northern Africa (Algeria/Egyptian), but most especially in Shakespeare's time the superpower Ottoman Empire. It was common at the time to refer to anyone of brown complexion as "black", as true sub-Saharan Africans were nearly unknown in Europe. Even the less-used term "blackamoor" was used to describe an especially swarthy Turk, while "white Moor" was understood to be one with paler skin.

The Ottoman Turks were engaged in a centuries-long struggle with Venice and other seagoing Christian states for control of the Mediterranean, and Venice especially had no qualms about hiring experienced opponents as mercenaries. In exchange for extremely generous monetary compensation, they merely had to profess conversion to Christianity and fight on behalf of the Venetian council. Othello certainly fits this profile.

Act II, sc 1 - Iago warns Roderigo that Cassio "with his truncheon may strike at you". He is referring not to a club, but to Cassio's baton signifying his rank. The warning makes a direct reference to being physically struck, but also a reminder that Cassio could inflict punishment by virtue of his position.

Act V, sc 2 - There is lots of violence in this show, but perhaps the most dangerous bit is the smothering of Desdemona. Check back in the combat section for tips on how to do this safely.

Once again, however, Shakespeare has an impossible death. She is smothered, but then speaks a few pages later that she has been murdered, and then dies. How can this be? Well it can't, so don't worry about it.

Romeo & Juliet

Although no specific year setting is mentioned in the script, we are given to understand that this story of star-crossed lovers takes place in about the mid-1400's, and of course in Verona, Italy. Forget any of the "historical background" which the modern town of Verona offers in order to entice tourists - the story and the characters are pure fiction. It was an old tale even in Shakespeare's time, but set in many cities and with many names. No matter - as always, Shakespeare's characters are all English men and women from the mid 1580's, so it is impossible to stage a "historically accurate" version of this show. Compromises will be made from the very first scene.

Act I, sc 1 - The play in fact opens with two very typical English youths discussing their prowess with the ladies and with the sword. When they spy two other youths from the rival household, the discussion quickly centers on the 16th century rules of the duel: who has a legal cause to begin a fight, etc. When the fight finally breaks out, "remember thy swashing blow" is a reminder to Gregory to use a good stout cutting motion rather than the finer thrust and parry of rapier fighting. From this we know that Samson and Gregory are sword and buckler men, not rapier duelists, and their swords were rather like short broadswords. It was the weapon of common soldiers and archers. The buckler is a very small shield, not practical for warfare, but light enough to have handy if a street brawl is anticipated. [The phrase "swashing blow" has been changed by some editors to "smashing blow" and by some to the ridiculous "washing blow", but this is both ludicrous and unnecessary, as the word "swash" means a full side-to-side slashing cut. The buckler is held in the left hand for defense, therefore such a fighter was known as a swash-buckler. Be kind to your audience. They aren't going to know about "swashing blows" or "washing blows", so just change the line to "slashing blow", a lovely, accurate and descriptive alternative.]

Tybalt and Benvolio are of more elevated birth than the first four serving men, so they would, by their stations, be expected to wear a rapier. In Shakespeare's time they would almost certainly also use a secondary weapon such as a dagger or cloak. [As we later learn that these are very hot summer days, we can assume that cloaks are not going to be used.] As long as they don't use the rapier by itself to block the swinging cuts of the stout swords, they could easily engage the servingmen in combat.

When the heads of the households arrive, at least one of them asks for the only sword with which someone of his generation would be familiar - the "longsword", the sword of war, what we term the broadsword, and not necessarily a two-handed variety. Since the broadsword is too heavy to wear on a daily basis, it is only natural that he would need to have someone fetch it.

As the townspeople attempt to put down the fight, they grab the nearest weapons they can. Bills and partisans are types of pole weapons used in war but also used by civilian armed watch, and are named by the crowd. Farm tools are not mentioned, but wouldn't be out of place.

The prince enters attended "with his train". That's all we know. He might be attended by advisors, by friends, by servants, by guards, or by the Rockettes. We just don't know.

Act III - Here in the "prince of cats" section we have a wonderful description of the rapier duelist when Mercutio describes Tybalt.

His point of view is strictly English, who generally despaired of widespread use of the rapier, that continental European weapon that killed men in peacetime and was useless in war. Yet, it was still necessary to have if for no other reason than someone who had one might pick a fight with you. Within Mercutio's speech is a reference to the almost mathematical precision of French dueling instruction, with its emphasis on learned patterns of feints (false attacks) before striking home with a thrust. "One, two, and the third in your bosom" would get a knowing if uneasy laugh from an English audience, at once in love with and in fear of this sneaky weapon used by sneaky people. Also subject to derision is the way that English youth would be taught not only fencing by these foreign masters, but also dancing, comportment, style, even to the point of how to stand, sit and walk with grace and elegance. Small wonder that he derides those who can no longer sit at ease on an old bench.

Mercutio also ridicules the use of Italian phrases used in swordplay instruction, mentioning specifically the *passado*, the *punto reverso*, and the *hay*. I should point out here that we no longer really know what these terms mean, but that doesn't stop scholars from trying to translate them. The most conservative translations of High Renaissance Italian would seem to indicate that the *passado* is a forward passing step (possibly combined with a thrust), the *punto reverso* is aiming or thrusting the sword to the outside of an opponent's guard, and *hay* is merely the shout given by the student as he attempts a strike (much like the "kiai" yell for modern karate students).

Later in the same scene, Mercutio pointedly refers to Tybalt as *alla stoccata*, which is a beautiful use of Italian that Tybalt can take either as a compliment or as a sly insult. *A la stocatta* literally translates to "by the thrust", but has more of the flavor of saying "in the style of quick tapping".

The fight between Mercutio and Tybalt is only briefly described. Mercutio himself says that he was hurt under Romeo's arm, which Benvolio confirms in his description of the fight to the Prince. From this we can assume that when Romeo rushes in to break-up the fight, he lifts up Mercutio's arms, exposing the belly to Tybalt's thrust. Benvolio also describes Mercutio's fighting, "with one hand beats cold death aside and with the other sends it back to Tybalt." From this we know that at the very least Mercutio fights with rapier in the right hand and some other weapon, probably a dagger, in the left. Fighting with only one sword would have been unusual in this period.

When Romeo later fights with Tybalt, does he use his own sword? Most productions like seeing Romeo unarmed before this scene, so often he is made to simply pick up the slain Mercutio's sword and kill Tybalt with it. Because this is a more impulsive fight, Romeo might not think to draw his knife. On the other hand, you could have him use only his knife and no sword at all. Or maybe he rushes at Tybalt with only his dagger. Completely your choice.

Act IV - When in Friar Lawrence's cell, it seems that Juliet pulls out a knife and threatens to kill herself. This is her own small dagger, not the one used later in the tomb. It is most likely a fairly small, narrow bladed knife, probably worn at the waist, but other locations, some hidden from view, are certainly common enough. [Comparing this scene with actions in the following act indicate that this is a childish outburst and not a real suicide threat. In that case, the size of the knife should reflect the lack of serious danger.]

Act V - Romeo and Paris are assumed to fight with rapiers, but there is no textual support for that supposition. We have no proof that Paris uses either rapier or dagger. We know that Romeo is wearing a dagger, and that he is holding a mallet *[mattock]* and a pry bar *[crow]*. Whether he uses any of these or any other items or for that matter any weapon at all is pure conjecture. Be very careful of the tool choices if you do incorporate them in the fight. A real crowbar, even if dulled, can do significant damage with even light accidental contact. There are some hollow alternatives available. I personally don't like to have Romeo wearing a sword in this scene, but only because I hate having to see him struggle with the scabbard when he has to be dead later in the tomb.

The final death (not counting Lady Montegue) is Juliet's. In this scene she truly commits herself to take her own life. She does not even consider using her small knife, but first looks to Romeo's vial of poison, and, finding it empty, takes his dagger. As such, Romeo's dagger has to look menacing but not have a blade so large as to make Juliet's suicide look comical. A blade length of ten inches should be the maximum considered unless your Juliet is an exceptionally long armed girl.

Helpful Hint: Juliet's death can still border on the comical if for no other reason that it is very difficult to pull off a suicide on stage. If what you are doing doesn't seem to be working, give the following a try:

First get a dagger with a blade length of no more than three quarters of Juliet's forearm length. If her sleeves are billowy, so much the better. Have her face full front to the audience, and have her hold the dagger with both hands on the handle and the blade pointed right at her stomach. Go ahead and let the hands be lower than the belly so that the audience gets a good picture of the lethality of the situation, or let the weapon be raised high if it gives everyone a better view. We want them to see the full blade pointing right at the center of her stomach. Just as she is trying to summon up the nerve to do the deed itself, she hears a noise - the others are about to enter! - she must kill herself now!

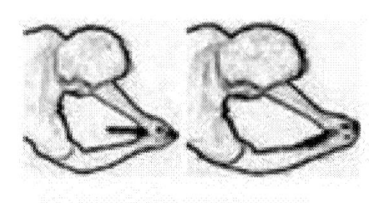

During that small moment is when Juliet can lift her hands slightly, which blocks the audience's view of the knife blade. Instantly she snaps the flat of the blade against her forearm, and then plunges her fists into her stomach. Depending on the knife, it might also be helpful to have the hand holding the knife to twist so that the palm is facing up. The last image the audience had of the knife was of the blade pointing at the belly, so that is where they think it still is. They will next look at her eyes for her reaction, further hiding the illusion. [If you really want to toy with the audience, have the thrust happen in two stuttering motions - the first move going only half way meeting resistance from the skin, then the full plunge immediately following.]

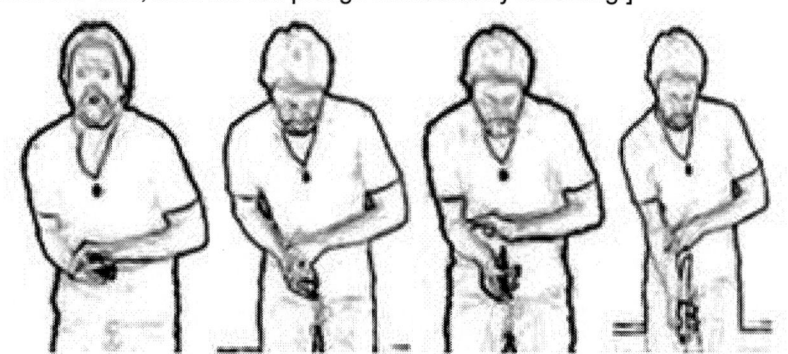

Here is the key to this simulation: withdraw the knife *slowly*, as though you have nothing to hide. Leaving the left hand on the belly, the right hand brings the knife out, all the while pushing the blade tip in towards the left hand. As it's coming out, the blade can even be slightly forced under the floating rib, so that with a little practice it can appear as though the blade is being pulled straight out of the belly - and right in front of the audience's view. The audience will not need any blood effect to believe that she actually stabbed herself.

Random art note: I often hear people justify Juliet's young age for marriage by noting that Lady Capulet was young when she wed and that, after all, everyone wed very young in "olden times". But that attitude shifts many times in different centuries. Lord Capulet himself is none too thrilled with the idea, perhaps from experience *["and too soon marred are those so early made"]*. More importantly, we can certainly assume that her youth would have been shocking for an Elizabethan audience. My own grandmother, in the old country, was married at the age of 14, but believe it or not in the England of Shakespeare's time the average age for a woman to marry was 23. The average male married at 26, so both Juliet and Romeo would have been considered far too young and immature for marriage. [Shakespeare himself required his father's permission in order to marry Anne Hathaway. At the age of eighteen, he was legally a minor.] It is very likely that for sixteenth century audiences this play wasn't so much a love story as a tragedy of juvenile impetuosity.

Taming of the Shrew

Act III, sc 2 - *Why, Petruchio is coming in a new hat and an old jerkin, a pair of old breeches thrice turned, a pair of boot that have been candle-cases, one buckled, another laced, an old rusty sword ta'en out of the town-armory, with a broken hilt, and chapeless; with two broken points;*

It is the sword, or more exactly the sheath for the sword, that is "chapeless", meaning that the brass bottom (the chape) of the leather sheath is missing. So the point of the sword is sticking out of the bottom of the scabbard. The sword is rusty, but not broken. The "two broken points" refers to the thin straps used to tie the hose onto the doublet. In other words, Petruchio's leggings are drooping. It has nothing to do with the sword.

Random art note: This, and the rest of the description, would to Elizabethan audiences be instantly recognized as the comic stereotype of the cuckolded husband. Will any modern audience understand this joke? Never. Nowadays the entire scene is just played as though Petruchio is trying to be outrageous, but it has really lost all of its original meaning. Modern productions can only play Petruchio as being a "wild man", even though what he is demonstrating is something more subtle. He's declaring that he knows what everyone is thinking, that he is going to be cuckolded, but that he wants to marry Kate anyway. Perhaps that's just as audacious and insulting, but is does add a little nuance to the scene, don't you think?

Another random art note: In England, Petruchio's name is pronounced just as it's written, with the "ch" sound. In the USA, our tradition is to use a hard "k". Who is right? In Italian the name was written *Petruccio*, so the double c should be pronounced as a "ch". It appears that the name was written in the play phonetically, to help the English actors in pronunciation. Unfortunately, in Italian the written "ch" is pronounced with the hard "k". We in the states have overthought this one, I'm afraid. The name should be pronounced as written, with the soft "ch". Say it out loud. There now, doesn't that sound a lot more Italian?

The Tempest

In Act II, sc 1 - Antonio says - *"Here lies your brother, ... Whom I, with this obedient steel, three inches of it, Can lay to bed for ever;"* A sword thrust need not penetrate too deeply to cause a fatal wound. A three inch stab and a person can quickly bleed to death. A similar observation is made in *Romeo & Juliet* with the death of Mercutio.

Titus Andronicus

As in all of Shakespeare's Roman and Greek plays, anachronisms abound. In this play, references are made several times to rapiers and scimitars, neither of which had been invented during the historic setting of the play. You may indeed choose to have Aaron wear a Turkish scimitar, and none in the audience will notice, but to have Demetrius and others wear a rapier while wearing the costumes of Ancient Rome is asking a bit much of their suspension of disbelief. When the characters speak of rapiers, just treat the word as a substitute for sword, and dress them in standard short swords of the period.

On the other hand, there is one specific reference that should be looked at a bit more carefully. Act II, sc 1 - *"Why, boy, although our mother, unadvised, gave you a dancing-rapier by your side, are you so desperate grown, to threat your friends?"* - What Demetrius is implying here is that, although Chiron may wear the sword of a man, such a weapon is nothing but swagger when worn by a boy. A sword worn as part of elegant dress for a court appearance or formal dance was called a dancing rapier, not seriously worn for self-defense. "Dancing-rapier" is not necessarily an insult, but is certainly used as one here. Demetrius follows up with an elaboration of the theme - *"Go to; have your lath glued within your sheath till you know better how to handle it."* - Actors of the time often wore prop swords made with blades of thin slats of wood [lath]. These "swords" were also sometimes rented out to lower nobility or social climbing merchants for social occasions, so the insult would have gotten a good chuckle from the audience.

A reminder that Aaron, like Othello, was probably imagined as a Turk, not an Ethiopian. Although both Aaron and his child are described as "black" or "blackamoor", those terms were used in Shakespeare's time to mean swarthy but not Negroid. Tamara, Demetrius and Chiron are Goths, so essentially German. Is any of this important for casting? No.

Twelfth Night

How much fighting we actually see depends on the director. Many productions do quite well without showing any sword contact at all. Just as Viola and Aguecheek have drawn their swords and stand shaking in terror, Antonio steps in and stops the action, quickly followed by the officers and the arrest. No pauses between any of the lines and no duel at all. On the other hand, I've seen some productions where the fighting rolls on and on, lasting a full five minutes, which is a huge time for uninterrupted fighting. In those versions, Aguecheek and Viola are allowed an extended comedic duel (in my estimation, the hardest fight to choreograph is one in which both combatants are cowards). After that, Sebastian steps in, but is taken on by first Toby and then Fabian. The officers briefly stop the action, but Sebastian takes them on as well, and soon is fighting off all four (sometimes five!) opponents in a daring piece of swashbuckling. Only when placed in a final hopeless situation does he give up and submit to his arrest.

There are many references to swords and fighting throughout the play, and most are very obvious, but on occasion some lead to small confusions, so let's clarify these:

Act III, sc 4 - *"on, or strip your sword stark naked; for meddle you must, that's certain, or forswear to wear iron about you"* Some people think that Sir Toby is telling Viola the same thing on both parts of this sentence, but it's a little more intricate than that. *"on* [go to Andrew] *, or strip your sword stark naked* [draw your sword and fight <u>me</u>]*; for meddle* [fight someone] *you must, that's certain, or forswear to wear iron about you* [never wear a sword again]*"*

Earlier in the same scene - *"He is knight, dubbed with unhatched rapier and on carpet consideration"*. Sir Andrew received his knighthood not from any battlefield exploit, but for some special service to the crown performed by himself or his father. These services might have been economic, diplomatic, cultural or even trivial, but were certainly of much less prestige than a knighthood for military service.

Shifting Weapons to Match Design Concepts

"How many ages hence
Shall this our lofty scene be acted over
In states unborn and accents yet unknown!"
    Julius Caesar - Act 3, Scene 1

The plays of Shakespeare are of course set in many times and countries, and it is common to re-set them in other periods and cultures. This makes it both more interesting for the artists (many of whom may have been in six or seven productions of Twelfth Night and so are grateful to get out of having to wear pumpkin breaches again) and also can help the audience see the story being told as dealing with universal themes.

I love seeing the costume designs for these retelling of old stories. The designers face interesting challenges in translating, as it were, the nature of Shakespeare's late Renaissance characters into people of other times and places. The props master has her work cut out for her as well, for weapons will have to be true to both the costume design and to the fight requirements.

Some conflicts are bound to occur. The most common is how to justify the wearing of weapons in times when weapons are not worn. While formal duels with the sword might have been common in 1865, civilians simply did not wear swords. Wearing a weapon when out on the street in Shakespeare's time was completely normal and non-threatening. But sticking a knife or gun on a character in a modern setting instantly makes that person look sinister. Then there are the more subtle difficulties of translating Elizabeth themes into modern equivalents. How do you express the generation gap between rapiers worn by youths and stout swords preferred by the older crowd?

What follows is an example of the weapons that we at Weapons of Choice have sent out for different productions of Macbeth, or "The Scottish Play". Those with a superstitious bent might refer to Macbeth that way, but by whatever name, it is always a powerful experience for an audience. Naturally, it has a special place in our hearts because of the number of times we outfit this show each year. Interestingly, we send broadswords to only about half of the productions, since this is one of those wonderful shows that responds so well to different settings.

The most common request is for "period" swords, although that usually requires a few follow-up questions. Macbeth's historical period (1040-1057 AD) is, of course, much different from Shakespeare's, (who never worried about historical accuracy) and well researched productions set in this period use a mix of Scottish and Viking single hand edged weapons, with short spears doing the brunt of the fighting.

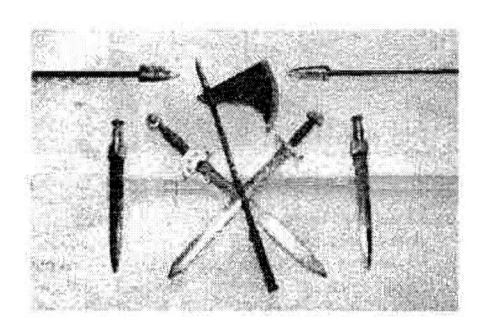

The swords of Shakespeare's day were quite different, anachronisms really, but when the costume plot is set in the 1500's, the corresponding weapons match the dialogue exactly. Big two handed broadswords, halberds, maces, all of the fun bashing stuff for the final scene, with some light swords for the more Anglicized nobles, are all appropriate.

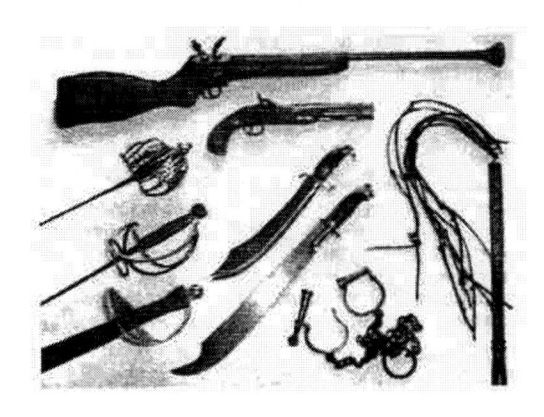

Always a delight to perform and watch is the Caribbean Macbeth, with voodoo priestesses instead of witches from the heath, and the ghost of Banquo is of course a true Zombie. Buccaneers and privateers involved in intrigue with petty local governor/mayors, and a blend of swashbuckling cutlasses and rapiers.

The most challenging for us are the post-Apocalyptic styles. Each will have it's own spin on what might be acquired after the big one drops (mostly found objects turned into bashing implements) or after society simply implodes on its own (a mix of weapons: low-tech, high-tech, and futuristic). Bag-ladies with shopping carts as witches? Shown are some fantasy weapons which we have created to fit different productions.

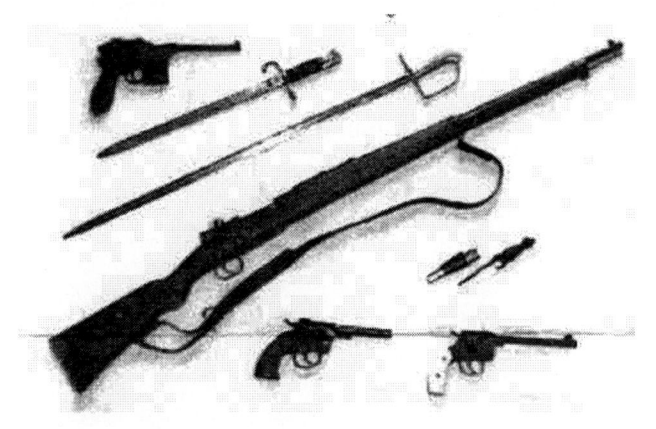

Our favorite? Not done often enough is the Victorian/Edwardian setting. All of those great drawing room suits and smoking jackets, fabulous gowns and jewelry, doughboy uniforms and WWI-style rifles for the soldiers, pistols and dress sabres for the officers. The use of the Gothic and morbid themes in art and literature, the toying with spiritualism so prevalent among the upper class can add a séance feel to all of the witches' scenes.

A unique spin to the above was to set the play in the Empire/ Napoleonic style of Europe. The witches were a band of Gypsies. Flintlock muskets to outfit an army attacking Dunsinane, and curved sabres for the final two fights.

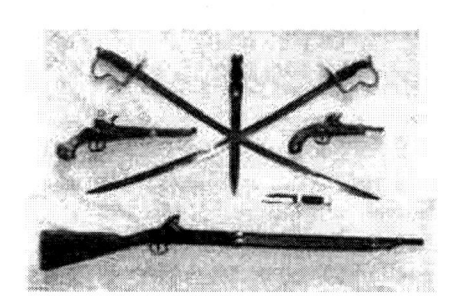

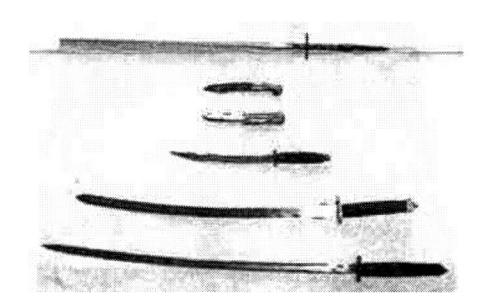

Speaking of curved blades, the "Shogun Macbeth" is a very powerful approach to the text. The Noh style movement merely adds to the grandeur of power and the depths of despair, and makes the bizarre elements of the script more, not less, plausible. Fantastical witches can be at once awe inspiring and repulsive; geisha witches both beautiful and unsettling. Assassins could be ninjas or peasants.

Modern dress productions now seem to take their cue from television news coverage of Iraq (Cuba used to be the model). Battle fatigues and business suits meet the shattered refugees of war on the heath, who slip a hallucinogenic brew to help Macbeth "see" the future.

No matter what period is selected, be very careful about using firearms as an automatic substitute for the sword. You can certainly outfit whatever soldiers you have with the latest weaponry, but the fights between important characters pose their own problems. A rapier or broadsword can only control the immediate space around the user, so even when pointed at an unarmed person it is always both a threat and an *invitation* to fight. The challenged person can always run away. Drawing a gun commands all of the distance in front of the barrel, so is only a threat and assault, not an invitation. You can't run away from a bullet.

Those other plays

The transcription of performed plays to the printed page come to us from two traditions. The ancient tradition was to write down plays as though they were poetry, for indeed the distinction between playwright and poet is relatively modern. The Greek and Roman plays, the works of Shakespeare and Moliere, are presented to us without any but the barest of stage directions. We just get the requisite "*enter*"s and "*exeunt*"s so we know who is onstage, and the occasional "*he dies*", which is also very handy to know. But for the most part the director and actors are on there own, forced to use their brain power to decipher the true meaning of each phrase. Obviously, this horrendous oversight has meant that no one ever performs Shakespeare, and that it is impossible to do anything creative with it.

The other tradition is much more modern, that of publishing the script in nearly the format of a novel. Along with the spoken lines, full stage directions, place settings, even line readings are included in the script in parenthesis. With these parentheticals already given, the reader can imagine a fully realized production from the very first reading. As a reader, I love it, for I have absolutely no confusion as to what any given bit of dialogue is supposed to mean, and I get a chance to get more of the author's perspective on the piece:

> (Late afternoon, a few clouds. A bird flies overhead, possibly a wren, but we cannot see or hear it. The smell of honeysuckle is in the air, mixed with a bit of neoprene. It rained three days ago, so the ground is soft. It might rain again in another day or so, so no need to set out the sprinklers. Just be sure to water the flowers on the porch. And pick up the mail if you get a chance.)

MORINA
(speaking as if to a peplum) What do you think about getting some sushi tonight? (deliberate pause, as though the air in the room had suddenly become thick with undulation) If we go now, we can get back before sundown. (Morina crosses upstage and picks up her sweater, pausing briefly to notice that one of the cuffs is slightly frayed. It probably had always been.)

SALFORTIO
(looks out the window) It looks kind of dark outside, (looks at his watch) but I think we have time. (looks at her sweater) Hey, is that your sweater?

MORINA
(indefatigably) Yes. (maladjustedly) Do you have your wallet?

SALFORTIO
(with two fingers of his left hand adjusts his right sleeve) (hesitant, but mangrovish) What?

MORINA
(predispositiously) Your wallet. (lifts her chin slightly to the right, hyper-splenic but not pyelogramic)

SALFORITO
(rectilinearly) Yes. (leans against bookshelf) (enucleatingly) Are you ready?

MORINA
(deeply fimbrinated) Sure. (chancellerious, but nasal) I'll just put on my sweater. (puts on her sweater, left arm first) (remittally, with a hint of basil)

```
Let's go. (she crosses to him, coniferous and dispensary.)

SALFORITO
(idiomorphically) OK. (they step down center in a slight arc so as to miss trip-
ping over the ottoman, which was purchased by the previous owner, then cross left
to exit through the front door, which is hinged on the left.)
```

Ok, I'm obviously exaggerating, but not by much. And honestly, I don't really care if publishers feel compelled to make the plays more descriptive and readable. I completely understand that they need to make money, and including a goodly amount of non-spoken narrative make the published work more accessible to the non-theatre audience.

The problem I see in this form of playwriting is that not enough of our nation's actors and directors know how to read a script and separate the wheat from the chaff. I can't tell you how many rehearsals I've sat through, biting my tongue and averting my eyes while the director and the actors slavishly follow every single stage direction in the script. There have been rare moments of brilliance where a brave actor will want to try a change in the described action, or say a line with a completely different tone, only to be shut down by a boorish director who always follows the parentheticals as though they are the one true gospel.

When you get a modern script, it went from the writer to you in one of two very different routes. If you aren't paying much in royalties, then it's more than likely a self-promoted play that didn't see a successful Broadway, off-Broadway, or even off-off-Broadway run. There are a lot of these that are performed every year by high school drama departments and community theatre troupes. Every word spoken and every stage direction given came from the writer directly onto paper, and then to the publisher. These are not terrible pieces, but nor are they great works of literature. As such, reading what's in the parenthesis might be the only way to figure out what is happening in the play. And there is certainly no reason to believe that the playwright was an exceptional actor, and that his work can't be helped considerably by trying different interpretations of the same lines. Good actors can make pedestrian scripts good merely by freeing themselves of the mediocrity of the delivery.

The other route is when a new play is a hit, gets a decent run, and the publisher makes arrangements to put the play in bookstores. Now, editors know that scripts change a lot during the rehearsals leading up to opening, so they don't want the playwright's copy. Instead, they take the stage manager's version - the performance copy with all of the corrections and final line corrections. Along with that is going to be all of the blocking that was performed for that now famous show. But if you try to recreate that same show using all of the stage directions and line readings, you are doomed to failure. For even if you know that an actor said one line "angrily", you don't know why she said it that way, or if that was even the only way she said it. And maybe she said it that way because of what the actor did just before that. A different partner, and she might have said it a completely different way. Uta Hagen in her book *Respect for Acting* has a great anecdote about rehearsing for *The Country Girl*. She had trouble finding the right tone for a particular moment, and one day she accidentally got tangled up putting on a sweater right at that point in the script. The frustration of dealing with the sweater brought up just the right emotional response for her. So she kept the bit and it helped her in performance as well. Years later she was shocked to see another actress trying to do the same bit of business. It seems that the struggle with the sweater was dutifully noted in the stage manager's script and was carefully included in the published play. She was aghast to think that now other actresses had to deal not only with the lines of the play but also an arbitrary bit of business that worked for her but couldn't possibly have any meaning for anyone else. The sweater for her was a way to connect with the scene, but for everyone else now is a bit of shtick that they have to somehow make meaningful. All because of useless stage directions.

And it's not just the "acting notes" that writers include that can get actors in trouble, but also the specific actions relating to violence. Some of those descriptions are ill-stated, and some are just wrong. Some describe what the Broadway version did, which even those actors would not repeat if working in a new space or under a new director. So in almost all cases, you are usually better off getting the gist of what is supposed to happen, and then figuring out your own moves to get there. The script may call for a slap, but what if a shove seems to work better? What about no movement at all? You can't tell if you don't try.

By the way, the same goes for those props lists and costume plots that are in the back of the script. Just because the production team was very diligent in writing down every article and item that was used for the Broadway version does not mean that you can or even should attempt to duplicate it. You have no way of knowing how any particular item got on that list. Perhaps an extra halberd was put on a wall to hide a hole where a carpenter's hammer went through the flat. Perhaps a character needed a stool to sit on in Act III because the actor playing him had a sore leg. Just make up your own list from what your production requires.

In truth, there are only two ways for directors to handle the scripted stage directions:

1) Read the play once through to find out what the general flow is, and to pin down any vital bits of action. Then get a heavy black marker and block out every bit of non-critical stage direction. Get rid of them, banish them. That must include every line reading, every mood indicator, every pause, and every blocking note. Explore this play, the one that's being created for the first time using the talents and abilities of all of the members of the production crew. Challenge each of the actors to find a different way to say each line every time you run the scene. Ninety percent of it won't work, but sooner or later there will be some fascinating discoveries made. And that ten percent that does work is gold, because it will come out of trying to make a connection with the real people on stage from the real life of the script, not just the ghost of Broadway past.

... or ...

2) Keep and follow every single stage direction you see. This must be done without exception when the director has neither talent nor intelligence. By following the line readings and pre-recorded blocking, the actors will not accidentally find any moment of real emotional honesty, which would clash with the rest of the production. Instead, you will have nice little automatons carefully parroting a lifeless version of a theatrical production. With plenty of false sentiments and declamatory pronouncements, they will hit each of their lines with whatever pre-ordained adjective was provided (*angrily, quietly, agreeably, quickly, tenderly, wildly,*) and convince themselves that they were acting.

Specific Scenes from a Mix of Plays

Aida - Elton John/Tim Rice Musical

You might want to go back to the first section and re-read the section on Egyptian fighting. Then you are going to have to toss all of that info aside and just use whatever will make the director happy. Even if you do happen to find a good compromise sword/dagger that looks vaguely Egyptian, you are still stuck with the fact that even the soldiers never wore their weapons, so more compromises need to be made. Since there is no point in trying for historical accuracy in this musical, don't worry about it. Whatever you pick (bronze age, medieval, fantasy) will work fine for this show.

Aida - Verdi Opera

If this is staged with greater respect for Egyptian culture, this gets much harder to prop, for the same reasons mentioned above. Usually it's simply easier to go with Greek/Roman weapons and call it a day.

Annie Get Your Gun

An expensive prop show if done faithfully to the Broadway script, but even if shortcuts are made, start saving your pennies well in advance of mounting this show.

The historic Annie Oakley used several types of rifles and pistols for her sharpshooting. Her favorite was not a lever-action rifle at all, but a Marlin repeating rifle, 22 caliber. It was the Broadway musical which had her and Frank use lever-actions, so that is what we are used to seeing. [In her song, *You Can't Get a Man With a Gun*, there is a reference to her "Remington", but this is mere songwriters' license and doesn't mean that you have to find a Remington rifle for the show. Anyway, there is no specific look to a "Remington" any more than there is to a "Chevrolet".] There is no doubt that she was a tremendous marksman, perhaps the finest that ever lived. But it should also be noted that for some of the trick shots, especially firing at balloons, some of her rifles were loaded with special cartridges filled with sand instead of a lead bullet. The sand expands in flight and covers a wide area which can easily pop a balloon or even shatter a shot glass, a trick still used in movie westerns. It was also done for some of the specialty numbers of the original Broadway version, but is so dangerous that no theatre would be allowed to do that today. Remember that until recently most guns shot onstage were real weapons loaded with blanks.

Again, the Broadway tradition has Frank and Annie using lever-action rifles, but simple semi-auto repeaters are also correct. The cost comes not just with the rental cost of each rifle, but the number of firing rifles required for the last scene, where Annie keeps "missing" with each rifle she picks up. So how can you reduce costs for this show?

1] Have the gun cases open away from the audience's view, so they never get a chance to see what is inside. That way the same two or three guns can be exchanged yet it can seem as though there are half a dozen inside.

2] Use cheaper guns. One production went so far as to use revolvers instead of rifles for the shooting match and was able to cut the overall weapons costs to one quarter of what it might have been.

3] Take a page from the latest Broadway remounting of the show and have the drummer do rim-shots instead of having the guns fire at all. I love this alternative, for it eliminates the inevitable headaches from misfiring and jamming guns, eliminates the danger to all the actors on stage, and drops the cost to a tenth or less of what it might ordinarily have been.

In the earlier scenes, Annie is introduced using her old hunting rifle. As the historic Annie was born in 1860 and started shooting at age 9 (1869), this old gun should be a percussion lock or perhaps even a flintlock rifle. The family couldn't have afforded a cartridge rifle, and the lever-action hadn't been invented yet.

The competition against Frank Butler took place in 1876, when she was sixteen years old. He might have had one of the newfangled lever-action rifles, but they were certainly state of the art machines, and prohibitively expensive for her to have even seen, let alone handled, one. Annie and Frank joined Buffalo Bill's Wild West show much later, in 1885, by which time she was a widely recognized expert in shooting any type of firearm.

Random art note: This show, with one number insulting to Native Americans and the entire script generally demeaning to women, is still popular enough with no sign of it dying away. Modern versions of the show usually try to add a tongue in cheek eye-rolling slant on the final scene so that it is a little less degrading, but as in *Taming of A Shrew*, you can't get around the words that are there. But why was the show even written this way? Especially since the historic Annie was a strong, independent woman, and the Wild West Show always treated her as a star of higher rank and respect than any of the other performers.

Annie Get Your Gun first opened in 1946, just after WWII, at a time when thousands of newly discharged soldiers were returning home to find that most of their pre-wartime jobs had been filled, and competently performed, by women. The War Department applied tremendous pressure to make sure that women relinquished those jobs (or were fired from them) so that the returning veterans would more easily slip back into their civilian roles. To have a show such as this that depicts a woman of accomplishment willingly slide back into subservience was comforting and appealing at the time.

Anything Goes

The "broadsword". It seems from the script that the sword here is from the British definition of broadsword, which is a heavy infantry straight sabre of the 18th century, not the medieval broadsword.

The Tommy Gun in a Violin Case. I'm sorry to tell you that a complete Tommy Gun doesn't fit inside any instrument case, let alone that of a violin. Only the dismantled parts of the weapon were ever transported this way, and even then it had to be the stripped down version with no buttstock and certainly not the distinctive round drum that holds the bullets. The gun would be reassembled once the gangster was in a safe or hidden location, but it was impossible to simply open the case and start using the gun. No, this moment in the show is pure fantasy, so a modified truncated Tommy Gun and a special case will have to be found or built.

Arcadia

A "rabbit pistol" is called for, but as far as I've been able to find out, there is no reference to such an item outside of the world of this play. We can safely assume that it is a small caliber flintlock or percussion lock pistol, but not a fancy heirloom piece. The term is probably similar to the modern "squirrel gun" or "deer rifle", just an offhand way that the owner of the firearm describes the primary purpose of having the weapon. Someone shooting at rabbits with a pistol is not trying to hunt down dinner, but is just "joy shooting" - the equivalent of playing a video game.

Also in this play is a reference to a Barlow knife, which is merely a brand name for a popular small folding pocket knife of the period.

Arthur
>see "Camelot"

Assassins
>I am using the caliber descriptions on the guns only for identification purposes, but the fact that we happen to know what the caliber was for a specific weapon shouldn't dissuade you from using a similar looking gun with a different number. Remember that caliber refers to the internal barrel diameter, so if you find something that looks OK which is 6/100's of an inch larger than the historical gun *no one will <u>ever</u> see the difference.*

>John Wilkes Booth   1865   A Philadelphia single-shot Derringer was used to shoot Lincoln, so in the final tableau, and in the opening scene, this should be the gun he holds. He also had with him a good sized Bowie knife that he brandished before jumping. The Two-shot hadn't been invented at the time of the assassination. It was still twenty years and a completely different firing system away. Booth fired the only shot he had from his blackpowder Philadelphia, then had to fight Major Rathbone (who was sitting in the balcony with Lincoln) using a large knife. During the scuffle, the useless pistol was dropped to the ground, which is why we know what he used. It was recovered and is now in the possession of the National Park Service.

>Colt 1851 percussion six-shooter, for the shoot-out and suicide in the barn. Booth actually had two revolvers and a carbine rifle with him at the time of his death, but only fired his Colt revolver. Whether he shot himself or was shot by one of the posse was never satisfactorily established.

>Guiteau 1881   British Bulldog .44 cal, silver handled.
There really is no such thing as a silver handle for a gun, and the script describes it as "silver mounted", an interesting phrase that defies easy explanation, for the term is used for sword hilts but not gun grips. Many assume that the reference is to a silver or nickel plated gun, but that's not really the same thing. Be that as it may, the script has it wrong on several counts. After his arrest, Guiteau told reporters that he felt it a shame that he wasn't able to get a gun with an *ivory* grip, feeling that the gun would look better when it would be seen by millions in a museum someday. He actually ended up purchasing a plain black version of the gun with a rough wooden grip. [The gun itself no longer exists, but a clear photograph of it is in the Smithsonian archives.]

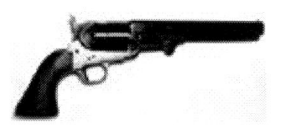

>Czolgosz   1901   Iver-Johnson .32 cal, owls on the side, black grip.
The owl was the logo of Iver-Johnson Firearms Company, and is set into the pattern of the grip mold. Even when holding the gun in your hand, it is awfully difficult to see the logo. Certainly the audience can never see it. Don't sweat over this minutia which is completely insignificant. [I hate details like this that are thrown into scripts but provide no benefit to the production.] The Iver-Johnson was a five shot top-breaking revolver, meaning the frame was hinged at the bottom of the frame. This allowed the barrel and chamber to swing down to expose it for loading, just like a break open shotgun.

Can you see the owl logo on the pistol grip? Neither can your audience.

IMPORTANT! It can be dangerous to use any firing pistol, stage-safe or real, for Czolgosz if you follow the stage directions and history. Stage guns usually have blocked barrels, which prevent any discharge from flying out of the barrel, and this is the only kind of firing gun that should ever be used onstage. Since Czolgosz is usually standing down center to shoot the invisible McKinley, pointing straight out at the audience, then of course there is no option but to use a gun with a blocked barrel anyway. But he is also supposed to wrap his gun in a handkerchief - it's how he got it past the receiving line, and it's mentioned in the lyrics. Guns that fire must vent in some direction, and the guns with plugged barrels generally vent through the side or the top of the gun. If that vent is blocked with a handkerchief, it can easily burn the fabric, starting a fire and/or injuring the actor's hand. You have three options:

1] go to black-out and have an off-stage gun provide the shot.

2] go to blackout and make sure that Czolgosz completely removes the handkerchief before firing. He doesn't have much time.

3] use a very well fireproofed handkerchief. Even then only loosely wrap the fabric around the gun. A tight wrap could cause a secondary pressure explosion directed back to the actor's hand, in a worst-case scenario sending the blast through the actor's fingers.

Zangara   1933   cheap 5-shot .32 cal revolver, does not fire until final scene.

The gun is very similar to the Iver-Johnson above, nickel-plated with black rubber grips, but this gun has an exposed hammer and a different logo on the grip. There is a reason why the gun looks so much like Czolgosz's. Iver Johnson also made a line of very cheap handguns, and marketed them under the name "U.S. Revolver Co.", so as not to hurt the Iver Johnson brand name.

Ozwald   1963   Mannlicher-Carcano bolt-action rifle with scope and .38 cal revolver.

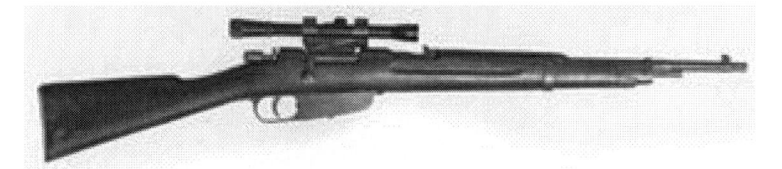

Just as with Booth, one gun, the rifle, was used for the assassination and another, the revolver, was with him when he was arrested/cornered.

Sarah Jane Moore   1975   nickel-plated .38 cal Smith & Wesson revolver; 4" barrel length.

Moore's gun most likely had the thin grip as shown, but could instead have had a more standard military grip, although it would have made handling and concealing the gun more difficult.

The same gun is supposed to be able to fire several times and also be loadable onstage. That presents some difficulties, since most theatres need to keep the sound down to a manageable level, which means .22 caliber. Those blanks are less than a quarter inch wide, so can easily fumble through the actor's fingers. You can get blank fire guns that are of larger caliber, but you'll need to get specially loaded blanks that are quiet enough for actors to use without earplugs. The script asks for something even more difficult, namely that Sarah be able to open the loaded gun and accidentally let the bullets fall out of the chamber and onto the floor. What follows is a very funny bit, but blanks that are of the correct caliber usually stick to the chambers of stage guns pretty well and don't fall out that easily. Real bullets for real revolvers do, but of course you're not going to do that. The best way to go with this is to have her palm a handful of dummy bullets and let them drop instead. This is better than dropping the blanks anyway, for the dummy rounds can be much larger and easier for the audience to see what President Ford is doing after he comes into the scene.

Lynette Squeaky Fromme   1975   Colt semiautomatic .45 cal pistol, model 1911, leg holster.

Apparently, her gun was a full-sized semiauto, so she is going to have quite a hefty bulk on her leg. An ankle holster usually can't provide enough support for any except smaller framed guns, so you might have to have her have this holster strapped much higher up on her leg, probably above the knee or at the calf.

[It was noted that when the police recovered the gun, it had four rounds in the clip but the chamber was empty.]

Byck   .22 cal revolver. No specifics that I've been able to find. Newspaper accounts of the time only mention that he had stolen the gun from a friend, but we are not told what kind it was.

Hinckley   22 caliber short-barreled revolver, Rohm RG-14

In the final scene all of the assassins face the audience and fire simultaneously directly at it. In most theatres that is simply going to be too much sound, so you will need to reduce the number of guns that are actually loaded to just a few of the actors. Also, if any of your guns have open barrels and there is any chance that some of the discharge is going to travel towards your audience, don't fire those guns. All you need is to have a tiny spark make it to someone's face and you have instant lawsuit.

In the "gun song", many directors have the actors dry fire their guns throughout the number. That's fine, but remember that dry-firing ("clicking") will sooner or later cause the hammer to break off. If you have rented the gun, you've just doubled the props cost for the show if even one of the guns break. If you have purchased the gun, you are in for a hefty repair bill.

Batboy; the Musical

A deer rifle is mentioned, but the character comes in having bagged a couple of geese. Well, he didn't do it with a rifle unless he's the next Annie Oakley, and if he did it with a *deer* rifle there wouldn't be much goose left. But, what, you're worried about plausibility in a show called *Batboy*?

The Bear

  SMIRNOV. [Examining the pistols] You see, there are several sorts of pistols. . . . There are Mortimer pistols, specially made for duels; they fire a percussion-cap. These are Smith and Wesson revolvers, triple action, with extractors. . . . These are excellent pistols. They can't cost less than ninety rubles the pair. . . .

  These lines get some people a little confused. Smirnov has not brought out any Mortimer pistols. He's not saying that there are Mortimer pistols in his hands, but that in the world there exist several types of guns. He starts off talking about pistols in general, and tosses out the term in a vain show of knowledge in order to impress the young lady. [A Mortimer pistol was a very distinctive single-shot percussion pistol that was in fact designed for target shooting, never for duels.] What he has brought out are two identical revolvers.

  The specific guns that we do see are described as being Smith and Wesson and having certain attributes - triple action, and having an integrated ejection rod ("extractors"). Triple action in this case refers to the mechanical-action capability of the hammer and its interplay with the trigger, and the audience is never going to see that. Neither can Smirnov, because it is not something that can be seen. He is either bluffing about his knowledge or he really is a minor expert in guns and their attributes. Be that as it may, the only part of the full description that is visible is the ejection/extractor rod. It's the part of Western style guns that looks like a thin barrel riding underneath the regular gun barrel, but is actually a push rod that allows the user to push out the spent brass cartridges from the cylinder after the gun is fired. It is a small detail that very few in the audience will know about, so if your prop gun doesn't have one, I wouldn't lose too much sleep over it. As for them being Smith and Wesson, the company made over a dozen distinct revolvers during this period, and the description in the script gives no indication of what the profile of the gun looks like, so you have a good chance that whatever gun you find will look like one of the Smith and Wesson's from the turn of the century.

  [In another of his works, a short story that takes place in a gun shop, Chekhov uses the same two gun references. Apparently, he had picked up these two bits of information somehow, and used them in his writing when he had the chance. They seem to be the sum of his gun knowledge.]

Big River
  see Tom Sawyer

Brigadoon

  With the exception of anglicized nobles in the 17th and 18th centuries, Scots never wore the sword off of the battlefield, but that won't stop directors from wanting many in the cast to wear them. And of course you'll need some swords for the sword dance. But which sword? The unmanageable two handed Claymore or the basket hilt single hand sword of the 17th century? As the time period for this show is fantasy, the weaponry choices for the Highland dance can be anything you want. The costuming suggests using traditional Scottish swords, but I've noticed that even modern Highland dancers from Scotland don't use Scottish swords when they perform or compete. Scottish two-handed broadswords (Claymores) with their very long and broad blades are simply too large to carry or dance over. Single-handed basket hilts swords are more manageable, but the three-dimensional hilts lift one side of the blades up from the floor by a couple of inches. Dancers can easily catch their toes on the raised blades and kick the weapons flying out into the audience. For that reason modern Highlanders tend to use very flat hilted society swords that can lay flat against the floor. I strongly suggest that this is the way to go on this show. Let the non-dancers wear the basket hilts.

By the way, the dance is traditionally performed with two cross swords, but there is no reason why it can't be done with a crossed sword and scabbard.

The show also needs a knife to be drawn and pointed, and you have a choice in terms of traditional Scottish daggers, but don't compromise on this. A long bladed dirk with no hand protection was worn at the waist - not the leg. The Scots did have a small knife tucked into the fold of their high wool socks, but this is not a dirk but rather the three inch bladed Skean Dubh. This little thing is just too small to be a credible threat, assuming that the audience can even see it. Don't try putting the larger dirk on the ankle or in a boot - it just doesn't work for the style nor the period nor for the comfort of the actor.

Book of Days

A very specific description of one of the two shotguns is in the lines. Ruth let's us know that it's a "custom made J. Purdey and Sons, British, side-by-side, engraved full sidelock". What does all that mean?

J. Purdey and Sons was a British firm that made shotguns and rifles, and specifically double barreled side-by-side shotguns from about 1890 to 1940. There is nothing particularly distinctive about the shape of a Purdey shotgun, so even a gun collector wouldn't necessarily spot one immediately. The gun would have internal hammers, rather than exposed, but so do shotguns of several companies. Ruth probably noticed the manufacturer's mark on the gun frame. Custom made shotguns might have a buttstock specially cut to fit the owner's arm length and upper body contours, but this could also have been an after-market adjustment. Engraving on a rifle or shotgun is a very expensive addition. And it is true that Purdey shotguns have an especially high value amoung collectors, so her estimate of thirty to fifty thousand dollars is spot on, assuming that the gun is in nearly mint condition.

So here's a case where the playwright has done all of his homework and gotten all the details right. Unfortunately, he picked quite an expensive piece to try to replicate for stage. Good luck trying to find a double barrel recessed-hammer shotgun without a trace of rust and with engraving covering the center "box" section (the sideplates). Better perhaps to just find whatever two double barreled shotguns you can and simply polish the heck out of at least one of them.

Bullshot Crummond

Just a word here about the sword fight near the end of the play. Naturally, this is a live-action cartoon, so whatever the fight looks like is fine so long as it's funny. That is the first and last consideration for this play. But if you really feel compelled to add some "historical accuracy" or character delineation to it, read on.

Otto lets it be known that he studied at Heidelberg (we would have expected nothing less) so that means that he is well versed in that college's distinctive style of sabre fencing - very different than the style Bullshot would have studied at Cambridge. Crummond would fight in Olympic sabre fencing (very quick snap cuts to the head and thrusts to the body with a very light, flexible and blunt sword while protected with a mask). Von Brunno would be skilled in the Mansuer style (cuts only to the face using a heavier, stiff, and razor-edged sword - and no mask!). Of course, the swords are Otto's, so they are the heavier style (the schlaeger blade). But, again, why put realism in this show anyway?

At one point in the fight Bullshot describes a move he has made as a "parry vitesse", which by the way is not a real fencing term. Roughly translated, he seems to be saying that it was a "quick block" or "parry at speed" (as though one would ever do a *slow* parry?). More interestingly, he describes this parry that occurred at the end of his own attack sequence, which means that the last move was an attack by Otto, parried by Bullshot. Then Otto asks if he should do an "attack vitesse" (speed attack). Again, no real meaning here. There are ways to choreograph this so that it matches the words and also makes physical sense, but don't rack your brains too much trying to make sense out of this. The author didn't so why should you?.

Camelot

Ah, Camelot. That lovely mythic tale about English knighthood. Written from a Victorian perspective. Translated from French-Norman-Renaissance sources. About a post-Roman pre-Saxon king.

The Arthur legend is a fairytale fantasy, so a "historically accurate" production is both laughable and doomed to failure. It has no relation to any real time period, so you can design it in that Disney/Medieval neo-thirteenth century storybook setting and feel comfortable that that is what the audience expects. The legend has always been popular, and much like the Robin Hood tale keeps gathering the attributes of the people who have taken it close to heart, so it is no coincidence that we see so much of Victorian Romanticism in the present incarnation.

The true Arthur would have been a Celtic/Briton warrior chieftain, leading a relatively small tribe by his position as the best warrior of the group, not because of his lineage. His fellow warriors would have numbered between a dozen to usually no more than a hundred men. They had horses but no stirrups, and no broadsword and certainly no code of chivalry. But, like so many myths, the name of a strong warrior survived hundreds of years, through the Roman occupation, the Saxon invasions, the imposition of the Dane law, conversion to Christianity, and the Norman Conquest. When the Normans developed their own culture of the sword and spur, romantic tales of early "knights" were created around extant stories of famous warrior kings. That's why the cast of characters' names are a mix of French, Anglo and Celtic, and elements of each passing religion get attached to the story, each group adding something to the tale.

Many moderns enjoy trying to peg the story of the round table and Camelot onto one of several "Artvr"'s that did exist, a mix of Celtic petty chieftains and later Breton/Roman warlords. But these are just flesh and blood markers on which to hang an illusion. [Even trying to find someone with the name Arthur is an error, for Arth is Celtic for bear, a warrior's sobriquet, but never used as a given name until long after the Saxon domination.] So there can be no "historical accuracy" when trying to design this show. Arthur belongs to the time of Sleeping Beauty and Snow White, a fantasy of knights in armor no different from that concocted by Don Quixote's fevered delirium.

As for Excaliber, whatever you imagine that sword to be is exactly what it should look like.

Carmen

The typical firearms for the period are all single-shot muskets and pistols, and it is right during the time when European armies are switching from flintlock to percussion lock, so you can get away with either style. The sidearm is a standard military sabre, but no pistols yet. Pistols were used by irregular units, and were not part of regulation armament.

For the knife fight, the typical Gypsy weapon would be the Navaja, a single-edged slightly curved folding knife which makes a ratcheting sound on opening. Unfortunately, Navajas are no longer imported into the United States, and no one manufactures them here, so a reasonable alternative is any large folding knife or a medium sized fixed-bladed knife.

Carnival

There is a sword box illusion required for this show. Most theatres won't have access to a large magic house in order to rent one, so will have to build their own. There is nothing complicated about this illusion, but there are two ways of doing it.

Version A: The easiest is actually the flashiest. An assistant steps in the box, immediately the swords are thrust in, and then the top and sides of the box are all folded down, showing all of the swords and ... the assistant has disappeared! Usually through an escape in the back of the box and then through a curtain, but sometimes through a trap door on the bottom of the box and into an impossibly smaller box on which the sword box is resting. The assistant has to curl up into a tiny ball, convincing the audience that no human could possibly fit inside that minuscule space.

Version B: Much riskier, but a wonderful illusion when the audience is right on top of or surrounding the action. This time the box is on top of a completely open frame, absolutely no chance of an escape. The assistant steps into the box, the magician says something to her/him, and she/he answers loudly. The swords are thrust into the box, *with the assistant still talking from inside the box!* The box is spun around, the swords removed, and the assistant steps out, none the worse for wear, and the sides drop down showing that there was no escape possible. This illusion requires very careful planning and quite a bit of glow tape inside the box, for the assistant has to contort into a very specific shape so that the swords will slide through the empty spaces. Each sword goes in in a prescribed order, so that the assistant can press her body against each sword blade in turn to create the next clear space. The glow tape is merely to mark where the first couple of swords are going to go.

Cherry Orchard

Two guns are shown in Act II, a rifle with a sling for Charlotta and a revolver for Epikhodov. Since the play was written in 1902, and the revolver obviously has to fit easily in a pocket, something like a British Bulldog or really any snub-nose revolver will do. The rifle is a slightly harder choice. Bolt-action rifles were available, but were primarily military weapons. Would this family have one? The common sporting rifles of the time would have been lever-action or simple repeaters.

Clue: the Musical

The show follows the tradition of using the six weapons of the British boardgame, designed in 1948: candlestick, knife, lead pipe, revolver, rope, and wrench. The problem comes when trying to match the knife and revolver.

The gun is a "pepperbox" style percussion pistol of 1837, not technically a revolver, but rather a multibarrel pistol. Why the gamemakers decided to use a firearm already over a hundred years old when the board game was invented is beyond me. Even stranger is the choice of knife - a bronze aged dagger of the style found in ancient Mesopotamia. These two items are not impossible to find, just difficult, as they are not standard items in most props cabinets.

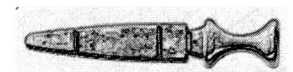

Columbinus

The four guns used in the high school tragedy are very specific, but remember that you only need to match the profile of the guns. Don't stress too much about getting the exact brand and model number unless you really want to spend hundreds (even thousands) of dollars on the rental.

a) Savage-Springfield 67H pump-action 12 gauge shotgun. The key here is "sawed off" and "pump action". Nothing else is important.

b) Hi-Point 995 Carbine 9 mm semi-automatic rifle with thirteen 10-round magazines. This one is going to be tougher to find. It's really a pistol retrofitted with a rifle butt stock, elogated barrel and foregrip to match. 10-round clip[s are fairly short; only about four inches long.

c) 9 mm Intratec Tec-9 Semi-automatic handgun with one 52-, one 32-, and one 28-round magazine. Two "long" clips ("magazines"), that's easy. As for the pistol, the main distinguishing feature is that the clip is in front of the trigger.

d) 12 gauge Stevens 311D double barreled sawed-off shotgun. This one is a bit odd in that it is a really old-fashioned weapon, basically Grandpa's old barn shotgun cut-off at the barrel and buttstock. One has to re-load after every two shots. Finding this item at a reasonable cost is going to be your biggest headache.

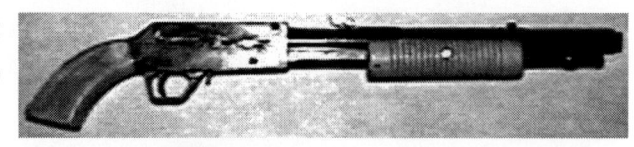

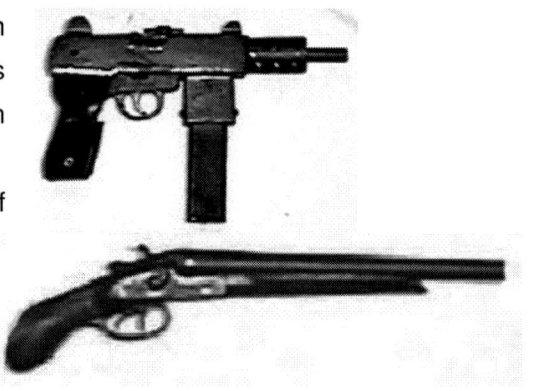

Corpse!

The gun is a revolver, and for this show must be the most reliable you can find, even at the expense of good appearance, for the order of the shots is crucial to the plot. In case of an early misfire, the actor can't simply try to fire again. One other problem is that the gun must be loaded in plain view of the audience. Unfortunately, that can limit your choices to fairly large caliber guns using hefty and costly blanks. The more affordable .22 caliber shells are hard for the actor to manage and the audience to see.

One option, and the script suggests this, is to use a dummy gun to load in front of the audience, and then a twin firing version that is switched out for the appropriate shots. Switching out is difficult, but not impossible. The tough part will be in finding the identical guns. When the script was written it was fairly common practice to use modified real guns with full chambers.

For the sword fight, the weapon is described as a sabre. But it is not the military sabre, rather the light Olympic style fencing sabre that is required here. A particularly gruesome effect is called for at the very end of the play, as Powell is exposed, not only impaled on a sword, but also stuck into the cabinet wall. If the Major is already wearing a light harness under his shirt, a dummy sword hilt can be screwed onto the front, and a short length of thick high tension wire (already connected to the wall) can be clipped onto his back. When the cabinet is opened, the Major can lean forward, making the wire taut, and for all the world it looks like the blade has gone through him and he's now stuck to the wall. He can even gently swing slightly side to side. Creepy.

But it is the killing of Powell before he is shut up in the cabinet that has actually caused more headaches for several productions. In order to make the last impaled bit work, many choreographers think that the audience needs to see him run through dead center. In order to do that, they need a collapsible sword. They don't really. All they need to do is position the final run-through so that the actor is in profile at that moment, or better yet in motion so that the run through and the closing of the cabinet can happen in one rushing action. The audience will put two and two together when the cabinet pops open later.

Actually, I talk about "those" choreographers, but to be honest, I was in that number for many years. I always used a collapsible whenever I choreographed this show. For each production I actually built four swords - two regular swords for the combatants, one duplicate collapsible for the final thrust home, and then a complete hilt with a stubby threaded four-inch bolt where the blade should be that could be screwed into the hidden harness. Since the regular sabres were outfitted with epee blades, a manual extendable car antenna made a great blade for the collapsible. I would work the choreography so that towards the end of the swordfight there would be a brief disarm of Evelyn, his sword going behind a sofa, where the switch to the collapsible could be conveniently made. There were a couple of drawbacks to this. The first is that the car antennae made a very weak blade, so that sword could only be used for a very few moves at the end of the fight, namely some very light deflections of thrusts by Powell. It was certainly far too weak to take even light cuts. Another problem is that the last section of these antennas is very thin and can be easily bent, and once bent, easily broken. So the end had to be carefully pushed in a few inches before the prop was pre-set behind the sofa, and Evelyn had to be very careful during his killing thrust. The last problem is that I was putting my actors in danger. If the antennae should ever have failed during that thrust, the actor playing Powell could have been seriously hurt. Even with that not happening, I still had to make sure that my Powells leaned forward at the moment of the kill, to prevent the tip from skimming off their chests and flying up toward their faces. I am no longer that cavalier with my actors' safety.

The Country Wife

Written and set in 1675, a pistol is fired. Ostensibly this is the squire's gun, but in this period pistols are still quite long and are really only military weapons, the flintlock pistol having just been invented that same year. The earlier pistols were mostly wheellocks, and very expensive, impractical for civilian defense and wildly inaccurate for hunting. The author was obviously keen on getting one of these contraptions in his play, but remember that the pistol was nearly unknown off of the battlefield. Some of the wealthy owned one or two as novelty pieces and for some delusional sense of home protection. [To the audience of the time, this would have had some of the shock value of seeing a modern middle-class homeowner pull out an assault rifle.] Although some civilians might have had a full-sized rifled musket for hunting, anything shorter lacked a true practical purpose unless one was firing at something only a few yards away. Even if you should be able to track down a wheellock pistol, feel free to use any flintlock pistol replica for this show, since the real item is so large that it just looks silly to modern audiences.

The Crucible

In Proctor's house, scene 2, we see him threaten to whip his servant, but it would be a mistake to think that a conventional whip is the most appropriate item for this show. A farmer in this part of the world would have had no need for the full length whip. Whether riding a horse or to impel a recalcitrant ox in front of a plow, a shorter stock whip with a very broad and flat slapping surface was probably what he would have used. A thin whip breaks the skin and can lead to infection and is very bad animal husbandry. On the other hand, a traditional whip looks a lot more brutal, so a director's choice is needed here. In any case, why does Proctor even own a whip? He mentions that he has just come from plowing, yet he only brings in his "gun". The whip has been in the house all day. Apparently it was included by the playwright purely as a theatrical device.

Later in the same scene, he uses a gun to hold off those who come to arrest him. The matchlock musket known as the Spanish musket is the strict historic choice, the later flintlock known as the Brown Bess is a close second, and perhaps even the far earlier arquebus is a possibility. I would suggest staying away from the blunderbuss at all costs. Although it has become something of a Thanksgiving Day icon to see a pilgrim bearing one of these flared barreled firearms, it was not used by farmers or hunters, and indeed creates an automatic laugh from the audience since it makes Proctor look like Elmer Fudd. Blunderbusses were used rarely in the colonies before the late 1700's, and none were in the Plymouth area before this time.

Why does Proctor have his gun with him when he has been plowing all day? Plowing is hard work and requires two arms to control the plow while the oxen drives forward, so where would he put the musket? Are we to think that he wore it on his back while working? Completely impractical. That he left it leaning against a tree while he plowed, ending up hundreds of yards away from it? Then it would be of no use to him in case of an animal attack. No, Proctor returns with the gun because we, the audience, need to believe that the gun might be loaded, which would not be the case if it had been in the house all day.

Whatever gun Proctor has would of course not have been left loaded, for the powder left in the barrel would attract moisture and quickly corrode the steel. Even walking with a musket can cause the powder and ball to shift away from the ignition point, which is why guns for hunting were loaded only once the quarry was sighted and the hunter could stand, load, and shoot without further traveling. The Spanish matchlock takes about three to four minutes to load and prep the lit fuse before firing, and the Brown Bess also takes about a minute to load, so anyone seeing Proctor pick up a gun and point it at them would know that it is not a credible threat. Arthur Miller took some artistic license, and who are we to argue.

No one else needs a gun in this play. Some productions like to have guards standing by with muskets or truncheons in the court scene, but this is not only inaccurate (there was no standing army nor even a constabulary) but it takes away from the powerful and more frightening concept of terrible injustice occurring by the sheer force of public panic rather than force of arms. Even in scene 2, when men come to arrest Proctor, there is no need for guns, for these are his neighbors and friends. The dramatic tension is actually heightened when they are unarmed, for Proctor's choice becomes a terrible one of becoming a murderer and outlaw or trusting that his town will finally come to his defense.

In the final scene, we see the prisoners shackled. Just a note here: shackles were difficult and time-consuming to place and remove and the better ones were built with a turn-key and threaded bolt rather than a modern switch-key lock. But key and lock shackles were uncommon, and most were built without a lock at all. They were cold riveted closed by a blacksmith, and you remained shackled until a blacksmith would cut them off. By the way, prisoners were charged for their own shackles and for the cost of food and housing while they were in jail. Even if found innocent of all charges, they still had to remain in jail until all costs were paid for by the family of the prisoner. So when Procter is led off in scene 2, he is worried not only about proving his innocence, but about the very real chance of economic ruin.

Cyrano de Bergerac

The real Hercule Savenion de Cyrano de Bergerac arrived in Paris at the ripe age of sixteen, and died at the age of thirty-one. His personal weapon would have been the cut and thrust rapier and he almost certainly would have used a secondary weapon in the left hand. But the author Rostand specifically describes the attributes of a much lighter weapon - the smallsword of the early 1800's. The duel in rhyme especially makes reference to moves only used in this later style of swordplay, and trying to make the fight conform to the historically correct sword blade is an unnecessary headache. No mention is ever made of a left handed weapon, and it just feels wrong to have him use one. The very light and quick style of swordplay of the nineteenth century, concentrating on finesse moves of the wrist, will help to show off the dazzling superiority of Cyrano's swordsmanship far better than will a heavy cut-and-thrust fight of the 1600's.

This play, written in the grand emotional romantic style already out of fashion at the time it premiered in 1885, was nonetheless wildly successful. Rostand wrote using the same swashbuckling clichés made popular by Dumas and Sabatini. Audiences did not demand historical accuracy, and it is usually a mistake to try to force it onto a fantasy such as this. Do what is exciting.

The duel itself is only roughly laid out, but there are some clues as to what the audience might see. Cyrano bates Valvert mercilessly until he can take no more. At "so be it", it almost seems inescapable that he draws his sword at this time. Cyrano does not, not until he describes the moment in the ballad "then out swords, and to work withal." Does the fight begin here? There's no reason why it cannot, with the rest of the lines coming in and around the fight moves. Or some choreographers may choose to delay the crossing of swords until after the first "thrust home". There is no right or wrong, merely a directorial choice. The only truly specific fencing terms used in the poem are "... beat, pass ... ", beat meaning a tapping of the opponent's blade to provoke a response, and pass simply a walking (crossing) step forward or back, as opposed to an advance or retreat. Less directly, the line "... note how my point floats, light as the foam..." is suggestive of some very tight point work which eludes Valvert's attempt to engage Cyrano's blade with his own.

It's easy to forget that there is only one fight shown in the play. Some directors like to put in a staged "fight against the hundred" in between Acts 1 and 2, but this is a grave mistake. Unless you actually have one hundred fighters on stage, the fight becomes ridiculous, the audience obviously seeing that you're using the same actors over and over. More importantly, a fight that exists in the audience's imagination will always be superior to whatever can be choreographed, so let the words of Act 2 provide the excitement of what they have <u>not</u> seen.

The battle scene in Act IV of course does not actually have a battle, although many directors will want to have a Spanish army overrun the stage. When that is the case, it is better to use a heavier blade on the swords that can survive the bigger bashing moves required. You'll risk a lot of broken blades if you stick with the lighter dueling epee blades.

The soldiers of Cyrano's unit are cadets, therefore not full soldiers. Perhaps someday they will be Musketeers, but not yet. It is likely that they have swords but that their primary battle weapon is a pike or halberd. Since for this scene they have been besieged for some time, it can easily be justified that as other soldiers have died, muskets, arquebuses, crossbows, lances, all in various states of disrepair, might have been scrounged together by individual soldiers and all have found their way onto this scene. By the way, the entire concept of a cadet is another anachronism that must be ignored. The term "cadet" has changed over time. Whereas now [and in Rostand's time] it means a student at a military college [and those didn't exist in Cyrano's time], from 1650 to

1775 it meant a younger son of a noble family who entered the military to try and establish a career there. But in Cyrano's time, cadet merely was the general term for a younger branch of a noble family or specifically the youngest son of a nobleman.

One last note. Even before the Gerard Depardieu version, many directors and choreographers have had Cyrano win the Act I duel by the end of the poem, but magnanimously not kill Valvert, only to have the horribly embarrassed Valvert try to sneakily run Cyrano through when his back is turned. Cyrano miraculously escapes and in a brilliant counter move, dispatches Valvert, but with regret and almost against his will. Very dramatic and touching, and adds a level of compassion and humanity to Cyrano. This helps directors soften Cyrano's image as a cold-blooded killer. I have found that this is not because of any squeamishness on the director's part, for these are usually the same people that want to put in three or four extra fights in the show. No, they make this change out of their belief that a hero would never choose to kill someone unless pushed to extremes.

This is a lovely thought, but is not supported by the script. That species of compassion is an alien concept to any but those of the mid to late twentieth century. Cyrano does not duel with the meddler because the meddler is of the common class. When the noble-born Valvert challenges him, Cyrano offers him every opportunity to back away from the fight, even while publicly insulting him. But once Valvert draws his sword, it is acknowledged that one or the other will die. Diminish that in any way, and Cyrano is not a man to be feared.

True Stage Weapon Story: Much like Hamlet, the role of Cyrano is often given to an experienced and mature actor, well versed in lyric poetry but sometimes a bit beyond his better years of athleticism. In a production in San Francisco, a very well regarded actor in his sixties tried to recreate the role that gave him local renown when he was in his late thirties. Alas, his earlier performance should have stayed as fond memory, rather than as a cruel point of comparison. The final *"as I end the refrain...thrust home!"* was usually so off the mark that most nights poor Valvert had to fling himself onto the blade if there was to be any chance of his dying. The effect was less a demonstration of Cyrano's skill than that of a confused and weary Valvert playing the noble Roman and falling on the sword so as not to offend Cyrano.

Dangerous Liaisons
[see Les Liaisons Dangereuses]

Deathtrap

The following is from an e-mail that we received at Weapons of Choice from a harried props master:

"I'm not sure what you might have in the realm of guns, the prop list called for a Smith and Wesson 38 snubnose with blanks and a Smith and Wesson 38 long barrel with blanks. We also need a dueling pistol, large with a light brown finish. All of these are working models.

As far as set dressing purposes, the props list calls for a Smith and Wesson 38 long barrel, a German Luger, 5 small antique pistols and 2 muskets.

For knives, I need a black handled knife and a gold handled dagger, these are "working" props, although obviously I assume that means they fold over or something as to not hurt the actor.

We also need a curved sword and three knives with sheathes for set dressing.

We need 2 crossbows (one as cover) three garrotes, (one a "working" model), and a spring plunger crossbow bolt (whatever that is). Also a screw on crossbow bolt and 3 regular crossbow bolts (one used, two dressing.)

For set dressing, we need a sickle, cleaver, four pair of leg irons, two pair of antique cuffs and a decorated Indian stick with metal rod."

It was my great joy to let her know that she needed very few of these things.

If you are about to do this play you've already been confronted with the massive props list in the back of the script (the above e-mail actually referenced only a few of them). Please don't feel that you have to find all of those items. Remember that that is merely a list in which someone from the original production very carefully notated every item used as either a practical prop or as set dressing. It in no way should be taken as a mandatory list for your show. Most of it can be ignored - just make sure that the walls are covered with a nice assortment of fun and frightening weapon replicas. Even the practical weapons that the technicians of the original show found may not be what you need for yours. Remember: your job is not to recreate the Broadway version. Your job is to tell the story in the most efficient manner. So your list of practical props may include some very dangerous ones as it is. Stripped down to the basics, here is truly what you need:

- Two blank-firing guns, and it is helpful if they have different looks, but that could merely be a difference in barrel length. Revolvers are always preferred over semi-autos because of their greater reliability.
- Trick-release manacles or handcuffs. Only the stage directions refer to them as "Houdini-style", so if the old style proves hard to find, you can easily switch to the more modern police style.
- A mock garrote, and a blood effects garrote. There are a few out there, which ooze out fake blood from a reservoir in the handle, but if you can't find one, you can always have the victim palm a blood pack, reach for his own throat and apply the blood himself. Here's how, using a real makeshift garrote - that's right, a real wire. After the wire is wrapped safely around the victim's neck, let the attacker simply rest his forearms against the victim's back. The victim can then press forward into the wire as far as he feels comfortable. After two seconds, the victim would naturally grab at his own throat to try and release the wire, right? That's when he brings up the small blood pack that he has palmed during the "struggle". There should be plenty of places on the desk to hide it. Once the blood pack pops against the wire, the blood oozes creepily through the victim's fingers. Very effective.
- A firing crossbow, which no matter what you do is a ridiculously dangerous weapon. A standard crossbow has a draw strength of about 250 pounds, and even though some theatrical varieties have only a 50 lb. draw strength, the force of the low velocity projectile causes severe damage when it hits soft tissue. Assume that the crossbow can and will fire without warning, and so must always and forever be pointed in a safe direction. There are some trick crossbows that don't fire the bolt [arrow] but instead when the trigger is pulled the bolt drops into a hidden compartment in the stock. If you can find one, use it for your show.
- A thin bladed knife, a stiletto. Used to jimmy the lock in the desk. This is a pantomime movement, so the knife need not be especially sturdy.
- A log from the fireplace for hitting over the head. Make it out of foam rubber, not Styrofoam, with a thin wooden core if the director insists on actually hitting the actor on the head, although I hate the idea and think that a clubbing technique as described in the earlier chapter is a better way to go. *"I've got news for you; Styrofoam hurts."* No kidding; a clubbing to the head can even cause a concussion and minor cerebral bleeding..
- Likewise, I don't like using a retractable bolt (arrow) for the stabbing. No retractable item is ever safe, nor is stabbing anything into a "protective" guard placed underneath the costume on the actor's chest. People have died this way, and for what? For a *show?!?*. Here's one way around that. On the plus side, crossbow bolts are fairly short, so hiding the stab is a lot easier than it would be with, say, a medieval dagger. You can always use

a blunted regular bolt, and use the attacker's arm as the collapsible. Holding the bolt with the downstage hand so that at least half of it is showing, the stab is done straight in, allowing the bolt to actually strike the victim. The attacker's hand is kept very loose, which allows the bolt to slide up the forearm, hidden from audience view. The attacker's hand can slide all the way up to the victim's chest. With a little practice, you can even do a quick "relax and grab" during the pull out. The bolt floats in air for a second as the hand withdraws slightly, and grabs the bolt at the original position. It can look great even in close up, so long as the forearm covers the bolt at the moment of the stab.

- A bolt (crossbow arrow) that somehow can be stuck into Clifford. The simplest is to have him wear a strap underneath his shirt that has a threaded nut built into it, and a bolt with a matching threaded end. He can simply screw in the bolt before coming back on stage. Make sure that this fake bolt is a bit shorter than the real bolt fired from the crossbow.

Desert Song

French Foreign Legion (actually Spanish, but we shouldn't quibble), therefore the soldier's weapon is the bolt-action rifle.

Diary of Ann Frank

At the final scene, "Nazi's" come to arrest the Van Dams and the Franks, and history gives us some specifics here. One uniformed SS sergeant and three (perhaps four) Dutch security police in plainclothes would have been a standard detail dispatched for the action. The weapons they carry should match the way they are costumed. A traditional German officer would have a pistol - a Lugar or Walther semi-automatic. While it's possible that uniformed or non-uniformed Dutch collaborators might have the same, it is far more likely that they would have generic 4" barreled revolvers. The security forces of German allies were usually given older guns, the newer and more highly powered weapons going to German frontline troops.

Escanaba in Da Moonlight

This play, and the pre-quel, *Escanaba in Love*, deals with deer hunters of the Upper Peninsula area of Michigan. Their weapons are bolt-action rifles, not shotguns or lever-action rifles or semi-automatic rifles.

Why? When hunting any animal, the idea is to kill it in one shot, because chasing after even a mortally wounded animal is going to be extremely difficult. It will probably still run faster and further than you can. And it is a hunter's obligation to put the wounded animal "out of its misery". Therefore a hunter needs to carefully aim at a spot on the deer that will kill it within a few seconds of being hit.

So the rifle has to be of a caliber sufficiently large to do the job. Shotguns, which fire a scatter spread of pellets, would cause the animal to slowly bleed to death; lever-action rifles are usually of low caliber and have poor range due to their short barrels, and semi-auto's are too dangerous for sportsmen in the field.

Eugene Onegin

The opera was written in 1879 by Tchaikovsky, but from a Pushkin lyric poem of 1833. Costume settings for the opera therefore tend to be set in either of these two times, and that will affect the choice of the pistols for the duel. Those that are set in 1833 need to use single-shot pistols, but those set in 1879 can get away with revolvers.

Evita

Rifles and pistols pop up in several scenes. Although Argentina produced most of its own armaments, the styles follow the same pattern as weapons found throughout Europe and the US, although usually a generation behind. Rifles for this period would be bolt-actions very similar to the German Mauser, while pistols cover all of the styles found during the mid-20th century.

Random art note: Every single production that I have seen, including the original, got the dancers' and tango singer's costumes wrong, putting them in a sort of ruffled sleeved conga/rumba/flamenco outfit and dancing some Cuban/Brazilian thing. It also doesn't help that the song he sings is not a tango. These are not trivial issues for this show, as it shows a lack of understanding of what the Argentines felt was their isolation in the twentieth century, a feeling that allowed a charismatic figure like Peron to sweep into power.

Argentina created the tango, but only for the citizens of the capitol city, Buenos Aires. It was they who danced the tango, who sang the tango, who lived the tango. Almost always in a minor key, with a driving 4/4 beat that pulls the dancers along in an eight step march to a relentless and bitter destiny. The dance itself is not rigid, and both the dancers and musicians are free to improvise in a fruitless effort at breaking away from the coming downbeat. The dancers especially try to create a sanctuary within their dance, the man choreographing, the woman improvising, ever searching for a place of safety, of escape, of something in the midst of their passionate embrace that can save them from the darkness in which they live. The closeness of their bodies becomes a desperate attempt to create a single entity, a vain attempt to create something stronger than either one alone, something that can overpower life, overpower the night, overpower death. But even as they try to sustain the intimacy of a pause, to brighten the moment with a flourish, the music plunges them back into the painful reality of a life cruel and uncaring. It is the music of people trapped in the poverty of a large city, and even the happy tangos carry an undercurrent of loss and melancholy, of disenfranchisement. Here is no joyous celebration of life as one finds in the music of Brazil or the Caribbean, and the male tango dancers and singers would only wear the uniform of the city, the two piece suit made for prowling the streets at night looking for solace. These are people who feel that they are lost Europeans, living thousands of miles away from civilization, surrounded by a vast continent that they would rather ignore than embrace. Buenos Aires was and still is an island unto itself.

The Fantastics

Make sure that the props master and the director are on the same page as to what sword you want. There have been so many times at our rental company where we'll get an order for one type of sword, only to get another call one a week later when they find out it won't fit in the trunk. Seems silly to have to remind people of this, but there you are.

Fiddler on the Roof

The show is set in 1905, so the rifles carried by the Russians, if any, should be bolt action rifles similar in style to the Mausers of WWI. No one in this play, even the police chief, needs a sword.

Forza Del Destino

This opera calls for a gun to be thrown to the floor, which then fires and kills the Marquis. First problem: no gun, real nor replica, can survive being dropped to the floor. This is especially the case for these single shot pistols of the 18th century, because the hammer is very exposed and most of the frame is wood. Second problem: No gun can be made to fire reliably when dropped to the ground. Yes, it can happen, but the gun has to turn in such a way so that the hammer would hit the ground first, with the force being directed forward, not back or down, and even then it's hardly a sure thing. Third problem: the drop has to be controlled so that the barrel is pointing directly at the Marquis when it hits the ground. If that doesn't happen, the audience laughs because it is so obvious that he couldn't have been shot.

What to do? First, buy a bunch of very cheap replica pistols, because most are going to break. If you buy very expensive sturdy guns, you're just throwing money away. Second, use an offstage sound for the gunshot. There is no safe way to get the gun to fire on impact, and absolutely no way to create a safe discharge down the barrel of such a thing. Third, practice that drop so that the barrel always ends up pointing exactly where you want. Good luck.

God's Country

Some very specific automatic weapons are mentioned in the props list, but not in the lines of the play, so all you need are some very scary assault weapons. The problem comes in the scene where we are supposed to see a gun rather expertly dismantled and reassembled in the process of cleaning it. There is nothing easy about this, no matter what gun or replica you get. I've seen actors blow this and accidentally send springs and parts flying across the stage (one time into the audience). You'll need to rent a (costly) real rifle that has been made safe for theatre, and then get expert training for your actor. Expert.

Grapes of Wrath

In the latest stage version, Tom disarms a deputy sheriff who has accidentally shot a woman in a crowd. The gun is described in the stage directions as being a semiautomatic pistol, and that Tom removes the clip and then chambers out the remaining round. Please don't feel that slavish adherence to the stage directions is necessary, or even wise. As you may have read elsewhere in this book, semi-auto's are notoriously unreliable as well as too loud for most theatres, so go ahead and change the pistol to a revolver. Tom can still open the gun and empty it of its "bullets", so the moment need not be lost. And don't let the gun drop to the ground. It will break.

Hedda Gabler

In the course of the play, Hedda produces what we are told are her father's pistols. Single shot dueling pistols are what most directors want to see, but percussion revolvers would actually have been more common considering the time period in which her father would have made the purchase.

I Hate Hamlet

The fight between Barrymore and Andrew can and should be as elaborate as you can imagine, and this is a great chance to throw in every movie swordfight cliché ever seen. Barrymore is, after all, not only provoking Andrew into fighting but also teaching him how to be a swashbuckler. Jumping over the sword, slicing the candle on the mantle, going body-to-body for the dramatic lines, as well as every cheap sight gag in the book should be in this fight.

The swords are Barrymore's of course, and as such are either his own practice fencing weapons or theatre/movie props from one of his shows or films. No matter which, the blades should be light fencing weight, such as the epee, for movie swordplay in Barrymore's time was based on Olympic fencing (even the "broadsword" fights were elaborate versions of sport fencing).

Huck Finn
    see Tom Sawyer

Into the Woods

The two princes are usually costumed wearing swords, and there are two ways to go with these, depending on how they are going to be costumed. Believe it or not, there are two fairy tale traditions from which to choose, and the best way to visualize these are to look to the Disney animated classics for examples. If the look is "medieval fairy tale" such as Sleeping Beauty, then a very light version of a straight edged broadsword would be the right sword to use. If the look is more "folk fairy tale" like Cinderella, then one should go with gently curved sabres.

Jekyll and Hyde

The novella was written in 1886. There is a gun in the play, and in the novel it is merely described as an "old" gun. So, how many years before 1886 is "old"? Well, the first practical cartridge revolvers are developed in the mid-1870's, only ten years before this story. Therefore it is not unreasonable to infer that he is referring to a blackpowder percussion revolver, a ball and cap six-shooter.

A sword cane is called for, and this poses a problem for the many states in which such weapons are illegal. In those cases, I'm afraid the only remedy is to try to build one yourself.

For the throat slitting, I always advise against using a blood effects knife. Better to go with a preset blood pot and have the actor apply the blood exactly when needed (see the stage combat section, page 390, for a couple of ideas).

Kentucky Cycle

What a prop and costume budgeting nightmare! To do the show right will take several thousand dollars to provide all of the period specific items called for. On the other hand, there is some doubling that you can do without breaking historical accuracy.

From 1775 to 1860, the United States Department of War didn't spend much on new weaponry. The same flintlock rifles that worked fine for the revolution were used for the War of 1812. Even during the first years of the Civil War, large quantities of these same flintlock muskets were simply retrofitted with percussion locks and put into use until the newly built percussion rifles could be shipped out to the troops. Be that as it may, you should probably use percussion lock muskets by the time you get to *God's Great Supper* (play 5).

So it is in the first half of the play that you can save the most money. In the second half, gun evolution progresses too quickly to allow for any doubling.

The King and I

Directors often want "palace guards" to wear elaborate scimitars. Sorry, wrong continent, but for this fluff musical you can probably get away with it. This show, and the book from which it is derived, strays so far from historical accuracy that you should feel free to put in just about anything that enters your imagination. (Traditionally, soldiers would have had short spears, not swords, and there doesn't seem to be an indication that there was a standing unit of palace guards or royal bodyguards. Certainly by the time of this play, soldiers would have had percussion muskets. Muskets were part of the Siamese armament from the late sixteenth century.)

Laura

The show requires a walking cane, which is also a firearm. *("He gives his stick a sudden twist, removes the bottom part. The rest is a gun. 'You see, it has a short barrel. It has, in effect, the same spread as a sawed-off shotgun.' ")* For something to have a "spread" it means that it is firing multiple pellets from a single cartridge, not a single bullet. So the gun/cane is loaded with a shotgun shell, although the barrel width could be that of any regular pistol. Shotshells made so that they can fit into regular short barrel guns are common, and actually come in many calibers. The cane itself would look like an ordinary cane, except for a recessed trigger that would only pop out when the gun is disengaged from the rest of the cane. All of this means that you can use any walking cane that can come apart easily enough and then look as though it has a hollow barrel. It helps if it has a shaped handle rather than being a simple walking stick.

Les Liaisons Dangereuses

Taking place in the mid 1780's, the fighting style of the duel in the penultimate scene should be in the smallsword style - truly the pinnacle of single weapon dueling complexity.

In the stage directions for Act 2, scene 8, it calls for a case for the "epees" to be carried out for the duel held on the misty open field. But such a case doesn't exist in history, at least not in the 18th century. More manageable would be a plush fabric bag, something similar to the soft carriers used to transport silverware. So why is there mention of a case? What I believe happened is that the playwright or author may have come across the phrase "case of rapiers", which actually refers to two rapiers built to be sheathed in one scabbard but used one in each hand, for true two-handed fighting. It has nothing to do with a case to put swords into, and in any case was not ever done for smallswords, but there you are. These kinds of errors abound in literature.)

After Danceny's first line, the stage directions refer to "this breach of etiquette". The conceit here is that it is understood among gentlemen that the combatants would not speak to each other before the duel, and that all concerns are handled through the seconds.

After Valmont's response, the stage directions have him lay his sword on the ground while he removes his coat and puts on his glove. No one who owns a sword would ever lay it on the ground, especially on a "misty December morning". The dew from the grass is an invitation to rust, which can ruin the blade. Why did he not just lay the sword back on the case or have Azolan hold it for a moment? Who knows, except that that's what happened in the London performance, and the stage manager dutifully noted all of the action in the script that later went to the publisher. The script by Christopher Hamton as published by Samuel French is one of those unfortunate examples of every frown and glance performed by the original cast having been faithfully entered into the published script - to the detriment of all future actors and directors trying to create their own production. (If such line readings and trivial specific actions had been included in Shakespeare's time, his work might not have survived past his lifetime.)

By contrast, for the specific moments of interest in the fight, at first reading there seems to be interesting stage directions concerning this duel. But a closer reading offers no true description of the fight itself, for there are no directions, just a vague emotional description that reads more like a novel than a script. The choreographer is supposed to translate "some piece of inattention very close to carelessness" into a series of moves that the audience can follow and comprehend. Simple in a film, but way too subtle for stage. And it explains nothing. Is he merely distracted? Does Danceny win the fight due to his skill? Why is it necessary for Valmont to be wounded in the middle of the fight? Does it change him?

Make the fight your own, as you would for *Romeo & Juliet*. Tell a story. Let the audience see a change in Valmont, one that commits him to a path that leads to his death. If the audience doesn't see the change and understand why he does what he does, the fight is a useless delay to the end of the show.

If you do have Valmont wounded in the middle of the fight, there is a break in the action in which the script says that he and Azolan have a "murmured consultation", afterwhich the fight resumes. What are they talking about?

Part of the duty of the seconds is to ensure that protocol is maintained and that honor is satisfied. One common understanding is that he who draws first blood can be considered to have won the duel. Valmont could simply walk away here and both men would have their honor intact. That Valmont returns to fight means that merely drawing blood will no longer suffice to finish this duel. If he wounds Danceny now, it is meaningless. No, Valmont has committed both men now to fight a duel to the death. One or the other must be carried off the field.

Les Miserables

A sabre as a side arm for a military man is standard, but a gendarme officer in full uniform would wear one as well. But then again, full dress uniform would only be worn for ceremonial occasions. Civilians at this time have given up the sword as an item of dress. So there is really no point in this play at which Joubert would be wearing his sword.

The firearms used by the citizenry at the barricade would be a mix of whatever they could lay their hands on. So it is reasonable to see a variety of percussion lock and flintlock muskets and even some single shot pistols. As the first revolvers are just being developed, it is unlikely that anyone in this scene on either side would have access to such a cutting edge item, so only single shot firearms should be used. The percussion firing system for both pistols and muskets had just been brought into limited manufacture, and even most armies had not yet begun to shift over from their stock of flintlocks. [By the way, young actors love to "go method" in this scene, especially if they get to be shot. They will smash the props if given half a chance, using the muskets to absorb their fall to the stage. This is a great way to destroy your props in just a few rehearsals, so be sure and set aside a portion of one rehearsal to teach them how to fall without trashing the guns or themselves.]

The action at the barricade is fairly well described in the script and the libretto, but is quite different from what happens in the Victor Hugo book. So enjoy the book as a research tool to bring nuance to the characters, but remember that our job is to bring life to the script as we find it. Both the novel and the script describe fights similar in tone, but not in specific actions. The script directions refer to some complicated manoeuvering on the other side, and if the actors are agreed as to what is happening offstage it just might help the audience as well. So some background: the soldiers are trained to be able to fire and reload their muskets within 16 seconds. The citizens at the barricades, even if some of them have had military experience, will need from 30 to 45 seconds between shots. Why? The soldiers all have identical muskets and are carrying pre-measured cartridges to allow for quick loading. The citizens have a variety of weapons, non-standard bullets, no training for battlefield conditions, and gunpowder brought loose in pouches or bags. Even knowing this, the officer in charge on the other side made an early, critical mistake. At the first sign of the barricade going up, the soldiers should have rushed the position in a bayonet charge. At a full run from even 80 yards away, they would realistically have faced only one round of largely ineffective gunfire from the unorganized insurgents. The citizens would not have had time to reload before the soldiers would have been on top of them. The soldiers could then have fired once at close range, and then quickly disperse and dispatch the remaining rebels with bayonets. [Artillery and grenades were available to the army and several attacks from a cannon are vividly described in detail in the novel, but again, not in the script, so we are going to assume for our purposes that a decision was made not to use them in a densely populated urban environment].

Instead, the officer treats the situation as the taking of a fort. He sends in a small company of sappers protected by a small company of infantrymen. Sappers were the engineers of the army, specialized in tunneling under enemy walls and in setting explosives. Whatever the sappers have planned for this situation, they are carrying tools instead of firearms, and that's why the infantrymen are accompanying them.

The citizens fire, and although their light sporting arms are underpowered compared to the soldiers' muskets, they are very accurate, and most of the bullets can find their targets at these limited ranges. Although the infantry try to provide covering return fire, they and the sappers take too many casualties and must retreat. The troopers' smoothbore firearms are very powerful, but these soldiers are not marksmen, and if they are more than 50 yards away cannot expect to hit a single man standing in an open field, let alone semi-hidden figures behind a barricade.

But there are a company of soldiers who are trained to do just that. Fusiliers, armed with rifle-barreled muskets even more accurate than the citizens' sporting rifles, can act as snipers in such situations, taking positions from windows and rooftops up to 200 yards away. So a little later, when the bullets start coming from a strange angle and landing inside the supposedly safe area behind the barricade, everyone rightfully panics. It is Valjean's coolness under fire that allows him to be able to evaluate the situation, spot the sniper, and use his own excellent return fire to kill him.

But the eventual outcome of this situation was a foregone conclusion as soon as the barricade was constructed. The army, with nearly unlimited replacements and supplies, moves in closer and closer with every engagement, and soon the shear volume of fire from the regular infantry compensates for accuracy. For the young revolutionaries, the heady optimism of romantic ignorance is replaced by cold deadly reality.

Lion in Winter

Even the nobility in the middle ages would never wear their swords unless actually approaching a field of battle, but this play specifically has several characters wearing their broadswords, so we go with it. Henry actually uses (draws and raises) his sword at the end of the play, and in most productions it strikes the ground or is even thrown across the set, so get the sturdiest sword you can find.

A great line in the play refers to the fact that everyone wore a dagger in the Middle Ages, and if we include general purpose utility knives, that is very true. Daggers were also fairly large, but remember that in the dungeon scene you need to hide those knives in a covered tray or platter, so depending on the tray size, you may need a second set of smaller knives for this scene, or perhaps choose smaller daggers for the earlier scenes. Or get a big platter.

A Little Night Music

As this show is set during the turn of the century, the only appropriate guns should be revolvers, not single shot dueling pistols. (After all, how can you challenge someone to Russian Roulette with a single shot pistol?)

Little Women

Even though some swords are called for when the sisters put on their amateur theatrical, we have from the text of the novel a very clear idea as to the nature of the props used.

" Being still too young to go often to the theater, and not rich enough to afford any great outlay for private performances, the girls put their wits to work, and necessity being the mother of invention, made whatever they needed. Very clever were some of their productions, pasteboard guitars, antique lamps made of old-fashioned butter boats covered with silver paper, gorgeous robes of old cotton, glittering with tin spangles from a pickle factory, and armor covered with the same useful diamond shaped bits left in sheets when the lids of preserve pots were cut out ... .Jo played male parts to her heart's content and took immense satisfaction in a pair of russet leather boots given her by a friend, who knew a lady who knew an actor. These boots, an old foil, and a slashed doublet once used by an artist for some picture, were Jo's chief treasures and appeared on all occasions."

So at best, there should be one old foil, and then whatever else the girls would have found or built (fireplace poker, sticks, what have you).

As the musical version actually has the stories come to life, actual swords should of course be used, but keep in mind that these are still fairy tale recreations, filtered through Jo's 1800's sensibilities. These fantasy swords should be very light and no more than three feet long, more presentation than practical.

Lovers and Executioners

Written in 1667-68, the sword used would be the transitional rapier, still a cut and thrust weapon, so a heavier blade than modern fencing weapons. The use of a weapon in the non-dominant hand has passed, so parries are done with the attacking sword. The true riposte is born in this period.

The American translation of this French play has one troublesome phrase in the middle of one of the comic duels. *Constance: "What was that move?" Don Lope: "A fully extended, left-lead passado"*. The phrase has no specific definition, so we have to break it down and provide our own. Passado meant simply a forward passing step, but with time has come to mean a forward passing step combined with a thrust. If we use the more modern definition, a left-lead passado seems to mean that Don Lope was standing with his right foot forward and presumably with the sword in his right hand. He then passed his left foot forward while thrusting. That part is fairly clear, but what about the "fully-extended" part? Try fully extending either leg and see which one you like best. If you straighten (extend) the right (trailing) leg, you get a nice opposite lunge - a very strong look. But if instead you straighten the left (leading) leg, you get a solid attack that still keeps the torso back and away from danger. It is also a wonderfully foppish look, especially if you allow the torso to lean back and the left hand to rise above the head. Very silly, which is why I love to use it in shows like this.

Lucia Di Lammermoor

This opera is set vaguely in the latter part of the 17th century. The Walter Scott novel on which it is based combined some factual incidents from 1669 and 1683, but Donizetti leaves the specific date open. Either way it leaves us with two choices to make concerning the swords that your cast will wear. We're right in the middle of a transition period for the civilian sword: the bulky rapier is considered something of a dinosaur but the ultra lean smallsword has not yet become common, even among the high nobility. Generally speaking, older users would tend to stick with the sword of their youth. To that add the distinctly Scottish view that any civilian version of the sword, whether rapier or smallsword, was unmanly. They never took to it the way the British did, using instead the basket-hilted broadsword in both war and in peace.

Those within the nobility who wanted to emulate French fashion eschewed the broadsword in favor of the elegant smallsword. But wearing such a sword also made a political statement. The French had at least weakly supported Scotland against England several generations before, but as the English nobles also copied French fashion, the wearing of the smallsword could be taken as submission to English rule. Confusing? Yes it is, and so it was back then as well. So it can make for interesting character choices to outfit each person on the sliding scales of Scottish vs. English vs. French and basket hilt vs. rapier vs. smallsword.

To aid in those choices, take a cue from your costumer. If traditional Scottish dress is used, stay with the basket hilts for everyone. If the dress is continental with nary a kilt in sight, then go with smallswords for the younger characters and rapiers for the older folk.

Man of La Mancha

Beyond the challenges of setting up the scenes of violence in this show, don't add another - trying to faithfully follow the stage directions. Honestly, are you really going to cast one of the Muleteers simply because he can do a handstand? Are you really going to demand that the central fight include a ladder just because the Broadway version used one?

As with all plays, better to read the stage directions once to get a feel of how the scene is supposed to flow, and then use a felt-tip pen and block it all out. Create your own fight according to your vision and the capabilities of the cast.

Mikado

When Gilbert and Sullivan wrote this, they were intending a realistic representation of the Japan of the time, the silliness of the script notwithstanding. So that doesn't explain what they possibly could have meant by the weapon called the "snickersnee". In their time, snickersnee was English slang for a cut and thrust weapon (from old Dutch: steken = stick; snijden = cut), but it was a lower-class term for a lower-class item, a cutting weapon larger than a common knife but shorter than a sword. I suppose the nearest Japanese equivalent might be the wakizashi, but that might be overthinking the bit. It's possible that there was a funny and lightly insulting joke of having a nobleman call his own weapon by a vulgar name. It probably got a good laugh from British audiences of the time, but modern audiences aren't going to get it. Better to simply give the character a normal katana and ignore the joke.

Moon Over Buffalo

There are several weapon issues for this show. First is the snippet of a sword fight across the room and over the couch. The style of stage swordplay for this period demands a very light blade and a great deal of point finesse. [It is helpful to keep the blade length at a less than standard length of 28" for the ease of the actors.] When we see "Cyrano" later in performance, the same light bladed weapon should be used, not a heavy rapier, for during the 1950's there would have been no thought given to historical accuracy.

"Patton" wears and fires his sidearm, but be careful. It is easy to assume that he should wear the standard issue US combat Colt 45 semiautomatic pistol Model 1911, as every other Army general wore, but Patton was a case apart. He used his own ivory handled western-styled Colt Peacemaker revolvers - in some photos just one, in other photos wearing two. Although it was a non-issued revolver, he used standard issue army holsters. A lot of people still remember him, so all of this is important. By the by, it was an ivory-handled gun - not pearl handled. He made it clear that no serious man would ever consider owning a pearl handled gun.

Musical Comedy Murders of 1940

The properties list in the script is nicely clear and comprehensive, but there are a couple of items that might get you into trouble. The action calls for a struggle during which the Lugar is to be dropped to the floor, and you'd be lucky to get more than a couple of drops before the gun [any gun] will crack. A rubber replica can be used, but the sound when it hits the floor doesn't sound very realistic, so if you use a plastic or metal replica try blocking the scene so that the pistol can drop into the seat of an overstuffed chair. One production worked it out so the gun "fell" onto the top shelf of a bookcase. The replicas are getting harder to find in most states, and you can't afford to replace the real items, so it behooves you to find an alternative to the bit as written.

An earlier bit describes a sword having been removed from a mantle during a blackout and then impaling someone through an easy chair. Please folks, common sense should tell you that one prop cannot do all that. The blackout allows for the sword on the wall to be removed and hidden, and a duplicate, shortened, dummy sword to be inserted into a specially drilled out chair. Unless you can rig up a pop-up blade that's strapped onto the dead actor (please don't waste your time), just turn the chair slightly upstage so that the impaling is implied but not fully seen.

My Favorite Year

The year in question being 1954, scrupulous attention to historical accuracy was just as important in the entertainment industry as it was in Shakespeare's time - that is to say, not at all. So the sword that Swann would have for the television show would be anything that the production department would have found a few days before, and that would most likely have been any sport fencing foil. Anything you find will be appropriate.

Noises Off

Not a fight show, but plenty of slapstick. In the second act, a backstage fireman's ax is needed. Please consider using a hollow or plastic headed ax here, for wielding a real ax in the close quarters and speeded timing of this scene can get away from even the most conscientious actor. Even with a light ax, be sure that each actor is slightly off-line of other actors whenever the ax is swung. In other words, the implied swing of the ax will be slightly upstage or downstage of the victim.

Gary has to tumble down the flight of stairs in the third act, and so just a reminder to go back to the movement section for tips on how to control this. Also, consider using the boxes to help start the tumble. For example, he could trip over them into a seated position first, allowing the tumble itself to start from a low squat instead of from standing (much easier).

Random art note: I've seen eight different productions of this show at every level of professionalism, and it never fails to be a huge hit with audiences. But there is one tiny moment that in every single case has stopped the laughter dead in its tracks. At first I though it was my imagination, but the last few times I've been able to predict it and it always happens.

In Act II, Lloyd comes rushing onstage in a panic and says, *"What the fuck is going on here!"* Up until that moment, the audience has been completely caught up with the fun, and then that single word comes out of nowhere as a slap to the face. Neither Lloyd nor any other character uses profanity at any other point in the script, and invariably the audience becomes silent. The rules have suddenly changed for them, and they don't know what to do with that new information. It takes about a page or two for the momentum to start to climb again. So, for the sake of the laughs, change the word. Even *"bloody hell"* can still have all of the force of the original, and especially American audiences can laugh with it.

Of Mice and Men

Only one gun is specifically mentioned - the Lugar pistol that ultimately is the one that George uses. The Lugar is a German manufactured semiautomatic pistol with a distinctive "swept" grip and exposed barrel. As written, the final scene is very dangerous for Lenny, for the Lugar is supposed to be pointed directly at the back of his head at point-blank range and then fired. There are several options available to try and make this a little safer.

First, and best, use a completely fake replica and use taped sound or an offstage starter pistol for the noise. If that is unacceptable, there are some block-barreled replicas that are blank-fire, so at least there is no discharge going directly down the barrel and straight into Lenny's head. Unfortunately, the sound can still be deafening, and if the director wants a good solid sound, it can leave the actor with permanent hearing loss. Ear protection should be worn by both actors.

If a blank-firing Lugar proves too difficult to find, you can always change the reference in the script to another brand ("Rugar", perhaps? It's a real brand) and then use any long-barreled blank-fire stage safe revolver.

In another scene in the play, several of the workers rush to get guns in order to hunt down Lenny. There are no specifics, so it can be a mix of hunting rifles, shotguns, and pistols.

There are two instances of physical violence in the show. When Lenny kills the girl, just remember that she should be doing all of the work. Lenny is there to make it look good, but she must be in control. Special attention must be taken to protect her head and neck at all costs, so no lifting by the head.

An early fist fight between Lenny and Curley is fairly basic, although a nice touch is to have Curley use the bareknuckle boxers stance described back in the unarmed stage combat chapter.

Oklahoma!

It is easy to forget that this show is set in 1906, for the costuming and sets are usually given a Hollywood generic cowboy treatment that look a lot more like 1877. If you want to stay a bit more true to the actual history, you should aim for a Mild West feel rather than Wild West. From even before the turn of the century, no one would wear a gun in town. For a gathering such as the box social, people would be dressed in their "Sunday-go-to-meetin'" best. So even cowhands would put on their best version of a three piece suit and bowler hat. On the other hand, it is a musical, and a grim adherence to historical reality takes a lot of the fun away from these shows. As for the weapons, you can go simple or costly. Some productions have every male character wearing a revolver, but the bare bones version takes two firing pistols, one knife, and one shotgun. As a matter of fact, if you really need to, you can get away with just one revolver and one knife.

All of the pistols should be Western style full-sized revolvers. Curly and Jud both need to have firing models, since they fire off one round each in the smokehouse scene.

Some productions save even more money and add to the dramatic tension of the smokehouse scene by having Jud and Curly share one gun. Here's how it's usually staged: Just before Curly enters the smokehouse, we see him take off his holster and pass it to some passing cowhand. The audience easily recognizes in this gesture that Curly is stepping into Jud's domain in a completely non-threatening manner. Later, Jud in a rage shoots his revolver and then stares at Curly while holding the gun in his hand. Curly then uses the bit about shooting through the knot hole not as a show of bravado, but as a way of easing the gun out of Jud's control. It makes for a tense and dramatic moment.

During "The Farmer and the Cowman", Aunt Eller shoots something, but it is not identified in the script. Usually it is a revolver pulled from someone's holster. It is wise to use a much louder blank for this scene than the kind used for the earlier quiet smokehouse scene. In this scene, the gunshot has to be louder than a full orchestra playing at fortissimo and forty feet stomping on a wooden stage.

Carnes holds a double barreled shotgun on Ali Hakim, but there is no real reason why it cannot be a western rifle. I realize that the old joke being played upon here is that of a "shotgun wedding", but if a shotgun cannot be found, a simple line change later for Ali to something like "looking down the barrel of a thirty-thirty" easily keeps the tone of the joke.

The Little Wonder - what is it, and did it ever really exist? There were some novelty items of the period and even through the 1920's, about four or five inches long, tube shaped, with an eye piece on one end and a glass reflector on the other. Look into one end and turn the other to a light source and you could see a good-quality photograph in fine detail and in seemingly large size. On occasion they were famous landscape shots, but far more commonly female nudes. That Jud found one that also has a spring loaded spike in it is not impossible, just not mentioned from any other source.

At the climactic fight between a knife-wielding Jud and an unarmed Curly, Jud dies having been impaled [fallen?] on his own knife. A retractable knife is sometimes asked for, but is both unwise and unnecessary, for a regular knife [dulled, of course] is far safer. Once the combatants separate, Jud needs only to be found lying on the ground with his back to the audience. We don't have to move him as the sheriff can merely examine Jud from upstage of the body. We also don't need to see the knife - the sheriff tells the assembled crowd what has happened and that is all we, the audience, need to know.

Oliver!

Near the end of the show Bill Sykes is shot at by one [or more] policeman. Actually, the stage notation uses the term "Hussar", which is a lightly armed (originally Hungarian) light cavalry. Since someone riding in on horseback would be quite a distraction during that scene, most productions stick to one or two generically uni-formed soldiers. The standing civilian police force of the time carried only nightsticks and wooden rattles - no firearms, no whistles. In Dicken's time, the uniformed and well armed soldiers took care of the serious threats. And yet, many directors decide to go with a vaguely "Bobby" police look, thinking that having soldiers appear would be confusing to the audience, and they're right.

Either way, as *Oliver Twist* was written in 1838, the only handgun available would have been a single shot percussion pistol. You might want to consider using a revolver instead. Yes, it is an anachronism, but if you are going to use live gunshot for the sound it is comforting for the actor doing the shooting to know that, if anything goes wrong, he can pull the trigger two or three times until something goes BANG. Consider it, at least, for if the single shot pistol fails to fire, someone will have to march up and strangle Sykes, for Bill Sykes must die.

Our Country's Good

The only weapons seen here are going to be for the British soldiers, so historically they would be the long flintlock musket called the Brown Bess. The scene calls for one of them to fire. If a true flintlock can be found, it looks wonderful to see the flash in the pan and then the muzzle flash a half second later, but the misfire rate is very high, as is the danger factor. Consider using a percussion musket, or better yet a block-barreled blank firing replica if possible.

Pajama Game

The old vaudeville knife throwing act is called for. You find a full explanation of how to set up the bit back in the end of the Edged Weaponry section of the Staged Violence chapter.

Pentecost

Set in an unnamed eastern-bloc country in modern times, we need not know any more specifics than to know that the soldiers in the final scene should have AK-47's during the assault. Officers might have a pistol as a military sidearm, which could be a generic semi-auto pistol, most likely a Makarov look-alike, a rather small frame semi-auto. The refugees, although from many countries, would only have access to what could be stolen locally or available on the black market.. Hunting rifles, surplus WWI and WWII rifles, and knock-off AK's would certainly be the first choice. Stay away from UZI's and M-16's. These would be far too costly for refugees and the ammunition would always be difficult to find.

Peter Pan

The toughest part of this show's weapons concerns is what to give to Peter. He definitely carries a dagger in the scenes before the pirate ship, but if it is a dagger of regular length, it makes the duel with Captain Hook very difficult. So some choices need to be made, starting with Hook.

Our poor captain usually is wearing a heavy and restrictive costume, heavy boots, a difficult wig and a precarious hat, and has one hand squeezed into a bell hook. Then he is stuck on a set filled with rigging, levels, pirates, Indians and lost boys, and expected to fight a duel with someone with a wire coming out of his/her back. Being kind, the fight choreographer will choose a very light-bladed sword and no scabbard, or at least have one of the pirates slip off the scabbard prior to the fight. If your actor is right-handed, put his hook on the left. *"But the story has Hook's hook in the right hand!"* Yes, but with all that going on onstage you'll want him to have complete control of that sword, so put the sword in his right and the hook on the left, and change the one line in the script.

For Peter then, much will center on the style of fighting desired. More finesse requires a matched sword, which Peter can snatch from one of the other pirates onboard. A more slapstick broad comedy fight can take more advantage of whatever flight capabilities you have, and also the chance to use a much shorter sword or even his own dagger. However, the greater the disparity in blade lengths means that Peter will have to jump back and forth that much more just to maintain appropriate distance, which may be difficult since at this point he is rigged for flying. I repeat: Peter need not use his dagger for the fight. Before the duel he has already dispatched a couple of pirates, so could easily have one of their swords in his hand when he reveals himself to Hook.

We have seen a lot of variation on the look of Peter's weapon. If he uses a pirate sword, then of course the look is a simple cutlass, but his own dagger can range from an early Greek look (he is, after all, the "Pan"), all the way to a simple cross made of wood such as a child would fashion from sticks and twine.

The Physicist

One gun in this show is called a "Browning revolver". Sorry, but there is no such firearm. All Browning pistols were and continue to be semiautomatics; not a revolver in the bunch. The erroneous term has been common in England since the first semiautos were produced at the turn of the century, although in this case the culprit was a translator's error.

Pippin

Another play that traditionally requires a collapsible knife. Since those are hard to find nowadays, you'll have to use a fixed dagger and some creative stage combat techniques. Check the stage combat section concerning stabbing with the knife. If done right, it can look better than using a trick knife.

Pirates of Penzance

The choice of swords for the pirates can vary depending on how elaborate the choreographer and director want to get. If minimal, than merely sturdy replicas are fine, either of standard cutlasses or more ornate rapiers, although certainly fight-worthy blades are needed if there is going to be sword to sword contact. This might happen if for example the choreographer has some of the pirates playfully fencing in the *"I Am a Pirate King"* number. But if the swords are only to be used in a brawl against the Bobbies at the end of the play, then sturdy but costume grade blades are fine against the wooden billy clubs.

Rashomon

As the play was written from the 1950 movie of the same name, and the screenplay was written in part by the director, we should not stray too far from the choices Kurosawa made. He has the samurai use the traditional katana, the curved double handed sword of the noble class. What is often unnoticed is that the bandit, on the other hand, has a Chinese singlehand straight sword, a dao. It is an interesting choice, although certainly as a thief he could have a katana as well. While it is possible that the thief is a disgraced *ronin*, a masterless samurai, there is no indication from the script or the movie to verify that.

In the translation of the play, the nobleman's sword is described as having a silver "handle", and this leads to some confusion. This play was translated into British English, not American. The Japanese term used in the screenplay is "tsuba", which in American English translates as "guard", the metal piece that keeps the hand away from the blade. British English translates the same word as "handle", because in England all of the sword hilt (everything that isn't the blade) is referred to collectively as the handle. Therefore the metal part that protects your hand is part of the "handle" in England, but it's called the "guard" in the USA, and "tsuba", in Japanese. The part that you actually hold onto is called the "grip" in England, but it's called the "handle" in the USA, and "tsuka", in Japanese. You can see how it gets confusing, but rest assured that for this sword the *handle* (the grip) is not made of silver, only the *guard*. Change the word for your production unless you are playing to a houseful of Brits.

Finally, the knife used by the wife is not her own, but is rather her husband's tanto, a sixteen inch curved battle knife. How it is that it's in her possession is not explained.

References to Salvador Dali Make Me Hot

The script refers to a 9mm revolver, but what is required is a semi-automatic pistol. The playwright (wrongly) used the term revolver for pistol, and then assumed (wrongly) that 9mm means semi-automatic. The gun is supposed to be American military, so it must be a semi-automatic pistol.

Rivals

This was written in 1775, so the swords need to be smallswords, not rapiers. It doesn't matter that the director invariably asks for rapiers - the look is completely wrong, something like doing West Side Story with machetes.

Robin Hood

Merry Robin, prince of thieves, noble born champion of the peasants against Norman oppression, finest archer in the realm, faithful subject of King Richard the Lionheart. I would not dare harm one iota of Robin's mythic persona, but I thought a little background on the development of the legend might be of some interest.

In the search for the birth of the Robin stories we go not to 1190 and Richard I but much later, to about 1370 and Edward III, a time of plague, costly foreign war, and domestic strife. The plague had reduced by half the population of England, which increased the value of each surviving laborer, but laws were still in place that froze the salaries of workers. Those who traveled to new towns for higher wages were declared outlaws, and those who accepted the low legal payment were unable to pay their taxes, and quickly run afoul of the shire reeve (sheriff).

With not enough workers to provide a steady source of food to major population centers, many went hungry and some resorted to petty thievery and poaching. More dangerous were bands of soldiers, returned from France, who found that it was easier to kill and steal than work and buy.

Here the first stories of Robin Hood are combined with the earlier 12th century French ballads of a petty thief who outsmarts the sheriff at every turn. A simple peasant, he takes a sly delight in making the nobles appear foolish, gives to the poor at times but has little scruple in murdering and pillaging himself should the occasion present itself.

With the civil war that followed, the longing for a time of peace under the rule of one legitimate monarch took private thoughts to the time of Richard the Lionheart, and soon the Robin myth settled there. It is at this time that Robin acquires his band of men, not so merry because they are wandering gangs of unemployed soldiers who would rather steal than work. When Henry V ascends the throne, the legend of Robin goes to work for the ruling class. He becomes for the first time a dispossessed noble (for only a noble can rule over others, rabble or not). He and his band are outlaws only because an "illegitimate" threatens the throne; they remain intensely loyal to the true crown.

There was a very practical side to this appropriation of the peasant tale. It promoted the practice of archery. The finest arm of the English army was its superior light infantry in the form of longbow archers. Other nations had crossbows, but crossbows could take a full minute to reload. In the hands of a trained archer, twelve arrows could be fired in that time, each with enough force and accuracy to pierce the stoutest armor at 200 yards. When fired in volley they had an effective battle range of 800 yards. This was an accuracy of rapid fire not again attained by infantry units until the development of breech loaded rifles of the 1890's.

The major problem with the longbow is that it requires constant practice to develop the strength and accuracy needed. Henry VIII went so far as to decree that men of fighting age had to practice every Sunday after morning religious service. The idea of having young lads attempt to emulate the exploits of a popular hero must have appealed greatly to the military leaders, while softening Robin's motivation by making him a wronged landowner and not another revolting peasant would soothe the nerves of the political leaders. Exactly how it was that this nobleman developed the skills of an archer-infantryman is tacitly ignored.

The animosity between Anglo-Saxons and Normans inherent in the story also had a practical use. The Anglo-Saxons made better archers because of their larger size.

An interesting footnote is the creation of the secondary characters. Little John is famous for his cudgeling of Robin by using his quarterstaff. Its use is very similar to some of the skills required for handling a bill or halberd in battle. Friar Tuck is a rascal of a monk who is also able to handle a sword. Tuck is the anglicized form of the Norman-French word "estoc", which is a longsword with no true cutting edge, used for thrusting only. It also had a 13th century meaning, to "reprove" or "upbraid". (The meaning of tuck as in "to eat heartily" did not come into use until the late 19th century.)

If a "historically correct" production of Robin Hood is desired, the sword types are limited to single hand broadswords with simple guards. The sword would only occasionally be gripped with two hands to deliver a powerful "baseball" swing or a finishing thrust when the opponent is down. Foot soldiers often used the falchion, a short, heavy meat-cleaver of a weapon that required little practice to put to deadly use. Archers had a short sword as a sidearm in battle, but they wore no armor. The sword was only used as a weapon of last resort, for an archer's best use in war was to take a long-range position behind the lines and fire into the enemy.

If your idea of a "traditional" Robin Hood (as mine) is Errol Flynn, a sturdy but light blade is needed instead of a broadsword blade. This keeps the moves dashing rather than bashing.

The longbow presents a different problem altogether. It is a wonderful weapon, made of a uniform single cut of yew and about 6 feet tall, with the arrow almost a yard long, but unfortunately wasn't used by the English until the late 14th century, about two hundred years later than the reign of Richard the Lionheart. The simplest way around the dilemma is to ignore it.

Rosencrantz & Guildenstern are Dead

Sorry, but this is another one of those shows that seems to require a retractable knife, and unfortunately it is nearly impossible to find one which is realistic enough. Add to that the fact that the liability is so large for a retractable on stage that American insurance companies won't cover a show that uses one.

But don't despair. A close reading of the script reveals that a retractable knife is never actually mentioned, only that the Player King realistically "stabs" himself and then shows that it was merely an illusion. If the actor can perfect the stage combat version of the stab described in an earlier section of this book, the moment concerned can be just as effective as using a retractable knife, and far safer to the actor.

The Rover

As the play was written in 1677, we're in an interesting time in terms of the type of sword that is most appropriate. We're in the transition period here between the rapier and the smallsword, and in general the swords were still the bulkier former rather than the ultra-light latter. You don't get any help from the script, which refers to merely the "sword". There is a passing reference to the Spaniard having the longest sword, and this was a common stereotype of the period, the Spanish having the reputation of carrying swords a little too large and too ornate, but not being able to handle them well.

Blunt has a rusty sword and buff belt. Although he is a gentleman and we would expect him to have a light courtsword or transitional rapier, he is an English *country* gentleman, and city wits never missed a chance to denigrate their country brethren as being hopelessly out of date. So his weapons should be an old fashioned full cup hilted rapier.

The addition of the pistol is interesting in that it would have to have been a wheellock pistol, an extraordinarily expensive item for a civilian to have.

Scarlet Pimpernel

Here is yet another show in which the sword choice for the final duel must be made within a range of possibilities. The action takes place in 1792, so noble-born civilians would use the smallsword in the light and fast fighting style of the late 1700's. The military soldiers and even the lower and mid-ranking officers would use a heavy-bladed sabre, and these two swords cannot fight each other for long without the smallsword blade shattering at the first or second clash. It seems that the Scarlet Pimpernel takes a sword from one of the soldiers, so this would normally lead to a bashing sabre duel, very rustic, brutal and ungentlemanly. But the original play was written in 1905, and the fight would have been a very fast version of Olympic style fencing - very Barrymore. The Broadway version made a compromise and used a sturdy schlaeger blade on a military sabre hilt, thereby increasing the strength of the blade but losing some of the finesse of the period. Other productions have made other choices, none of them incorrect.

No matter what the blade choice, don't let the nationalities of the characters influence the hilt choice. In this era, style is more affected by class than geography. The French soldiers would definitely have stout looking sabres; the English nobles would have individualized thin smallswords.

Seven Brides for Seven Brothers

The show is set in 1851, so the rifles and shotguns will all have the same look - percussion and flintlock blackpowder muzzleloaders. Sorry, no lever-action rifles and no break-open shotguns, double-barrel or otherwise; they hadn't been invented yet.

Shenandoah

Just a reminder that when the Civil War began, both sides had nearly identical firearms. When the war suddenly flared up and more and more men were thrown into action, huge numbers of old style flintlock muskets were quickly retrofitted with new percussion locks until newly manufactured rifles could arrive. During the final year and a half of the war, the Southern army had almost no manufacturing capability and had to scramble to purchase rifles. As the war dragged soldiers had to make do with any and all muskets and rifles that they could scrape together. The weaponry would show the same kind of long use and wear and a certain level of randomness as should the uniforms.

Sherlock Holmes

The firearms used by Holmes and Watson are only mentioned in stories covering the early part of

Holmesian fiction, roughly from 1879 to 1903. There are many references to guns, but few specifics, and although Holmes and Watson are both supposed to be knowledgeable concerning firearms and their use, the author of the stories was not. Although Conan-Doyale was a gun enthusiast, he was not a very dilligent researcher. Many inaccuracies abound, but we can still get a general idea as to the guns Sir Arthur had in mind.

Watson, we know, has an "old service revolver", so more than likely would be similar to a Webley with a four inch barrel. Yes, I know that there is a specific reference to an "Eley's No.2". But Eley Bros. didn't make a No.2 model; Webley did. Either way, neither type of pistol was standard military issue during the time that the fictional Watson was in the service. And Holmes specifically tells Watson to slip the revolver into his pocket; again, not practical with the true service revolvers.

Holmes himself preferred a revolver with a short barrel, perhaps only two inches. This would be something with decent stopping power but could also easily fit in a coat or pants pocket, or in one story the pocket of his dressing gown. Something similar to the British Bulldog, more than likely.

One last thing about Holmes, we know that he has tremendous muscular strength belied by his thin build. We also know that he has trained (and we suppose has become a master of) the art of Baritsu. This was a real martial art form which was something of a sensation for upper class Victorian London men. It only flourished from 1899 to 1903. It combined boxing, wrestling, fencing, judo, jujitsu and most especially the application of attacks and defenses using a standard cane, walking stick or even a folded umbrella.

Sound of Music

Only Rolfe specifically has a pistol in a later scene of the play, and a good look is a Walther P-38 or the Lugar P-08. Although there are other guns that also might be appropriate, these two have an instant Nazi look that most audience members will recognize.

For the other soldiers chasing after the Von Trapps, simple bolt-action rifles are just fine.

Sleuth

This show has one of the scariest moments you will find in theatre - not for the audience, but for the actors. A critical plot point has one actor execute another with a point-blank shot to the back of the head. It violates every rule we have on gun safety, but there it is in the script, so what can you do?

The first thing is to try to get as much distance as you can between the shooter and the victim. Even moving the gun an extra 6 inches away can reduce the danger level dramatically. Although it may sound strange, in this case the one thing you should not do is have the shooter aim slightly upstage of the victim. If you are using a block-barreled gun (as you should) the hot gasses from the blank are going to go off to either side of the gun, so in this case the victim is in slightly less danger if the barrel is pointed directly at him. But don't get me wrong; the danger level here is still extremely high.

The only way to protect the victim is by isolating him completely not only from the discharge but also from the sound. That's right, the sound. At point-blank distance the sound from even a quarter load 22 caliber blank can lead to permanent hearing loss.

Luckily the victim is dressed as a clown in this scene, and therein lays the key to safety. As part of the costume, construct a clown wig on a light helmet (the detachable linings for construction hard hats work great), and attach built-in ear muffs (get at least 23 decibel protection). The entire helmet can be hidden by the wig. Finish by completely fireproofing the wig and the upper portion of the clown costume with a suitable liquid theatrical fire retardant.

Sweeney Todd

The story of Sweeney Todd originally "occurred" in 1805, although the Sondheim musical is set in 1835. Either way, the type of gun Anthony uses at the insane asylum would be a single-shot flintlock or percussion pistol. If you do want to have the gunshot come from the gun rather than a sound effect, I suggest using a blank-fire multishot revolver instead. It's out of period, but if anything goes wrong the actor can simply keep pulling the trigger until the shot occurs.

There are some special effects houses that make the bleeding razor required for this show, but in order to keep the razor of manageable size the blood reservoir has to be seperate from the razor. That means that the squeeze bulb with the blood and the long tube connect it to the razor has to be hidden up the sleeve of the actor. Not a very elegant solution, but a bit better than the oversized handles which hide a very small bulb. No one style seems to be any more effective or reliable than another.

Three Musketeers

I'm going to spend a little more time on this show, so bear with me, please. It has happened so many times that a theatre company will choose to do this play or the musical in the hopes of having a blockbuster show, only to have the final product be vaguely disappointing. I don't think that it is a problem with the scripts.

It is not without reason that so many films, plays, and novels are written of the swashbuckling era of rapiers and musketeers. Visually lush and thematically exciting, many are the acting companies that have even set their productions of several Shakespeare plays in the mid-1600's instead of the late 1590's. And certainly we have all thrilled to the musketeers on the big screen, and we hope to recreate that excitement on stage when we reproduce the period.

Unfortunately, many productions have fallen far short of the expectations that caused the selection in the first place. Most often, the excitement of the novel or film is simply lost on stage. Part of the problem may be in not fully understanding which period is to be truly represented.

Most of us start by closely examining the art, philosophy, science, and culture of the year in which the play is set. Unfortunately, this may not have been in the author's mind at all when the play was written. In works such as *Cyrano* or *The Three Musketeers*, the authors were writing in the middle of the Romantic period, in which huge sweeps of emotion were sought and enjoyed by the audience.

The music, architecture, art and dress of the time expressed this larger than life passion, an explosion of human vitality that we dismiss as being melodramatic but they viewed as being intensely "heartfelt". The popular works of art of the time reflected this, and one can feel the powerful, almost soaring drive of the time in hearing the music of Glinka, for example.

Just as Dumas wrote for 19th century sensibilities, so did filmmakers of the 1930's and '40's provide breathless excitement for audiences hungry for grand passion to forget the harsh realities of the depression, and later to bolster their courage for the frightening task of fighting another World War. When they watched Errol Flynn as Captain Blood or as Robin Hood, they were looking for an emotional sustenance that could get them through the difficult times ahead. Surely this is just as romantic a view of life as was the earlier period.

Small wonder that filmmakers borrow from the romantic period when attempting to create an action movie. *Star Wars* composer John Williams knew that the most viscerally effective music for the space-based swashbuckling film would be a "heroic" theme drawn on the operatic overtures of the 1800's. (Interesting that jazz works so well in the bar scene. Any type of rock music would have been grossly inappropriate.)

Just as the right music, be it from Rossini, Berlioz, or Williams, automatically creates excitement, so too can the set, costumes, and acting style further propel the audience into the passion of the piece. Vibrant colors, sweeping movement, visual excess on an operatic scale, these can provide a great deal of support to modern actors who, trained in subdued realism, often feel lost in the fiery world of grand passion and mistake it for melodrama.

As far as the simulation of violence is concerned, I am going to take a minority view and suggest that creation of a historically correct fighting style, though certainly just as exciting, is not necessarily what the audience has paid to see. I would suggest looking at the films of the 30's and 40's to get an idea of what worked best, as well as studying a bit about the fencing style that was used onstage in the mid-1800's. Even a review of the original *Star Wars* trilogy will show that many of the moves in the light-sabre fights are quite similar to those in the lively broadsword fight of Flynn's *Robin Hood.*

The best style source for the period is from the paintings and sculptures of 1820 to 1880. Browse through an art book while listening to the overture from *William Tell* or *Tristan et Isolde.* Look at the scenic designs of operas and plays produced at the time. Read a Superman comic book while listening to the theme from *Star Trek: The Next Generation.* Dance a waltz taking leaps instead of steps, and do it to the waltz music of the movie *The Addams Family.*

Pure melodrama, grand passion, driving energy and comic book violence - what more could you want from theatre? This show is sometimes difficult for American actors to embrace because they feel self-conscious in trying to perform in an acting style that celebrates the joy of expressing emotions for their own sake. This is opera on the grand scale, and anything that gets in the way of the actors or the audience to experience that rush of excitement must be excised form the production. There is nothing in this show that should be a slave to history, and nothing in the acting or directing that should come from a tradition of method acting. Realistic, yes; naturalistic, no. All of the actors must believe that these people lived this large every day of their lives.

A few anachronisms should be noted, though not necessarily corrected onstage. Depending on which script you use, the muskets themselves may need to fire more than once relatively rapidly. Of course, the real muskets couldn't do that, nor could you actually aim and fire the gun as a marksman would with any degree of accuracy. The real muskets were braced against the chest, not shoulder, in order to better absorb the shock, and they were quite heavy and simply could not be held in one's arms for firing. Every musketeer carried a four-foot forked pole onto which he would rest the musket before firing. But this is all harsh realism that we must blithely ignore.

Likewise, because the swords for these musketeers were also historically heavy, we need to make them light for dynamic and energetic fight sequences. It should be noted that most recent movie versions use a historically correct heavy sword, and then have to speed up the film during the fights. Stage actors will need some help in order to keep the fights exciting, even if that means using different swords for different scenes. There is certainly no harm in having a light fencing blade for the dueling type fights and then identical hilts outfitted with heavy cutting blades for the big brawling mass scenes.

The latest stage version, written by Ken Ludwig, has a couple of prop challenges. D'artagnan's sword is supposed to be broken each night. The most reliable thing to do is have two swords, one complete and the other with a pre-broken blade which is barely tack-welded at the point of the break. If the weld is made to be brittle, it should break easily each night. Of course that also means that the blade must be re-welded before each show. Brasing will not be strong enough, nor will any type of glue. The only alternative is to make a fake blade out of wood, which won't sound very convincing.

That script also calls for the Countess DeWinter to pull a "17th century switchblade" from her bodice. That from the stage directions. Such an item is of course a fantasy piece, and one was built for the Broadway version but you are not going to be able to find one anywhere. Unless you build your own (good luck) it is easier to have the countess use a regular fixed-bladed stilleto. The reason that the Ludwig version used a switchblade was to maximize the size of the weapon, since there isn't much room in a bodice to hide a knife, and a fold-out knife has no menace. One nice way around this problem is to have M'lady appear to pull out an impossibly large full length dagger from the bodice with the right hand while her left hand tugs at the top of the bodice. You guessed it: the dagger is hidden in the sleeve of her left forearm. The bit gets a great laugh and provides a decent sized knife for the fight.

Lastly, this is a show that begs to be underscored. Challenge your sound designer to have music playing for every moment of the play, for your actors need the support in order to create and maintain this world of grand passion.

So we allow historical accuracy to take a back seat to the emotional accuracy of the later period in terms of acting and fighting styles, set design, and music choices. The stunning theatricality of the swashbuckling films of the 1940's is a fitting testimony to the effectiveness of an eclectic, emotional, exciting approach as opposed to a scrupulously researched and all too often lifeless realism found in many modern productions.

Tom Sawyer

If we take at face value Samuel Clemens' assertion that the incidents in the book are all based on real events from his boyhood in Hannibal, Missouri, we can assume that the stories are set no earlier than 1845 and no later than 1848. That means that any shotguns or rifles are going to be simple single barrel muzzleloaders, identical to each other in outward appearance. The only pistols that would realistically be seen at this time and place would be single shot percussion style. Revolvers had been invented, but were not widely available until after 1848.

Tosca

Just as in Carmen, the typical firearms for the period are all single-shot muskets and pistols, and it is right during the time when European armies are switching from flintlock to percussion lock. If you want the muskets to fire and you want a flame coming from the barrel, make life easier for everyone and use percussion rather than flintlock muskets.

The sidearm for soldiers of the period is a military sabre, not a pistol. Pistols in the military were mostly used by irregulars.

Twelve Angry Men

Also now commonly called *Twelve Angry Women* or *Twelve Angry Jurors* or *Twelve Angry Citizens*. A "unique" spring-loaded switchblade is called for, but the problem in this day and age is that switchblades are illegal in the United States. When the play was written, switchblades could be purchased at any corner drugstore, but those days are long gone. One way around the problem is to try to use a modified novelty switchblade comb, although it is a fragile prop, far too fragile to attempt anything like the stab into the table. Oh, no, what do we do? Use the prop but just don't stab it into the table. There, was that so hard?

Some directors really don't want to give up on the stab into the tabletop bit, so they have the set designer work out a table that has a piece of Styrofoam built into it. If you have a sturdy real switchblade (don't tell me how you got one) that works fine. If you only have the novelty switchblade comb conversion, it will simply collapse after the first stab.

Another possibility is to use a butterfly knife, but the action of opening one isn't exactly what is called for in the script. Besides, the likelihood is high that the handles of the knife will flop down comically once the knife is stuck in the table, so this isn't a very elegant solution. The point may be moot, as these are becoming more and more restricted as time goes by and more "fear laws" are passed.

Uncle Vanya

In Act III, here is what the stage directions call for: *Helena tries to wrest a revolver from Voitski. He frees himself and rushes in, looking for Serebrakoff. He shoots at him. He flings the revolver on the floor, and drops helpless into a chair.* Great. This is about the worst combination one can do with a gun onstage. Wrestling with a loaded gun means that if the gun goes off during the struggle (it happens) someone gets a face-full of burning gunpowder. Throwing a gun on the floor means that sooner or later your firing gun is going to be a bunch of scrap metal.

There are some ways around the danger points, though. If the brief struggle between Voitski and Helena takes place just outside of a doorway, a quick turn by Voitski so that he is partially hidden again by the door frame provides a moment where he can swap the dummy gun with which they had been struggling with the firing gun. A simple hand-off can be done by an stagehand. As for flinging the gun to the ground, just cut the action. He can collapse into the chair and *then* let the gun gently drop to the floor from just a few inches, or better yet let it drop into the chair first. Don't fling the gun into the chair - it'll bounce out.

The Unexpected Guest

A slightly confusing prop is described in the script, and in the novella from which it was derived. A gun is described as being a continental war souvenir, possibly WWI or WWII, a service revolver that has an external safety. The British army did in fact use revolvers as their sidearms, but on the continent (Germany, Italy, etc.) the pistols were almost always semiautomatics. Don't worry too much about that. Since the turn of the century, the English have had a bad habit of referring to any multishot pistol as a revolver, regardless of how the gun operates. Either get a British military revolver of the period, or change the line from *revolver* to *pistol,* and use an appropriate continental semi-auto.

The Visit

When the townsfolk go out late in the play to hunt the "tiger", they could have mostly rifles, not necessarily shotguns. A few fowling pieces mixed in is no problem, and although it is true that to bring down a large mammal, feline or human, a rifle is more appropriate, the whole point is that people have grabbed whatever lethal instrument is near at hand. Don't sweat it, and give the actors whatever you can find.

West Side Story

Switchblade knives are mandatory for this show, but nowadays are completely illegal to manufacture, sell or transport - and a felony offense, so we aren't talking parking citation here. What to do? Well, you could use other forms of one-hand-opening knives if permitted in your area, but they won't have the same side-swing-out look so perfect for the 1950's. Regular fixed bladed knives can be used, but they lack the added sense of menace and flash that switchblades have. A final choice has the best look, but is a headache for the actors and properties master, and that is the aluminum switchblade combs sold in novelty shops. The plastic comb can be removed and a thin piece of metal put in its place, but this will always be a weak prop, subject to early failure. Keep several on hand for the run of the show, for you'll use them up quickly.

At the final scene, Chico's gun is a small framed revolver. Semi-auto pistols, although period correct, would be too expensive for Chico to have acquired.

True Stage Weapon Story: Every show that uses a blank-firing gun has a story about what happened when the gun didn't go off. This isn't that story. In one production of this show, poor Tony struggled bravely through the performance even though he was suffering from a fairly nasty flu. Notwithstanding, he was doing a very good job of keeping himself together. Finally, during the last scene, at just the moment where he was supposed to get shot by Chico, Tony's stomach told him that he shouldn't be onstage for what was about to happen. So off he ran back into the wings and safely through the side stage door to a place where he could privately lose his dinner. The actors who remained onstage simply waited patiently - all except for one. Chico, unaware of Tony's exit, had timed his dramatic second story balcony appearance, gun in hand, to the exact second that Tony would call out for Maria in time with the underscored music. Out sprang Chico and pointed his gun at .... no Tony! As Chico searched the stage (and audience) for some trace of the leading man, who should make her entrance but the leading woman. "Oh, well," thought Chico, "at least it's a principal" as he pointed his gun at the perplexed Maria and shot her. Maria, after very briefly considering yelling out "Ha! You missed me!", took the line of least resistance and promptly fell to the ground. It was at this precise moment that our Tony came rushing back in, too late for his own funeral but apparently just in time for someone else's. He rushed to Maria's side and tried to shake her to consciousness, but Maria was too crafty to fall for that old ploy, and resolutely stayed dead. To his credit, Tony sang the song that Maria was supposed to sing to him - "There's A Place For Us" - and then, realizing that the rest of the cast was too terrified to approach the chaos and remained rooted to their spots upstage, he lifted Maria and carried her off.

Who's Afraid of Virginia Woolf

A shotgun is produced at one point in the play that shoots out a parasol with the American flag on it. All of this information is in the stage directions - *but not in one word of the dialogue.* So you don't need to track down a parasol-shooting shotgun. And there is no deep meaning in the fact that it is an American flag that pops out. The only reason the stage directions are so specific is because that's what they had in the original Broadway 1962 production. [They had simply rented one of the props guns left over from the 1959 run of *Gypsy*. Those guns no longer exist, but they were rented out for decades. Unfortunately, the barrel diameter had to be so large to accommodate the umbrella that the shotgun looked ludicrous.] For this show, any rifle that shoots out any kind of a gag will work just fine.

There is a quick reference to the item being Japanese. Nothing special there. During the early 1960's most novelty items sold in the US were made in Japan, as were a wide range of cheap, mass-produced items. At the time, to say "made in Japan" would get a quick knowing chuckle from the listener. The joke is now lost on modern audiences.

Helpful hint: there is also a bottle-breaking moment in the show, and breakaways can cost you a bit of change. To save some money, have the bit occur <u>behind</u> the bar, and place a small crash box there for the sound.

You Can't Take It With You

The Russian ballet instructor Kolenkhov does some sort of judo move on Mr. Kirby, and if your actors have gymnastic ability this can be quite showy. If their only experience is in judo or wrestling or none at all, then don't let them work something out on their own. Their techniques assume some sort of cushion on which to fall - without that, even experienced athletes can hurt themselves. Instead, use a stage combat technique that will keep both actors injury free. Here are three possibilities - one simple, the others more advanced. Either way Kirby initiates the movement by putting his hands gently in front as if saying, "very flattering, but, no, not really".

a] With his right hand Kolenkhov takes Kirby's right wrist. Kirby spins to the left simulating being twisted around until his right arm is behind his own back. The simulation can end here or ...

b] ... Kolenkhov places the top of his foot behind the calf muscle of one of Kirby's leg, simulating a leg sweep, as both actors perform a combined sit fall.

c] Just as in variation A, Kolenkhov takes Kirby's right wrist, but Kirby performs a forward roll as Kolenkhov pantomimes giving him a "spinning wristlock". You've probably seen this move in a lot of movies and television shows. The aggressor, in this case Kolenkhov, gently pretends to twist the victim's wrist around in a circle as the aggressor spins in place. Normally this move would leave the victim with his own arm held against his back, but we're going to push the simulation to allow for Kirby to take that forward roll. Kirby only has to worry about doing the forward roll. It is Kolenkhov's job to make it seem as though he is maintaining contact with Kirby's wrist and leading the movement. Should this bit of pantomime prove difficult, Kolenkhov can forget about doing the spin and merely pretend to crank Kirby's arm once as though it were a handle from an old water pump. The audience will buy it because it is a very old gag.

After Kirby lands, Kolenkhov steps upstage and pantomimes a drop to the floor on his [arbitrarily] left side while the right leg "lands" on Kirby's stomach. Of course, Kolenkhov's right knee is bent so there is no contact with Kirby, merely bridging over the stomach, but the right foot can make a resounding stomp on the floor to simulate the impact.

Zorro

The sword of California in the early 1800's was actually two swords, one military (the sabre) and the other civilian (the smallsword). While the sabre is a strong battlefield weapon meant to cut off limbs, the smallsword was designed not for handling strong cutting motions but rather for the very quick deflection and thrust movements seen in modern swordplay.

Which sword would Zorro use? If we assume that he must fight soldiers armed with the sabre, he needs to either have a sabre himself in order to block a sabre cut, or quickly run-thru his opponent with a smallsword before the soldier's sabre comes crashing down. The smallsword simply cannot block a sabre.

So if Zorro has a smallsword, he can only kill and run, since "swordplay" against the heavy sabre is impossible. If Zorro has a sabre, he can hack away broadsword-style, but certainly cannot make his trademark "Z" very quickly. How do we get around this conundrum?

In *"The Mark of Zorro"* with Tyrone Power and Basil Rathbone, they simply used different blades on look-alike sword hilts depending on the necessity of the scene. In fights with the soldiers or cutting through a two-inch rope, Zorro's sabre blade was straight but broad. In his duel with the villain, it transformed magically into the thin straight epee blade of the smallsword. Either way, the hand guard was the modern Olympic sabre, as it was for *"Zorro, the Gay Blade"* with George Hamilton. In the newer *"Mask of Zorro"* with Antonio Banderas and Anthony Hopkins a more delicate compromise was made. Zorro uses a 17th century transitional rapier, just slightly ahead in time of the sword of the Three Musketeers, still a cut and thrust weapon with a straight blade, but with a leaner look. Keep in mind that the quick moves needed for finesse "point moves" are still as impossible for this weapon as it would be for the sabre, but it at least lowers the plausibility threshold somewhat.

This means that whatever you should happen to choose will also be a compromise, so the best advise I can give is to make two separate decisions. First, find out what fighting style is going to be used for the show. If it is going to feature fast fencing-style moves, go with a light blade. If heavy cutting motions will predominate, then a sturdier blade will be more suitable. Then, decide what look you want for each of the characters. Most sword makers can match any hand guard style to any blade width.

Zoo Story

I'm sorry that this show is so popular, for it requires a prop that is now giving nightmares to prop masters throughout the United States. Albee wrote in a knife that needs to retract, stay stuck in the actor's chest, slowly bleed during an interminable monologue, and then be able to be removed with the blade exposed. If you've read other sections in the book you already know how I feel about retractable blades, so you can guess that I'm no fan about shows that require one, especially one as complicated as this. I strongly suggest here that the stab be performed using the stage combat techniques described earlier, and then pull the knife out immediately - before the monologue. Reasonably intelligent actors and directors can make it work.

Some Final Words

This book has been about art and violence. Many people believe that the two should never be mixed, that exposure to visual violence can only lead to more actual violence and should therefore never be allowed onstage or on the screen. Although I appreciate the sincerity of those who hold this opinion, it fails to take a couple of points into account.

Violence is a storytelling device. We as theatre artists are required to tell a playwright's story to the best of our ability, and sometimes that includes expressions of the less noble of humanity's attributes, including our capacity for physical brutality to members of our own species which surpasses that of other animals. To ignore those aspects is to be dishonest, and ultimately does a disservice to the very art we serve.

Staged violence serves two purposes. It progresses the story and it stirs the emotions of the audience. The former is our obligation, but the latter can be crucial to the ultimate purpose of art, namely to move the audience to experience, albeit vicariously, something outside of daily life. That vicarious experience may be revulsion or exhilaration, but it is the catalyst that can push past the intellectual barrier the audience brings in when they see a show. They know they are going to be challenged, and they willingly leave themselves open to our efforts, with the understanding that we have a very good reason to play with their emotions. For us to ignore our part of the bargain insults them.

Having those high-minded ideals doesn't ignore the fact that violence is also entertainment. There is a thrill there that has always excited audiences. Stories told around prehistoric campgrounds begot tribal heroic legends begot staged revenge tragedies begot action/adventure films begot video games - all pandering to the same desire. They may have an exalted motive or merely look for approval or wealth, but those storytellers would have no audience if it weren't for a deep need that brings listeners around the campfire.

That the majority of those who approach and stay for the bloody bits are male is probably no accident. In almost all societies, males from a very early age are taught that the world is a dangerous place and that their measure of worthiness will be in how they confront those dangers. In play, those activities that allow them to "win" against superior odds are the most popular. In entertainment, violent battles against overwhelmingly powerful opponents are not only invigorating but also comforting, creating an inner image of being somehow powerful as well. In a way it is much like the visualization techniques used by Olympic athletes. By seeing yourself win, it is possible to practice winning. By seeing heroes bravely engage in battle, it is possible to counteract the more natural impulse to flee when faced with physical danger. It is interesting that modern-day soldiers before going into battle receive solace and courage by watching war movies, putting themselves in the roles of the victors and by extension being victorious.

Certainly there are and have been a great many female warriors, just as fearsome in battle as their male counterparts. Certainly the number of superb female athletes who excel in every field of athletic competition grows each year. But it still remains true that violence for its own sake seems to have a greater appeal to the male portion of the population, and especially young males.

It is no secret that military leaders need to have their recruits be as young as possible. They understand that not only can young soldiers' bodies be trained to be at their peak of physical condition, but that their minds are more easily molded by training to accept orders unquestioningly. After a certain age, critical judgment is much harder to break down. Older recruits are more likely to consider the consequences of actions when deciding what actions should be performed. Twenty-six years of age is usually the dividing line. Interesting that twenty-six is also the minimum age that rental car companies will allow someone to rent a car. Younger drivers simply engage in too much reckless behavior for its own sake.

Cultural conditioning might explain part of the affinity, but not all. The human brain begins its development before birth, but all parts of the brain do not finish growing at the same time. The very last part to make all of the electrical connections necessary for smooth functioning is the very one responsible for critical judgment. When does that happen? At about the age of twenty-six. Wisdom in the young is not only rare, it might be physically difficult.

It may also be that human males are pre-wired to enjoy seeing and committing violence. It is already well known that in males, testosterone levels spike dramatically when they are engaged in violent physical activity, be it war or confrontational sports such as football or soccer. It has also been demonstrated that even the male *spectators* of these events experience the same testosterone spike. Now it makes sense that the warriors or athletes can use the extra testosterone, since the hormone increases aggression as well as lessens fatigue, builds muscle mass, and helps in recovery from injury. But then why should the *viewers* need the extra push?

A long-term study measured the testosterone levels of soccer fans in Italy as they entered and then exited soccer stadiums on game day. As expected, testosterone levels were dramatically higher after the game, but mainly for the fans of the winning team. Fans of the losing team not only had testosterone levels lower than the others, but unexpectedly lower than their *own* pre-game levels. Being associated with the losers literally took the fight out of them, or at least reduced their ability to fight.

In a larger tribal setting, we can see how this can translate into a useful survival strategy. Remember that in pre-"total-war" societies, only a comparatively few warriors battle while the rest of the tribe observes. As soon as one tribe begins to show dominance in battle, the winning observers get pumped-up and are more likely to join the warriors, whereas the observers on the losing side are more likely to retreat and concede a loss. Were it not for this outcome-driven hormonal shift, the outcome of the conflict might degenerate into a total donnybrook, to the detriment and perhaps annihilation of both tribes.

Sports fanatics identify completely with "their" team, and so naturally feel this effect far more than the casual sports fan. And we see that in the US especially, it is the "winning" fans who are the ones who vandalize local cars and businesses surrounding the stadium, not the losers. Likewise, viewing an adventure movie or playing a video game invites the audience/participants to identify intensely with the protagonist, indeed even to become the protagonist. It would not surprise me if a future study shows the same spike in testosterone levels, with the concomitant rise in both elation and aggression. Small wonder why "chick flicks" are not popular with male viewers, as crying and empathy with loss are depressing in a physical sense and leads to a self-identification of weakness. Interestingly, the exceptions are those viewers who consciously reject the stereotype or who already feel weakened or marginalized by the prevailing male profile.

In describing the above I am not implying that violence is good nor bad, just that it exists. I myself believe that it is impossible to ignore, and can even be helpful in telling a story. We should not shy away from using images of violence so long as we are being honest with ourselves as to why we are doing so, and are willing to constantly reevaluate our use of it in every project we work on. When that violence does not serve the art nor the community, it should be deleted.

I am not ever going to ask that someone shortchange their own artistic impulse for the sake of trying to be non-controversial, and I would never advocate any type of censorship. Artists should be absolutely free to do anything they want to in the name of art. But they should also be willing to support the right of the audience to perform its function and duty - to either praise or denounce those works which they have witnessed. Instead, many artists become defensive and blame the audience for not "understanding" their work.

[Now is when I start my rant.] Artists today are too afraid of criticism ("*I never read reviews*", is the common refrain of the insecure), but criticism is merely market research. It makes us better performers, not worse. So just suck it up, read the reviews, let people picket your theatre, allow all the voices to be heard, take it all in and learn from it. If they find your "vision" offensive, that just means that the audience responded viscerally to your product. Isn't that what you wanted? And if they call for others to boycott your product, accept that as another honest response.

But a special word to the apologists of violence and crudity. Another common saying among those in the biz is that "*art elevates us*", followed closely by "*art cannot hurt people*" - well, come on now, you can't have it both ways. If it is true that people respond to what they see, that experiencing a work of art can effect a profound change deep in someone's psyche, then it is only wishful thinking to believe that that change is either only for good or is effect-neutral. If compassion breeds compassion, if demonstrations of forgiveness breeds forgiveness, then it follows that violence breeds violence and crudity merely spawns more crudity.

"*But violence has been in entertainment forever*", and the more specific "*Shakespeare's plays are full of violence* ". Yes, of course, all of that is true. But remember that live theatre was and is mainly an adult form of communal entertainment, rare and expensive enough so that even in a densely populated capital city such as London very few people would see more than two or three shows a year. No film, no television, no radio, just a couple of live shows. The memory of the show would live long after the event, and would be discussed among friends in great detail. Even as late as the 1950's, few people would see more than one movie per month, the vast majority of the population seeing only a handful in a decade, and that was the extent of entertainment to which they would be exposed. Most of whatever people learned about life they did so by living.

Compare that with the incredible volume of images that floods in through the television set every day. The average American has seen more depictions of violence by the time he is four years old than his counterpart fifty years ago would have seen in his entire life. By the time he or she is ten years old, that average American will have witnessed 547 realistic murders on television alone. And now with the explosion of cable channels and the internet, even the most violent shows are available virtually twenty-four hours a day. It's not just the programming. Take an evening and look at how many commercials use violent actions in order to sell their products - and we don't even think twice about it. Violence is being drummed in at a rate never imagined before - to a very passive and receptive audience.

"*Everyone I know has seen violence since we were kids, and we are not mass murderers*". True enough, but that isn't to say that we aren't becoming a more violent society as a whole. Especially in the United States we've gotten sucked-in to the idea that complex problems can be solved with the simple expedient of resorting to violence (in thirty minutes for a comedy, one hour for a drama, an hour and a half if we have to blow things up). We've become desensitized to its consequences, and if not violent ourselves we give a tacit approval to those who use it to solve their problems. If not violent ourselves, we allow our government to resolve issues by proxy, using violence instead of negotiation. If not violent ourselves, violence is viewed as strong, negotiation as weak, taking us right back to our early insecurity of not being real men unless we can battle toe-to-toe against whatever we fear.

We seem to have the capacity to use our reason so as not to choose violence as our first response to a threat, and yet we also tacitly allow it under an ever expanding set of circumstances. Juries consider an increasingly broader range of violent actions as being justified. We no longer look down on people who act brutish, we allow youths to take on the attributes of bullies in speech, dress and manner. We are not shocked by people cutting us off on the freeway, flipping us the finger while talking on a cell phone. We are maddened, yes, but not shocked. And we demand no change. We have even accepted abusive speech and violent action and call it freedom.

"*Violence in not harmful when the message of the work is anti-violence*". Sorry. I would love that to be true, but studies have shown that children are immediately more predisposed to use physical force when confronted with conflict after they are exposed to any image of violence. That includes cartoon images, news images, and "educational" images. [Were the ancient Greeks right in thinking that violence on stage wasn't necessary for the performance and probably harmful to society?] So direct is this correlation that I strongly urge educators not to teach stage combat to children at anything below the high school level. The younger children simply do not have the maturity skills necessary to dispassionately judge the effects of even these pretend actions. If needed for a specific show, teach how to do the simulation to just the child involved. But stage combat workshops for young actors, although profitable, do more harm than good in the development of acting skills.

So where does that leave us? I've spent two thirds of my life teaching people how to sell violence to an audience, so I'm not in a position to advocate that we remove all violent imagery from art, nor would I want to. But at the very least I want us not to be ignorant nor self-delusional about what it is we do. I would like for us to talk openly about the necessity of using violence to promote our art, and maybe find a way to pull back from levels with which we have become all too comfortable.

Any carpenter arrives at a worksite with all of the tools he might need for the job. Hammer, saw, level, tape measure, plane - he is expert in their uses and applies each as each specific task requires. He may go days without using a crowbar, but doesn't feel cheated at not showing off his full abilities. The focus is on doing the job well, not in adding actions where none are called for.

In martial arts it is necessary to engage in combat with sudden and total effort. Sometimes to effectively generate this energy it might be necessary to develop almost a fury. But this fury must be one that springs not from the heart, but rather from a persona we use in order to succeed in that moment. We know that it is not real, but the damage that it can cause is. When the threat is gone the persona, the fury, is put away. It is called the mask of the tiger, and it is accepted that it has only a very limited usefulness. So it should be for us. We are not warriors, and neither should we be panderers. We are, first and last, storytellers, sometimes playing the clown, sometimes the lover, sometimes donning the kingly crown, and on rare occasion wearing the mask of the tiger. As with any tool in our toolbox, we must use it well and wisely.

Index

A

Africa 14, 16, 19, 38, 39, 96, 393
Anglo-Saxon 53, 57, 135, 434
Arab 17, 35, 38, 41, 393
Argentine 80, 120
attack targets 306, 322
ax 110, 111, 119, 121, 123, 125, 163, 168
Aztec 20

B

Babylon 35
back fall 271, 275
balestra 317
Baroque 68
bayonet 43, 72, 75, 78, 94, 111, 130, 136, 142, 337, 350, 425
bite 262
blade 112, 147, 148, 154, 156, 158, 165, 323
blank-fire 112, 189
blanks 112, 177, 180
BLED 301
block
    263, 283, 295, 310, 311, 313, 345, 352, 443
blood 147, 348, 395
  cleaning from costumes 371
  effects 369, 370
  mixtures 371
  pack 370
blood groove 121, 156
blunderbus 78, 113, 415
Bobbies 102, 432
bottle 171, 357
bow
  archery
    14, 19, 20, 21, 24, 25, 27, 35, 37, 54, 61, 66, 70, 113, 213, 434
  courtesy
    22, 36, 41, 51, 56, 59, 63, 66, 69, 73, 77, 80, 82, 88
  en passant 69
  Japan 30, 145, 340
boxing 22, 292
breakaway 171, 360, 442
broadsword
    17, 23, 42, 66, 77, 114, 125, 131, 160, 305, 312, 313, 337, 406
buckler 23, 61, 67, 68, 114, 136, 356
bushido 22, 27, 29
butterfly knife 115, 168, 349, 440
Byzantium 62

C

carbon steel 156
Cavalier 68, 77
Celtic 54, 120, 124, 390, 412
center of balance 151, 161, 163, 303
center of percussion 161, 311
China 16, 24, 26, 96
choke 246, 247, 248
choreography 228, 231, 333, 372
Civil War 86, 127, 435
club 16, 19, 20, 21, 22, 48, 112, 117, 126, 136, 141, 358
collapsible knife 432
corps à corps 327
count coup 20
crossbow 25, 60, 62, 66, 70, 109, 117, 215, 419
crusades 39, 58, 63
cut 151, 163, 296, 307, 310, 311, 312
cutlass 79, 117, 161, 337, 400

D

dagger 118, 132, 165, 335
dancing sword 68, 118, 386
demi-volte 321
duel 31, 54, 60, 67, 74, 81, 83, 85, 95, 110, 119, 295, 303, 304, 305, 364, 386

E

edge 155, 157, 295
Egypt 35, 39, 101, 119, 124, 127
elbow to spine 261
elbow to stomach 260
Elizabethan 64, 139, 160, 165
Empire 79, 401
en guard 304, 322, 338, 340
epee 119, 159
Ethiopia 35, 398
evasion 320
Excaliber 53, 412

F

face scratch 262
fall 271, 276
feudalism 25, 27, 51, 55
fight call 226, 232
fight choreographer 222, 225
fight director 222
flail 116, 120, 218, 360
flintlock 20, 75, 86, 120, 209, 364, 365

foil 120, 158, 387
foot stomp 248
forward roll 273, 275
found object 170, 357

G

gangster 89, 366
gladiator 48, 141, 359
Gothic 58
grab 242
Greece 43, 120, 337
grip 122, 153, 164, 302, 341, 343
groin kick 265
guard 122, 153
gun 171, 173, 176, 189, 362, 363, 366

H

Hamlet 386
handcuffs 103, 122, 213
handle 123, 152
Hawaiian 22
head butt 262
head to wall 269
Heavy Cavalry 13
Heavy Infantry 13
hilt 124, 148
Homer 45
hunter/gatherers 15

I

improvise 145, 221, 224
Inca 21
India 16, 22, 109, 130, 156
Israel 35, 141

J

jab 249, 250, 264, 292
Janissary 40
Japan 26, 277, 305

K

katana 24, 27, 31, 124, 149, 303, 340, 433
kick 264, 286
knees to floor 271
knife 124, 165, 166, 342
knighthood 59

L

Light Cavalry 13
Light Infantry 13
lunge 308, 309, 318, 321

M

machete 95, 126, 161, 162, 337

manacles 103, 127, 213
martial arts 220, 224, 277
Maya 20
Medieval 55, 58
Mesopotamia 34
Middle East 16, 17, 24, 38, 134
Minie bullet 86
Moor 64, 79, 393
moulinet 339
musket 42, 68, 71, 109, 127, 210, 363
musketeer 71, 75, 159

N

nightstick 103, 128
non-gun 190
Norman 53, 55, 56
Nubia 35, 37, 101

O

Ottoman 39

P

parry 295, 299, 313, 314, 320
passata soto 321
percussion 82, 85, 129, 202, 205, 207, 366
Persia 22, 39
pirate 78
pistol 71, 106, 129
polearm 129, 168
police 101, 359, 366, 431
Polynesia 21
pommel 130, 151, 324
Pre-History 14
pull 244, 245
punch 237, 282
punto reverso 317, 325
push 243

Q

quarterstaff 67, 130, 350
quillon 131, 154

R

rapier 66, 70, 131, 303, 304
rehearsal 230
rehearse 329
Renaissance 62, 64
retractable 166, 343, 346
revolver 85, 365
rifle 66, 133, 364
riposte 299, 309
Rococo 72
Rome 45, 101

S

sabre 134, 159, 303, 312, 338, 406
salute 67, 75, 76, 85
samurai 26, 124, 134, 302, 305, 339
schlaeger 132, 135, 160
scimitar 42, 135, 161
seiza 30
Shaka Zulu 17
Shakespeare 65, 295, 378, 386
shield 136, 356
shortsword 45, 48, 160, 337
shotgun 85, 103, 136, 201, 364
slap 221, 253, 257
slash 318
smallsword 74, 81, 137, 159, 295, 304
smothering 246
spank 257
SPAR 234
squibs 370
stab 166, 343, 345
stage directions 235
stunts 223
Sudan 16
Sumerian 35
sword 140, 146, 147, 148, 150, 157

T

tackle 275
tang 140, 155
throw 275
throwing
   sword 327
thrust 308
trip 244
Turkey 39

V

Viking 53
VINO 234
volte 321

W

war 13
watch 101, 102
whip 142, 216

Z

Zulu 17, 18